VULNERABILITY AND THE LEGAL ORGANIZATION OF WORK

This book uses the concepts of vulnerability and resilience to analyze the situation of individuals and institutions in the context of the employment relationship. It is based on the premise that both employer and employee are vulnerable to various social, economic, and political forces, although differently so. It demonstrates how in responding to those complementary institutional relationships of employer and employee the state unequally and inequitably favors employers over employees.

Several chapters included in this collection also consider how the state shapes, creates and maintains through law the social identities of employer and employee and how that legal regime operates as the allocation of power and privilege. This unique and fundamental role of the state in defining the employment relationship profoundly affects the respective abilities and degree of resiliency of actual employers and employees.

Other chapters explore how attention to vulnerability and resilience in assessing the employment relationship can raise fundamental questions of social justice and suggest new avenues for critical engagement with labor and employment law. Collectively, these pieces articulate a framework for imaging what would constitute an appropriately "responsive state" in the employment context and how those interested in social justice might begin to argue for it.

Martha Albertson Fineman is Robert W. Woodruff Professor of Law at Emory University. A leading authority on family law and feminist jurisprudence, Fineman is the founding director of the Feminism and Legal Theory Project, an interdisciplinary scholarly project she began at the University of Wisconsin in 1984. Since 2007, she also directs Emory's Vulnerability and the Human Condition Initiative, an interdisciplinary project housed in the Laney Graduate School. Her scholarly work focuses on various aspects of the legal regulation of intimacy and on the social, cultural, and legal implications of human dependency and vulnerability and includes *The Neutered Mother, The Sexual Family and Other Twentieth Century Tragedies* (1995) and *The Autonomy Myth: A Theory of Dependency* (2004).

Jonathan W. Fineman is an Associate Professor at Florida Agricultural and Mechanical University's College of Law. After earning his JD from Columbia University, he practised law as a business litigator in San Francisco. He writes about employment law and the workplace, focusing on private ordering and contract. He also publishes and speaks about vulnerability theory.

Gender in Law, Culture, and Society

Series Editor
Martha Albertson Fineman, Emory University School of Law, USA

Gender in Law, Culture, and Society will address key issues and theoretical debates related to gender, culture, and the law. Its titles will advance understanding of the ways in which a society's cultural and legal approaches to gender intersect, clash, and are reconciled or remain in tension. The series will further examine connections between gender and economic and political systems, as well as various other cultural and societal influences on gender construction and presentation, including social and legal consequences that men and women uniquely or differently encounter. Intended for a scholarly readership as well as for courses, its titles will be a mix of single-authored volumes and collections of original essays that will be both pragmatic and theoretical. It will draw from the perspectives of critical and feminist legal theory, as well as other schools of jurisprudence. Interdisciplinary, and international in scope, the series will offer a range of voices speaking to significant questions arising from the study of law in relation to gender, including the very nature of law itself.

Other titles in the series:

Gender, Truth and State Power: Capitalising on Punishment
Anette Ballinger
ISBN: 978-0-754-67478-8 (hbk)

In Search of Common Ground on Abortion: From Culture War to Reproductive Justice
Robin West, Justin Murray and Meredith Esser
ISBN 978-1-4724-2045-9 (hbk)
ISBN 978-1-472-42046-6 (pbk)

Sister Wives, Surrogates and Sex Workers: Outlaws by Choice?
Angela Campbell
ISBN 978-1-409-43521-1 (hbk)
ISBN 978-1-138-24723-9 (pbk)

Exploring Masculinities: Feminist Legal Theory Reflections
Edited by Martha Albertson Fineman and Michael Thomson
ISBN 978-1-472-41511-0 (hbk)
ISBN 978-1-472-41512-7 (pbk)

VULNERABILITY AND THE LEGAL ORGANIZATION OF WORK

Edited by Martha Albertson Fineman and Jonathan W. Fineman

Routledge
Taylor & Francis Group
LONDON AND NEW YORK

First published 2018
by Routledge
2 Park Square, Milton Park, Abingdon, Oxon OX14 4RN

and by Routledge
711 Third Avenue, New York, NY 10017

Routledge is an imprint of the Taylor & Francis Group, an informa business

British Library Cataloguing-in-Publication Data
A catalogue record for this book is available from the British Library

Library of Congress Cataloging-in-Publication Data
Names: Fineman, Martha, author. | Fineman, Jonathan W., author.
Title: Vulnerability and the legal organization of work / Martha Albertson Fineman, Jonathan W. Fineman.
Description: Abingdon, Oxon [UK] ; New York : Routledge, 2017. | Series: Gender in law, culture, and society | Includes bibliographical references and index.
Identifiers: LCCN 2017014251 | ISBN 9781138698604 (hardback) | ISBN 9781138698826 (pbk.)
Subjects: LCSH: Labor laws and legislation. | Industrial relations. | Collective labor agreements. | Labor unions—Law and legislation. | Migrant labor—Legal status, laws, etc. | Discrimination in employment—Law and legislation.
Classification: LCC K1705 .F53 2017 | DDC 344.01/88—dc23
LC record available at https://lccn.loc.gov/2017014251

ISBN: 978-1-138-69860-4 (hbk)
ISBN: 978-1-138-69882-6 (pbk)
ISBN: 978-1-315-51857-2 (ebk)

Typeset in Bembo
by Apex CoVantage, LLC

CONTENTS

FIGURES AND TABLES

Figures

Tables

INTRODUCING VULNERABILITY

Martha Albertson Fineman[1]

I. Introduction

The authors in this collection use the concepts of vulnerability and resilience to analyze individuals, institutions, and the role of law in the context of employment and work relationships. The following chapters generally recognize that those people or entities we categorize as the employer (the one who directs work or is "worked-for") and the person we call the employee (the one who does the directed tasks or is the "worker") are engaged in a relationship that exists within and has implications for the larger society, as well as for those particular individuals. Within this socio-economic relationship, both employer and employee are susceptible, although differently so, to changes in social, economic, and political contexts. These changes can have both negative and positive implications for those individuals, the work relationship, and the economy.

Legal rules and regulations governing work and employment can and do address the potential consequences of such changes, while also reflecting how the politician and policy maker understand and define the public's interest in work and employment. Those rules also reveal how the perceived needs, entitlements, contributions, and returns of both employer and employee have been noted, assessed, and valued in and by law. For that reason, a vulnerability approach suggests that the very existence of laws and regulations concerning work and employment substantially undermines the prevalent notion that conditions of work and the nature of the employment relationship are predominantly private matters to be negotiated and bargained for by relatively unfettered individuals within an open and free labor market. Indeed, a vulnerability approach proceeds based on the realization

1 Robert W. Woodruff Professor of Law, Founding Director of the Vulnerability and the Human Condition Initiative, Emory University.

that the employment contract is in fact an integral part of a broader social contract, with the regulation of work and the employment relationship forged within the confines of the assumptions, beliefs, norms, and values governing society as a whole. Law absorbs those norms and values and the resulting rules, mandates, prohibitions, and regulations shape the complementary – but often contending – identities of employer and employee. In doing so law typically enfolds social and legal power and privilege within those identities, affecting not only the options and aspirations of each individual, but the wellbeing of society as a whole. Often the allocation of that power between employer and employee is uneven, and sometimes it should be seen as unjust when viewed according to prevailing norms and values.

Recognizing this process of the legal construction of identities within the social organization of work, we can assess how the state inevitably plays an active and ongoing role within the employment relationship. What is particularly disconcerting and conceptually distorting in contemporary policy approaches to the employment relationship are the ways in which the role of the state has been obscured in political and legal culture. As a result, inappropriate and unrealistic assumptions and beliefs about the nature of work, the characteristics and capabilities of workers, and the power dynamics of the employment or work relationship abound in political and policy discussions. Employers and employees are assessed as separate, transacting, and contracting individuals, equally capable of bargaining and agreeing to terms of employment reflecting their respective best interests. Society's interest in the terms or potential consequences of the relationship so formed appears to be minimal, mostly found in regulations addressing health and safety or certain forms of discrimination and harassment.

By contrast, when considering possible disruptions or failures in the employment relationship, such assumed equality is discarded. Political and policy assessments tend to focus on perceived institutional, economic, and market vulnerabilities of employers in the face of uncertainty and change, often ignoring corresponding detriments to employees' wellbeing and their potential implications for society. Inequitable and uneven attention to the corresponding vulnerabilities of employees versus employers can raise fundamental questions of social justice that suggest new avenues for critical engagement with labor and employment law. These questions concern not only the effect of the organization of work on the lives of workers and their families, but also the implications for society and its institutions when the employment relationship breaks down for an employee and the state is forced to play a social welfare role. The laws addressing work and the employment relationship must consider the limitations and realities of complementary social arrangements, such as the family, and reflect the reality that work is only one part of a comprehensive and complicated web of institutional relationships governed by law.

To take the broader approach of a vulnerability analysis is not to idealize the possibilities of using law to achieve social justice in the workplace. As several of the following chapters demonstrate, law has its limits, and the classifications and parameters it constructs can be manipulated, weakened, and even avoided by employers seeking to evade regulation and responsibility. This should not suggest a retreat from law, however. Rather, it mandates an ongoing, active, and consistent critique and engagement. Vulnerability theory begins its engagement with law by asking a fundamental question: who is the subject of law? The legal subject is an all-inclusive and universal construct – the "idealized ordinary." The laws we craft will reflect the assumed needs, capabilities, and characteristics of that contrived subject and will form the social institutions and relationships that meet those needs.

Our contemporary understanding of the legal subject is an impoverished one, built on an ideology that values liberty over equality and manipulates contractual concepts such as choice and consent to justify relations of exploitation and inequality to the benefit of some at the expense of others in society. This fundamental structural inequality in our perception of the legal subject in turn distorts and constrains the law's analysis and the concepts it uses to organize work and construct the social identities of both employer (worked-for) and employee (worker).

II. Vulnerability

Western systems of law and justice have inherited a political perspective that imagines a "liberal legal subject" as the ideal citizen – this subject is an autonomous, independent, and fully-functioning adult, who inhabits a world defined by individual, not societal responsibility, where state intervention or regulation is perceived as a violation of his liberty. Social arrangements and institutions with significant effects on everyone's lives, such as the family, are deemed "private" and their operation and functioning relegated to ideologies of meritocracy and the free market.

Vulnerability theory challenges this dominant, static, and individualized legal subject, and argues for the recognition of the reality of the human condition as finite and fragile, as well as socially and materially dynamic. We are embodied beings who are inexorably embedded in social relationships and institutions over the life course. Vulnerability theory rejects the limited and abstracted subjectivity constructed in the liberal imagination. We acknowledge instead the complex and changeable condition of the "vulnerable legal subject" – a political vision of how the human condition is profoundly shaped by an inherent and constant state of vulnerability across the life course from birth until death. This complex and empirically informed subjectivity should be our guide to the ways in which we understand and define individual, institutional, and state responsibilities. It provides a conceptual basis to question and critique current allocations of responsibility for individual and societal wellbeing.

A. The embodied human being

The label of "vulnerability" is often associated with specific instances of victimhood, deprivation, dependency, or pathology and negatively contrasted with idealized notions of autonomy and independence that are deemed characteristics of members of the larger society. For example, public health discourse refers to "vulnerable populations," such as those who are infected with HIV/AIDS. Groups of persons living in poverty or confined in prisons or other state institutions are often labeled as vulnerable populations. Children or the elderly are prototypical examples of more sympathetic vulnerable populations.

By contrast, the basic, foundational premise in a vulnerability approach is that human vulnerability is universal and constant – there can be no position of invulnerability. Vulnerability IS the human condition. Our vulnerability is located in the fact that humans are embodied beings. As embodied beings we are continuously susceptible to change or alteration – both positive and negative – in our physical or biological wellbeing, as well as in our needs and circumstances. Further, this understanding of human vulnerability and the human needs it reveals must be at the heart of our concepts of social justice and state responsibility.

When vulnerability is normalized within the human body and thus freed from its limited and negative associations, it proves a powerful conceptual tool. Vulnerability has the potential to help us define state obligation in richer and more robust terms than is currently afforded under concepts such as antidiscrimination and equal protection of law. Vulnerability can act as a heuristic device, exposing the hidden assumptions and biases that have shaped social and cultural meanings, raising new issues, posing different questions, and opening up new avenues for critical exploration. Most significantly, acceptance of human vulnerability supports the demand that we need a political and economic system that reacts in a responsive and supportive way to that vulnerability.

The second major point about embodiment has to do with differences in real, living bodies. Importantly, while it is built on understanding human vulnerability as universal and constant, the approach also recognizes particularity across individuals by incorporating two forms of human difference or variation into the analysis. Taking a life course perspective, a vulnerability approach highlights human differences that are developmental or biological (vertical differences over time for any individual). By contrast, the autonomous legal subject is static, reflecting only an idealized (and often unrealized) age-specific point in the life course.[2]

In addition, there are differences between or among individuals living in society at any particular time (horizontal differences across groups of individuals). These variations in embodiment we classify with labels such as race, sex, gender, ability, and so on. The state has found it necessary and important over time to respond to these differences and currently protects those with certain characteristics from

2 One way to think about this is to recognize that the state does not consider some developmental stages of life as warranting full legal subjectivity, with childhood being the most obvious example. Different, often "protective" rules apply and this difference in treatment is not considered inappropriate discrimination.

discrimination.[3] Antidiscrimination laws emphasize the importance of inclusion and are based on principles of civil rights and equal treatment.

In addition to providing the basis for antidiscrimination laws, differences in embodiment (both horizontal and vertical) should also highlight the need to focus on the ways in which law affects or shapes the nature and functioning of the social institutions and relationships that respond to human vulnerability on a day-to-day basis. This institutional focus provides a second prong or wing of a vulnerability analysis. Because our physical or material bodies have needs and wants that must be satisfied, we are all inevitably dependent on social arrangements over the course of our lives. In other words, our *embodied* beings are inevitably *embedded* in social institutions and relationships.

Human vulnerability therefore has a social or relational component, as well as a physical manifestation. Human beings are innately dependent on the provision of care by others when we are infants and often when we are ill, aged, or disabled. This social dependency is also continuous throughout the life course, although the institutions and relationships on which we depend may change. Our social vulnerability is reflected in our creation of societal institutions such as the family, the school, and the workplace.

Differences are also important in regard to the social or relational aspects of human vulnerability. Equally vulnerable individuals will have widely varying experiences within society. The ability to mitigate, compensate, or manage vulnerability will vary according to the quality and quantity of resources that individuals possess or can command. While society cannot eradicate human vulnerability, it can and does provide mediating structures or institutions that can allow us to live with vulnerability.

III. Resilience

Importantly, the primary emphasis of vulnerability theory is not our human vulnerability, although the theory begins there. Significantly, the counterpoint to vulnerability is *not* invulnerability, for that is impossible to achieve, but the resilience that comes from having some means with which to address and confront misfortune. When vulnerability is understood as a universal constant, the task then becomes to explore the strategies by which we can mitigate this vulnerability.

The inequality of *resilience* is at the heart of vulnerability theory because it turns our attention to society and social institutions. Human beings are not rendered

3 There are also protective laws for young and old. These are not antidiscrimination laws, but are based on the need for protective differences in treatment. Because they are built on difference, such laws are often resisted as being paternalistic or denials of agency and carrying stigma. This type of response to conferral of state protection underscores the strength of the idealized autonomous and independent legal subject and the way it can propel individuals and groups to resist exactly the kind of state responses to vulnerability that we all need.

more or less vulnerable because they have certain characteristics or are at various stages in their lives, but they do experience the world with differing levels of resilience. Importantly, no one is born resilient. Rather, resilience is produced within and through institutions and relationships that confer privilege and power. Those institutions and relationships, whether deemed public or private, are at least partially defined and reinforced by law.

Resilience is measured in part by an individual's ability to survive or recover from harm or setbacks that inevitably occur over the life course. Resilience has implications for individual and social progress as well. Resilient individuals are able to form relationships, undertake transactions, and take advantage of opportunities or take risks in life, confident that if they fail the challenge or meet unexpected obstacles, they are likely to have the means and ability to recover. In other words, resilience allows us to respond to life – to not only survive, but thrive within the circumstances in which we find ourselves.

Accepting the premise that the reality of our universal fragility and susceptibility to change has played a significant role in the design and construction of our societal institutions necessitates that the effectiveness and justice of those institutions be measured by their responses to that vulnerability. The societal institutions that have grown up around vulnerability are interlocking and overlapping, creating layered possibilities of opportunities and support, but also containing gaps and potential pitfalls. These institutions collectively form systems that play an important role in mitigating, ameliorating, and compensating for vulnerability. Together and independently they provide us with "assets" – resources in the form of advantages or coping mechanisms. There are at least five types of resources that societal organizations and institutions can provide: physical assets, ecological or environmental assets, existential assets,[4] human assets, and social assets.

Physical assets are physical or material goods that determine our present economic quality of life and provide the material basis for accumulation of additional sustainable resources in the form of savings and investments.[5] Ecological assets can be conferred through our position in relation to the physical or natural environments in which we find ourselves. We live in the context of external factors and sets of physical conditions that interact with us and profoundly influence our needs, as well as shaping the circumstances of our wellbeing.[6] Existential resources are provided by systems of belief or aesthetics, such as religion, culture, or art. These resources can help us to understand our place within the world and allow us to see meaning and beauty in our existence.[7]

4 In the context of existentialism: involved in or vital to the shaping of a person's self-chosen mode of existence and moral stance with respect to the rest of the world.

5 Certainly tax and inheritance laws impact the distribution of physical assets and are part of this system, but so also are banking rules and regulations, and credit policies.

6 The natural environment has been greatly altered and affected by human activity and institutions, only some of which are beneficial, and laws, regulations and agencies have grown up around efforts to protect natural resources from further deterioration.

7 Governmental policies subsidize religious and cultural entities through tax policy and more direct means.

The forms of resources most obviously relevant when talking about employment relationships are human and social assets. Like physical assets, human assets also affect material wellbeing. If we define human assets as the innate or developed abilities for us to make the most of a given situation, they provide on an individual level for the accumulation of human capital or "capabilities." These assets are largely dependent on our experiences within the general health and education systems and are expended, as well as developed, within employment systems. Human assets are those skills and training that facilitate participation in the market and make possible the accumulation of material resources that help bolster individuals' resilience. Such assets are also necessary for an individual's ability to form and support family and other relationships.

Social assets are networks of relationships from which we gain support and strength. The family is a major institution providing social assets, particularly for the young. Social assets are conferred through other associations, such as political collectives in which individuals bolster their resilience by joining together to address vulnerabilities generated by the market. In the context of work and employment, these collectives historically included trade unions and political parties and also encompass professional organizations and associations.[8]

This description of various types of assets in relation to the institutions that provide and distribute them suggests a link between those assets and state responsibility. The institutions providing resources to us are brought into legal existence only through state mechanisms. Entities such as firms, corporations, families, or churches are legitimated and given a status that confers on them benefits and protections by law. Their very content and meaning is defined through state processes. The social and economic relationships they contain, such as that between employer/employee or those-who-are-worked-for/worker are also structured by and legitimated through law. In other words, the idea that institutions can naturally be divided and sorted according to the labels "private" and "public" is deeply flawed. At best we have public and quasi-public institutions, with the latter category being relatively more insulated against regulation. To the extent that these institutions and social arrangements are also distributing significant social goods and justifying privilege, they should be monitored by the state.

This need for monitoring is intensified by the realization that social institutions and arrangements should also be understood as vulnerable entities in and of themselves. We know that societal institutions are not consistently stable, even in the short-term. They may fail in the wake of market fluctuations, changing international policies, institutional and political compromises, or human prejudices. They can be captured, corrupted, or become unwieldy and bloated. Their effects on the individual and society can change as conditions evolve. Even the most established institutions when viewed over time are potentially unstable and susceptible

8 In recent decades, a sense of community organized around identity characteristics, such as race, ethnicity, and gender, has constituted powerful networks of affiliation and belonging. Interest groups forming around those identities have impacted employment law through uncovering inappropriate discrimination in hiring and firing.

to challenges from both internal and external forces. Further, this institutional vulnerability is almost always obscured and those in control of institutions have a powerful interest in disclaiming the appearance of any vulnerability. Riddled with their own vulnerabilities, society's institutions cannot eradicate, and often operate to exacerbate, our individual vulnerability and social harms. This present and persistent possibility gives rise to the demand that the state ultimately must be responsive to vulnerability.

IV. Conclusion

In conclusion I want to review some of the points made above and emphasize what vulnerability is *not*, at least what it is not within a vulnerability analysis. The approach taken in developing this theory employs the term vulnerability as a term of art. Its choice reflects the empirical and experiential reality that, unlike the concepts with which it is often confused, there is no contradictory or dichotomous pairing for vulnerability. There is no position of human invulnerability in which we are not susceptible to change in our physical and social wellbeing.

Generally, the designation of "vulnerability" in a vulnerability approach to a social problem or issue is not simply a substitute term for "dependency on care." Nor is it or its theoretical and conceptual potential exhausted in concepts such as weakness, fragility, precariousness, or being "at-risk" (these are terms usually found in dualistic combinations – weakness/strength; precarity/stability, and so on). As we know intuitively and experientially there is no position of invulnerability – there is only resilience.

Particularly important in the context of work and employment, vulnerability is not just another way of talking about discrimination or signaling disadvantage. Vulnerability is not merely one among many possible "identities" traditionally adopted or assigned in arguing for equality and civil and political rights. In addition, recognition of vulnerability does not reflect or assert the absence or impossibility of agency – rather, it recognizes that agency, in the form of resilience, is socially produced over the life course and is limited and constrained by the resources and relationships available to any specific individual. Vulnerability theory asserts that agency or autonomy – like the concept of resilience (and unlike vulnerability) – should always be understood as particular, partial, and contextual.

Furthermore, theorizing vulnerability as both universal and constant means that it should not be used as a variable or a comparative concept. No individual or group should be considered more or less vulnerable, uniquely vulnerable, or specifically or especially vulnerable. Rather, we can think about spaces, places, and positions or relationships as indicators of the proximity of, exposure to, or probability for vulnerability to be manifested or realized in the form of dependency. By the same token, we can think of these same spaces, places, and positions as sites for the production of resilience – these are and should be thought of as sites of state responsibility.

This last point underscores the theoretical point that it is not human vulnerability that is socially produced or created. Certain social situations may reveal our vulnerability in ways that are hard to ignore. So, while we may recognize that childhood is a stage in which our shared vulnerability is most evident, it is theoretically important to always refer to the universal in the first instance. We refer to the *vulnerable subject as a child* and do not position childhood as creating a somehow uniquely vulnerable subgroup of beings – a "vulnerable population." In the same way, we do not think of the vulnerable worker (which some might use to distinguish some categories of workers from others), but focus on the situation of the vulnerable subject at work or as a worker.

In other words, vulnerability is the constant aspect of the human condition, present throughout our lives and in all social circumstances. We are not rendered more or less vulnerable because of certain characteristics or statuses *or* life stages (even as children), but we are more or less resilient. That inequality of resilience is what is often produced within and through social institutions and relationships of privilege defined and reinforced by law. Similarly, we can talk of different probabilities that vulnerability will be realized in the form of dependency on others or on institutions. This could take the form of risk assessment, with the realization that the increased risk was not located within the individual, but in the social and institutional contexts in which he or she was located.

The legal and political organization and structuring of these vital social institutions often provokes political disagreement and always presents significant policy choices. But these disagreements and choices should be confronted and decisions made, not obscured, by a rhetoric seeped in individualism, independence, autonomy, and choice that ignores how society and its institutions actually work, with each human being profoundly embedded within webs of relationships. The conceptual pairing of institutional relationships, such as employer/employee; parent/child; and corporation/shareholder, should be examined and understood as examples of interlocking and overlapping legally-shaped identities in need of constant attention and reexamination in a state responsive to human vulnerability and attentive to social justice.

It is important to conclude with the observation that a vulnerability approach does *not* mean that different treatment, even the conferral of privilege or advantage, is never warranted. It does mean that if the state confers or tolerates institutional conferral of privilege or advantage, an affirmative obligation exists to provide justification for the disparate circumstances. Privileging must be both transparent and explained. This type of process would certainly change political discourse and the terms under which legislators and legislation are judged. Vulnerability analysis can be thought of as defining what constitutes ethical political and legislative behavior. It is an attempt to articulate a more self-conscious and aware egalitarian political culture; one that more robustly adheres to the promise of equality of opportunity. Given the centrality of work to the accumulation of financial, social, and sustainable resources of resilience and the significance of work-based resilience to wellbeing across the life course, the state should be particularly attentive to this arena of social ordering.

V. This collection

This collection is organized into four parts. The first, Vulnerability and work, introduces us to vulnerability theory in the context of the organization of work and also some of the other major approaches to work and law. Part II, Law and social welfare, considers the relationship between work and social welfare institutions. The third part, Marginalized workers, explores some of the ways in which legal classifications can work to fragment those who work into marginalized or deviant categories denying them the full protections of employment law and the resilience it can provide for the vulnerable subject at work. The final part, Limits of law, looks at some of the limitations of law when it comes to the organization of work.

Acknowledgements

We are deeply grateful to all of the talented scholars who have contributed their outstanding work to this volume. Their individual pieces on labor and vulnerability bring a diversity of national backgrounds and perspectives to bear on the issue, giving this collection a depth and richness that would be impossible from one author alone.

We would also like to thank: Kirsten Widner for project management and copy editing; Rachel Ezrol for editorial support; and Brenda Huffman for formatting and administrative support.

PART I

Law and vulnerability

This section begins with the application of vulnerability theory to the existing organization of work in the US. It addresses the transformation of work and the working relationship over time, although certainly one constant across legal cultures and over time remains the need for the state to respond to change. Today, forces such as globalization and technological innovation can render historically settled doctrines governing the organization of work unhelpful, ineffective, or incoherent. How are we to think about the needs of employers and employees and the society, the state and its institutions in the face of such change? What factors, principles, perspectives should guide the next generation of law reform in the organization of work and the working relationship?

The first chapter articulates the problems with the notion of private ordering in which the role of the state is viewed as only responding to specific crises when and if they arise, rather than realizing that law is always actively involved in structuring both work and the relationship between employer and employee. Two basic principles of vulnerability theory are (1) that all individuals and institutions are constantly and universally vulnerable – susceptible to changes in their physical and societal wellbeing, whether those changes are positive or negative in result, and (2) that given the role of societal institutions in providing the resilience that will determine if individuals and social arrangements survive, endure, or thrive, the state must be responsive to vulnerability.

In placing work and the relationships inherent in working within a larger societal context, vulnerability theory highlights the significant interests that exist in the socio-legal organization of work and the working relationship. It also illuminates how questions and concerns raised by considering the respective vulnerabilities of employers and employees are inherently political and ideological.

While there may be similarities in the conceptions of work and working relationships across countries, the legal apparatus for implementing and monitoring those conceptions may differ. Are there preferred methods of regulation and response? How do we judge what is preferable? Whose interests do we consider and what outcomes do we prefer? Can we rehabilitate existing doctrines and principles, fashion novel arguments from centuries-old legal rules? Can we reach back to even more ancient concepts, religious principles historically argued to present a moral frame for governing relations between and among societies, individuals, and institutions?

In the opening chapter, "A vulnerability approach to private ordering of employment," co-editor Jonathan Fineman argues that US labor law's reliance on the idea of employment as a private contract ignores the role and interests of society in the structuring of work, and therefore fails to provide a coherent conceptual framework for changing needs and circumstances. He suggests that vulnerability theory can provide a flexible, but robust and comprehensive approach to employment law that is context-specific enough to accommodate adjustments as employment changes over time. In particular, he argues that the concept of resilience, and the state's obligation to ensure a minimum level of resilience in the face of vulnerability, may serve as a guiding principle to think about all areas of employment law.

Katherine Van Wezel Stone's piece, "Green shoots in the labor market: a cornucopia of social experiments," describes changes that have taken place in employment practices and regulation in advanced industrial countries. Stone shows that job security and the other features of the standard contract of employment are fading, and describes measures undertaken in some countries and regions to try to protect workers and to ameliorate the insecurity that present practices generate. The chapter concludes by considering what countries can learn from ameliorative policies and programs in other countries.

In her chapter, "The constitutional right to organize," Rebecca Zietlow uses vulnerability theory to make the case that workers do indeed have a constitutional right to organize. She notes that when we move beyond the traditional autonomous, independent liberal subject, we see that ability to organize and bargain collectively is essential if we hope to equalize the power imbalance between employers and employees. She proposes that the strongest argument in favor of a constitutional right to organize is that such a right is embedded in our constitutional culture, and thus finds the right not in court rulings but in the years of political advocacy of workers supporting that constitutional vision.

In "Labor rights as natural rights," Sean Coyle traces the origins of natural law arguments in Catholic theology and finds support for the right to meaningful work and to collectively bargain as principles of natural law. He describes how the Church's traditional characterization of the human nature and the need for a responsive state parallels and lends support to vulnerability theories core principles and its application in the labor context.

1

A VULNERABILITY APPROACH TO PRIVATE ORDERING OF EMPLOYMENT

Jonathan W. Fineman[1]

This chapter discusses rules of American employment law, including the employment at-will rule and the US' response to various forms of contingent labor practices. One purpose of the chapter is to demonstrate how vulnerability theory can provide a unique perspective and guiding set of principles for approaching regulation of a complex system. Although this chapter focuses on American law, the principles can be applied to jurisdictions with different specific rules about private ordering. Moreover, it appears that the current trend in many jurisdictions is towards a more American style, at-will approach to employment regulation and increased use of contingent labor (Bredgaard et al., 2010; Countouris et al., 2009). The problems faced by workers in the US may be instructive even in those jurisdictions that have traditionally followed another regulatory path.

I. A comprehensive perspective on the employment relationship

Much has changed in the actual experience of the employment relationship over the last several decades. Katherine Stone (2004) has argued that the old "psychological contract" between employers and employees (loyal service in exchange for lifetime employment) has been largely replaced by a culture in which employees no longer value or respect the same things. The workplace has also been transformed by the decline of unions and the withering away of job security in general (J. Fineman, 2013b). All of this has been accompanied by a rise in contingent labor (Befort, 2002; Stone, 2004). Also important are changes in the economic and societal contexts in which the employment relationship is played out, including

1 Associate Professor, Florida Agricultural & Mechanical University College of Law.

globalization, privatization of government functions, rapid and far-reaching technological changes, the 2008 financial crisis, and alterations in basic societal arrangements such as those within the family.

A. The need for a flexible but comprehensive theory of employment

In the face of changes in the workplace, we need a flexible, but robust and comprehensive approach to employment law that is context-specific enough to accommodate adjustments as employment changes over time. Without such a theoretical base, revisions undertaken today will inevitably present yet another set of problems in a few years' time. Society and the nature of the employment experience inevitably shifts, often in ways that will require yet another recalibration.

The changing nature of the employment relationship suggests the importance of considering the possible impacts of inevitable change on other (symbiotic) societal relationships and institutions. Essentially, a forward-looking, adaptable reassessment of employment law must also anchor the employment relationship in a larger societal context. Employment law establishes the terms of the relationship between employers and employees, but its effects do not stop there. It impacts interests and relationships well beyond those of the employers and employees who are parties to employment contracts. It also affects families, communities, and society at large.

Employment law is relevant to the functioning and wellbeing of societal structures and institutions, such as the family. It also profoundly affects the ability of society to address persistent social problems, such as poverty. Employment laws and the bargains they shape also affect or influence educational policy, thus the opportunities provided for the next generation. Employment has implications for public health and wellbeing, particularly as it shapes governmental responses to child or health care.

We need a theory of employment law that is clear about its objectives, one that would allow policy makers to deal with today's problems and challenges, as well as the inevitable changes that will surely come. The theory should address not only the objectives to be accomplished, but also the underlying assumptions about the respective interests, obligations, and capacities of the parties to the employment relationship and those third parties (including society) affected by that relationship.

B. The need for an alternative to private ordering

Currently, the primary theoretical understanding of employment in the US is private ordering. The employment relationship is considered a contractual relationship, and in large part it is governed by the same set of rules and principles as any other contract (Story, 1995). As such, the terms of the employment relationship are assumed to be a matter of private, rather than public, concern. The parties are generally free to determine the structure and terms of the agreement.

As discussed in more detail below, policy makers have at various points in time recognized the need to regulate employment contracts. For example, lawmakers passed Title VII of the Civil Rights Act of 1964, prohibiting employers from discriminating on the basis of race, sex, national origin, and religion, based on a public interest in eliminating discrimination (Henson, 2012). However, there is no common theoretical underpinning to the way we understand the public interest in employment contracts. Nor is there an agreed basis for discussing the effects of employment law on the rest of society. Even within a single exception to the at-will rule, such as antidiscrimination law, there appears to be no principled reason why, for example, federal law prohibits discrimination based on gender, but not sexual orientation.

This lack of theoretical coherence about social policy objectives extends beyond the exceptions to the at-will rule to other areas of employment regulation. Laws governing the workplace are passed based on different, often unrelated reasons. For example, the minimum wage and overtime provisions of the Fair Labor Standards Act (FLSA) were originally enacted in order to stimulate the economy during the Great Depression, while workers' compensation laws were established as a way to limit tort claims brought by injured employees against their employers (Pierce and Dworkin, 1988; Vance, 2002). In addition, innovations based on common law rules, such as implied contract claims and public policy torts, are inconsistently adopted and applied in large part because there is no coherent agreement as to the justifications for or appropriateness of such rules.

The theoretical rationale behind programs such as Social Security, created early in the 20th century and justified by the crisis of the Great Depression, has not been significantly reformulated. There are, however, significant contemporary political challenges to its continuation in conditions perceived very differently from those existing over seventy years ago. The rationale for such historic compromises may not make much sense to today's politicians and are often inadequate to capture the very different and specific needs of employees and employers (or the state) today.

In sum, we have a patchwork system of rules and exceptions adopted in response to a specific crisis or a particular confluence of interests between stakeholders and the general public. Private ordering continues to govern in the significant space between the patchwork regulations.

II. Private ordering of the employment relationship in the US

Historically, neither the individual states nor the federal government in the US have been as protective of employees as their counterparts in Europe and elsewhere around the world. Instead, the US takes a rather unique approach to employment regulation that positions employers and employees as conceptually autonomous equals, defers to the needs of the marketplace for flexibility and self-regulation, and is suspicious of governmental interference and control. As a result, there are far fewer regulatory protections for US employees than in many parts of the world (Rasnic, 2015).

A vulnerability approach disrupts the American assumption that employment is a private contract between the employer and employee. It allows us to harness the idea that work and production are structured to privilege employers, and this privilege might appropriately be accompanied by some reciprocal responsibility by the employer for addressing the analogous vulnerability of the employee. In addition, because employment law is a system of rights and responsibilities created by the state, the state has an obligation to protect employees' resiliency, as well as that of employers. The state's responsibility is based on the fact that law shapes the employment relationship, and the state's involvement means that the employment relationship should not be considered simply private. In reality, the employment relationship, which is recognized as one of the most complex and important relationships in modern society, constitutes a social arrangement or compact that implicates the obligations of a responsive state to consider the interests of all the stakeholders, including society, when regulating employment through its law.

A. Employment at-will

The at-will rule has been the basic foundation of American employment law since the late nineteenth century (Feinman, 1976). The at-will rule provides that each party to an employment relationship of indefinite term is able to unilaterally terminate the employment without notice at any time for any reason. It positions the employer and employee as equals within a bargaining relationship and is couched in terms of freedom of contract and individual liberty.

The ability of the employer to terminate the employment relationship at any time also means that it may unilaterally change the terms of the relationship for any reason without notice. There may be some specific limitations on the employer's ability to set the terms and conditions of work provided by measures such as the requirement of a statutory minimum wage. Apart from these specific areas of substantive regulation, however, employers are positioned by the at-will rule to effectively control all of the terms and conditions of employment (J. Fineman, 2013b).

The at-will rule has not been the only principle that governs the employment relationship. Employers and employees can contract around the at-will rule, most commonly by agreeing that employees can only be fired for good cause. Such an agreement can be express or implied-in-fact in many jurisdictions (J. Fineman, 2008). In addition, state and federal legislatures have adopted statutes that limit employers' discretion in some respects, and the courts have also acted through common law doctrines. The primary exceptions to employers' right to terminate or take other adverse employment actions are antidiscrimination statutes, public policy claims, and implied-in-fact contract claims (J. Fineman, 2013b).

Importantly, however, these exceptions do not displace the at-will rule. Rather, the exceptions merely identify certain designated unlawful reasons for termination that allow an employee to bring a wrongful termination claim. Unless an employer chooses to contract around the at-will rule or its actions fall within one of the specific exceptions, it is still free to terminate employees for any reason without notice (Estlund, 2002; Schwab, 1993). The exceptions do not change the basic perception of employment as privately ordered. The contract aspect of employment is still emphasized over its social implications.

1. Employment as a private contract

Hundreds of books and law review articles have been devoted to the at-will employment rule (Bird, 2004). While the overwhelming majority of scholars criticize the at-will rule, the criticisms have had little effect. The rule is still widely followed, and may have even gained strength in the last few decades (J. Fineman, 2013b). There is also a vocal minority who defend the at-will rule (Dimatteo et al., 2011; Frantz, 1997; Freed and Polsby, 1989; Harrison, 1984; Larson, 1986; Maitland, 1989; Posner, 1989; Power, 1983). The seminal defense of the at-will rule is the 1984 article by Richard Epstein entitled "In Defense of the Contract at Will." Professor Epstein argues "the importance of freedom of contract as an end in itself" (p. 953). Employees are perceived as competent enough to understand and enter contracts of their own free will, and it is thus argued that they should be free to enter into at-will employment relationships on equivalent terms with the employer if they so choose. Consistent with the abstract ideal of freedom of contract, Epstein argues that a hypothetical typical employee will "choose" to be employed at-will because they want the reciprocal "benefits" of that arrangement, especially the ability to terminate the employment relationship at any time. Therefore, the prevalence of employment at-will reflects what would be the voluntary complementary choices of both employer and employee.

Epstein also describes what he sees as the objective benefits of employment at-will over the alternative of a just cause rule. Privileging the position of employers, he argues that the at-will rule is necessary to provide employers with the ability to motivate workers and make sure they are productive; the threat of termination prevents employees from taking advantage of employers. Conversely, the ability of employees to quit at any time prevents employers from taking advantage of employees, who would choose to leave if the burdens of employment outweighed the benefits. In addition, the flexibility of the at-will employment relationship is posited to allow both parties to respond to changing conditions and imperfect information.

Epstein asserts that the increased costs and reduced flexibility of a "just cause" rule would "hamper general mobility in labor markets" (p. 972). Employers would be worried about the possibility of lawsuits and therefore would not be as willing to hire. Other scholars have expanded this argument to claim more broadly that employment at-will is the most efficient system (Freed and Polsby, 1989; Harrison, 1984). Employers are posited as being more willing to hire in times of growth and invest in labor instead of capital improvements if they know they can jettison employees if it does not work out (Dimatteo et al., 2011). Furthermore, the costs associated with processing and protecting themselves against claims will take up resources that could be directed towards the enterprise or given to employees (Posner, 1989).

Finally, Epstein argues that market forces will naturally prevent employers from abusing whatever superior bargaining position they are argued to have under the at-will rule because if an employer terminates an employee arbitrarily or for some improper reason, that employer will have a difficult time retaining and recruiting other employees who might perceive the employer as unfair. Failing to explain how such information will be made available to potential employees, he sees further restraint in the fact that the employer would also bear the costs of selecting and training a new employee.

Criticisms of the at-will approach are based on a few different grounds – inequality of power (Bouffard, 1986), fairness to employees (St. Antoine, 1988), human rights or ethics (Phillips, 1992), and social consequences. Many critics also disagree with the efficiency arguments raised by Professor Epstein and others, arguing that costs to employers from a just cause system are outweighed by increases in productivity provided by job security (Leonard, 1988).

The assumed alternative to replace an at-will employment model is "just cause" protection, like the one that has been applied in many jurisdictions in the world outside the US. Under a "just cause" system, an employer must have a good reason to take an adverse employment action, usually evidence of either non-trivial employee misconduct or underperformance, or a substantial economic or other business-related reason (Libenson, 2006).

Instituting a "just cause" system would prevent employers from making certain types of decisions that are currently allowed. Most obviously, employers could not terminate an employee arbitrarily. Neither could an employer act for a non-business-related reason, for example, replacing a competent employee because of nepotism or personal dislike. In addition, a "just cause" system may make it more difficult for employers to act even when they believe the decision to be justified, because the decision will be second-guessed by a court, arbitrator, or other adjudicative body. An employer may not take action against an employee unless and until the employer is able to gather enough evidence to support the decision to the adjudicator, which may slow or even prevent some decisions altogether (Estlund, 2002; Frantz, 1997).

The way criticisms have been structured around the European alternatives have cast the debate as a binary choice in which either at-will survives in its current form or it is done away with completely by statute or by being swallowed by its exceptions. The US does not have a robust employee rights or human rights framework with which to vanquish employment at-will, and such an all-or-nothing approach has deterred the development of more moderate, but potentially politically acceptable alternative lines of reform. The arguments about the at-will rule and its implications for balancing the interests of employers and employees are not constructive in their current form; the debates for the most part simply restate polarized opinions and accomplish little in terms of reconciliation of interests for either side.

What few changes have been made in the application of at-will rule are arbitrary and substantively inconsistent. Dealing with discreet issues through the crafting of exceptions, as important as they may be, has not led to the fashioning of a comprehensive and coherent approach to the existing inequality of power inherent in the modern employment relationship. On the other hand, the grand aspiration of a European-style "just cause" standard seems unrealistic. The resulting patchwork of exceptions offers limited protections for only some workers in a haphazard system that pleases neither employers nor academic critics of the at-will rule. As articulated by Professor Joseph E. Slater:

> [T]he best description of the at-will rule today is that it embodies the worst of both worlds, with exceptions so numerous and unclear as to frustrate employers but too small and narrow to protect employees in the vast majority of circumstances.
>
> *(Slater, 2007, p. 98)*

2. Reconceptualizing the employment at-will debate

Instead of continuing to engage in efforts to eliminate the at-will rule, it might be more fruitful to discuss how to reform the American system to provide additional benefits and protections for workers. Such an approach would begin by addressing why it is imperative in the 21st century that employers assume some responsibility for the negative consequences their decisions have on not only on their employees, but also on society.

To achieve this type of more balanced or socially equitable end, we do not need to completely rethink the employment relationship. In some respects, we can think of employment as *partially* a private or individual contractual relationship between employer and employee, recognizing the ability of the respective parties to shape their relationship to their mutual advantage. But recognizing the *possibility* of individualized negotiation does not mean that the contract aspects of employment relationships should dominate the approach to regulation. Employment is a social relationship that needs to be governed with a view towards social implications, not just private concerns.

Nor should recognizing that individuals can form contracts mean that employment law should impose an unrealistic and forced form of egalitarianism on the respective positions of the parties, assuming they are operating from exactly the same vantage points and, thus, face similar or equivalent constraints and consequences. The law must recognize there are relevant and significant differences between the positions of and possibilities for employers and employees both in their ability to bargain with each other and in their ability to successfully respond to such things as economic dislocations, market fluctuations or distortions, and disruption of "business as usual."

What has been muted by the focus on private ordering is the recognition that the employer/employee relationship reflected in employment law is also the manifestation of social policy embedded within and inseparable from the interests of society at large. This has significant theoretical importance. Actual employment relationships not only reflect an agreement arising from bargaining on the part of the parties to that contract, but also reflect the realities and significance of employment law. It is law that forms the actual framework of most employment relationships by defining the default rules regarding the nature, limitations and consequences of that relationship for both employer and employee. In this way, the state plays a vital role in the shaping of all employment agreements and the nature of the subsequent relationships they enable.

Employment agreements should be further understood to address social relationships of interdependence – the interdependence of employers and employees upon each other, as well as the interdependence of society and its institutions on the successful operation of the fundamental societal relationships embedded in employment. European societies use human rights principles to give substance to the interconnectedness of societal interests with the employer/employee relationship. The US has not ratified these approaches, making it imperative to search for some alternative theoretical framework with which to address the employment relationship and its implications for society.

3. Regulating the social implications of employment in the US

The state has regulated the employment relationship to address social concerns in the past, although not pursuant to a larger theoretical framework. There are two ways in which the law has responded to threats to employees' and society's wellbeing: the provision of social welfare benefits and direct intervention into the terms of the employment relationship.

For example, the Great Depression, with its resulting massive unemployment, hunger, poverty, and need, led to the creation of the modern US welfare state, with programs such as Social Security addressing vulnerability to aging and disability. Aid to Families with Dependent Children responded to the needs of the family when the head of household or wage earner was unavailable or unable to provide for them. Such social welfare provisions generally responded to hunger, dispossession, and other harms related to poverty.

State response during these times of national crisis also set the stage for certain interventions into and regulation of the employment relationship. For example, the Fair Labor Standards Act responded to the possibility of the employee being exploited by the employer. In structuring a concept of employer responsibility for the meeting the needs of the employee, the state did not only address temporary situations, but put permanent response mechanisms in place.

The state has directly intervened into the employment relationship by prohibiting some terms and conditions of employment, like discrimination on certain bases. The state has also set parameters or standards that employers must follow, like a minimum wage and safety regulations. Although these regulations do provide some limitations on private ordering, they do not challenge the basic presumption that the employer can structure the workplace how it wants.

Programs such as workers' compensation and unemployment insurance can be understood as reflecting a policy choice that mandated employers share the costs of disruption in employment, at least to some extent. These measures provide an income after dissolution of the employment relationship or, in the case of injury, simultaneously acted to relieve or supplement the programs of the newly-responsible welfare state. These measures spread to the employer some of the costs of their business decisions resulting in unemployment or physical injury that otherwise would be borne solely by the employee. Importantly, however, workers' compensation and unemployment benefits are conceptually designed not to limit the employer's choice or undermine the idea of at-will employment. Rather, they merely attach some consequences to the exercising of the employer's choice in certain circumstances. If an employer chooses to put workers at risk of injury or fails to provide adequate safeguards, it will be responsible for the employee's medical bills in case of injury. If the employer chooses to terminate an employee without just cause, its payments to the unemployment system may be affected.

Although perhaps not substantial, these publicly-imposed regulations and cost-sharing systems do have real economic consequences for the employer as well as benefits for the employee. They demonstrate that, at least in some situations, society recognizes the significant social dimensions of the employment contract and the reality that workers are too unevenly and negatively affected by the decisions of their employers. They suggest there are productive ways to refocus the law to consider larger implications, incorporating public as well as private interests and equitably balancing the uneven power relationship between employer and employee.

Unfortunately, because employment is still considered primarily a matter of private ordering, employers often attempt to avoid these rules by reorganizing their labor practices to circumvent these hard-won protections. There is little benefit in mandating a system of workers' compensation, for example, if employers can avoid the system by designating their employees as independent contractors. The next section discusses some of the contemporary ways in which employers use private ordering to avoid rules designed to promote social interests.

B. Contingent labor

The rise in contingent labor has captured both headlines and political attention. It is a phenomenon both nationally and internationally. The number of contingent workers in the US has increased dramatically in the last few decades, especially since the financial crisis of 2008 (Glynn, 2011). According to some projections, contingent workers will constitute as much as 40% of the American workforce by 2020 (Cunningham-Parmeter, 2016). The current understanding of the contingent labor relationship is also one deeply rooted in the concepts of contract and private ordering.

There is no single agreed definition of the term "contingent labor." I use a broad definition that includes long-term independent contractors, temporary employees, leased employees, and on-call employees. I also include outsourcing or subcontracting arrangements (McGinley & McClure, this volume). The common characteristic in these forms of employment is that the relationship between the person doing the labor or work (traditionally the employee) and the entity for which the work or product is ultimately performed or produced (traditionally the employer) is not a direct, traditional employment relationship. As a result, workers in these arrangements may lose some of the benefits and protections associated with the traditional employment relationship.

1. Private ordering and the failure to regulate

As Congress and the states began to enact laws protecting workers and regulating the workplace, they did not place any substantive restrictions on employers' ability to utilize contingent labor. Most of the laws, including the FLSA, National Labor Relations Act (NLRA), workers compensation laws, and antidiscrimination laws, predicated protections and liability on the existence of an employer/employee relationship (Glynn, 2011). Congress also failed to provide an adequate definition of "employee," creating uncertainty about the scope of protection under the law (Carlson, 2001).

a. Defining the employee

The best statutory definition of employee is from the 1938 FLSA, which defines an employee as an individual who is employed by an employer, and an employer as one who acts in the interest of an employer in relation to an employee (29 USCA §§ 203(d); 203(e)). Although there is some evidence suggesting that Congress intended the definition to be broad, the courts found it too vague to be of use, and instead turned to principles of agency law to define the term "employee" (Carlson, 2001). In particular, courts first used the "right of control" test and then the "economic realities" test. These tests are designed to distinguish employees from independent contractors for purposes of determining whether the principal is liable for the agent's negligent actions. The primary consideration in both tests is the amount of control exercised by the employer over the purported employee, but courts now also consider other factors such as whether the purported employee appears to be engaged in an independent business and whether the work performed is an integral part of the employer's business (Carlson, 2001). In the past eighty years, Congress has not stepped in to provide a more specific definition of employee or change the widespread use of the agency test. This same test is used for almost every type of workplace action.

Critics have rightly noted that the agency test might not be the best method for determining employment status for all purposes. The policy implications in determining who is an employee for antidiscrimination purposes is different from determining liability of the principal for a tort action brought by some injured third party. In addition, the agency test is based on factors that are largely within employers' control, allowing employers to unilaterally modify their employment practices in an attempt to achieve desired results (Griffith, 2009).

b. Who defines employment?

It is the idea of private ordering that allows employers to manipulate the system through misuse of contingent labor. Because we conceive of an employment relationship as a private contractual relationship, an employer can disrupt an employment relationship by disrupting the contract.

First, an employer can change the terms of the contract to specifically disclaim an employment relationship. A contract of employment, like any other contract, is based on mutual assent. In enforcing contracts, courts will usually seek to uphold the intent of the parties. By establishing some form of relationship other than traditional employment in the contract, employers may attempt to avoid the imposition of an employment relationship.

Second, employers can remove workers from the contract altogether by contracting with another party to get the very same services. If there is no contract at all between the employer and the worker in question, it is often difficult to establish an employment relationship. The new contractual relation between the third party and the worker becomes the contract of relevance, usurping and transforming the relationship between the employer and the individual actually performing its work.

c. Limits on private ordering

Of course, there are limits on employers' ability to disclaim employment relationships. First, the law might prohibit certain types of employer actions, and private ordering is subject to the law. But unless there is some specific, applicable provision of law, employers generally have the freedom to act how they wish. Legislatures are slow to pass specific limitations on employers' ability to engage in contingent labor practices. As employers have reorganized the workplace, avoiding (intentionally or not) protections embedded in previous employment regulation, the law has not kept pace with the changes.

A second limitation on employers' ability to disclaim employment relationships is the inherent limitations of the classifications they attempt to utilize. Courts and administrative agencies usually do not simply accept an employer's classification of workers at face value, but will instead look at the "reality" of the situation. For example, employees or government agencies may challenge an employers' designation of a worker as an independent contractor using the economic realities test. Since 2010, the Obama administration has cracked down on and increased penalties for employers who misclassify employees as independent contractors. These efforts have led to greater accountability for misclassification, but have by no means eliminated the problem (United States Department of Labor, 2016; McGinley and McClure, this volume; Rogers, 2010). Similarly, in triangular employment relationships involving a subcontractor or staffing agency, courts and administrative agencies might examine whether the company hiring the subcontractor or staffing agency exerts sufficient control over the worker to be an employer despite the intermediary.

Despite these limitations, the use of independent contractors and triangular employment relationships continues to grow. This is due partly to the use of the economic realities test as the primary basis for determining employment status, a test that is subject to manipulation since many of its factors are within the control of employers. The economic realities test is only relevant to certain types of contingent labor practices, and then only in those situations where the employer retains a significant degree of control over the work performed. Also, in order for the economic realities test to matter, workers must recognize that they might have a claim and then actually pursue that claim before a court or administrative agency. Many workers are either unaware of their rights or are unwilling or unable to pursue them (Cunningham-Parmeter, 2016).

On the whole, the regulation of contingent labor can best be described as an absence of regulation. Even when the law does react, it is not based on any principled, theoretical framework. As discussed previously with respect to the at-will rule, the presumption of private ordering is strong. When it comes to employment, private contract is the default position that makes oversight and regulation more difficult. A glaring social harm may be enough (depending on political circumstances) to override the default position. However, there is no comprehensive theory with which to challenge the logic of private ordering generally.

We are left with a system where employers mostly can choose the type of labor they want to utilize. Although employers do sometimes have to worry about a court or administrative agency second-guessing their decision, they use an outdated, one-size-fits-all definition to make that determination. There are no legal remedies for workers unless they can prove that the employer misclassified them. Employers have fundamentally changed the nature of employment, and the protections built around the idea of an interdependent employment relationship.

2. *Misuse of contingent labor*

To be clear, there is nothing inherently problematic about contingent labor practices as such. Each has a logical foundation, and in many situations it makes sense to distinguish workers on this basis and treat them differently from regular employees. As an illustration, suppose a manufacturing company hires a consultant with specialized expertise for two weeks to help it solve a design problem for a new product. No one would question that the consultant is an independent contractor, nor would anyone question the need to treat the consultant differently from the company's regular employees, at least in some respects. For example, unless there was an express agreement to the contrary between the company and the consultant, the company should not have to pay the consultant's payroll taxes, provide health benefits to the consultant, or be responsible through *respondeat superior* for the consultant's negligent actions.

Many modern contingent labor practices are problematic because employers misuse the categories, displacing the protections of the employment relationship by manipulating the existing rules. "Misuse" in this context includes three concepts. First, employers may stretch the categories beyond their traditional, reasonable definitions to encompass the type of workers who previously would have been described as employees without question (Cunningham-Parmeter, 2016). Second, while the traditional use of contingent labor usually involved a choice on behalf of both the employer and the worker to enter into a non-traditional work arrangement, companies increasingly make the choice unilaterally for workers who have no other option. Third, many employers seem to be choosing contingent labor practices not because the structure of the relationship matches the labor needs of the company, but rather for the specific purpose of avoiding costs, regulation, or rules protecting employees (Cunningham-Parmeter, 2016; Glynn, 2011).

For example, instead of reserving independent contractor status for a short-term consultant, a company might use the independent contractor label for long-term workers who do the same job as its regular employees (*Vizcaino v. Microsoft Corp.*, 1996). Uber's whole business model is built on replacing the traditional employee model with an entire workforce of independent contractors, thereby saving costs and undercutting traditional competitors (Cunningham-Parmeter, 2016). Similar forms of misuse are common with leased employees, outsourcing, and the other types of contingent labor.

Employers avoid a range of protective regulatory measures designed to benefit employees by using contingent labor rather than the traditional employment model. Without an employment relationship, employers are not liable for violations of most employment statutes, including the FLSA, NLRA, and antidiscrimination laws (Rogers, 2010). Employers may also reduce the costs of employment by avoiding paying payroll taxes, provision of health insurance under the Affordable Care Act, workers' compensation benefits, and unemployment insurance benefits (Glynn, 2011; Rogers, 2010). Employers can also use contingent labor practices to avoid regulations designed to ensure that pre-tax health benefits are provided equally to all employees, or to avoid laws protecting the right of employees to unionize. Some employers also use contingent labor practices to outsource illegal or questionable behavior, such as hiring undocumented aliens.

Workers, on the other hand, are often worse off as a result of contingent labor practices. On average, contingent workers earn less than regular employees, have less job security, and are less likely to have any health or retirement benefits. The negative consequences of contingent labor fall disproportionately on low-wage and minority workers (McGinley and McClure, this volume).

There are also significant consequences for society in the expansion of contingent labor. As discussed above, many workplace laws and regulations were designed to address specific social problems where Congress recognized the need to infringe on private ordering of the employment relationship to achieve public or social benefits. Congress recognized the social implications of the employment contract, treating it in some respects less as a private contract than a policy choice. With the rise of contingent labor, employers are essentially using the concept of private contract to disengage the social aspects of the employment relationship and return it to a fully private system where the employer does not have to consider the social implications of its actions. The presumption of private ordering obscures the fact that employers are using private contract to undermine public policy, avoid obligations to their workers, and shirk their responsibilities to contribute to social programs like Social Security.

The tremendous growth in new forms of employment and the projected continuation of that trend demand a reconceptualization of the nature of the employment relationship that is more inclusive and comprehensive than the old model. It is necessary to develop an innovative model to capture the situation of those now standing outside of the formal status of employee. Importantly, the focus should not only be on the behavior or motivation of the employer and employee, but also on consideration of the nature, extent, and allocation of the costs and benefits associated with an employment action.

III. Applying the vulnerability thesis to the employment relationship

Vulnerability theory recognizes that institutions, as human creations, are vulnerable, and this vulnerability extends to the employment system and its structures as well as to the state. These institutions are the sites for the production of human resilience – the locations where individuals can accrue the resources essential to survive and thrive in the face of human vulnerability. Resilience allows us to both confront life's challenges and to have the courage and ability to take advantage of life's opportunities and enjoyments. Understanding resilience highlights the central role of societal organization in addressing human vulnerability. No one is born with resilience; rather resilience is produced over time and within webs of societal institutions and relationships. The role and functioning of those institutions and relationships are both reflected in and defined by law. It is this role of law in the process and structure of resilience that defines state responsibility.

Employment is a fundamental nexus for resilience. Employment is the means by which most people earn money, which is essential for family formation, health, future economic security, and other aspects of resilience. In addition to financial resilience, employment is also central to individual identity and being a productive member of society. Employment creates social and economic stability for the country and enables the consumer economy, affecting the ability of all individuals, corporate entities, and institutions to build resilience. Considering the importance of employment, it is essential that the state take seriously its obligation to regulate the relationship.

Several aspects of a vulnerability analysis are useful in considering how to regulate the modern employment relationship. First, a vulnerability approach shifts the focus to legal and institutional arrangements, and contextualizes individuals in their roles as employers or employees. Second, the theory looks to how those social roles of employer and employee work to allocate power and privilege or advantage within the employment relationship as constructed in law. In addition, recognizing the role of law in this process compels the conclusion that the state is always at least a residual actor in forging the employment contract and therefore there is a state responsibility to ensure employment law is equitable and structures the employment relationship in a just and fair manner.

Although both employers and employees are vulnerable, they are not equally or similarly vulnerable. Their vulnerabilities may be different, but they are also intertwined because they are both part of the complex employment relationship. As such, within the larger financial and economic climate, they are both reliant on the success of that relationship and both will be harmed if it fails. In certain situations, the interests of employers and employees may contradict each other. In those cases, employment law has to balance the interests and needs of the parties to the relationship and resolve the contradiction in favor of one or the other. This resolution should be seen as the conferral of a benefit or advantage to one party to the employment relationship and undertaken only with a comprehensive balancing of the potential costs and benefits to both parties and a clear understanding of the potential social and economic implications for society.

Through the concept of resilience, vulnerability offers a cohesive theoretical framework because it provides a unifying set of principles for employment regulation. First, when considering regulation (or lack of regulation), policy makers should consider as a guiding principle the effect on employers' and employees' ability to maintain resilience. Second, we must consider employment in a larger social context, rather than as a matter of private ordering, because of the effect that employment has on the resilience of family and other social institutions. Finally, vulnerability defines the proper role of the state as a responsive one, with the obligation to regulate fairly to maximize resilience among all of the affected stakeholders. Moreover, vulnerability is a universal theory that can be applied to all areas of law, not just employment. Fitting employment regulation into a larger theoretical framework might help lessen political problems associated with special interest advocacy.

A. The vulnerable employee

Employment has become increasingly insecure for American workers over the last few decades; fewer employees are protected by contractual or statutory job protection provisions (J. Fineman, 2013b). More workers are "underemployed," with not enough work or not enough pay to support their families. The consequences of this insecurity to employees are serious and can be long-lasting. Lack of work may cut off employees' access to and opportunities within employment, force them to use existing resources to replace lost wages and benefits, and impair their ability to continue to build the resources necessary for the future.

1. *Effects of job insecurity on workers*

Loss of employment often results in eroding or diminishing of other resources an employee has accumulated, such as savings or investments, further undermining his or her resilience and, hence, ability to meet challenges going forward. Loss of employment can also have implications for existing social resources. Just as accumulated financial resources may be consumed when there is no paycheck or an insufficient paycheck, family relations and feelings of self-worth and dignity can be eroded and there can be serious impacts on families. Studies have shown that employees who are fired from their jobs have an increased likelihood of suffering from depression, substance abuse, illness, and suicide. Their families also are often harmed: evidence shows that spouses also suffer effects similar to those experienced by the terminated employee (Greenberg, 2011). In addition, unemployment is linked to increased levels of divorce, child abuse, and infant mortality (Moomaw et al., 2009). Further, unemployment affects the health and future prospects of the family and its members, with potentially serious intergenerational implications. The inability of one generation to adequately provide for their children in terms of providing education, child care, and basic necessities has long-term implications for the ability of these children to succeed when adults.

Unemployment also contributes to poverty and crime (Melick, 2003). For every 1% increase in unemployment, there are increases of 5.7% in homicides, 4.1% in suicides, and 1.9% in heart, liver, and stress-related diseases and disorders (Bird, 2005; Schliebner and Peregoy, 1994; Waters and Moore, 2002).

2. *Employer control of the terms and conditions of work*

The threat of losing one's job is not the only potential source of harm resulting from private ordering of the employment relationship. Flexibility is also a rationale for ceding control over the terms and conditions of employment to the employer. The employer has (with a few restrictions) the unilateral ability to set pay, hours, and benefits. Its control also extends to determining the form and nature of the work and the environment in which the work is performed. This control is not necessarily related to employers' economic interests in the employment relationship and, belying the rhetoric of an employment contract negotiated between equals, can actually reflect hierarchical, perhaps subordinating social arrangements.

For example, while it is obvious that physical conditions at work can profoundly affect the health and economic wellbeing of employees, employer actions may also affect the social and psychological wellbeing of employees. Workplace bullying can have devastating effects on the ability of an employee to adequately perform tasks, perhaps even leading to his or her resignation. If the employee belongs to a protected class, perhaps some relief may be forthcoming. But the question is why an employer's responsibility to discourage or discipline bullying should be limited to only employees who occupy select identity categories, and not be generally based on the nature of the employment relationship and a duty to provide a safe, secure, and civil work environment.

Even seemingly innocent workplace rules can convey the message that employees are inferior and untrustworthy beings in need of employer surveillance and control. Some dress or uniform requirements may fall under this category. Requiring permission to use the restroom outside of scheduled breaks reduces employees to the status of kindergarteners and is an affront to their dignity. The employer can also limit or structure the interactions of employees on the job in ways that might result in depriving employees of the opportunity to build positive working relationships. As with the other categories falling under conditions in the workplace, with only a few exceptions, the employer has the unilateral ability to determine the rules of the game.

B. The vulnerable employer

As business and corporate structures, employers are also vulnerable to harm, decline, and demise. They too must be understood as vulnerable, and the state has an obligation to address their vulnerability. The vulnerability of the employer is qualitatively different from that of the employee, however. In addition to the risks and rewards of the market and threats from competitors, the employer must negotiate legal regulations when they apply to its operations. Firms do go out of business or can be taken over, but that sort of "demise" is not the same as the death of a human individual and may, in fact, result in a more vigorous resurrected entity through bankruptcy and reorganization.

Similarly, while loss of profits resulting from natural or market disasters can hurt and weaken the employer as an entity, those harms are economic rather than corporal, as the business is an artificial legal construct, rather than an embodied living creature. As such, the employer has a different set of concerns about vulnerability, which are largely financial in nature. Significantly, there are typically vast differences in the nature and quantity of economic resources that an employer can muster as contrasted with the average employee when facing risks and opportunities. In other words, employers tend to be far more resilient than employees when it comes to the possibility of failure of an employment relationship.

Using a vulnerability approach, private ordering of the employment relationship should be seen as a privilege granted to employers that allows them to maximize resilience. By letting employers control most aspects of the workplace and the employment contract, the law gives employers the ability to be flexible and protect against possible economic harm. Law and policy makers have been much more willing to address employers' vulnerability in law. Law is a major source of resilience for employers. Further, the vulnerability of corporate or business institutions to start-up costs, operating costs, or costs associated with maintaining ongoing production schedules are routinely evoked to justify subsidies, whether they take the form of tax policies, come in the form of direct transfers and investments, or are delivered through facilitating access to mechanisms of state authority, such as law.

If we assume that private ordering is the natural or default method of organizing the workplace, any restrictions or benefits mandated by law must be justified as sufficiently important to overcome that presumption. Such protections or benefits are seen as a special privilege or concession. However, if we view employer control as a privilege conferred through employment law, rather than as natural and inevitable, we approach workplace regulation in a different light. Perhaps we should ask employers to justify their privilege, rather than asking employees to justify their protections.

This chapter cannot examine all aspects of applying vulnerability theory to employment. That will require a wide variety of detailed and extensive inquiries over time. Such further examinations of the employment relationship should outline the factors that should be weighed and balanced and ask some basic questions suggested by the vulnerability framework.

1. Justifying employer privilege

As indicated earlier, the major rationales for employer control over the employment relationship and the workplace are economic, i.e. based on the need for flexibility and efficiency. It has been argued that employers who are free to act unencumbered will be able to maximize profits and remain competitive, and this happy result will confer benefits on society in terms of jobs and prosperity. These justifications resonate in American notions of capitalism and free market ideology.

Considering the potential severity of costs to the individual and society that can follow from employer activity, a vulnerability approach raises the question of whether we should routinely examine the general justification for employer privilege to see if it can appropriately be stretched to cover a specific manifestation of control. Some employer actions (or inactions) cause unwarranted harm and confer unnecessary costs on the employee and may also be inconsistent with generally accepted societal norms. Perhaps the first question for policy makers and regulators to ask in considering a specific practice is whether it is in fact encompassed within and consistent with the justification for employer privilege.

Here, we should make a distinction between the privilege itself and actions that are taken under protection of the privilege. In some instances employer discretion should be subjected to political and societal scrutiny and not left solely up to the employer. Decisions involving public safety or health fall into this category. As to the vast number of decisions, however, there should also be limitations on employers' actions with the potential to cause harm to employees or social objectives. Conceding the general right of employers under employment law to generally control their enterprises does not mean that their control can or should be absolute.

There may be some particular exercises of employer discretion that do not fall within the scope of the justification establishing the blanket privilege. Tolerance for a coercive or bullying work culture and environment is one example. Since the justifications for employer's control over the workplace revolve around the need for freedom to make business decisions, there are questions that should be asked when the business motivation for a decision is not evident. What business need provides justification for an employer decision to allow harassment in its workplace?

Of course, there would be costs to the employer associated with addressing harassment, but those are not likely to negatively affect its economic success or interfere with production. Production might even increase. On the other hand, the potential costs visited on employees subject to bullying are substantial. And there may be societal interests that are affected by allowing employers to maintain a workplace where harassment can be considered appropriate behavior. Perhaps health and safety standards for the workplace can be expanded to include regulatory protection for mental and emotional health. Alternatively, Title VII provisions on sexual harassment could be expanded and deepened to include private remedies for bullying not associated with sex or other protected categories.

2. *Allocating the costs of employer privilege*

Even if many employer actions can and will be justified under the terms of the business rationale, that should not end the analysis. Vulnerability directs our attention to the costs to the employee's resilience and general wellbeing that can result from an exercise of the employer's privilege of control. One significant problem with the current focus of employment law and the issue of employer control over the workplace is that there is insufficient attempt to address the issue of allocation of costs or consequences that flow from employer decisions.

In the case of termination of employment, unless it is one of those rare instances where the employer is found to have violated one of the exceptions, the costs are allocated to the employee and whatever existing programs can help cushion the blow. In other words, the focus on at-will has largely limited the debate to the issue of the necessity for employer choice, rather than the question of whether society should address the consequences or costs of those choices through employment or other areas of law. Perhaps, in some circumstances, the employer should share in the costs accruing from its exercise of the privilege of control.

To recognize that the costs associated with termination are significant and generally borne by the employee and the state (through safety net programs) is not to suggest that the employer should be responsible for *all* of the costs. The process is one of balancing interests and needs. Employers are also vulnerable, particularly economically, but they should not be exempt from the costs of their actions on others for that reason alone. It is unfair to shift all the costs to the employee and, potentially, to society. But some parity is surely not too much to demand. Employees and local communities do not have the right to demand that employers preserve jobs or keep factories open in times of economic uncertainty. They are able to shift few of the communal costs of failure in the face of economic uncertainty onto the employer without its full consent.

The costs and benefits of employment decisions should be of public concern, not in the least because often the public ultimately shoulders the costs for these "private" decisions when employees must resort to social welfare programs. The tendency to perceive these issues to be solely private arrangements when they have significant public implications must be challenged. Considering the range of vulnerabilities inherent in the employment relationship as it is played out in its full social and economic contexts will extend analysis beyond the idea of the employer and employee as autonomous beings, to include societal costs. This more inclusive approach also allows us to focus on the ways in which the law has responded to vulnerabilities in the employment relationship and consider whether those responses are appropriate and balanced.

Certainly some balancing of interests, risks, losses and benefits should take place. The fact that the employer will receive significant benefits from the control conferred by private ordering in terms of flexibility, planning, mitigation of harm, and control is a compelling reason for allocating to it at least some of the costs of potential failure.

Some employer responsibility for the costs of termination has already been legislated, as we have seen with programs such as Workers Compensation. Perhaps the law should require the employer to provide some form of severance package that could include continued health insurance coverage for a period of time after termination, as well as severance pay. Other less expensive reforms might include making employers responsible for providing assistance to help the employee obtain another position. It is well documented that opportunities in employment are largely dependent on education and training. In situations of termination, further education or training could prove beneficial to the employee. Assistance with job search and access to human resource personnel could also be helpful. At a minimum, employers should be required to provide sufficient notice of intent to terminate and a paid waiting period so the employee has some chance to mitigate the damages of termination. We might also conclude that employers should contribute more to social welfare programs, unemployment insurance, or other programs that counteract negative effects of employers' business decisions.

These suggestions are not outrageously idealistic. Some are already provided voluntarily by some employers. They could be arranged through a public/private partnership model. The state has programs to help terminated employees that could be expanded and enriched by adding private resources. Unfortunately, however, employment law remains structured in such a way that the default rule is that employees bear the costs of termination, with the state acting as an often inadequate and stigmatized safety net. The relative insulation of the employer from the individual and social costs associated with the risks of inevitable economic instability is inequitable. This is particularly apparent when we consider the benefits they gain from the very flexibility that exposes both the employee and the state to additional burdens and losses. Employment law should strive for a more equitable distribution of the risks and costs of economic uncertainty between the individual, the state, and the employer.

3. *State responsibility*

It would be unreasonable to suggest that employers should bear the entire burden of employment law regulation, but the current system is unbalanced in favor of employers. A reasonable and more sustainable solution would involve a balancing of the risk, burdens, and restrictions on both sides of the employment relationship. Employers' interests in retaining flexibility and avoiding economic vulnerability are both real and important. After assessing all relevant interests, it may be quite reasonable to conclude that employers are entitled to retain at least some of the privileges of private ordering and that employees retain at least some of the risks and costs associated with employment decisions. But the assignment of risk is only part of the issue.

To the extent employment regulation encompasses private ordering and leads to job insecurity and underemployment, vulnerability theory suggests that the state has an interest in addressing the impact on employee resilience that system may cause. When employment law places certain risks and costs on employees or privileges the interests of employers over employees, it may be justified, but it also places some responsibility on the state. Specifically, the state has an obligation to provide robust social welfare or safety net provisions to assist people who are unable to obtain sufficient resilience due to private ordering of employment.

IV. Conclusion

The metaphor of private contract should not be used to describe the essential social relationship of employment. The idea of contract focuses our attention on the wrong things. Employers and employees are not autonomous, independent individuals negotiating a private arrangement. Rather, they are social beings operating within socially defined roles of employer and employee in contexts that have significant social implications. The idea of private contract cannot be used to isolate this relationship and its implications from legal regulation by the responsive state. It is time to recognize that the employment contract is not a private contract at all but a social compact implicating and defining a significant role for a state responsive to the needs of both a vulnerable employee and a vulnerable employer.

This chapter argues for a shift in focus away from private contract, not necessarily a total and permanent abandonment of private ordering. I believe that vulnerability theory and its application to employment law warrants further exploration. Employer advocates have been very successful in arguing against regulation. They point to free market principles and economic arguments that resonate strongly with law makers, judges, and the public. Employee advocates need a theoretical basis to support new rules (and hold on to old ones) that is consistent and persuasive. The concept of resilience, and the state's obligation to ensure a minimum level of resilience in the face of vulnerability, may serve as a guiding principle when thinking about all areas of employment law.

2

GREEN SHOOTS IN THE LABOR MARKET

A cornucopia of social experiments

Katherine Van Wezel Stone[1]

Over the past two decades, there has been a transformation in the nature of work in industrial countries, a transformation that will have profound ramifications for decades to come. For most of the 20th century, the concept of "employment" meant a steady job with a decent wage, an expectation of regular incremental raises, and clear pathways for promotion. In some places, job security was so iron-clad that it was practically impossible for workers to lose their job, even when their employers faced imminent economic catastrophe. Moreover, the standard employment contract ensured that workers had not only jobs of open-ended duration but also an ample package of benefits and dependable social insurance. Although varying country by country, workers who had jobs typically received pensions, health insurance, industrial accident insurance, vacation benefits, maternity leave, death benefits, and other social welfare protections from their employer or the state. The combination of steady jobs, reliably rising incomes, and a package of social protection made the lives of most workers stable and their life courses predictable.

Yet, since the late 1970s, that standard model of employment has been declining throughout the industrialized world. Job security and rich benefit packages have disappeared from the workplace along with typewriters and dictaphones. Firms have repudiated long-term employment relationships and turned to other types of employment arrangements instead. The result is that today, having a job does not mean having job security or benefits – it means having a relationship with an employing entity that involves exchanging labor time for a wage for a finite and uncertain period of time. Even if the job continues over time, there is no assumption or reasonable expectation that it will do so.

1 Arjay and Frances Miller Distinguished Professor of Law, UCLA School of Law.

These changes in the nature of employment are undermining the current labor regulatory arrangements throughout the industrialized world. The institutions and laws that organized and governed employment relationships for the past century are being dismantled. Those laws that remain are no longer adequate to address the issues and needs of large sectors of the population. Precarious work in all its guises is increasing rapidly, generating instability, insecurity, and frustration for individuals, and threatening disruption in the social fabric.

This chapter describes the changes that have taken place in employment practices and regulation in advanced industrial countries. It first canvasses employment trends to show that job security and the other features of the standard contract of employment are fading. It then describes some measures undertaken in some countries and regions to try to protect workers and to ameliorate the insecurity that present and human resource practices generate. It concludes by considering what countries can learn from ameliorative policies and programs in other countries.

I. The standard contract of employment

The standard contract of employment became the norm in large manufacturing firms throughout much of the 20th century. This form of employment did not emerge fully formed. It was created by large manufacturing firm human resource practices, bolstered by pressures from unions, and fortified by the various labor law regimes in the industrial nations. Gradually, over the first half of the 20th century, legal regimes that regulated employment emerged in various countries that adopted the standard employment model as their template. As a result, by the mid-20th century, most industrial nations had labor law systems that provided extensive protection for job security by statute, contract, or custom. Most countries also had laws fostering company or industry level collective bargaining between companies and unions whose members who had long-term jobs. Most countries also had laws that limited the types of permissible employment contracts and placed strict limits on the ability of firms to utilize temporary workers, short-term workers, or independent contractors.

Although the basic shape of the standard employment contract was similar in the various countries, the legal regimes that emerged to support it differed markedly from country to country. In some countries, the state mandated job security by statute, in others, job security was negotiated as part of a state-supported system of collective bargaining, and in others, it was a product of custom reinforced by legal mechanisms. Moreover, in some countries, the state used tax revenues to provide a broad spectrum of work-related benefits such as skills training, employment insurance, job placement centers, and day care, as well as universal benefits to workers and others, such as health care, social housing, and education. In other countries, many of these benefits were provided by employers, under compulsion of law, in response to pressures brought by unions through collective bargaining, or as part of a strategy to recruit and retain a loyal and productive workforce.

To be sure, the standard employment contract was never universal. In each country, it covered different portions of the workforce, and within the workforce, different sectors and segments. It was more characteristic of large manufacturing enterprises and the public sector than it was of small enterprises or the service sector, more likely to cover men than women, and more available to well-established populations than recent immigrants or racial and ethnic minorities. Nonetheless, allowing for all these variations, the standard employment contract was both the paradigm that informed much labor policy and practice and the ideal to which these aspired.

In the past two decades, the standard employment contract has declined in importance. Many industrialized countries have deregulated their labor markets, repealed labor laws, relaxed employee protections, and reduced state-provided or state-mandated benefits of all kinds. In part, these changes have coincided with changes in the global political economy. Market fundamentalist ideology, trade liberalization programs, and fiscal austerity measures have attracted the support of governments, political parties, academic thinkers, and policy communities across the developed world. In part, they have coincided with major changes in the strategy and ideology of management.

Globalization has driven many of these changes. As current trading regimes took shape in the 1980s and 1990s, firms that had stable market shares found their market positions challenged by foreign competition. The drive to capture markets and cut costs led firms to rethink their human resource strategies. In doing so, they repudiated the stable long-term employment relationships they had maintained and instead sought to streamline their operations by making their workforce, as well as their product offerings and supply sourcing, flexible.

Technology has enabled many of these changes. Firms are responding more quickly to a wider variety of market signals, replacing human operatives with digitized machinery, and dispersing operations down a supply chain of local and offshore feeder firms. Each of these developments has had obvious implications for the way workforces are recruited, trained, managed, and disposed of – and for the relevance of the standard employment contract.

Technology has also driven change. Firms engaged in a determined quest for a competitive edge in a globalized world believe that they must enhance their capacity for innovation. Innovation requires that, at any given moment, firms must be able to mobilize an array of relevant skills to perform new tasks at a cost that gives them a competitive edge. Given rapidly changing technology and markets, skill requirements shift quickly, frequently requiring differently skilled employees and making incumbent ones unnecessary.

These changes have created a new and constantly evolving international division of labor, as low-skill, low-wage functions are relocated to the developing world, while those requiring greater sophistication or proximity to head offices are retained in more advanced economies. In such a scenario, long-term, locally based employees – the beneficiaries of the standard employment contract – often come to be seen as a costly burden rather than an asset. In general, flexibility has replaced stability in the lexicon of corporate managers.

Because of globalization and new technological developments, firms have repudiated long-term employment promises and instead have developed a variety of short-term, episodic employment relationships (Stone and Arthurs, 2013). For example, the percentage of workers on fixed-term – i.e. temporary – contracts more than doubled in Spain, France, the Netherlands, and Italy between 1985 and 2003. There were also substantial increases in the percentage of temporary employment in Germany, Finland, Sweden, and Portugal during the same period (Schmidt, 2008). The percentage of casual employment in Australia also nearly doubled between 1982 and 2004 (Campbell and Peter Brosnan, 2005). A similar trend was apparent in Japan, which experienced a 25% increase in the ratio of non-regular workers to regular workers in the five-year period from 1999 to 2005, so that overall, approximately one third of the Japanese workforce is currently in non-standard employment (Japan Institute for Labour Policy and Training, 2006).

Concomitantly, there has been a sea change in individual employees' experiences and career expectations. Most individuals are no longer employed by a single firm for their entire career. Many older workers are forced to change jobs, despite their earlier expectations of career stability, or forced into early and often poorly pensioned retirement. Many younger workers expect to, and do, change jobs more frequently than their predecessors (Kurz, 2008). Most also recognize that they have to retrain periodically in order to remain employable. Many workers, especially younger workers, see themselves as free agents who sell their knowledge, skill, and talent in a fluid labor market. Just as firms no longer demonstrate long-term attachment to their workers, many workers have no expectation or desire to spend their entire lives with one employer. They may, in fact, end up staying with a single firm for a long period, but this is not their initial, nor their ongoing, expectation.

The result of these changes is that, for an increasing number of workers, employment is no longer the open-ended long-term relationship of the standard employment contract, but rather a temporary, episodic arrangement that might or might not be renewed from time to time. For example, in Australia, the categories of full-time casual work and part-time permanent work *each* grew by more than 200% between 1992 and 2007 (Campbell et al., 2009). In most countries in Europe, the changes were equally dramatic. Temporary employment in France and Italy increased from under 5% of the workforce to nearly 15% between 1985 and 2009. In Germany, it went from 10% to 15% in the same period. In the Netherlands, temporary employment as a percentage of the workforce increased from 8% to nearly 20%, and in Spain, it increased from 15% to 25%. Only in the UK and Denmark, did the percentage of workers in temporary employment decline in that same period (European Commission, 2004; Stone and Arthurs, 2013).

The statistics reflect a change in life experiences for a large percentage of the population. For example, the number of young persons who have permanent employment has declined markedly in most advanced countries. Individuals today can expect a series of jobs throughout their work lives and a series of relationships to the labor market. They move between firms, between employment and unemployment, in and out of self-employment, and in and out of training. Employees no longer expect job security from their employers, and firms no longer hire for life and train from within. Rather, they hire specific skills on an as-needed basis from the external labor market. Furthermore, firms increasingly use temporary workers, short-term workers, leased workers, and independent contractors in lieu of regular employees. The new labor market rewards skill, flexibility, adaptability, and entrepreneurial self-marketing. It no longer seeks, nor does it value, long-term, stable employment relationships.

II. The regulatory vacuum

Throughout the latter half of the 20th century, most countries in the industrialized world had labor law regimes that supported the standard contract of employment. Different countries used different mixes of regulation, bargaining, and custom to provide workers with job security, steady incomes, social insurance, and other benefits. Despite numerous variations and many shortcomings, domestic labor law in the industrialized world protected workers by making employment conditions stable, reliable, and predictable. The labor law systems were one aspect of the prevailing Keynesian approach to economic policy, and they operated to raise wages and stabilize aggregate demand.

The labor law regimes reflected prevailing human resource theories that counseled firms to organize work into stable, long-term relationships arranged in internal labor markets. These theories were developed by Frederick Winslow Taylor, the US engineer who fathered "scientific management," and the personnel management theorists of the early 20th century (Jacoby, 1985; Stone, 1975, 2004). The theories spread throughout the industrialized world, influencing employment practices from Europe to Japan and Australia (Merkle, 1980).

The labor law regimes that emerged varied from country to country, but almost all of them were based upon employees having long-term, stable employment contracts with a single employer. For example, in the US, the New Deal labor law – the National Labor Relations Act – organized collective bargaining rights according to stable bargaining units within firms. The law assumed employees had long-term employment relationships and facilitated unionization for employees in large firms that offered long-term employment (Stone, 2004). Although the US does not have any statutory protection against unjust dismissal, most unions negotiated "just cause" protection in their collective agreements, thereby providing job security to those workers, usually in large firms, who successfully unionized.

In parts of continental Europe such as Spain and France, unfair dismissal laws were enacted that made it nearly impossible to dismiss employees, giving them *de facto* job tenure. In other parts of Europe, including Germany, extension laws made collectively bargained job security arrangements applicable to whole sectors of the economy. And in Japan, a culture of long-term employment that developed after World War II was reinforced by judicial decisions granting protection against dismissal. The only major exception was Australia, where there was no culture or law providing job security and enterprise-level bargaining was uncommon. Instead, the

Australian arbitration and award system provided sector-wide uniform employment terms that offered not employer-based, but sector-based job protection.

In addition to encouraging long-term employment, most legal regimes discouraged or even prohibited any other forms of employment. For example, in Japan short-term employment was heavily regulated. The Labor Standards Law (LSL) enacted in 1947 only permitted employers to hire employees on fixed term contracts lasting up to one year in duration. This law was not relaxed until 1998. Similarly, until 1985, the Japanese Employment Security Law (ESL) prohibited, as "illegal supply projects" any arrangement by which a worker is hired by one entity and performs work under the supervision of another. The type of relationship the law proscribes is the triangular employment relationship typical of temporary help, employee leasing, and worker dispatching industries. Thus, Japan did not merely regulate third party employment relationships, such as temporary agencies, it prohibited them (Araki, 2002).

In the late 20th century, these labor laws came under attack as the intensified competitive environment created by liberalized trade regimes and new production technologies put pressures on firms to streamline their operations, downsize their work forces, and hone their product offerings to a fickle and unforgiving marketplace. In their efforts to make these changes, firms found domestic labor laws to be a major impediment. Furthermore, the eclipse of Keynesianism by supply-side economic theories undercut the rationale for regulation that fostered a high-wage middle class. By the end of the 20th century, pressures from the business communities converged with changing attitudes amongst the public, inducing politicians to dismantle labor protections and revise the labor laws.

Accordingly, over the past two decades, the labor laws in industrialized countries have changed in tandem with changes in work practices. Countries have relaxed their dismissal protections and expanded the types of non-standard employment relationships that are permissible. For example, Japan has enacted several laws in the past few years that together have created an external labor market to enable firms to hire laterally for skills that they cannot obtain in-house. Beginning in 1985, a series of laws relaxed the prohibition on use of temporary employment. And since 1998, it has expanded the ability of employers to hire workers on fixed-term contracts. In addition, Japan has legalized private job placement services to enable workers to initiate mid-career job moves. New court decisions have relaxed the circumstances in which firms can dismiss workers for economic reasons. Another new law has modified the previous rigid limitations on working hours and facilitated the use of incentive-based pay. In addition, in 2004, the Diet created a new dispute resolution tribunal that enables individual workers to bring claims when they feel that their employment rights have been violated. Subsequently, in 2007, the Diet enacted an individual employment contract law that gives workers the ability to negotiate individual employment terms. Also in 2007, Japan revised its minimum wage law to eliminate the role of collective bargaining in establishing industry minimums. These and other changes make it an open question whether Japan's longstanding tradition of secure, lifetime jobs with seniority-based pay will survive.

Similarly, dramatic changes have occurred in Australia. In 2005, Australia abandoned its longstanding employment arbitration and award system after a fifteen-year process in which the system had been gradually diluted. The award system had made Australia one of the most egalitarian societies in the industrialized world for one hundred years. The modifications began in the 1980s and gained strength in the 1990s by measures that permitted awards to be superseded by collective bargaining and individual employment contracts. The 2005 Work Choices Act not only dismantled the award system, it also radically individualized the employment relationship. It contained measures that made it a crime to engage in collective efforts to set employment terms. After the election of a labor government in 2007, Australia embarked on a process of revising its entire regulatory regime. The new labor laws enacted did not reinstate the former award system, but instead enacted a new system that combined collective bargaining with a set of universally applicable individual employment guarantees.

Throughout Europe, the issue of flexibility and labor law reform are currently a subject of intense dispute, both within the European Union (EU) and individual nations. The EU has recently adopted measures to grant employers increased flexibility to use non-standard workers and make it easier for employers to terminate workers in the event of business exigencies. At the same time, the EU has strengthened some forms of job protection in an effort to devise a new set of policies that combine flexibility with security (Muffels, 2008).

Tensions between flexibility and security are also playing out inside the EU member states. For example, in France in 2006, the government proposed new forms of flexible work contracts that triggered widespread demonstrations in opposition. The proposed legislation would have enabled employers to dismiss an employee under the age of twenty-six during the first two years of employment without having to go through the cumbersome and expensive dismissal proceedings required by French labor law. Over 2.5 million workers and students went on strike in protest. Although the protests caused the government to withdraw that legislative proposal, similar legislation to make work flexible and relax restrictions on dismissals has been enacted in recent years.

In the past two decades, Germany has relaxed its legal restrictions on the use of short-term contracts and temporary agency work. It has also relaxed its dismissal protections. In the early 2000s, it enacted a series of reforms to the unemployment system, called the Harz reforms, which had the effect of expanding the low-wage sector and pushing many jobless workers into the precarious, low-wage labor market. It also created a new category of work, called "mini-jobs," which usually pay poorly and carry no right to social insurance benefits.

In Italy, a law was proposed in 2002 that which would have relaxed dismissal protection for workers in small establishments. The law would have permitted employers with less than fifteen employees to dismiss their workers without the extensive "just cause" protection required by Italian labor law. The purpose of the law was to give small employers flexibility so that they would have an incentive to hire more employees. Over three million workers struck in protest, and the proposal was rescinded (Henneberger, 2002). Nonetheless, the following year, Italy enacted a major revision to its labor laws. The Biagi reforms created over forty new types of lawful types of employment contracts in Italy – a big change from the former one-size-fits-all standard open-ended employment contract of the past (Tiraboschi, 2005).

In Spain, until 1984, it was a fundamental legal principle that employment contracts had to be open-ended. Temporary or fixed-term contracts were forbidden except for a small number of discrete types of tasks. In 1984, a significant change to the law made it possible for employers to utilize temporary workers for any task for up to a maximum of three years. The 1984 law also created special fixed-term contracts for training young people and for launching new activities. Subsequent changes relaxed the job security of "permanent" workers. In 1994, a major change to the labor law made it easier for firms to dismiss regular employees for economic reasons. That year, a reform also legalized temporary employment agencies for the first time. As a result, employers have greatly expanded their use temporary contracts. Currently, Spain has the largest percentage of its workforce in temporary employment of any country in Western Europe (Hernandez, 2008).

In Sweden, where industrial relations are primarily a matter of negotiated agreements rather than legislation, there have been attempts to enact legislation to permit more flexibility, especially by relaxing protection for job security. Further, there have been changes in the law to permit increased use of fixed-term employment contracts, and there are proposals by the government to further liberalize the use of short-term temporary workers (Nyström, 2006). In addition, two court decisions in 2003 and 2004 by the Swedish Labor Court permitted employers to substitute contract workers for regular employees despite legislation and collective agreements to the contrary (Danhard, 2006).

As the labor laws have changed, employers' use of temporary agencies, short-term contract workers, on-call workers, and independent contractors has accordingly expanded. For example, between 2004 and 2007, the amount of temporary agency work increased 53% in Germany, 48% in the Netherlands, 70% in Sweden, 27% in Belgium, 40% in Ireland, and a whopping 133% in Greece (European Foundation for the Improvement of Living and Working Conditions, 2009). Similarly, the number of temporary agency workers in Japan skyrocketed once legal restrictions on temporary work were relaxed in 1998, more than doubling in numbers between 1998 and 2006 (Japan Ministry of Labor, Health and Welfare, 2006). So too has the use of outsourcing, in-sourcing, and subcontracting, all contributing to the demise of the standard employment contract.

These changes in employment relations obviously have different consequences in countries where workers are dependent on their direct employer for benefits and job security than in countries in which the state provides extensive benefits directly to workers or requires employers to do so. In the former countries, unions have been weakened through changes in labor laws as well as through the decline in working class identity, culture, and solidarity. In the latter ones, changes in the global political economy and in local political cultures have led governments across the political spectrum to weaken programs designed to buffer workers from the consequences of unemployment and other job-related misfortunes.

The combined effect of these developments, at least in the advanced economies, is that workers have experienced flat or declining real wages, reduced social protection, diminished political influence, and a declining capacity to defend their own interests through industrial action. According to the OECD (2007b), the wage share of national income in the OECD countries has dropped from 67% to below 60% between 1975 and 2005.

III. Dismantling job security and shifting employment risks

Countries throughout the developed world have enacted new labor laws in order to provide firms with flexibility in their work forces so they can reduce costs, foster innovation, and respond nimbly to fast changing product market trends. However, the regulatory changes have diluted the preexisting mechanisms for job and income security. Some of the changes have been the following:

- dismantling or relaxing employment security protections,
- permitting numerous types of short-term employment,
- expanding the use of temporary workers and independent contractors,
- breaking the norm of uniformity in pay and benefits, and
- changing compensation systems so that pay is aligned with market rather than institutional factors.

One consequence of the new employment regimes has been a rise in precarious employment. More and more, workers are hired on temporary or fixed-term contracts, without any hope of regular employment. The new "precariat" move in and out of the labor market, earning low wages when they have work and putting strains on public welfare and health care systems when they do not (Standing, 2011; Thornley et al., 2010). In Japan, it is estimated that up to a million young people have lost hope of long-term job prospects and have retreated entirely from social life, staying at home and in their bedroom alone for months or even years (Kremer and Hammond, 2013).

The rise of precarious employment has been accompanied by a growing chasm between regular employees and non-regular ones. This is the phenomenon known as "labor market dualism," a condition in which a privileged group of workers has well-paid secure jobs, while the rest of the labor force has intermittent, low-paid work in dead-end jobs. As many countries in Europe have discovered, extreme labor market dualism threatens social cohesion. Often the non-regular employees are members of marginalized groups, such as youth, immigrants, racial, ethnic, or religious minorities, the elderly, and women. In some parts of Europe, growing labor market dualism has dovetailed with tensions about immigration, religion, and ethnicity to create an explosive mix of social problems.

For individuals, the new labor practices mean that they bear many risks that used to be borne by the firm. Workers now face increased risk of job loss, and with it, the loss of those forms of social insurance that are employer-based. In many countries, therefore, job loss means loss of health insurance and pensions. Moreover, workers who have jobs face the risk of uncertain pay and promotion prospects, making it difficult to obtain credit or start a family. All workers risk the loss of the value of their labor market skills because as jobs are redefined, skill requirements shift. The previous training mechanisms no longer suffice to keep workers up-to-date, so incumbent workers can no longer compete with newcomers.

Another consequence of the changing nature of work is a decline of unions. In the 20th century, unions in most countries were organized to represent workers in stable jobs with long-term employment. As work practices become precarious, unions – as we have known them – decline. Union decline affects not only workplace-specific concerns – it also affects the quality of democratic governance. Unions provide workplace voice and their presence enables workers to experience at least a modicum of participation in their everyday life. Without participation and voice, civic engagement is diminished.

The decline of unions also contributes to growing income inequality. As firms abandon institutional and union-negotiated compensation practices and shift to market-based and performance-based pay, wage differentials escalate. The use of benchmarking – a practice that imports external labor market wage differentials into the firm – testifies to the increase in market measures rather than internal institutional measures for establishing pay (Capelli and Neumark, 2001). Furthermore, the decline of unions also means that the wage compression effect of unions is no longer operative.

Labor market policies are unlikely to return to the protective regimes of the 20th century. Pressures from international competition and globalized production are transforming employment relationships in ways that make the labor protections of the past unworkable. Rather, it is necessary to invent a new regulatory framework that can promote fairness at work and a new type of social safety net to address problems associated with the contemporary labor market.

IV. Green shoots

In addition to its destabilizing tendencies, the process of globalization has opened up policy space for experimentation in the area of employment regulation at the national and subnational levels. Countries are reconsidering their longstanding regulatory frameworks, and in so doing, permitting new ideas, approaches, and considerations to take root. Thus, there are a number of "green shoots" of policy experimentation in a number of places. Some countries, regions, and sub-regions, as well as some theorists, are devising or proposing new approaches to labor regulation that can facilitate flexibility and innovative economic performance for firms without sacrificing worker security.

Some of the labor policy green shoots involve mechanisms to assist people during work-life transitions, such as new types of social safety nets that provide for assistance for transitions into, out of, and within the labor market. Others involve new regional institutions to offer employers flexibility while providing new types of protective labor market measures for employees at the local and regional levels. Yet others involve new forms of worker activism and representation that engage multiple employers across multiple sectors of the economy. Some involve new types of worker training and unemployment programs. Still others involve new types of dispute resolution that enable individual workers to enforce employment rights in tribunals that are located outside the workplace. These and other green shoots are attempts to find more efficient and flexible regulatory strategies that nonetheless can plausibly claim to produce results for workers comparable to those they enjoyed under the old employment arrangements.

In 2010, Harry Arthurs, Canada's leading labor law scholar and I brought together labor experts from ten key countries to compare and evaluate institutional innovations in labor markets in advanced economies. With the help of the Rockefeller Foundation, the Russell Sage Foundation, Osgood Hall Law School, and UCLA Institute for Research on Labor and Employment, we held a conference at the Rockefeller Conference Center in Bellagio, in September 2010. There, nineteen scholars in eight different fields and from ten countries explored changes in the nature of work and new regulatory approaches to address the new challenges in each of the ten countries represented. The results of our collaborative work were published by the Russell Sage Foundation Press in February 2013 in a book entitled "*Rethinking Workplace Regulation: Beyond the Standard Contract of Employment.*"

In the book, each author reported on experimental forms of regulatory intervention in their national settings to rebalance firm flexibility and worker security so as to retain the dynamism of flexible work practices while also maintaining social stability and a legitimate social order. Not all the experiments discussed were successful. Failures can be as instructive as successes in their power to reveal previously unknown complexities and practical limits. Indeed, failure and success are interlinked and necessary aspects of any new strategy. Below I describe some of our findings.

A. The emerging plural forms of employment contracts

As explained above, until recently, most European countries placed strict limitations on the lawful forms of employment contracts. They required that all employment take the form of a standard open-ended contract with iron-clad protections against dismissal. But in recent years, several countries have introduced other types of permissible employment contracts that relax job security protection but add new features in its stead. For example, in Italy, there are forty different lawful types of employment contracts, some of which give workers some employment protection while also giving employers flexibility to redesign employment relationships. These include training contracts, transitional contracts, provisional contracts, and contracts with graduated security, amongst others. Some countries have developed a new legal category, variously called "quasi-employee," "freelance worker," or "dependent contractor," which expand employment protections to non-regular and heretofore excluded categories of employees (Caruso, 2013).

Oxford Professor Mark Freedland (2003) has proposed a further development – that we adopt a concept of a contract for intermittent employment as a mechanism to provide some employment protections even when workers make transitions in their working lives. The new forms of contracts are designed to provide firms with flexibility to utilize short-term workers and project workers. In that sense, they have the potential of impairing job security and degrading labor standards. For example, the new German "mini-jobs" permit employers to hire short-hours workers and avoid paying full social benefits. Mini-jobs offer workers no protection against dismissal, the jobs tend to be low paid, and they are the fastest growing part of the German labor market (Kemmerling and Bruttel, 2006).

Despite the weakening of job security characteristics of most new types of employment contracts, some have provisions that are designed to provide workers with another form of security known as "employability." For example, some forms of employment contracts available for younger workers mandate that the employer provide training, so that workers receive skills that can serve them throughout their careers. In Italy, the government gives tax subsidies to firms that agree to provide worker training to young workers. Another type of reform is a contract that subsidizes retraining for workers who become technologically unemployed so they can obtain skills in new, rising industries. Overall, the new forms of employment contracts promote a variety of employment arrangements that depart from standard full-time employment, such as probationary employment, combinations of work with training, voluntary work, and unpaid work experience placements.

In the main, unions have opposed most, if not all, the new forms of employment contracts precisely because they fail to provide job security. Nonetheless, when such contracts are coupled with training mandates, they can help workers at all ages and career stages weather the winds of change.

Several countries have also attempted to transform the employment contracts of atypical workers by mandating that atypical workers receive the same terms of employment as regular workers. For example, amidst the rapid increase in the number of part-time workers in the Netherlands, the Dutch legislature passed a statute called the Prohibition of Discrimination in Working Hours Act in 1996 that required employers to provide part-time workers with the same pay and benefits (pro rata) as full-time workers (Visser, 2013). Subsequently, in 1999, the EU adopted the Fixed Term Directive that required member states to enact mechanisms to give fixed-term workers equal pay with open-term employees. These kinds of measures help regularize atypical employment by giving atypical employees the same aspects of the emoluments that typical employees enjoy. However, they do not ensure that atypical workers have job security or adequate annual incomes.

B. Flexicurity

At the same time that the job security protections and centralized bargaining systems in Europe are breaking apart, Europe has become a laboratory of experimentation and diversity in the area of employment regulation. While some of the reforms are designed to assist employers by making labor markets more flexible and thereby remove impediments to job creation and economic efficiency widely attributed to 20th century social protections, some of the reforms attempt to preserve the livelihoods of citizens who are threatened by changing corporate human resource practices. These latter efforts are often grouped under the general heading of "flexicurity."

The EU advocated flexicurity policies in its 2007 and 2008 *Employment in Europe* reports. The reports defined flexicurity as "a high level of employment security, that is the possibility to easily find a job at every stage of active life and have a good prospect for career development in a quickly changing economic environment" (Keune, 2007). As the definition makes clear, the goal of flexicurity is not to foster a continuous job with a particular employer, nor to recreate the job security systems of the past. Rather, the goal of flexicurity is to devise new employment relationships that combine flexibility for employers with livelihood security for employees. The reports called for new institutions and governance in both labor relations and labor markets that develop employees' labor market prospects throughout their working lives.

Flexicurity is a deliberately vague concept that is meant to encourage local diversity and experimentation. In recent years, several European countries have attempted to implement the flexicurity mandate. Some countries have attempted to provide flexicurity by relaxing restrictions on working hours, revising entitlements for leave, and requiring lifelong education and training. For example, in several countries, employers and workers can agree to establish "time banks" by which a worker can work longer hours than otherwise permitted for limited periods of time in exchange for shorter hours or time off at another time. German unions have negotiated "working time corridors" with employers to escape the rigid restrictions imposed by overtime rules, thereby enabling employers and workers to restructure their working time to meet production or personal needs (Haipeter, 2013).

The best known example of flexicurity is the approach to employment regulation and social protection developed by the Nordic countries of Denmark, Sweden, Norway, and Finland. While each of the Nordic countries differs, their employment systems have several common features, including high union density, strong unions committed to solidaristic wage policies, centralized wage setting devices, relatively egalitarian wage structures, and the use of collective bargaining rather than legislation to set most terms of employment. The Nordic countries devote vast sums to education, worker training, and public welfare programs. They also provide workers with a high level of unemployment benefits combined with labor market activation measures to assist unemployed workers during labor market transitions. For example, Denmark's unemployment system gives unemployed workers approximately 80% wage replacement coupled with extensive labor market activation measures that require unemployed workers to undergo training to upgrade their skills. The system also provides unemployed workers with job opportunities and pays for education, training, relocation, and other job-related expenses. Thus while Denmark does not provide its workers with statutory protection for job security, Danish workers have assurances that they will have adequate incomes and valuable training when they change jobs. As a result, Danish workers change jobs more frequently than do other workers in Europe, and Danish companies are able to automate and change workplace practices without engendering opposition from the national unions.

Another well-known example of flexicurity is found in the Netherlands. There, flexicurity has been directed toward facilitating part-time work opportunities, particularly for women with child care responsibilities who previously had been either excluded from the labor market or relegated to marginal jobs. A series of laws and national-level agreements between the unions and employers' associations eased the transition from non-work to part-time work and enabled part-time workers to increase and decrease their hours to adapt to care work demands. There were also laws that regularized the pay and benefits of part-time workers by requiring employers to give part-time workers parity with full-time workers, as mentioned above.

Flexicurity has also been furthered in the Netherlands by the use of minimal terms and framework collective bargaining agreements. These forms of agreements permit unions and management to negotiate plant-level terms that deviate from uniform terms set nationally. By decentralizing collective bargaining, unions and management can negotiate a variety of measures at the plant level to give firms more flexibility over issues such as working time and sickness and accident leave (Visser, 2013).

C. Redesigning unemployment insurance and severance pay

Some countries have made adjustments to their public programs for unemployment compensation, severance benefits, and labor market reentry after child rearing in order to enable individuals to move between jobs and between jobs and non-work statuses. At the same time, many countries have made access to unemployment assistance conditional on participation in work or training programs. Some further couple unemployment compensation with relocation assistance to enable workers to assume new types of jobs and careers. Others have restructured systems that provide severance pay. Severance pay is designed to assist workers who lose their jobs, but in the past, payments have often been structured to discourage job changing and hence lock workers in to dead-end jobs in declining industries. To combat these rigidities, Austria implemented a new severance pay scheme in 2003 that was designed to facilitate job mobility by removing penalties for frequent job changers and enabling all workers to build up rainy day savings.

As with the new forms of employment contracts, the changes to benefit systems have been controversial. And as with the new types of employment contracts discussed above, the devil is in the details. For example, the Hartz reforms to the German unemployment system in the early 2000s engendered bitter opposition and conflict because they not only curtailed the duration of unemployment benefits, they also pushed workers into low-wage jobs. Nonetheless, as the Danish example shows, some types of unemployment insurance programs can provide workers with enhanced career opportunities and facilitate upward rather than downward mobility.

D. New forms of transition assistance and new types of social insurance

In many countries, health benefits, old age assistance, and other forms of social insurance are linked to employment, and as a result, they fail to address the needs of today's mobile workers. For example, in the US, neither the social welfare laws nor the labor laws have focused on the problem of transitions. Moreover, US unions do not negotiate with employers to provide post-employment assistance because once workers lose their jobs, they also lose their union membership and their contract rights.

Because most workers today can expect to experience discontinuities in their labor market experiences, we need social assistance programs that provide for workers and their families during gaps and transitions in their labor market experience. The inevitability of gaps in employment means that any such program must be part of a new type of social safety net, one that is delinked from any particular employer and that provides protection for workers during periods of transition and for those workers who have atypical or discontinuous labor market affiliations (O'Donnell, 2013). The new safety net will have to offer portable health benefits and provide lifetime training and retraining opportunities, universal and adequate old age assistance, and other forms of assistance for individuals who are moving between jobs, between jobs and unemployment, between jobs and training, and during periods of care work.

Australia has developed the beginnings of such a new safety net. Its social assistance program provides a generous means-tested, flat rate benefit to those out of work for any reason. Eligibility does not depend upon a specific period of time spent in the labor market, and the amount of benefits is not pegged to prior earnings. The benefits are also tapered once a recipient has a job, so they do not provide a disincentive for taking a job. The benefits are financed from general tax revenues. Because the Australian tax system is highly progressive and because the benefits are means tested, they have a redistributive impact. However, because most people can expect to draw on the benefit at some points in their life course – for child rearing, unemployment, retraining – the system acts as an income-smoothing device.

The issue of transition assistance has been actively considered in Europe. A group of distinguished labor relations experts was convened by the European Commission in 1999 to consider the implications of the changing nature of work. The group, chaired by French labor law professor Alain Supiot, was charged with considering the impact of changes in the workplace on labor regulation in Europe and to devise proposals for reform. In 2000, the group issued a report, known as the Supiot Report. The Supiot Report contained a number of suggestions for changes in the institutions regulating work to provide active security, of which the most visionary proposal was for the creation of "social drawing rights" to facilitate worker mobility and to enable workers to weather transitions. Under the proposal, an individual would accumulate social drawing rights on the basis of time spent at work. The drawing rights could be used for paid leave for purposes of obtaining training, working in the family sphere, or performing charitable or public service work. It would be a right that the individual could invoke on an optional basis to navigate career transitions, thereby giving flexibility and security in an era of uncertainty. Social drawing rights, its proponents claim, would smooth these transitions and give individuals the resources to retool and to weather the unpredictable cycles of today's workplace (Supiot, 2001).

The Supiot Report did not address the question of who would pay for the social drawing rights. One possibility is that it be paid out of general tax revenues. Another is that it be paid by employers as a form of mandatory paid-in leave.

Australia has long had a form of leave that resembles the Supiot proposal for social drawing rights. In Australia, employees are entitled to long service leave after they have been with the same employer for a fixed period of time. The particulars of long service leave are set by each state or by awards and collective agreements, and the time requirement for eligibility is between seven and fifteen years. Employees who reach the requisite time are entitled to a period of time off – usually three to six months – at regular pay (FairWork Ombudsman, 2014; O'Donnell, 2013). Although long service leave is currently designed to reward continuous service with a single employer, it is a concept that could be adapted to current employment practices. If individuals were able to accumulate leave time by working for a number of employers and tacking together their various stints in the labor market, then long service leave could become a vehicle to enable individuals to periodically retool and reinvent their careers.

In the US, there are precedents for the concept of paid time off with reemployment rights to facilitate career transitions or life emergencies. There are well-established precedents for paid leaves for military service, maternity, jury duty, union business, and other socially valuable activities. Some occupations also offer periodic sabbatical leaves. The concept is also built into the idea of temporary disability in state workers compensation and other insurance programs, which provide compensation and guarantee reemployment after temporary absences. These programs acknowledge the importance of subsidized time away from the workplace to enable employees to make a greater contribution to the workplace. They could serve as the basis for developing a more generalized concept of career transition leave, or to use more familiar parlance, a workplace sabbatical. Indeed, it could take the form that is currently used for unemployment compensation, where employers contribute to a fund which workers can draw on once they satisfy the eligibility criteria (Stone, 2004).

E. New regional labor market institutions

In the past fifteen years, there have developed new local and regional institutions that attempt to protect labor rights and at the same time strengthen local economies. One such institution, found in Italy, Spain, the UK and some other European countries, are local and territorial social pacts (Regalia, 2013). The pacts are established as a result of negotiations between local labor groups, local employers, and local government officials. They set local labor market policy, addressing issues such as unemployment insurance arrangements, worker training programs, and other labor market measures. In some cases, the territorial pacts are negotiated not only by the traditional social partners – employers' associations and trade unions – but also with participation by civic groups and other organized local constituencies. The territorial pacts receive funding from the EU structural funds as well as their national governments to invest in infrastructure and regional economic development. As Italian legal scholar, Bruno Caruso (2001), writes:

> [Territorial employment pacts in Italy have] fostered territorial bargaining in the so-called economy of "districts" . . . which often correspond to sectors traditionally featuring small firms or craftsmen (textiles, furniture, building, tourism). . . . [Territorial bargaining has involved a] bilateral partnership but at a territorial rather than industry or plant level, to support the competitiveness of micro firms by injecting a heavy dose of flexibility (as regards working hours, wages, and geographic location) into both the internal and external labor market. These measures are almost always accompanied by others supporting income levels if not permanent employment security.
>
> *(p. 210)*

There is some debate about the effectiveness of local forms of bargaining, but many observers acknowledge that they are a promising means to improve local economic performance while at the same time providing employment protection to local populations (Regalia, 2013).

In addition to territorial pacts, another territorially based labor market institution has emerged in some parts of France and Italy, where employers have formed cooperative associations to share their workforces. These associations are formed by employers who have seasonal or variable production schedules and flexible staffing needs, yet require workers with particular skills that they do not want to lose when they institute layoffs during slack periods. In France, the associations, known as the *groupments d'emploi* (GdE), employ workers on behalf of all the member firms in a localized geographic area. Each employer in the GdE can utilize workers from the association as needed without establishing a direct employment relationship with any individual worker. The worker has an open-ended employment relationship with the GdE, and the GdE itself is the employer for purposes of labor rights and benefits. Sometimes the GdE also provides the workers with training.

The GdE is similar to a US union hiring hall in that employers only hire on an as-needed basis and workers do not have ongoing relationships with a particular employer. And, like a hiring hall, the wages and benefits of the workers are set uniformly for all the firms, so that the firms do not compete with each other over wages. However, unlike a hiring hall, the workers in a GdE have steady jobs with steady income and benefits. The GdE, not the particular firm, gives workers a standard contract of employment. The worker thereby receives substantially more job, wage, and benefit security than they would either in a hiring hall or in the unmediated labor market.

F. Resolving disputes in a new world of work – new modes of workplace dispute resolution systems

Workplace dispute resolution systems evolved in an era of mass production industry, strong unions, and stable employment relationships. For example, the privatized labor arbitration system that developed under the Wagner Act model of collective bargaining in the US was responsive to the world of work of its era. Arbitration was developed as a mechanism to enable unions and employees to enforce the types of rights against their employer that were specified in collective bargaining agreements – rights to job security, pay raises, pensions, vacations, sick leave, and health benefits. These rights pertained to the working conditions and terms provided within a single employing unit. They were important to long-term employees who expected to stay with that employer for a long time (Stone, 2004).

As the organization of work has been changed in recent decades, these dispute resolution institutions are becoming outdated. As unions have declined, today's workplace disputes are primarily brought by individuals and involve individual claims of unfair treatment. Today, many disputes arise at the hiring stage, when individuals are either refused employment on allegedly discriminatory grounds, or are offered employment as temporary workers, independent contractors, or some other status that is inferior to that of a firm's "regular" employees. Many other disputes arise at the time of an employee's exit, when employers want to impose post-employment restrictive covenants in order to restrict its employees' ability to use intellectual property the worker acquired on the job. Other common disputes involve claims of unfair treatment on the job – the denial of a bonus or promotion to which an employee felt entitled. All advanced countries have experienced a large increase in individual workplace disputes of these types in recent decades (Colvin, 2013).

In response to the mushrooming of individual workplace disputes, many countries have revised their workplace dispute resolution institutions. The Anglo-American countries (the US, Canada, the UK, Australia, and New Zealand) have been the sites of a range of different institutional approaches. In the US, the most important development in workplace dispute resolution is the growth of a system of management-initiated privatized arbitration tribunals in non-union workplaces. These tribunals adjudicate claims of alleged violations of statutory employment rights in important areas of statutory regulation such as civil rights and minimum employment standards. By contrast, in the UK, an increase in the statutory regulation of employment has been accompanied by a system of public employment tribunals that are seeing increasing caseloads. Meanwhile, the recent enactment of major labor law reforms in Australia includes the establishment of an independent umpire structure, dubbed "Fair Work Australia," and a public Fair Work Ombudsman.

There have also been new directions in established dispute resolution institutions in some of the European countries. For example, the German system of labor courts has until recently received less attention than that country's works councils and codetermination systems, but their caseload for individual claims has mushroom in the past two decades. In response to the massive increase in termination cases brought to the Labor Courts, the Diet revised the Dismissal Protection Act in 2003 so that firms can now avoid judicial proceedings by offering severance payments to employees who agree to refrain from filing claims with the Labor Court.

In Japan, a new public system of labor tribunals was established in 2004 in order to give employees a mechanism to vindicate their individual employment rights outside their specific workplace. The system is designed to provide an alternative to the previous one in which the primary mechanisms for vindicating workplace rights were enterprise-specific and relied on enterprise unions. The new tribunals extend employment protection to employees who are not part of the lifetime employment system. Each tribunal comprises one judge and two lay judges – one appointed by the major union federation and the other by the major employer association. The tribunal holds three sessions in which it gathers facts, attempts to mediate the dispute, and failing that, conducts a hearing and issues an award. Parties then have two weeks to reject the award and take the case to the civil courts. If they do not do so, the award becomes binding.

The Japanese employment tribunals went into operation in 2006. In its first four years of operation, nearly 85% of cases either ended with an arbitral award to which neither party objected, or were settled by the parties. Only 15% went to the civil court. Moreover, the average time for the entire case from filing to completion was about two and a half months, far less than a proceeding in a civil court (Araki, 2013).

Across these various national systems, there are common themes: increasing dispute levels in the context of growing individualization of employment relations, and a shift from collective bargaining terms and conditions of employment to greater reliance on a basket of minimum rights provided by statutes. Many past workplace dispute resolution systems were tied to an individual employer. A major issue in the new world of work is to fashion workplace dispute resolution systems that can respond effectively to disputes involving multiple employers who jointly employ workers, such as subcontractors or networked models of production, and to address issues that arise for workers in the course of careers that span multiple employers.

G. New forms of collective bargaining to reconcile individual bargaining with collective rights

In their classic study of collective bargaining in the 1990s, "Converging Divergences," Harry Katz and Owen Darbishire (2000) reported that collective bargaining systems were undergoing revision throughout the developed world. The changes involved devolution away from centralized bargaining structures and the relocation of collective bargaining to the plant and even, in some cases, to the individual level. The decentralization process Katz and Darbishire described has continued into the present, but with some new permutations.

In Germany, starting in the late 1990s, some national sectoral agreements contained clauses that permitted local works councils to bargain with their individual companies on issues of incentive wages and working hours. Since then, it has become common for national unions to negotiate framework agreements and permit local works councils to negotiate terms that derogate from those in the applicable national or sectoral agreements. In addition, some industry agreements permit firms to negotiate with individual workers and to conclude individual agreements on wages and hours that vary from the terms of the collective agreements. To prevent a total erosion of collective agreements, the chemical workers' union and the metal workers' union developed standards for derogations and imposed coordination rules that give the national union final authority over which ones are approved (Haipeter, 2013).

The German experience of devolution of bargaining to the local and individual level and the derogation of collective terms by individual agreements is mirrored by similar new forms of bargaining in some sectors in Italy, Belgium, the Netherlands, and other places. For example, in the Netherlands, since the 1980s, unions and employers have expanded the types of collective agreements they negotiate. Previously they negotiated standard agreements that set terms and conditions either for a single company or a sector and did not permit deviations from the terms. Since the 1980s, they began to negotiate two other types of agreements – minimal term agreements that permit plant-level bargaining for upward deviations in favor of employees, and framework agreements that permit both upward and downward deviations by means of local bargaining. Some industry agreements have both types of provisions for particular specified areas. Some have a provision that permits individual workers to give up some money in exchange for reduced working time or paid leave (Visser, 2013).

The European experience of derogated bargaining has similarities to "embedded contract bargaining," which is used for craft workers in the entertainment industry in the US. In that industry, craft-based unions representing trades such as lighting design or sound engineering negotiate framework agreements with multi-employer groups. Once a worker is hired for a job, each makes their own bargain above the minimum specified in the framework agreement. The collective agreements do not offer workers job security, but they do provide them with a floor of minimum terms for each project and contributions to their benefit funds. Some of the unions also negotiate provisions that require employers to contribute to funds to training programs so the union members can keep their skills up-to-date (Stone, 2004).

These new forms of collective bargaining provide a mechanism to enable employers to avoid rigid one-size-fits-all employment terms and adapt employment hours and other conditions to changing operational needs. In the German case, some analysts have argued that these kinds of carve-outs represent the weakness of unions and the erosion of collective bargaining (Streeck, 2010). However, German labor sociologist Thomas Haipeter (2013) argues that there has been an unforeseen consequence of the devolution of bargaining to the plant level in Germany. He chronicles the growth of "local alliances" between management and works councils that have enabled works councils, now heavily dominated by the unions, to have input into new issues, including ongoing training, task qualification, the development of criteria for wage classification, and the use of teamwork. Even more significant, he claims, is the fact that the shift of the locus of bargaining to the local level has forced unions to encourage rank-and-file participation, which they have done by instituting grass roots mobilizations and conducting short-term strikes. Some unions have used their new-found clout at the local level to get employers to agree to innovate, make investments in research and development, and institute training and apprenticeship programs.

These new forms of bargaining, while risky for unions and still in experimental stages in many places, may provide a mechanism to reconcile individual bargaining with collective rights, thereby giving employers flexibility to individualize employment relationships while enabling workers to retain some of the benefits of having collective representation.

H. New forms of unions and employee organizations

In light of the decline of worker-firm attachment, workers need organizations that further their joint interests but that are not pegged to a particular employer. Because workers move between firms throughout their working lives, they need a mechanism that enables them to deploy their collective power in order to protect their terms and conditions across multiple employers. At the present time, some new types of labor organizations are forming that do just that. For example, in many US cities, unions have formed coalitions with community groups to enact living wage ordinances to improve labor standards for low-wage public sector employees citywide. Presently, there are living wage ordinances in over forty US cities. In addition, unions and community groups in Los Angeles, San Antonio, and some other cities have formed coalitions to negotiate agreements, called "community benefit agreements," with city authorities and private developers. These agreements obligate developers to create jobs and provide job training, local hiring preferences, affordable housing, social services, public parks, and other community improvements in exchange for the coalition's political support for development projects. There has also been organizing amongst immigrant workers within particular sectors. In many cities, worker centers have developed to inform low-wage workers, often immigrants, of their legal rights (Stone, 2013; Stone and Cummings, 2011).

In Japan, there has also been an explosion of non-traditional forms of labor organizations. In some urban areas, there are city unions that pressure employers in an entire metropolitan area around work-related concerns. There are also women's unions organized to further interests of women workers, and ethnically specific unions to assert pressure on behalf of specific ethnic groups. Unions of immigrant workers, organized by their country of origin, have also become prevalent in Japan. For example, there is a large union of Peruvian immigrant workers in a major working class suburb of Tokyo.

A particularly dynamic form of non-conventional unionism in Japan is the community union. These unions include part-time workers, temporary workers, immigrant workers, and others who are generally excluded from the traditional enterprise-based unions. In 1990, the Community Union National Network was formed to bring together seventy-two community unions that were operating in thirty different prefectures. These unions have continued to grow in membership and numbers, and some have affiliated with the National Confederation of Trade Unions or the Japanese Trade Union Congress. Community unions pressure local governments to adopt labor-friendly policies and they participate in community assistance organizations. They also advocate for policies to promote employment of the handicapped and elderly and provide a meeting place for retired union members. Some have advocated improvements in school lunch programs in order to improve the employment opportunities for women with children.

One particularly important role that community unions play is to advise individual workers who have job-related problems about how to resolve them in union committees, labor tribunals, or the courts. In some cases, the community union provides representation to individual workers in the new employment tribunals described above (Nakamura and Nitta, 2013).

The labor laws in most countries do not easily accommodate area-wide multi-employer, multi-sector bargaining, particularly when it involves union-community partnerships on one side, and multiple employers and city agencies on the other. However, organizations that engage in such efforts could provide important benefits for workers in today's labor market. Although workers change jobs more than in the past, a majority find new jobs in the same geographic area of their previous jobs. Hence, it would be desirable for labor laws to be designed to facilitate area-wide bargaining on such issues as minimum pay levels, health and pension benefits, leave policies, safety standards, job training programs, job transfer rights, and employment benefits at the local or regional levels.

V. Conclusion: legal transplantation and the prospects for cross-national legal learning

This chapter has described numerous initiatives that together comprise not one but a cluster of green shoots that have emerged in different countries in response to the challenges posed by the end of the standard employment contract and the spread of precarious, unpredictable, and non-standard forms of employment. It remains to ask whether any of these can be transplanted across national boundaries. It is a bedrock principle of comparative labor law that one cannot simply transfer an industrial relations system from one country to another. However, countries can learn from each other's successes and failures. Moreover, the experience of the EU's "open method of coordination" demonstrates that some policy convergence can be achieved within a regional economic union without achieving precise conformity. Harry Arthurs (2013) has addressed the problem of policy transplants and the possibilities for transnational legal and policy learning. He outlines the difficulty of applying lessons across national boundaries given the unique nature of national and regional political economies, legal systems, and sociocultural environments. Despite these difficulties, he shows that it is useful to think of transnational learning as not an outcome, but a process. To be sure, in that process, policy makers and theorists are bound to encounter structural, epistemological, and methodological barriers that are every bit as real as those posed by the differing legal systems, histories, and cultures of the countries that might otherwise learn from each other. Nonetheless, Arthurs contends, globalization itself has created conditions that are conducive to transnational learning and policy transplantation. The integration of national economies across the globe and the convergence in trade, monetary, and fiscal policies have made it possible for policy makers to imagine and even construct social policies and programs that are somewhat detached from their national origin. In this setting, transplanting aspects of labor and social policy may be more possible today than it was in the past.

Here, I have described a number of policy "green shoots," without prioritizing them or insisting that each one is either effective or transplantable. I do so in the spirit of enabling the creation of a transnational dialogue and fostering the spread of "best practices" for protecting employee rights while retaining the benefits of flexibility. It is hoped that by uncovering and sharing these green shoots, we can foster a transnational learning process.

3

THE CONSTITUTIONAL RIGHT TO ORGANIZE

Rebecca E. Zietlow[1]

This chapter explores the role of a worker's right to organize into a union in constitutional law and constitutional politics. This right has been contested since workers began to claim it in the mid-19th century, but the right to organize is currently under direct attack. In 2011, the state legislatures in Wisconsin and Ohio, two states with historically strong union traditions, both enacted measures which effectively eliminated the right to organize of most state employees. Legislatures in the historically pro-labor states of Michigan and Indiana have enacted "right to work" measures, aimed at undermining the power of private sector unions (Slater, 2013). Unions and their supporters have fought back against these measures, with limited success. What is notable is what opponents of these measures in all states have *not* argued – that the statutes deprive workers of the fundamental right to organize under the United States Constitution. While the right to organize is protected by statutes, including the federal National Labor Relations Act (NLRA), there is also good reason to believe that it has constitutional dimensions, based in the First and Thirteenth Amendments. Courts have been open to some limited First Amendment based arguments, but they have been resistant to broader arguments based in the Thirteenth Amendment. However, courts do not act in a vacuum; rights often develop in constitutional politics before they are adopted by courts. This chapter joins the growing body of work on popular constitutionalism – constitutional law outside the courts, which plays a crucial role in defining and developing constitutional rights. The debate over the constitutional right to organize is a particularly rich example of politics influencing rights consciousness and constitutional law. As recent developments reflect, the debate pitting the right to organize against the right to work has played out primarily not

1 Charles W. Fornoff Professor of Law and Values, University of Toledo College of Law.

in courts, but within our constitutional culture. Underlying this debate is a struggle over the meaning of worker's freedom. Opponents of the right to organize invoke individual autonomy, while its supporters claim that the right is necessary for true worker autonomy. The question of whether there is a constitutional right to organize hinges on the ongoing battle, in courts, and in the political realm, over collective rights in constitutional law.

The right to organize plays an important role in vulnerability theory because it provides a means of empowerment for vulnerable workers and facilitates the full inclusion of disempowered outsiders in our political and economic realm. The right to organize is crucial to improving the economic and political status of the vulnerable worker in our society. Vulnerability theory recognizes that all workers are vulnerable because vulnerability is universal and constant. Individual workers lack resilience in the face of that vulnerability because they have far fewer resources than their employers and are thus limited in their ability to negotiate for wages and benefits. The ability to organize and bargain collectively helps to equalize this power imbalance. This is evident in the fact that the widening gap between rich and poor in the US in the past several decades has coincided with the decline in union membership. Opponents of the right to organize champion "the autonomous and independent subject asserted in the liberal tradition," but vulnerability theorists recognize that the autonomous, independent subject is a myth (Fineman, 2008, p. 2). Collective rights, such as the right to organize, provide a voice for the vulnerable subject, and a means to achieve political and economic goals. The right to organize is a crucial tool for remedying class disparities in our society. Vulnerability theorists understand that there is much at stake in this debate over collective constitutional rights.

What would a constitutional right to organize look like? At the very least, the right to organize would include the right of workers to form an organization to advocate for their interests (Slater, 2000). In the US, the NLRA provides a statutory right to join a union, bargain collectively, and to strike. Unions need not bargain collectively and strike to fall within the definition of a "union." Nonetheless, a robust right to organize would encompass all three components. Labor leaders have long claimed a collective right to freedom of expression that could only be protected through collective action. Responding to their advocacy, courts have recognized only that the first dimension of the right to organize, the right to join a union, is protected by the First Amendment. Courts have not recognized the other elements of the right to organize, the rights to bargain collectively and to strike, as constitutional rights. The argument in favor of those rights is based in constitutional history and politics.

A broader theory of the right to organize has its roots in the Thirteenth Amendment's prohibition against involuntary servitude. The Thirteenth Amendment establishes a positive right to free labor, which arguably includes the collective right to contract and the right to strike. The Amendment reflects the broad free labor ideology of the antislavery activists who formed first the Free Soil, Free Labor Party, and then joined the nascent Republican Party (Vandervelde, 1989).

Litigators and courts have largely overlooked the Thirteenth Amendment as a source of union rights. However, generations of activists have argued in favor of the right to organize, some framing it in constitutional terms. Labor leaders in the late 19th century seized on that aspect of the Free Soil ideology to claim that the Thirteenth Amendment protected the individual workers' right to organize (Pope, 1997). Members of Congress returned to those arguments during debates over the NLRA, evoking a vision of fundamental rights for workers based in the Constitution.

Vulnerability theory tells us that the state is not sufficiently responsive to the needs of the vulnerable subjects that make up our society. This is due in part to the liberal ideology, which is based in the myth of autonomy (Fineman, 2004). But it is also the case that powerful interests in our society oppose legal measures, such as the right to organize, that would empower people and upset the status quo. During the mid-20th century, labor activists struggled for decades against Lochner Era rulings enforcing liberty of contract (Forbath, 1991). Labor activists insisted that collective rights were essential to workers achieving true autonomy and freedom of contract. As soon as the NLRA was enacted, its opponents began their own political campaign to limit that right. They asserted their own ideology of worker's autonomy. The business interests behind this campaign viewed the right to organize as a dangerous threat to the status quo. Yet they too couched their campaign as one protecting workers – the liberty of workers *not* to join unions – and some individual workers joined their cause (Lee, 2014). Thus, even though *Lochner* was overturned long ago, individual liberty-based rights pose a great challenge to collective vulnerability-based rights. While there may be a collective right to organize, that right is in constant tension with the individual right *not* to organize. In recent years, the counter-narrative of the right not to organize has prevailed in the political process, and in the courts.

Therefore, if there is a constitutional right to organize, it is not because of court rulings identifying that right, but due to the years of political advocacy of workers supporting that constitutional vision. The strongest argument in favor of a constitutional right to organize is that such a right is embedded in our constitutional culture. If there is no constitutional right to organize, it is due not only to the courts' resistance to those rights, but to the political success of those opposing those rights, which has altered our constitutional culture and contributed to the demise of collective rights in constitutional law.

I. The importance of the right to organize

Since the passage of the NLRA in 1935, federal law has recognized a right to organize for private employees. A network of statutes also recognizes such a right for public employees, both state and federal (Slater, 2004). Given that the right to organize is protected by statutes, why bother to consider whether there is also a constitutional right? The first reason is that many workers do not benefit from the statutory right. State workers are exempt from the NLRA. Some of the most disadvantaged workers in our society, including domestic, agricultural and home health care workers, are excluded from the protections of the NLRA. Courts have cut back significantly on the protections afforded by the NLRA (Pope, 2004). The remedies for violating the NLRA are limited, far more so than the remedies for violating a constitutional right would be likely to be (Slater, 2007). In addition, while many government workers enjoy a statutory right to organize, many others do not. Recent developments in states such as Ohio and Wisconsin serve as reminders that workers cannot be complacent about their protections under state law. Finally, and most importantly, there is a symbolic value to framing a right as a constitutional right. Historically, this has been an effective tool for political advocacy. The right to organize should be evaluated as a constitutional right because it is a fundamental and important source of resilience for the vulnerable subjects who make up our society.

A. The right to organize and vulnerability theory

Vulnerability theory is "concerned with privilege and favor conferred on limited segments of the population by the state and broader society through their institutions" (Fineman, 2008, p. 1). The right to organize regulates the relationship between workers and their employers, altering the balance of power in that relationship to favor the workers. Through collective action, workers can advocate more effectively to improve their wages and working conditions. Job protections negotiated through union contracts can protect workers from being arbitrarily fired. Collective bargaining agreements furnish an avenue of redress to improve conditions of employment and to address harassment and other bad treatment that might not reach the level actionable through civil rights statutes. Collective bargaining agreements also can serve as a means of equalizing pay scales, thus diminishing gender- and race-based gaps in wages and compensation. Thus, the right to organize provides resilience against the vulnerability of the individual worker (Fineman, 2004).

Vulnerability theory also explores the role of the state in addressing the needs of the vulnerable subject. The right to organize empowers workers to exercise agency on their own behalf. By recognizing the right to organize, the state enables private bargaining to establish the wages and conditions of work. Thus, the right to organize is a means for our society to "mobilize around a concept of shared, inevitable vulnerability" and "enable us more easily to build conditions among those who have not benefitted as fully as others from current societal organization" (Fineman, 2008, p. 17). The right to organize is a collective right, enabling the collective empowerment of vulnerable workers. A state that recognizes that right makes a commitment to the collective welfare of low-wage workers in our society.

This chapter asks not only whether the state should recognize the right to organize, but also whether it is required to do so as a matter of constitutional law. Martha Fineman points out, "The state is not mandated to respond to those inequalities, nor does it have to establish mechanisms to ensure more equitable distributions of either social goods or responsibilities between individuals, groups and institutions" (Fineman, 2008, pp. 2–3). Fineman is undeniably correct that in general our Constitution is one of negative, not positive, rights. It is a constitution that protects individual liberty from state interference, but does not guarantee basic social goods, such as housing, education, or health care. However, the right to organize is not a basic social good, but instead a right to process that arguably fits more comfortably into our constitutional tradition. The right to organize does not guarantee a decent job or decent wages, but instead guarantees to workers the ability to advocate effectively for those goods. Moreover, the right to organize sounds in liberty as well – the liberty to work free of undue coercion and to exercise collective action to achieve these goals.

The right to organize is based in both equality and liberty, but not individual liberty. The collective nature of the right to organize distinguishes it from other constitutional rights. In the US, the aspiration for equality has been balanced against the ideal of individual autonomy and liberty (Fineman, 2008, pp. 2–3). Notably, in recent years in the US, "the possibilities for a robust and expansive vision of equality seem to have eroded" as the ideal of individual autonomy has been ascendant. This "freedom has resulted in a diminishing of options and autonomy for many as our society has become more and more unequal" (Fineman, 2010, p. 14). The myth of autonomy and independence not only "fails to reflect the vulnerable as well as dependent nature of the human condition," but also serves as an effective rhetorical tool for opponents to collective rights (Fineman, 2008, p. 19). Thus, vulnerability theory shows that the ideology of individual autonomy is a barrier to those advocating for collective autonomy, and a stumbling block for those advocating for collective constitutional rights. This is evident in the ongoing legal battle between the collective right to organize and the individual right *not* to organize.

B. The right to organize as an international fundamental right

The right to organize is recognized as a fundamental right under international law (Weiss, 2009). The Universal Declaration of Human Rights provides that "[e]veryone has the right to form and to join trade unions for the protection of his interests." The right to organize is also recognized in the International Covenant on Civil and Political Rights, as well as the International Covenant on Economic, Social, and Cultural Rights. Recently, the Supreme Court of Canada recognized the right to organize as a fundamental right, protected by the Canadian Constitution. The right to organize fits within all of these rubrics because it reflects the intersection of economic and civil rights. Under international law, economic rights include "the right to an adequate standard of living" and "the right to work, including non-discrimination, decent work, and fair wages" (Weiss, 2009, pp. 259, 264). Union membership is an important means for workers to achieve those goals and achieve self-actualization as effective members of society.

The right to organize into a union, bargain collectively, and to strike, is a fundamental human right because it facilitates the formation of communities of workers who benefit economically, socially, and politically. The right to organize enables workers to use collective action to achieve economic and political gains. Belonging to a union empowers workers, not only in the workplace, but also in the political arena, because unions are a strong political force. Workers who join unions are more likely to feel invested in their communities and to engage in political action (Cohen, 1990). Thus, the right to organize facilitates democratic governance.

In addition, the right to organize furthers human autonomy. Under the authoritarian tradition of master/servant, workers can be cowed, both psychologically and socially, and intimidated to work under difficult conditions. Belonging to a union gives workers a mechanism to demand respect from their employers and enforce that demand. Thus, the right to organize furthers not only economic wellbeing and political engagement, but also personal autonomy and fulfillment. For all of these reasons, the right to organize is a fundamental human right, and important to vulnerability theory.

II. A constitutional theory of the right to organize

Of course, many fundamental human rights are not protected by the US Constitution. This section considers the argument in favor of a constitutional right to organize. There are three components to that right – the right to be a union member, the right to bargain collectively, and the right to strike to influence the bargaining process. Courts have found that the First Amendment protects the first component of the right, the right of an individual to be a member of a union. The court has emphatically rejected the second component – the right to collective bargaining – and has by and large ignored the third constitutional argument in favor of the right to strike. Both of those components find constitutional support in the Thirteenth Amendment, which has largely been enforced not by courts, but by collective action in favor of constitutional values.

The Thirteenth Amendment protects a broad array of rights of the free person, including a positive right to free labor. Slavery was a system of exploitation of labor, made possible by the racist ideology that slaves were less than human. Ending slavery would end the exploitation of labor without pay, but incorporating slaves into society required comprehensive affirmative measures. In the 20th century, labor leaders invoked the First and Thirteenth Amendments, arguing that they had a constitutional right to organize into unions and to engage in strikes and boycotts. Those leaders recalled the days of civil disobedience by abolitionist ministers. This antislavery tradition influenced their unionist methods as well as their ideology (Forbath, 1991). While no court has ever adopted those arguments, members of Congress echoed them when enacting the NLRA. Thus, there is a strong constitutional tradition that provides a solid basis for a constitutional right to organize.

A. Freedom of association and the right to join a union

Labor leaders have long argued that they had a First Amendment right to belong to a union. They claimed that the First Amendment right to assemble, and to petition, includes the right to assemble in labor unions and petition collectively. The Supreme Court has recognized the First Amendment rights of union members in a series of cases. Lower courts have found that workers' freedom of association, protected by the First Amendment, encompasses the right to organize. However, the courts have defined that right narrowly, as merely a right to belong to a union.

1. Constitutional activism

Labor activists have long argued that the right to organize is an expressive right that should be protected by the First Amendment. During the 19th century, activists invoked the Declaration of Independence to support their claims of workers' autonomy (Wilentz, 1984). In the 20th century, labor leaders linked the right to organize to democracy and claimed that it was a right of citizenship. They saw that workers' right to join a union furthers their "active participation in determining their collective destiny and with a loyalty to the nation that transcended individual prosperity" (Wilentz, 1984, p. 23). Activists such as pro-labor radical Eugene Debs advocated unions as a means to extend basic civil and political rights into the realm of production and the market sphere. In 1920s Seattle, teachers' unions seized on this argument and maintained that the right to organize was a fundamental right of citizenship that could not be denied by states (Lichtenstein and Harris, 1993). For constitutional support, these activists claimed a First Amendment right to engage not only in the political process, but also to participate effectively in the economic realm. They claimed the First Amendment's protections of freedom of expression and association (Pope, 1997).

Labor's democracy and First Amendment based claims were successful in the political realm. In the period immediately following World War I, industrial democracy and citizenship rights were linked to union membership in the public mind, and over a million new workers joined unions (Lichtenstein and Harris, 1993). Labor's arguments gradually gained mainstream acceptance. "By the 1920s, senators and congressmen frequently complained that the courts had defined the rights of property so as to threaten workers' constitutional freedoms and to erode the first and thirteenth amendments" (Forbath, 1991, p. 141). A decade later, during congressional debates over the NLRA, supporters of the Act argued that it would promote freedom of expression and association. For example, Robert Wagner, the sponsor of the Act, argued that members of Congress had recognized that "full freedom of association and self-organization among workers was desirable" and would be furthered by the Act (78 Cong Rec 12017 (June 16, 1934)). Labor activists continue to argue that union membership is an expressive right, in the political realm and before the courts.

2. Court response

Courts have accepted the argument that the right to join a union is protected by the First Amendment. In *Hague v CIO* (1939), the Supreme Court found that union organizers had a First Amendment right to speak about the rights of workers and about the NLRA. The court held that the freedom to assemble peaceably and disseminate the information were a privilege or immunity of citizens of the US. In *Thornhill v Alabama* (1940), the court held that a union organizer had a First Amendment right to picket in connection with an ongoing strike. The court noted that "[t]he safeguarding of these rights to the ends that men may speak as they think on matters vital to them . . . is essential to free government" (p. 95). In *Thomas v Collins* (1945), the court found that the state of Texas violated the rights of freedom of speech and free assembly of a union organizer when it issued a restraining order prohibiting him from soliciting members in the United Auto Workers Union. The court rejected Texas' suggestion that a state could distinguish between the rights of free speech and assembly for one engaged in "business activities" and others exercising those rights. The court concluded: "Of course espousal of the cause of labor is entitled to no higher constitutional protection than the espousal of any other lawful cause. It is entitled to the same protection" (p. 538).

In these cases, the court upheld the First Amendment rights of union organizers to engage in pro-union advocacy. These cases are significant because they treat the speech of union organizers with the same level of respect as political speech. The court recognized that economic advocacy contributed not only to the wellbeing of workers, but also to the effective functioning of democracy. However, as we shall see, the court has since strayed from this attitude, imposing restrictions on the political speech of unions.

In another series of cases, the court has found that government employees have First Amendment rights. In *Garrity v New Jersey* (1967), the court held that a government employer cannot compel a confession to what could be a crime under threat of discharge. As the court explained, "policemen, like teachers and lawyers, are not relegated to a watered down version of constitutional rights" (p. 500). The same year, the court held that a New York law requiring college teachers to certify that they had not been communists violated the First Amendment. Overruling prior precedent, the court held that public employment could not "be conditioned upon the surrender of constitutional rights which could not be abridged by direct government action" (*Keyishian v Board of Regents*, 1967, p. 605). In later cases, the court established a balancing test for public employee speech cases. These cases also laid the groundwork for the First Amendment right to join a union. In *Smith v Arkansas Highway Employees Local 1315* (1970), the court held that the First Amendment protects a public employee's right to speak in favor of a union.

Lower courts have held that the free speech rights of government employees include their right to join a union. In *American Federation of State, County, and Municipal Employees, AFL-CIO ("AFSCME") v Woodward* (1969), the Eighth Circuit Court of Appeals held that the right to join a union is protected by the right of association in the First Amendment. The court noted that "the guarantee of the 'right of assembly' protects more than 'the right to attend a meeting; it includes the right to express one's attitudes or philosophies by membership in a group or by affiliation with it or by other lawful means.'" Only a "paramount public interest" could justify infringing on the employee's right to join a labor union (pp. 139, 140). Similarly, in *McLaughlin v Tilendis* (1968), the Seventh Circuit held that a teacher who was dismissed because of his membership had a First Amendment right to form and join a union. The court noted that the Supreme Court had just held that a teacher's First Amendment rights were violated because she was fired for criticizing the local school board. The court opined, surely teachers also have the right to "form and take part in associations to further what they consider to be their well-being" (p. 289).

In *Atkins v City of Charlotte* (1969), a District Court struck down North Carolina statutes that prohibited government employees from becoming members of national labor organizations as violating the First Amendment's protection of freedom of association. According to the court, "there is no valid state interest in denying firemen the right to organize in a labor union." The court continued: "It is beyond argument that a single individual cannot negotiate on an equal basis with an employer who hires hundreds of people. Recognition of this fact of life is the basis of labor-management relations in this country" (p. 1075). Thus, the *Atkins* court recognized the power differential between employees and management in negotiating contracts, and held that the differential justified the worker's right to be a member of a union.

Most recently, in *Wisconsin Education Association v Walker* (2013), plaintiffs alleged that the provisions of Act 10 which eliminated bargaining rights for all "general" employees of the state of Wisconsin, with the exception of the right to bargain about "total base wages" violated the First Amendment. Act 10 imposed such onerous obligations on unions representing public employees that it would be difficult for those unions to continue to function. Plaintiffs argued that those restrictions violated the First Amendment because they infringed on the workers' freedom of association. The District Court agreed, and struck down those provisions. However, the Seventh Circuit Court of Appeals overturned the trial court, holding that the impact on freedom of association was insufficient to violate the Constitution.

Thus, courts have held that the First Amendment protects the individual right of a worker to join a union, under the doctrine of freedom of association. Courts have also recognized the link between union membership and democratic participation. However, due to the state action doctrine, the First Amendment only applies to government employees, and it does not protect the collective right of union members to join together and bargain collectively with their employers. While the right not to be fired due to one's union membership is clearly significant, the First Amendment right alone has limited utility in improving the material conditions of union members.

B. Freedom of contract and the right to bargain collectively

The second component of the right to organize is the right to bargain collectively with one's employer. The courts have not been nearly as receptive to this argument, but it is based on longstanding constitutional tradition. The ideology of freedom of contract dates back to the Free Soil, Free Labor antislavery tradition (Foner, 1995a). Free Soilers claimed that slavery violated the right of employees to contract with their employers over wages and conditions of labor. Slaves had absolutely no power whatsoever over their conditions of labor and lacked any shred of individual autonomy. Because they were competing against workers who were not paid, poor free workers found it hard to negotiate with employers for decent conditions and wages. Thus, the disempowerment of slaves hurt all workers, by bringing down the floor of conditions of labor (Vandervelde, 1989). Ending slavery would enable all workers to bargain more effectively for improved conditions and wages. The Thirteenth Amendment arguably establishes a constitutional right to do so.

1. Constitutional activism

Supporters of the Thirteenth Amendment believed that slaves had certain fundamental human rights that would be restored when the peculiar institution was abolished. Shortly after the Thirteenth Amendment became law, they acted to protect those rights. The Reconstruction Congress gave substance to those rights in statutes enforcing the Amendment, including the 1866 Civil Rights Act and the 1867 Anti-Peonage Act. The 1866 Civil Rights Act protects the right to be free of race discrimination in contracts. The 1867 Anti-Peonage Act establishes the right to be free of coercive employers, prohibiting both voluntary and involuntary peonage (Soifer, 2012). Supporters of the Anti-Peonage Act made it clear that the goal of the Thirteenth Amendment was not only to end slavery, but also to improve the lives of all workers. While these measures do not establish a right to organize in a union, they do provide the building blocks for that right – the right to contract and the right to leave one's employer. They also left open the possibility that those rights would be exercised collectively.

In the late 19th and early 20th centuries, some labor activists argued that the Thirteenth Amendment protected a collective right to contract, to be enjoyed by workers who organized in unions. They claimed that without the robust right to organize, workers were no better than slaves. They insisted that in the industrial age, an individual worker lacked the power to bargain effectively with his employer if he bargains alone. True freedom of contract requires workers to be able to join unions and bargain collectively, because only then can they effectively exercise their fundamental right to contract. More broadly, these activists advocated for worker autonomy and control over their lives, which could be possible only if workers could band together to exert that control effectively. To these activists, true workers' freedom could only be enforced through collective action.

Notwithstanding the Supreme Court's Lochner Era rulings, the collective ideology of freedom of contract flourished in the labor movement during the first half of the 20th century. As Jim Pope describes it, "[u]nionists did not wait for judicial approval to put their constitutional vision into practice. Having declared laws unconstitutional, they endeavored to strike them down through noncompliance and direct action" (Pope, 1997, p. 943). Labor leaders continued to argue that workers could only be free if they were allowed to join unions and bargain collectively. Some of these leaders invoked the Thirteenth Amendment, claiming that workers were no more than slaves if they lacked the right to organize. Others invoked the liberty protected by the Due Process Clause of the Fourteenth Amendment, in a direct challenge to the court's libertarian interpretation of that provision. As AFL President William Green told a congressional hearing in 1935, "We are looking to Congress for help, if we want to make the word 'freedom' a real vital force; freedom for the workers; freedom for them to organize: freedom for them to bargain collectively; freedom for them to mobilize their economic strength; and freedom to use it in accordance with their own judgment" (Labor Disputes Act: Hearing on HR 6288 Before the H. Comm. on Labor, 74th Cong. 1 (1935) (testimony of William Green, President of Am. Fedn of Labor)).

Members of Congress eventually seized on this theory as they debated the NLRA, which protects the right to collective bargaining. The Act's sponsor, Robert Wagner, said that the right to organize was "a veritable charter of freedom of contract," and argued that without the right to bargain collectively, "there would be slavery by contract." Wagner continued, "The fathers of our nation did not regard freedom of contract as an abstract end. They valued it as a means of insuring equal opportunities, which cannot be attained where contracts are dictated by the stronger party" (Speech by Senator Wagner, Conference of Code Authorities, Washington DC, March 5, 1934; printed in 78 Cong Rec 3678). Years later, Ken Keyserling, Wagner's legislative aide, recalled that Wagner always said that the purpose of the act was "to make the worker a free man" (Casebeer, 1987, p. 329). Many of Wagner's congressional allies agreed. For example, Nebraska Representative Terry Carpenter insisted that "[t]he worker can exercise his God-given faculty of freedom only through a system which permits him to choose freely his representatives in industry" (78 Cong Rec 9061 (May 17, 1934)). The Senate Report on the Wagner Act explained that it would establish equal bargaining power, "which is a prerequisite to equality of opportunity and freedom of contract." By enacting the NLRA, Congress emphatically embraced the unionists' view – that the freedom of contract required measures to ensure the equality of bargaining power. Though these members of Congress did not base the NLRA on their power to enforce the Thirteenth Amendment, they made clear they believed that they were protecting a fundamental right that sounded in constitutional terms.

2. *Court response*

In the only rulings in which it has recognized a constitutional right to contract, the court adopted a libertarian vision of the right that is directly contrary to the collective vision held by the labor movement. The court enforced solely the right of the individual employer to bargain with an individual employee. For example, in *Lochner v New York* (1908), the court struck down a New York state law which prohibited bakers from working more than 10 hours a day or 60 hours a week. The court held that the law violated the freedom of contract of the employer who wanted to hire workers for longer hours, and of the employees who wanted to contract to work longer hours. This libertarian view of the right to contract directly conflicted with the collective view advocated by the labor movement. Indeed, the court struck down numerous statutes protecting the right of workers as violating the freedom of contract (Forbath, 1991).

Most notably, the Lochner Era Court struck down both state and federal laws that protected the right to organize as violating the freedom of contract. At issue were "yellow dog contract" laws, which prohibited employers from conditioning employment on an employee's agreement not to join a union. The court found that the laws violated the right of employers and employees to contract with each other. In *Adair v US* (1908), the court stated that "[t]he right of a person to sell his labor upon such terms as he deems proper is, in essence, the same as the right of the purchaser of labor to prescribe the conditions upon which he will accept such labor from the person offering to sell it" (p. 174). The court rejected the argument that unions empowered workers to exercise their freedom of contract effectively. Instead, the court focused only on the workers who were willing to agree not to join a union as a condition of employment. "In all such particulars the employer and the employee have equality of right, and any legislation that disturbs that equality is an arbitrary interference with the liberty of contract which no government can legally justify in a free land" (p. 175). The court was not receptive to the contention that the right to join a union was part of the freedom to contract, asking rhetorically in *Coppage v Kansas* (1915): "[I]s the employee's right to be free to join a labor union any more sacred, or more securely founded upon the Constitution, than his right to work for whom he will, or to be idle if he will?" (p. 13). The court responded: "Conceding the full right of the individual to join the union, he has no inherent right to do this and still remain in the employ of one who is unwilling to employ a union man" (p. 19). The employee had the liberty to quit his job. That is all the Constitution required.

Finally, the laws could not be justified on the grounds that they equalized bargaining power between the employee and the employer. Said the court in *Coppage*: "And, since it is self-evident that, unless all things are held in common, some persons must have more property than others, it is from the nature of things impossible to uphold freedom of contract and the right of private property without at the same time recognizing as legitimate those inequalities of fortune that are the necessary result of the exercise of those rights." This argument only proved that "an interference with the normal exercise of personal liberty and property rights is the primary object of the statute . . . such restriction is the very thing that is inhibited by the Amendment" (pp. 17, 18).

Congress resoundingly rejected the court's freedom of contract jurisprudence by enacting the NLRA and other legislation protecting workers' rights and regulating the employer-employee relationship. The court also overruled its Lochner Era jurisprudence, holding that there is no constitutional right to contract. However, the courts have never accepted the argument that workers have a constitutional right to bargain collectively. In *Smith v Arkansas State Highway Employees*

(1979), the court held that a state employer was not required to negotiate with a union that represented its workers. The Arkansas State Highway Commission had a policy of not considering a grievance unless the employee submitted his written complaint directly to the designated employer representative. The union representing the employees sued, arguing that this procedure prohibited the union from submitting effective grievances on the employees' behalf, and thus violated the First Amendment. While agreeing that the First Amendment "protects the right of associations to engage in advocacy on behalf of their members," the court continued, "the First Amendment is not a substitute for the national labor relations laws" (p. 464). The court acknowledged that the First Amendment prohibited employers from retaliating against employees for their union activism. "But the First Amendment does not impose any affirmative obligation on the government to listen, to respond or, in this context, to recognize the association and bargain with it" (p. 465). The Highway Commission's practice might have constituted an unfair labor practice under the NLRA if the Act applied to state employers, but the practice was not unconstitutional. "[A]ll the Commission has done in its challenged conduct is simply to ignore the union. That it is free to do" (p. 466).

Thus, the Supreme Court has repeatedly rejected the argument that workers' freedom of contract entails some equality of bargaining power. The argument in favor of a collective freedom of contract depends on popular constitutionalism, not court rulings, for its support. History shows that workers will obtain their collective vision of freedom of contract only through political activism.

C. *Freedom from involuntary servitude and the right to strike*

The third component of the right to organize is the right to strike. Such right may be protected by the Thirteenth Amendment, which provides that "neither slavery nor involuntary servitude shall exist." Arguably, workers who lack the right to strike are subject to involuntary servitude. At the very least, the Thirteenth Amendment protects "the inalienable right to quit work" (Pope, 2010a, p. 1478). Thirteenth Amendment based anti-peonage statutes, and cases interpreting those statutes, recognize the right of employees to change their employers. More contested is the question of whether the Thirteenth Amendment protects the collective right to leave a job temporarily to protest wages or conditions of work – that is, the right to strike. Like the right to bargain collectively, the right to strike is linked to worker autonomy. Workers strike to exercise control over their conditions of employment and influence the bargaining process. Just as collective bargaining is more effective than individual bargaining because it equalizes power dynamics, the collective right to strike is more effective than the individual right to quit.

1. Constitutional activism

During the early part of the 20th century, labor leaders argued that the right to strike was protected by the Thirteenth Amendment (Pope, 2010a). In December

1919, the American Federation of Labor issued a statement proclaiming that "[t]he right to strike . . . meant the difference between voluntary and involuntary servitude, between freedom and slavery." In his speeches, AFL President Samuel Gompers repeatedly insisted that the right to strike was necessary to prevent slavery (Pope, 1997, pp. 959, 1001). The constitutional arguments made by these labor activists were consistent with the free labor vision of the Reconstruction Congress that enacted the Thirteenth Amendment and measures enforcing that Amendment.

Prior to enacting the Thirteenth Amendment, leading Republicans argued that the distinction between a free labor and slave system was the capacity of the system "to ensure that the laborer could enjoy the rewards of his own labor" (Pope, 2010a, p. 1535). Consistent with the Free Soil ideology, some workers took matters into their own hands. In 1860, 20,000 Massachusetts shoemakers staged the largest strike in history and proclaimed that they "would not be slaves." Speaking in Connecticut, then presidential candidate Abraham Lincoln said: "I am glad to see that a system of labor prevails in New England under which laborers can strike when they want to, where they are not obliged to work under all circumstances, and not tied down and obliged to labor whether you pay them or not!" (Pope, 2010a, pp. 1535, 1559). This is evidence that the supporters of the Thirteenth Amendment understood the right to strike as part of the rights of free men. Others have argued that Lincoln really supported no more than the right to quit. However, during the war, Lincoln regularly expressed support for striking workers. Other influential Republicans, including Horace Greeley and E. L. Godkin, also endorsed labor organization as linked to effective labor freedom. Thus, there is evidence that northern workers during the Civil War "might reasonably have thought that the right to strike was part of a free labor system" (Pope, 2010a, pp. 1535, 1560).

During Reconstruction, members of Congress continued to articulate a free labor vision, enacting measures to empower workers who had not been enslaved along with those who had. This is most clearly evident from the fact that the Thirteenth Amendment prohibits not just slavery, but also "involuntary servitude." In March 1867, Congress enacted an Anti-Peonage Act, which prohibited "the holding of any person to service or labor under the system known as peonage." Peonage was defined broadly, as "establish[ing], maintain[ing], or enforce[ing], directly or indirectly, the voluntary or involuntary service or labor of any persons as peons, in liquidation of any debt or obligation, or otherwise." The Act went beyond the language of the Thirteenth Amendment, barring not only "involuntary" but also "voluntary" peonage, that is peonage relationships entered into freely by the worker. Speaking in support of this measure, Pennsylvania Senator Charles Buckalew explained that terms of debt service were "always exceedingly unfavorable to [the laborer], and the system degrade[d] both the owner of the labor and the laborer himself" (Cong Globe, 39th Cong, 2d Sess, 1572 (1867)). The sponsor of the bill, Massachusetts Senator Henry Wilson, explained that the bill would elevate the status of all workers because in areas where peonage had been eliminated, such as New Mexico, "peons who once worked for two or three dollars a month are now able to command respectable wages" (Cong Globe, 39th Cong, 2d Sess, 1571 (1867)). These measures did not address the ability of workers to act collectively in strikes, but they laid the groundwork for that constitutional argument. These members of the Reconstruction Congress showed that they believed that the Thirteenth Amendment protected the autonomy of the worker to leave his or her job, autonomy that was necessary to improve working conditions.

The Reconstruction Congress enacted two other anti-peonage measures. The first was the 1874 Padrone Act, which prohibited the practice of bringing children from Italy to large cities, isolating them and exploiting their labor. The second measure was a joint resolution conveying authority upon the US military to "reclaim from peonage" women and children being held in that condition "in the territory adjacent to their homes" and on the Navajo reservation. These measures reflect the desire of the Reconstruction Congress to protect workers from exploitative practices regardless of their race or prior condition of servitude and to foster a measure of worker autonomy.

Congress has also amended the 1867 Anti-Peonage Act twice to expand its scope. In 1948, Congress amended the Act to replace the phrase "slave trade" with "involuntary servitude," and to make it a crime to hold someone in a condition of involuntary servitude. Most recently, Congress amended the Anti-Peonage Act again with the 2000 Trafficking Victims Protection Act (TVPA). The TVPA is a measure addressing the international and domestic trafficking of workers, which the bill's supporters described as "one of the largest manifestations of modern day slavery internationally" (146 Cong Rec 22,044). The bill expanded the definition of coercion outlawed by the Act to include psychological, not just physical coercion. Like the 1948 Amendment, the TVPA protects individual, not collective rights. However, these measures also empower vulnerable workers to act on their own behalf to improve their conditions of labor.

In the beginning of the 20th century, labor leaders seized on the abolitionist tradition to argue that anti-strike rulings by courts violated their Thirteenth Amendment based right to strike. Those leaders invoked the infamous *Dred Scott* decision to oppose court intervention. They claimed that the courts' treatment of workers' rights as property rights violated the Amendment's prohibition against slavery, and that the Amendment therefore protected the right to strike. Labor leaders argued that they had a constitutional right to resist anti-strike injunctions, and opposing injunctions became a central tenant of their political strategy (Forbath, 1991). They argued that the Thirteenth Amendment gave them the right to strike, and testified before Congress that anti-injunction legislation should be based in Congress' power to enforce the Thirteenth Amendment. They achieved their goal in 1932, when Congress enacted the Norris-LaGuardia Act, which prohibits federal courts from issuing injunctions in labor-management disputes. However, notwithstanding the pleas of the labor leaders who testified before Congress, including AFL lobbyist Andrew Furuseth, Congress did not base the legislation in its power to enforce the Thirteenth Amendment (Forbath, 1991). The 1935 NLRA includes the right to strike as one of the activities that is "protected" under section 7 of the

Act. Again, some labor representatives asked Congress to base the legislation in Congress' power to enforce the Thirteenth Amendment (Forbath, 2001). While members of Congress chose the commerce clause instead, many of them invoked the Amendment's promise of freedom when speaking in favor of the Act.

The Anti-Peonage Acts and the NLRA are consistent with the Thirteenth Amendment's protections of worker autonomy, and the Free Soil recognition that workers need to be able to leave their job to improve their conditions of labor. The right to strike is a collective means of exercising that autonomy to achieve those goals. Thus, the right to strike may fall within the protections of the Thirteenth Amendment.

2. Court response

Courts have been reluctant to recognize a right to strike. It is true that in *Wolff Packing Co. v Court of Industrial Relations* (1923), the Supreme Court held that workers have a constitutional right to strike under the Due Process Clause of the Fourteenth Amendment. In that case, Justice Taft said that the workers' right to strike was "a most important element of freedom of labor" because it gave him a "means of putting himself on an equality with his employer" (p. 540). However, the *Wolff Packing* ruling has been ignored, due in part to its substantive due process basis. Moreover, the court has issued numerous rulings inconsistent with this principle, including cases upholding the privilege of employers to hire replacement workers, sustaining a ban on secondary strikes, and up-holding a prohibition of employee strikes (Pope, 2010a).

The most persuasive precedent in support of a constitutional right to strikes is Justice Robert's Jackson's opinion for the court in a 1944 case interpreting the Anti-Peonage Act, *Pollock v Williams* (1944). In *Pollock*, the court held that a Florida law that made it a misdemeanor to leave an employer after promising to work for the employer and receiving compensation for the promised work effectuated involuntary servitude in violation of the Anti-Peonage Act. In his opinion, Justice Jackson explained that employment relationships are generally presumed voluntary because "the defense against oppressive hours, working conditions, or treatment is the right to change employers." Justice Jackson elaborated: "[W]hen the master can compel and the laborer cannot escape the obligation to go on, there is no power below to redress and no incentive above to relieve a harsh overlordship or unwholesome conditions of work" (p. 18). Jim Pope has persuasively argued that the *Pollock* standard is the correct standard for interpreting the "involuntary servitude" clause of the Thirteenth Amendment, reflecting a positive goal of completely free and involuntary labor throughout the country (Pope, 2010a). If that is so, then the right to strike would probably be protected by the clause. The right to strike is an essential means of exercising the "power below" to ensure that employers bargain fairly with workers. If workers truly enjoy the right to strike, this greatly diminishes the employer's authority to be a "harsh overlord." To put it simply, effective exercise of the workers' right to quit requires that they be able to exercise it collectively. Only the right to strike can empower workers to bargain with employers on an equal basis (Pope, 2010a).

To the extent that workers have enjoyed a constitutional right to strike, it has been greatly reduced by Supreme Court rulings undermining the job security of striking workers. While the court ruled long ago that employers could replace striking workers, employers have only been willing to do so with impunity in recent decades. The following section discusses the reason behind this development – the ascendance of the "right to work" movement, and the right *not* to organize.

III. Collective versus individual rights and the right *not* to organize

The battle over the constitutional right to organize is a struggle over the salience of collective rights in constitutional law. The arguments for and against the constitutional right to organize have played out in courts and in the political realm. From the Lochner Era to the present day, courts have limited collective rights with rulings championing individual liberty. Since Congress recognized the right to organize with the NLRA, opponents have attacked that right and raised a conflicting vision of the constitutional rights of workers. They have argued that the right to organize violated the individual rights of workers and championed the right to work free of union membership (Lee, 2014). This conservative vision pitted the individual rights of employees to bargain on their own behalf against the collective rights of employees to band together and bargain collectively. Anti-union advocates champion a libertarian vision of workers' rights that evokes Lochner Era freedom of contract. Vulnerable workers are caught up in this ongoing struggle of liberty versus equality in the law of workers' rights.

The struggle over workers' rights is a constant battle between the individualist and collective vision of rights. While workers have scored victories for collective rights in the political realm, courts have often and repeatedly cut back on those rights. Even in the political realm, however, the conservative individualist vision often prevails in the battle over constitutional rights for workers. Even as pro-union advocates promoted a constitutional right to organize, opponents of unions sought to establish a right *not* to join a union. The opponents have been quite successful in doing so. While framing political rights in constitutional terms is indeed an effective tool for political advocacy, it can also be dangerous to the rights of vulnerable subjects to try to constitutionalize the political debate over workers' rights.

A. *The right to work campaign*

Immediately after Congress established a statutory right to organize with the NLRA, right-wing opponents began to mount a challenge to its collective promise. In 1937, a group of southern Democrats drafted a "statement of principles" which they called the "Conservative Manifesto," reaffirming their devotion to states' rights, liberty of contract and the property rights of owners of capital (Forbath, 2001). The Conservative Manifesto harkened back to the Lochner Era freedom of contract ideology. It was directed against President Franklin Roosevelt's Economic Bill of Rights, which would have established the original right to work – the right to gainful employment. Southern segregationists saw FDR's right to work as unduly threatening to the southern way of life, which depended on the economic exploitation of Black agricultural and domestic workers. They had insisted that agricultural and domestic works be excluded from the protections of the NLRA (Forbath, 2001). The Conservative Manifesto presented an alternative approach to the right to work – one rooted in individual freedom to oppose collective rights. Over the years since then, the right to work movement has gained momentum and has come perilously close to trumping the collective right to organize.

In the 1940s, conservatives coined the term "right to work" as the right of an individual employee not to belong to a union. Noted movie director Cecil De Mille was part of a "cadre of conservative activists" who claimed an individual right not to belong to a union or pay union dues (Lee, 2014, p. 59). They relied on pre-New Deal Era precedent, claiming that their right to contract, and to earn their livelihood, trumped federal labor laws. They focused their early attack on the "closed shop," a unionized workplace where the employees were required to be union members. Notwithstanding the Supreme Court's repudiation of *Lochner*, some lower courts agreed with these arguments and issued injunctions against unions based on the right to work (Lee, 2014, p. 59). But the right to work campaign was far more successful in the political realm. On his radio show, De Mille campaigned for the right to work, claiming that it was "endowed by God" and in the Declaration of Independence and Bill of Rights. De Mille also drew an analogy between closed shops and American slavery, arguing that workers needed a "second emancipation proclamation" against unions (Lee, 2014, pp. 59, 71, 73). His campaign had a significant impact. In 1947, Congress enacted the Taft Hartley Act, which prohibits closed shops, and allows state to pass "right to work" statutes. This was a major victory for De Mille, who called his effort the conservative civil rights movement. Fourteen states immediately adopted right to work statutes (Lee, 2014, p. 59).

Congress amended the NLRA again in 1950, to authorize union shops (shops in which eligible workers were required to join unions). However, the right to work movement continued to grow in the 1950s and 1960s. They framed the right to work as the right to earn a living "with or without union membership," and they claimed that it had constitutional dimensions. By the 1950s, the right to work movement had some powerful support, including the investment of General Motors, the National Association of Manufacturers, and other major businesses (Lee, 2014, pp. 59, 117, 120). Like their union opponents, the National Right to Work Committee raised free speech and free association claims. They called union members "forced followers" (Lee, 2014, pp. 59, 124). This use of language is ironic, since "[i]n right to work states, employees who wish to form a union were effectively forced to subsidize the provision of union benefits to coworkers who refuse to support the union," including higher wages, better working conditions and procedural rights under collective bargaining agreements. Thus right to work laws enable employees to be free-riders, and strain the resources of the unions (Fisk and Chemerinsky, 2013, pp. 1032, 1033).

In the 1950s and early 1960s, union membership was at its peak in our nation's history, and labor had political clout. The right to work movement sought to exploit a union's obligation to represent its members under the Duty of Fair Representation rule to split alliances between labor and the civil rights movement. The National Association of Manufacturers sought to make alliances with conservative Blacks, focusing on union discrimination to solicit Black voters and alienate racial liberals' support for labor. By the 1970s, disputes over affirmative action and union dues had emerged, and the right to work movement had gained strength. From 1965 to 1971, leading Senators Everett Dirksen and Pete Dominici repeatedly introduced legislation which they called a "laboring man's bill of rights," which included both right to work and antidiscrimination measures. Resisting unions had become a more mainstream business position. The election of Ronald Reagan for president in 1980 was a victory for the New Right, a coalition of Goldwater Republicans and next generation conservatives who strongly supported the right to work (Lee, 2014).

In August 1981, President Reagan fired over 11,000 striking air traffic controllers, citing a law that prohibited government workers from striking if it endangered public safety. The President's action had an incredible symbolic importance, signaling that it was permissible for employers to fire striking workers (Slater, 2013). Unions became less effective and suffered a decline in membership. Union membership has now dropped to below 10% of the workforce (Lee, 2014, p. 257). Meanwhile, the right to work campaign is alive and successful. Half of the states in the US, including the industrial union stronghold states of Indiana, Michigan and Wisconsin, are now right to work states. Thus, the decline of collective rights in our constitutional consciousness is not a coincidence. It results, at least in part, from a concerted political campaign against those rights, invoking a libertarian ideology that is increasingly salient in both the political and legal realms.

B. Limits on the First Amendment rights of unions

Although the Supreme Court has recognized that unions and union members enjoy First Amendment rights based on freedom of expression and freedom of association, both Congress and the courts have limited the scope of those rights. Congress amended the NLRA to restrict labor picketing, and the court upheld those restrictions. The right to organize empowers workers to act collectively in the economic and political realms. Unions play a democracy-enhancing role in the workplace and in the political sphere (Fisk and Chemerinsky, 2013). The court has recognized that union membership furthers the freedom of speech and association of union members. Nonetheless, the court has also limited the freedom of expression enjoyed by unions to speak on behalf of their members. The court rulings restricting the expressive rights of unions and their members arguably undermine the claim to a constitutional right to organize.

Although the NLRA protects the right to strike, the Taft Hartley Act amended the law to impose limitations on picketing by unions. The statute bars violent or intimidating picketing and secondary boycotts. The court has not only upheld these limits against First Amendment challenges, but it has interpreted the limits to broadly restrict any expressive activities of union members that are not directly related to economic issues and collective bargaining. Moreover, the court has held that states may enjoin picketing expressing a viewpoint that is contrary to state policy. These restrictions are notable given that the court has extended First Amendment protection to other picketers, even when they threaten violence or engage in offensive picketing against state policy (Garden, 2011). As a result, "labor unions receive less protection than other social movement groups . . . sometimes less protection than even commercial speech" (Garden, 2011, p. 17).

In series of cases involving the use of union dues for political purposes, the court has drawn a line between the economic and political speech of unions. In *Abood v Detroit Board of Education* (1977), the court held that non-union public sector workers in unionized workplaces can be required to pay union dues to support collective bargaining, but they cannot be required to support union political activities. The court held that requiring government workers to fund union political activities would violate those workers' First Amendment rights. Thus, the First Amendment required the unions to allow employees to opt out of paying dues for political purposes. In *Communications Workers v Beck* (1988), the Court extended the *Abood* ruling to private sector workers as a matter of statutory interpretation. These cases limit the ability of unions to use funds to pay for political advocacy, and impose an administrative burden on unions to ensure that the funds are used appropriately. Remarkably, in these cases the court only considers the First Amendment rights of the dissenting workers, and not those of the majority of workers who support the union and its political speech (Fisk and Chemerinsky, 2013). The union dues cases represent a direct conflict between the individual rights of dissenting workers and the collective rights of union members. In these cases, the court has made it clear that individual liberty trumps collective liberty, at the expense of the First Amendment rights of unions and their members.

C. Union dues and the right not *to organize*

In the union dues cases, the courts have robustly enforced the right *not* to organize, at the expense of unions and their members. Thus, courts have not only limited the First Amendment rights of union members, but also have enforced the First Amendment rights of employees in unionized workplaces who do not wish to belong to unions or support their activities. More recently, the court has threatened to overrule *Abood* and hinted that requiring anti-union government employees to pay any union dues may violate their First Amendment rights.

Abood and *Beck* reflect a compromise ruling which authorizes "union security agreements" – contracts that require all employees, whether union members or not, to share the costs of negotiating and administering collective bargaining agreements. The plaintiffs argue that requiring them to pay dues is a form of compelled speech, violating their First Amendment rights. In *Abood*, the court agreed, but held that such compulsion was justified as a means of maintaining labor peace and overcoming the free rider problem. Though paying agency fees did intrude on the First Amendment rights of anti-union employees, the court held that the government interests served by union security agreements outweighed this burden. However, the government could not justify requiring dissenting employees to pay for political expenditures by unions (Sachs, 2012). This is the basis for the distinction between dues paid for economic and political issues discussed above. It enables unions to function within the workplace in exchange for restrictions of their political activities.

The challengers in *Beck* and *Abood* were funded by the right to work movement, and sought to achieve the same goals (Lee, 2014). Like right to work laws, the decisions limiting the use of union dues reduce the amount of money that unions have to spend on First Amendment activity. They tax the resources of unions and limit their effectiveness overall. Recently, the court has expanded the rights of dissenting workers and indicated that it might be willing to strike down the payment of *any* union dues by non-union members.

In *Knox v SEIU* (2012), the court held that the First Amendment prohibited public sector unions from using dues for political expenditures unless employees had affirmatively opted in. Knox represents the first time that the court has held that an opt-out system is not sufficient to protect non-union employees from compelled speech. The court gave no weight to the First Amendment rights of the union, or the majority of the union members who wanted to express a political message. Instead, the court focused entirely on dissenting members (Fisk and Chemerisnky). Most notably, Justice Alito's majority opinion appears to suggest that requiring any non-union worker to pay union dues might violate the First Amendment. Justice Alito opined: "[B]y allowing unions to collect any fees from non-members and by permitting unions to use opt-out rather than opt-in schemes when annual dues are billed, our cases have substantially impinged upon the First Amendment rights of non-members" (p. 2295). This dicta suggests that a majority of the court may be considering a holding that bargaining based on majority rule exclusivity is unconstitutional "even if it is done on a free rider basis" (Fisk and Chemerinsky, 2013, p. 1074).

In *Harris v Quinn* (2014), the court held that the state of Illinois could not require home health care personal assistants, who chose not to be members of the union representing such assistants, to pay any dues to that union. The court held that the *Abood* rule did not apply to the plaintiffs in *Harris* because they did not fall under the definition of public sector employees. In his majority decision, Justice Alito again questioned the portion of the *Abood* ruling which allowed unions to require non-members to pay dues to support collective bargaining. Alito opined that the *Abood* court had failed to appreciate the difference between public and private sector workers, arguing that the context of public sector employment made it too difficult to distinguish between economic and political issues. But the court was also skeptical of union security agreements in general, questioning why the union needed the dues of dissenting employees to operate effectively when it presumably had the support of the majority of employees.

After *Harris*, it appeared that the court was poised to overrule *Abood* and find that union security agreements violate the First Amendment rights of public sector employees. In 2015, the court heard the case of *Friedericks v California Teachers Association*, a case which provided another possible vehicle to overrule *Abood*. The death of Justice Scalia prior to the court issuing its ruling in Friedericks leaves the status of public sector unions in doubt. The status of *Abood* hangs in the balance, depending on the next Justice to join the Supreme Court.

Like right to work laws, the union security clause rulings have the effect of limiting the financial resources of unions, and restricting the ability of unions to engage in political activity. The dicta in these rulings suggesting that the court go even further is frightening. Though these rulings would appear to be limited to public employees due to the state action doctrine, it is possible that the court would apply the rule to private sector employees as a matter of statutory interpretation, as it did in *Beck*. Thus, the union dues cases threaten the very existence of unions. In these cases, there is a danger that the dissenting employee's individual right not to organize may trump the majority employees' collective right to organize.

IV. Conclusion

Do recent political developments and case law preclude the argument that there is a right to organize? Maybe, but maybe not. Rights have proven to be incredibly resilient in our society – when people continually assert them, eventually the law adopts them. Thus, politics matters more than case law. If workers come to believe that they lack the right to organize, and stop advocating for the right, then it will be extinguished by political developments. There is a constitutional right to organize, despite decades of court rulings hostile to the collective aspects of the right. The future resilience of the right to organize depends not only on court precedent, but also on the strength of that right in our constitutional culture.

4

LABOR RIGHTS AS NATURAL RIGHTS

Sean Coyle[1]

This chapter examines the question of labor and of workers as a problem of social justice. Liberal free market societies in the West are overwhelmingly orientated toward the ideals of personal autonomy and unlimited economic growth. The first of these ideals has long been associated with the withdrawal of "the state," and the limitation of the competence of government to intervene or interfere in the lives of its citizens. Privacy and freedom of choice, the two great demands of modern times, result in a society in which the vast majority of interactions are transactional and anonymous. The second ideal, of economic growth, requires more direct and substantial intervention by government; for the very "freedom" of the market which is regarded as necessary for unending growth is not a natural product of economic activity but the result of careful regulation: the manipulation of interest rates, control of inflation, protection of intellectual property, prohibition of insider and criminal practices, and so forth. But the necessity of control places government in the position, not of master, but of servant to the economy and its corporations. Hence political understandings of the question of justice in the context of labor are too readily hijacked by the very liberal capitalism they seek to constrain, at a time when workers' unions have lost their power (with the disappearance of the class struggle). I argue that a coherent response to the question cannot stem from an ideological perspective.

The modern view of labor understands it as a commodity, a product that can be bought and sold at market rates. Given the overall scarcity of jobs, workers must increasingly adapt their expectations about remuneration, working conditions etc. to the varying levels of market demand for their skills (i.e. to the demands of employers). Whilst the commodification of labor is of benefit to the skill-mobile, who are no longer confined by circumstances of birth or class, it compounds the essential

1 Professor of Jurisprudence, Birmingham Law School.

vulnerability of those whose skills or situation – such as family or other commitments, health issues, etc. – are less transferable. The necessary moral criticism of the market cannot come from politics, for the political fortunes of governments rest with successful economic indicators, nor from economics, for the market cannot be considered apart from its political interpretations. It must come from a properly radical criticism, from outside the political and economic perspectives that are in question: from the non-political and non-ideological moral demands of "natural law,"[2] as presented above all by Aquinas and articulated as demands by the Catholic Church.

It may seem strange to modern ears to *contrast* moral reasoning with ideals, used as we are to using these terms interchangeably: the attempt to amend actions and practices, to cure injustices, is to judge them in the light of, or move them toward, "moral ideals;" ideals of justice. But it is of fundamental importance to distinguish between the position of the inquirer into the nature of the "just state," or "good *polis*," and the ideologue who treats all questions of morality as "value judgments" in the modern sense of that term, in which they appear either as subjective valuations in opposition to the real world, or as the projections of an ideal world that ignores the real obstacles of recalcitrance and self interest that characterize the real world. Plato and Aristotle were not ideologues, indulging subjective valuations in opposition to reality. Their efforts to describe the character of the just state were part of an objective inquiry into the nature of reality (see Voeglin, 1957, p. 83; Finnis, 2010, p. 246). As such, "ideals," considered as aspirational guides to excellent conduct, must be contrasted with the *duties* that structure moral action in the present, considered as baselines or demands.[3]

The Church's critique of labor markets comes from the only possible place: from outside the system of politics and economics as such. It directs its demands at *all* political and economic systems, and gives special priority to none of them. Its fundamental concern is truly with human vulnerability, firmly committing itself to the situation of the worker because it is a "church of the poor" (Encyclical *Laborem Exercens* of Pope John Paul II, 14 Sept 1981 §8). I consider the detail of the Church's position in section II. First, I will spell out the underpinning framework of practical reasoning about moral matters as drawn from Aquinas. Readers in a hurry could possibly proceed to section II, if they are content with the above explanation and sufficiently familiar with the Thomist standpoint on practical reason which underpins the Church's teachings.

I. Practical reason and moral good

In modern times we are used to the suggestion that our grasp of moral ideas is dependent upon our acceptance of, or unconscious immersion in, some or other

2 "Natural law" is for these purposes an entirely secular idea, grounded in claims as to what is reasonable. Aquinas's arguments typically run from what is reasonable and *therefore* natural, rather than vice versa: see *Summa Theologiae* [hereafter *ST*] I-II.71.2c; I-II.94.3 ad 2.

3 On the distinction between a morality of aspiration and a morality of duty, see Fuller (1969), chapter 1.

ideology. But the suppositions involved in our moral judgments – which are statements of, and not about, our beliefs concerning what is true – and of sciences such as anthropology, in fact reveal that this grasp is grounded in an understanding of what is good for human beings; the intelligibility of quite diverse human practices, from handshakes to human cannibalism, arises from their aiming, sometimes incompetently or grotesquely, at human goods, such as life, bravery, sociability, and security. Our grasp of such goods, and the scientific objectivity of comparative anthropology, depend in no way upon prior ideology, for ideology is among the data being compared. So the question to ask is not whether, but *how*, practical reason arrives at a grasp of moral ideas.

Aquinas tells us that the *first* precept of practical reason is that good is to be done and pursued, and evil avoided (ST I-II.94.2c).[4] "Good" has here the intelligibility of "end" [*finis*], so that *whatever* practical reason naturally apprehends as good belongs to the idea of "to be done," and defines the objects of action – the things to be pursued – whereas those things that are contrary to good are singled out by reason as to be avoided. This principle is the foundation for all practical thinking because good in this generic sense is the first thing to fall within the unrestricted grasp of the mind when reasoning practically: for every possible principle of action acts for the sake of some end, and the end has the intelligible character [*ratio*] of good (ST I-II.94.2c).

The equation of "good" with "end" must, of course, eventually meet with some restriction if any intelligibility is to be given to the idea of objects contrary to good [*malum*]. But the necessary restrictions upon what the mind can authentically consider as good do not need to be derived from any ideology or political stance. For, according to the classical and medieval typology, whereas some things are good because they are useful for some further end [*bonum utile*] and others because they are pleasurable [*delectabile*], some good things are good both self-evidently [*per se nota*] and in themselves [*honestas*], without reference to any further end (ST I.5.6). Air travel is a good (if it is a good) only because of its serviceability for further ends, the objects of one's travels; perhaps these include the delightful contemplation of celebrated landmarks, yet the delight experienced is itself adjunct of something that is good merely in itself and for no further reason. If we say that travel broadens the mind, it is because a broad mind – the accumulation of knowledge of things, or direct aesthetic experiences – is deemed to be good, not only in virtue of possible uses of such knowledge and experiences, perhaps as future conversation pieces, but because they are worth having in their own right, and intelligible, sane objects to pursue even in the absence of further more remote goals.

The identification of *bona honesta* derives in the first place from those natural inclinations that human beings share with all beings, such as the inclination to preserve one's own being and to ward off threats and dangers. In common with other animals, human beings also share the inclination to generate and educate offspring,

4 "*bonum est faciendum et prosequendum et malum vitandum*".

but there is additionally in human beings an inclination to those goods identified according to reason. Aquinas gives as examples of *bona honesta* such things as knowledge and the social friendship between humans, "as well as other things" (ST I-II.94.2). Such goods can be grasped by the intellect prior to any moral considerations and devoid of any idealistic, ideological or further practical commitment.

Late scholastic commentaries on Aquinas elaborated a further distinction within the category of *bonum honestum*, with the aim of clarifying Aquinas's theoretical intentions. Accordingly one can distinguish possible objects of pursuit that are good in themselves when contemplated simply from the perspective of fulfillment of human inclinations [*bonum naturale*] from ends that are properly morally good [*bonum morale*]. In drawing this distinction, the Thomistic interpreters could plausibly claim to be faithfully transmitting the sense of passages upon which Aquinas apparently or explicitly relies and clarifying Aquinas's meaning where he speaks generically of the *honestum* or merely the *bonum humanum*.[5] Both the Aristotelian and Stoic sources from which Aquinas draws his arguments understand the *honestum* [uprightness, nobility] as associated with intellectual fulfillment, in contrast to the pleasurable, which pertains to bodily satisfactions such as the quenching of thirst. This seems to accord with Aquinas's treatment in the *Summa Theologiae* I-II.94.2. Though he distinguishes between those inclinations, and thus goods, that belong to rational nature and those which are shared with "other animals" and "all substances," his further remarks make clear that the agent's possession of rational nature transforms the character of those other ranges of goods. For example, he states: "All inclinations, from whatever aspect of human nature, belong to the natural law insofar as they are ruled by reason" (ST I-II.94.2 ad 2) and, "[a]lthough reason is a discrete thing, yet it directs all things concerning the human being; thus whatever can be ruled by reason, falls under the law of reason" (ST I-II.94.2 ad 3). The *honestum* thus includes a number of natural goods, some of which are mentioned by Aquinas, including life and knowledge, which are related to propriety and virtue even if not exclusively moral in the modern sense of that term. But the focus (focal meaning) of the *honestum* pertains to "noble" goods: proper behavior, peace-seeking, avoidance of error and false belief etc. Reason lifts the subordinate ranges of natural goods into properly moral goods: sexual appetite into the generation and rearing of children, sociable nature into a requirement to seek peace, stability and cultural capital, and so on.

It does so for it grasps these goods precisely as *human* goods [*esse bona humana*]: not merely as good for myself personally, but good for others insofar as their nature resembles mine. To act in ways that erode or threaten those goods, or in ways that fail to secure or at least allow for the participation of others in those goods, therefore constitute moral wrongs.

5 Suarez, *De Legibus* II.7.5; see also II.7.4: "the natural law embraces all precepts or moral principles which are plainly characterized by the goodness necessary to rectitude of conduct, whereas the contrary precepts plainly involve immorality and wickedness. This is the opinion of Saint Thomas." See also II.15.2, and *Disputationes Metaphysicae*, X.

One can thus identify duties of justice or, more precisely, the grounds of those duties by reference to human goods (and "bads") that can be apprehended by the intellect prior to the development in one's mind of any specific political, historical, cultural, or ideological theses. The particular historical or material circumstances of a community, or even community of nations, may well define more precisely what is due, as a matter of justice, to persons, for as Aquinas goes on to say, "[t]he natural law is the same for all concerning its general principles [*prima principia communia*], both as to their correctness and knowledge of them; but in the case of conclusions from those principles, pertaining to certain matters of detail, their validity and knowability is the same for all only in the majority of cases [*ut in pluribus*], and in some few cases they may fail altogether, either as to validity, by reason of certain obstacles . . . or as to knowledge, since reason in some cases can be deflected by emotion, or evil habits or dispositions" (I-II.94.4; see also 94.6). There is, in other words, no one particular form of regime that constitutes the right way to live, but *all* regimes are held accountable against standards of justice and reasonableness, standards which owe nothing to ideology, for they are the measure against which ideologies are judged and which determine a bedrock or baseline from which no society can legitimately deviate.

In modern times, Aquinas's treatment of the *bona humana* has been reinterpreted and elaborated by "new natural lawyers" such as John Finnis. Finnis (1980/2011a) seeks to give an exhaustive list of the *bona humana* (which he calls "basic goods") on the basis of Aquinas's discussion above: (1) knowledge and appreciation of reality; (2) skillful performance, in work or play, for its own sake; (3) bodily life, and the components of its fullness (safety, health etc.); (4) sociability, meaning harmony, association, and friendship between persons; (5) marriage as a lifelong union and basis for the generation and education of children; (6) practical reasonableness and order in one's intellectual and emotional life; and (7) religion, the contemplation of ultimate meanings, and the attempt to follow the mode of life they indicate (Finnis 2011b, vol. 1, 244n).

Though Finnis clearly regards the basic goods as *bona honesta* (Finnis 2011a, 76), in fact they are closer in character to the *bonum naturale*, and thus not *honestum* in the focal sense. However that may be, as human, rather than merely personal, goods, they form the subject matter of moral judgments as being in some sense *due* to persons, without qualification, so that transgressions against these forms of good or failure to open them to pursuit by others, constitute injustices. Finnis considers the list of seven basic goods as exhaustive, in that any further imaginable form of human good, if it is *genuinely* good, will turn out to be either a mode of engagement with one of the basic goods, or else some amalgamation of numerous such goods.

My purpose here is to explore a form of human good that is the substance of a natural right, which is not mentioned anywhere by Finnis, and which does not, in my view, reduce to any of the "basic goods" enumerated by him. I am referring to "meaningful labor."

II. Labor as a natural right

In a wide sense, all practical reasoning concerns reason directed to a work and the identification of things to be pursued through work [*opus*]. But it is in the narrower sense of labor as a mode of productive and remunerated employment, including self-employment, "earning a living," or "making one's way in the world" that it is proper to speak of labor as a natural right. It is in this narrower sense that labor is to be identified as a human good, something which ought to figure in every human life to some degree, and which, as a demand of justice, requires the protection of positive law. Here I will confine myself to outlining some of the attributes of labor as a natural right, without pretending to exhaust all that might be said in explanation or defense of it.

As a form of good, meaningful labor is distinct from the good of skillful performance, for it is not the sheer activity that is in issue, though this aspect of good may undeniably form an incident of work. Similarly, it is distinct from knowledge, though of course knowledge is required for the carrying out of laborious tasks. Its goodness for the agent lies in its genuine productivity, the fact that it is, for want of a better word, "honest" labor, as distinct from work that is (a) pointless or unproductive, designed merely to eat up the worker's time, or (b) exploitative either of the worker or of others, or otherwise directed to some unedifying end, such as a dishonest or criminal enterprise. To these characteristics we should also add that the work is appropriately remunerated, or in some other way contributory to the worker's own ends or interests, as well as freely undertaken, as distinct from slavery or the workhouse.

In common with the other basic goods, meaningful labor is self-constituting activity – it contributes to the agent's development of capacities, potentialities, and realization of ends. But it is distinguishable from the other forms of good in being directed, if indeed meaningful, particularly toward the common good, as a contribution to the community's "cultural capital," including, for these purposes, monetary or material capital. Modern ethics in general, but powerful strains of Kantian moral philosophy in particular, have laid great emphasis upon the principle that persons must be treated as ends-in-themselves rather than as means to further ends. That this principle gives expression to an important dimension of human dignity should not be doubted. But modern ethics entirely overlooks an equally important principle: that there is a certain dignity in the agent's own determination to serve as a *means* to the common good of the community – that is, to be of use, to live a life that has significance, to avoid being a mere wastrel or drain on collective resources. There is a moral necessity in living for others and not only of oneself: an aspect of a good life that is genuinely good also for the person who makes themselves an instrument for others. Recall for example the remarks of the bystanders at Scrooge's grave site in *A Christmas Carol*.

It is perhaps the assumptions of capitalism on the one hand, and of socialist central planning on the other, which have obscured for modern ethicists the understanding that such determination on the part of the agent is a genuine aspect of the agent's *own* flourishing. For the human being is defined not least by the work that he or she does. Amongst modern sources, it is only the Church that has given expression to the ideas I am here raising. Across a number of documents, from *Rerum Novarum* ("new things" relating to capital and labor) in 1891, to *Laborem Exercens* (1981), *Economic Justice for All* (1986) and *Centesimus Annus* (1991), the Church has articulated its staunch defense of labor unions and workers' organizations, and has challenged the idea of labor as a commodity; work is for the worker, not the worker for the work. From these documents can be extracted two thoughts in particular: (1) work must be understood as a human good, insofar as it forms part of the self-development of the individual, and is thus a fitting subject for rights, for "the self-realization of the person is the measure of what is right and wrong" (*Laborem Exercens* §6);[6] and (2) the needs of workers extend beyond remuneration and contractual conditions, but reach into the value of the work itself; they must have a share in the responsibility and creativity of the work process, not feel themselves to be cogs in a machine moved from above (*Laborem Exercens* §15).

Rerum Novarum (Encyclical of Pope Leo XIII, 15 May 1891), can easily be mistaken for a political document. Its subject matter is the position of the worker under free market capitalism and under communist central planning. But the encyclical actually carries on the Thomist tradition of the Church in asserting moral demands from *outside* these political systems – and indeed all political systems – as criticisms of any political or ideological system which fails to respect basic demands of justice (*Quadragesimo Anno*, encyclical of Pope Pius XI, 15 May 1931, §§14, 42). The theme of the encyclical is the "hardheartedness of employers," "greed," and "rapacious usury" that obtain under circumstances of "unchecked competition," and the tendency of the open market to concentrate matters pertaining to the hiring of labor and the conduct of trade in the hands of the relatively few. Socialist planning, on the other hand, works upon the poor person's envy of the rich, so that much that ought to be private passes into public ownership, and this naturally but significantly erodes the power of persons to dispose of their remuneration as they please. Socialists thereby deprive the worker above all by divesting all workers of the liberty to dispose freely of their wages in the hope and possibility of increasing their resources and bettering their condition in life (*Rerum Novarum* §§5-6). Neither private property nor profit, nor even inequality itself is contrary to human good (*Rerum Novarum* §§8–13) – natural law does not demand a "flat" society devoid of differentiation between persons (*Rerum Novarum* §17). The key duties of employers are to ensure opportunities for earning an *honorable* livelihood, not to misuse workers as *mere* means to profit, or as mere "resources" to be consumed, and to avoid exposing workers to "corrupting circumstances" or "dangerous occasions" (*Rerum Novarum* §20).

Virtuous and properly remunerated work – what I am calling meaningful labor – is understood by the Church to be a vital matter not only for spiritual

6 Extant translations of the encyclicals have been followed except in a few cases.

wellbeing but also the temporal and earthly interests of persons. The Church is emphatically a church of the poor and the wretched (*Rerum Novarum* §28-30). Throughout its social justice encyclicals, it speaks very clearly the language of vulnerability. It desires to penetrate the realities of injustice that lie behind formal considerations of equality or of freedom, and it recognizes the need for a collective effort to respond to the plight of the vulnerable, not only by the Church but by "all human agencies," preeminently the State itself (*Rerum Novarum* §§31–32; *Quadragesimo Anno* §§25–27, 78, 80–82).

Subsequent encyclicals have reinforced and elaborated these demands. The Church has not ceased to point out specific injustices which, across the years, have arisen from the mistaken belief that "the economic and moral orders are so distinct from and alien to one another that the former depends in no way upon the latter" (*Quadragesimo Anno* §42). It is "reason itself" which, through its assessment of the capacities of the human body and mind, and of natural resources, determines the limits of productive human effort, the rationality and morality of means and ends.

Quadragesimo Anno, and subsequent encyclicals, are not short on specific advice and detail in relation to the rights and duties of workers and employers. The economic and moral good of the community are considered as inextricably linked. Thus, although the teachings are structured around basic principles, the principles are elaborated in the light of prevailing socio-economic problems. "[T]he remuneration of work is not something that can be left to the laws of the marketplace," asserts *Laborem Exercens*, "nor should it be a decision left to the will of the more powerful. It must be determined in accordance with justice and equity; which means that workers must be paid a wage which allows them to live a truly human life and to fulfill their family obligations in a worthy manner" (*Laborem Exercens* §15). But what do justice and equality actually demand? Amongst other things,

> [i]n determining the amount of the wage, the condition of a business and of the one carrying it on must also be taken into account; for it would be unjust to demand excessive wages which a business cannot stand without its ruin and consequent calamity to the workers. If, however, a business makes too little money, because of lack of energy or lack of initiative or because of indifference to technical and economic progress, that must not be regarded a just reason for reducing the compensation of the workers. But if the business in question is not making enough money to pay the workers an equitable wage because it is being crushed by unjust burdens or forced to sell its product at less than a just price, those who are thus the cause of the injury are guilty of grave wrong, for they deprive workers of their just wage and force them under the pinch of necessity to accept a wage less than fair (*Quadragesimo Anno* §§72, 74).

But many other factors also enter into the assessment of a just wage, for example:

> the effective contribution which each individual makes to the economic effort, the financial state of the company for which he works, the requirements of

> the general good of the particular country – having regard especially to the repercussions on the overall employment of the working force in the country as a whole – and finally the requirements of the common good of the universal family of nations.

Remuneration is not the only consideration that pertains to the worker's dignity as a worker, as opposed to a mere asset or slave. Further considerations include, but are not confined to, the question of working conditions. Some *active* involvement in the shaping or direction of the work, and of the broader concerns of which it may be part, are necessary:

> The capital at the disposal of management is in part the product of the labor of those who have toiled in the company over the years, including currently employed workers. As a minimum, workers have a right to be informed in advance when such decisions are under consideration, a right to negotiate with management about possible alternatives, and a right to fair compensation and assistance with retraining and relocation expenses should these be necessary. Since even these minimal rights are jeopardized without collective negotiation, industrial cooperation requires a strong role for labor unions in our changing economy (*Mater et Magistra,* encyclical of Pope John XXII, 15 May 1961 §71).

In a similar way, Pope John Paul II observed that the needs of workers extend beyond remuneration and contractual conditions, but reach into the value of the work itself: they must have a share in the responsibility and creativity of the work-process. "They want to feel that they are working for themselves – an awareness that is smothered in a bureaucratic system where they only feel themselves to be 'cogs' in a huge machine moved from above" (*Laborem Exercens* §15).

Throughout its teachings, the Church displays a concern not only with the rights of workers, but also the character of the labor itself. In a sense, these concerns are the same: the recognition of *meaningful* labor as a human good involves a recognition of the right of the worker not to be exploited, but neither to be made an *instrument* of exploitation.[7] It embodies an understanding of work as "the immediate expression of a human personality, [which] must always be rated higher than the possession of external goods which of their very nature are merely instrumental" (*Mater et Magistra* §107). This amounts to a clear recognition of meaningful labor as a *bonum honestum*, and thus as an object or ground for a set of natural rights.[8]

7 Pastoral letter on Catholic social teaching and the US economy, "Economic justice for all" (1986), §303. See also *Mater et Magistra* §99.

8 *Laborem Exercens* §9: "Work remains a good thing, not only because it is useful and enjoyable, but also because it expresses and increases the worker's dignity. Through work, we not only transform the world but are ourselves transformed, becoming more human in our being."

Such rights do not derive from political or economic starting points or from ideological perspectives, for workers' rights "cannot be doomed to be the mere result of economic systems" (*Laborem Exercens* §17). Instead, "the thing that must shape the whole economy is respect for the rights of workers within each country and all through the world's economy" (*Laborem Exercens* §17). It is therefore entirely "right to struggle *against* an unjust economic system that does not uphold the priority of the human being over capital and land" (*Centesimus Annus* §35, encyclical letter of Pope John Paul II, 15 May 1991, emphasis added). All must recognize that work is for the worker and not the worker for the work. "Work itself can have greater or lesser objective value, but all work should be judged by the measure of dignity given to the person who carries it out" (*Laborem Exercens* §6). Above all, "[w]e must pay more attention to the one who works than to what the worker does. The self-realization of the human person is the measure of what is right and wrong" (*Laborem Exercens* §6).

The encyclicals, along with other documents of the Church's social teaching, contain many other pronouncements on the position and situation of workers, some understood as articulating general standards of justice, demands of morality to which there are no possible exceptions (i.e. baseline rights), and others which are more specific, in relation to particular evils of capitalism or socialism to which a response is morally urgent. Taken together, the encyclicals represent a penetrating criticism of the treatment and general position of workers, one that proceeds not from any specific political or ideological standpoint, but remains critical of all such standpoints.

The Church's teachings on labor rights exhibit exactly the structure of Aquinas's treatment of practical (non-ideological) reasoning. They proceed from the intellect's initial grasp of human goods as objects to be pursued, to the question of how such goods are to be secured, precisely as *human* goods, even in a world of recalcitrance and self-interest. The most basic demands of justice generated by the recognition of meaningful labor as good for human beings, embody general principles that are intelligible to all persons, and morally bind everyone without exception. The further implications of these duties, as they arise in relation to specific circumstances (economic, historical, social etc.) are subject to a certain variation, though they are definite enough to be rationally apprehended as demands in most situations [*ut in pluribus*]. These are not ideals to be obtained, but duties of justice in the here and now.

We do not thereby escape the difficulties involved in opposing the vested interests of the recalcitrant or conspirators against the common good, or in overcoming the enthusiasms of the ideologues. But the perspective of natural law furnishes a standpoint from which the errors, deceptions, and empty justifications of those who exploit the vulnerable subject, or remain silently complicit in the face of such exploitation, can be soberly, relentlessly and above all finally, exposed.

PART II

Work and social welfare

The second section of this book examines the state's role in providing for the wellbeing of its citizens. Vulnerability theory envisions a responsive state that has a duty to act to ensure its citizens have an adequate measure of resilience. The most obvious way that a responsive state can provide for the welfare of its citizens is through direct, publicly-run social welfare programs. But these public social welfare programs operate in connection with private systems, and both need to be analyzed together as a single system of social welfare. The authors in this section discuss some of the "private" means to achieve resilience through employment, such as wages, retirement benefits, and health insurance.

When establishing and maintaining public welfare programs, the state often assumes that many citizens will be able to achieve resilience through the workplace, with the public systems operating as a "safety net" in case the private systems fail individual citizens. Vulnerability theory suggests that it is ultimately the state's responsibility to ensure the welfare of its citizens, whether the means is public or private. If the state chooses to modify, privatize, or discontinue a public welfare program, it has an obligation to ensure that the change does not have an undue effect on the resilience of the affected parties. Likewise, the state impacts the ability of workers to obtain resilience at work through regulation (or, just as importantly, failure to regulate), and therefore the state has an obligation to ensure that the private systems are fair.

The chapters in this section discuss the tension between private and public ordering of social welfare. The authors describe situations in which states cast social welfare as an issue of private contract or individual rights, which often leads to an abdication of responsibility by the state. The authors in this section highlight the importance of thinking about welfare as a collective issue, rather than an individual one. Thinking collectively affects decisions about public benefits and also suggests new areas of regulation that would improve resilience through private institutions and employment. At the end of the day, workers should have a decent income, a dignified life after retirement, and a means to obtain quality health care, whether these things are provided by the state or through a "private" system that is regulated by the state.

In "Paid care work, gendered labor law and the vulnerability of community," Lydia Hayes examines how labor law and privatization can undermine the community building aspects of social welfare programs, such as home care for the elderly. Through stories drawn from interviews with caregivers, she demonstrates how traditional legal conceptions of home and business as "private" spheres undermine the resilience of both workers and service-users, and how a vulnerability approach helps us to understand the social and institutional context in which care work occurs.

In her chapter, "Vulnerability, workfare law and resilient social justice," Camilla Sabroe Jydebjerg examines the way that Denmark provides resilience by securing economic assistance to people who are jobless. She argues that the Nordic Welfare States previously approached the role of the state in a way consistent with vulnerability theory, viewing the state as responsible for providing resilience to its inhabitants, but this view is being challenged by a workfare agenda. She closely analyzes provisions in law concerning people that are currently outside the regular workforce and receiving social security assistance and assesses the degree to which these provisions offer resilient social justice for people receiving assistance.

In "Contract as public law: the public nature of collective bargaining agreements," Risa Lieberwitz examines the importance of statutory rights to unionization and collective bargaining in achieving the public values of the welfare state and analyzes the way that exercise of these rights promotes values of democratic participation and economic redistribution. She argues that collective bargaining has been central to creating greater workplace equality while at the same time raising employees' wages and benefits, improving working conditions, and providing increased job security, and discusses the obstacles to broadening the scope of unionization and the redistribution of wealth and power.

Susan Bisom-Rapp and Malcolm Sargeant's chapter, "Acknowledging but transcending gender at work: applying the model of lifetime disadvantage and vulnerability theory to women's poverty in retirement," illustrates how the disproportionate rates of poverty experienced by women in retirement are produced by multiple factors connected to gender and how the disadvantage produced by many of those factors is cumulative. They argue that addressing women's systemic lifetime disadvantage requires a coordinated approach rather than the piecemeal, disjointed incrementalism that often characterizes changes in employment law. They suggest that vulnerability theory can be used as a normative frame for developing regulatory solutions that account for but move beyond gender to provide resilience in the face of the economic insecurity experienced by all working people.

Finally, in "Laboring freedom: neoliberalism, the jurisprudence of Obamacare, and the welfare state left," Jack Jackson examines the Affordable Care Act through both Marxist analysis and vulnerability theory. He finds that while the law is flawed and incomplete, it also represents a significant step towards separating the provision of necessary services from its long-standing connection to labor, enhancing the freedom of workers.

5

PAID CARE WORK, GENDERED LABOR LAW AND THE VULNERABILITY OF COMMUNITY

LJB Hayes[1]

I. Introduction

This chapter suggests that the vulnerability of "community" is impacted by the gendering of labor law. Its assessment draws on interview research I conducted with homecare workers in England, women who are employed to provide essential support to older and disabled people living in their own homes.[2] Central to the discussion is the narrative of a research participant to whom I have given the pseudonym "Sophie." Like many other homecare workers with whom I spoke, Sophie was just days away from losing her job. The public sector local authority for which she had worked for almost a decade was closing down its homecare department and transferring work to almost fifty separate private sector organizations with which it had entered into service delivery contracts following a process of cost competitive tendering. Sophie's story, set out in the following section, sheds light on what it means for an individual homecare worker and her service-user to physically experience the relocating of care services from the public to the private sector.[3] It draws attention to the apparent ease with which care services can move from one paradigm to another through the legal metaphor of contract, and its dissonance with the human experience of deep trauma as a consequence of service transfer.

1 Lecturer in Law, Cardiff University, Wales, UK.

2 With thanks to the *Journal of Law and Society* for funding the junior research fellowship which enabled me to conduct the study 2013–2016. It is the basis of my monograph, *Stories of Care, A Labour of Law: Gender and Class at Work.* (London: Palgrave Macmillan, 2017).

3 All data has been anonymized and research participants gave written consent to take part in the study and for their comments and opinions to be published once their identity and those of their service-users was disguised. For information about methods and the research study, see Hayes 2017, Chapter 1.

Inevitably, vulnerability is a constitutive feature of caregiving. However, I use Sophie's narrative to account for state-funded social care as being both a physical and existential resource which anticipates and accommodates human vulnerability. It not only supplies the material support necessary to sustain life in the face of adversity, disease and physical dependency, but also helps us to understand our place in the world and see beauty and meaning in the vulnerability of our shared existence (see Fineman, 2010, pp. 269–272). I argue that understandings of community have been produced and promoted through the provision of state-funded care in the private homes of older and disabled people. This draws attention to ways in which social care expresses the capacity of the state to support notions of community which mediate, compensate or lessen human vulnerabilities. Engaging in a vulnerability analysis requires that we move beyond a narrow view of Sophie and her service-user as being conceptually marooned within the confines of the domestic home. Instead of conceiving of paid care work as the product of an individuated interaction, we can recognize the labor of state-funded paid care workers as a potentially progressive expression of community. Yet Sophie's narrative also opens our eyes to ways in which the physical and existential qualities of state-funded care have been undermined by contractual processes of privatization and service transfer. Notions of community, established ways of being, shared understandings of what counts and what matters most, caring relationships and personal hopes, quality of life, and forms of identity have been lost in the relocation of services.

It is my argument that this undermining of the qualities of paid care work has been facilitated by the gendered inadequacy of labor law. The legal protections made available by the state in relation to employment do not adequately recognize the validity of paid care work as employment. They have failed to uphold the integrity of homecare workers' employment contracts in the context of service provision change, they do not protect homecare workers' pay from the negative influence of sex discrimination, and instead justify the contractual imposition of unpaid labor (endemic across the private sector homecare industry) by failing to recognize, in full, care workers' working time for the purposes of statutory minimum wage protection. The state has actively crafted its privatization agenda in pursuit of large reductions in labor costs and appears ambivalent about the labor standards entitlements of homecare workers (Atkinson and Lucas, 2013; Hayes, 2015, 2017; Lewis and West, 2014). As a consequence of the state's unwillingness to protect the employment of paid caregivers and, moreover, the tenacity with which it has exploited gendered labor market vulnerabilities, the state has undermined the fabric of what it means to be part of a resilient community.

II. Sophie's story

Homecare workers give personal care to older and disabled people, visiting them in their own homes to provide assistance with washing, dressing, continence/incontinence and basic nursing care. Their caregiving also supports people at the end of life by maintaining discreet routines and promoting personal dignity. In line with demographic changes seen in many other parts of the world, the UK population is aging. Rising demand for elder care has prompted the state to shift financial resources away from institutional care and towards the provision of care in people's own homes. State funding accounts for about 80% of the service volume of the entire UK homecare sector (Holmes, 2015, p. 10). It is especially evident since the labor market restructuring which has followed the financial crisis of 2008 that the homecare industry has become a major source of low-wage employment for women without formal educational qualifications – a demographic who face an increasingly restricted range of employment options (Hayes, 2015). There are approximately a million jobs in which workers provide care at home to older and disabled people, and the size of the workforce is expected to double within a decade. However, wages are by far the largest component in the cost of service provision and the price of services purchased from the private sector is about half the average cost of public sector homecare provision (UKHCA, 2010). Since 2010, the UK government has implemented an austerity program in which state spending on public services has been severely reduced. Concerns about the inadequacy of public spending on adult social care pre-date the UK's austerity program, yet adult social care is the largest category of local authority expenditure and has been a principle casualty under conditions of austerity. Local authorities have redoubled their efforts to purchase care from private sector contractors at ever lower prices and applied stricter criteria to individuals seeking care and support. About a third of elderly people who would previously have been eligible are now unentitled to state-funded care (Age UK, 2015).

In the interview research I conducted with homecare workers between 2012 and 2014, I engaged with women who were employed in both the public and private sectors, as well as those who were self-employed or working informally on a cash-in-hand basis (see Hayes, 2017). However, over the past two decades, homecare workers in public sector employment have become increasingly few in number.[4] When I spoke with Sophie, she told me she was to lose her job the following week and felt "devastated." As has happened in local authority areas across the UK, Sophie's public sector employer had decided it was no longer economically viable to directly employ a homecare workforce. Her job was consequently redundant and her labor replaced by workers employed at lower cost, working for contractor

4 In Scotland and Northern Ireland, approximately two-thirds of jobs lie outside of the public sector; in Wales, four-fifths of homecare employment is no longer with local authorities (Holmes, 2015). The privatization of homecare is a process for which there is no foreseeable possibility of reverse, it is most pronounced in England where it seems likely that only 3% of jobs remain with public sector local authorities. Between 1993 and 2011, the proportion of state-funded homecare delivered by the non-public, "independent" sector (some charitable, but mainly private companies) rose in England from 5% to 90% (HSCI, 2012. Community Care Statistics, Social Services Activity, England, 2011–2012, Final Release, p. 46). From 2011 to 2015 the number of direct caregiving jobs with local authorities fell by a further 32%; (HCSI, 2016. Personal Social Services: Staff of Social Services Departments, England, as at September 2015).

organizations that Sophie referred to as "agencies" to reflect the transient, insecure and casualized forms of employment that were on offer to newcomers.

While employed by the local authority, Sophie was able to work full-time in a homecare job which provided regular, guaranteed hours of work, fell within the scope of national structures of public sector collective bargaining coverage and, consequently, benefitted from an occupational pension, sick pay and, most recently, the local implementation of an equality-proofed job evaluation scheme. Homecare was accordingly classified as a skilled job and was paid at rates equal to those of men employed by the local authority in comparable work, as is required under equal pay law. Sophie had many regular service-users and made scheduled visits to their homes of either 30, 60, or 90 minutes' duration, according to a strictly timed rota. However, Sophie talked with particular passion about an older woman named Mavis, of whom she was particularly fond and had been visiting as part of her work schedule for over ten years.

Mavis had dementia, recently she had also been diagnosed with lung cancer. Each morning, Sophie visited Mavis at 8.45am. After so many years, their relationship was not only emotionally close, but it also carried symbolic meaning because Sophie's initiative and caring skill had sustained Mavis' living at home well beyond all initial expectations. Sophie and Mavis were incredibly proud and appreciative of one another. Some time ago, Sophie had deduced that Mavis' confusion was ameliorated if she was woken prior to Sophie's arrival by classical music. She had set a preprogrammed clock radio at Mavis' bedside to play soothing tracks from 8am and reassure her that Sophie would be arriving before the music ended. Sophie and her colleagues also kept a journal for Mavis. Each new day warranted a fresh page entry with a schedule detailing how Mavis' care visits would be arranged and who was coming to visit her. The journal was kept next to a television magazine in her lounge so that Mavis could try and understand where she was in the day, according to what was on the TV.

When homecare was privatized, the work of looking after Mavis was part of a package contracted out to a care agency. The older people for whom Sophie cared were not all transferred over to a single organization as part of that package, but were instead randomly divided between various service delivery contractors. From a labor law perspective, this fragmented form of contract allocation was significant because it prevented Sophie from being able to claim entitlement to retain her job with a transferee organization under legal provisions otherwise available in the event of service provision change (Transfer of Undertakings (Protection of Employment) Regulations, 2006; Hayes, 2017, p. 105–106). However, at an experiential level it meant that Sophie did not know the identity of the organization, nor the care worker, with future responsibility for Mavis' care. Yet in the week prior to the switch, Sophie was required to show her unknown replacement how to care for Mavis. Sophie explained:

> The management turned round to us and said that because [Mavis] was privatized then basically we had got to work with the agency in Mavis'

> home to show the new homecares what needs to be done. As soon as we had told the new girls what they are doing, we are out of the door! We have had to train them, showing them how to do our jobs and then we are gone. It's not fair. But then at the end of the day we have to do it for the families and for the service-users because it's them that will suffer if the new workers don't know how to look after them.

Hence the relational nature of homecare work was used to justify a management instruction to Sophie and her colleagues that they must guide and support workers who were drafted in to their service-users' homes as part of a privatization initiative specifically designed to undercut public sector labor costs. It did not pass without Sophie's attention that the cost of agency labor is lower on the assumption that homecare work can be done without any prior training or experience, via casual employment contracts which lie outside of the scope of public sector collective agreements, and on the basis of terms and conditions which are often set at no more than legally permissible minimum levels. Nevertheless, despite feelings of indignation and deep sadness, Sophie turned up at Mavis' house at 8.45am on the day the handover was to happen. For Mavis' sake, she put on a brave face, acted as though it was nothing but an ordinary day, and waited to show the agency worker the ropes. When no agency worker turned up, Mavis began to get agitated because her routine was not running as she was accustomed. In the circumstances, Sophie decided it was best to begin bathing Mavis on her own, to make her bed, to put her makeup on for her as she normally did and to brush her hair. Just like every other morning, she sang the songs that made Mavis smile and laugh as she gave her medication, while she made her a cup of tea and as she helped Mavis eat her breakfast.

By 9.45am, and still with no agency worker in sight, Sophie was getting very worried on Mavis' behalf because today was the last time she was employed to care for her. Although Mavis didn't vocalize her awareness that Sophie's care was about to be removed from her life, Mavis communicated her sense of loss by staring directly at Sophie with tears rolling down her cheeks. Sophie telephoned the agency directly. She said, "Look, I'm a [local authority] homecare. I've been waiting for over an hour for one of your agency girls to turn up and she hasn't." They replied, "Oh yes, sorry about that but the person who was supposed to come has phoned in sick this morning." Sophie was so cross that she found it hard to contain her feelings. No one had phoned to let Mavis know she was not forgotten; no one had let Mavis know that they cared. To Sophie, the experience indicated that her caregiving relationships, however fundamental they were for her service-users, were utterly invisible within the privatization process.

I spoke with many homecare workers who experienced the feelings of fear and anxiety Sophie expressed so powerfully in her concern for Mavis as a "forgotten about" person. They also shared in Sophie's realization that privatization treated their presence in service-users' lives as insignificant. The decisions taken by the local authority, through which care had been bundled into tradable units in order to be transferred within the legal metaphor of a service delivery contract, failed to take any account of the value of Sophie's longstanding relationship with Mavis and what it meant to both their lives. Instead, Mavis' health and wellbeing, and Sophie's sense of confidence and achievement, were reduced to the abstract concept of an appointment to be fulfilled by any person so employed, for a fixed fee, as part of a service delivery arrangement. As previous UK studies of homecare work have evidenced, formal organizational strategies seeking efficiency and profit in the context of care-contracting fail to capture the relational complexities of homecare work (Bolton and Wibberley, 2013; Rubery et al., 2015).

Both Sophie and Mavis are vulnerable to being hurt and feeling loss as a consequence of privatization because it is their relationship with one another that makes them both feel safe and secure, albeit in different ways. The high quality of the caring bond between them is a product of their co-vulnerability. In Sophie's realization that the state considered caring relationships to be a drain on public resources, rather than as an essential component of social care, she understood how paid care had been reconfigured as a commodity which the state had reprogramed, repackaged, transposed and traded away. It is apparent that social care provision relies upon management, coordination and cooperation between large numbers of actors, a continuity of resources, the predictability of organizational order and timely access to knowledge, equipment and personnel (Bowden, 2000). In my conversations with local authority employed homecare workers, state-funded social care was frequently referred to as "the only link to the outside world" for otherwise isolated service-users. State-funded homecare workers, whether employed by local authorities or by private sector contractors, represent the *outside world* as they deliver the state's responsibilities for ensuring welfare and wellbeing (see Barnes, 2012, p. 118). This is a very important rejoinder to imaginings about paid caregiving as the enactment of closed relationships within private homes.

Although her paid caregiving was clearly based on a personal relationship, Sophie's story represents the idea that state-funded homecare work communicates notions of "community." It is a counter to reductive assumptions about the private and familial qualities of caregiving, through which paid care work is perpetually undervalued in the labor market. Social care has transformed private homes such as Mavis' into accessible places of welfare by opening up the domestic sphere as a receptacle space for caregiving and a place where public priorities are made manifest. In order for the state to systematically address vulnerability, caring for the elderly must be accepted as a collective, as well as a personal, responsibility (Tong, 2013). It requires that we account for paid caregiving as being about so much more than an individual interaction between a worker and a service-user (Milligan and Wiles, 2010). Social care is an essential tenet of community and it follows on from a recognition by the state of its central role in creating the conditions by which human contact and relationships can produce communal forms of resilience to the vulnerabilities of aging, of ill-health, as well as those of employment. In addition to its manifestation within family structures, the formal and social provision of paid care is the foundation of the state's human infrastructure (Boydston, 1990; Glenn, 2010; Kessler-Harris, 1982).

A challenge to understanding paid care work within a collective context is that much academic writing focuses on care as an individualized practice, as an individual experience, and as an individuated relation between caregiver and care receiver. In feminist theory, caregiving is frequently perceived as a dyadic relationship and this tendency is also apparent in industrial relations literature in which homecare workers are typically discussed as individuals performing intimate personal tasks in a relationship with individual service-users. An excessive focus on caregiving relationships as individualized encounters denies the communal "being-ness" of homecare work and fails to appreciate its collective coordination.

Individualizing the substance of homecare work relies upon gendered conventions which assert that what goes on "behind closed doors" is "private." It misreads "home" as a privately owned domain and misconceives of people in receipt of state-funded social care as proprietary actors. At the level of lived experience however, the relationship between a homecare worker and service-user is not private and does not rest upon a one-to-one connection. Caregiving activities are a basis of community, in the sense that communities are forged in the social and cultural reproduction of what it means to be a human being in a particular time and place (Anderson, 2000). It is people, rather than places, which are central to understanding how care expresses solidarity. Communities are not sterile geographic locations but exist within social relationships, through intergenerational linkages, and they are experienced as mental frameworks of imagination and emotional sensation (Anderson, 1983; Pahl, 2005; Studdert, 2006). It was amply described in the research I undertook that homecare work transported meanings of "community" from home to home. Some of these meanings are undoubtedly local in the sense that they reflect a shared local history and knowledge of customs, local traditions, or an appreciation of local dialect or food preferences. However, the work of state-funded paid care workers also transmits meanings of national community and is profoundly rooted in understandings of public duty. A key difference between the unpaid caregiving provided by families and the work of state-funded homecare is that paid caregivers, whether employed by local authorities or contracting organizations, carry public priorities, public duties, and public policy into domestic environments.

Homecare work is particularly susceptible to being undermined as a public duty or a social good because it is located in private domestic homes. Despite the shaping of family life by taxation and legal norms and the shaping of living spaces by social welfare and housing policy, there is a commonplace regard for domestic homes as private, personal places where people live so-called private lives. Similarly, despite the investment of the state in education, transportation, infrastructure, and the general conditions which enable private businesses to thrive, economic markets are considered private, in contradistinction from the state. Regard for paid care as a public good seems incommensurate with understandings of both the home and the marketplace as private spheres. Furthermore, caregiving at home is culturally associated with unpaid family responsibilities, typically shouldered by women. Social expectations of care as the natural, freely available and inevitable outcome of families, marriage, and having children, sit uncomfortably with the economic reality of homecare as a multi billion pound industry. The privatization of homecare work has mixed the economically private realm of the market, together with the socially private realm of the home. The consequence is a concoction in which ideas of public service, state responsibility, democratic accountability, and even adherence to labor standards in law seem out of place.

Sophie's experience of privatization heralded a world in which she sensed all certainties had collapsed, and her intense fear of the future was felt by others similarly impacted by privatization. The threat which privatization presented to their way of life, and to that of their service-users, drew on a collective knowledge that homecare workers weren't worth much in economic terms to the outside world. The impoverishment of women as caregivers has a history that stretches back over generations. It has fueled anxiety about the annihilation of the homecare service and the perils to which service-users would be exposed. From the perspective of local authority homecare workers, privatization was, and is, the antithesis of regard for social care as a form of community resilience in relation to human vulnerability. The trauma inflicted by privatization was a community trauma, understood by them as a finality that warranted grief for the loss of the community foundations of the service in which they worked.

Vulnerability is a universal condition of human existence across the life course. Martha Fineman's (2008) vulnerability thesis draws inspiration from the failures of that which is commonly referred to as "equality law." Ironically, it is a body of law which does not actually seek to produce equality, but rather aims to remove discrimination; a very different purpose, and indeed a partial one, since law provides a range of opportunities for discrimination to be lawfully justified. Undoubtedly, homecare workers have faced longstanding detriment and discrimination in an employment context because of the gendered nature of the tasks they perform, their structural location within private domestic homes and the individual characteristics of the people who typically occupy homecare jobs. However, Fineman has taken issue with legal interventions designed to offer protection to people who fit within a necessarily narrow range of identity characteristics (such as sex, race, disability, religion, age, etc.) which serve as formally recognized proxies of disadvantage (Fineman, 2013b). It is a strategy that has failed to remedy inequalities of wealth and power and is bound to continue to fail because the discrimination model of equality law enables an account of inequality which does not disrupt an assumption at the heart of liberal legal theory; namely, that all human beings, irrespective of context, are equal in law regardless of position or possibilities (Fineman, 2010). Legal recognition of discrimination, therefore, seeks to remedy inequality as though it were a distortion of normative human experience. By way of contrast to the identity-driven conception of discriminatory disadvantage, Fineman's emphasis shifts debates about individual and societal inequality towards the capacity of the state to produce comprehensive conditions of advantage.

Yet a vulnerability approach to inequality and the meeting of human needs ought not simply replace one view of the individual subject of law with another. Instead, it can usefully accommodate understandings in which the vulnerable subject is both an individual and a collective human entity. A vulnerability-centered view enables consideration of the individual in a social context and of the range of social institutions and structures that protect us against some vulnerabilities and expose us to risk in relation to others (Tong, 2013). Understood fully, vulnerability denotes human fallibility and weakness, but it also generates our motivations to reach out to others, to form relationships, and to build institutions (Fineman, 2013c). Vulnerability is a basis for human innovation, growth, creativity and, important for the argument here, it is a basis for notions of community.

Sentiments and concerns about a loss of community values and the discontinuation of historic patterns of social life, social relationships, and behavioral routines are typically attached to narratives of deindustrialization, such as those that chart the loss of male manual work in heavy industries like mining, steel production, or motor manufacturing (Walkerdine, 2010). When we think of large scale redundancies and of industries closed down, we tend to think of men losing jobs they have lived and breathed for decades and of the decimation of *their* communities and of *their* associated loss of pride and tradition. However, Sophie's story testifies that the loss of homecare work to the private sector has blighted the lives of individuals and inflicted community harms which are just as real as those borne of deindustrialization. Sophie said that being expected to show a rival worker how to do her job made her feel "like I'd been slung in the trash."

Yet in social policy, in judicial commentary, and in some strands of academic debate, there is an inclination to conceptualize paid care work on the basis of individual relations between care workers and service-users. In my view, this reflects a conceptual flaw that closes down a vulnerability approach to understanding what it means to provide social care in private homes as a basis of paid employment. Indeed, it dissuades us from thinking about caregiving as a form of paid work at all. Denied a collective industrial identity, and without the credit of public service, the location of homecare work within the domestic sphere is wrongly taken to confirm the separation of homecare labor from the mainstream world of work. This is a gendered representation in which "home" symbolizes a lack of economic worth and the notion of a private realm is used to justify the absence, removal, or ineffectuality of legal rights.

Taking a vulnerability approach to studying the impact of labor law as it actually exists requires us to recognize that labor law cannot remove the condition of vulnerability which is inherent to human experience within the employment relationship. We can posit, however, that the promise of labor law lies in its emancipatory potential to free working people of many of the burdens of vulnerability, either by ensuring that employment risks lie with an employing organization which is more able to sustain those risks than are atomized individuals, or by assuming part of the risk as a collective responsibility via the state through measures such as state funding of maternity pay for small business and national insurance schemes to support statutory sickness pay or unemployment benefits.

Yet, when individualized understandings of care work show up in judicial comments in relation to labor law claims, the effect is often to deny homecare workers access to the benefit of legal provisions. For example, in *Cumbria County Council v Dow* (2008), Justice Elias decided that a homecare worker claimant could not make a valid equal pay comparison with a male worker in receipt of a productivity bonus.[5] His reasoning suggested that homecare workers were not "productive" because they lacked control over their work rate. He said:

> A care worker who works properly is subject to the demands and requirements of the patient and cannot sensibly dictate the speed of working.
>
> *(p. 145)*

Justice Elias' formulation of what it means to be a paid care worker overlooks the presence of an employer controlling the homecare workers' schedule and requiring her to take responsibility for deadlines. There is a significant distance between this judicial view and the homecare industry's heavy reliance on time restraint and cost control and its obsession with productivity measurement (Hayes and Moore, 2016). In Justice Elias' picture, the claimant's relations of employment are obscured and her legal status as a paid worker is rendered barely visible. The ease with which the employee-employer relationship is overlooked in social policy making about care services has been previously explored in research seeking to understand the regulation of homecare quality as a human resources issue (Rubery and Urwin, 2011). However, the appearance of the same phenomenon in this example of legal doctrine sheds light on the stereotyping brought into play when paid care work is assumed to be individualized and unproductive. It is claimed that a homecare worker works "properly" when she has no control over her own work rate. The use of the word "sensibly" suggests it would be folly for a homecare worker to try and influence her rate of work at all. The image of a homecare worker properly subject to the demands of the "patient" invokes notions of women's subservience and gendered expectations of women as selfless carers in a domestic context.

Perceptions of homecare workers as isolated caregivers reflect a sexist impulse to align them with the idea that women best belong in private domestic spaces where their interests are subordinate to the personal needs of others. This is not to deny the reality that homecare workers are a distinctive occupational group, different from factory or retail workers, for example, because they lack a central or regular place of work in which to interact with one another. Indeed, a homecare worker with 25 service-users to see in a week has 25 different workplaces and might work with no one else but those service-users. This does not mean, however, that those relationships are freestanding or individually contingent. The contact that service-users have with homecare workers represents the relation of service-users to the state, not only as the subjects of the state's welfare provision

5 See also *Gibson v Sheffield City Council* (2010), in which homecare work is discussed by the Court of Appeal as "work which is not measurable" in an industry where productivity is "beyond control."

but also as citizens to whom the state is accountable. While privatization has relocated the delivery of care away from the public sector, it has been facilitated by social, organizational, and legal factors that enable homecare workers to be characterized as low cost, expendable, and easily replaced. Privatization has stripped homecare workers of their identity as public servants and, echoing traditions of women's unpaid labor as wives and daughters in domestic settings, has (re)asserted that caregiving is built on individualized (and often demeaning) relations of gender. Meanings of community and public duty have changed in accordance with revised public priorities. The spatial markers of gendered social difference, by which the private domestic domain is set apart from the wider labor market, are reaffirmed. By reconstituting relations of employment, privatization is the state's signal that caring relationships and the forms of community resilience which they enable, are no longer a public policy priority. Indeed, they are crafted as excessive and unvalued by-products. When state recognition of paid care work is reduced to recognition only of an individuated commercial exchange, caring relationships are fractured and effectively erased from consideration. Through the privatization of social care provision, established forms of community have been ruptured. Both workers and service-users have faced the consequential dismantling of caregiving relationships that had previously offered continuity and communal security in otherwise uncertain, insecure, and socially-excluded lives.

Studies of labor law frequently take the individual subject of law as both the start and end point of consideration. This is particularly so in relation to studies of sex-based inequality, since the law conceives of discrimination as being as an individualized harm, albeit one which is inflicted as a consequence of group membership. Yet by taking a vulnerability approach it is possible to connect the inadequacies of labor law at an individual level to the collective significance of its gendered inclinations. A growing body of empirical evidence points to connections between the deregulation of homecare employment and worsening standards of care (Bessa et al., 2013; Bolton and Wibberley, 2014; Koehler, 2014; Lewis and West, 2014; Rubery and Urwin, 2011). The relocating of the homecare workforce from the public to the private sector over two decades has effectively removed a large cohort of low-waged women from access to legal protection against discriminatory pay, from entitlement to those employment rights which stem from being engaged under a contract which is legally recognized as a contract of employment, as well as from the benefits of provisions set out in collective agreements covering public sector workers.

Employment is a special form of contractual relationship. It is evidently different from a standard commercial contract because the relationship created by an employment contract is one to which the state is willing to extend particular protections. Common law and statutory provisions erect a boundary around a limited selection of employment relationships, in order to craft them as arrangements into which normative expectations of protection and minimum standards may be imported and legally enforced. However, the impact of legal reasoning and statutory framing is to skew the allocation of employment protection towards forms of employment typically associated with men. The privileging of contractual arrangements which tend to reflect male experiences of paid work also serves to actively disadvantage individuals in forms of employment typically associated with women. This suggests that employment protection law communicates key messages about the inferiority of working class women and reproduces gendered subordination in the organization of homecare work.

Where local authorities were previously direct employers with clear legal responsibilities to homecare workers, they are now commissioners and financiers at the head of a complex care market in which obligations and responsibilities for terms and conditions of work are fragmented across contracting chains (Rubery et al., 2012; Rubery and Urwin, 2011). This has led to the effective deregulation of homecare employment. Wages have plummeted, pensions and occupational sick pay have evaporated, and terms and conditions of work now follow the contours of statutory minima (Koehler, 2014). Even so, there are continued difficulties for homecare workers seeking the protection of law. The statutory framing of minimum wage rights, for example, is not sufficiently inclusive as to communicate that care work is as valuable as any other. What counts as "work" according to legal findings of fact in minimum wage claims testifies to harmful assumptions of gender and class that strip homecare work of value. National minimum wage rules mirror, and hence communicate state approval of, the gendered association of caring labor with unpaid work. When applied by the courts, minimum wage law reinforces the expectations of informality and self-sacrifice by female caregivers that have exacerbated the employment vulnerabilities of the homecare workforce post-privatization. The National Minimum Wage Act 1998 fails to extend the right to minimum pay protection when non-family care workers are treated "like family."[6] Furthermore, judicial interpretations of national minimum wage law silence attempts by homecare workers to pin the descriptor "work" on much of the caring activity that they undertake. Higher hurdles are imposed on care workers than are imposed on workers in traditionally male forms of employment such as security work. Minimum wage law fails to ensure that all working time is waged time and employers are not legally expected to pay workers for all the hours they contractually require of them. Hence minimum wage law serves as a source of social justification for organizing homecare work around notions of productive and unproductive time. By providing succor for gendered understandings of care work as lacking in monetary value, the impact of national minimum wage law in homecare has been to introduce new avenues through which earnings can be reduced and unpaid time constructed as legitimate.

A lack of employer and state regard for minimum labor standards in the social care sector is commonplace (HM Revenue and Customs found half of the homecare companies it inspected in 2013 to be non-compliant). In England alone, the pay of hundreds of thousands of private sector homecare workers is so low as to

6 For a full discussion of homecare workers' national minimum wage rights see Hayes, 2015 and Hayes, 2017, pp. 135–152.

be unlawful in relation to national minimum wage law (Gardiner, 2015; Public Accounts Committee, 2014). The impact is not only widespread, but economically significant. On the few occasions that action has been taken against offending employers, HM Revenue and Customs reports that the average underpayment to workers in the homecare sector is four times higher than the average amount across all sectors (National Audit Office, 2016). There have been repeated calls for local authorities to attend to their commissioning practices in relation to minimum labor standards. Nevertheless, government intervention has been slow to materialize, and the most recent statutory guidance falls short of imposing a requirement that local authorities ensure the pay of homecare workers employed by contracting organizations meets legal minimum standards (Department of Health, 2016).

Employment protection law offers stronger protection in some parts of the labor market than in others. In the privatized homecare industry, it is especially weak. This suggests that the state is unwilling to protect the type of employment relationships in which homecare workers are now most often engaged. In legal adjudications over employment protection rights, some work activities and forms of employment are interpreted as being different from those which attract protection in law. Empirical evidence suggests that the poor working conditions which prevail in those jobs reflect the identity of the workers who typically participate in them. Across the UK labor market, a large majority of insecure and undesirable jobs are filled by women (Gregg and Gardiner, 2015). Sex-based subordination is embedded in low-waged industries, and the composition of the contemporary working class is largely female. It is not simply paradoxical that workers in good quality jobs have access to stronger legal protection than workers who are most likely to be exploited or badly treated; it exemplifies that subordinations of gender and class are perpetuated in law.

Judicial doctrine focuses protection on forms of employment in which men have been, and continue to be, typically engaged. The legal reasoning upon which this doctrine is based offers justification for under-protecting forms of employment which do not satisfy standards set against benchmarks of male participation in the labor market, such as full-time, long-term work arrangements with regular hours in clearly demarcated locations. Excluded forms of labor market activity are typified as those most likely to be undertaken by working class women. Consequently, when homecare workers are subject to the judicial preferences and tests established in doctrine, the ensuing interpretations of their work activities, work patterns and contractual relationships are especially likely to position them outside of the boundaries of employment protection law. From a legal perspective, precarious employment is viewed as a contractual issue rather than as a public policy or a social justice concern. However, an interpretation of individual contractual status is merely a first step in establishing eligibility to lay claim to rights associated with employment status because such rights are almost always accompanied by length of service criteria.

Parliament has recently drawn firmer demarcations of entitlement in the post-financial crisis context of falling wages and living standards across the economy.

It has restricted access to the benefit of legal rights in ways that reassert the alignment of available state protections with male interests and to the disadvantage of homecare workers. For example, in relation to unfair dismissal protection, section 108 of the Employment Rights Act 1996 previously required employees to have a year of continuous service with their current employer. In 2012 it was amended to introduce a two-year continuous service qualification (Employment Rights (increase of limits) Order, 2011). The Beecroft Employment Law Review, commissioned by government, had recommended an extension of the qualification period and claimed this could improve the health of the labor market because, under the twelve-month rule, employers "dismiss employees about whom they are uncertain after eleven months because they don't want to face the hassle of the process of dismissing someone after the unfair dismissal rules come into play" (Beecroft, 2011, p. 4). The irony of this argument is to suggest that making workers less secure in law will make them more secure in practice. The outcome is to render women's employment less secure than forms of employment in which men are typically engaged because women are more likely to have a shorter length of service than men.

When we consider that 42% of all homecare workers have been in their current job for less than 12 months (Skills for Care, 2015), we can immediately appreciate the deepening of employment insecurity which has followed from extended length of service criteria. Yet if we layer on top of this the realization that a large proportion of new starters with one homecare provider will have come straight from employment with a rival homecare provider within the same local authority area, we can question qualification periods as a systemic injustice. By denying protection of employment on the basis of non-continuous working, the law provides justification for practices within the homecare industry which result in a high turnover of labor. Employment protection law plays a role in creating the material circumstances through which homecare workers are unable to meet the (now extended) criteria necessary to gain the benefits of employment protection. The contractual basis of work typically available within the homecare sector marks out homecare workers as being the legal inferiors of those to whom employment protection is normatively supposed to apply.

Although employment protection law applies equally to all men and women in the labor market, in the context of homecare it is particularly apparent that labor law communicates an implicit presumption that low-waged women are less capable, less committed, and less deserving than other labor market participants. The lack of employment protection available to homecare workers signals their institutionalized separation from the work and forms of employment relations in which other workers are engaged. It also signals that inequalities in the labor market have not been created by immutable economic forces but are shaped by legal rules that have yet to be reimagined and reapproved as appropriate for a labor market in which women are able to gain full protection and the respect of the state for their participation. The current failure of the state to extend full recognition of paid caregiving as work in minimum wage law, as well as the state's refusal to provide statutory protection in the forms of employment in which homecare workers are typically engaged, is a harm to the integrity, stability, and resilience of notions of community which are generated as a result of the existential and material qualities of social care.

III. Conclusion

In this chapter I have taken a vulnerability approach to make quintessential connections between the gendering of labor law and the capacity for social care to support notions of community resilience as expressed in social relationships, hopes and aspirations, emotional sensation, and human interaction. The significance for labor law scholarship is to attend to the contribution that "individual" employment rights make to the social relations we understand as "community." By taking a vulnerability approach it is possible to connect the inadequacies of labor law at an individual level to the collective significance of its gendered inclinations. Vulnerability is a socially contingent concept. It arises from the possibilities, encounters, and happenstance of life as it is lived. Scholars of law, labor, and work might usefully engage further with nuanced appreciations of the vulnerability of community, recognizing where labor law in its current form contributes to the unequal allocation of social and economic power between men and women.

A focus on advantage rather than disadvantage gives rise to questions about how states might reimagine and recreate labor laws that give both men and women the full advantages that come from entitlements which enable people to mitigate the consequences of the vulnerability that is inherent to the experience of employment. With a focus on advantage, we must recognize that inequality of access to statutory protection at work is not a product of the market, but of an imbalance in law which undermines the fabric of community resilience.

6

VULNERABILITY, WORKFARE LAW AND RESILIENT SOCIAL JUSTICE

Camilla Sabroe Jydebjerg[1]

> *Let us be deliberately simplistic: Either there is work, or there isn't. If there is a structural necessity making it such that there is no work – or very little – one must say so and give an account of what the structure produces. If, on the contrary, there can be work – but in a reformed, if not transformed, structure (organization of capital, meaning or direction of "growth", energy needs) – then one must make it happen. But either way, it will be necessary to make room for what is irreducible: not work, nor capital, but people, all of us together.*
>
> *(Jean Luc Nancy, 2015, p. 4)*

I. Introduction

Being jobless is a state that can manifest our vulnerability and lessen our resilience due to loss of wages, loss of possibilities for education and training, and loss of the relationships and sense of belonging and purpose that a job can provide. Jobs may provide these things but do not necessarily do so. Jobs can also make our vulnerability manifest through bad working conditions, low wages, no training possibilities, low job security, and harmful social and societal relationships. This is important to point out because the dominant political discourses about work seem to associate employment with resilience and unemployment with vulnerability and need. This is a juxtaposition that glosses over the many ways in which dependency on precarious, low paying, exhausting, stress-inducing, or dangerous jobs for wages realizes our vulnerability rather than our possibility for resilience. However, being jobless, at the very least, manifests our vulnerability in the sense of financial insecurity and makes us dependent on alternative sources of income, rather than a salary. One of the ways that the state can provide resilience in this situation is to make sure that such an income is available. In this chapter I examine

1 Lecturer, Department of Social Work and Administration, University College Zealand, Denmark.

the way that Denmark as a Nordic welfare state provides resilience by securing economic assistance to people that are jobless. I suggest that the Nordic welfare states were, for a time, in line with vulnerability theory's assertions about the responsibility of the state to provide resilience to its inhabitants, but this responsibility is being challenged by a workfare agenda. I examine provisions in law concerning people who are currently outside the regular workforce and receiving social security assistance. The aim of the investigation is to determine if and how these provisions constitute resilient social justice for people receiving assistance. By resilient social justice I mean the possibility of making legal decisions that take into account the particularity as well as the universality of the embodied and embedded vulnerable subject in a way that fosters resilient states of being.

In Denmark, the state provides social security assistance to people who are out of work and unable to provide financially for themselves. Social security assistance is publicly funded monetary assistance to cover the cost of living for people who are unable to do so themselves. To be eligible for social security a person must not be eligible for unemployment insurance[2] and be unable to provide for him- or herself due to a "social occurrence" – most often unemployment (other "social occurrences" could be divorce, death of a spouse or cohabitant, and illness) (Act on Active Social Policy § 11). Furthermore, the person must not have a spouse who can provide for him or her. Denmark is a Nordic welfare state. It could be argued that the Nordic welfare states, with their comprehensive system of publicly funded benefits, universal and free education and health systems, and tradition for user involvement and cooperative movements, are providing their inhabitants with the necessary assets to be socially, politically and economically resilient (Bjørnholt, 2013). The Nordic welfare states can be said to be shaped around an admission of our vulnerable condition and a wish to counter this vulnerability. Social welfare laws in the welfare state are put into place with the purpose of cushioning and alleviating our meeting with situations that expose our vulnerability, such as unemployment, disability, illness, or old age. The Danish social welfare laws provide for a host of universal (e.g. child care, family allowance, maternity/paternity leave, and old age pension) as well as need-based benefits (e.g. social security, support in case of illness, or disability, home care, etc.) designed to counteract most situations during a lifespan in which a need is present. These laws have the explicit purpose of preventing life events from leading to social problems and marginalization.

The understanding of the subject as vulnerable, embodied, and embedded can to a certain degree be found in the traditional Nordic welfare understanding developed in the post World War II years, which in Denmark saw its legal heyday with the Act on Public Assistance in 1976. The Act on Public Assistance entailed

2 Unemployment insurance benefits requires a membership of a union as well as a certain amount of paid hours on the "regular job market." After two years on unemployment insurance benefits you lose the right to this benefit and have to re-earn the right by working "regular" jobs for a certain amount of hours.

a comprehensive regulation concerning sickness, unemployment, disability, age, etc. The Act provided that help should be provided on the basis of individual need, with the purpose of making sure that people were supported through life events so as to not be put in a significantly worse position by life events such as unemployment or sickness (Hornemann Greve, 2002; Møller, 2004). The bill specifically stated that its purpose was:

> to make it possible to provide help that would give families and individuals the possibility to maintain the standard of living even in times of troubles no matter what the cause of the troubles might be. Hereby ensuring that illness or other changes to an individual's living conditions or earnings does not entail a progressive deterioration of the person's or family's situation.
>
> *(Greve, 2002, author's translation; Rasmussen and Hansen, 2015, pp. 27–28)*

However, the politics of workfare or active labor market policies that are found in most OECD welfare states has also become more and more pervasive in Denmark from the 1990s onward, individualizing social problems, as well as framing unemployment as the main social problem that a person can have (Caswell et al., 2010; Hoff, 2009). Workfare laws have gradually implemented a duty for everybody receiving social assistance to participate in activation measures as a condition of receiving assistance – an obligation to work for welfare (Møller, 2004). Activation measures can consist of work-related schemes, such as internships, education and training, or a combination of these. The workfare laws have also led to increased attempts at curtailing social worker discretion by standardization of procedures. One such standardization is a system of categorization to assess a person's work capability. In this chapter, I examine what measures such as work capability assessments mean to the understanding of the legal subject as vulnerable and how it matters for the way a person can be embodied and embedded in law.

Vulnerability theory contributes greatly to legal studies by giving the body a legal shape that is as material as it is discursive by anchoring the legal subject in its inherent and structural embodiment and embeddedness. I attempt to contribute to this theory by bringing forth the material register of laws in my analysis, as I investigate how certain kinds of being takes shape within law, as well as law's resilience fostering potential, and discuss the concept of social justice concerned with social welfare law and the practical application of law in social work in everyday praxis. In this analysis, this chapter further takes inspiration in the philosophy of Jean Luc Nancy. First, I take inspiration in Nancy's claim that being is always being with; we depend on each other for resilience (Nancy, 2000). "Existing is first of all living in the world with others" (Devisch, 2011, p. 3). I further draw on Nancy and Tataryn to examine how the concept of exscription can challenge us to think about how and under which circumstances bodies are made to count in their particular lived vulnerability and what kinds of being and what kind of bodies are written out of the law and practice of workfare laws (Nancy, 1993; Tataryn, 2015).

Finally, I suggest that the provisions of social welfare law contain space for creating resilience in an acknowledgement of our shared vulnerability, despite a strong tendency of workfare laws to focus on individual responsibility and autonomy. I suggest that the various degrees of discretion in social welfare laws deliver such a space, not only for social worker agency, but also for social worker responsibility and obligation. I further suggest that this space can allow for the bodies that have been written out of the law's text to touch the meaning of law and to remind us of their being.

II. Discretionary decisions of administrative law

Social security law in Denmark is administrative. First instance decisions about the right to social security and the duties entailed with this are made by the local government of the municipality where the applicant resides. It is prescribed by law that all municipalities must have a job center to administer "active employment measures." Active employment measures are different kinds of activation or training/education that a person receiving social security must participate in as a condition of receiving public assistance. Social welfare law in Denmark is traditionally the domain of social workers. Social work education includes education and training in administrative law and social welfare law. Job centers, however, have a high ratio of case workers who are not social workers and seem to have changed recruitment of staff, replacing trained social workers with staff trained as clerical or administrative workers (Avisen.dk, 2016; Larsen, 2013). Case workers who are not social workers may or may not be trained in law.

Danish administrative law ascribes to the continental view on the legality principle to ensure administrative justice, largely defined as fairness and absence of arbitrariness. The legality principle entails that "any use of public power has to be based on regulation" (Andersen, 2013; Tollenaar and De Ridder, 2010, p. 309). A decision must refer specifically to the law in which it finds its legality. However, social welfare laws are formulated with various degrees of discretion; that is, they are not precise regulation where a social worker can find an exact prescription on how to act in a particular case. The wording is often (more or less) purposefully left vague and elastic and requires further interpretation or use of discretion by the administrative body (Andersen, 2013; Schultz, 2004). Discretionary provisions specifically aim at making it possible to act on an individual basis, adjusted to the individual need for help (Schultz, 2004). The provisions contain a more or less precise description of criteria according to which the social worker must make an individual assessment in each case, based on the factual information about the person in need of a benefit and the law. An example of this is Article 13, subsection 8 in the Consolidation Act on Active Social Policy, about being exempted from the duty to participate in activation if you have problems that make you less capable of taking a job, for example, illness, addiction, or disabilities. According to this rule the municipality must assess if there are factors that should make a person exempt from activation. There is a list of possible reasons for exemption such as illness in subsection 7, but apart from these reasons the municipality can decide that other reasons not stated by law can exempt a person from activation. The law leaves room for discretion in which a social worker can adjust the decision to a local context based on individual facts and circumstances. In this way many provisions of social welfare law allow for the case worker and the person applying for help to work with the law to adjust legal decisions to the individual being in the local context taking into consideration this being's specific lived experiences.

III. Vulnerable beings and law

The scholarship and practice of legal liberalism has largely based its interpretations on the notion of a rational autonomous liberal subject. This subject has individual legal rights and can use these rights to address inequality and wrongs through the legal justice system. In her work on vulnerability and in opposition to what she describes as the myth of autonomy, Martha Fineman conceptualizes the vulnerable legal subject. The vulnerable subject is not to be seen as in opposition to an invulnerable subject, singling out special categories of legal subjects with a minority status rendering them vulnerable and, as such, in need of special rights protecting them and helping them with access to a society of rational autonomous legal subjects. There are no invulnerable beings in vulnerability theory. All embodied beings are vulnerable (Fineman, 2008, 2013b; Fineman and Grear, 2013; Grear, 2013). Vulnerability is a universal condition of an embodied being in the sense that all embodied beings are susceptible to illness, injury, harm, and misfortune. Vulnerability is also particular in the sense that each being is embodied and situated differently in relation to social, economic, and institutional realities, and thereby lives a vulnerability that is expressed and experienced particularly and differently (Fineman, 2008, 2013b; Grear, 2013). Vulnerable beings are always both embodied and embedded in lived actualities and material conditions (Grear, 2013). Embodiment and embeddedness – the fact that our being is always vulnerable and always socio-materially dependent, is what makes us the same and also differentiates us. We are all vulnerable bodies, but different bodies living different vulnerabilities with different "ontological loads" (Fuller and Goriunova, 2012, p. 161).

To counter the inevitable vulnerability of all beings, we have only resilience to rely on. Resilience is always particular. It is founded in the assets and resources of the individual being and this being's interactions with and connections to other beings and societal institutions (Fineman and Grear, 2013). We depend on each other for resilience. This condition accentuates our being-with as our ontological starting point. "Existing is first of all living in the world with others" (Devisch, 2011, p. 3). The societal institutions that we create in response to vulnerability should be resilience-fostering, and they should create "possibilities of opportunities and support" providing us with "assets – reservoirs of capabilities, advantages and coping mechanisms" (Fineman, 2013b, p. 22). Embodied beings' lives are "intricately dependent on their interactions within the institutions and political structures society has constructed" (p. 24). The state shapes institutions and structures individual and institutional relationships through law (Fineman, 2008; Selberg and Wegerstad, 2011). Law plays a role in reforms, and laws are therefore important in fostering resilience. Laws must be shaped around the vulnerable subject, recognizing material, cultural, and social imbalances, and "fashioned around a complete, comprehensive vision of the human experience if they are to meet the needs of real-life subjects" (Fineman, 2008, p. 10). The question for legal scholarship must then be what kind of law takes into account the particularity as well as the universality of the embodied and embedded vulnerable being in a way that fosters resilient states of law and of being of law. We must also be asking what kind of law takes into account that existing is "being-in-common" (Nancy, 1991).

By anchoring the legal subject in its inherent and structural embodiment and embeddedness, vulnerability theory gives the body a legal shape that is as material as it is discursive. Vulnerability can be accentuated or lessened by law. Laws are not neutral; law promotes, produces, and reproduces particular understandings of how to be human, of society, of family, of equality, and of inequality (Fineman, 2008). These promotions matter not only in the sense that they promote hegemony and privilege some understandings before others, but also in the sense that certain kinds of being take shape within law that could have taken shape otherwise within other kinds of law. This is not just a matter of privileging certain kinds of thought or knowledge but of privileging and thereby giving shape to certain kinds of bodies, of materiality, of being, and of becoming (Fletcher et al., 2008). Law and the power law represents brings being into existence (O'Brien, 2005). Law matters not just for its actual content in words, but for its materiality and for the affect it has on human beings, the affective register it brings forth, the way that a book of law will make us pause, its heaviness not just its physical mass, the heft of it, its emotional weight, the sense of gravity, the seriousness of opening the computer program of laws and legal interpretations, and turning to authority. Only case workers – decision makers entrusted with power – have access to the program on the computer, the service applicants do not. Authority is made tangible by the letters, by the computer screen on a desk, by the concentration and silence while searching for "the law," by the sound and the fingertip sensation of the tapping on the keyboard.

Law is not just law on the books, finished and static once they are written down and passed. Law is also the people and the institutions that realize law (Selberg and Wegerstad, 2011). Social welfare law is used, read, understood, interpreted, construed, analyzed, and expounded by social workers in municipalities in their encounters with other embodied beings embedded in their specific socio-material conditions. The bodies that law regulates push back at law and affect law (Barad, 1998, 2008; Hekman, 2008). Neither bodies nor law are static or enclosed within themselves, they cannot be neatly separated, but exist in a continuous interaction, in a "mix of political and social practice," which has "material, political and ethical dimensions" (Alaimo and Hekman, 2008a, p. 8). Bodies interpret and create law, and the law interprets and creates bodies (Ahmed, 2010; Brøgger, 2015). Human bodies and bodies of law interact to make, unmake and remake becomings of law. Paraphrasing Nancy (1993), we have no more made the law, than it has made us. The continuous onto-epistemology of law and of being and becoming of law (Barad, 2008) is accentuated in social welfare law by the vague and elastic wording of the legal texts of social welfare law making room for various degrees of discretion. Despite discretion, the legal texts still play a powerful agentic role. The wording of the provisions depict particular versions of reality, a gallery of things and conditions recognized by law. The words inscribe particular kinds of being, making it harder or impossible to recognize others.

IV. From solidary beings to individual beings

The view of the welfare state as a matter of sharing the burden of whatever conditions the humans inhabiting the state found themselves in as a result of their shared vulnerability and the room for individual assessment and solutions rooted in the particular life conditions of the individual in need of assistance has been challenged by competing considerations, particularly by the politics of workfare that have become more and more pervasive from the 1990s onward. The move towards workfare policies has shifted the aspiration from social solidarity via redistribution of resources and is gradually replacing it with individual responsibility, individualizing social problems and making them a matter of unemployment (Carr, 2013; Hoff, 2009). Work has become the defining relationship between a person and society, and marginalization is mainly defined by whether a person is in "regular" paid employment in the labor market or not. The move towards workfare is a fundamental change in both the meaning and understanding of social welfare rights and the administration of social welfare, turning the exclusion from work into the center of the relationship between society and people experiencing the need for assistance from the state (Handler, 2004). The policy of workfare has brought a host of changes to the social welfare laws, including a reduction in assistance, a reduction of the period of unemployment assistance which makes more people dependent on the lower social security assistance, ever-increasing conditionality concerning social security assistance, and an increase in obligations attached to welfare rights (Handler, 2004). For each of these statutory changes the rhetoric of law and the view on the person in need of help has also changed. In the forefront of these changes is "the disappearance of the class struggle, a refusal to recognize the collective nature of the problems that affect the poor. Instead focus is on individual rehabilitation" (Handler, 2004, p. 120 (quoting Procacci)). This is also seen in the way case workers on the ground level prioritize. A study conducted in 2001 and 2008 by Larsen and colleagues shows that the focus of case workers has changed. In 2001, case workers described their most important objective as to "fully consider the individual circumstances facing social assistance recipients and to use training and education to help them qualify for jobs." In 2008, the top priorities were to impose activation requirements, to apply sanctions, and to use activation as work-ability testing. "The majority of the respondents also prioritized the needs of the labor market higher than the individual wishes and needs of persons receiving social assistance" (Larsen, 2013, pp. 114–115).

The Act on Active Social Policy was passed in 1997 as part of a social welfare law reform that substituted the previous social legislation, the Act on Assistance of 1976. The social welfare law reform of 1997 entailed an ideological shift to a greater emphasis on the individual responsibility of the person in need. Obligations outweigh rights, and the emphasis is on equal possibilities rather than equality (Møller, 2004). The Act at the same time extends the obligation to participate in activation to everybody receiving benefits, no matter what problems people may have, and implements a host of sanctions directed at persons who do not participate (Carstens, 1998; Hansen, 2015). In the bill on active social policy that was part of the reform, it is specified that the purpose of the bill is to emphasize individual responsibility (Nr LSF 230). Personal responsibility is further accentuated by being the headline of the first chapter of the law (Carstens, 1998). Personal responsibility was also a headline in the Act on Assistance, but the first headline was "Public Responsibilities for the Individual" (p. 79).

V. Becoming a rational entity

The tendency towards individualization can also be found in the rules concerning communication between the social worker and the person applying for help. When obligations to talk to and listen to the person applying for assistance were first introduced into Danish law in 1964 and later strengthened in 1987, this was grounded in the need to protect the person in contact with the administration from the arbitrary use of power, as well as the desire to secure correct decisions and create trust in public administration (Hansen, 2006; Gottrup, 2011; Hielmcrone and Schultz, 2007; Jydebjerg et al., 2016). Part of the reform of 1997 was a new act with rules concerning case handling in the municipalities (Consolidation Act on Legal Protection and Administration in Social Matters). The Act not only applies in cases about social security, but also in most other cases about help and support decided by local government, such as aid and financial support for people with disabilities, help and support for children and their families etc. The Act contains a rule (§ 4) about communication between the local government (represented by the social worker) and people having cases processed by local government. The objective of Article 4 is wider than securing correct decisions, since the person applying for help must also be involved to solidify the autonomy of the person and to make sure that the person takes an active responsibility for his or her own situation (Andersen, 2013; Nr LSF 228).

Furthermore, the focus on the power discrepancy between the state and the person applying for help from the state is toned down. The focus is now on a partnership between the state and the person in need of assistance (Jydebjerg et al., 2016). Collaboration is required, and plans and contracts have to some extent replaced traditional adjudications, blurring the line between collaboration and decision (Andersen, 2003). The legal subject of social welfare law has become the rational autonomous subject of private law. Entering into the unemployment system today, one of the first things you must do "in collaboration" with your social worker is make a plan called "my plan." The text of the law about these plans makes it sound as if these plans are agreements between the person receiving assistance and the social worker. The plan must state the person's "employment goals," but these goals must be in accordance with the needs of the labor market.[3] The right to assistance entails a host of duties other than making a plan, of which the most prevalent is the duty to participate in activation. Activation is called "job offers" in the law though neither a job nor an offer is involved. The decisions about activation and the content of activation is closely linked with an assessment of the work capability of the person receiving assistance. This decision about work capability also relates to other duties for the person, such as the frequency of meetings,[4] and the obligation to look for jobs and to register in a job seeking system (Klausen et al., 2015). The work capability assessment is made on the basis of a standardized system of classification into categories. The statutory changes of workfare policies have included a move away from discretion in particular through standardization and categorization.

VI. From vulnerable bodies to workable bodies

Classification in social welfare law was originally a matter of being deserving or undeserving poor. However, the social reform of the 1970s, culminating with the Act of Assistance, to a large degree did away with this distinction as the purpose of the Act was to provide help without focusing on the reason that help was needed. The focus instead was on society's responsibility in relation to needs on the basis of "social occurrences" in a person's life. The law of assistance was based on a principle of discretion trusting that local decisions made close to the person in need of assistance would be providing the best help tailored to the individual or family in need (Greve, 2002).

Following the legislative changes due to workfare policies the language of law has changed from a focus on vulnerability and structural explanations to a focus on work potential and the inherent (but perhaps yet uncovered or unrealized) resources of persons applying for help (Caswell et al., 2010, Eskelinen et al., 2010; Nielsen, 2015a). Legislative changes have also led to increased attempts at curtailing social worker discretion by various standardization procedures. Currently it seems that

3 The plan should describe how the case worker estimates that the possibilities for the person receiving assistance to re-enter the labor market can be bettered (Consolidation Act on Active Labor Market Measures § 27). The plan must list what activation placements the person will get. If the activation is not targeted to an area with a lack of labor, an explanation for the choice of activation must be given in the plan (§ 27). One or more "labor goals" must be described for the individual and entered into the plan. These goals should target areas where there is a lack of labor. If a person is assessed ready for activation but not for jobs the plan can also include activations with a purpose of stabilizing and bettering the person's physical, psychological, or social conditions (§ 28).

4 People receiving social assistance must participate in a number of meetings with the social worker during their unemployment period, the minimum number of which is specified by law. These meetings are called job interviews (though there is no job).

there is a tendency to minimize discretion by implementing standardizations in many areas of social work (Schultz, 2004). Standardized methods have been implemented within many areas of social work in the municipalities. The methods entail a classification of problems, problem areas, and ways of examining a case. One of the standardized methods that has been introduced is a system of categorization of people receiving social security. The system requires that all municipalities classify receivers of social security into groups according to their work capability. One of the reasons given for the introduction of a system based on categorizations was the variation and unpredictability of municipal case work and decisions (Nielsen, 2015b). The first categorizations that were introduced in 2000 in a guide from the ministry to the municipalities were concerned with problems of the person receiving assistance (Nielsen, 2015b). The problems mentioned in the guide to categorization were varied and connected to the person's socio-material being.

Particularly the two "last" groups, groups 4 and 5, are concerned with the person's health and what is termed "social disadvantages," which include crime, and lack of relations and social competences. It is worth noticing that these social disadvantages, poverty, and other structural disadvantages, are all portrayed as characteristics of the person (Ministry of Social Affairs, 2001). In 2004, it became mandatory to categorize people receiving social security into five groups measuring how far away the case worker estimated the benefit recipient was from a job (Ministry of Labor, 2004; Nielsen, 2015b). The categorization system has been changed twice since. The changes share a focus on the person's abilities in connection to the labor market. The categorizations measure the person in accordance with how far the person is understood to be away from a "regular" job. Each change has made the goal of matching the person with the labor market more predominate, and the language has changed so that the focus is now on resources, abilities, and potentials rather than on problems (Caswell et al 2010; Eskelinen et al., 2010; Nielsen, 2015a, 2015b). In the first three systems the kinds of socio-material conditions that would be taken into account in the assessment of what category a person should be placed in were more or less well described. All three systems also had a category for people who were not able to participate in the labor market or in activation activities at all due to their socio-material circumstances (Agency of Labor, 2009; Ministry of Social Affairs, 2001; Ministry of Labor, 2004). These persons could be exempted from the obligation of activation without losing their social security assistance.

The newest categories are from 2014 introduced in connection with yet another revision of the benefit system. This revision contains only two categories. You can either be ready for work or ready for "activities" (activation). You are ready for a job if the social worker estimates that you will be able to take a job on the regular job market within three months – the job market notwithstanding. This means that readiness is measured on the facts of the person and not the facts of the job market. The assessment of the person will be the same no matter the state of the market, the number of available jobs, or the economic conditions. It is the hypothetical matter of whether a person could take a job if such a job was there. If you are not assessed ready for a job you will be assessed ready for "activities." There is no longer a category for not being ready; only a state of being of readiness is imagined (Nielsen, 2015b). Whereas the earlier categorization systems all had more or less detailed descriptions of what kind of socio-material conditions would matter in the choosing of category for an individual, this system is oddly silent about the body in question. Apart from the measurement of three months we seem to get very little information about what kind of socio-material conditions will place a person closer to or further away from the labor market. In guidelines given by the ministry in connection with the reform, it is mentioned that the problems that people who are not "job-ready" have can be vocational, social, or medical (Agency of Labor, 2013). In a way you can say that the body has disappeared, as has the specific socio-material conditions of the person and the way that he or she is connected to society. The actual physical and material experience of joblessness is removed from recognized categories of unemployment (Tataryn, 2015). The focus on resources has eliminated problems from the law, and thereby largely made vulnerabilities invisible (Nielsen, 2015a). Bodies are now only measured against a standard of work capability. After having been categorized, the "my plan" is made "in collaboration" between the social worker and the person receiving assistance. It can be difficult to ascertain because of the language of compliance (activation measures are called "job offers" in the text of the law), but the decision about what kind of activation a person must participate in, as a requirement for receiving a benefit, is made by the social worker. The job offer should be given based on an assessment of the wishes and circumstances of the person, but job offers must, if possible, be aimed at areas where there is a lack of labor, and the job center can establish the job offer taking the needs of the labor market into consideration (Consolidation Act on Active Labor Market Measures § 22). It is no longer the person receiving assistance who has needs, it is the labor market. The labor market asks, and the bodies must answer. The law now only seems to recognize ready bodies. Ready for work, education or at least activation (Nielsen, 2015a). Bodies must work, but working or striving to work is not enough, bodies must also be ready for the needs of the market. You might say that it is not enough for the body to be (or strive to become) work-capable, rather the body must be work-able, ready to be shaped and bent and folded into whatever need arises in the labor market. Bodies must conform, bodies must get up in the morning, bodies must be ready, bodies must be workable. Bodies that do not conform have been written out of the legal text as has embodied and embedded vulnerability. The actual lived lives of human beings slip through the cracks between categories, not able to settle securely into any set category (Tataryn, 2015). The bodies are written out of the law; vulnerability, dumb luck, blind chance, the precariousness of the body, the wear and tear of bodies, and the different ontological loads carried by different bodies are written out (Fuller and Goriunova, 2012; Tataryn, 2015). So much life is left in the margins outside the categories, in the lived actualities. However, these bodies are still in the job center, they still participate or do not participate; their non-conformity, non-readiness, and non-workability displays a daily challenge to the reality as described by the law (Tataryn, 2015).

VII. Being exscribed to the margins of law

Jean Luc Nancy's concept of exscription may give us a terminology to understand some of what happens in this interaction between non-conforming human bodies, relegated to the legal grey areas and bodies of law always trying to work them into that which is inscribed by the letters of the law (Tataryn, 2015). Nancy (1993) makes the point that "writing exscribes meaning every bit as much as it inscribes significations. It exscribes meaning or, in other words, it shows that what matters . . . The existence of everything, that is in question in the text . . . is outside the text." (p. 338). The concept of exscription may therefore challenge us to think about what is written out of the text of the law (Tataryn, 2015). The inscription of human bodies in work capability, the demand for bodies to be workable for the needs of the labor market, means that human beings are recognized and categorized based on their ability to work, on the possibility of their economic contribution, and their ability to become self-supporting, non-dependent rational subjects, making sound choices free from the fragility of the body and the environment in which they live. Unemployment becomes a question of readiness and will, not of available jobs that pay a livable wage and do not wear down your body. The categories of work capability are an inscription that signifies bodies by distinguishing bodies by their ability to work on the labor seemingly encompassing the totality of these being's relationship to work (Tataryn, 2015). This makes it seem like the distance between a person and the labor market is one of simple measure, never contesting the demands of the (labor) market or the fairness of the measure. The needs of the beings must bow to the needs of the market. Perhaps it is this very inscription that makes workfare policies travel seemingly unquestioned across countries and otherwise rarely crossable political divides uniting left and right-wing parties in presenting every change as a helping hand to bodies that would otherwise stagnate into unreadiness or inflexible unworkability. "Too many get social security in years without receiving the right measures to move on to jobs or education. To them social security has become a condition of life" (Mette Fredriksen, Social Democrat and previous Minister of Employment, Agency of Labor, 2013). Changes in the laws on social security are presented as a way to lessen (labor market) marginalization, yet economic inequality has risen in Denmark since the mid-nineties (Hansen, 2004; Hansen et al., 2015; Møller, 2004). The same is evident in most other OECD countries (OECD, 2015). It could also be argued that many of the workfare schemes, such as job trials, internships and utility jobs, designed to help people with access to the regular labor force can be understood as non-standard jobs. According to OECD (writing about non-standard jobs, not workfare schemes[5]), non-standard jobs are, adding to economic inequality due to low wages (and I would add sometimes no wages but benefits), job insecurity, poor access to training, and slow (or no) wage growth. Exscription might help to explain how the welfare state "denies what it exscribes away from itself" (Tataryn,

5 In fact, OECD widely advocated workfare policies in the 1990s (Larsen, 2013).

2015 p. 97), telling a story of inclusion and the working against marginalization, while the extreme focus on labor and work capability excludes bodies that are not able to become workable and sets up new exclusive agendas (Tataryn, 2015). At the same time, the welfare state keeps silent about the structural and socio-material actualities of the bodily materialities of the day-to-day interactions in the job center, or makes these bodily realities something to be overcome in order for all bodies to become rational and workable. Workfare has reduced multiplicity and imprisoned being into identities of categorizations. However, though it will seem that the law desires to shape fit, rational, and workable subjects, law must also come to grips with that which it tries to represent (Meurs and Devisch, 2015). That which is left outside, resisting signification, must still touch the meaning of law (Morin, 2012). People meeting the categorizations of law are not merely reduced to their significations by being exscribed. "Exscription is not in opposition" (Tataryn, 2015, p. 96), but rather it reveals the limit of thought, the limit of writing (Morin, 2012). It reminds us of that which weighs outside of thought or, perhaps even more, "it presents itself exscribed" (Nancy, 1993, p. 339). It presents itself in its absence by "inscribing the uninscribable in inscription itself" (Derrida, 2005, p. 298). The coming to grips with bodies happens in the job center in the daily practice of discretionary laws that only in the most rudimentary of forms will state the conditions connected to the decisions made. It is here sense must be made. Sense in Nancy's work is a "privileged name for being" (Librett, 2015, p. 213) or "being presenting itself to us" (Meurs and Devisch, 2015, p. 49). Sense in Nancy's understanding is not a matter of signification, but rather sense challenges or (re)opens our closed representations and challenges the categorizations made to make sense by law (Meurs and Devisch, 2015; Nancy, 1997; Tataryn, 2015). If law is to matter to social justice at all it must recognize the beings coming before it. Thought and thing must touch each other (Morin, 2012), beings of law and human beings much touch and interact to create resilient states of being in law.

VIII. Discretion revisited: a space for resistance

How is it even possible to talk about social justice, let alone believe in it, in the job center in a time when social welfare law seemingly fits uncontested and without discrepancies with rising inequality, where difference in socio-material and bodily resilience is translated into a matter of the will to transform oneself into a workable body? When the needs of the market weigh heavier than the needs of people? Where vulnerability as a constituting factor of being as well as of social welfare law has seemingly disappeared? On the other hand, how can we not? This is, after all, the law that social workers and people receiving assistance from the state have to interact with in their daily life in the job center. While social workers as well as lawyers should certainly work for law reforms of a formal kind in the form of law revisions that will not enhance economic and political systems that tolerate and justify unequal distributions of resilience fostering opportunities, such a law reform does not seem to be impending (Fineman, 2013b). However, law reform does not only come in formalized versions from elected governments, but can come just as much or perhaps even more from the daily interactions of bodies of law and human bodies. It is in this interaction that the bodies gain their full and ever-changing materialities. I will therefore follow the lead of Archana Parashar (2008) and look for a space for agency and responsibility, and I suggest that the possibility of discretion delivers such a space, not only for social worker agency, but also for responsibility and obligation.

Discretionary provisions specifically aim at making it possible to act on an individual basis adjusted to the individual need for help. In a guide from the Ministry of Social Affairs to the municipalities it is thus emphasized that the meaning of discretionary provisions is to make it possible for legal authority to help individuals and families in meeting with specific cases. Discretionary rules are discretionary because law makers are not able to or do not want to describe every situation exhaustively (Ministry of Social Affairs, 2006). Thus, the provisions should allow for the legal decisions to adjust to the individual subject in the local context taking into consideration this subject's specific lived experiences. The possibility to take into account the individual being's embodiment and embeddedness in discretionary decisions is accentuated by one of the fundamental ethical principles of social work, which is the obligation to treat each person as a whole and to recognize all aspects of a person's life (IFSW, 2012). This principle is also a part of the Danish social welfare law (the totality principle). The totality principle requires that the individual being must be understood in terms of the individual being's relations to others as well as the material, social, and cultural resources the individual has (Guldager, 2011). This means that a case worker must assess a person's needs broadly in accordance with all of the law's possibilities, as well as offer counseling and guidance to the person concerning these possibilities. The case worker cannot just look at whatever the person him- or herself is asking about or applying for, but must also tend to other needs that the case worker ought to recognize from the facts of the case. If the totality principle is not followed in a case, a decision may be considered invalid and must then be made anew by the municipality upholding the principle (Andersen, 2013; Schultz, 2004). The latest law reform has an increased focus on coordination in adherence to the principle of wholeness (Agency of Labor, 2013). While every decision is thus particular, a decision is never just a matter of the individual case, since decisions create a practice that will inform coming decisions, which in turn are also informed by previous decisions.

It has been and still is contested in legal and social work studies whether discretionary provisions or prescriptive provisions are preferable.[6] The argument against discretion is that discretionary provisions can make it harder for the person in

6 The distinction between interpretation and discretion is gradual and not easily made in practice but is dependent on how vague and imprecise the wording of the provision is (Andersen, 2013). Though much discussion in legal theory is about this distinction, I have not distinguished sharply between them in this chapter. They share the connectedness to practice and the opening towards practice that make law happen when the text is enacted in praxis.

need of help as well as for the social worker to predict and asses the state of law and their legal standing, and that discretionary provisions cause an irregular legal practice, treating people unequally before the law (Greve, 2002; Hansen, 2015; Klausen, 2002; Schultz, 2004). This has also been the reason for the introduction of the standardized methods of categorization of work capability and a succession of other standards of social work practice. The possibility to adjust decisions to the particularities of a case carries an inbuilt tension between particularity and law's promise of universality, which is meeting all cases equally, objectively and impartially, powerfully displayed by the symbol of the blindfolded Justitia with the weights to weigh all equally. Yet law is determined with praxis. It is impossible to capture life in all its multiplicity by language in legal texts. This is what discretion knows and acknowledges. The letter of the law must be interpreted by praxis; the legal "answers" do not materialize until the body of law interacts with the human bodies. This meeting is never predetermined, and in that sense the answer will always be a surprise even to law itself. The tendency to minimize discretion through standardization and detailed regulation in order to be done with difference in adjunction in the name of equality and impartiality impedes justice. For social justice to be resilient it must hang in the (im)possible balance between the one and the many and between decision and uncertainty. Justice must always trouble the decision, but it can never justify the decision fully. This obliges the social worker to a state of being of necessary and permanent uneasiness, risk, and responsibility, having to leave the excuse of law behind but never leaving law behind completely (Bankovsky, 2012; De Ville, 2011; Sokoloff, 2005). Justice can therefore not be merely a matter of measure – the distance between the text and the body, nor the distance between the body and the labor market. Justice must be more nuanced than measuring against the same, more nuanced than looking for sameness, more nuanced than measuring and weighing bodies against a standard of equality in the meaning of likeness, and more nuanced than measuring bodies against a standard of workability. Bodies are not equal though they are worth the same. Social justice must come to grips with the vulnerable beings it interacts with. Justice must therefore be a matter of meetings rather than measures. Being treated justly is being met in one's particular embedded embodiment. The social worker, the person needing assistance, and the law must come together (Devisch and Wynn, 2010).

The absence of a fully determinate content in discretionary provisions "calls for a responsive opening" . . . "to the possibility of being otherwise" (Matthews, 2015 p. 122, (quoting Fitzpatrick, 2004)). Laws can never just be read in one way. Even hegemony doesn't present itself coherently (Parashar, 2008). Legal text (and that of the accompanying guidelines) is filled with tensions and contradictions, filled with vague and elastic concepts and concepts that contradict each other. Law is no more autonomous and rational than people. The law seems to embrace the rational workable body on one hand and a renewed focus on coordination in adherence to the principle of wholeness on the other (Agency of Labor, 2013). This openness and indeterminacy leaves a space for agency and for that which is left out of the text to remind us of its being. Neither the needs of the market nor being work-capable are closely defined, and though they certainly come with strong hegemonic ties to ideologies of autonomy, self sufficiency, and independence, as well as a seemingly total lack of focus on structural, socio-material and societal explanations for unemployment, they also come with a discretionary space, where assessments must be made in praxis, and in that sense they are still open to everything that exceeds them (Crowley, 2014). To acknowledge that law happens not just in legal texts but in praxis does not make legal texts less consequential. Law matters with its words, it just does not matter alone, and praxis matters too. Praxis matters to law precisely because law is never done but is always enacted in particular practices together with the beings that it interacts with. This understanding allows for a focus that does not underemphasize law nor practice but is observant of the connections between state, law, social workers and their socio-material conditions, people receiving assistance and their socio-material conditions, and how power is dispersed (Parashar, 2008). Neither law on the books nor law in practice is "real" law. Law happens when text and practice meet. This view makes the making of law a responsibility not just of the politicians (though certainly of them), but also of the social workers (and all other legal decision makers) (Parashar, 2008). It is a responsibility not (merely) for using the law "right" but for owning one's share in the becoming of social law, for the consequences that flow from these becomings, and for one's role in what is inscribed and what is left out. The world is created in each decision, and each decision is a possibility for challenging the validity of an established "just measure in the name of the incommensurable" (Morin, 2012, p. 111; Nancy, 1993). Perhaps Nancy's thinking about sense as a praxis can aid us in this responsibility. "Thinking . . . means being sensible or passable for sense, being capable of the shock of sense. . . . To be passible is not just to be passive, but to act, to wonder . . . before that which presents itself" (Devisch, 2006 (quoting Nancy), p. 67). Perhaps in wondering before that which is before them and they who present themselves, social workers can be open to those who have been left out of the text. It is important to stress that though the decision is made for the particular being coming up against the law, the decision is at the same time creating a world for everyone by the legal knowledge practices it brings into the world (Parashar, 2008).

7

CONTRACT AS PUBLIC LAW

The public nature of collective bargaining agreements

Risa L. Lieberwitz[1]

Under current economic and political conditions, examining the potential of contract as public law presents a potentially effective means to push back against the forces of privatization. The relentless attack on the welfare state has made it ever more difficult to achieve public interest legislation that increases economic well-being for all, including improvements in worker rights and workplace conditions. In the face of privatization, however, the collective bargaining agreement (CBA) provides an important model for private contracts that provide for public welfare. Although corporations, through their disproportionate control over Congress, can block labor-friendly legislation, employees can collectively oppose corporate power by unionizing and thereby obligating their corporate employers to bargain for a CBA.

In the US, of course, workers face enormous obstacles due to employer hostility against unionization and collective bargaining. Corporate attacks on unions are reflected in the continuing decline in the rate of unionization in the private sector. Recently, public employers have sought to capitalize on these trends by weakening state collective bargaining laws in an attempt to reverse the growth in public sector unionization. Nevertheless, statutory rights to unionize in both the private and public sectors continue to hold the greatest potential for employees to redistribute wealth and power through negotiations for CBAs that provide for higher wages, better benefits, safer working conditions, and protections such as "just cause" requirements for discharge or discipline.

This chapter examines the public nature of the process of collective bargaining and the content of CBAs. Both have been instrumental in bringing democratic values and practices to the workplace through the redistribution of wealth

1 Professor, School of Industrial and Labor Relations, Cornell University.

and power. Although there are important critiques of the reliance on contract to achieve public values, at this moment, collective bargaining retains its potential for promoting the public interest. Further, while there are important critiques of the labor movement's continued lack of diverse leadership, unionization and collective bargaining have proven essential to improving working conditions and increasing democratic participation of women and people of color at the workplace.

Section I sets forth the current social and economic context of growing inequality in the distribution of wealth and power. This ongoing trend resulting from privatization and global capitalism has been accompanied by the decline of unionization rates in the US. Against this background, Section II examines the importance of statutory rights to unionization and collective bargaining in achieving the public values of the welfare state. This discussion analyzes the way that exercise of these rights promotes values of democratic participation and economic redistribution. This section of the chapter identifies the democratic values promoted by both the collective bargaining process and the content of CBAs. This study reveals the central role of the CBA in redistribution of wealth and power by creating greater workplace equality while at the same time raising employees' wages and benefits, improving working conditions, and providing increased job security. Section III addresses the obstacles to broadening the scope of unionization and the redistribution of wealth and power. This discussion explores the structural legal constraints created by the National Labor Relations Act (NLRA), the limits of "business unionism," and the problem of hostility by employers to unionization and collective bargaining. Section IV moves to the more recent anti-union attacks by public sector employers through statutory changes initiated by Republican governors and state legislatures, including severe restraints on collective bargaining and impairment of CBAs. These aggressive attacks by state governments reveal the impact of the ideology of individualism and privatization, which seeks to eliminate collective power that employees gain through unionization and collective bargaining.

I. Growing rates of inequality and declining rates of unionization

The current dearth of democratic political participation in the US is certainly related to the growing inequality of wealth. It is likely that causality goes in both directions; that is, inequality of political power leads to inequality in the distribution of wealth, which in turn, results in increasing inequalities of power. The well-known statistics bring home the reality that workers have been steadily losing power and wealth as inequality has grown. In 2010, the top 10% in the US controlled 77% of all wealth, leaving the bottom 90% with only 23% (Mishel et al., 2012, p. 376). In that same year, the first year of the economic recovery, 93% of the income gains went to the top 1% of Americans (Porter, 2012). Despite the 69% growth in productivity from 1979 to 2011, median hourly compensation (wages and benefits) grew only 7% (Mishel et al., 2012, p. 7). In 2010, typical employees earned roughly the same wage per hour as in 2000.

Thus, employers are using the recession as a pretext to increase inequality by shifting employee wages to corporate profits. Corporate social responsibility has not accompanied the greater corporate power that comes with deregulation, as witnessed by the parade of corporate scandals in the late 1990s and early 2000s (Borrus, McNamee and Zegel, 2002) and the bank and investment corporation bailouts since 2008.

The growth in inequality in the US reveals the failure of public policy that restricts the role of the state in providing for the public welfare. This approach places employment at the center of individuals' ability to meet their needs, whether through wages or employer-provided benefits. The US system of "private welfare" (Munger, 2004, pp. 550–551) or of an "employee welfare state" (Charny, 1996, p. 1601) focuses on the private employment relationship rather than a public welfare state to provide for basic needs. In practice, therefore, much of employees' social protection is contingent on employment contracts or employers' voluntary actions. This amounts to a public policy that substitutes employment-related benefits for a governmental obligation to ensure that all individuals have a minimal level of food, housing, health care, paid sick leave, child care, and paid vacations. As labor economist Thomas Kochan and legal expert Beth Shulman have noted, this "*laissez-faire* benefit model" is based on the 1930s New Deal expectation that benefits would be linked to a "long-term, relatively stable employment relationship" (Kochan and Shulman, 2007, p. 6). This expectation, in turn, depends on employees having a meaningful right to unionize. After World War II, the 35% private sector unionization rate created a strong base for collective bargaining for higher wages and benefits (Kochan and Shulman, 2007, p. 2). For example, unionized employees "are 18.3% more likely to have health insurance, 22.5% more likely to have pension coverage, and 3.2% more likely to have paid leave" than non-union workers (Mishel et al., 2012, pp. 272–273). Further, with a sufficient level of unionization in a healthy economy, even non-union employers would feel pressured to provide these social protections to their employees (Charny, 1996).

In the context of globalization, increased capital mobility has shifted manufacturing facilities from high-wage industrialized countries to low-wage developing countries (Silver, 2003). The effects of globalization hit US workers hard, with the loss of jobs in industries with high union density, including the steel, automobile, appliance, and high technology industries. The loss of these higher paid union jobs and the shift to a largely non-union service economy also meant the loss of social protection through benefits won in collective bargaining. Employers in the service economy, covering a wide range that includes retail stores, hospitals, nursing homes, hotels, and restaurants, have actively resisted employees' efforts to unionize. Further, with the loss of the unionized industrial base, workers are increasingly vulnerable to employer efforts to restructure the employment relationship in the name of gaining flexibility in the competitive global market. This redefinition has entailed an increase in contingent employment, including a growth in the use of part-time and temporary employees and independent contractors. In the case of temporary employees, employers often distance themselves further from the employees by "leasing" them through temporary employment agencies (Lieberwitz, 2005, p. 328). The rate of contingent employment increased dramatically in the 1990s, with estimates that contingent employees now make up at least 25% of the workforce (de Haas, 1998; Duncan, 1999; Lieberwitz, 2005, p. 328; Rodgers et al., 2014; Walpole-Hofmeister, 2001).

By creating a "second-class of subordinate workers" (Sukert, 2000, p. 448), employers have found an effective mechanism for avoiding unions, lowering wage rates, and cutting back on benefits. Part-time and temporary employees are difficult to unionize (Raday, 1999). With the private sector unionization rate at less than 7%, workers lack the bargaining power to demand that employers share their profits and to oppose reductions in wages and benefits, job losses, and shifts to part-time work (Mishel et al., 2006/2007).

As unemployment rates have grown along with the low-wage, non-union service economy, poverty rates have also been increasing (Tavernise, 2011). Under the federal official poverty threshold, 15.1% of the US population is in poverty, which comprises more than 46 million people (Mishel et al., 2012, p. 420). This rate increased from 12.5% in 2007. These increases in poverty rates have a disproportionately negative impact on women and people of color, with African Americans having the highest poverty rate at 27.4%, followed by Hispanics at 26.6% and whites at 9.9%. Defining poverty is closely related to, though not synonymous with, defining the "working poor." Given the unrealistically low threshold defined by the federal official poverty threshold, many low-wage workers are poor but do not meet the government's definition of poverty. When the numbers are calculated in terms of inadequate income to meet basic needs, in 2011, 28% of workers earned poverty-level wages of $11.06 or less an hour (Mishel et al., 2012, p. 432; Cauthen, 2007, p. 1).

Several societal factors explain the rise in poverty even in the financially flush period of first part of the 2000s. One important factor is the high percentage of low-wage jobs. Since wages make up about three-fourths of family income in the US, changes in wage levels will determine most families' financial conditions (Cauthen, 2007). Some progress was made in reducing poverty-level wage jobs in the late 1990s, but this trend ended in the early part of the 2000s. Since 2002, "there has been no progress in reducing the share of workers with low earnings" (Cauthen, 2007, p. 7). Currently, 25% to 30% of the workforce hold low-wage jobs that keep them in poverty level conditions. Almost half of minimum-wage jobs are in the retail and hospitality industries. As Nancy Cauthen notes, "such jobs typically offer few of the employer-sponsored benefits – such as health insurance, paid sick leave, retirement plans, and the flexibility to deal with family needs – that higher-income workers often take for granted" (Cauthen, 2007, p. 1). Yet, most low-wage workers do not receive public benefits, due to underfunding of programs for eligible low-income workers, or because their low-wage income is still higher than the eligibility threshold. "Many such families are merely one crisis – a serious illness, job loss, or divorce – away from financial devastation" (Cauthen, 2007, pp. 2,

11–14). Some groups are disproportionately represented, with women, Blacks, and Hispanics significantly more likely to earn poverty-level wages than white men.[2] In general, women, minorities, and immigrants are overrepresented among low-wage workers (Mishelet al., 2006/2007).

During the period of economic growth in the mid-1990s, it was primarily the wealthy who enjoyed the benefits of productivity growth. As the Economic Policy Institute has emphasized, increased inequality in income is a key factor that explains the continued poor conditions of low-wage workers, as "the link between economic growth and broadly shared income gains [was] broken" in the 1990s (Mishelet al., 2006/2007, p. 4). During this period, wealth flowed from the bottom to the top of the income ladder, resulting in "levels of concentration [of wealth] not seen since the latter 1920s" (Mishelet al., 2006/2007). One example of the growing income gap is the skyrocketing of executive compensation even as wages and benefits dropped for the working class. In the late 1970s, CEOs were paid about 30 times more than a typical worker; this disparity has grown to the current level of CEO pay at more than 200 times that of a typical worker (Mishel et al., 2012, p. 175). In 2011, the median chief executive in the top-paid 100 CEOs in the US was paid $14.4 million, in stark contrast to the average annual American salary of $45,230 (Singer, April 2012).

The 2000s exacerbated the financial conditions of the working class as "most families experienced stagnant or falling real incomes" during "the longest jobless recovery on record" after the 2001 recession (Mishelet al., 2006/2007, pp. 3, 9–10). This period had a negative impact on low-wage workers, as the value of the minimum wage fell steadily in real terms from 2000 until 2007, when it was raised for the first time in more than a decade. This decline in the value of the minimum wage caused low-wage workers' earnings "to seriously fall behind" not only the wealthy, but also all other workers (Mishelet al., 2006/2007, p. 9).

II. The role of unionization to promote democratic values

A. *Unionization and collective bargaining as democratic participation*

Unionization and collective bargaining provide an important route for bringing democratic values into the workplace and reducing the current extreme inequalities of power and wealth. Given the continued drive toward privatization and away from the welfare state, it is becoming more difficult to achieve legislation that increases worker rights and economic wellbeing. Even in the face of legislative stalemate or hostility, employees can collectively oppose private corporate power by unionizing and thereby obligating their corporate employers to bargain

2 In 2011, nearly 25% of male workers, nearly one-third of women workers, 23.4% of white workers, 36% of Black workers, and 43.3% of Hispanic workers earned poverty-level wages (Mishel et al., 2012, pp. 193–194).

for a CBA. At this moment, then, the CBA provides an important model of collective action to achieve contracts that provide for public welfare.

Unionization imports democratic rights and values into the authoritarian workplace hierarchy. The NLRA promotes equality by giving collective power to private sector employees to negotiate with their employers for CBAs. It is worth remembering that section 1 of the NLRA, "Findings and Policies," links employees' freedom of contract with their freedom of association:

> The inequality of bargaining power between employees who do not possess full freedom of association or actual liberty of contract and employers who are organized in the corporate or other forms of ownership association substantially burdens and affects the flow of commerce.

Even apart from the content of the CBA, the rights to unionize and collectively bargain are inherently valuable in promoting democratic rights of meaningful employee participation at the workplace. The NLRA creates democratic rights at multiple stages of the process of unionization and collective bargaining. Section 9 of the NLRA contains the provisions dealing with representation issues, including the union's ability to file a petition for an election. Section 9 also states the principle of majority rule, where a majority of employees in a bargaining unit may select a union as their exclusive representative for purposes of collective bargaining. A union selected by a majority of employees in a bargaining unit becomes the exclusive bargaining representative for all the employees in that bargaining unit.[3] The employer may bargain only with the exclusive bargaining representative concerning working conditions in that bargaining unit. Given the power of exclusive representation, the union has a duty to fairly represent all the employees in the bargaining unit, including those who may have voted against the union.

If employees do unionize, section 8(d) of the NLRA requires that the employer and union bargain in good faith over "wages, hours, and other terms and conditions of employment." Mandatory subjects cover a broad range of issues, such as wages, benefits, "just cause" requirements, promotion processes, safety provisions, pensions, and grievance/arbitration procedures. Collective bargaining over working conditions is a democratizing process, as the union negotiating team, which includes bargaining unit employees, bargains as an equal across the table from the employer. This process provides the employees with the collective power to decide their priorities in bargaining, rather than leaving it to the employer to decide what is good for the employees.

The collective bargaining process promotes democratic values of openness and transparency. It opposes the culture of secrecy and confidentiality that employers

3 29 USC §159 (a). In an election, the union wins if selected by a majority of bargaining unit employees voting. If a voluntary recognition process is used, the majority is based on the number of employees in the bargaining unit.

often create concerning wages, benefits, and other "perks" to individual employees. Employers are obligated to provide information relevant to collective bargaining if requested by the union, including information about employees' wages, benefits, and job classifications (Truitt, 1956). Employers who claim they cannot afford to meet the union's proposals must provide financial records that support their assertion if requested by the union. Unions conduct membership votes at important stages in this process, including strike votes and votes on contract ratification. The resulting CBA creates transparency in informing all bargaining unit employees of their terms and conditions of employment. Contract enforcement continues this democratic process, primarily through the grievance/arbitration dispute resolution process contained in the CBA. The US Supreme Court has emphasized that unionization, collective bargaining, and the enforcement of collective bargaining agreements constitute a dynamic process for democratizing the workplace:

> [T]he grievance machinery under a collective bargaining agreement is at the very heart of the system of industrial self-government. . . . The processing of disputes through the grievance machinery is actually a vehicle by which meaning and content are given to the collective bargaining agreement. . . . The grievance procedure is, in other words, a part of the continuous collective bargaining process.
>
> (*United Steelworkers of America v Warrior & Gulf*, *1960, p. 581)*

B. Unionization and collective bargaining as a means of redistribution of wealth and power

Unionization and collective bargaining promote democratic values of providing for the common good. The NLRA builds this concept into the rights described in section 7, which includes the right of employees "to bargain collectively through representatives of their own choosing, and to engage in other concerted activities for the purpose of collective bargaining or other mutual aid or protection." The Supreme Court has described the value of employees acting collectively for their mutual benefit. In 1944, the court explained that collective bargaining represents employees' decision to forego their potential individual advantages in favor of negotiating gains in wages and benefits that are shared by employees in the bargaining unit (*J.I. Case v NLRB*, 1944). The court emphasized the redistributive nature of collective bargaining, stating:

> The practice and philosophy of collective bargaining looks with suspicion on . . . individual advantages. . . . They are a fruitful way of interfering with organization and choice of representatives; increased compensation, if individually deserved, is often earned at the cost of breaking down some

> other standard thought to be for the welfare of the group, and always creates the suspicion of being paid at the long-range expense of the group as a whole.
>
> *(p. 339)*

Thus, unionization and collective bargaining bring democratic values to the workplace through a more equal distribution of wealth and power in two ways: vertically, between employers and employees; and horizontally, by spreading negotiated gains throughout the bargaining unit. The concept of "mutual aid or protection" can entail collective bargaining for different levels of wages and benefits to take account of factors such as seniority and skill level. But the equalizing impact is still present through the use of objective measures to distribute wages and benefits in an evenhanded fashion, rather than through highly subjective measures unilaterally controlled by the employer.

The CBA may contain a wide range of provisions, including economic matters such as wages, raises, paid sick leave and vacation, employer-paid insurance, pensions, and other benefits. Health and safety provisions and antidiscrimination provisions may be negotiated as conditions of employment that build on the floor of statutory regulations. Due process protections take various forms in CBAs, incorporating criteria for transparency and objective criteria in decision making. Seniority is the norm for determining the order of layoffs and recalls. Promotions clauses usually provide for open bidding processes that use the objective measure of seniority along with more subjective measures in judging qualifications. Perhaps most distinctive about the CBA is the provision requiring employers to use "just cause" in decisions about discipline or discharge of bargaining unit employees. Almost all CBAs in the US include grievance/arbitration provisions to resolve contract disputes, including discipline and discharge (Garden and Leong, 2013). The union and employer negotiate for the grievance procedures, which usually entail two or three pre-arbitration steps to resolve disputes informally. If these steps are unsuccessful, the grievance can go to an arbitration hearing before a third-party arbitrator or arbitration panel mutually selected by the union and employer.

In arbitration, the employer bears the burden of proving "just cause" in discipline or discharge cases, which requires the employer to prove both procedural and substantive due process in carrying out the discipline or discharge. The significance of this requirement becomes apparent when contrasted with the legal background in the US of the common law doctrine of "employment at-will," which has influenced the legislatures and courts since at least the 19th century (Ballam, 1996). Under the familiar litany of employment at-will doctrine, an employer may hire or discharge an individual for "a good reason, a bad reason, or no reason at all," emphasizing employers' unilateral power to decide whether to initially employ or continue to employ an individual. In other words, the employer has no obligation to make rational hiring decisions or to discharge employees only for just cause (Player, 2004, pp. 85–95). The CBA thus brings democratic values of due process into the workplace by holding the employer to this objective standard in discipline or discharge cases and by placing the burden on the employer to prove just cause. The "just cause" provision increases fair treatment and job security by applying basic values of procedural and substantive due process.

C. The limits of collective bargaining to promote democracy

Although CBAs import democratic values into the workplace, they have also been critiqued as a means to maintain the private nature of employment relations by reinforcing the contractual basis of employees' wages, hours, and working conditions. In collective bargaining, employees gain improvements in their conditions of work through a *quid pro quo* process of compromise. Further, the traditional means of enforcing the CBA through grievance/arbitration procedures creates a private system of workplace justice, where the union and employer hire a private arbitrator to hear evidence and decide the grievance (Stone, 1981). A more public means of establishing employees' rights to higher wages and benefits and better working conditions would be through legislation that applies to all employees, rather than through CBAs that apply only to the employees in the particular bargaining unit. Such legislation would reflect a stronger welfare state, as in Europe, where unions play an important political role in labor parties to elect legislators who will promote a labor rights agenda.

Given the continued drive toward privatization and away from the welfare state, however, it is becoming more difficult to achieve legislation that increases worker rights and economic wellbeing. At this moment, then, the CBA provides an essential model for contracts that provide for the public welfare and the common good. Unionization continues to hold the greatest potential for employees to shift wealth and power from employers to labor through negotiations for CBAs that provide for higher wages, better benefits, safer working conditions, and protections such as "just cause" requirements for discharge or discipline. If union density increases, this will give the labor movement greater power to win better collective bargaining agreements, which will put pressure on non-union employers to raise wages and benefits.

At the same time, it should be recognized that the labor movement in the US plays an important role in political action to enact legislation that increases the floor of economic rights for all workers, such as minimum wage increases, health and safety protections, antidiscrimination laws, and universal health care, and more recently, for immigrant rights (Garden and Leong, 2013). Greater union density, thus, will also make the labor movement a more powerful force to pressure the federal and state governments to adopt legislation providing higher wages and benefits universally. Such political power by unions would not reduce the need for unionization at the workplace. As discussed above, unions create collective power for employees to engage in meaningful workplace participation.

Through collective bargaining, unions can build on economic benefits provided by statute. As importantly, they can press for redistribution of decision making about work process and business-related decisions.

III. Obstacles to unionization and collective bargaining

Given the benefits to employees of unionization and collective bargaining, why is union density in the private sector of the US so low, currently under 7%?[4] The reasons range from structural legal constraints created by the NLRA, to social conditions of limited internal union democracy, to the deep and active hostility by government and employers to unionization.

A. *Structural obstacles in the NLRA*

Several aspects of the NLRA, as written and interpreted, have particularly strong limiting effects on union organizing. One aspect is the restriction on unions' ability to organize on a broad industrial basis. Section 9 of the NLRA describes the structure of bargaining units within a specific business, rather than through industry-wide collective bargaining. There may be multiple bargaining units at one place of business, but the National Labor Relations Board (NLRB) will not find a bargaining unit appropriate if a union seeks to represent employees from different employers in a single bargaining unit. The NLRB, in effect, conditions the union's use of the NLRA election processes on the union's organizing on a firm-by-firm basis. This seriously impedes unions' ability to organize broadly on an industrial or occupational basis across employers (Edwards and Seitz, 1998; Rogers, 1990).

In the case of temporary employees, who are made up disproportionately of women, it is particularly difficult to unionize where the temporary employees are hired by a "user employer" through a temporary employment agency (TEA). The NLRB has decided that unions must obtain the consent of the user employer and TEA to a mixed bargaining unit of temporary employees supplied by a TEA and regular employees of the user employer's business. If the user employer and TEA refuse to consent to a mixed bargaining unit, the union is left to organize the temporary employees in a separate unit, with the TEA as the employer (H.S. Care LLC, d/b/a Oakwood Care Ctr., 2004). The more liberal NLRB under the Obama administration recently signaled an interest in reconsidering this approach, inviting *amicus* briefs on whether employers' consent should be required for such bargaining units (Miller & Anderson, Inc., 2015). On the heels of this development,

4 In 2014, the union membership rate in the US private sector was 6.6%, with a higher rate in the public sector, at 35.7%. The number of employees represented by a union in 2014 was 16.2 million, which comprises union members (14.6 million) and employees who are not union members, but whose jobs are covered by a collective bargaining agreement (1.6 million). Bureau of Labour Statistics, www.bls.gov/news.release/union2.nr0.htm.

the NLRB issued a decision that makes it easier to establish joint-employer status, including TEA-user employer relationships (Browning-Ferris Industries, 2015). The board described its revised standard as reflecting "changing economic circumstances, particularly the recent dramatic growth in contingent employment relationships" (p. 2). Expanding unions' options in organizing recognizes the economic realities of the user employer's control over the temporary employees and the common interests of the temporary and regular employees (Lieberwitz, 2005).

Another aspect of the NLRA narrows the statutory definition of "employee," which excludes many employees from the right to unionize and collectively bargain. The NLRA excludes all supervisors from the definition of employee under the Act. Congress created this exclusion in the Labor Management Relations Act of 1947 (Taft-Hartley) amending the NLRA. This legislative change, decreasing the ranks of labor, was consistent with the anti-union motivation underlying this and other provisions of the Taft-Hartley Act. The exclusion of supervisors was based largely on Congress' view that employers should be able to demand undivided loyalty from individuals employed to carry out supervisory duties (Seitz, 1984). The scope of the section 2(11) exclusion of supervisors, though, is very broad, defining supervisors as any individual who exercises any one of twelve supervisory duties in the interest of the employer, including assignment or direction of work, as well as duties with greater authority, such as recommending wage increases or employee discipline.

In recent years, the Supreme Court has expanded the reach of the NLRA section 2(11) exclusion of supervisors with an especially negative impact on professional employees. The Taft-Hartley Act had softened the blow of section 2(11) by adding section 2(12), which explicitly defined and included "professional employees" within the category of employees covered by the NLRA. In two recent cases, though, the Supreme Court severely restricted the ranks of labor in the health care profession, by rejecting the NLRB's legal test for determining the supervisory status of nurses (*NLRB v Health Care and Retirement Corp. of America*, 1994; *NLRB v Kentucky River Community Care Inc.*, 2001). The Supreme Court's holdings and the subsequent NLRB application of the Supreme Court's decisions will affect professional employees well beyond the health care field. Given the growing importance of the service sector in the US economy, the negative impact on the labor movement is critical. As the two board members stated, in dissenting from the NLRB's broad definition of supervisory status, "Today's decision threatens to create a new class of workers . . . who have neither the genuine prerogatives of management, nor the statutory rights of ordinary employees. Into that category may fall most professionals" (*In re Oakwood Healthcare, Inc.*, 2006, pp. 700–709).

Even if employees do unionize, the NLRA reduces labor power by confining unions to a narrow scope of bargaining (Rogers, 1990). The employer and union have a duty to bargain over "mandatory subjects," consisting of "wages, hours, and other terms and conditions of employment." Mandatory subjects cover a broad range of "bread and butter" issues, but do not include "permissive subjects," about which the employer and union may bargain, but there is no duty to bargain. For example, "permissive subjects of bargaining" would include decisions viewed as part of "managerial prerogatives," such hiring decisions,[5] decisions about business investments, advertising, restructuring a business, closing part of a business, or relocating it due to non-labor costs (*Dubuque Packing Co.*, 1991; *First National Maintenance Corp. v NLRB*, 1981). Employers would also argue that issues concerning the work process are permissive subjects. Professional employees may be particularly affected by these definitions if they seek to bargain over issues of importance to their profession. For example, nurses seeking to bargain over the level of staffing or the quality of hospital equipment may face an employer argument that this is only a permissive subject of bargaining.

B. The limits of "business unionism"

Whether or not this is a causal relationship, the NLRA constraints of organizing at the business firm level and bargaining only for mandatory subjects are consistent with the American Federation of Labor and Congress of Industrial Organizations' (AFL-CIO) traditional organizing model. Unionization of an industry could be accomplished by organizing a sufficient number of firms to create significant union density, which enabled unions to accomplish broad unionization of heavy industry such as steel and automobiles, where CBAs provided significant gains in mandatory subjects of bargaining. This model, however, also has significant drawbacks. Described as "business unionism," unionization came to mean collective bargaining for "bread and butter" issues (Crain and Matheny, 2001, pp. 1771–1788). Once the employer-union relationship became stable and long-term, the union's focus narrowed to negotiating contract renewals and "servicing" the bargaining unit through contract enforcement.

The tunnel vision of business unionism contrasts with a vision of unions as a social movement for societal justice and democracy in ways that extend beyond negotiating for higher wages and benefits. The success of business unionism in increasing union density in the 1950s, however, led the AFL-CIO unions to cut back on organizational campaigns in non-union workplaces (Milkman and Voss, 2004). This meant that unions were not expanding to organize in other occupations, including those filled predominately by women and people of color. Stereotypes that women and people of color were not "organizable" because they were not interested in unionization became rationalizations for organizing and servicing only in occupations held predominately by white men (Milkman, 2007). Combined with the exclusion of women and people of color from unionized occupations such as steelworkers and construction, the result was that unionized workplaces and union leadership remained the domain of white men.

With the deindustrialization of the US in the 1970s and 1980s and the shift of the US to a service economy, union density has steadily decreased to its current

5 However, promotions processes, including the weight placed on seniority, are mandatory subjects of bargaining.

low point of less than 7% in the private sector. On a more positive note, though, new blood has been pumped into the labor movement as the AFL-CIO has been forced to confront questions of its very survival (Rooks, 2004). Factors such as the more progressive leadership of the AFL-CIO since the mid-1990s led to greater commitment of union resources to organizing employees in professional service jobs, such as nurses, and in low-wage non-professional jobs, such as hotel cleaning staff, aides in hospitals and retirement homes, and laundry workers. Given the high percentage of women and people of color in these occupations, such organizing campaigns expand the diversity of the labor movement (Waldinger et al., 1998).[6]

These changes have led to important gains for women. Unions are more likely to win an election in bargaining units where women predominate (Bronfenbrenner, 2005). In fact, women have been the majority of new unionized workers each year since the mid-1980s, and growth of unionization has been especially strong among Black women. In bargaining units where women predominate, the collective bargaining agenda prioritizes issues of particular importance for women, such as child care subsidies, flex-time, and paid leaves (Cobble, 2007; Drago and Fazioli, 2003; Grundy and Firestein, 1997). In one study comparing hourly workers who take family and medical leave, 46% of unionized workers compared to 29% of non-unionized workers received full pay while on leave (MacGillvary and Firestein, 2009, p. 3). This same study found that unionized workers are 50% more likely than non-unionized workers to have paid personal leave that can be used to care for sick children. Further, companies with a unionization rate of at least 30% are five times as likely as companies with no unionized workers to pay the entire family health insurance premium. Female-majority unions have been at the forefront of collective bargaining for LGBT rights and benefits and for lobbying for state and federal legislative changes for paid family leave and child care subsidies for all workers, whether unionized or not (Firestein and Dones, 2007; Hunt and Boris, 2007).

Despite these gains, many organizational campaigns continue to take place in workplaces where women are in the minority (Bronfenbrenner, 2005). Further, although women currently make up almost half of union members, women's views of unions reportedly grew increasingly negative during the late 1990s and into the early 2000s (Nussbaum, 2007). Moreover, even with the growth of women union members, union leadership is still mostly male, including in unions representing traditionally female occupations (Bronfenbrenner, 2005; Nussbaum, 2007).

C. Employer and governmental hostility to unions

The 1980s drop in union density was linked not only to the deindustrialization of the US, but to the right-wing shift in US politics, which included hostility to

6 In 2005, the SEIU and six other unions left the AFL-CIO to form the Change to Win Coalition, based on concerns that the AFL-CIO was not adequately committed to expanded organizing efforts (Gross, 2005/2006).

unions as part of a program of privatization and pro-business decisions by federal agencies such as the NLRB (Nussbaum, 2007). The mid-1990s election of progressive leadership to the AFL-CIO came at the same time as the election of a Republican majority in Congress and the growing inequalities in income and wealth in the US. Hostility by the Republican Congress came to a head with the Senate's refusal to consider the Obama administration's pro-labor nominees to the NLRB, leading President Obama to make three recess appointments in January 2012. In its 2014 decision in *NLRB v Noel Canning*, the Supreme Court upheld an employer challenge to the constitutional validity of these appointments. The unanimous court concluded that Senate was not in recess in January 2012 when the Senate convened every three days in *pro forma* sessions. Further, a recess of three days is too short a time to trigger the President's power to make recess appointments. Following the court's decision and after new appointments were confirmed by the Senate, the NLRB unanimously ratified all actions taken by the board during the period of close to two years when it did not have a quorum (NLRB, August 4, 2014).

Employer anti-union attitudes and actions are not new. Employers resist the redistribution of power and wealth that unionization entails. That is, employers are hostile to challenges to their unilateral control over decision making and over distribution of profits. Employers engage in active anti-union campaigns designed to persuade or coerce employees to vote against the union in secret ballot elections (Compa, 2000; Weiler, 1983). During these campaigns, employer tactics include delivering anti-union speeches at "captive audience" meetings with employees, while also barring the union from the employer's property. Given the employer's economic power over employees, the employer has enormous potential influence over the employees' votes – even if the employer uses only lawful anti-union propaganda.

Further, the weak remedies under the NLRA and the delays in NLRA enforcement do little to deter employers from engaging in unlawful conduct (unfair labor practices (ULPs)) prior to a union election. Through these ULPs, such as threats of discharge or threats to close the plant or department if the employees unionize, employers exploit their power over employees' economic futures. An employer's cost-benefit calculations may lead the employer to conclude that it will ultimately be less costly to violate the law in an attempt to discourage unionization and avoid the higher costs and loss of total control resulting from collective bargaining (Block, 1997). In all likelihood, an employer committing ULPs during a union organizational campaign would face only a remedial order to cease threatening employees or an order to reinstate discharged employees with back pay reduced by the employee's interim earnings. Even if the union wins the election and becomes the exclusive bargaining representative, the legal remedy for bad faith bargaining is simply a slap on the wrist, consisting of an order to bargain in good faith. Such a weak remedy provides no deterrence to employer misconduct. Nor does it make the employees whole for the loss of increased wages and benefits during the period of bad faith bargaining and litigation.

IV. Privatization and the attacks on public sector unionization and collective bargaining

Since the 1960s, about two-thirds of US states have enacted public sector collective bargaining statutes (about 33 states). As union density in the private sector has been steadily dropping, public sector unionization rates have risen to reach their current rate of 35.7% (Bureau of Labor Statistics [BLS], January 23, 2015). Due to this high level of public sector unionization, overall union density in the US has been maintained at about 11% (BLS, January 23, 2015). Privatization trends have had significant negative effects on the public sector through the reduction of public services and public sector employee layoffs (Dannin, 2012). The privatization philosophy has also imported the anti-union ideology of the private sector. Having succeeded in weakening the power of unions in the private sector, corporations and right-wing politicians have turned their attention to undermining unions in the public sector. These political attacks draw caricatures of public sector unions as organizations that have become so powerful that they have forced public employers to agree to CBAs that are causing financial crises in state government. Public employees are portrayed as overpaid and underworked, marking time until they can enjoy a retirement supported by an inflated pension, all guaranteed by CBAs. These images thus portray public sector unions and employees as acting against the public good. The attacks on public sector CBAs, wages, and benefits are designed, as well, to create resentment by non-union private sector employees who do not have good wages, benefits, or pensions. Given the low level of private sector unionization, this attack seeks to divide the interests of union and non-union employees.

Despite the repeated refrain that public sector employees are overpaid and underworked, the evidence supports a different conclusion. Studies comparing public and private sector employees find that public employees are paid less than private sector employees with similar credentials in similar jobs (Slater, 2012). A national study by the Economic Policy Institute concluded that, on average, full-time state and local employees are paid 3.7% less than similar private sector employees (Slater, 2012, p. 201). These findings were similar in states with significant levels of unionization and strong public sector collective bargaining laws. The accusation that public sector collective bargaining exacerbates state deficits is also not supported by the evidence. States with public sector collective bargaining, on average, have smaller deficits (14%) relative to their budgets, than states that prohibit public sector collective bargaining (16.5% deficit). As Slater notes, Texas and Nevada, states without public sector collective bargaining, are among the states with the largest state budget deficits. In contrast, Wisconsin, Ohio, and Iowa, states that have (or in the case of Wisconsin, had) strong public sector collective bargaining laws, have smaller than average deficits. The gap between accusations and evidence strengthens the conclusion that the attack on public sector workers and unions is ideological, rather than a matter of necessity to address state budget deficits.

Particularly since 2010, supported and lobbied by right-wing organizations like the American Legislative Exchange Council (ALEC), Republican governors and legislatures have amended statutes and enacted new laws that use three major tactics to weaken public sector unions: restrictions of the scope of public sector collective bargaining; impairment of existing CBAs; and undermining the financial viability of unions. As discussed below, these legislative restraints on public sector unions and collective bargaining have been adopted in states with a high level of unionization, including Wisconsin and Michigan. In seeking to weaken public sector unions and collective bargaining, these new statutes also weaken public values of democratic workplace participation and redistribution.

A. State laws limiting the scope of public sector collective bargaining

The legislative battles in Wisconsin and Ohio in 2010 and 2011 are characteristic of the level of hostility against public sector unions and collective bargaining. In taking on Wisconsin, Republican Governor Scott Walker and Republican state legislators made a direct attack on public sector unionization in a strongly unionized state that in 1959, enacted the first public sector collective bargaining law. The "Budget Repair Bill" signed by Governor Walker in 2011 eviscerated the public sector collective bargaining laws. Prior to this amendment to the law, Wisconsin public sector collective bargaining statutes covered state, local, and county public employees. The amended law eliminates collective bargaining rights completely for some employees, specifically, University of Wisconsin (UW) system employees, employees of the UW Hospitals and Clinics Authority, and certain home care and child care providers. For all other government employees, except for police and firefighters, the new Act imposes severe restrictions on the scope of collective bargaining, which is now limited to bargaining about wage increases. No other issues may be negotiated in collective bargaining. Even bargaining about wages is restricted to an increase no greater than the percentage change in the consumer price index (Artz, 2012; Slater, 2012). Another severe attack on unions in the new Wisconsin law is an "unprecedented" requirement that unions must be recertified in an annual election by a vote of 51% of employees in the bargaining unit (Slater, 2012, p. 204).

The shocking level of the right-wing attack in Wisconsin led to an extraordinary surge of collective protest by public sector employees, union members, and supporters from Wisconsin and other states who joined together to occupy the state house. Democratic Wisconsin state legislators left the state and went into hiding in an attempt to block the vote on the bill. Ultimately, though, the bill was passed and signed into law. Collective action continued, including the recall gubernatorial election, which Governor Walker survived.

The story in Ohio also involved a draconian law to eviscerate public sector collective bargaining. Fortunately, political protests and activism were successful, with a state-wide referendum in November 2011 that repealed the new public sector collective bargaining statute (Slater, 2012). Like the new Wisconsin law, SB 5 would have eliminated collective bargaining rights entirely for certain employees, including most college and university faculty, lower level supervisors in police and fire departments, and employees of charter schools. SB 5 would have limited the bargaining rights of some other employees, who would have been able to bargain only if the public employer agreed to bargain. SB 5 would have barred collective bargaining over specified benefits and working conditions, including employer-paid employee contributions to retirement systems; health care benefits (except the amount of premium the employer and employees pay); contracting out of public sector work; overtime payment exceeding the federal Fair Labor Standards Act rate; and the number of employees required to be on duty. SB 5 would have eliminated the right to strike for public employees who can bargain and would have eliminated, as well, the right to binding interest arbitration to resolve collective bargaining impasses.

B. State laws impairing the enforcement of public sector CBAs

Another form of attack on the integrity of CBAs is through legislation providing for the impairment of contracts. In Michigan, the 2011 Local Government and School District Fiscal Accountability Act, known as the "dictator's law" (Artz, 2012, p. 133), gives the governor the power to appoint an "emergency manager" for local governments experiencing a "financial emergency" (Slater, 2012, p. 209). The manager can reject, modify, or terminate any terms of public sector CBAs. Legal challenges were filed alleging that the emergency manager law violates the US Constitution (Livengood and Ferretti, 2014; Slater, 2012, p. 209).

Similarly, in Ohio, SB 5 would have enabled a public employer in a state of fiscal emergency or under "fiscal watch" to terminate, modify, or negotiate a public sector CBA (Slater, 2012, p. 208). As noted above, SB 5 was repealed by referendum.

C. State "right to work" laws

Recent enactments of state "right to work" laws are designed to weaken unions as organizations. The symbolic value of such legislation is particularly important as highly unionized states such as Michigan and Wisconsin are added to "right to work" southern anti-union states. Currently, 24 states have right to work laws, including additions of Wisconsin, Michigan, and Indiana during the past two years (Fink, 2012). The Michigan law was especially shocking in the heart of the unionized auto industry (Fletcher and Sullivan, 2012). Further, the Michigan right to work law was enacted following the defeat by voters of a state constitutional amendment to guarantee collective bargaining rights. In Wisconsin, the right to work rules, which are part of the new public sector collective bargaining law, apply to all public employees except those in "protective occupations" (primarily police and firefighters) (Slater, 2012, p. 204).

The impact of right to work laws on unions is both financial and symbolic. These laws prohibit unions and employers from negotiating union security clauses, which generally consist of "agency shop" clauses or "fair share" clauses. Agency shop clauses require bargaining unit employees to pay to the union, as a condition of employment, the amount of union dues, whether or not the employees are union members. Fair share clauses are similar, but limit the obligated payment by non-members to that portion of their dues which goes to representing the bargaining unit in matters related to collective bargaining. These union security clauses spread the costs associated with collective bargaining by avoiding the free rider problem. Thus, employees who are not union members, but who are represented by the union, are obligated to pay a fair share of the costs of collective bargaining for the benefits they receive in the CBA. Collection of dues under the union security clauses is usually done through automatic payroll deduction.

Right to work laws express governmental hostility to unions by creating obstacles to negotiating for CBA provisions important to the financial support of unions' collective bargaining functions. Such laws paint unions as self-interested organizations that are concerned primarily with employees' union dues. In Wisconsin, the law goes even further in creating obstacles to unions collecting union dues by making it illegal for an employer to agree to automatic payroll deductions even for employees who wish to pay dues (Slater, 2012). In a related development, the US Supreme Court recently considered whether to overrule its 40-year precedent upholding the constitutionality, under the First Amendment, of public sector agency fees (*Friedrichs v California Teachers Association*, 2016).

V. Rising from the ashes?

These are hard times to feel hopeful about a potential phoenix rising from the ashes of the devastation of the labor movement in the public and private sectors. Nevertheless, there are some inspiring collective actions by workers fighting back against corporate greed and privatization. In the private sector, these actions have been through non-traditional employee organizations, such as OUR Walmart (Organization United for Respect at Walmart) and Fast Food Forward, which engaged in strikes against Walmart and the fast-food chains such as McDonalds on Black Friday prior to the Christmas shopping season since 2012 (Greenhouse, November 2012; Harkinson, 2014; Woodman, 2012). These organizations, which are supported by unions such as UFCW and SEIU, are important grass roots claims for respect, dignity, and a collective voice against corporate power. Similarly, workers' centers such as Domestic Workers United have been important organizations to provide a collective voice to workers excluded from legal rights to unionize and collectively bargain (Hill, 2010; Poo, 2011).

In the public sector, despite their defeat in Wisconsin, union supporters made a valiant stand against the new anti-union public sector collective bargaining laws.

In Ohio, the unions won this fight with the referendum repealing SB 5. Another important example of public sector activism is the Chicago Teachers Union's strike in 2012 (Cunningham-Cook, 2012). The success of this strike was based in the mobilization by new union leadership of Black women teachers, with grass roots organizing and community alliances against privatization of the public schools. This is an inspiring example of the melding of democratic values and collective bargaining defined broadly in terms of improving working conditions and working for the public interest.

8

ACKNOWLEDGING BUT TRANSCENDING GENDER AT WORK

Applying the model of lifetime disadvantage and vulnerability theory to women's poverty in retirement

Susan Bisom-Rapp[1] *and Malcolm Sargeant*[2]

I. Introduction

Women comprise close to half of the labor force in the US, and make up slightly more than 50% of the US population (Ms. Foundation, 2013). Despite these numbers, women workers suffer multiple disadvantages during their working lives, which result in significantly poorer outcomes in old age in comparison to men (US GAO, 2012). In fact, in the US, the poverty rate of women 65 years old and older is nearly double that of their male counterparts (Banerjee, 2012, p. 13; O'Brien et al., 2010). Older women of color are especially disadvantaged, living in poverty at significantly greater rates than those who are white (Ms. Foundation, 2013).

The US is not unique in this respect. On the global scene, the International Labour Organization (ILO) notes that women suffer cumulative disadvantages during their working lives due to multiple factors. These include discrimination and "high numbers in unpaid, low-paid, part-time, frequently interrupted, or informal economy work" (ILO, 2008, p. 4). Women around the world are less frequently entitled to pensions, and when they do have pension rights, their pensions are typically lower than men's because of "lower earnings and shorter contribution periods."

How best to capture and address cumulative, temporally-amplified, gender-based disadvantage is the subject of this chapter. More specifically, we argue that capturing the social ill in a descriptive sense requires attending carefully to the way gender plays out across the lives of girls and women. To that end, our "model

1 Associate Dean for Faculty Research and Scholarship and Professor of Law, Thomas Jefferson School of Law, San Diego, California, US.

2 Professor of Labour Law, Middlesex University Business School, London, UK.

of lifetime disadvantage," which we created in our previous work, is offered (Bisom-Rapp and Sargeant, 2014, 2016). The model illustrates that the difficulties experienced by many women in retirement are produced by multiple factors connected to gender, some directly and others less so. Additionally, the disadvantage produced by many of the factors is cumulative and is best understood through a life course approach.

However, in crafting legal and policy solutions, a paradigm addressing but not limited to ameliorating gender disadvantage is necessary. Economic insecurity has become endemic to working life for most people in paid labor in the US. Meeting the needs of women workers thus requires more than attempting to place them on equal footing with men. Rather, the conditions confronting male and female workers must be assessed.

Vulnerability theory provides a potential framework for thinking through the regulatory challenges of addressing women's lifetime disadvantage. Vulnerability theory acknowledges the inherent fragility of and dependence within the human condition, and places responsibility on the state for individuals' resilience in the face of inevitable, capacity-limiting events (Fineman, 2008). Such an approach may resonate with a broad-based, populist political movement and avoid some of the pitfalls attendant to identity politics.

This chapter proceeds in several parts. Part II describes the model of lifetime disadvantage created by the authors to explain women's relative poverty in retirement in comparison to men. Part III of the chapter argues that addressing women's systemic lifetime disadvantage requires a coordinated approach rather than the piecemeal, disjointed incrementalism that often characterizes changes in employment law. Moreover, regulatory solutions should be framed in ways that account for but move beyond gender given significant increases in economic insecurity experienced by all working people. Vulnerability theory is explored as a normative frame for that task. The chapter ends with Part IV, which is a short conclusion.

II. Conceptualizing women workers' disadvantages through a model

How should we conceptualize issues affecting women, including their condition in retirement, when a prohibition of sex discrimination in employment has been on the books for half a century? How should we account for differences among working and retired women based on race, ethnicity, national origin, age, and socioeconomic status, among other characteristics? Finally, at a time when changes in work and the structure of the labor market affect men as well as women, does it make sense to focus only on gender disadvantage?

The answer to all three questions is, "It's complicated." As an initial and descriptive matter, women's elevated risk of falling into poverty in retirement clearly tracks gender lines, and cannot be understood apart from the gender dimension. Developing legal and policy responses to one day vanquish this social ill requires recognizing that circumstances affect girls and women over the course of their lives, creating suboptimal results for them in their later years. It is not by chance that the poverty rate for retired women in the US is greater than that for retired men. This is a social problem present not only in the US but also in other countries – a problem the ILO has observed on the global level.

Gender-conscious analysis must be employed, at least for descriptive purposes, to comprehend the challenges women face in preparing for and living in retirement. Eschewing an analysis sensitive to gender would eclipse what Martha Fineman refers to as women's "gendered lives," lives that are influenced by "material, psychological, physical, social, and cultural" experiences that may be similar to those of men and yet remain distinct (Fineman, 1995, pp. 47–49). Understanding working women's disadvantage fifty years after sex discrimination in employment was prohibited through Title VII of the Civil Rights Act of 1964 requires acknowledging significantly unequal outcomes for women in retirement and determining what produces them. The systemic, cumulative, and sweeping nature of this harm cannot be conceptualized apart from gender.

That said, an intellectually robust descriptive analysis explaining why many women fare poorly in retirement must acknowledge and incorporate, *inter alia*, two significant phenomena: the changing nature of work; and differences among women based on a multiplicity of other important characteristics beyond gender. Mindful of this, our multi-factored model of lifetime disadvantage incorporates non-standard work and intersectionality as important aspects of women's lives that must be assessed.

Regarding the first factor – the changing nature of work – the model recognizes that work in the 21st century is organized and performed differently than it was half a century ago. Standard employment relationships are declining and non-standard forms of working seem to be proliferating (Stone, 2013). The changing nature of work is especially important to the model since workplace statutory protections and rights generally hinge on there being an employment relationship between a worker and a firm (Glynn, 2011). Moreover, even where such a relationship can be established, women's tendency to occupy certain non-standard categories – for example, American women are twice as likely to work part-time as men (US Dept. of Labor, 2011) and comprise two-thirds of the part-time workforce (Maloney, 2010) – may place them outside the protective ambit of certain laws (Bakst and Taubman, 2010). Finally, across a broad range of occupations, part-time workers, a category occupied by a large majority of women, have over time seen their earnings deteriorate in comparison to their full-time counterparts. By one estimate, the wage penalty for working part-time increased from 39% to 46% between 1979 and 2012 (Bernhardt, 2014). In other words, part-time workers earn a median wage 46% lower than that of full-time workers, and their position vis-à-vis full-time workers has changed for the worse.

The second factor – intersectionality – is important to the model because some women workers occupy statuses or have characteristics that complicate the way they are viewed, and subject them to exclusion or disadvantage not experienced by women as a whole (ILO, 2007; Sheppard, 2011). While an intersectional approach is necessary to fully grasp this phenomenon, the model's authors realize the concept has limitations in addressing disadvantage through equal employment opportunity law. This is due to the difficulty some victims may have in identifying this form of discrimination when they are subject to it, doctrinal and evidentiary barriers to evaluating such claims, and judicial skepticism (Bisom Rapp and Sargeant, 2014, 2016; Moore, 2007). Thus, for descriptive purposes, intersectionality is important to acknowledge, and is no doubt essential to evaluating necessary policy changes, but it has proven to be a difficult concept to shoehorn into traditional employment discrimination law.

Turning to our model of lifetime disadvantage, we consider the major factors that, on average, create unequal outcomes for working women at the end of their careers. First, gender-based factors, concern phenomena directly connected to social or psychological aspects of gender, such as gender stereotyping and women's traditionally greater roles in family caring activities. Second, what we call "incremental disadvantage factors" are connected to gender, but that connection is less overt, and the disadvantage they produce increases incrementally over time. Factors in this second category include non-standard working (part-time work, temporary work, etc.) and career interruptions. The model is illustrated below:

TABLE 8.1 Model of lifetime disadvantage

Gender-based factors	*Incremental disadvantage factors*
Education and training	Pay inequality
Stereotyping	Occupational segregation
Multiple discrimination	Non-standard working
Caregiving roles	Career breaks
Career outcomes	Retirement and pensions

A. Gender-based factors

The model first describes a set of gender-based factors, which from a very early point in their lives link girls, and later women, to particular characteristics, traits, interests, and roles, and ultimately impact the trajectories of many women's careers, as they encounter the so-called maternal wall and glass ceiling. Those characteristics, traits, interests, and roles are in some cases further complicated, and some girls and women further disadvantaged, by multiple discrimination on the basis of race, ethnicity, disability, religion, and sexual orientation, among other statuses. Regarding multiple discrimination, aging, in particular, affects women differently, more negatively, and earlier than men. Moreover, law and policy has proven of limited utility in ameliorating the gender-based factors' lifetime effects on women, a fact evident when one examines women's career outcomes.

1. Education and training

The model begins in girlhood, with a view to understanding formative experiences in education and training that might place girls at a disadvantage in their later years. A nuanced view of gender-related trends in education is necessary because in access, attainment, and ambition, girls and young women fare very well. Girls are more likely than boys to anticipate working in high status careers; they score better in reading and a little less well in math (US Dept. of Commerce and Executive Office of the President, 2011, p. 20). Yet it is in educational attainment where young women clearly outpace their male counterparts.

Women in the US earn 57% of college degrees and make up the same percentage of the undergraduate population. The catch is that these degrees are far less likely to be in the science, technology, engineering, and medical (STEM) fields. This is a concern because there is a smaller gender wage gap in those fields than in other occupations (Beede et al., 2011).

2. Stereotyping

Stereotyping, associated with implicit bias, is the second factor in the model. Beginning in the classroom and extending into the workplace, gendered beliefs about the differing characteristics of males and females may lead to differential treatment. Thus, in the classroom, boys tend to receive more praise than girls, and boys' contributions to class discussions are more frequently accepted (Bohan, 2011; Sadker et al., 2009). Research reveals that girls are more likely to be rewarded for quiet and compliant behavior (Cantalupo, 2012). Despite the long-standing prohibition of sex discrimination in employment generally and sex stereotyping specifically, descriptive and prescriptive stereotypes continue to pervade the workplace as well (Bartlett, 2009). These biases may infect the way a job is typed, and the way employment decisions are made, and have enormous ramifications for women's occupational advancement over time (Bisom-Rapp and Sargeant, 2014, 2016).

3. Multiple discrimination

The third factor in the model is multiple discrimination. This phenomenon is known more commonly in North America as intersectionality. Simply stated, women may occupy statuses that further complicate the way in which they are viewed, treated, and function. One significant complicating factor for working women is the issue of aging. Older workers are seen as less competent, more difficult to train, and more expensive than younger workers (Blaine, 2013).

Moreover, research reveals three predominant ways that women are stereotyped as they age. First, women are seen as aging sooner than men (Canetto, 2001). Next, compared with older men, older women are seen as even less intelligent and capable. Finally, the image of the grandmother has a bearing on how older women are viewed. More specifically, older women are seen as being more nurturing and warmer than older men. Aging has also been found to affect women psychologically more profoundly and negatively than men (Grant, 2011). Of course, women also may occupy other statuses that further complicate their identity and position in the workplace, including minority race, ethnicity, or religion, disability, and sexual orientation, among others.

Employment discrimination law, however, has proven especially ill-suited as a tool for redressing multiple discrimination. A 2011 study found that "both intersectional demographic characteristics and legal claims are associated with dramatically reduced odds of a plaintiff victory" (Best et al., 2011, pp. 991–992). Research in the UK points to another problem associated with multiple discrimination claims. A 2007 study revealed that victims themselves often have trouble identifying the specific effects of multiple characteristics (Moore, 2007).

4. Caregiving roles

Women's traditional role as caregivers to children, partners, parents, and others is the fourth gender-related factor in the model. Included within this factor is pregnancy, a precursor to caregiving for most mothers. No doubt balancing caregiving with paid employment is as daunting for men as for women (Bornstein, 2012). Men, however, while increasingly assuming caregiving roles, are still less likely to do so than women. Moreover, when they embrace caregiving, men on average spend less time at it (Bisom-Rapp and Sargeant, 2014, 2016). Men are also less likely than women to drop out of the labor force or reduce their paid labor as a result of their caregiving responsibilities. Over their life's course, women potentially face three overlapping periods of caregiving: (1) when women parent their own children (Livingston and Cohn, 2010); (2) when women care for elderly or sick family members or friends, including partners Bisom-Rapp and Sargeant, 2014, 2016); and (3) when women care for their grandchildren (Kitchen, 2011; Livingston and Parker, 2010; Weaver, 2013).

Caregiving responsibilities, which affect some men but are disproportionately assumed by women, often place caregivers at a disadvantage in the workplace because caregivers face conflicting demands on their time (Porter, 2010). Most workplaces are not designed with caregiving in mind; working hours may be long, inflexible, or unpredictable. Attendance policies may be rigid. Finally, in the US, law and policy related to caregiving and pregnancy is insufficient, and so-called family responsibilities discrimination is widespread. Aggrieved workers must attempt to craft protection from a patchwork of "legal theories [based] in federal and state law – for example, as sex discrimination, discrimination based on association with a person with a disability, or violation of state or federal family and medical leave laws" (National Alliance for Caregiving and AARP, 2009; Williams et al., 2012, p. 2).

5. Career outcomes

Given the gender-based factors detailed above, it is no surprise that career outcomes, the model's fifth factor, are adversely affected. Women's occupational mobility is affected by the so-called "glass ceiling" – the unseen, impenetrable barrier that prevents women from advancing to the upper ranks of their chosen occupation. Relatedly, many hit a "maternal wall," which diverts or even derails career trajectories when women become pregnant, become mothers, or choose to work in part-time or flexible work arrangements (Williams and Segal, 2003).

B. Incremental disadvantage factors

Having delineated a set of gender-based factors, the model turns to a series of five factors that incrementally and increasingly produce disadvantage for women over time.

1. Pay inequality

First among the incremental disadvantage factors is pay inequality. Gender-based pay inequality reflects the subpar state of women's opportunities for financial progress, wealth accumulation, and retirement planning. Across the Organisation for Economic Cooperation and Development (OECD) countries, women's wages fall short of those of men. An Ifo Institute (2013) report noted that the pay gap between male and female full-time worker median earnings is in OECD countries between 10% and 20%. The US scored poorly in this study with a gap of 18.8%.

No matter how one measures the pay gap – and there are many ways – white male workers make significantly more money than do white women and women of color (Nat'l Equal Pay Task Force, 2013). That gap persists when controlling for occupation, education, and experience. Overall, 97% of women full-time workers serve in occupations where women earn less than men (Glynn and Wu, 2013). Moreover, these pay differentials are enormously consequential over time. Estimates vary concerning losses that accrue during women's careers, but the US Department of Labor pegged the cumulative earnings loss at $380,000 (Manzano-Diaz, 2011). Another estimate posited that the cumulative gender-based earnings loss for a woman college graduate is $1.2 million (Murphy and Graff, 2005).

The reasons for pay inequality are complicated. They include that women and men work in sex-segregated occupations, reward mechanisms affect female and male workers differently, women's skills and work are undervalued, few women occupy leadership positions either in policymaking or in the labor force, gender roles and traditions shape educational choices and working patterns, women on average carry greater family responsibilities and so work fewer hours than men, and women are the victims of discrimination (European Commission, 2013). The legal and policy responses to pay inequality fall short of what is necessary to address this complex web of disadvantage. Although pay equality legislation has existed for more than a half century, the strictures of equal pay law render it unequal to its task.

Two statutes, Title VII and the Equal Pay Act (EPA) (29 USC § 206(d)), dating to 1964 and 1963 respectively, may be used to address pay discrimination. When Title VII is used, the plaintiff might frame her claim using disparate treatment theory, which requires that she prove that the employer acted with a discriminatory state of mind; in other words, the employer must intentionally have paid her less money because she is a woman. Yet as Professor Deborah Eisenberg (2012) notes, this conception of how the pay discrepancy came about "ignores the complex, subtle realities of pay discrimination," which often occurs because of highly discretionary pay systems that allow supervisors to assign different pay for employees doing the same work (p. 233). Many employers do not consciously desire to pay women less than men even though the end result is that women are paid less than their male counterparts.

Unintentional discrimination might be addressed under Title VII's disparate impact theory, a theory that allows a plaintiff to challenge a neutral practice, like subjective decision making on pay, by demonstrating that the practice produces discriminatory outcomes. Unfortunately, however, the US Supreme Court, in *Wal-Mart Stores, Inc. v Dukes* (2011), eviscerated the theory's broad use in the class action context.

The EPA is similarly lacking in utility. Under the EPA, the plaintiff need only show she is compensated less well for equal work; the employer's state of mind is not relevant. Even so, courts have so strictly construed the "prima-facie standard of substantial equality between compared positions . . . so . . . as to exclude most working women . . . from the Act's coverage" (Eisenberg, 2010, 2012, p. 236). Moreover, the EPA's "factor other than sex" defense has been employed broadly by courts to shield employers from liability for pay disparities. Additionally, the EPA does not permit class actions, inhibiting groups of women from challenging their employer's pay policies collectively.

2. Occupational segregation

Linked closely to pay inequality is the second incremental disadvantage factor: occupational segregation. While the labor market has changed greatly in the last half century, including significant increases of women entering paid work, many occupations continue to be occupied primarily by women or by men (Hegewisch et al., 2010). Importantly, there is a negative relationship between the wages an occupation pays and the share of women who engage in that occupation. The National Equal Pay Task Force (2013, p. 27) estimated that "every 10 percentage point increase in female [occupational] share [is] associated with a 4% decline in average wages."

Feminized occupations – those occupations filled predominantly by women – are linked not only to disadvantage regarding pay but also to poorer outcomes in terms of power and prestige for women and men working in those occupations (Jarman et al., 2012). Regression analyses disturbingly reveal, however, that within feminized occupations, women's pay is impacted more greatly than men's pay. As Professor Marianne Kulow notes, women in feminized occupations "are twice disadvantaged – first by being in a 'female' field and second by being a woman in that field, since men make more than women even in 'female' fields" (2013, p. 404).

In the US, almost 20% of women workers are concentrated "in just five occupations: secretaries, registered nurses, elementary school teachers, cashiers, and nursing aids" (US Dept. of Commerce and Executive Office of the President, 2011, p. 33). In 2012, more than half of American women working full-time worked in low-paying positions in administrative support, service, and sales, occupying jobs "such as secretaries, cashiers, retail sales persons, maids, child care workers, and customer service representatives" (Nat'l Equal Pay Task Force, 2013, p. 4).

Race and ethnicity add complexity to the gender-segregated American landscape. Women of different races and ethnicities display divergent occupational patterns (Hegewisch et al., 2010). More specifically, "White and Asian women are more likely to work in higher-paying management and professional jobs" (US Dept. of Commerce and Executive Office of the President, 2011, p. 33). African American women and Latinas "are more likely to work in lower-paying service occupations and significantly more likely to be among the working poor" (Nat'l Equal Pay Task Force, 2013, p. 7). Yet even when they work in professional jobs, women are over-represented in the lower-paying fields of education and health care.

Occupational gender desegregation in the US has stalled since the late 1990s (Hegewisch et al., 2010). Lack of progress in integrating occupations is manifest in jobs requiring a four-year university degree, as well as for jobs with lesser educational requirements. Occupational segregation is even stronger for younger working women at the present time than it was at the start of the 21st century. One study surmised that significant occupational desegregation would not resume without women gaining significant ground in traditionally male blue-collar jobs and in STEM fields (Blau et al., 2012).

In terms of law and policy, in order to break down occupational segregation, the Obama administration is committed to enforcing existing law, which has proven a blunt instrument for bringing about what would need to be massive change in the labor market. The government also recommends educational efforts to encourage girls and women to consider non-traditional jobs. The two most promising legal strategies to address occupational segregation – comparable worth and affirmative action – are presently controversial and therefore likely not viable in the US (Kulow, 2013). Comparable worth, which would seek to equalize pay across occupational categories that are gender segregated, has largely been rejected by the courts.

3. Non-standard working

The third incremental disadvantage factor is non-standard working, which was addressed at the beginning of this section by noting that in the US standard employment relationships are declining and that one form of non-standard work – part-time work – is dominated by women. Not only does women's cumulative income suffer when they work part-time, since they log fewer hours in paid labor, there is also a wage penalty for working part-time that appears to be increasing over time.

Legal regulation to protect part-time workers is sorely lacking in the US. Those who work less than 1000 hours annually (about 20 hours per week) may be excluded from employer-provided pension plans (Bakst and Taubman, 2010). Those who work under 1,250 hours per year (about 24 hours per week) are not covered by the Family and Medical Leave Act. Some states exclude part-time workers from unemployment compensation coverage. There is no federal legislation requiring proportional pay for part-time workers. While there are federal proposals to require employers to pro-rate benefits for part-timers, the political viability of such legislation is questionable (Folbre, 2013). The Affordable Care Act requires employers with 50 or more employees to make health insurance available to their employees, but those working less than 30 hours per week are not covered by the employer mandate.

4. Career breaks

Fourth among the incremental disadvantage factors is career breaks. Put simply, women in general are more likely than men to exit the labor market due to childbirth or caring for a special needs child or an elderly or sick adult (Feinberg et al., 2011; Miller and Alderman, 2014; National Alliance for Caregiving and AARP, 2009; Omori and Smith, 2006). The existence of a wage penalty for intermittent employment is well-documented and has implications for women's ability to save for retirement (Hotchkiss et al., 2011). A frequently cited US study found that the pay of women who temporarily exit the labor market not only lags upon their return to work but never catches up (Jacobsen and Levin, 1996). The penalty remains evident more than two decades after the end of the final career break. More specifically, women whose last gap occurred over 20 years ago earn between 5% and 7% less than women who have not had breaks in their work history. This, of course, is money lost in addition to forgone wages during the career break itself. In fact, career breaks are significant contributors to the pay differential between women and men (Hotchkiss et al., 2011).

5. Retirement and pensions

The final incremental disadvantage factor is retirement and pensions. It is within this arena that women's systemic disadvantage is most keenly felt. For many women who have worked for pay, retirement is hampered by the conditions that preceded it – significantly lower lifetime earnings, resulting in the accumulation of fewer assets, and periods of "unemployment, part-time employment, and absence from the labor market," which are linked to conflicts between paid labor and caregiving (Estes et al., 2012, p. 2). Such disadvantage for the retired is especially notable among women of color. As one report put it, "For too many women, retirement is the culmination of an entire career – an entire lifetime – of pay and income inequality" (Estes et al., 2012.). Add to these factors that elderly women have greater longevity than men and are more likely than men to live alone, and it is hardly surprising that they are at greater risk of falling into poverty, having depleted any retirement savings they may have amassed (GAO, 2012).

In the US, financial support in retirement is supposed to come from three sources: private pensions, government retirement payments through the national Social Security program, and private savings and investment (DeWitt, 1996). As noted above, it is more difficult for women to save for retirement than it is for men. Additionally, the private pension picture has a gender dimension. Women are far less likely to receive private pension income than men. One report noted, for example, that "only 28% of women age 65–74 receive pension income compared to 42% of men" for the same age group (Estes et al., 2012, p. 3). When they do contribute to employer pension plans, women's rates of contribution are significantly lower than those of men. A US Government Accountability Office (2012) report highlighted three factors that account for women's lower participation in and contribution to private pension plans as compared with men: women are more likely to work part-time, to have less on-the-job tenure, and to be single parents. This deficit can be assessed in bottom line terms: the median income of American women age 65 and over is 25% lower than that of men, and women are almost twice as likely to be living in poverty as a result.

As a result of the shortfall in access to private pensions and savings and investments, women aged 65 and over are generally more dependent than men on state-provided Social Security retirement benefits. Indeed, over 26.5% of older women rely on this state pension system "for 90% or more of their family income, compared to 20% of older men" (Shelton, 2013, p. 5). Women's reliance on the program is greatest among widows, for whom Social Security is close to the sole source of income for more than one-third, and divorced women, of whom 27% are almost entirely reliant.

However, many older minority women – more specifically those who are Asian or Hispanic – are ineligible to receive benefits either due to immigration status or, for naturalized citizens, lack of sufficient years of work to qualify for benefits. Moreover, while Social Security retirement benefits are credited with keeping close to 40% of white, older women out of poverty, in comparison to 32% of their male counterparts, the program is far less effective for forestalling poverty among minority women. In fact, of concern, and related to all older women, "extreme poverty rates increased significantly for women 65 and older to 3.1% in 2012 from 2.6% in 2011 . . . [and] for older women 65 and living alone, to 4.7% in 2012 from 3.6% in 2011" (Entmacher et al., 2013).

Social Security provides full retirement and disability benefits to older workers with 40 quarters (ten years) of work (Estes et al., 2012). While the work credits may be earned at any time over the course of a lifetime, the disability portion of the benefits requires that an individual must have been employed half of the decade preceding the disability in order to receive disability benefits. In gender terms, 91% of men are fully insured for retirement benefits and 81% are insured for disability benefits; for women, 85% qualify for full retirement benefits but only 74% are eligible for disability benefits.

Social Security is an old program, established in 1939, and the benefits it provides have attempted, to some extent, to take account of women's life course. Thus, married women may qualify for benefits either on their own earnings or be eligible for payments as a spouse or widow based on the earnings of their husbands. Yet qualifying for such benefits requires that the marriage lasted at least a decade, and many women, especially those among the "Baby Boomers," begin retirement without having had a marriage of that duration; others have never been married. For such women who have had caregiving responsibilities for children or elderly parents – responsibilities that may have taken them out of the labor market for significant periods of time – there is no credit toward retirement for that important societal work.

The result of years of lower earnings than men when they do work and years spent outside the labor force providing uncompensated care work take a substantial toll on the annual income provided to older women through Social Security. While, in 2009, the average annual government provided income to retired men was $15,620, retired women received an annual income of only $12,155. Moreover, those who do receive spousal benefits experience a 33% to 50% reduction in benefits upon the death of the spouse, an occurrence that can produce significant financial hardship.

Modeling women's lifetime disadvantage reveals the complex factors women encounter over the course of their lives, which leave many in poor conditions in retirement compared with men. An effective, comprehensive regulatory approach could help compensate for these factors. Yet legal and policy efforts in the US are not able to prevent women's systemic disadvantage. This is in large part because these efforts are produced by policy making that fails to articulate overarching goals, takes small rather than grand steps, and produces responses lacking in coordination. Confronting women's lifetime disadvantage, however, requires acknowledging at the outset the outcomes sought and the justifications for them. Below we consider vulnerability theory as a normative construct that might ground a comprehensive, effective regulatory response to women's lifetime disadvantage.

III. Vulnerability theory as a normative framework for crafting a regulatory response to women's lifetime disadvantage

The model of lifetime disadvantage is a descriptive account of the elements leading to the retirement ills of many women, and a starting point for thinking about possible legal and policy reforms. As the model illustrates, the factors confounding women's ability to accumulate resources for retirement are complicated, directly and indirectly related to gender, and poorly addressed by existing law or policy. Such a complex problem defies easy legislative or policy fixes. In other words, tackling this multifaceted phenomenon requires more than tinkering around the margins, as is often the case when employment law reforms are attempted. An effective regulatory response requires a coordinated approach accounting for the life course of many women. Such coordination, however, should not be undertaken without a sound theoretical grounding, one presently lacking in the American approach to the employment relationship (J. Fineman, 2013b).

More concretely, the US leaves many facets of the employment relationship to the workings of the market. The legal protections for American workers are thin in comparison with the protections afforded workers in other countries. Insecurity and stagnant wages are common features of standard as well as non-standard jobs. A retirement crisis looms and potentially impacts many men as well as women. Thus, reforms aimed only at equal treatment of or equal outcomes for women workers will fall short of providing equitable conditions for them and their male counterparts. Thus, while equality – conceived in its formal or substantive forms – is a necessary component of envisioning women's place in the labor market and correcting women's lifetime disadvantage, it is not sufficient for the promotion of social justice for working people and retirees (Bisom-Rapp, 2011).

Moreover, as Martha Fineman has noted, relying on a traditional equal protection approach to equality to correct social injustice "has set up a perverse dynamic that often results in pitting one protected group against another . . . as well as generating a politics of resentment and backlash . . . [by] those who perceive" they are excluded from such a strategy (2010, p. 253). At a time when the American economy is flourishing but the distribution of resources has become alarmingly unequal, meaningful responses require theoretically reframing the debate. To this end, Fineman and a number of other scholars have developed vulnerability theory as a mechanism for describing the relationship between the individual, the state, and society's institutions. That theory and its application to our model is discussed below.

A. Vulnerability theory described

Law and policy in the US is tied to a political discourse of liberty and autonomy, which prizes individuality over social rights (Fineman, 2012). At the center of the discourse is the "autonomous liberal subject," a hypothetical construct who is self-reliant, makes independent choices, and values the right to contract. The role of the state in this discourse is restrained, limited, and non-interventionist; the state exists to protect the freedom and independence of the individual (Fineman, 2010). Government efforts aimed at enhancing social welfare are thus often construed in political terms as antithetical to the proper role of the state.

In such a system, vulnerability and dependence are deviant, often stigmatized conditions applying, for example, to the young, the old, the ill, and the poor, who are subjected to the state's discipline and control (Fineman, 2012). The vulnerability of the autonomous liberal subject remains invisible and unacknowledged. Reality, however, gives the lie to the myth of self-sufficiency. Aimed at what is hidden or overlooked, vulnerability theory seeks to reconfigure the political subject in order better recognize the broad range of aspects of the human condition, and set the stage for the state to respond better to the needs of its people.

Vulnerability theory has as its touchstone a "universal vulnerable subject" rooted in the human experience (Fineman, 2010). As humans, we are all potentially subject to malady or harm, representing the physical aspect of vulnerability. Yet when the inevitable befalls us, "economic, employment, or family relationships" may be adversely affected as well (pp. 267–68). For example, if one falls ill, he or she may not be able to work for pay, which has economic implications for that individual and his or her family. Family members, in turn, may be called on to play caregiving roles to an individual who is ill and becomes dependent, and this responsibility may interfere with their activities as well, rendering them derivatively dependent. As humans, our vulnerability makes us dependent on one another and on societal institutions and programs. Through the mediating devices of institutions and programs, society alleviates vulnerability and promotes individual resiliency.

Importantly, the theory is not merely attentive to the individual at one point in time but throughout the life course. In this regard, the vulnerable subject is very much in harmony with our theory of women's lifetime disadvantage. Indeed, vulnerability theory accepts that "economic and institutional harms can accumulate" in an individual's life and that these effects may relate to "social groupings" and classes, including "race, gender, ethnicity, or religious affiliation" (p. 268).

Regarding law and policy, vulnerability theory conceptualizes a "responsive state" that operates for the common good by monitoring and adjusting societal institutions and programs to ensure that resiliency is promoted for all and that no one group is privileged by institutional or programmatic structure while other groups are disadvantaged. This conception of state responsibility potentially indicts US law and policy regarding the ability of women to plan for and live in retirement. As our model of lifetime disadvantage demonstrates, a host of factors over the life course hinder many women in assembling sufficient resources for sustenance in old age. To correct this imbalance, vulnerability theory would require a restructuring of institutions and programs to account for women's gendered lives.

B. Vulnerability theory and the workplace

Many of the reforms required to correct women's lifetime disadvantage would of necessity be changes related directly and indirectly to the law of work. More specifically, reform is required to create regulatory and institutional structures responsive to women's experiences with paid labor. The goal or outcome must be fostering women's resiliency over the course of their lives to ensure they accumulate sufficient resources to live in dignity in retirement.

Vulnerability theory may assist in framing how this enormous task might be accomplished. While it exceeds the scope of this chapter to discuss in detail what would obviously take years of legislative and regulatory work to accomplish, we will attempt to sketch out some thoughts about how policy makers might begin the process.

Jonathan Fineman (2013b) has produced the first treatment of the application of vulnerability theory to employment law and work. Focusing on the power imbalance inherent in the employment relationship, especially in light of the employment at-will rule, which allows either party to terminate the employment relationship at any time without cause, he exhorts the rule's critics to abandon attempts to defeat it. Instead, he recommends the state create laws, systems, and structures to promote the resilience of employees in the face of employer action or inaction.

In thinking about how the state, through law, has historically responded to worker vulnerability, Jonathan Fineman discerns two mechanisms: (1) the creation of social welfare benefits, such as those in Social Security aimed at the disabled and aged; and (2) intervention into some of the terms of the employment relationship, such as those related to wage and hour law, and requirements that employers pay at least some of the costs associated with decisions made or conditions created that are adverse to employee interests, such as mandating that employers pay for Workers Compensation insurance for the protection and maintenance of injured employees.

While he views the overall protections as thin and inadequate, he notes that the productive way forward is not to abandon employment at-will but instead, through vulnerability theory, to focus on the "equitable allocation of costs and consequences of termination among the employee, the employer, and the state" (p. 309). Those costs are presently inequitably allocated, and, in terms of vulnerability, fall disproportionately on individual employees.

Justified by a perceived employer need for flexibility and efficiency, US employment law presently privileges employer resiliency over that of the employee. This privilege is neither natural nor inevitable but is conferred by the state through employment law. Moreover, exercise of the privilege often results in significant and severe consequences for individual employees. The state, Jonathan Fineman argues, must account for such outcomes, and make adjustments accordingly, in some cases by requiring the employer share in the costs of its decisions. Such responsiveness by the state is requisite in order to meet its obligation to provide a minimum level of resilience to its people.

Applying Jonathan Fineman's insights regarding employment law to the multifaceted problem of women's lifetime disadvantage yields some interesting insights. Tying potential regulatory solutions to the principles of vulnerability theory provides a starting point for possible reform.

C. Bringing vulnerability theory to bear on women's lifetime disadvantage

In previous work laying out our model, we consider women's lifetime disadvantage as a global phenomenon. We also survey the regulatory field in the UK, the US, and elsewhere to better understand how law and policy might ameliorate women's lifetime disadvantage. Not surprisingly, we find legal provisions in the EU-influenced UK significantly more protective of and responsive to the lives of women (Bisom-Rapp and Sargeant, 2014, 2016). Regulations in the UK that aim to cushion the vulnerability of women workers fall into four categories:

(1) measures aimed at tackling sex discrimination and unequal pay; (2) measures to facilitate working time flexibility and to protect non-standard work from second class status; (3) measures protecting women during pregnancy and periods of maternity leave; and (4) efforts specifically geared to help women in retirement.

To be certain, results in the UK are far from perfect. Indeed, despite much stronger law, empirical reality – in terms of pregnancy discrimination, pay inequality, implicit bias, and retirement disadvantages, among other problems – is still very problematic for British women. We hypothesize that this is due in part to policy making that is disjointed and incremental and that fails to be driven by overarching goals. Vulnerability theory teaches that the responsive state must monitor and adjust institutions and programs so that all people are resilient and no one group is structurally advantaged. Men in the UK continue to be advantaged in the labor market during their working lives, and so vulnerability theory carries some lessons for policy makers there. Vulnerability theory instructs UK policy makers to further strengthen law and policy in light of working women's continuing suboptimal experiences across the life course. Discussion of the specific steps that should be taken in the UK exceeds the scope of this chapter but is addressed at some length in our book, *Lifetime Disadvantage, Discrimination and the Gendered Workforce* (Bisom-Rapp and Sargeant, 2016).

In the US, however, we might wed our model and vulnerability theory along the following lines. As noted above, we would advocate a regulatory approach to women that has as its goal fostering women's resiliency throughout their lives so that they amass sufficient resources to support a dignified retirement. Regarding law in the first and third categories above – law prohibiting sex discrimination/ mandating equal pay and measures protecting women during pregnancy/ maternity leave – legal provisions exist but fall far short of what is necessary to cushion women throughout their lives. Hence, as in the UK, vulnerability theory would require policy makers to strengthen and adjust existing law and policy because working men are better positioned than working women.

Unlike the UK, however, the US lacks provisions in categories two and four above – measures to facilitate working time flexibility/keep non-standard work from second class status and robust efforts to assist women in retirement. It is here that vulnerability theory might help reframe the justifications for regulatory change. This chapter frames the argument for the adoption of legal provisions regarding flexible working time, broadly defined, so that employees may better adapt to changing circumstances in their lives. It uses vulnerability theory to argue for: (1) national law requiring employers to provide employees with paid sick leave and paid family leave; (2) outlawing or limiting just-in-time scheduling; and (3) creating a right of employees to request flexible working arrangements, including telecommuting, modified work schedules, and the like.

In the US, the need for employer flexibility and responsiveness to changing conditions is a primary justification for at-will employment and, in contrast to other countries, only a very thin menu of legally-required terms and conditions of employment (J. Fineman, 2013b). Advocates for the current legal framework argue that without this flexibility, employers would be far more economically vulnerable. Yet when it comes to flexibility for working people, the law provides scant refuge and women, as more frequently responsible for caregiving than men, may be doubly disadvantaged. No national law mandates paid sick leave or paid leave to care for family members who are ill. No national law limits just-in-time scheduling, a practice in which work shifts are assigned and cancelled with little notice. There is no right to request a flexible working schedule from one's employer in order to meet one's responsibilities outside of work.

The rigidity of many employees' working schedules, and the unpredictability of just-in-time scheduling for others, makes responding to the dependency of family members a difficult proposition. US employment law does not honor, as it does for employers, the need for employees to have a modicum of flexibility in order to respond to changing conditions. The resulting decrease in employee resilience is significant. In fact, many women drop out of the labor force due to the lack of flexibility in paid labor, which conflicts with their caregiving responsibilities to children and elderly parents (Bisom-Rapp and Sargeant, 2014, 2016). These career breaks, as noted above, are costly occurrences for women in terms of pay, certainly impact career outcomes, and may act as a drag on women's ability to amass resources for retirement, all aspects of our model of lifetime disadvantage.

Vulnerability theory might highlight the unilateral privilege afforded American employers either to maintain incredibly rigid or extremely unpredictable shift scheduling, and to refuse, as many do, to provide paid sick or paid family leave to their employees. Since such working conditions impose great costs on employees in terms of their ability to respond to changing conditions, can they be justified? Interrogating the economic justification behind the freedom to rigidly schedule – that it is needed to maximize business profitability – may reveal that occasional employee absence due to illness or caregiving responsibilities does little to affect business profitability. Yet failing to provide paid sick or paid family care leave exacts a huge toll on employees and their families. A more equitable allocation of the costs of rigid scheduling may be in order. If employers wish to maintain rigid schedules for their employees, they are responsible for some of the costs inherent in doing so. The law might respond by requiring paid sick or paid family leave policies be maintained by employing entities.

With respect to just-in-time scheduling, the claim that scheduling and cancelling work shifts with little notice is necessary to hold labor costs to a minimum is unlikely to withstand scrutiny. In fact, research demonstrates that these scheduling mechanisms lead to high quit rates. Employers with high quit rates will incur significant increases in employee replacement costs (Boushey and Glynn, 2012; Ton, 2012). In short, the use of such scheduling strategies does not grow a business. In light of this, and in contrast to rigid scheduling, a legal solution rooted in vulnerability theory might require intervening with the terms of the employment relationship and, in order to provide a minimum level of resilience to employees, prohibiting or greatly limiting the practice of just-in-time scheduling.

But what about employees who wish to restructure or modify their working time? Might vulnerability theory assist in framing an argument that employees should be given a legal right to request a change in their working hours so they can, for example, meet their responsibilities to school-age children or an elderly parent in declining health? Here too, there may be a business case for arguing that working time flexibility does not significantly affect the employer's bottom line. As such, a law akin to one in the UK, which affords employees the right to request such flexibility, may be in order (UK Flexible Working Regulations, 2014).

The Flexible Working Regulations in the UK permit employees with at least 26 weeks of service to petition their employers for a change in working hours or flexibility in working time. Complex rules take into account and attempt to balance the costs associated with granting the request; those rules may protect an employer's denial of a request as well (Bisom-Rapp and Sargeant, 2014, 2016). While protecting those with care responsibilities, the regulations go beyond that and cover any eligible employee who desires working time flexibility. Embracing such a law in the US, while far more inherently intrusive to employer prerogative than requiring paid sick leave or paid family leave, would still leave intact employment at-will so that an employee working flexibly who fails to be a productive member of the employer's team might easily be terminated. At the same time, such a law would promote employee resilience in the face of caregiving responsibilities, potentially allowing caregivers, many of whom are women, to remain attached to the workforce, and thereby enhancing the ability of women to accumulate resources sufficient for retirement.

IV. Conclusion

Working women lead gendered lives within a system that creates lifetime disadvantage and results in poorer outcomes for them in old age. Our model of lifetime disadvantage details the major factors contributing to those results. Vulnerability theory, however, may help us begin to think about how to refashion a system that is neither natural nor inevitable. This chapter has used vulnerability theory as a framework for arguments that the conditions illustrated by our model must be corrected, and that it is incumbent upon the state to act.

One important aspect of our vulnerability theory-inspired arguments is that they are responsive to women's gendered lives, and hence attentive to our model of lifetime disadvantage. Nonetheless, the solutions we advocate in this chapter are gender neutral in operation, and thus address the vulnerability-creating conditions confronting women *and* men who work for pay. Legally mandating paid sick and paid family leave, outlawing or limiting just-in-time scheduling, and enacting a right to request flexible working time are regulatory steps the state might take that would assist all employees. In this sense, vulnerability theory, when paired with our model of lifetime disadvantage, assists in imagining a reconfigured workplace that acknowledges but transcends gender.

9

LABORING FREEDOM

Neoliberalism, the jurisprudence of Obamacare, and the welfare state left

Jack Jackson[1]

> *Of all the checks on democracy, federalism has been the most efficacious and congenial . . . it is the only method of curbing not only the majority but the power of the whole people.*
>
> *(Lord Acton)*

> *The wider the range of activities covered by the market, the fewer are the issues on which explicitly political decisions are required.*
>
> *(Milton Friedman)*

I. Introduction

The ascendancy and the sprawl of neoliberalism in recent decades has been met with many declarations of ends: the end of the welfare state and social democracy (Judt, 2010); the end of the law (ended either by a lawlessness hitched to capital *or* by an infestation and subordination of the law by neoliberal instrumentalization *or* by some sequential combination of the two) (Fiss, 2001; Klein, 2007); the end of non-market ends (Harvey, 2005); and the end of liberal democracy (Brown, 2005). One is tempted by an array of political facts to affirm the rightness of these declarations. How easy it is to imagine the end of the law at the hands of neoliberalism, for example, with the fast rise

1 Assistant Professor of Politics, Whitman College. This chapter is a condensed and revised version of an article published in *Theory & Event*. The full cite for that article is: Jack Jackson, "Not Yet an End: Neoliberalism, the Jurisprudence of Obamacare, and the Welfare-State Left," *Theory & Event*, 19, no. 2 (2016). Earlier versions of this chapter encountered thoughtful suggestions, questions, and criticisms from colleagues when presented at the annual APSA conference, the Emory Law School at the invitation of the Vulnerability and Human Condition Initiative, and the Politics colloquium at Whitman College.

of law and economics as an adjudicatory rationale, with the rapid proliferation of conjoined JD/MBA programs (rather than JDs earned in conjunction with graduate degrees in divinity or ecology or political philosophy), with the emergence of the most "business friendly" Supreme Court in three or four generations (Liptak, 2013), and perhaps most notoriously with the transformation of corporate power into juridical personhood in First Amendment jurisprudence (*Citizens United v FEC*, 2010).

But it is with this litany of professed neoliberal ends that the principal opinions in the landmark constitutional case of *NFIB v Sebelius* (2012) break: one break being intentional (in affirming democratic power over the market), the other break being ironic in its consequences and unintended in its origin (in weakening the necessary coercive power of the neoliberal state in the name of neoliberal freedom). Moreover, the legislation that gave rise to the litigation of the case also signals, in key parts, a welcome departure from the logics of neoliberalism. Against the neoliberal trifecta of "deregulation, privatization, and withdrawal of the state" from social welfare (Harvey, 2005), the Affordable Care Act (ACA), colloquially known as "Obamacare," stands as a rebuttal with its renewed regulation, redistribution, and welfare state expansion in the service of more accessible health insurance and medical care. The ACA intensifies regulation of the private insurance industry by mandating a higher percentage of expenditures be spent on providing care and by blocking insurance companies from denying individual coverage based upon preexisting conditions. Private insurance survives, but the logic of privatization is unwound via a redistributive regime of subsidies for those purchasing insurance on the newly created and regulated insurance exchanges. Perhaps most importantly, the law produces the largest expansion of Medicaid since its inception in 1965. The law extends Medicaid eligibility to adults earning up to 138% of the poverty line. Of those without insurance at the passage of the ACA, over 50% are now eligible for coverage under Medicaid (Kaiser Family Foundation, 2013).

The ACA's expansion of the welfare state in the provision of health care should be read as something other than "compensatory social policies" for neoliberal policy failures or as a sign of liberalism's limits (Unger, 1998, p. 53), and instead be reconsidered as a critical component of a variety of emancipatory political projects, including partial emancipation from the scene of wage labor and its constitutive dominations and exploitations (Jackson, 2016). Additionally, the law constitutes an important reassertion of the primacy of collective democratic power over the "market," and it offers a vision of the state as responsive to the needs of labor, labor understood here as a class "embedded" in a particular material, legal, and social relationship (Fineman, 2015).

To develop these arguments, this chapter begins with an analysis of *NFIB v Sebelius*, turns next to a defense of the law and the welfare state from the perspective of laboring freedom, and then concludes with a consideration of how the foregoing defense of the welfare state in the name of freedom converges with key insights from the emerging field of vulnerability theory.

II. The jurisprudence of *NFIB v Sebelius*

The case of *NFIB v Sebelius* centered upon a contestation over the meaning of two constitutional provisions: the Commerce Clause (Congress' power to mandate the purchase of health insurance by individuals) and the Spending Clause (Congress' power to compel the states to accept conditions upon receiving expanded Medicaid funds). The Supreme Court split deeply on both issues. A shifting majority limited the federal government's power on both fronts, but the fifth vote in the case, that of Chief Justice John Roberts, rescued the individual mandate via the taxing power and preserved the potentiality of Medicaid expansion but without its primary enforcement mechanism. That unexpected threading of the needle proved indispensable for the survival of the ACA, but theoretically it is less interesting than the chasm between two visions that emerged on the court between Justice Ginsburg on the one hand and the joint dissent of Justices Scalia, Kennedy, Thomas, and Alito on the other.

This chasm represents a reopening of the great constitutional battles of the New Deal era. In the early 20th century the Supreme Court invoked multiple constitutional provisions to curb social welfare legislation. For example, when individual states established limits on the hours of labor in a workweek, the court declared that such laws violated the "liberty of contract" possessed by both employer and employee, or more accurately by "master" and "servant" (*Lochner v New York*, 1905). And when the federal government attempted to prohibit the transportation and sale of goods produced by child labor, the Supreme Court held that the Commerce Clause should be interpreted narrowly so as to deny Congress this regulatory power (*Hammer v Dagenhart*, 1918). Following this path, the court transformed the economic crisis of the Great Depression into a constitutional crisis of first rank when it struck down a federal law regulating the hours (setting a maximum) and wages (establishing a minimum) in the coal industry on a juridically invented distinction between "production" and "commerce." The court reasoned that since the law regulated the site of production it was not really in the government's power to regulate because commerce, according to this theory, only begins after production (*Carter v Carter Coal Co.*, 1936). With political pressure and new Roosevelt appointed jurists on the bench, the court reversed positions in the late 1930s to early 1940s and affirmed the basic architecture of the modern regulatory state (see *Wickard v Filburn*, 1942).

Justice Ginsburg's opinion in *Sebelius* harkened back to this era of constitutional history. First, Justice Ginsburg eschewed a narrow legal formalism (as to an imagined formal line between economic activity/inactivity with regard to the individual mandate) and reminded the court of a legal realist tradition that centered "practical" considerations and "actual experience" at the heart of Commerce Clause jurisprudence (p. 2616). Experience alone, however, can offer no guide for judgment unless there is a normative commitment against which to measure that experience. "Practical considerations" could easily be tethered to neoliberal ends. However, Justice Ginsburg understood democracy to be pitted against free market fundamentalisms and sought to preserve the power of "the people's representatives" to pass social and economic regulation (p. 2628). In a second and related turn against neoliberal rationality and to New Deal era history, Justice Ginsburg warned of a return to a period when the Supreme Court "routinely thwarted Congress' effort to regulate the national economy in the interest of those who labor to sustain it" (p. 2609).

In the wake of a long tradition of a critique of rights one can forget the first "right" of democracy is the collective right to govern. Of course rights-based politics can generate a logic of atomization, and it is true that even the right of democracy has been imagined in hyperindividualistic terms, as with the Supreme Court's established principle of "one person, one vote" (*Reynolds v Sims*, 1964). Yet, the Declaration of Independence, in theoretical contrast to the Bill of Rights, declared the "unalienable Rights" of liberty and happiness in terms that prioritized collective political action rather than individual claims to this or that right, including the right to property or even security. Tyrants do not threaten property, they threaten self-government; tyrants do not threaten the individual qua individual, they disestablish the conditions of assembly and rule.[2] Right cannot be exhausted by singularity even if singularity must be a component of the concept of juridical right.

In conjunction with the critique of rights as too individualistic is the critique of rights as too immaterial and thus divorced from the corporeal inequalities of everyday life; such a disjunction in fact secures these inequalities. Marx's (1843) early critique of the constitutional state exemplifies, if not inaugurates, this perspective: "the consummation of the idealism of the state was at the same time the consummation of the materialism of civil society . . . political life declares itself to be only a *means*, whose end is the life of civil society" (pp. 44–45). More precisely, in his reading of the Declaration of the Rights of Man and certain 18th century constitutional provisions of the various US states, Marx argued that property in particular stood at the center of "civil society" and that this is what the concept of rights built a fortress around. Contemporary skeptics of the "rights-revolution" of mid-20th century jurisprudence developed and deepened both lines of thinking, seeing the turn to rights as a turn away from collective power and incapable of confronting the political facts of capital (see Tushnet, 1984).

Many are unaccustomed to thinking of the Commerce Clause as vital wellspring of democratic political power, a primary constitutional source of the right to democracy, but the peculiarities of the US Constitutional tradition have rendered it so. It is important that the "right" of those who labor endorsed by Justice Ginsburg is envisioned as a collective right, the right of labor as labor to govern

2 The Declaration of Independence (1776) itemizes the tyranny of the king against political life: "He has refused his Assent to Laws, the most wholesome and necessary for the public good . . . He has refused to pass other Laws for the accommodation of large districts of people, unless those people would relinquish the right of Representation in the Legislature, a right inestimable to them and formidable to tyrants only. He has called together legislative bodies at places unusual, uncomfortable, and distant from the depository of their public Records, for the sole purpose of fatiguing them into compliance with his measures." This is but a sample of the indictment.

the material conditions of their existence. It is a right to power rather than an individualized shield from it; thus it revives a strand of New Deal thinking that, at least partially, engages with the critique of rights in early Marx even while, admittedly, not addressing the logics of production in later Marx. It exceeds our narrowed understanding of current liberal politics if liberalism is understood as primarily an order of rights against political power rather than as a claim to it, and it is a conceptualization of democracy that neoliberalism works with fury and force to disembowel (Harvey, 2005).

Despite the important shifts in constitutional law during the 20th century that Justice Ginsburg draws upon in *Sebelius*, the Constitution of the US is no friend of democracy. The Constitution deliberately thwarts the coming together of democratic power by dispersing it temporally and institutionally, and it secures these anti-democratic tendencies by erecting high barriers to constitutional change via normal democratic processes (Jackson, 2012; Levinson, 2006). Thus it is no surprise that Milton Friedman (1962) turns to the US Constitution as a model for protecting neoliberal "freedom" from the unfreedom heralded by the presence of democratic political power:

> How can we benefit from the promise of government while avoiding the threat to freedom? Two broad principles embodied in our Constitution give an answer that has preserved our freedom so far . . . First, the scope of government must be limited. Its major function must be to protect our freedom both from the enemies outside our gates and from our fellow citizens . . . The second broad principle is that government power must be dispersed. If government is to exercise power, better in the county than in the state, better in the state than in Washington.
>
> *(pp. 2–3)*

In their dissenting opinion, Justices Kennedy, Scalia, Alito, and Thomas sought to nullify the ACA in its entirety and vindicate these two constitutional principles. They repeatedly returned to the "structural protections" of liberty, "notably the restraints imposed by federalism and the separation of powers" (p. 2677). For them, the mandate was unconstitutional because it *compelled* economic activity rather than regulated it, and thus portended the transformation of the Commerce Clause into a general power to solve national problems. The threat to withhold all federal Medicaid funding from states that did not agree to expand their programs in accord with the federal statute raised the specter of Congress "trampling on State's sovereignty" and degenerating into a dreaded "parliament of the whole people" (p. 2648). Rather than defer to democratic power in the realm of social and economic welfare legislation, the dissent imagined the role of the court as stern schoolmaster of the Republic:

> Structural protections . . . are less romantic and have less obvious a connection to personal freedom than the Bill of Rights or the Civil War

> Amendments. Hence they tend to be undervalued or even forgotten by our citizens. It should be the responsibility of the Court to teach otherwise . . . Today's decision should have vindicated, should have taught, this truth.
>
> (NFIB v Sebelius, *2677)*

Neoliberal citizens are, apparently, ignorant and stubborn, and in need of constant reminders and tutorials that the acquisition of their individual freedom demands the surrender of their political power.

In light of the dissent's constitutional theory, how then does this constitute a departure from neoliberal ends? Recall that Milton Friedman's hostility to centralized political power offered a gradation of judgment about governmental power when governmental power was called for: county rather than state, state rather than federal. Unlike Medicare, which is administered by the federal government, Medicaid is a joint project between the states and federal government, an example of "cooperative federalism." Any state could withdraw from Medicaid and leave the poor in grave distress; no action by this or that state can threaten the distribution of health coverage provided by Medicare. And as Justice Ginsburg pointed out, the constitutionality of Medicare is on sound constitutional footing; it does not prod the states, it bypasses them via the Taxing and Spending power. By rendering federal attachments to federal funds constitutionally suspect, the dissent comes near to creating an either/or logic with respect to future federal action: spend directly or do nothing. When doing nothing ceases to be a political option, nationalized public health care will be the surest legal path; after all, why risk the constitutional challenge when you can simply avoid it? Ironically, the dissent undermines federalism in the name of federalism and thus turns neoliberalism against itself.

Individual liberty and limited government are considered to be neoliberal virtues, but limited government in neoliberal governance in fact means limits in some domains but real and robust power in others. As Wendy Brown has astutely noted, neoliberalism does not fight state power *per se*, but turns state power toward the creation of new neoliberal orders: "the state is not without a project in the making of the neoliberal subject" (2005, p. 43; see, also, Passavant, 2005). Chile's simultaneous experience of neoliberalization and rightwing dictatorship helped set the historical mold for realizing Friedman's ordering of economic freedom as preceding and grounding other practices of freedom and for unleashing the state as a productive force in building a marketized society. Following Brown's lead, we can see that the Pinochet dictatorship did not represent the emergence of a libertarian order of the state policing a naturally functioning market, but instead signaled an active neoliberal state of intervention and social engineering. A key policy triumph of the neoliberals in Chile was the privatization of the public pension system under the Pinochet dictatorship. The minister of labor in charge of that project, José Piñera, would also come to co-chair the Cato Institute's Project on Social Security Privatization in the US. Chile replaced public pensions with "individually-owned, private investment accounts." The law established a "*mandatory* minimum savings level of 10% of wages," and all "new entrants to the labor force *were required to enter* the PSA system" (Piñera, Testimony before the Subcommittee on Social Security, House Ways and Means Committee, 1997 (emphasis added)). Workers, however, were "free to choose" which financial services company they wanted to manage their mandatory individual pension savings account.

To translate this into the language of the *Sebelius* case, the state has issued an individual mandate that all workers must purchase financial services products. The state does not disappear here, it simply appears in neoliberal form. But this appearance is precisely what the right-wing dissent in *Sebelius* held to be constitutionally impermissible. If the state can not only regulate economic "activity" but in fact can *compel* it, have we not then crossed the Rubicon from limited government into its very opposite? As the dissent put it, if the power of regulation includes the power to compel that which is regulated, "then the idea of a limited government power is at an end" (p. 2566). The capacity of the federal government to privatize Social Security along Chilean lines is thus constitutionally blocked. The dissenting opinion sings with neoliberal poetry only to potentially thwart a longstanding neoliberal dream. It has wandered into that vexing predicament where "neoliberals have never been able to live with, or without, the state" (Peck, 2010a, p. 20).

III. The welfare state left

If neoliberals have never been able to live with or without the state in general, a parallel on the political Left has been its inability to live with or without the welfare state in particular. Even as the welfare state has been under sustained assault, and even as that assault has generated fierce resistance from the Left, it has simultaneously remained an object of leftist suspicion and anti-subordination critique. Those critiques have been indispensable to rethinking what constitutes emancipatory politics and have also contoured the engagements of those politics with the welfare state. Critics have identified the racial exclusions in early Social Security legislation (Quadagno, 1984); the gendered norms of many mechanisms and logics of welfare state distribution (see Gordon, 1992); the aims of social control rather than social justice in some relief programs (Piven and Cloward, 1993); and the failure of the welfare state to forge a "commitment to emancipating the realm of production" (Brown, 2005, p. 55). In short, there is a leftist tradition that views the welfare state as a source and site of unfreedom, as primarily a network of disciplinary power (a regime of social workers and case managers producing, distributing, and policing norms) or as a distraction from postcapitalist tomorrows and a deflection of the revolutionary fervor required to get us there. The *locus classicus* of the latter argument remains Marx's (1850) insistence that social democrats should be greeted with absolute "mistrust" (p. 507) as they hope to do nothing more than "bribe the workers" into accepting a mere "change of social conditions" and thus prevent a transformation of "the whole of society" (pp. 504–505).

These criticisms have been marginal in the broader conflicts over welfare in US political discourse. Historical waves of state repression and cultural "red scares" silenced the Marxist critiques and left only isolated thinkers here and there in the academy or in small and mostly unread journals. The primary public debate has progressed along other lines: traditionally, the libertarians have claimed the mantle of "freedom" to argue against progressive schemes of taxation and redistribution. On this account, the freedom of the wealthy is unjustly violated by taxation and the freedom of the recipient of the entitlement is hobbled by dependency. By contrast, welfare state advocates have more often invoked values other than freedom such as a desire to "protect the weak" (Goodin, 1988, p. x) or to ensure social stability (King and Ross, 2010) or to defend the principle of equality or to strengthen the bonds of citizenship (Marshall, 1965) or to generate a humanitarian floor below which no citizen can fall. In some other instances, justification for the welfare state is rooted in the grammar of economics and technocracy. The current democratic-socialist candidate for US President recently proposed universalizing Medicare on the grounds that the state, through economies of scale, is able to manage health care "more efficiently" than private industry (Eskow, 2015). However, at the most basic level, political disagreements have been normative rather than technocratic (although there is a certain neoliberal normativity in the appeal to the technocratic measure of efficiency), with individual freedom counterpoised to the equality of the welfare state.

One thing should be clear: the welfare state is neither necessarily synonymous with freedom nor freedom's singularly proper end, but it is a mistake to render it *per se* alien, exterior, or antagonistic to freedom as matter of historical practice or theoretical principle. To open up our thinking, perhaps it might be useful to begin considering the question of freedom and welfare from the shores of the marginalized Left critiques. Indeed the variety of critiques themselves invites us to think of the welfare state from a number of different angles and thus further pluralize our understanding of emancipatory politics (Jackson, 2016).[3] Linked with a hesitation to speak of the Left in the singular, or in singular contradistinction to liberal politics, should be a hesitation to speak of the "welfare state" as a singular entity in the present with only one organizing principle. The latter is particularly important as the politics of the welfare state in the US is too often thought exhausted by the politics of "welfare" for only the very poor.

Our judgment about the welfare state should be particularized, but one must move outward to see it in broader terms; we should recall that the US welfare state includes: Social Security Disability Insurance, socialized old age pensions, socialized public education, Medicare coverage for the elderly, food stamps, TANF (Temporary Aid to Needy Families), Head Start pre-school programs, and a Medicaid program that now extends eligibility to adults earning up to 138% of the poverty line via the ACA. By 2022, Medicaid could add over 20 million new

3 This chapter considers the welfare state from a laboring perspective, but the original article more fully engages with feminist and Foucaultian critiques.

enrollees (Kaiser Family Foundation, 2013). All of these programs constitute the "welfare state" in the US but they are reducible to no single political principle other than one: the collective right of democracy to govern the material conditions of "civil society" and the political right to establish new property rather than simply police extant forms.

The ACA thus represents first and foremost the freedom of democracy over the prerogatives and presumptions of libertarian market freedom, an important reaffirmation of democracy in a period defined by its increasing fragility – as we witnessed in the jurisprudence of *Sebelius* (Brown, 2015). But other freedoms are enabled too, including a freedom of exit for workers,[4] a freedom that in this instance moves both with and against central currents of Marxist thought.

A. Wage work and freedom

The claim that "the Left has traditionally stood for a set of values and possibilities qualitatively different from those of welfare state liberals" (Brown, 2005, p. 55) should be reconsidered when we take into account the extent to which the welfare state assists, or may assist, in freedom vis-a-vis "the realm of production." The welfare state helps to partially sever the dependency of the individual upon a particular employment relationship. It facilitates a partial breakage of the old iron-clad logic of survival under capitalist orders for the working class, "a class of labourers, who live only so long as they find work, and who find work only so long as their labour increases capital" (Marx and Engels, 1848, p. 479). An acceleration in the de-linking of a social good and necessity from the power dynamics of the employer/employee relationship offers support for emancipatory political practices and projects with regard to that relationship. As an example, the Social Security program emancipates many from the requirements of wage labor during old age or injury without dooming them to ghastly poverty and misery. To illustrate: the percentage of Social Security recipients over the age of 65 in West Virginia who live in poverty is 9%; without Social Security it would be 52%. In Mississippi the poverty rate for that group is 12%; without Social Security it would be 55%. In Vermont the poverty rate for that group is 8.5%; without Social Security it would be 49% (*AARP Bulletin*, 2013).

As Justice Ginsburg noted in *Sebelius*, the legislative aim of the ACA was "the interest of those who labor." The ACA tends to the interest of workers as workers by defending and materially supporting a freedom of exit. There are at least two different dimensions of this freedom interest in this instance: the freedom to exit one job for another, and the freedom to exit the wage labor force in meaningful ways prior to old age. The expansion of Medicaid coupled with income-based subsidies for the purchase of insurance within regulated market exchanges empowers workers who are in a condition of "job lock." Job lock binds a worker to a particular job. Prior to the ACA many workers with employment-based insurance

4 Workers in the labor market; work that does not receive a wage is outside the scope of this chapter.

could not leave the job they held due to the fear of losing health insurance for themselves and their families. The potential loss of insurance was closer to fact than fear for those who had preexisting health conditions. In response to this, the ACA forbids insurance companies from refusing coverage of preexisting conditions and socializes the cost within the insurance exchanges. Consequently, workers are now more free to exit their current employment arrangement than they were prior to the passage of the law.

Marxist theory has been more critical than appreciative of this freedom to exit. As Jon Elster (1983) has noted, Marxists have claimed that this particular freedom "tends to generate the illusion that the worker is free not only with respect to the individual capitalist, but with respect to capital as such" (p. 284). However if capitalism is rendered conceptually and historically plural, then the particulars of this or that moment of capitalism are in fact "capital as such." The condition of job lock is a material unfreedom that recalls pre-capitalist feudal forms. To borrow from Faulkner, the past has never been entirely in the past in the present tenses of capitalism. Karen Orren's (1991) exploration of the endurance of feudal practices and norms in US employment law well into the twentieth century highlights this fact. And it is noteworthy that Orren identified an entire apparatus around employment designed "in a manner to bind the worker to his job and ward off interlopers" that stood in contrast to the popular image of the "free labor calculating his day-to-day advantage, ready to pick up and follow the highest bidder" (p. 13). Mobility is thus a freedom contra feudalism *and* contra capitalism when the former inhabits the latter as matter of practice, and when practice refuses to yield to the dictates and demarcations of periodization. Additionally, such mobility must be defended as something other than an illusion to be discarded at some future moment of anti/postcapitalist emancipation lest the freedom of the worker be entirely devoured by a collective "social power" that produces the conditions whereby the individual is immediately and inexorably conscripted into "industrial armies" (Marx and Engels, 1848, p. 490) at the moment of freedom.

The rhetorical conflation of emancipation with the establishment of industrial armies by Marx and Engels signals continuity across the frontiers of capitalist norms into communist imaginaries: both place work at the center of life and the latter locates work at the center of freedom. As labor becomes the realization and signature of humanity, exit from labor – whether organized via the wage labor system of capitalism or the socialized armies of labor of Marxism – as an act or precondition of freedom becomes suspect. Even when the Marxist tradition has envisioned emancipation from work and a life outside of it, it has done so in contradiction to its own theoretical premises. Hannah Arendt (1998) noted this contradiction in Marx's thought: "in all stages of his work he defines man as an *animal laborans* and then leads him into a society in which this greatest and most human power is no longer necessary" (p. 105). In the 20th century the contradiction was resolved in favor of the "productivist imperative" in Marxism, and two options emerged as dominant: "socialist modernization" which emphasized "more work," and "socialist humanism" which emphasized "better work" (Weeks, 2011, pp. 81–83). Thus the worker in both capitalist states and communist societies dwelled in the realm of labor and discovered that emancipation was contingent upon and coterminous with the normalization and internalization of a simple truth that there was no alternative to that realm. On all paths potentially leading somewhere else stood signs stating simply, "no exit." Worse, the normalization of the work imperative became so entrenched that it occurred to fewer and fewer to even seek out or contemplate such paths.

Understanding capitalist work structures to be at their heart ones of domination or exploitation (and for most who labor, both) and envisioning human beings as something other than *animal laborans* requires freedom to be reconceptualized as unhinged from simply democratizing or revolutionizing the conditions of work even if and when freedom demands that revolution of democratization. Freedom requires less work and thus a criterion of judgment about the existence and expansion of the welfare state should be the extent to which it transforms that goal into a material reality. In the words of political theorist Kathi Weeks, the aim is "not for a liberation of work but a liberation *from* work" (p. 97). Of course, one could be thrown out of work and into the teeth of bare existence and thus reminded of Marx's point that when survival is linked to laboring for a wage the absence of labor turns existence into a question. Indeed, a hallmark of neoliberalism has been the emergence of an economy bereft of full-time, long-term employment and overflowing with short-term contracts providing minimal benefits; work precarity rather than labor monotony defines the neoliberal present and may be one reason that the call for emancipation from work currently lacks traction. Nonetheless, the task is to resist the impulse for a politics of herding people into labor (however "free") and instead to embrace contingency freed from the rule of hyperscarcity, competition, and anxiety.

As neoliberalism evacuates from public life social meanings, political vocabularies, and normative reference points other than those drawn from economics (including the concept of "public life" itself), the pride of place once given to the "citizen" in liberal democracy has been increasingly supplanted by the model neoliberal actor, the postcitizen *par excellence*, the "entrepreneur." Perhaps ironically or perhaps as a measure of neoliberal hegemony, some politicians explicitly referenced the "freeing" of the entrepreneur as a reason to support the ACA. After all, if job lock stymies risk then the inventor of the next magical technowidget may not pursue their creative impulses; in a sense, job lock does to the entrepreneur in the economic marketplace what Mill once worried "opinion" did to the speaker in the political marketplace: it changes the calculation about action and produces a stillness and quietude in the individual. Creative destruction thus compels the dissolution of the neofeudal bond within contemporary US capitalism even if that entails the expansion of the welfare state to accomplish it and even as a neoliberal discourse circulates around the expansion. Thus it is not surprising that the liberal Speaker of the House of Representatives who shepherded the ACA towards enactment said afterwards, "we see it as an entrepreneurial bill" (Chait, 2015).

One might be tempted to stop at this elevation of entrepreneurship and see in it an indictment of the limits of the legislation, the limits of the political discourse deployed to defend it, or the end of freedom beyond the contours of a neoliberal order in which "contemporary neoliberal governance operates through isolating and entrepreneurializing responsible units and individuals" (Brown, 2015, p. 129). Without discounting such possibilities, it still might behoove us to think more intently about how the ACA creates the possibility for some people to exit not just their particular job but the labor market entirely. Discursively, another figure appeared in the ACA debates as a potential alternative to the heroic entrepreneur: the artist. In the same moment she was praising entrepreneurship, Speaker Pelosi also defended the ACA as enabling "the pursuit of happiness" in other directions. She celebrated "people having the freedom to be self-employed, play music, write poetry, wherever their aspirations or talents take them" (Brooks, 2012). Unsurprisingly, the political Right mocked and pilloried her for this justification (see, e.g., Goldberg, 2014). Equally unsurprising but perhaps more disappointingly, some liberals insisted that the key point being made by Pelosi was an entrepreneurial one and that "Democrats are *not*, of course, proposing to provide some kind of welfare dole to individuals who wish to create art rather than work" (Chait, 2015).

Happily, the ACA did, in fact, create a welfare program that has enabled some number of individuals to leave the wage labor market and create art. What some cite as a failure of the ACA should be revalued as a triumph: the ACA has reduced "the number of hours worked by the equivalent of 2.5 million jobs" (Congressional Budget Office, 2014). The ACA has been described as a "tremendous blessing" to actors, painters, poets, and musicians since "not having health insurance has long been part of the life of an artist, even though health problems can have a particularly debilitating effect on artists' careers" (Karlamangla, 2014). The availability of socialized health insurance helps negate the necessity of choosing between performing unfulfilling work or living life as an artist. As numerous testimonials from artists illustrate, the ACA "makes it easier to carve out the time that makes it possible" be an artist. One example among literally hundreds of thousands is Karin Abromaitis who at the age of 61 had received only eight years of employer-provided health care and had confronted a perpetual choice in life of selecting a job for insurance or opting out of wage labor to make ceramic bowls and teapots (Cunningham, 2014). The ACA protects the second option as a viable one.

This freedom to exit the labor market, either entirely or in large measure, is more than a "bribe" to workers; it is a victory born of political democracy by workers for the right to be something other than workers. And while making art may be a form of work, it is also an activity of autonomy, leisure, and non-work. Karl Marx's son-in-law Paul Lafarge celebrated the vital space of life, art, and pleasure when he offered up garlands of praise to bestow upon "O, laziness, mother of the arts and the noble virtues" (Weeks, 2011, p. 98). The poet, actor, and musician appear today as strange subjects of freedom by contrast to the entrepreneur or the worker, but political theories and practices of freedom would be enriched by encouraging them to take the stage and taking the time to hear them perform without necessarily envisioning them as ideal or model human types or as freedom's vanguard subjects.

B. Freedom and vulnerability

This understanding of the welfare state as both partially emanating from and potentially undergirding a set of intertwined freedoms – the collective freedom of labor as a political power, the freedom of the individual worker to leave her specific job, the freedom of an individual to possibly (and this possibility will of course be informed by intersecting social differences) leave the wage labor market, and the freedom of artists to secure less precarious time to be artists – both diverges from and converges with some of the key arguments in the emerging field of vulnerability theory. Vulnerability theorists such as Martha Fineman (2013) offer a critique of the foundational assumptions beneath liberalism's "political and legal subject" for being mistakenly and misleadingly abstract and immaterial. Put succinctly, Fineman contends that abstract autonomy fails to recognize our embodiment, and immateriality elides the ways our subjectivity is situated or embedded in a variety of institutions and relationships. In contrast to liberal legal and political theory, Anna Grear (2013) insists that the "vulnerable subject is both *fully embodied and ineluctably embedded* in lived actualities and material conditions" (p. 49).

One could make this move against the foundations of liberal theory and then take it in at least two directions: one could say that if subjectivity exists only in the contingencies of lived actualities then foundationalism itself is suspect, *or* one could attempt to install vulnerability as a new foundation for law and politics. Fineman embraces the latter option: "vulnerability should be recognized as *the* primal human condition. As embodied beings, we are universally and individually constantly susceptible to harm" (2015, p. 614). Grear agrees: "the vulnerability thesis . . . is to be understood as being emphatically universal in scope – as an intrinsic, ineluctable characteristic (or given) of the human condition itself" (2013, p. 43). Vulnerability may be a component of human existence, but it is also true that radical difference defines humans and their conditions such that it may be simply impossible (and perhaps ultimately undesirable) to establish the primacy of any condition as *the* human condition. Assertions about the human condition often tell us more about the particular social and political conditions within that epoch than they do the eternal and universal truth of the human condition.

For example, when Aristotle stated that nature has "endowed man alone among the animals with the power of speech," we come closer to knowing something true about life in the polis of ancient Athens than we do to establishing *the* human condition. Similarly, when Marx argued that humans "begin to distinguish themselves from animals as soon as they begin to *produce* their means of subsistence" (1978, p. 150) the centrality of capitalist production in nineteenth century Europe reveals itself to us even as *the* human condition remains elusive. The emergence of "vulnerability" as a potential foundational condition could be seen in this succession: we today are beset by precarity and vulnerability born from relentless exposure to the vicissitudes of neoliberalism and globalization, and thus some leading political and legal theorists (including Fineman and Grear) are responding by centering vulnerability in their thinking – theory too is always embedded within historical time and material practices.

Although both Fineman and Grear embrace singular foundationalism in theory and as fact, they also insist that it is "important to understand that the concept of vulnerability is deployed . . . as an avowedly heuristic device" (Grear, 2013, p. 43) that enables us to "examine hidden assumptions and biases folded into legal, social, and cultural practices" (Fineman, 2013b, p. 20). As a heuristic device, it has indeed facilitated a detailed critique of the omissions and limits of liberalism, opened vital new lines of inquiry for law and politics, and brought forth a raft of policy proposals to address precarity and vulnerability in the present. Further, the heuristic turn opens up productive avenues of engagement with political projects beginning from different theoretical origins. One can arrive at many of the political conclusions of vulnerability theory without affirming vulnerability as *the* human condition or without claiming any foundational attachments at all. Vulnerability theory may thus be seen as both an invitation to think in a serious and sustained manner about the multiple ways we can be vulnerable and an incitement to generate a set of values far "more egalitarian and collective in nature" (Fineman, 2013, p. 26) than the atomized and economized values under current neoliberal orders.

This chapter's defense of the ACA and the welfare state finds numerous points of convergence and agreement with some of the central ideas developed in vulnerability theory. First, vulnerability theorists draw our attention to the impoverished thinking of a legal regime that understands the threat to equality and freedom primarily as formal exclusion from institutions and state action in policing it (or inaction in remedying it). As Martha Fineman has pointedly put it: "this means the state and its actors and institutions can treat individuals poorly, just as long as they treat them the same" (2015, p. 610). The scenes of laboring unfreedom we have encountered in this chapter cannot be addressed within an antidiscrimination paradigm focused on the discreet and insular identities of equal protection jurisprudence; the problem is not discrimination at work, but the nature of work itself. A second point of convergence is that in this critique, as with vulnerability theory, the market or civil society is not taken here as a natural, ahistorical original home for freedom that precedes political intervention; economic life has a history that is always already caught up with political actions and decisions. A third and final point of convergence involves a reconceptualization of the state. Anna Grear argues that one implication of vulnerability theory is that "the state (and politics) should attempt to reassume some kind of resistive role in challenging the stranglehold of capitalist economic hegemony at both the national and international levels" (2013, p. 59). In accord with vulnerability theory, the desired state in this chapter is active (it rejects *laissez-faire* fantasies), democratic (it responds to the laboring multitude rather than the oligarchic few), and socialist (it embraces social democracy *without* being antagonistic to more radical egalitarian incursions into capitalist property rights and regimes of governance at work). In sum, the political and legal aims of vulnerability theory can find zones of thick overlap with post-foundational theories of freedom. Each can enrich the other.

IV. Conclusion

The passage of the ACA marks an important challenge to the policies and logics of neoliberalism. In writing as a friend of the law, however, I do not intend to suggest that the statute is without failures, omissions, or exclusions: its exclusion of undocumented people is a crime in xenophobic times, its continuation of the Hyde Amendment's prohibition of federal monies for abortion is in contradiction to the meaning (even if not the current jurisprudence) of equal protection of the laws, and its fragmentation of distribution weakens basic principles of solidarity. But the vices of the law are not necessarily born from its many virtues and, indeed, the latter may well provide cure for the former. As an example, the exclusion produced by the Hyde Amendment is cognizable only because of the existence of the Medicaid program, and the repair of the injury both presumes and demands the public distribution or subsidy of health care. This is inclusion born of socialized material expansion rather than liberal inclusion into a right of competition, inequality, and market-based reward.

Any reading of the ACA must take note of its flaws, but those flaws should not blot out the ways in which the law potentially abolishes job lock and lessens the necessity for wage labor. More generally, Justice Ginsburg's eloquent reminder that the welfare state can be the assertion of democracy's primacy over the so-called "market" by those who labor in it should today compel a reconsideration of the theoretical bifurcation witnessed in multiple traditions of political thought between "welfare" and "freedom."

PART III
Marginalized workers

The third section of this book examines specific groups of workers who are frequently referred to today as "marginalized:" immigrants, victims of human trafficking, migrant domestic workers, ex-prisoners, and contingent workers. Compared to "mainstream" workers, these groups (among others) are argued to more likely perform undesirable work, earn less, endure difficult working conditions, and have little job security. In part, this is because legal protections designed for mainstream workers do not always reach these groups. The authors in this section discuss how legal definitions, distinctions of citizenship, and decisions about enforcement contribute to the problem.

Using concepts of vulnerability, the authors in this section also add another dimension to the analysis. To truly understand and address the issues of marginalized workers, we have to place them in a larger system of work and workplace regulation. These "marginalized" groups are not complete outsiders, but rather part of the system of low-wage workers that also includes and may disadvantage "mainstream" employees. Many of the challenges faced by the marginalized groups are structural problems that affect all low-wage workers. Recognizing the nature of universal and constant vulnerability and the relationship between work and resilience, the authors suggest that the solutions to these problems involve broad questions of state regulation and state responsibility, not just inclusion of marginalized groups in existing employment protections or specifically tailored regulation directed at each group.

In his chapter, "The productive subject in immigration law," Silas Allard uses vulnerability analysis to expose the ways in which US immigration law confers privilege and protection on some while tolerating the disadvantage of others. He argues that US immigration law attempts to address the need for immigrant labor and the fear of immigrant vulnerability by creating categories of desirable and undesirable immigrants. He concludes that the extensive benefits reaped from immigrant labor by US society create an obligation to care for all such laborers, regardless of their official status.

In the next chapter, "The wages of human trafficking," Rana Jaleel argues that our current legal definitions of human trafficking are vague and lack clear theoretical underpinnings about what we understand human trafficking to be, why we prohibit it, and in turn, what it means to be free. Using vulnerability theory as a tool for understanding the wrong of human trafficking, she argues that the heart of the crime is the exploitation of workers through forcing, coercing, or deceiving people into performing work – including commercial sex acts – under intolerable, illicit, or degrading conditions. She asserts that human trafficking law should not be understood solely as a corrective to state failure to manage migrant workers, but also as a lens through which to see the connections between migrant exploitation and the exploitation of domestic low-wage workers.

In their chapter, "Migrant domestic workers and decent work standards: exclusions, exemptions and rights," Siobhan Mullally and Clíodhna Murphy examine recent changes to UK laws relating to migrant workers. They position the changes as one example of states' resistance to advocates' efforts to use human rights law to address the nexus between migration status, access to safe migration routes, and the enjoyment of rights. They demonstrate that the empowering process of enacting rights in courts and through political activism is difficult and uncertain when the reforms secured are contingent and reversible, as they were in the UK case.

Kristin Bumiller's chapter, "Bad jobs and good workers: the hiring of ex-prisoners in a segmented economy," addresses the complex barriers to sustainable workplace participation faced by people who were formerly incarcerated. Through a unique study involving interviews with employers who do hire former prisoners, she shows that most of the employment opportunities that do exist for them are in non-contractual low-wage jobs and that this precarious employment offers too few benefits and not enough support to sustain many if not most persons leaving prisons. While these employers treat their workers with a modicum of humanity, their gestures are unlikely to counteract the overall failure of social support.

The final chapter in this section, "We are all contingent: fighting vulnerability in the US workforce," by Ann C. McGinley and David McClure, argues that nearly all Americans' work is contingent, and that what we call "contingent" work has become the norm in American workplaces. It explains why the literature on contingent work does not always capture the essence of conditions in American workplaces and offers a broad range of solutions to build resilience in American workers.

10

A DESIRED COMPOSITION

Regulating vulnerability through immigration law

Silas W. Allard[1]

> *It is likely that the last hands to hold the blueberries, strawberries, peaches, asparagus, or lettuce before you pick them up in your local grocery store belong to Latin American migrant laborers.*
>
> *(Holmes, 2013, p. 48)*

> *We know, then that "ideal" bodies are desired for undesirable labor and that those bodies cross borders all the time, even as their movements are increasingly policed. We know as well that the work these bodies perform often is quite literally disabling and that subsequent recourse to national support systems is absent.*
>
> *(Markotic and McRuer, 2012, p. 168)*

I. Introduction

In his ethnography *Fresh Fruit, Broken Bodies*, anthropologist and medical doctor Seth Holmes describes Triqui Mexican farmworkers who enter the US outside of the formal immigration process to work in the fruit and produce fields of Washington and California. Holmes describes immigrants who perform disabling labor so that they and their families can survive. But it is also, and equally, true that these immigrants' labor is the backbone of the US agricultural system. Holmes recounts the words of Samuel, a 31-year-old farmworker:

> We dedicate everything to the fields, we are field workers. We are workers; ever since we're born we're planting. . . . Poor people from Oaxaca come here; we come here to give away our strength and everything and they don't do anything for us. . . . Because of our will this government survives.
>
> *(2013, p. 30 (ellipses in original))*

1 Associate Director and Harold J. Berman Senior Fellow in Law and Religion, Center for the Study of Law and Religion at Emory University.

As Holmes notes, reflecting on Samuel's story, "They dedicate everything to the fields in the US, their labor and skills, their energy and time, and their identities and reputations, as well as their minds and bodies" (2013, p. 30).

This is one story, among millions, of people – immigrants – upon whom American society and the American economy have come to depend (Singer, March 2012). Recent data indicates that immigrants make up around 16% of the total labor force (Bureau of Labor Statistics (BLS), 2014, p. 1)[2] and undocumented immigrants make up around 5% of the total labor force (Passel and Cohn, 2015, p. 5). Immigrants are overrepresented in certain essential sectors, including agriculture, construction, food service, and hospitality (Passel and Cohn, 2015, p. 5; Singer, March 2012, p. 5). The sector with the highest immigrant representation is private households (49% of all workers are immigrants), where immigrants cook, clean, and otherwise engage in care work (Singer, March 2012, p. 5).

These trends of significant immigrant participation in the labor force and divergent patterns of participation by industry are not new aspects of the US economy, but part of a long story of immigration and labor. Immigrant laborers have always filled certain gaps in the labor force. While those gaps have changed over time from manufacturing to agriculture to, increasingly, service industries, the immigrant laborer is an enduring member of the American economic and social community, if not the American political community.

In order to participate in the labor force, immigrants must either pass through or bypass the highly regulated immigration system. Even at the dawn of immigration regulation in the late-nineteenth century, when the era of open borders came to a close – and long before the confusing alphabet soup of visa categories that characterizes contemporary immigration law – the exercise of regulatory power was expansive (Fairchild, 2003, pp. 14–16). How movement over the political borders of the US is regulated is intimately tied up with the role of immigrants as laborers. The structure and function of the immigration law and its enforcement reflect certain constructions of immigrant and non-immigrant subjectivity, which determine who is admitted, who is excluded, and who arrives outside the formal channels.

Martha Fineman and others have encouraged scholars to consider how universal human vulnerability challenges extant legal and institutional structures (Fineman, 2008, 2010; Fineman and Grear, 2013). By paying attention to the vulnerable subject – the human subject that, embodied, is always and universally susceptible to harms ranging from the minor to the catastrophic – and how that subject fares in society and social institutions, we can observe "the ways in which societal resources are channeled to see if the result is to privilege and protect some while tolerating the disadvantage and vulnerability of others" (Fineman, 2008, pp. 20–21). While vulnerability analysis helps uncover exploitative and unequal social

2 The Bureau of Labor Statistics uses the term "foreign born," which includes all persons born as non-citizens outside the US who are resident in the US, including naturalized citizens, legal permanent residents, temporary residents, and undocumented immigrants. This definition is generally followed in compiling data on immigrants in the labor force.

arrangements, the universality of human vulnerability also forms the basis of a critique of such institutions, by asking why, if we are all vulnerable, some should be protected while others are not. As Fineman elaborates:

> At a minimum the vulnerability approach would be premised on the idea that it is inappropriate for the state and its institutions to protect and privilege some, to shield them or to mediate their vulnerability through the creation and maintenance of societal institutions, and it would force us to uncover the ways the state allows some to struggle with vulnerability and dependency.
>
> *(2008, p. 21, fn52)*

In this chapter, I am interested in how the state structures the institution of immigration law and its enforcement to mediate vulnerability among citizens and non-citizens. Expanding the scope of state responsibility beyond citizens is necessary to take account of vulnerability as a universal human condition in those contexts where the state inevitably encounters non-citizens, such as in the context of immigration. As Ruth Gomberg-Muñoz (2011) points out in a critique of calls for closed borders and mass deportations:

> [T]he issues that are brought up by a theorization of undocumented labor migration – globalization, capitalism, racism, nativism, marginalization, class exploitation – are complex problems. . . . Further, these problems are not only complex, they are international – created, transformed, and intensified by globalized interactions. International problems are not likely to have nationalist solutions.
>
> *(p. 135)*

In our globalized world, attention must be paid to the non-citizen because the vulnerabilities of the citizen and the non-citizen are deeply intertwined; the non-citizen cannot be understood as a distant and disconnected other. As Anna Grear has noted, "[I]t is an intrinsic implication of vulnerability theory that the embodied subject is always and everywhere an inherently international subject" (2013, p. 57), and this implication follows from the recognition that vulnerability is a relational characteristic that "positions us in relation to each other as human beings and also suggests a relationship of responsibility between state and individual" (Fineman, 2010, p. 255). Because, as Gomberg-Muñoz says, our relationships inherently extend beyond the national, our analysis must consider how the state mediates the vulnerability of all those over whom it exercises power.

In what follows I argue that US immigration law is, in many ways, structured around perceptions of vulnerability in order to "privilege and protect some while tolerating the disadvantage and vulnerability of others" (Fineman, 2008, pp. 20–21).[3]

3 Though my analysis is limited to the context of the US, I suggest that similar dynamics are at play in other predominately receiving countries, and in some countries with more mixed sending and

The way in which immigration law mediates vulnerability is bound up with the category of "labor" and, specifically, who is sought, who is tolerated, and who is excluded. To conduct this analysis, I use the heuristic categories of need, fear, and desire: US immigration law attempts to address the *need* for immigrant labor and the *fear* of immigrant vulnerability by creating categories of *desire*, or desirable and undesirable immigrants. By applying a vulnerability analysis, we can also observe that in the preoccupation with immigrant vulnerability the vulnerabilities of a predominately receiving society, such as the US, are laid bare.

It is not my intention to suggest a comprehensive theory of either migration or immigration law. As labor, work, and economics are not the only operative factors in the decision to migrate (Castles and Miller, 2009, chapter 2; Portes and Borocz, 1989), neither are they the only operative factors in determining admission and exclusion. Throughout the history of US immigration law and continuing into the contemporary period, factors including nativism (Higham, 2002) and racism (Ngai, 2004) have played profound roles in shaping US immigration law. In a more positive vein the US has – by comparison with other predominately receiving countries – maintained relatively generous policies on family reunification and refugee resettlement. Acknowledging the complexity and multiplicity of migration's causes and regulations, this chapter takes the opportunity to investigate the particular role of labor in forming immigration law and, using a vulnerability analysis, to shed some light on this important factor.

II. History

A brief survey of US immigration law's development will provide some necessary context and an introduction to legislation that will be discussed throughout the chapter. Prior to 1875, the US maintained an essentially open border, meaning that movement across the political borders of the US was generally not policed, and laws did not regulate who could come and go as a matter of admission or exclusion at the border. As Aristide Zolberg has shown, the absence of immigration laws did not mean that immigration was unregulated, but it was controlled through other means, such as shipping regulations and foreign policy (2006). These regulations were intended to promote immigration in some cases, such as efforts to remove exit barriers in eighteenth century Europe, and to restrict immigration in other cases, such as shipping regulations that raised the price of passage and deterred immigration by the poor (Zolberg, 2006). Until the late-nineteenth century it remained unclear whether immigration was to be regulated at the federal or state

---

receiving migration patterns. Where economics and demographics create labor shortages, either generally or by sector, there is increasing recourse to migrant labor with regulatory schemes that function to maximize the benefit of such labor for the receiving country while minimizing that country's exposure to immigrant vulnerability, leading inevitably to situations of exploitation. Similar patterns can also be seen in some places with significant internal (or intra-state) labor migration, as was famously chronicled in John Steinbeck's *The Grapes of Wrath*.

level, and states enacted some restrictions on immigration principally intended to exclude criminals and paupers; however, because the restrictions were not adopted comprehensively, they posed minimal barriers to immigration as ships would simply land in neighboring states (Zolberg, 2006).

Early federal laws regulating immigration were based on the principle of individual exclusion. In theory, immigration to the US was open – anyone could come and no caps on total immigrant numbers existed – with the exception that certain categories of persons were defined as excludable. The first federal immigration statue, the Page Law, was passed in 1875 and excluded convicts and prostitutes. The Page Law was followed shortly by the Chinese Exclusion Act of 1882, which served principally to exclude Chinese laborers, but also excluded "any convict, lunatic, idiot, or any person unable to take care of himself or herself without becoming a public charge" (Gordon et al., 2004, §§ 2.02–04). Thus, there was no numerical limit or cap on admissions and those persons admitted to the country were, for immigration purposes, undifferentiated. This regime lasted – with the number and variety of exclusions growing over time – until 1921, when the Emergency Quota Act placed the first comprehensive limit on admissions.

With the passage of the Emergency Quota Act, the principle of individual exclusion was replaced with a quota system whereby immigration would be numerically restricted as a first principle. Exceptions to the quota system (including, importantly, the entire Western Hemisphere) and continued exclusions (grounds for non-admission of an immigrant who would otherwise have been admitted within the cap) functioned within the governing logic of the restrictionist quota. The Emergency Quota Act was shortly replaced by the Immigration Act of 1924, which laid the foundation of the national origin quota system that would remain in place until 1965. The national origin quota system restricted immigration from any given country to 2% of the total nationals of that country recorded in the 1890 census (later amendments would change the census year used as reference point). The 1924 Act created a restrictionist regime governed by a nationalist logic of prior admissions, the intent of which was to restrict overall immigration while also maintaining the "racial" balance of the country by reducing immigration from non-European countries to a nominal amount (Ngai, 2004, pp. 25–29).[4]

The national origin quota system came to an end in 1965 with the Hart-Cellar Act, which repealed all national origin quotas. The Hart-Cellar Act kept a restrictionist regime in place by continuing to limit total immigration to the US, but altered the rubric of admission. Instead of regulating admission on the basis of nationality, the Hart-Cellar Act created preference categories for family-based immigration (persons immigrating to join a lawfully present alien already in the US) and employment-based immigration (persons immigrating to fill a job opening in the US). Thus, the Hart-Cellar Act could be described as establishing a

4 Natalia Bronshtein has created a helpful visualization of the national origin quota system's impact on immigration trends using legal permanent resident data. The visualization can be found at http://insightfulinteraction.com/immigration200years.html.

restrictionist regime governed by a preference logic, where the preferences reflected values written into the immigration system, namely family unity and labor needs. Although the particular preferences and numerical limits have changed over time, the scheme established by the Hart-Cellar Act remains the governing logic of immigration law today.

III. Regulating immigration: needs, fears, and desires

A fundamental tension exists in US immigration law between laws of admission that respond to the need for immigrant labor and laws of exclusion that respond to fear of immigrants. This tension is longstanding, dating from the earliest efforts to limit immigration in the nineteenth century (Fairchild, 2003, p. 11), and it is reflected in contemporary discourse around immigration, including the language of "brokenness" that is so prominent in debates about immigration reform today. When pundits and politicians refer to our broken immigration system they are referring to either the inability of current laws to accommodate the admission of sufficient immigrant laborers, or the inability of current laws to effectively exclude undocumented migrants. Sometimes, they mean both things simultaneously, as did President Obama in his November 2014 address to the nation on immigration:

> [T]oday, our immigration system is broken – and everybody knows it. Families who enter our country the right way and play by the rules watch others flout the rules. Business owners who offer their workers good wages and benefits see the competition exploit undocumented immigrants by paying them far less. All of us take offense to anyone who reaps the rewards of living in America without taking on the responsibilities of living in America. And undocumented immigrants who desperately want to embrace those responsibilities see little option but to remain in the shadows, or risk their families being torn apart.
>
> *(para. 4)*

The principle purpose of President Obama's November 2014 address was to announce his proposal for Deferred Action for Parents of Americans and Lawful Permanent Residents, or DAPA, which would suspend deportations of certain undocumented immigrants: long-term residents with American citizen or legal permanent resident children who did not have a criminal record (United States Citizenship and Immigration Service (USCIS), 2015). In the course of his remarks, however, the President also noted two additional actions he was taking: (1) improving the speed and access to immigration for "high-skilled" immigrants "as so many business leaders have proposed," and (2) providing "additional resources for our law enforcement personnel [at the border] so they can stem the flow of illegal crossings" (Obama, 2014, paras. 11–12). According to President Obama, addressing our broken immigration system means finding some answer to the unresolved status of the eleven million undocumented immigrants currently in the US (or at least some subset of that population), but it also means bringing in more laborers who are in high demand and doing a better job of excluding those who migrate outside the formal channels of immigration law. What Obama did not say is that those who make up the "flow of illegal crossings" are also in demand as laborers, just not as neighbors and fellow citizens. In what follows, I want to explore how we arrive at this perspective: why are some immigrant laborers valorized and others stigmatized?

A. Need: economic dependence and commodified laborers

The need and ability to recruit immigrant labor is a longstanding determinant of immigration policy. Even prior to formal immigration laws, Zolberg (2006) has shown how the US utilized foreign policy to end exit restrictions and create access to sources of immigrant labor from Europe, China, and Japan in response to domestic labor shortages and the demands of westward expansion. Amy Fairchild has demonstrated that the immigrant medical exam administered at ports of entry such as Ellis Island, Angel Island, and Brownsville, Texas, between 1890 and 1930 served not so much to deny entry to immigrants as to form newly arriving immigrants in the disciplines of industrial labor or, in Fairchild's words, to form industrial citizens (2003, p. 14). Even during the period of declining immigration from 1930 to 1965, the period marked by the most restrictionist policies, the immigrant population remained in excess of 9 million persons and nearly 5% of the total population (Migration Policy Institute, n.d.). Importantly, this period of declining immigration corresponded with the period of the Bracero program (1942–1964), which brought millions of Mexican workers to the US as part of the largest guest worker program in US history (Ngai, 2004, p. 138). Thus, an active and intentional program of temporary labor migration offset the effect of declining permanent migration to the US.

Immigration law does not only function to create access to labor, nor does it serve principally to restrict immigration; rather, the purpose of immigration law is to control immigration (Fairchild, 2003, p. 13), and, thereby, to produce economic and social realities. If labor has been commodified in the global market economy, immigrants are subject to this phenomenon in a particularly profound way, whereby it is not their labor but the immigrant body as a laboring body that is commodified and selected for or against in the regulatory process of admission (McGovern, 2012, pp. 486–487, 491–492). Thus, immigration becomes, in part, a source of economic prosperity that is adaptable to changing conditions, and the immigrant body enters American society, if it enters at all, subject to this rubric. Fairchild (2003) describes how this process functioned at the turn of the twentieth century through the immigrant medical exam:

> Like industry's scientific managers, federal immigration officials would concern themselves primarily with the so-called 'dumb ox' variety of immigrant favored by industry: those with strong backs but lacking the capacity

> to manage their own labor. Within a new context of assembly-line production and industrial management, the laborer became an expendable cog in a vast machine.
>
> *(p. 15)*

Because the burgeoning industrial economy needed a growing workforce, the immigrant medical exam excluded very few immigrants, and those it did exclude were excluded on the grounds that they lacked the physical or mental integrity to participate in the new industrial workforce (Fairchild 2003, p. 33).

The changing and adaptable nature of immigration control can be seen as labor-intense manufacturing began to decline following World War I. As labor needs changed, a concomitant shift in the structures of migration regulation occurred. As Mae Ngai describes, "[B]y 1920, the country simply no longer needed the same levels of mass immigration. . . . [because] industrial capitalism had matured to the point where economic growth could come more from technological advances in mass production than from a continued expansion of the manufacturing workforce" (2004, p. 19). The commodification of the immigrant laborer meant that as demand fell, supply could be curtailed, and in response to the changing economy Congress restricted immigration by establishing a numerically capped quota system under the Emergency Quota Act of 1921 and the Immigration Act of 1924.

While the need for *industrial* labor was shrinking in the inter-war years, the exception for Western Hemisphere migrants written into the 1924 legislation reveals the continuing necessity of immigrant labor to the US economy, now focused on the agricultural economy. As Ngai notes, the Western Hemisphere exception was created "in deference to the need for labor in southwestern agriculture and American diplomatic and trade interests with Canada and Mexico" (2004, p. 23). The shift from a regulatory scheme designed to secure European laborers for industry to one designed to secure Mexican laborers for agriculture also reflected the nature of the work. Immigration officials believed – mistakenly in many cases – that Mexican workers would come for seasonal work but not settle permanently in the US (Ngai, 2004, pp. 50, 147–148). Agricultural work, unlike industrial work, did not need a workforce resident near industrial centers, often located in the upper Midwest and Northeast; rather, for southwestern agricultural work, seasonal recruiting from nearby Mexico with admission on a temporary basis was a viable alternative system.

While the period after 1965 saw a steady rise in immigration, as well as a rapid and significant diversification of immigrant countries of origin (see Bronshtein, n.d.; MPI, n.d.), trends in immigrant labor continue to depend heavily on undocumented migrants from Mexico and Central America, especially for difficult, dangerous, and poorly compensated jobs in agriculture, construction, caregiving, and hospitality. Taking the agricultural sector as an example, Holmes reports that estimates place the share of US farmworkers who were born in Mexico at 95%, with 52% of those being undocumented immigrants (2013, p. 40). These trends have caused the US agriculture industry to depend on the presence of immigrant workers, including undocumented workers. In 2011, the State of Georgia passed a controversial law known as HB 87, with the explicit aim of making the state inhospitable for undocumented immigrants. The passage of HB 87 was effective insofar as both documented and undocumented immigrants left the state fearing harassment, discrimination, and possible deportation. The resulting labor shortages are estimated to have cost Georgia agriculture producers $140 million dollars, largely in unharvested produce (Powell, 2012).

As President Obama noted in his November 2014 address, there is also a current need for immigrant labor in the technology sector. As noted previously, immigrants are overrepresented in sectors including agriculture, construction, and caregiving, but they are also overrepresented in information technology and high-tech manufacturing (Singer, March 2012, p. 5). These dual labor market needs have not, however, led to dual labor market recruiting efforts. Instead, there is an increasing bifurcation in US labor recruiting, as there is globally. As Patrick McGovern (2012) notes:

> [G]overnments have become much more selective about skill levels as they try to restrict labour market competition from low-wage, semi-skilled migrants. Highly skilled migration programmes have gained in popularity for reasons that include shortages of skilled labour, the fact that the admitting country has substantial control over the selection process, and, increasingly, because there is a "global war for talent" within the new "knowledge" economy.
>
> *(p. 488 (internal citation omitted))*

In the next section I will discuss how perceptions of immigrant vulnerability contribute to this result.

B. Fear: a flood of the poor, needy, and dependent

Susanna Snyder has argued that when it comes to migration, western societies operate in an "ecology of fear" (2012, chapter 5). "Immigrants," Snyder argues, "particularly asylum seekers and those without documents . . . are seen as a prime threat. While fear and the perception of newcomers as threat are not inevitable, talk of a migration crisis is widespread and in 'virtually every world capital, the flow of people is regarded with alarm'" (p. 87).[5] Xenophobia is a complex phenomenon, irreducible to a single issue or bias. As many other scholars have noted, a persistent racism operates in immigration policy, especially with regard to immigrants from Latin American and the Caribbean (see, e.g., De La Torre, 2009; Holmes, 2013; Ngai, 2004). Furthermore, issues of race and class are intimately connected, and perceptions of poor immigrants are shot through with

5 Quoting Weiner, 1995, p. 1.

race-based stereotypes. In what follows, I focus on fears around immigrant vulnerability and dependency, especially as they are written directly into the immigration laws, particularly because these fears are tied to ideas of autonomy and the need for labor.

The fear of immigrant vulnerability manifests in the persistence of dependency language as a ground of exclusion. From the earliest immigration laws, the need for immigrant labor was in tension with a profound fear of immigrant dependency. Thus, the exclusion of those likely to become dependents was part of the early state laws that attempted to regulate immigration (Zolberg, 2006) and was among the categories of exclusion from the earliest federal laws, including the Chinese Exclusion Act of 1882. As Fairchild points out, in the period following the industrial revolution, the goal of immigration regulation was to admit ideal laborers (conceived as a corporeal ideal) and to exclude those immigrants who were perceived as vulnerable and likely to become state dependents. Fairchild's work on the immigrant medical examination reveals how the examination served to form immigrants as industrial laborers, but it also served to screen for labor capacity and against potential dependency. The Public Health Service created two categories of medical exclusion: Class A and Class B. Class A included "loathsome and dangerous" contagious diseases, while Class B included conditions such as hernia, heart disease, or physical disability that were perceived as incongruous with industrial work and, therefore, likely to render the immigrant a public charge. As Fairchild says, "This new way of categorizing laborers, of categorizing both inability and ability to perform in the work force, elaborated on the formulation of what made a good industrial citizen: one who would remain healthy, be a useful worker, and not become dependent on the charity of the nation" (2003, p. 14). Thus, while the Public Health Service inspected more than twenty-five million arriving immigrants between 1891 and 1930, it only denied entry to some 79,000 (or 4.4%) on medical grounds, choosing instead to exclude immigrants principally "for causes related to economic 'dependency,' . . . most often as 'likely to become a public charge'" (2003, pp. 4–5).

While the language of "public charge" rings archaic, the exclusion remains an important part of contemporary immigration law. Section 212(a) of the current Immigration and Nationality Act permits the exclusion of any immigrant who, "in the opinion of the Attorney General at the time of application for admission or adjustment of status, is likely at any time to become a public charge" (8 USC § 1182(a)(4)(A)). In considering whether an immigrant is likely to become a public charge, the Attorney General considers the following factors: age; health; family status; assets, resources, and financial status; and education and skills (8 USC § 1182(a)(4)(B)(i)). In other words, the Attorney General will consider whether the immigrant is capable of working to support herself. Barriers to employment – whether corporeal, intellectual, educational, or financial – diminish the immigrant's potential admissibility. Nor is the US shy about invoking the public charge exclusion. A 2010 Congressional Research Service Report found that between 1994 and 2004, the principal ground of exclusion for immigrant petitioners was the public charge exclusion (Wasem, 2010, pp. 14–15).[6]

Fear rhetoric around immigration often comes accompanied by tropes of "floods," "hordes," and "masses," capturing perceptions of inundation, deluge, and overrun. Ngai notes with regard to the restrictionist quota legislation of the 1920s that "[a] crisis atmosphere surrounded discussion of immigration in Congress in 1920–21. The American Legion, the American Federation of Labor, and the patriotic orders warned that 'hordes' of impoverished people fleeing war-torn Europe were on the way" (2004, p. 20), and Fairchild notes the importance of metaphors of flood and deluge in describing immigrants as a force in need of control and discipline (2003, p. 47). Nearly one hundred years later, discussions of immigration remain enmeshed in such rhetoric, with flood metaphors appearing in news stories and opinion pieces across the media spectrum.

The rhetoric of hordes, masses, and floods operates to lump immigrants into an undifferentiated state of poverty and dependency. This hyperbole reflects a perceived vulnerability on the part of this country to all of the world's poor. It presumes the likelihood of immigrant dependency overwhelming social resources. Thus, this language supports the idea that there must be a bulwark against the poor immigrant; otherwise, there will be no way to stop the "flood" of poverty and need. This bulwark may be the public charge exclusion, or, as discussed further below, it may be the channeling of certain immigrants into informal or undocumented entry.

Ultimately, the fear associated with immigrants is tied up with what Fineman has characterized as the ideal of the autonomous liberal subject and the reality of the inherently vulnerable corporeal subject (2008). Vulnerability is a threat to the autonomous subject; it undermines the idea of autonomy. Thus, fear and vulnerability are tied together as the autonomous subject fears being vulnerable and being exposed to the vulnerability of others. In immigration, that fear can be exercised as a power of exclusion. If an autonomous subject is the ideal, then those who are not perceived as autonomous are likely subjects of the power to exclude.

C. Desire: balancing need and fear through regulation

Ngai has argued that "[i]mmigration policy is constitutive of Americans' understanding of national membership and citizenship, drawing lines of inclusion and exclusion that articulate a desired composition – imagined if not necessarily realized – of the nation" (Ngai, 2004, p. 5). While Ngai was writing with regard to the laws and policies that regulated the racial makeup of the US, her insight also holds for the construction of labor migration regulation. Certain immigrant

6 The use of the public charge exclusion has declined significantly from its peak usage in 2000, as the use of illegal presence and prior removal as grounds of exclusion has grown dramatically (Wasem, 2010, p. 19). The change reflects the rise of interior enforcement and deportation as principal methods of regulatory enforcement.

laborers are desired for inclusion in the American community, while others are not; regulation of this desired composition maximizes the benefit of immigrant labor while minimizing exposure to immigrant vulnerability.

The contemporary approach is, once again, prefigured by earlier regulatory schemes. In the industrial era, as Fairchild (2003) describes:

> [W]hile much of the public and federal discourse and even immigration law favored exclusion, the economy made exclusion impractical. Industry relied on a constant supply of labor to draw on at a moment's notice and then discard when the need for immediate production diminished, and Congress accordingly formulated immigration law "along conservative lines [in order to] avoid measures so drastic as to cripple American industry." . . . Immigrant laborers – more vulnerable than native-born workers to unemployment during the many periods of depression – had to learn that they were expected to remain fit throughout the inevitable spells of unemployment that they would be required to weather.
>
> *(p. 51 (quoting from Congressional Record (1902): 5763–64))*

While exclusion rates during this period were low, those immigrants who exhibited or manifested certain kinds of vulnerability, those perceived likely to become dependent on or charges of public services, were turned away. The tension between need and fear was negotiated through desirability. Some immigrants became desirable – young, healthy – and some became undesirable – the disabled, chronically ill, and elderly. In between these poles existed a spectrum of embodiment that may not have conformed to the ideal of the industrial laborer, but which could be trained into the desirable habits and expectations of industrial labor (Fairchild, 2003, pp. 51–52).

Economic conditions have changed over time, and with those changes the categories of desirable and undesirable immigrants have also changed. The industrial laborer is no longer the paradigmatic immigrant or the paradigmatic laborer. Rather, employment-based immigration is now bifurcated between sectors, with sectors such as education, management, and STEM (science, technology, engineering, and mathematics) falling into the desirable category and sectors such as agriculture, food service, and construction falling into the undesirable category.

The common parlance for this bifurcation is high-skill versus low-skill, but these categories are inaccurate and obfuscate the value determinations implicit in differentiating between these kinds of work. A skill is the ability to do something well, and thus we can speak of highly skilled workers in any field, i.e., those workers who perform well at whatever task they are assigned on the basis of whatever metrics measure success. As Holmes describes, it takes a high level of skill to pick fruit with the speed, efficiency, and care that is required of immigrant farmworkers, and despite "high-skill" training as both a medical doctor and an anthropologist, he was never able to pick the minimum requirement of fruit that was required of the immigrants he worked alongside in the fields of Washington and California (2013, pp.

34, 79). "High-skill" and "low-skill" are misleading and pejorative proxies for the value that is assigned to certain types of work. High-skill work generally requires formal education and is compensated well, while low-skill work requires informal education and is often poorly compensated, despite the essential nature of much "low-skill" work (McGovern, 2012, p. 489). Because these terms define the debate and are written into the law, I will employ them, but in quotes to acknowledge that skill is a misnomer and these categorizations reflect constructions of value.

The regulation of labor migration occurs in two ways: formally through the employment-based visa system and informally through the management of undocumented labor. The employment-based visa system is composed of five preference categories.[7] The vast majority of employment-based visas are reserved for management, technology workers, and other categories that fall into the "high-skill" designation. Of the five preference categories only the E3 visa would admit someone in a "low-skill" occupation through its provision for "other workers," defined as "immigrants who are capable, at the time of petitioning for classification under this paragraph, of performing unskilled labor, not of a temporary or seasonal nature" (8 USC § 1153(b)(3)(A)(iii)). The E3 "other worker" category is capped at 10,000 visas per year compared with ~40,000 per year for E1 and E2, and ~30,000 for the other E3 subcategories.

Insofar as "low-skilled" labor needs are addressed through the formal immigration system, it is principally through what are called non-immigrant visas that permit temporary residence in the US, commonly known as guest worker visas. The most common guest worker visas include the H-1B, H-2A, H-2B, L-1A, and L-1B (Immigration Policy Center [IPC], 2011, pp. 1–2). Even in these temporary employment visa categories, the bifurcation between desirable "high-skill" and undesirable "low-skill" employment is present. The H-1B, L-1A, and L-1B categories correspond to "high-skill" employment, and for each of these categories, the visa holder's employer may sponsor the visa holder for a permanent visa, giving the visa holder status as a legal permanent resident.[8] In contrast, H-2A, for temporary agricultural workers, and H-2B, for seasonal, non-agricultural temporary workers, are not eligible for sponsorship to a permanent visa. In 2013, ~132,000 visas were issued under the H-2A and H-2B categories, while ~153,000 were issued under the H-1B category alone (US Department of State, 2013, table VI).

7 These preferences are defined at 8 USC § 1153(b) and include the following:

- E1 – priority workers, including aliens with extraordinary ability, outstanding professors and researchers, and certain multinational managers or executives;
- E2 – aliens who are members of the professions holding advanced degrees or aliens of exceptional ability in the arts, science or business;
- E3 – skilled workers, professionals, and other workers;
- E4 – certain special immigrants; and
- E5 – employment creation, i.e., immigrant investors/entrepreneurs.

8 The H-1B visa is for highly educated foreign professionals in "specialty occupations" that require at least a bachelor's degree or the equivalent. The L-1A and L-1B categories are for managers, executives, and other positions involving specialized knowledge (IPC, 2011, p. 1).

Of course, formal employment-based immigration only captures a portion of the total immigrant population in the labor force. Passel and Cohn (2015) report that undocumented immigrants make up 5.1% of the total labor force, which represents approximately 8.1 million undocumented immigrants who are either working or looking for work. These workers tend to be employed in "low-skill" occupations. The occupations with the largest share of workers who are undocumented immigrants include farming, fishing, and forestry (26%); building/ground cleaning and maintenance (17%); construction and extracting (14%); and food preparation and serving (11%). Compared to their US-born counterparts, undocumented immigrants are overrepresented in the service industry (33% versus 17%); construction and extraction (15% versus 5%); and farming, fishing, and forestry (4% versus 0.5%). By contrast, the US-born are twice as likely to work in sales, office, and administrative support (26% versus 13%) and nearly three times as likely to work in professional, management, business, and finance (36% versus 13%) (p. 8).

If Ngai is correct that patterns of inclusion and exclusion reveal something about the desired composition of the country, then it is revealing that the formal structure of labor immigration, the employment-based visa system, is weighted heavily in favor of professional, managerial, and technology workers who are significantly more likely to possess higher levels of formal education and to belong to a wealthier economic class in their country of origin. Meanwhile, although there is a significant need for "low-skill" workers, access to migration for such positions is either on a temporary basis or through the informal (undocumented) path. These workers, unlike their counterparts who have access to the employment-based visa system, are generally more likely to have lower levels of formal education, belong to a lower economic class in their country of origin, and take jobs in the US that are likely to pay lower wages. Desirable immigrants look, on the surface, like the ideal of autonomous subjects, while undesirable immigrants are more exposed in their vulnerability. The immigration laws reveal a desire to include those perceived as less vulnerable and exclude those perceived as more vulnerable.

IV. Lessons from a vulnerability analysis of labor and immigration

In an effort to negotiate the need for immigrant labor and the fear of immigrant dependency, labor immigration in the US is structured so that some immigrants have access to formal procedures leading to legal permanent residence and the opportunity to naturalize as citizens, while other immigrants are granted only temporary access or no formal access at all. Importantly, this hierarchy of admissions, these modes of inclusion and exclusion, break along class lines. Better-educated and wealthier immigrants arriving through formal procedures are also those who have access to the full panoply of rights and services associated with membership in the political community. Those less well off who arrive on temporary visas or outside of formal procedures are shut out by law from access to many services such as unemployment benefits, food and housing assistance, and medical insurance subsidies, as well as limited in their access to other services such as police protection, public education, and hospital care by the stigma and fear that come with being undocumented or in an otherwise precarious status.

The vulnerability of undocumented workers and those on temporary work visas is compounded by the nature of the work performed. As Robert McRuer writes:

> We know, then, that "ideal" bodies are desired for undesirable labor and that those bodies cross borders all the time, even as their movements are increasingly policed. We know as well that the work these bodies perform often is quite literally disabling and that subsequent recourse to national support systems is absent.
>
> *(Markotic and McRuer, 2012, p. 168)*

The intense physical labor of occupations with large numbers of undocumented and temporary immigrant workers is often accompanied by increased risks of both accidental injury (Schenker, 2011) and chronic health conditions (Holmes, 2013, pp. 99–103). Holmes describes the general health conditions of immigrant farmworkers in the US, noting that the combination of working conditions, living conditions, and poverty mean "[a]gricultural workers have increased rates of nonfatal injuries, musculoskeletal pain, heart disease, and many types of cancer," as well as increased rates of chronic conditions including "malnutrition, anemia, hypertension, diabetes, dermatitis, fatigue, headaches, sleep disturbances, anxiety, memory problems, sterility, blood disorders, dental problems, and abnormalities in liver and kidney function" (p. 101).

The costs associated with immigrant vulnerability are largely not born by the US. Undocumented and temporary immigrant laborers have little access to social service resources, particularly those resources that are publicly funded. In addition, the ability to utilize what resources are available is often impeded by language barriers and constraints of poverty, such as lack of transportation or the inability to take time off from work. Furthermore, as Holmes notes, the costs associated with reproduction and education, as well as, often, old age and disability are born not by the US but by the immigrant's country of origin because migrants most often arrive in the US as young, healthy adults and frequently return to their country of origin in the event of old age, sickness, or injury (2013, pp. 12–13).

The current structure of employment-based immigration maximizes the benefit of the labor provided even by those who are formally excluded from the country, while minimizing or displacing the costs associated with their vulnerability. In this way, immigrants ameliorate the vulnerability of US citizens: immigrants pick our food, build our houses, and care for our children and parents; meanwhile, the immigrants' own vulnerability goes unaddressed to be born fully by the immigrants themselves or, perhaps, their country of origin.

V. Conclusion

The exercise of immigration authority to effectuate a desired composition for the country fails to acknowledge the web of interdependency that underlies the movement of people across borders. Ports of entry are not the first interaction between the US and immigrants. The relationship between the US and those who cross its borders preexists the act of migration and is reified through the act of migration (Ahn, 2014, chapter 2). As Ngai notes:

> [M]igration is an 'embedded,' 'temporally and spatially bounded' process that crosses these kinds of 'bridges' between sending and receiving nations. It is not, as conventional thinking suggests, a unidirectional phenomenon, in which the hapless poor of the world clamor at the gates of putatively disinterested wealthier nations.
>
> *(2004, pp. 10–11)*[9]

The high level of immigration to the US from Latin America and the Caribbean is not an accident. The annexation of northern Mexico by the Treaty of Guadalupe-Hidalgo, the Western Hemisphere exemption to the immigration restrictions of the 1920s, and the Bracero program all established networks between communities and family members, as well as employers and employees across borders (Ngai, 2004). Actions taken by US industry and the US military in Central America, South America, and the Caribbean throughout the nineteenth and twentieth centuries fostered conditions promoting out-migration from those countries (De La Torre, 2009). Free trade agreements including the North American Free Trade Agreement and the Central American Free Trade Agreement have displaced small farmers throughout Mexico and Central America while maintaining agricultural subsidies in the US that promote agricultural exports and create demand for farmworker labor (Heyer, 2012; Holmes, 2013). How the admission, exclusion, and treatment of immigrants is structured must take account of these relationships.

A vulnerability analysis challenges immigration law to take account of the full context of relationality between the US and the immigrants who come to this country through whatever channel they arrive. First, applying a vulnerability analysis challenges the immigrant worker as commodity. Commodification and expendability are a direct response to two vectors of vulnerability: the economic vulnerability of people living in an economic system that requires a steady supply of cheap labor, which is addressed through the commodification of immigrant labor as another raw material in the production process, and the embodied vulnerability of immigrant laborers, which is outsourced or ignored as immigrant laborers are perceived as expendable. Commodification must be rejected because it denies the human vulnerability of everyone involved. Second, taking both the vulnerability of citizens and the vulnerability of immigrant laborers

9 Quoting Sassen, 2000, pp. 135–37.

seriously means addressing their mutual vulnerabilities. The focus on promotion of "high-skill" immigration while ignoring the importance of immigrant labor in "low-skill" work masks the vulnerabilities and dependencies of the American economy. Taking vulnerability seriously means creating immigration policy that appreciates rather than ignores the full panoply of immigrant labor force participation. Third, the process of admission and exclusion must also appreciate our mutual vulnerability. While there may be a place for temporary worker programs, such programs cannot serve to permanently exclude immigrants from the political community. All temporary worker programs must provide some avenue to permanent residence and naturalization for immigrant laborers who choose to stay in the US over the long term; otherwise, temporary labor programs create a resident underclass who are limited in their capacity to voice grievances and affect change, to address their needs and desires. Likewise, there is simply no justification for excluding any immigrant, regardless of status, from essential social services and labor laws. To benefit from the labor of those who are unprotected by the laws and unable to receive the benefits of the value they produce is the very definition of exploitation. That the US economy, government, and citizenry all benefit from the labor of immigrants in all manner of statuses is an obligation to care for those who labor regardless of status.

11

THE WAGES OF HUMAN TRAFFICKING

Rana M. Jaleel[1]

I. Introduction

President Barack Obama has pledged a "zero tolerance" approach to human trafficking – a crime that, in his words:

> ought to concern every person, because it is a debasement of our common humanity . . . every community, because it tears at our social fabric . . . every business, because it distorts markets [and] . . . every nation, because it endangers public health and fuels violence and organized crime.[2]
>
> This stance is hardly controversial. Pundits and practitioners alike deplore the occurrence of human trafficking. Yet while President Obama's remarks may well reflect a growing national and international consensus, recent and conflicting reinterpretations of the elements of human trafficking have destabilized the definition of the crime and thus its scope and meaning.

The legal definition of human trafficking – which is remarkably consistent across US federal and international law – has been subject to wide-ranging interpretations. Pared to its core elements, human trafficking requires: (1) an act (the movement, recruitment, receipt, or harboring of men, women, or children); (2) a means (by force, fraud, or coercion); and (3) a purpose (at a minimum, involuntary servitude, slavery, or sexual or labor exploitation, which may include the removal of organs). While human trafficking was once viewed as functionally equivalent to criminalized sexual gender violence, recent scholarly and legal efforts

1 Assistant Professor of Women, Sexuality, and Gender Studies at the University of California, Davis. This chapter is excerpted from an article of the same name, first published in the *Brooklyn Law Review*, 81, no. 2 (2016): 1–65.

2 "Remarks by the President to the Clinton Global Initiative," September 25, 2012. https://obama whitehouse.archives.gov/the-press-office/2012/09/25/remarks-president-clinton-global-initiative.

have targeted labor-sector human trafficking, specifically migrant labor exploitation. This nascent focus on labor exploitation, while a step in the right direction, is nonetheless insufficient to address the global problem of human trafficking. Recent changes in how the US State Department interprets the federal anti-trafficking statute, the Trafficking Victims Protection Act of 2000 (TVPA), prove this point.

In 2012, the US State Department's Trafficking in Persons Office (TIP Office) declared that "many forms of enslavement" lie at the heart of the phenomenon of human trafficking – "[h]uman [t]rafficking can include but does not require movement" (p. 29). This eschewal of any movement or recruitment requirement has resulted in the elimination of any distinction between human trafficking and forced labor. This development, as well as the simultaneous equation of human trafficking with slavery, has far-reaching implications for human trafficking's meaning. In essence, these interpretative shifts have pulled the legal conceptualization of human trafficking in two directions. In the first, human trafficking is a *labor problem*, as the elimination of distinctions between trafficked forced labor and non-trafficked forced labor suggests. In the second, it is an *ownership* problem of a different sort: human trafficking is *slavery*.

These developments raise extremely pressing questions: how does the US enforce a "zero tolerance" approach to human trafficking if it has no clear, conceptual understanding of what the act of human trafficking entails? To put a finer point on it, what is human trafficking "more like:" a labor problem or a slavery problem? The stakes of these questions become readily apparent when we recognize the revocation of the movement requirement and the equation of human trafficking with slavery as indicative of an early, emerging split between US and international perspectives on human trafficking. While the US has characterized human trafficking as a problem of slavery, the international community has largely sought to preserve distinctions between the variety of acts encompassed by anti-trafficking instruments, including distinctions between slavery, forced labor, and an array of lesser labor exploitations (Chuang, 2014).

The urgency of the problem of human trafficking together with its doctrinal complexity demands a principled exploration of its limits. This chapter takes up the challenge by asking a seemingly straightforward question: what is the wrong of human trafficking?

In the sixteen years since the advent of contemporary human trafficking law, this question has yet to be addressed by legal scholars. Now it is time to ask the question anew. For while we may intuitively believe that we will "know it when we see it," the continuously transfiguring terrain of human trafficking law has only offered disparate examples of *what* human trafficking might be with no underlying theoretical account of *why* all acts prohibited by extant law are in fact actionable. While there are no fast and easy rules or tests to identify human trafficking, settling our conceptual approach helps ensure a more targeted, steady, and uniform forward course by establishing *what* we understand human trafficking to be, *why* we act against it, and in turn, what it means to be free. Accounting for the wrong of human trafficking is therefore no theoretical indulgence, but an operational imperative.

Accordingly, this chapter does not analyze human trafficking from within the familiar frames of transnational crime, sexualized gender violence, or human rights. Nor does it consider human trafficking to be best described as a problem of slavery or a problem faced largely by migrant workers. Each of these approaches fails to capture the core wrong of human trafficking. In the alternative, this chapter views human trafficking as a labor and employment problem that fits under what I call the new low-wage/vulnerable labor paradigm. In this account, human trafficking is wrong because it exploits worker vulnerability, regardless of migrant status, by forcing, coercing, or deceiving people into performing work (including commercial sex acts) under intolerable, illicit, or degrading conditions. Therefore, human trafficking law should not be understood solely as a corrective to state failure to manage migrant workers, but rather as a lens through which to see the connections between human trafficking and domestic low-wage labor markets. At the heart of human trafficking debates lies a single and often unarticulated question: irrespective of citizenship status, what do states owe their workers, and also, what do workers owe the states that employ them?

I use the term "vulnerable labor" to denote a methodological commitment to Martha Albertson Fineman's (2008) vulnerability theory. This approach departs from liberal legal and political analyses that view the legal subject as autonomous, rights-bearing, and self-sufficient. It instead depicts both human and state/institutional subjects as embodied and embedded – differentially marked by the uneven social, cultural, economic, and material cultural contexts in which they act and exist.

If human trafficking law is typically viewed as a corrective for state failure to confront the global sex trade or humanely manage migrant workers, a vulnerability approach to human trafficking law provides a necessary alternative perspective. Vulnerability theory, simply put, allows us to examine not only the individual subject, but also the web of relationships that form it. In the context of global human trafficking, a vulnerability approach foregrounds the relationships between workers and states, as well as the geopolitical relationships between states themselves – relationships that are structured and sustained in part through transnational criminal anti human trafficking legal instruments. Vulnerability theory is a lens through which to see the connections between human trafficking, typically understood as a global problem, and low-wage labor markets, generally understood as domestic ones.

Vulnerability theory provides a new window into current human trafficking debates that offer the separate, but overlapping paradigms of slavery and labor migration as palliatives to dominant criminal gender violence approaches. These debates are conceptually caught between construing the wrong of human trafficking as a violation of equality (with a slavery paradigm positing a discriminatory dimension to a problem of ownership) or as a violation of labor rights (understood in the classic sense as collective rights that govern structural relationships between employers and employees and not solely as the provisioning of equal treatment for exploited migrant laborers). That view, what I call the *labor migration paradigm*, focuses on affording migrant workers the same protections as non-migrant workers in order to end exploitative working conditions. Recent empirical research, however, has thrown the general conditions of the US low-wage labor market, and the efficacy of existing labor and employment protections, into question.

While a labor migration paradigm helpfully emphasizes how *cumulative* labor conditions characterized by subtly coercive and deceptive employment practices can also cross the threshold into human trafficking (International Labour Organization, 2009; Shamir, 2012), it cabins the full import of that claim by limiting its analysis to migrant workers and often identifying "sectors prone to human trafficking" – from agriculture, home health care, service, begging, domestic work, and manufacturing, to name a few (United Nations Office on Drugs and Crime, 2009) – as the target of their interventions. In contrast, the new low-wage/vulnerable labor paradigm's more general emphasis on *the conditions of low-wage and vulnerable work* prevents a too-narrow focus on job sectors or categories, whose susceptibility to human trafficking may change over time.

In this way, the new low-wage/vulnerable labor paradigm prevents us from ignoring how contemporary conditions of low-wage work – including unenforced or under-enforced employment law – not only *enable* human trafficking, but *continue to exploit* those who survive their trafficking only to enter an, at times, equally exploitative low-wage labor market. Cambodian workers who are "rescued" from sex work only to enter into the infamously perilous garment industry are emblematic of this tension (Moore, 2015).

Therefore, the new low-wage/vulnerable labor paradigm does not foreground movement/recruitment as the heart of the offense and would caution against axiomatic separations between, for example, trafficked forced labor and forced labor. That hard distinction rests on the fallacy that non-trafficked forced laborers inevitably have more control or agency than non-trafficked workers – an assumption that empirical research and on-the-ground observation have since undermined. Anchoring the wrong of human trafficking in a low-wage/vulnerable labor paradigm thus mitigates the too-narrow focus on migrant labor, while also correcting for the overwhelming emphasis on sex sector human trafficking that still dominates legal efforts to quell the crime.[3]

The new low-wage/vulnerable labor paradigm also does not understand all human trafficking as crimes of enslavement. The wrong of human trafficking lies less in its proximate relationship to slavery than it does in the systemic problems that inhere in low-wage labor. Therefore, and perhaps most importantly, understanding the wrong of human trafficking as a low-wage/vulnerable labor one will help ward off the conceptual collapse of human trafficking and slavery by fostering principled discussion over where we now want to draw the line between exploitation of all stripes and what constitutes the impermissible ownership of persons as a *jus cogen* norm and a crime of universal jurisdiction.

Finally, in advocating a low-wage/vulnerable labor approach to human trafficking, I do not mean to suggest that all low-wage labor abuses should be found to constitute human trafficking, or that human trafficking law alone should be

3 Despite an increased interest in labor, prosecutions worldwide remain fixated on sex sector human trafficking. The US 2014 Trafficking in Persons Report reports that in 2013, the 44,758 trafficked persons identified worldwide resulted in only 7909 prosecutions and 3969 convictions. Only 478 of these were related to labor trafficking while the rest were related to sex trafficking (p. 45).

responsible for remedying widespread domestic workplace violations. Rather, I seek to establish a conceptual framework for human trafficking that locates the problems of domestic low-wage labor markets at its very core. Acknowledging the continuities and overlap between human trafficking and domestic low-wage labor violations is not only necessary for a clear conceptual understanding of the wrong of human trafficking, but is also *intentionally and doctrinally supported* by the expansive definition and remedies offered by our anti human trafficking federal statutes and international legal instruments.

For example, the UN Trafficking Protocol, the TVPA, and other anti-trafficking legal instruments provide remedies for trafficked persons beyond those offered by employment law. These include, for example, the TVPA's "T-visa," which enables some trafficked persons to remain in the country. The TVPA also allows trafficked persons to enforce payment of wages that exceed the federal minimum wage, which the Fair Labor Standards Act (FLSA) does not provide. Additionally, the FLSA does not cover all workers. Most relevant to this discussion, perhaps, the FLSA does not cover forced prostitution. For these reasons, a human trafficking legal framework has the potential to bridge migrant and non-migrant worker exploitation and provoke a broader discussion about labor, immigration, and general low-wage and vulnerable labor exploitation in the US and around the world. The human trafficking legal framework also has the potential, as Kathleen Kim and Kusia Hreshchyshyn (2004) as well as Theodore R. Sangalis (2011) have noted, to consider these questions through civil as well as criminal frameworks.

For these reasons, understanding the wrong of human trafficking as a low-wage/vulnerable labor one best describes anti-trafficking law's broad scope, while preserving the integrity of related legal concepts. This approach allows us to see human trafficking for what it is: a problem of how we value workers and how we recognize, categorize, and manage work and vulnerability.

II. The parameters of human trafficking law

Contemporary human trafficking law begins at the turn of the millennium with the passage of two legal instruments: the UN Protocol to Prevent, Punish, and Suppress Trafficking in Persons, Especially Women and Children (2000), and the US TVPA (2000). The UN Trafficking Protocol has since, and with notable consistency, served as the template for all subsequent anti human trafficking law. In the intervening years, as Anne T. Gallagher (2009) has noted, this law has mushroomed into an international legal system comprising regional treaties, a range of policy instruments, and a canon of state practice. According to the United Nations Office on Drugs and Crime's 2014 *Global Report on Trafficking in Persons,* the UN Human Trafficking Protocol has been ratified by 162 countries, and is nothing short of a "success story."

The UN Trafficking Protocol and the TVPA detailed new definitions of human trafficking that ushered the issue to international prominence by virtue of their capaciousness and their calculated association with transnational organized crime. From the start, the definition of human trafficking has hardly been exact. For the sake of consensus, the elements of the emerging crime of human trafficking were left intentionally vague. The elements of the means component (force, fraud, and coercion) are not defined under international law. Under the UN Trafficking Protocol and the TVPA, the question of what degree of coercion or abuse of power satisfies this definitional prong remains an open one (Kim, 2009). These instruments also codify a distinction between sexual exploitation and labor exploitation. This framework has contributed to the gendered, hyper-sexual focus of much human trafficking law, policy, and discourse, despite that fact that no reputable research has ever demonstrated that women are more vulnerable to human trafficking, sex sector or otherwise, than men (Agustín, 2007; Chang and Kim, 2007; Dottridge. 2007; Tien, 2013).

Moreover, the UN Trafficking Protocol and the TVPA each neglect to define the new term "exploitation" in a targeted way, and subsequent case law and legislation provide little guidance. In fact, the ILO Global Report (2009) notes that "for the legal concept of exploitation, which underpins the definition of [human] trafficking . . . there is almost no precedent in international law, nor is there much national legislation" (p. 6). These omissions foster uncertainty as to the conditions under which exploitation amounts to human trafficking. As a result, both the UN Human Trafficking Protocol and the TVPA as written are amenable to vast interpretative shifts, requiring a continual recalibration of both focus and scope. The adjustments, which affect the legal recognition of human trafficking, also implicate a broader geopolitical landscape, given the specific enforcement mechanisms authorized by the TVPA.

While the TVPA and the UN Trafficking Protocol are compatible by letter of the law, the US influence and ability to set the legal and policy terms of the global anti-trafficking debate are, as Janie Chuang (2006) and others have observed, difficult to overstate. The TVPA is infamous for the reach of its unilateral global sanctions regime. The TVPA's congressional sponsors believed that the eradication of human trafficking into the US depended upon *other* countries' behavior – namely their explicit cooperation with US anti-trafficking efforts. The resulting, codified unilateral sanctions regime empowers the US government to deny non-humanitarian, non-trade-related foreign assistance to any government perceived as non-compliant with US defined anti-trafficking "minimum standards." In applying the US minimum standards, the State Department considers and classifies countries as either origin, transit, or destination countries, issuing an annual *Trafficking in Persons Report* (TIP Report) that details the state of human trafficking in countries across the world. Notably, the US did not assess its own human trafficking issues and include them in the TIP Report until 2012.

It is against this backdrop that efforts to move human trafficking beyond the criminal prostitution reform debates that characterized its infancy occur – a backdrop where countries' prior classifications as origin, transit, or destination countries linger, even as new, expansive, non-sex sector, labor inclusive interpretations of human trafficking are deployed – even as the operational parameters of what constitutes human trafficking shift. This landscape has complicated the recognition of lesser labor offenses that may constitute human trafficking while keeping legal efforts too tightly focused on migrant labor.

III. The labor migration paradigm of human trafficking

A. The rise of a labor approach to human trafficking

Recent US and international human trafficking law and policy have quietly steered anti human trafficking efforts beyond prostitution reform debates. The George W. Bush Administration viewed prostitution, voluntary or otherwise, as a correlate if not a cause of human trafficking, asserting that "where prostitution has been legalized or tolerated, there is an increase in the demand for sex slaves" (US Department of State, 2004). By 2010, however, the Obama Administration effectively reversed the Bush Administration's equation of voluntary prostitution with sex slavery and human trafficking. As the US State Department's 2010 TIP Report states, "[p]rostitution by willing adults is not human trafficking regardless of whether it is legalized, decriminalized, or criminalized" (p. 8).

Meanwhile, on other fronts, the International Labor Organization (ILO) has attempted to exert new authority within human trafficking law through its close association with forced labor, a bailiwick of the ILO. In recognition of the prevalence of human trafficking and other "modern forms of slavery," in 2014, the ILO adopted a new and legally binding Protocol to ILO Convention No. 29, the 1930 Forced Labor Convention.

The ILO's interest human trafficking as a form of forced labor serves as a corrective to its notable absence in the discussions that culminated in the drafting and adoption of the UN Trafficking Protocol (International Labour Organization, 2001), while simultaneously changing the tenor of the legal debates over what human trafficking essentially *is*. The entrance of the ILO into these deliberations moves the wrong of human trafficking towards a labor paradigm. A rebuke to the Bush Administration's interpretive lens of gendered morality, a labor paradigm for human trafficking promotes collective action and collective bargaining, protective employment legislation, and context specific standard setting in sectors vulnerable to human trafficking (Shamir, 2012). However, the current labor paradigm has been built on the legal architecture of extant human trafficking law to troubling effect. As a transnational criminal issue, human trafficking law has collapsed distinctions between consensual economic migration and the act of movement – an act once thought necessary to support a charge of human trafficking. While the Obama Administration and the ILO thus recognize a labor wrong (among others) at the heart of human trafficking, they adopt a specific species of labor as the object of their best efforts: migrant labor.

B. Construing labor as migrant labor

The turn to migrant labor as the object of human trafficking law is also reflected in an emerging consensus among both labor and human trafficking legal scholars, who contend that a labor paradigm attuned to the vulnerabilities of migrant labor best recognizes and addresses the harms of human trafficking (Bravo, 2009;

Gallagher, 2013; Shamir, 2012). This paradigm casts human trafficking as largely the lot of the poor and the foreign who find themselves funneled into commercial sex work, construction, food service, home health care, agricultural work, or other forms of low-wage, poorly regulated labor with little recourse to the labor and employment protections enjoyed by native born or citizen workers.

To stem the tide of human trafficking, some human trafficking and labor scholars advocate a general, broad-based strengthening of the complex of laws (labor, criminal, and private) that affect structural relationships between employers and employees (Keren-Paz, 2013; Shamir, 2012). Others, like James Gray Pope (2010b) and Karen Bravo (2009), suggest that the prohibition against "modern slavery," typically understood as extreme, often collectivized migrant labor abuse, should incorporate support for "selected labor rights" that would afford migrant workers the same protections provided to citizen workers, including the right to change employers, the right to bargain collectively, and the right to freedom of association, among others.

Yet how recent interpretative changes in the conceptual meaning of human trafficking affect the operational parameters of human trafficking law is not assessed or explained in these works. Where human trafficking begins and lesser exploitation ends remains, in the words of Janie Chuang (2010, pp. 1656–1657) "hotly contested" – especially with the absence of any movement requirement and the simultaneous reordering of all human trafficking as slavery. Setting the wrong of human trafficking as a low-wage/vulnerable labor one helps shift the parameters of human trafficking debates towards the free approach advanced by these scholars while integrating the labor conditions of native/citizen workers more firmly into analyses of exploitation – what it is and how it operates.

As discussed, the act of movement or recruitment was at the onset considered uniquely critical in isolating and recognizing a specific population thought to be particularly susceptible to exploitation: namely *migrants* or internally displaced persons. From the first, anti human trafficking laws targeted the harms and vulnerabilities associated with migration, aiming to protect the least protected persons for whom migrants served as the model: those people without or unable to access home state protections, people in flux. Debates about the movement requirement remained debates about how to best protect, first and foremost, if not exclusively, this at-risk population. As the ILO explained its early adherence to the movement requirement, trafficked forced laborers are "probably worse off" than non-trafficked victims, who were thought to exercise greater degrees of agency and control over work conditions (quoted in Andrees and van der Linden, 2005, p. 64).

Recognizing how labor paradigm advocates have focused on migrant labor – for legal, strategic, and ideological reasons – illuminates how this position has not kept pace with transformations in how we interpret the elements necessary for a criminal or even civil charge of human trafficking. Other scholars have understood these developments as an "unmaking" of human trafficking law – as the destruction of the legal integrity of the crime of human trafficking (Chuang, 2014; Gallagher, 2013). Instead, these shifts indicate the tension at the heart of the definition of human trafficking, inscribed within the codified split between labor and sexual exploitation, between economic and equality (non-discrimination) interests, whose meanings are themselves susceptible to the paradigms adopted for their interpretation.

In this way, a labor migration paradigm – while undoubtedly promoting the collective rights of workers – nevertheless carries within it an embedded equality argument rooted in group identity; it understands the rights of migrant workers as uniquely diminished within the global market. Migrant workers are not treated as equals to citizen workers, who are understood as largely protected by domestic law and enjoying access to shared sociocultural resources. This dichotomized view of labor exploitation – whether freely entered into by the worker or not – casts migrant worker treatment as an affront to a liberal notion of freedom premised on equality, while the low-wage/vulnerable work conditions that engender their exploitation remain beyond legal attention.

The labor migration paradigm has, however, resulted in several significant improvements in how we address human trafficking. Understanding the wrong of human trafficking as a labor wrong that predominantly befalls migrant workers allows us to see several significant harms that criminal, human rights, and assorted gender paradigms obscure. By framing human trafficking as a migrant labor issue, the labor migration paradigm foregrounds the movement of workers of all genders and persuasions across borders or to otherwise non-native locales. Doing so reveals the vulnerabilities and interdependencies that inhere to the human condition – particularly human *working* conditions – while retaining a focus on the unique vulnerabilities of those who work beyond the borders of their homelands or place of origin. A labor migration paradigm thus offers a particular portrait of the inner workings of power – one where the struggle lies in perfecting the balance of power in citizen and non-citizen labor arrangements, in sectors thought to be susceptible to human trafficking.

Unqualified comparison between *all* migrant work and *all* work performed by a state's citizenry, however, may not be the best metric for producing sound law or policy. Differences across work sectors, industries, and job categories may complicate categorical claims that migrant workers are necessarily more exploited than other workers, particularly when the legal threshold for exploitation includes not only forced, but also psychologically coerced labor, as well as deceptive or fraudulent recruitment practices that may cumulatively rise to the level of actionable exploitation. Is the wrong of human trafficking, then, best described through an unremitting, if not legally prescribed, focus on migrant labor? What harms would be made visible if states understood migrant labor in ways that also assessed the conditions of low-wage work more broadly, without recourse to worker citizenship status as an unacknowledged template for the violation? In other words, how would we understand the wrong of human trafficking if we reframed human trafficking debates as issues of domestic low-wage/vulnerable work and employment conditions?

Before turning to an exploration of the new low-wage/vulnerable labor paradigm, it is worth noting how the increasing willingness to recognize and address non-sex sector labor exploitation as legally actionable human trafficking has been accompanied by a tendency to deemphasize any movement requirement and instead spotlight exploitation as its core harm. Theoretically, this should push against the notion that anti human trafficking efforts should focus almost exclusively on migrant exploitation. Yet the assumption that trafficked labor is largely, if not exclusively, migrant labor lingers within legal descriptions of human trafficking, even though the scope of anti human trafficking law is less than ever limited to migrants. In other words, the abuse that constitutes actionable exploitation has been legally sundered from its foundational motivation: the susceptibility of migrant workers to various forms of organized exploitation perpetrated by international criminal syndicates.

What persists, however, are the old ties of movement, migrancy, and criminality. To illustrate this claim, the following sections describe the impact of eliminating the movement requirement on legal interpretations of human trafficking law. These sections also explore how the transnational criminal paradigm has *conflated migrancy and movement with the harm of trafficking* in ways that keep extant labor critiques from looking beyond severe (migrant) exploitation and towards lesser exploitations also prohibited by law that impact migrant and non-migrant workers alike. Part of the exclusion of lesser labor exploitation from analyses of human trafficking turns on the equivalence of movement with migrancy and vulnerability, and simultaneously, citizenship with protection, access, and freedom.

IV. Fusing movement and migration

The focus on migrant labor has occurred even as the TIP Office has eliminated the movement requirement, demonstrating that the kind of isolation and lack of access to resources or remedies that characterizes human trafficking is not solely achieved by being physically moved, either across a border or within a state. A fusion of movement and migration as equivalent bad acts that befall human trafficking victims has resulted in case law that has been unable to capture the less severe forms of labor exploitation otherwise included in anti-trafficking law. Indeed, an understanding of movement as a prerequisite for a charge of human trafficking relies on an inaccurate perspective of the conditions of both migrancy *and* low-wage work.

A. The elimination of the movement requirement and the meaning of exploitation

The TIP Office's disavowal of any movement requirement is noteworthy because it is an explicit step towards integrating a labor perspective within the US legal approach to human trafficking. To satisfy the act element in the absence of a movement requirement, the TIP Office has adopted expansive interpretations of the enumerated act elements, including "harboring," "receipt," and "obtaining" (Chuang, 2014). The Obama Administration understands any of these acts alone as sufficient to support a charge of human trafficking – no movement or recruitment by a third party is required. In this way, prior distinctions between trafficked and non-trafficked forced labor have conceptually crumbled, allowing the Obama Administration to subsume all forced labor within the ambit of human trafficking.

Moreover, in the absence of a movement requirement, the exploitation element takes on new significance in ways that transform the relationship between the three elements (act, means, purpose) of the crime. With "exploitation" an element, early interpretations of the TVPA and the UN Human Trafficking Protocol were not understood to contain an explicit mandate to end human sexual or labor exploitation. They were categorized instead, as James C. Hathaway (2008) has observed, as "process orient[ed]" proscriptions (p. 10). These instruments were construed as singling out certain acts that engender exploitation for legal action, but not others. In other words, they were initially interpreted to only prohibit specific forms of *dealing* – the "recruitment, transportation, transfer, harboring or receipt of persons" per the UN Trafficking Protocol, and the "the recruitment, harboring, transportation, provision, or obtaining of a person" per the TVPA – by which people are exploited through force, fraud, or coercion.

Now that exploitation and not movement, however, has become central to the TIP Office's interpretation of human trafficking, the relationship between the act and purpose elements of human trafficking has changed. With the *act of movement* that once underpinned the meaning of "recruitment, harboring, transportation, provision, or obtaining of a person" removed, *exploitation itself* takes center stage. This has already changed the face of human trafficking case law and prosecutorial practice. In New York City, for instance, where state laws are not interpreted to require movement, the City Bar Justice Center (2014) reports that employers who exploit migrant workers who have already been in the country for some time are now routinely prosecuted – a fact pattern that was not always thought to indicate human trafficking.

As a result of the abandonment of the movement requirement, anti human trafficking instruments no longer function as strict process-oriented proscriptions. Instead, they now fall in line with anti human trafficking campaigns that aim to "end modern slavery." This, then, is the point where the TIP Office's move to classify (1) all forced labor as human trafficking, and (2) to view all human trafficking as slavery, with all its populist abolitionary appeal, converge: in an effort to move from much critiqued "process oriented proscriptions" to wholesale attempts to end exploitation.

A closer analysis of the relevance of movement to the recognition of human trafficking is illustrative in this regard. How human trafficking law has understood migration in relation to the movement requirement has led to problems in how the law identifies acts of human trafficking for both migrant and non-migrant workers. This in turn affects how the meaning and significance of migration, and therefore movement, shift with the paradigms applied to interpret human trafficking law – even if these shifts in meaning have been largely unacknowledged.

B. A critique of the movement requirement

1. Mistaking migration as the harm

The wisdom of requiring movement – not to mention what sort of movement counts, transborder or intra-state, and when the movement had to occur in order to count – has long been a site of debate. Paradigmatic shifts in the legal approach to human trafficking have driven, among other things, the debates over the significance of the movement to human trafficking. The debates over movement are in essence debates about what causes the underlying conditions that create and foster exploitation, and what those underlying conditions actually are. The early transnational criminal understanding of human trafficking has led to the notion that migration is in and of itself a harmful act, in ways that have inhibited the law's ability to recognize the full range of acts prohibited by our primary anti human trafficking instruments.

In the view of the early, transnational criminal paradigm, migration and victimhood are deeply entwined. The UN Human Trafficking Protocol and the TVPA conceive of human trafficking as a critical security issue deeply tied to transnational organized crime syndicates that facilitate clandestine, often illicit, migration and primarily target women and children. For US courts, trafficked persons' vulnerability was tied to their assumed status as unwitting victims far from home (Chuang, 2010).

Definitional ambiguities in the UN Trafficking Protocol fostered early, first stage debates on whether the crime of human trafficking necessitated transborder movement, either across state borders or within a single state. Indeed, equivocation over the meaning of movement/recruitment is tied to the conceptualization of the wrong. While authors and advocates of the UN Trafficking Protocol initially understood the movement requirement as essential to any *transnational criminal* legal definition of human trafficking (Chuang, 2014), others questioned the effectiveness of this approach. The issue of whether or not the UN Human Trafficking Protocol named the *internal* recruitment, transportation, transfer, harboring, or receipt of persons within a single state as actionable human trafficking fueled accusations that the human trafficking legal regime "while billed as key to the modern fight against slavery, has actually promoted a very partial perspective on the problem of modern slavery" (Hathaway, 2008, p. 4).

Assurances and clarifications in the legal meaning of human trafficking shortly followed. Intra-state movement debates were ultimately quelled by subsequent regional and state laws that explicitly included intra-state movement within the auspices of human trafficking. Yet the issue of the relationship between movement and human trafficking is not put to rest, even with the express inclusion of intra-state movement as an act that can trigger human trafficking law. This enduring tension is attributable to the worry that migration, often uncritically equated with *forced movement* – and not the labor structures and employment conditions into which migrants relocate – is itself the core harm and wrong of human trafficking.

Early debates on the scope of human trafficking law and the meaning of human trafficking demonstrate this slippage between migration, movement, and the core harm of human trafficking.

For instance, on January 29, 1998, a roundtable on "The Meaning of 'Trafficking in Persons': A Human Rights Perspective" was held in Washington, DC by the International Human Rights Law Group. Convened by the Women's Rights Advocacy Program (WRAP) of the International Human Rights Law Group with the assistance of the Harvard Law School Human Rights Program, participants included human rights activists, scholars, and professionals actively working to end the human rights abuses of human trafficking, while simultaneously seeking to define what precisely "human trafficking" could be (Miller and Stewart, 1998). All present roundly rejected any "crossing the border" requirement, be it international, national, state, or intra-state, noting that "the harm to victims can be the same whether they are moved two miles across a national border or 1,000 miles within national boundaries" (Miller and Steward, 1998, p. 14). For those present, certain "factors" associated with border crossing – not an actual border crossing – lay at the heart of human trafficking. These factors include: "movement to a foreign or unfamiliar milieu; victims having illegal or non-national status; language, cultural or other barriers; and separation from family and community" (Miller and Steward, 1998). Nonetheless, roundtable participants deemed it "unfitting and inappropriate that a change in status or conditions without any physical transport, movement or travel should qualify as [human] trafficking" (Miller and Steward, 1998, p. 15).

The rationales for this declaration are not elaborated in the record. What this assertion and omission indicates is the degree to which migration itself is viewed as a harmful act. Here, movement or *migration* becomes an act instigated (or enabled) by a wrongdoer that is both evidence of wrongdoing and in itself a kind of harm – this is the direct result of approaching human trafficking through a transnational criminal frame.

This slippage between the movement requirement, migration, and harm are made even more visible in early efforts to distinguish human trafficking from human smuggling. Human smuggling entails "the procurement, in order to obtain, directly or indirectly, a financial or other material benefit, of the illegal entry of a person into a State Party of which the person is not a national or a permanent resident" (UN Protocol against the Smuggling of Migrants by Land, Sea and Air, 2000). While the definition of human trafficking turns on the existence of forceful, coercive, or fraudulent dealings leading to sexual or labor exploitation, human smuggling has been historically understood as "a consensual and relatively benign market-based response to the existence of laws that seek artificially to constrain the marriage of surplus labor supply on one side of a border with unmet demand for certain forms of labor on the other side of that border" (Hathaway, 2008, p. 5). The transnational criminalization of human trafficking, however, revivified and entrenched aggressive state border securitization and policing strategies, resulting in the attendant criminalization of human smuggling, facilitating the passage of the UN Protocol Against Human Smuggling (2000). The UN Trafficking Protocol and its parent convention on Organized Crime sought to facilitate inter-state cooperation to stamp out human trafficking, intercept traffickers, and control borders through standardized practices that include information exchange, mutual legal assistance, and repatriation procedures.

By ignoring the market dynamics that put workers' bodies in migratory motion, and framing those efforts to work and survive as illicit criminal enterprise, the transnational criminalization of human smuggling is in essence, as James C. Hathaway (2008) observes, the transnational criminalization of a market responsive *labor practice.* Economic migration and the act of movement necessary for a charge of human trafficking thus became conceptually fused and, as such, became the subjects or targets of anti human trafficking law. As a result, subsequent paradigmatic attempts to correct for the excesses of the transnational criminal paradigm retain a heavy, if not exclusive, focus on migrant labor.

This emphasis, in turn, all but removes the non-migrant workers whose conditions of work might trigger a charge of human trafficking from legal attention and analysis. The weighty charge of transnational criminality also maintains a focus on more extreme forms of exploitation, keeping lesser exploitations prohibited by anti human trafficking law beyond legal purview. These tendencies are exemplified by the current labor analysis of human trafficking – the labor migration paradigm.

2. *Rethinking the relationship between movement, migration, and harm*

When migration is recognized as value neutral, as potentially chosen and compelled by a *desire to find work*, even "bad" work, the legal significance of movement changes. Movement becomes a cipher for a social or structural lack of access to resources or options instead of something imposed or instigated by bad actors on unwitting victims. Movement becomes a proxy, in other words, for isolation or an inability to access resources, not simply forced migration. Indeed, when confronted with the choice to seek protection as victims of human trafficking or portray themselves as workers fighting for their rights, RESPECT, a network of European migrant domestic workers, rejected the human trafficking framework, which they felt compromised their efforts to overcome "the feeling of powerlessness among the migrants" and failed to promote "the regularization of undocumented migrants as workers" (Schwenken, 2005, p. 11). In understanding irregular or illegal labor migration as integral to the global economy, RESPECT further alleged that the mainstream legal fight against human trafficking "delegitimize[s] and even destroy[s] safer mechanisms of irregular migration" (Schwenken, 2005).

If the differing relationships between migration, movement, and vulnerability seem subtle, they are nonetheless significant in legal diagnoses of human trafficking. As the members of RESPECT attest, vulnerability does not stem from migration, even irregular migration, but instead emerges from within the larger labor and immigration structures in which it occurs, if not the strictures of human trafficking law itself, when it is interpreted as a process-oriented proscription that focuses legal attention on some kinds of exploitation, but not others. In other words, it is the failure to enact and enforce basic labor protections and employment laws that create vulnerability and isolation, not the act of migration or movement.

Thinking through what differentiates trafficked forced labor from forced labor evinces this point. Are trafficked forced laborers inevitably "worse off," as the ILO once suggested, than non-trafficked forced laborers (Andrees and van der Linden, 2005, p. 64)? Perhaps not, or not always.

First, there is a temporal issue with the way that trafficked and non-trafficked forced labor has been differentiated. It is fairly noncontroversial that a migrant worker who is smuggled across a border or recruited by an agency or other intermediary into a textbook forced labor situation, where the worker's wages are withheld and the worker is compelled to labor under threat of violence, would be considered a victim of human trafficking. Indeed, second only to sex sector human trafficking, this is, for US courts in particular, the classic human trafficking scenario. If, however, a migrant worker is recruited by an agency, works for a period of months without incident, changes employers, and is then subject to the same sort of exploitation, should this count as human trafficking? Is the worker's migrant status the source of vulnerability? Or is it the working conditions that are at issue?

This scenario is far from a mere hypothetical. As mentioned earlier, in New York City, where state laws expressly disavow movement as a requirement for human trafficking, the New York City Bar Justice Center's (2014) Immigrant Women and Children Project reports that such is the case with many of their clients. This example demonstrates how, with the abandonment of the movement requirement, legal interpretations of anti human trafficking law are coming closer to understanding the wrong of human trafficking as a labor and employment wrong that that may befall migrant or non-migrant workers – even if this is currently unacknowledged and underexplored. When nothing in either the UN Trafficking Protocol or the TVPA limit their application to migrant workers, what but an unexamined fusion between migrancy and vulnerability – one that crowds out a robust examination of non-migrant worker vulnerability – can account for the current legal conceptual approach to human trafficking, which treats labor exploitation as almost exclusively a migrant labor problem (Andrees and van der Linden, 2005)?

As the next section details, however, the new low-wage/vulnerable labor paradigm begins a conversation to remedy these issues. In recognizing human trafficking's wrong as a low-wage/vulnerable labor one, the intuitive meaning of the movement requirement is preserved – namely, the vulnerability of living dislocated from institutional or social redress. Instead of rigorously inhering in the act of movement, however, isolation might also be achieved through the accumulation of poor working conditions and lack of meaningful avenues of redress, which, as the US context shows, affects migrant and non-migrant workers alike, albeit to varying degrees.

This is not to suggest that "forced labor [should] be equated simply with low wages or poor working conditions . . . [or] situations of pure economic necessity, as when a worker feels unable to leave a job because of the real or perceived absence of employment alternatives" (ILO, 2009, p. 5). Rather, the new low-wage/vulnerable labor paradigm is a first step towards recognizing the unacknowledged breadth of our contemporary anti-trafficking instruments. Crucially, the new paradigm is no lofty theoretical imposition, but rather is an analytic synthesis of new legal interpretations of the elements of human trafficking and social scientific research. Both advocate for more frequent and sustained legal attention to labor exploitation and working conditions in the context of human trafficking. For these reasons, the new low-wage/vulnerable labor paradigm best describes the core wrong of human trafficking.

V. A thin line: human trafficking and the new low-wage/vulnerable labor paradigm

The preceding sections provide two new, fundamental insights about the current legal approach to human trafficking: (1) dominant paradigms fail to capture the full range of acts prohibited by human trafficking's primary legal instruments; and (2) even the emerging labor approach, which does a better job of describing the wrong of human trafficking than the criminal law, gender violence, or human rights paradigms, hamstrings the full potential of human trafficking law through the unacknowledged use of migrant labor as a template for understanding human trafficking. The new low-wage/vulnerable labor paradigm not only addresses the shortcomings of prior efforts to interpret human trafficking law, but is also consistent with attempts to construe human trafficking law as mandating the end of exploitation.

A. *Human trafficking as a low-wage/vulnerable labor problem*

The low-wage/vulnerable labor paradigm proposes that the wrong of human trafficking may lie in the nature of low-wage work itself, depending on how we as a society choose to configure the relationship between equality, labor, and freedom. In this spirit, I use the word "vulnerable" in an inclusionary way. "Vulnerable" can both describe precarious low-wage labor and encompass acts that are not paid a wage or recognized as work, including prostitution or other commercial sex acts. Recourse to vulnerability theory also emphasizes how a worker's susceptibility to exploitation is both context specific and inherent in the human condition. As new sociological scholarship reveals, "[w]orkplace violations are not limited to immigrant workers or other vulnerable groups in the labor force – everyone is at risk, although to different degrees" (Bernhardt et al. 2009, p. 5). With this understanding, I reference vulnerability, following Martha Albertson Fineman (2008), as a methodological commitment to analyzing structural and institutional distributions of advantage and disadvantage that exceed a discrimination-based model's narrow focus on individual identity. In the present case, vulnerability theory compels an analysis of human trafficking that looks beyond legal status designations such as citizenship to interrogate the broader institutional and social arrangements that put people at risk.

Vulnerability theory complements recent labor law scholarship that aims to make the law responsive and reflective of the changing nature of work in a globalized economy. This scholarship reconceptualizes the foundations of labor law by basing the extension of social protections on labor-force membership status – not the employment relationship. Alain Supiot (2001) takes this position, locating labor-force membership status in work, which differs from activity because work "results from an obligation, whether voluntarily undertaken or compulsorily imposed" (p. 54). Foregrounding the wrong of human trafficking in this way captures the full range of offenses proscribed by human trafficking law, from labor performed pursuant to enslavement to deceptive or coercive exploitation. It does so by understanding that the wrong that binds this range of exploitative practices is a collective wrong that inheres in the inner workings of global labor markets and manifests in employment conditions.

To flesh out these potentials, the following section contrasts a recent report describing low-wage work conditions in the US with a 2009 ILO Global Report authored in conjunction with the EU. The ILO report focuses on how to recognize less extreme versions of human trafficking, listing combinations of acts or violations that alone would not suggest its occurrence, but that together, offer a vision of human trafficking as a cumulative accretion of workplace violations. Here, the trafficked person at issue belies the iconic image of the shackled sex slave or other worker trapped and forced to labor in slave-like conditions. Instead, the trafficked person more closely resembles someone trapped in the low-wage labor market.

Read in tandem, these two reports demonstrate the need for a thorough reconceptualization of the wrong of human trafficking as a baseline for developing targeted and effective action against it. This can be accomplished by recognizing how latent equality arguments are embedded within a labor migration paradigm in ways that draw a false distinction between trafficked migrant labor and other low-wage and vulnerable work. This division, while preserving the legal integrity of a vision of human trafficking defined by force, violence, and slavery, may in fact generate anti-trafficking efforts that fail to address "less extreme," but equally proscribed forms of human trafficking – or worse, actively contribute to their flourishing.

B. Cumulative labor violations as human trafficking

In "A Labor Paradigm for Human Trafficking," Hila Shamir (2012) writes that the majority of scholars and activists agree that a certain "seriousness" threshold must be reached before a detrimental employment practice may be deemed human trafficking. And yet the threshold requirements are anything but clear: "uncertainty remains as to what exactly constitutes [human] trafficking" (p. 86). Anne

T. Gallagher (2009), a preeminent human trafficking scholar and activist (and one of the drafters of the UN Trafficking Protocol), concurs, noting that beyond this seriousness threshold, "the lines [delineating human trafficking] remain blurred" (p. 791). The ambiguity surrounding what constitutes exploitation as well as the porousness of the means element of the definition have contributed to the definitional imprecisions of human trafficking.

Nevertheless, Shamir and others understand the means elements to have accrued certain content by experience and application in international and national contexts. In other words, the meaning of human trafficking has been determined by practice and experience – not necessarily through recourse to the plain language of the UN Trafficking Protocol or in accordance with its drafters' intention. Accordingly, physical coercion is decidedly *not* a threshold requirement for a practice to constitute human trafficking – other, less robust forms of intimidation have proven sufficient. Hila Shamir specifically observes that "[w]ithholding wages or identification papers, continually threatening to expose a worker's undocumented status to authorities, and using indebted labor (bonded labor or indentured labor) are all understood to satisfy the means element" (International Labour Organization, 2009; Shamir, 2012, pp. 86–87).

Relatedly and quite crucially, human trafficking may also arise in situations where workers have consented to travel for work – abduction and deception over the kind and conditions of work are not the sole actions proscribed by anti human trafficking law (Gallagher, 2013; Richards, 2004; Shamir, 2012). Instead, human trafficking can occur not only when the type of work one is compelled to engage in differs from what one was promised, but also when the worker has not consented to the working conditions themselves. Long working hours, illicit or excessive wage deductions, delayed payment, low wages, or restrictions on freedom of movement may support a charge of human trafficking (Shamir, 2012). Deceptive recruitment is therefore not perceived as essential to the violative essence of human trafficking. Instead, human trafficking emerges as "a combination of labor rights violations, where each one alone might not amount to [human] trafficking" (International Labour Organization, 2009; Shamir, 2012, p. 87). Under this configuration, a worker's migrant status may contribute to her vulnerability, but does it describe the core wrong of human trafficking? Perhaps instead the wrong is rooted in the employment conditions themselves.

C. The ILO's operational indicators of trafficking in human beings

The 2009 *Operational Indicators of Trafficking in Human Beings* report, discussed fully in the ILO 2009 Global Report, originated in a joint ILO and EC project to reach consensus among European experts on what indicators should be used to characterize the various elements of the definition of human trafficking for data collection purposes.

This report was not only an attempt to standardize human trafficking definitions and the meaning of relevant labor exploitation across Europe, but was also part of a broader effort to "strengthen freedom, justice, and security in the EU" (International Labour Organization, 2009, p. 2). In fact, the ILO-EC project was itself a sub-group housed within an expert group requested by the European Council's Hague Program and convened by the EC to assess the EU's policy needs for data on crime and criminal justice. In this way, the enduring transnational criminal paradigm subtly structures what labor perspective may most readily graft onto human trafficking law: one focused on migrant labor, one that commandeers labor issues and wraps them in the veil of state security, one that sees migrant labor (abuse) as a threat to state sovereignty. And yet the operational indicators describing trafficked work that emerge from the joint report do not only characterize the kinds of work conditions suffered by migrant workers in Europe – they also describe large swaths of the US landscape of low-wage work.

The report yielded four sets of operational indicators for adult and child victims of labor and sexual exploitation, respectively. Each set is a structured list of indicators that together reveal six dimensions of human trafficking: (1) deceptive recruitment, or deception during recruitment, transfer, and transportation (ten indicators); (2) coercive recruitment, or coercion during recruitment, transfer, and transportation (ten indicators); (3) recruitment by abuse of vulnerability (sixteen indicators); (4) exploitative conditions of work (nine indicators); (5) coercion at destination (fifteen indicators); and (6) abuse of vulnerability at destination (seven indicators).

For each of the identified six dimensions of human trafficking, a combination of strong, medium, or weak indicators can indicate a positive assessment, meaning that the dimension is present for the victim. A positive assessment can include: two strong indicators; one strong indicator and one medium or weak indicator; three medium indicators; or two medium indicators and one weak indicator. The final analysis involves combining all six elements to identify victims of human trafficking. Based on the results, migrants are classified as successful migrants (no deception, no coercion, no exploitation); exploited migrants (exploitation without deception or coercion); victims of exploitation and deception (without coercion); and victims of trafficking for forced labor (deception, exploitation, and coercion).

The 2009 ILO/EC report is therefore significant for two reasons. First, it offers a reputable model for how experts across a region can develop a working consensus on the parameters of human trafficking – a model that could prove useful as the scope of human trafficking law continues to be debated. Second, the report is valuable for the specific consensus of the experts that the accrual of labor violations can produce the type of exploitation prohibited by anti-trafficking instruments. Interestingly, although the report understands migrant workers to be the paradigmatic face of human trafficking, the acts and harms that give rise to the charge of human trafficking need not result from a worker's migrant status. The abuse workers suffer – the conditions of work that merit a charge of trafficked work – could be inflicted on many low-wage workers. This suggests that the wrong of human trafficking has less to do with the legal status of the workers than it does with the conditions of the work endured by workers and by the broader assignation of duties and responsibilities that workers and employers are thought to owe one another.

D. State of the low-wage nation – surveying US low-wage work conditions and the new low-wage labor paradigm

In the landmark 2009 report *Broken Laws, Unprotected Workers: Violations of Employment and Labor Law in America's Cities*, a team of expert policy analysts, researchers, and professors surveyed 4,387 low-wage workers in the three largest US cities – Chicago, Los Angeles, and New York City. By opting for a broad analysis of work conditions across low-wage industries and including vulnerable workers often missed in standard surveys, such as unauthorized immigrants and those paid in cash, this report departed from the majority of prior studies in significant ways.

The report found widespread and systematic violations of the most basic workplace protections – the sort assumed to have been long addressed by US labor law. Among the core labor protections routinely denied US low-wage workers are: the right to be paid at least the minimum wage, the right to be paid for overtime hours, the right to take meal breaks, access to workers' compensation when injured, and the right to advocate for better working conditions. Wage violations were exceedingly common. Of those surveyed, 26% had been paid below minimum wage the week before; 60% of these were underpaid by more than $1 an hour. One quarter worked more than 40 hours per week in "off the clock," unpaid labor; and 76% were not paid the legally required overtime rate. Workers with violations had put in an average of 11 underpaid or unpaid overtime. Moreover, of the tipped workers surveyed, 30% were not paid the tipped worker minimum wage, which is lower than the minimum wage in Illinois and New York.

Workers were also subjected to long working hours, at times without pay. One quarter of surveyed workers exceeded their work shift; 70% of these received no pay for extra work. In California, Illinois and New York, workers are required to receive documentation of their earnings and deductions, regardless of whether they are paid in cash or by check; 57% of workers in the sample did not receive this mandatory documentation and 41% of those surveyed also reported illegal employer deductions for damage or loss of work-related tools or materials or transportation.

When low-wage workers attempted to assert their labor rights, legal processes failed them. One in five workers surveyed reported either filing a complaint or attempting to form a union in the last year. Of those, 43% experienced one or more forms of retaliation, including termination, suspension, threats to cut hours or pay, and threats to call immigration authorities. Another 20% did not make a complaint even after suffering a serious workplace problem (e.g., no minimum wage, dangerous working conditions): 50% refrained due to fear of termination, 10% feared hour and wage cuts, while 36% thought it would make no difference.

This brief account of US low-wage work conditions evinces the continuities between erstwhile legal low-wage work and the kind of exploitative work that meets the legal definition of trafficked work. In this way, the new low-wage/vulnerable labor paradigm demonstrates how anti human trafficking law may cast a net wide enough to include a significant portion of workers within the US low-wage labor market. This is significant because it taps into the crisis inherent to human trafficking law itself: that of envisioning the act of human trafficking as befalling certain individuals and the alternative – understanding human trafficking as rooted in collective labor exploitation that does not discriminate by citizenship status.

Further, comparing conditions of low-wage work with conditions that meet the legal definition of trafficked work shows that attempts to rescue or rehabilitate trafficked workers will not end their exploitation – not when an exploitative low-wage labor market is the liberation that awaits them. A low-wage/vulnerable labor paradigm reveals how, from chronic wage theft to an increased vulnerability to on the job sexual violence, otherwise legal low-wage work can look the same as the kind of exploitative work that meets the legal definition of trafficked work – even if other elements of a human trafficking charge are not present and human trafficking itself is not a supportable charge. As such, understanding human trafficking as having more in common with low-wage and vulnerable labor abuse than slavery or criminal gender violence is both normatively and descriptively more useful than interpreting human trafficking through those current dominant paradigms, which also tend to view all human trafficking as rooted in migration problems.

VI. Conclusion

Contrary to the standards adopted by international agencies and other federal departments, the US TIP Office has attempted to (1) absorb forced labor beneath the banner of human trafficking via an abandonment of any movement/recruitment requirement for a charge of human trafficking, and (2) simultaneously reconceptualize *all* human trafficking as slavery. These transformations in the law have occurred as an international push to incorporate a labor perspective in human trafficking law has taken root. This emergent labor perspective, which uses migrant labor as a template, understands that the accumulation of poor labor conditions, which individually might simply constitute discrete labor violations, can cross the threshold into human trafficking.

The naming of human trafficking as modern slavery, while signaling the gravity of the act, fails to provide a full account of why all acts proscribed by human trafficking law, at the center and at the margins, are wrong. Moreover, the emerging labor migration paradigm, while usefully identifying human trafficking as a labor issue, analytically limits the would-be structural scope of a labor analysis of human trafficking by tacitly construing its wrong as an equality or autonomy wrong suffered by migrant workers. This labor migration perspective focuses on affording migrant workers the same protections as non-migrant workers in order to end exploitation.

Yet neither the slavery nor the labor migration approach describes the full range of exploitative acts prohibited by primary anti-trafficking instruments. Less severe exploitation, including the accumulation of poor labor conditions that individually would not constitute actionable exploitation, are also proscribed – and largely neglected. This discretionary oversight has left many migrant and non-migrant low-wage and vulnerable workers whose conditions of work might meet the requirements for a charge of human trafficking outside of legal analysis or attention.

As a corrective, this chapter argues that the core wrong of human trafficking is a low-wage/vulnerable labor wrong, where the conditions of work (which includes commercial sexual acts) are controlling, independent of the migratory status of the workers themselves. Theorizing the wrong of human trafficking in this way, through what this chapter calls a new low-wage/vulnerable labor paradigm, captures the full range of offenses proscribed by human trafficking law, from labor performed pursuant to enslavement to lesser exploitation. A low-wage/vulnerable labor perspective also allows for a structural perspective on the wrong of human trafficking, understanding it as engendered by global labor markets and not individual wrongdoers alone.

Approaching human trafficking law through the new low-wage/vulnerable labor paradigm not only provides a comprehensive account of *why* all acts able to be prosecuted as human trafficking are wrong, it also helps preserve the legal integrity of one of the most serious violations recognized by law: slavery. The new low-wage/vulnerable labor paradigm ensures that the seriousness of slavery is maintained, while also assuring that deeply concerning acts of human trafficking are not overlooked simply because they do not resemble the extreme conditions of traditional slavery. For these reasons, a theoretical exploration of the wrong of human trafficking is necessary to halt the continuously shifting interpretations of its legal definition. Settling the wrong of human trafficking will help establish a more cohesive understanding of the problem. Doing so will establish firm ground to locate and oppose exploitation and the misery that it brings to workers at home and around the world.

12

MIGRANT DOMESTIC WORKERS IN THE UK

Enacting exclusions, exemptions and rights

Siobhán Mullally[1] *and Clíodhna Murphy*[2]

I. Introduction

Domestic work, the provision of caring work in the intimate, domestic sphere, is work that continues to be undertaken primarily by women, and increasingly by migrant women (Galotti, 2009; Lutz, 200). The expected reduction in demand for paid domestic workers has not materialized, leading some to ask whether the emergence of "global care chains" should be assessed as a major defeat for feminist movements or as "unfinished business" (Fudge, 2012; Lutz, 2010). Combined with the movement of women into paid employment, the retreat from welfare state supports in Western Europe has produced care economies that are increasingly reliant on the outsourcing of intimate, reproductive labor (Anderson, 2000; Lutz, 2010). A range of factors have contributed to the demand for paid domestic labor, including population aging, changing household structures, increasing female participation in the labor market, difficulties in reconciling paid employment and caring for dependants, and the availability of a flexible, low cost, female (and mainly migrant) work force.

Human rights law has somewhat belatedly begun to address the inequalities and exclusions that structure the domain of domestic work. As in other areas of international law, it is primarily the moments of crisis that have captured the attention of human rights law. The "everyday" of workplace exploitation, exclusion from the protections of employment law and social security, and precarious migration status, have attracted less attention to date. Recent standard setting

1 Professor of Law, University College Cork.

2 Lecturer, Maynooth University. The authors would like to acknowledge the support received from an Irish Research Council Senior Fellowship Award. An earlier draft of this chapter was published in *Human Rights Quarterly* 36, no. 2 (2014): 397–427.

initiatives have attempted to address this gap and have included the adoption of the landmark 2011 ILO Convention Concerning Decent Work for Domestic Workers, a 2008 General Recommendation from the UN Committee on the Elimination of All Forms of Discrimination Against Women (CEDAW) on Women Migrant Workers (CEDAW General Recommendation), and a 2011 General Comment from the UN Committee on Migrant Workers and their Families on Migrant Domestic Workers (CMW General Comment). Against the background of this "justice cascade" (Sikkink, 2011), however, migration laws continue to function as limits to the transformative promise of such initiatives. Migration status adds yet another axis of discrimination to the intersections of gender, race and class for domestic workers (Anderson, 2000; Lutz, 2010). States remain reluctant, however, to recognize the "dissensus" that arises between "border norms" and evolving human rights standards (Bosniak, 2006).

The UN Special Rapporteur on Contemporary Forms of Slavery has identified a "net of dependency factors" that prevent domestic workers from leaving situations of exploitation, many of which include constructed vulnerabilities linked to migration status (Report of the Special Rapporteur, 2010). The exploitation of migrant domestic workers is often presented by states as the action of an aberrant and abusive individual employer. The role played by migration law in creating the conditions within which such exploitation occurs, and often goes unchecked, is not acknowledged. As Anderson (2010a) notes, however, migration law not only reinforces the unequal power relations between migrant domestic workers and their employers, it also provides unscrupulous employers with mechanisms of control they might not otherwise have.

This chapter examines the reforms introduced in the Overseas Domestic Workers (ODW) visa regime in the UK and the politics and practice of human rights that has surrounded these changes. The move towards a more precarious migration status for migrant domestic workers marks a rejection of the reforms secured through sustained political activism by domestic workers' advocates. It also highlights the contingency and instability of political moments that secure progressive change and legal recognition of migrant workers' human rights claims.

The reforms to the ODW visa follow on from the UK government's failure to support the 2011 ILO Convention on Decent Work for Domestic Workers and its ambiguous commitment to the expansion of EU anti-trafficking legislation.[3] These steps reflect a resistance to the "cascade" of human rights standards that have sought to overcome the limits of migration status as a prerequisite to the exercise of rights (Inter-American Court of Human Rights Advisory Opinion OC-18/03, 2003; Global Forum on Migration and Development, 2012a). A series

3 See statement to the House of Commons from Minister Damien Green, 22 March 2011, available at www.homeoffice.gov.uk/publications/about-us/parliamentary-business/written-ministerial-statement/eu-direct-human-trafficking-wms. The UK government did not initially opt in to the proposed Directive.

of cases before the European Court of Human Rights,[4] have highlighted the nexus between migration status and heightened risks of exploitation, as have the work of the CEDAW and Migrant Workers Committees. Limited access to secure migration status, however, remains the norm for many domestic workers. As the changes in the UK migrant domestic workers' visa regime reveal, states continue to invoke the "deportability" of migrant workers (Kesby, 2012).

The move by the UK government to introduce a highly precarious temporary status for migrant domestic workers and wider policy discourse on circular migration, mark a resistance to the expansion of human rights norms to the realm of domestic work and to migrants (Dauvergne and Marsden, 2012). This resistance is accompanied by appeals to protective norms that have shaped laws' engagement with migrant women. The Modern Slavery Act 2015, again, reiterates the government's commitment to combating human trafficking and modern slavery, yet leaves in place the reforms made to the ODW visa that have further entrenched the precarious position of domestic workers.[5] The normative compulsion of preventing abuse is again appealed to, as a justification for the failure to reinstate the full panoply of rights that had accompanied the ODW visa regime. Section 53 of the Act specifically allows for a right to change employer, but that it is available only to those who are referred into the National Referral mechanism and receive a positive finding that they are a victim of modern slavery or human trafficking (Ewins, 2015).

Following heated debate and proposals for amendment of the Modern Slavery Bill in the House of Lords, it was agreed that an independent review of the Overseas Domestic Worker Visa would be undertaken. That review was completed and published in December 2015. As the independent review notes, the visa tie and its impact on vulnerability to abuse of domestic workers, was central to most of the debate on reform. The review concludes that although it is difficult to quantify precisely the impact of a visa tie:

> the phenomenon is clear: the presence of a tie to a specific employer places both real and perceived restrictions upon an overseas domestic worker's ability to seek protection of her fundamental rights [. . .] which increases her risk of abuse.
>
> *(Ewins, 2015, para. 86.2)*

As is also noted, the exception provided for in section 53 of the Act only applies to slavery and human trafficking, not any other abuse on the continuum of

4 *Siliadin v France* (2006) 43 EHRR 16; *Rantsev v Cyprus and Russia*, Application No. 25965/04, Judgment of 7 January 2010; *CN and V v France*, Application no. 67724/09, Judgment of 11 October 2012; *CN v The United Kingdom*, App. No. 4239/08, Judgment of 13 November 2012.

5 Home Office, Draft Modern Slavery Bill, December 2013 Cm 8770. See also Joint Committee on the Draft Modern Slavery Bill, oral evidence 28 January 2014, available at www. parliament.uk/ business/committees/committees-a-z/joint-select/draft-modern-slavery-bill/ written-evidence/. (HC [1019], discussing the implications of the 2012 changes to the overseas domestic worker visa regime).

exploitation. While the review accepts that escaping slavery is not always as simple as changing employer, it notes, that "sometimes it is" (Ewins, 2015, para. 78). The key is to ensure that the migrant domestic worker has the possibility to remove herself from an abusive situation without risking becoming an irregular migrant. The deportability of the migrant is recognized as a key continuing chilling factor. Ultimately the review concludes in favour of a universal right to change employer for all migrant domestic workers, but only within the domestic work sector in private households. It also recommends the possibility of extensions of the right to stay for up to a two-and-a-half-year period, but without a pathway to settlement as such. It is a compromise, one that seeks to reintroduce an element of control and autonomy into the lives of migrant domestic workers, but the immigration control imperative remains, albeit not fully intact. Against this background, the "*jurisgenerative*" potential of human rights standards, heralded by many, continues to be limited.[6]

II. Decent work standards, expanding human rights norms: a justice cascade?

As Carens (2008) has noted, migrant domestic workers are "hard to locate on the map of democracy" (p. 419). The movement of migrant domestic workers across multiple jurisdictional boundaries, between states as well as from the "public" domain into the "private" domain of the home, is central to the experience of the domestic worker (Fudge, 2011). Law plays a dual role here, jealously guarding the public borders of the state through immigration laws while at the same time "reifying the private borders of the home" (Fudge, 2011, p. 243). The UN Special Rapporteur on the Human Rights of Migrants has pointed out that "the lack of watchdog mechanisms and inadequate monitoring by the Government in the country of destination, the recruiting agencies and even consulates, mean that migrant domestic workers are cut off and abuses remain unseen" (Report of the Special Rapporteur, 2004).

For some, the movement to establish decent work standards for domestic work is doomed to failure, given the historical legacy of low status, low pay and exploitation associated with such work. Legal reforms, it is argued, cannot fully account for the wider "realm of indignities" experienced by domestic workers or the dynamics of power played out on "concrete historicised bodies" that are gendered, raced and classed (Blackett, 2011, p. 43). Migrant domestic workers are situated in the isolating and devalued "privatised economy of household labour," where highly personalized and emotionally exacting work is undertaken in situations that are "heavy with the histories of racialised subordination" (Williams, 2010, p. 386). Lack of enforcement and application restricts the potential for human

6 The term 'jurisgenerative' is borrowed from Robert M. Cover (1982). See also: Benhabib, 2011; Cover, 1982; Dauvergne and Marsden, 2012; Fudge, 2012.

rights norms to disturb the ongoing reproduction of such histories (Schwenken et al., 2011). Against this background, the expansion of decent work standards to domestic work may provide a corrective, as Adelle Blackett (2011) has suggested, to the "abstract articulations" of rights that traditionally overlook exploitation of domestic workers. The refusal on the part of some Governments and employers to support this expansion of rights, however, continues to postpone what is a significant political moment for domestic workers.

A. The ILO Convention on Decent Work for Domestic Workers: beyond "noblesse oblige"

Reification (and exclusion) of the household was one of the key issues that emerged in debates leading up to the adoption of the ILO Convention on Decent Work for Domestic Workers. The 2011 ILO Convention on Decent Work for Domestic Workers (Domestic Work Convention) is the first dedicated international instrument to address the specificity of domestic work. As the report that preceded the Convention notes, it is intended to mark a transition from paternalistic conceptions of "good employers acting out of a sense of *noblesse oblige*" to respect for domestic workers' rights (International Labour Conference Report IV(1), 2010, p. 13, hereafter, ILO Report IV(1)). The Convention seeks to extend core decent work standards concerning fair terms of employment and working conditions to the realm of domestic work. States are required to ensure that domestic workers enjoy equality with other workers regarding working time, entitlements to minimum wage, healthy and safe working conditions, and social security protection, including maternity. States are also required to introduce measures providing for the regulation of employment agencies and for effective and accessible dispute resolution mechanisms for domestic workers.

The only specific provision in the Domestic Work Convention relating directly to migration is found in Article 8, which provides that national laws or regulations specify that written job offers or contracts of employment are provided to domestic workers prior to their departure to the country where the work is to be performed. The conditions under which migrant domestic workers are entitled to repatriation following the expiry or termination of their contract of employment are also to be specified pre-departure. This requirement, while important, is relatively weak. It requires only that such terms and conditions be specified, but does nothing to address the inequalities of bargaining power between worker and employer. Article 7 of the Convention adopts a similarly minimal approach, requiring that domestic workers be informed of the terms and conditions of their work – including, for example, the types of work to be performed and the remuneration – but without elaborating on the content of such terms and conditions. Article 9 requires members to ensure that domestic workers are "free to negotiate with the employer whether to reside in the household." Such freedoms remain illusory, however, where immigration restrictions including access to public funds (such as affordable or social housing programs) for migrants is restricted and where minimum wage protections are not enforced or applicable. The proposed model contract of employment for domestic workers, noted in the accompanying Recommendation, seeks to overcome the minimal approach taken in the Convention itself (ILO Recommendation No. 201, 2011, hereafter, ILO Recommendation Concerning Decent Work for Domestic Workers). Its inclusion in the nonbinding text of the Recommendation, however, reflects the reluctance of states to take concrete steps to realize the aspirations of a shift "from status to contract" for domestic workers. Even these limited requirements attracted opposition from states, however. The UK government argued that it was not, in its view, "the duty of a government to ensure that terms and conditions of employment were understood by workers" (ILO Report of the Committee on Domestic Workers, Provisional Record No. 15, 2011).

Despite the commitment to addressing disadvantage within the domestic work sector, the Convention's scope is deliberately limited. The specific difficulties facing agency workers, domestic workers in diplomatic households, irregular migrant domestic workers and workers categorized as au pairs were highlighted repeatedly in the submissions made during the drafting process of the Convention (RESPECT Network, 2009). These issues remain unresolved as the Convention continues to allow for "de-juridifications" that could render its expansion of rights meaningless for such workers. Allowing for the possibilities of opting out – that is excluding certain categories of domestic workers – was a concession to states and to employers' organizations, many of whom were opposed to the proposal to adopt a legally binding instrument (ILO Report IV(1), 2010). The position of the EU during the negotiating process, for example, was to support the adoption of a Convention supplemented by a Recommendation, but to ensure flexibility in the text of the Convention itself. This flexibility is found in Article 2 of the Convention, which allows for a sweeping measure of disentitlement with respect to "limited categories of workers in respect of which special problems of a substantial nature arise." These special problems are not specified. A requirement of consultation with employers, employees, and, where they exist, domestic workers' organizations is intended to provide a check on the process of opting out. The office of the High Commissioner for Human Rights had specifically expressed concern at the wide discretion allowed by Article 2, during the drafting process (ILO Report IV(2A), 2011). Despite its concerns, the provision remained in the final text, however, and is a significant concession to the pursuit of greater flexibility for employers and states in defining the content of rights enjoyed by domestic workers.

The ILO has specifically acknowledged the need to address a wide spectrum of actors, both state and non-state, if the objectives of standard-setting initiatives such as the Domestic Work Convention and Recommendation are to be met. Recruitment agencies are key actors in this process. Article 15 of the Convention specifically addresses the role of private recruitment agencies and notes measures required to safeguard against abusive practices by such agencies. This provision is particularly important for migrant domestic workers. The need for cooperation between states to address exploitative practices in the context of transnational recruitment is highlighted. However, the requirement of an "employment relationship" in Article 1 of the Convention itself potentially restricts the application of the Convention to domestic workers categorized as self-employed, or those who are recruited through private agencies. The specific role of intermediaries such as recruitment agencies is widely recognized as a matter of concern, given the vagaries of domestic employment legislation and its application to agency workers. Although Article 15 of the Convention requires members to adopt laws specifying the obligations of agencies towards domestic workers, considerable discretion is allowed for determining the scope of such obligations.

The regulation of employment agencies was one of the more contentious issues arising during the drafting process, with several non-governmental organizations (NGOs), workers' representatives, and governments highlighting the importance of close monitoring. The government members of the Africa group, represented by South Africa, specifically identified the role of private recruitment agencies as a key concern. Human Rights Watch in its submission pointed to the need to ensure that employment agencies did not charge domestic workers for recruitment costs incurred by employers, a practice that frequently leads domestic workers to forced labor and servitude (ILO Report of the Committee on Domestic Workers, Provisional Record No. 15, 2011). The issue of exorbitant fees charged by agencies was highlighted also by the Migrant Forum in Asia. Despite recognition of these risks, the Convention itself does little to directly address abusive practices by agencies.

The adoption of the Domestic Work Convention, and the global momentum that led to its enactment as the first binding ILO instrument in more than a decade, is an important political moment. However, it is one that is marked by an enactment of limits. The exclusions and exemptions that remain within the ILO text reflect the continuing reluctance by some members to acknowledge the domestic worker as a subject of rights and as more than a commodity or ingredient in an economic process. There is also a reluctance to acknowledge the imperative to re-draw gendered boundaries between public and private if international legal standards are to secure a movement beyond "*noblesse oblige*." Taking this additional step also requires recognizing the intersections of overlapping axes of discrimination – of race, gender and migration status.[7] Recognition of these intersections is evident in the work of UN human rights treaty bodies, which have somewhat belatedly begun to address the sphere of domestic work. This gradual expansion of multilateral standards to encompass the realm of domestic work has the potential to move beyond the limits of bilateral attempts at reform, where the predictable trade-off between access to jobs and workers' rights too frequently kicks in (Varia, 2011).

7 See written comments submitted by Interights to the European Court of Human Rights (pursuant to leave granted by the President of the Chamber in accordance with Rule 44 § 2 of the Rules of Court) in *Kawogo v UK*, para. 18.

B. Human rights at the intersections: recognizing the nexus with migration status

As Crenshaw (1991) has noted, "the intersections of racism and sexism [. . .] cannot be captured wholly by looking at the race or gender dimensions separately" (p. 1241). Addressing the intersections of both expands the possibilities of human rights law's potential to address discrimination. Migration status, however, is often excluded from the scope of race discrimination prohibitions and is frequently ignored in analyses of discrimination that adopt a "nationally insular approach" (Bosniak, 2006). Notably, the reluctance to extend non-discrimination norms to the migration context is evident even in the Migrant Workers Convention, which does not include migration status in the list of non-discrimination prohibitions. The 1990 International Convention on the Protection of the Rights of All Migrant Workers and Members of their Families (Migrant Workers Convention) has been described "as a beacon of what has not been achieved in the realm of rights," both because of its limited ratifications to date and the distinctions made between the rights of documented and undocumented workers (Dauvergne and Marsden, 2012). In the practice of UN human rights treaty bodies, including the Migrant Workers Committee, however, the significance of migration status as relevant to questions of racial and gender discrimination is increasingly probed, despite apparent textual exclusions from the treaty standards themselves (Committee for the Elimination of All Forms of Racial Discrimination, 2004).

The obligations of effective deterrence that arise from forced labor, slavery and trafficking prohibitions are enshrined in several international and regional instruments, including CEDAW, the International Covenant on Civil and Political Rights, the Palermo Protocol,[8] and the Council of Europe Convention on Action Against Trafficking (2005). Developing obligations of due diligence at regional and international levels have highlighted the nexus between states' positive obligations of prevention and non-discrimination norms, potentially of significance to migrant domestic workers. The European Court of Human Rights has repeatedly recognized that a state's positive obligations under the Convention go beyond the imposition of criminal sanctions and include policing and operative measures. In *Opuz v Turkey* (2009) the European Court of Human Rights, for the first time in Strasbourg case law, linked states' obligations to combat domestic violence to Article 14 ECHR non-discrimination requirements. More generally, the gradual expansion of indirect discrimination prohibitions suggests possible strategies for such challenges (*DH and Others v the Czech Republic*, 2006). The *Jessica Lenahan* (2011) case and the *Campo Algondero* case (*Gonzalez ("Cotton Fields") v Mexico*, 2009) before the Inter-American Court of Human Rights, and others, similarly point to the non-discrimination nexus. Given that the majority of domestic workers are women and many are migrants, a similar nexus between migration law,

8 Protocol to Prevent, Suppress and Punish Trafficking in Persons Especially Women and Children, supplementing the United Nations Convention against Transnational Organized Crime (2000).

positive obligations and non-discrimination norms arises. The Advisory Opinion of the Inter-American Court on the application of Non-discrimination and Equality norms to Undocumented Migrants points to the transformative promise that underpins human rights standards. Fitting into the discrimination paradigm is not without its difficulties, however, and is a strategy that brings many pitfalls, particularly when required to identify an appropriate comparator or when faced with the possibility not of a legal remedy, but of deportation (Edwards, 2010).

In its General Comment on Migrant Domestic Workers, the Migrant Workers Committee outlines the specific role that immigration law plays in disadvantaging particular workers. Overly restrictive immigration laws, they note, lead to higher numbers of migrant domestic workers who are undocumented or in an irregular situation, and thus more likely to suffer human rights violations. Similar disadvantages arise where migration laws tie a worker's migration status to the continued sponsorship of a particular employer, with the result that domestic workers may risk deportation if they leave an abusive employment relationship. Any such arrangement can "unduly restrict" liberty of movement and increase exploitation and abuse, "including in conditions of forced labour or servitude." Migration status may also limit access to rights such as family reunification. Where visa or work permit permissions impose limits on access to public funds, rights to education, health care, and housing remain illusory (Spencer and Pobjoy, 2011). The nexus between discrimination and migration status is also recognized in CEDAW's General Recommendation no. 26 on Women Migrant Workers. CEDAW notes that while states parties are entitled to control their borders and regulate migration, they must do so "in full compliance" with their international obligations. Those obligations include "the promotion of safe migration procedures and the obligation to respect, protect and fulfil the human rights of women throughout the migration cycle" (CEDAW General Recommendation, 2008, para. 3).

CEDAW has also called on states to ensure that visa schemes do not indirectly discriminate against women by excluding or limiting options for certain female-dominated occupations, such as domestic work. The changes introduced in the UK Overseas Domestic Worker visa regime, however, ignore this call, revealing the continuing willingness of states to circumvent human rights standards and resort to what Paul Berman (2012) has described elsewhere as "sovereigntist territorial prerogatives."

III. Migrant domestic workers in the UK: exclusions from rights

A. Limited recognition of domestic work: a concession

Until 1979, resident domestic workers in the UK came within the scope of the general work permit regime operating under the 1971 Immigration Act. In 1980, when the issuing of work permits for "unskilled workers" ended, a limited exception was made for domestic workers who had worked for their employers for at least 12 months prior to coming to the UK (Clayton, 2012). Given the important reproductive function carried out by domestic workers, allowing for such a concession was justified in the "national interest" so as to ensure that productive, highly skilled migrants would continue to choose the UK as a preferred destination.[9] Many years later, a similar rationale was to surface in the case law of the Court of Justice of the European Union on the free movement rights of EU citizens and their third country national spouses (*Carpenter*, 2002). Under the concession scheme, employers were permitted to bring domestic workers into the UK either as a "visitor" or as a "person named to work with a specified employer" (Anderson, 2000, p. 89). A degree of confusion surrounding the appropriate immigration status to be granted was evident in the varying statuses granted to domestic workers on entry. In general, however, it was presumed that the employment rights of domestic workers and their migration status were linked to their employer, increasing the potential for exploitation and abuse, despite the recognized "national interest" served through their work (Anderson, 1993).

B. Enacting rights: the ODW visa

In 1998, the newly elected Labour government announced a scheme to regularize the position of domestic workers who had entered under the concession scheme.[10] In 2002, the ODW visa scheme was introduced, following an extensive advocacy campaign by migrant domestic workers' NGOs, including the Waling-Waling, Kalayaan and Commission for Filippino Migrant Workers organizations. Under the ODW visa scheme, migrant domestic workers were permitted to change employers, a key element of the campaign for reform. Employment protections were also recognized as applying to domestic work and, as with other categories of migrant workers, domestic workers could apply to have their dependants join them in the UK. The possibility of qualifying for indefinite leave to remain was also recognized, subject to meeting generally applicable criteria such as the requirement of continuous employment. While these hurdles were not insignificant and could pose barriers to secure migration status, a route out of temporary residence was at least, in principle, available.

Labor market mobility for domestic workers on the ODW visa was, however, limited, as visa extensions were dependant on securing continuous employment in the domestic work sector,[11] thus limiting possibilities for moving out of a traditionally lower paid and undervalued employment sector. The eligibility criteria also limited the potential impact of the visa scheme; only domestic workers employed for one year or more in the house of their employer or a connected household, were eligible to apply. The requirement of no recourse to public funds meant that, in practice, many domestic workers had no option but to accept "live-in"

9 Lord Reay, HL Deb col 1052 (28 November 1990).

10 See announcement by Mr Mike O'Brien MP (Immigration Minister) on 23 July 1998. HC Deb col 611W (23 July 1998).

11 Para. 159EA of the Immigration Rules.

arrangements, thus exacerbating the isolated nature of the work and heightening risks of abuse. Thus, while the ODW visa provided important employment rights protections, it did not fully resolve the precarious status of migrant domestic workers.

In 2006, the Labour government proposed a new "Points Based System" of immigration, as part of which it was proposed that domestic workers would receive six-month non-renewable business visitor visas only and lose the right to change employers (UK Home Office, 2006).[12] Following an extensive campaign led by Kalayaan and other NGOs, the government agreed to postpone the introduction of changes to the ODW pending a review of the national anti-trafficking strategy (Oxfam and Kalayaan, 2008; UK Border Agency, 2008). The government also affirmed its commitment to minimizing risks of abuse or exploitation in any process of reform. In 2009, the House of Commons, Home Affairs Select Committee, in its *Report on Human Trafficking in the UK*, concluded that the retention of the existing ODW visa and the protections it offered was the single most important issue in preventing forced labor and trafficking of domestic workers.[13] Given the particular susceptibility of migrant domestic workers to abuse, the committee argued that the preservation of the ODW regime would be necessary for much longer than the two-year period proposed by government. In 2010, the United Nations Special Rapporteur on the Human Rights of Migrants specifically commended the effectiveness of visa protections for migrant domestic workers in the UK and recommended that its protections be extended to cover domestic workers in diplomatic households.[14]

C. Reform: enacting exclusion

The issue of reform, delayed by the previous Labour government, came to the fore again in 2011. In June 2011, a consultation paper on overseas domestic workers published by the Liberal Democratic-Conservative coalition government proposed abolishing the special entry route for domestic workers, abolishing the special ODW visa regime or significantly restricting its operation to a six-month non-renewable entry visa and removing the right to change employers (in effect, returning to the earlier Labour government proposals), noting that the UK was "more generous in its provision for ODWs than other EU countries" (UK Border Agency, 2011). This "generosity," it seemed, was not to be commended. Documented abuses as well as levels of unemployment in the UK domestic labor market

12 The proposals were raised in a Westminster Hall debate on Migrant Domestic Workers. HC Deb cols 101–107WH (10 May 2006).

13 House of Commons, Home Affairs Select Committee, Sixth Report of Session 2008–2009, *The Trade in Human Beings: Human Trafficking in the UK*, HC 23-I, 14 May 2009, para. 59.

14 UN Human Rights Council, Report of the Special Rapporteur on the human rights of migrants, Addendum: Mission to the United Kingdom of Great Britain and Northern Ireland, 16 March 2010, A/HRC/14/30/Add.3, at 15 and 16, and recommendation, para. 76.

were appealed to as support for the case to abolish the ODW visa. The announcement of the proposed reforms coincided with the UK government's decision to abstain from voting on the ILO Domestic Worker's Convention, a move that attracted significant criticism from domestic workers' advocates (Williams, F. 2011).

The stated rationale for the proposed reforms reveals the continuing characterization of domestic work as low-skilled and of little economic value (UK Border Agency, 2011). Continuing to allow "unrestricted low-skilled entry for an extended period" ran counter to the government's policy of seeking to attract highly skilled migrants and limiting access to settlement routes. This policy can also be seen to fit with broader trends at the EU level to encourage and facilitate preferential immigration routes for "highly qualified workers" and their family members (The Stockholm Programme, 2010). The categorization of skills levels in this context is potentially a highly gendered exercise. The stated concerns to protect demand-led labor migration ignore the continuing demand for domestic workers. The consultation paper pointed to the existence of the National Referral Mechanism as sufficient to identify victims of trafficking and responding to abuses experienced by domestic workers. A route to settlement, such as that offered by the ODW visa, was not considered an appropriate response. The level of documented abuses of migrant domestic workers was presented, in itself, as a reason to cease the operation of the ODW visa. This argument, in particular, seems difficult to sustain given the acknowledged protections that it offered to migrant domestic workers, including, in particular, the right to change employers.

Again, we see the reluctance to acknowledge the nexus between access to safe migration routes and states' positive obligations to deter and prevent human rights abuses. The proposed reforms were strongly resisted by NGOs, who argued that the changes would remove crucial protections from migrant domestic workers.[15] Central to the debates on the impact of reform proposals is the disputed role that immigration laws and policies are presumed to play. While advocates for the retention of the ODW visa regime highlighted immigration restrictions as likely to contribute to further abuse and exploitation of domestic workers, the government invoked controls on immigration as essential to curbing abuse by unscrupulous employers (Anderson, 2010). This argument was also made by the government in its response to the OSCE Special Representative's Report on her 2011 country visit.[16]

In the House of Commons debates on the proposed reforms, MPs arguing in favour of the retention of the ODW visa emphasized the critical role played by the right to change employer in limiting the potential for exploitation. The proposed reforms, it was noted, would lead to an increase in abuse and illegality, and

15 Kalayaan Statement, "Government Proposes Return to Slavery for Migrant Domestic Workers in the UK" (2011). See also Kalayaan "Response to Consultation – questions on MDWs" (5 August 2011).

16 Report by OSCE Special Representative and Coordinator for Combating Trafficking in Human Beings, following her visit to the UK, 7–10 March 2011, SEC.GAL/200/11, 18 January 2012, Appendix 1, p. 12.

would "dramatically increase the power that the employer has over the worker."[17] Despite these arguments, the government continued to refuse to recognize the links between migration routes, migration status, and susceptibility to abuse.

A series of changes to the Immigration Rules applicable to domestic workers came into effect on April 6, 2012. Against the trend of expanding human rights norms for migrant domestic workers, the reforms introduced significantly increase the precariousness of the migrant domestic worker's position. Domestic workers will now be permitted to enter and stay in the UK for a maximum period of six months only. Critically, the right to change employer is removed, as is the possibility of sponsoring dependants or seeking longer-term settlement in the UK. In introducing these changes, the government signaled its intention to align the domestic worker migration route with wider migration policies and to return it to its original purpose, "to allow visitors and diplomats to be accompanied by their domestic staff – not to provide permanent access to the UK for unskilled workers."[18] Central to the government's position is the view that the domestic worker's reproductive labor requires limited skills and is easily replaced. The intimate connections, relationships and caring skills involved in much of domestic work are denied, as are the wider protections afforded to other workers. The confinement to a temporary status, combined with increasing policy discourse on circular migration, facilitates further curbs on family reunification as the domestic worker is denied the possibility of claiming family unity rights.

Migrant domestic workers employed in diplomatic households have not enjoyed the right to change employer, even prior to the reforms introduced in 2012. Their migration status was and continues to be tied directly to their employment with a named diplomatic or international civil servant. In 2010, the UN Special Rapporteur on the Human Rights on Migrants specifically recommended that the UK government consider extending the right to change employers to domestic workers in diplomatic households as a safeguard against "abusive practices."[19] In 2011, the OSCE Special Representative and Coordinator for Combating Trafficking in Human Beings included a similar recommendation in the report on her UK country visit.[20] These recommendations were ignored, however. Instead, further limits on the rights of domestic workers in diplomatic households were enacted; the route to settlement that had previously been available after a five-year residence period has now been removed.

The changes to the ODW regime and the return to a highly temporary and tied status for domestic workers has been noted with concern in the UK evaluation

17 HC Deb col 101WH (10 May 2006).

18 Home Office Announcement, "Immigration (Employment-related settlement, Overseas Domestic Workers, Tier 5 of the Points Based System and Visitors)," 29 February 2012, p. 2.

19 UN Human Rights Council, Report of the Special Rapporteur on the human rights of migrants, Addendum: Mission to the United Kingdom of Great Britain and Northern Ireland, para. 76(a).

20 Report by OSCE Special Representative and Coordinator for Combating Trafficking in Human Beings, following her visit to the UK, 7–10 March 2011, SEC.GAL/200/11, 18 January 2012, Recommendation 5, p. 8.

report of the Group of Experts on Action Trafficking in Human Beings (GRETA, 2012). In its response, the government argued that the removal of the right to change employer will not affect its ability to take other positive measures to combat trafficking (GRETA, 2012).[21]

This argument, however, refuses to acknowledge the chilling effect that immigration controls can and do have on access to legal remedies. The GRETA report notes the limited engagement by potential victims with the UK's National Referral Mechanism on human trafficking and the view of NGOs that this lack of engagement is, at least in part, due to the absence of an immigration firewall and the ever present threat of deportation. Given the very temporary nature of the immigration routes, it is likely that an increasing number of migrant domestic workers will find themselves in an irregular situation when their visa expires (Mantouvalou, 2015). As Noll (2010) has noted, in such cases human rights law provides little assistance. The absence of a firewall between employment, social security or other legal remedies, and migration laws ensures that the disciplinary and punitive reach of immigration limits the claiming of rights.

D. Domestic work, the public and the private: work like no other

Prior to the final adoption of the ILO Convention, the UK government had signaled its commitment to a "workable convention" that could be ratified by as many states as possible and would protect "vulnerable domestic workers worldwide."[22] Despite this commitment, the UK government was one of eight states to abstain from the final vote on the Convention.[23] Ultimately, the government concluded that the Convention failed to acknowledge the specificity of domestic work or the particular difficulties concerning the application of labor rights in the domestic household.[24] Speaking in the House of Commons, the Minister for Employment Relations commented that the main sticking point for the government was the potential application of health and safety legislation to private homes.[25] Such a legislative disincentive to employment of domestic workers could, he argued, force elderly or disabled individuals into residential homes thereby undermining government policy to support independent living through direct payments to recipients of care supports.

In refusing to support the 2011 ILO Domestic Work Convention, the government was concerned to protect its own care and welfare policies, as well as to

21 UK authorities' comments on the report concerning the implementation of the Council of Europe Convention on Action against Trafficking in Human Beings by the United Kingdom, pp. 97–98, para. 19.

22 HC Deb col WA 469W (23 May 2011).

23 The other states that abstained from the vote were El Salvador, Malaysia, Panama, Singapore, Thailand, the Czech Republic and Sudan. See, Fiona MacTaggart MP, HC Deb col 269WH (29 June 2011).

24 As quoted by Fiona MacTaggart MP, HC Deb cols 269–293WH (29 June 2011).

25 HC Deb cols 288–289 (Ed Davey MP) (29 June 2011).

shield employers in the domestic sphere from what it argued were unnecessary and burdensome regulatory obligations. The shift towards direct cash payments has been a key feature of social care policy in the UK over the last decade, facilitating a trend towards outsourcing of care work to private actors, including migrant women. Direct payments in the social care system are cash payments given to service-users in lieu of community care services and are presented as facilitating greater choice and independence in sourcing care supports (Department of Health, 2009). A system of direct payments has been in place since 1996, premised on an increasing trend towards "personalization" of care, including allocation of personal budgets and direct payments (Department of Health, 2010). Williams, F. (2011) has argued that direct cash payments of this kind have encouraged the development of a particular form of care or domestic help: home-based, often low-paid, commodified, and generally accessed privately through the market. At the same time, the trend towards outsourcing of care, she notes, has expanded employment opportunities for newly arrived migrant women workers, creating yet another link in a wider transnational political economy of care. The employer-driven nature of the market for care workers, however, contributes to the potential for exploitation of migrant domestic workers particularly in a context where the usual decent work standards are deemed not to apply (Gordolan and Lalani, 2009).

The claimed specificity of domestic work, as work that takes place in the domestic household, was also central to the government's decision not to support the ILO Convention. Echoing sentiments expressed in earlier eras in the context of debates on domestic violence, the Minister for Employment Relations questioned why the government would wish to pass "quite an intrusive law," one that would give to health and safety inspectors a "new right to visit millions of homes?"[26] The evidence of the need for such a change, he argued, was weak – households being "low-risk in health and safety terms." The previous government had balked at taking such a measure and had continued to uphold the exemptions applicable to domestic households from the operation of the 1974 Health and Safety Act. The increased risks to domestic workers, the Minister argued, arose not from health and safety concerns but rather from the actions of individual employers that were already covered in other legislation.

This argument, however, ignores the legislative exemptions relating to domestic work that continue to operate in the UK and that provide a protective shield to unscrupulous employers. Domestic workers are excluded from certain aspects of the regulation of working time under the Working Time Regulations 1998, for example.[27] Deductions may be made from the minimum wage payment if

26 HC Deb 29 June 2011 cols 269–293WH.

27 Regulation 19, Working Time Regulations 1998 (No. 1833 of 1998), which provides that Regulations 4(1) and (2), 6(1), (2) and (7), 7(1), (2) and (6), and 8 do not apply in relation to a worker employed as a domestic worker in a private household. These regulations cover the maximum weekly working time, length of night work, health assessment and transfer of night workers to day work, and weekly rest period.

accommodation is provided,[28] effectively allowing for "in kind" payments for the live-in domestic worker (ILO, 2011). Perhaps one of the most striking of these exemptions has been that provided by Regulation 2(2) of the National Minimum Wage Regulations, which allows for payments less than the national minimum wage where a domestic worker is treated as "a member of the family."

A new provision introduced into the revised Immigration Rules is the requirement to provide written terms and conditions of employment as part of the preentry application process, and to commit to complying with the terms of the National Minimum Wage Act 1998 and supporting Regulations. The strengthening of preentry protections is a feature of the 2011 ILO Domestic Work Convention, which the government refused to support. Given this refusal, it is unclear how effective preentry clearance measures will be in practice or whether there is any political will to monitor their impact on the prevention of abuse. A previous report of the House of Commons Home Affairs Select Committee on Human Trafficking expressed scepticism as to the effectiveness of pre-departure interviews with domestic workers in preventing abuse, noting that enforcement was patchy at best.[29] Furthermore, the "family member" exemption from the operation of the minimum wage requirements continues to apply. And, as was noted by domestic workers' advocates, access to UK employment protections or remedies for failure to comply with minimum wage requirements, are greatly limited by the temporary and tied nature of the new visa arrangements. The family member exemption, perhaps more than any other, reinforces the public private divide that limits the enforcement of decent work standards for domestic workers (Kalayaan/Lalani, 2011). It is a line that is, of course, deeply gendered and reflects continuing categorization of domestic work as work "like no other."

E. *Just like one of the family: enacting exclusions*

A series of cases before the UK Employment Appeals Tribunal (EAT) highlights the difficulties that arise when the family member exemption is applied.[30] Where the work done could be characterized as similar to the everyday work that characterizes intimate domestic life, it was removed from the scope of employment law protections reserved for the public domain. In *Ms Julio v Ms Jose* (2011), the Employment Appeal Tribunal (EAT) accepted Ms Julio's evidence that she was not at any time paid the agreed monthly salary, but found that she was treated as "a member of the family as regards to the provision of accommodation, meals and the sharing of tasks and leisure activities" (para. 21). The family member exemption from the minimum wage regulations was therefore applicable. In the case of *Ms Nambalat v Mr Taher and Mrs Tayeb* (2011), the EAT found that there were distinct phases in the

28 Regulations 36 and 37 of the Minimum Wage Regulations 1999 (No. 584 of 1999).
29 House of Commons, Home Affairs Select Committee, Sixth Report of Session 2008–2009, *The Trade in Human Beings: Human Trafficking in the UK*, HC 23-I, 14 May 2009, paras. 116–118.
30 Appeal No. UKEAT/0553/10/DM, Judgment of 8 December 2011 ("EAT judgment").

employment relationship, during which Ms Nambalat's work duties varied widely. Despite these variations, the tribunal concluded that the family member exemption nonetheless applied. In the case of *Ms Udin v Mr and Mrs Chamsi-Pasha* (2011), variations in the working and living conditions of the claimant were found by the tribunal to have changed the nature of the employment relationship. Financial difficulties encountered by the employers had led to a downsizing of accommodation space and more difficult living conditions for Ms Udin for limited periods. For these periods only, the tribunal concluded that the family member exemption did not apply, and Ms Udin was therefore entitled to a remedy for the unauthorized deductions from her wages during this time.

On appeal, each of the claimants argued that the EAT had erred in its interpretation of the family member exemption. The narrowest possible interpretation, it was argued, should be given to this exemption so as to ensure consistency with the statutory language and compliance with the public policy good of eliminating gender and racial discrimination, given that the majority of domestic workers were women from minority ethnic communities. It was also argued that a narrow interpretation was necessary to meet the state's positive obligations under Article 4 ECHR, in line with the judgment of European Court of Human Rights in *Siliadin v France* (2006). The EAT did not specifically comment on the Article 4 ECHR arguments, but did accept that a narrow interpretation must be given to the family member exemption. The dignity with which the domestic worker is treated, the degree of privacy and autonomy afforded and the extent to which, if at all, exploitation occurs, were also relevant. The core question was whether the worker is "integrated into the family" (para. 45). If the answer is yes, then the limits of human rights protections appear to be reached. In each of the three cases before it, the EAT concluded that the family member exemption applied and the domestic workers (all of whom were migrants) were not entitled to payment of the national minimum wage (para. 58).[31] These findings were then confirmed by the Court of Appeal in respect of the two workers who had appealed the judgment of the EAT (*Nambalat v Taher & Ors*, 2012). Speaking for the Court of Appeal, Pill LJ approved the basic test as being whether the worker is "integrated into the family", although he noted that "there comes a point where the demands upon the worker are so onerous and extensive as to be inconsistent with the worker being treated as a member of the family" (para. 47).

That "integration into the family" could trigger an exemption from a core labor standard reveals a continuing reluctance, as the European Court of Human Rights has noted elsewhere, to apply human rights norms "within personal relationships or closed circuits" (*Opuz v Turkey*, 2009). Until recently, the UK Border Agency's Instructions to entry clearance officers noted that non-payment of the national minimum wage was not a valid reason for a refusal to issue an ODW

31 Appeal No. UKEAT/0553/10/DM, Judgment of 8 December 2011 ("EAT judgment"). In relation to Ms Udin, the EAT overturned the majority finding of the Employment Tribunal, concluding that in the overall context of the family's circumstances, the changing conditions did not result in Ms Udin ceasing to be treated as a member of the family.

visa. The House of Commons Home Affairs Select Committee, in its *Report on Human Trafficking in the UK*, criticized this practice commenting that it "makes a mockery of the concept of a legal minimum wage" (Home Affairs Select Committee, 2009).[32] Changes to the Immigration Rules introduced in April 2012 only partly address this criticism. Applicants for an ODW visa now have to demonstrate that the employer has agreed to pay the minimum wage in accordance with the National Minimum Wage Regulations (Immigration Rules). However, the family member exemption continues to apply, giving legal standing to the paradox inherent in many domestic work employment relationships; employers delegate intimate reproductive labor to domestic workers, expecting unconditional availability and care, while remaining unwilling to comply with decent work standards.

The Modern Slavery Act 2015 does not reinstate the right to change employer, or provide a route to long-term residence, despite a recommendation from the Joint Select Committee on the draft Modern Slavery Bill to reverse the changes to the ODW visa. This, they argued, would "at the very least allow organizations and agencies to remove a worker from an abusive employment situation immediately." It would also facilitate prosecutions of modern slavery, by removing the chilling effect of a fear of deportation (Joint Committee on the Modern Slavery Bill, 2014).[33] Concerning diplomatic domestic workers, the committee recommended that the government consider the merits of granting visas to diplomatic domestic workers only where they have contractual arrangements directly with the embassy or other diplomatic mission, so as to facilitate workers being able to secure remedies against diplomatic employers. Both of these recommendations were rejected by the government. Reiterating their determination to stamp out all forms of modern slavery, including slavery, servitude and forced labor faced by domestic workers, they conclude that the previous ODW visa arrangements potentially encouraged abuse by allowing for longer-term residence (Government Response to the Joint Committee on the Draft Modern Slavery Bill, 2014).[34] Pointing to the "substantial safeguards" that exist in the ODW route, as reformed, they note the requirement to comply with national minimum wage regulations, but do not acknowledge that such safeguards do not apply to live-in domestic workers who fall within the family member exemption. They also note that it is not government policy to facilitate "low-skilled" immigration to the UK.

There is in the government response no acknowledgment of the disputed categories of skilled/unskilled or of the appeals to rights standards in both oral and written submissions from domestic workers advocates. The responses to abuse of

32 House of Commons, Home Affairs Select Committee, Sixth Report of Session 2008–2009, *The Trade in Human Beings: Human Trafficking in the UK*, HC 23-I, 14 May 2009, para. 53.

33 Report of the Joint Select Committee on the Modern Slavery Bill, April 8 2014, para. 227, citing written evidence from Human Rights Watch, available at www.publications.parliament.uk/pa/jt201314/jtselect/jtslavery/166/16610.htm.

34 The government response to the report from the Joint Committee on the Draft Modern Slavery Bill: Session 2013–14 HL Paper 166 /HC 1019, Cm 8889, June 2014, p. 28.

workers, instead, continues to focus on prosecutorial strategy and enforcement of criminal law prohibitions. To date, the positive obligations jurisprudence of the European Court of Human Rights has also largely remained confined within this more familiar comfort zone of civil and political rights enactment, failing to address the everyday exploitation of migrant domestic workers.

IV. Litigating Article 4 of the European Convention on Human Rights

The Coroners and Justice Act (2009) introduced into the domestic law of the UK the offense of holding another person in slavery or servitude or requiring them to perform forced or compulsory labor. The introduction of this offense sought to remedy the legislative gap that arose in cases where trafficking had not occurred or the trafficking element could not be proven to a criminal standard (Crown Prosecution Service, 2009). A series of cases before the European Court of Human Rights highlight the inadequacies of the legal framework in place prior to the adoption of the 2009 Act and the challenges of enforcement of forced labor, servitude and slavery prohibitions, particular in a migration context. These cases build on the Court's evolving jurisprudence under Article 4, following the landmark *Siliadin* (2006) judgment.

In *Siliadin*, the Court recognized for the first time that Article 4 could give rise to positive obligations for states, including obligations to ensure that effective criminal sanctions were in place and enforced at domestic level. A key question that had arisen in the domestic legal proceedings was how to demarcate the boundaries of everyday intimate labor in the domestic sphere from working conditions contrary to Article 4. The French Civil Court of Appeal, in concluding that exploitation had taken place, was anxious to clarify that *Siliadin* was not a member of the family and was not treated as such (Van Walsum, 2012). The public tests of rights compliance could, therefore, kick in. In contrast, the court found that *Siliadin* had not been subject to working conditions that were "incompatible with human dignity." These conditions they noted were "the lot of many mothers" (para. 44). The court's presumption that the usual standards of human dignity could not apply, therefore, served to distinguish domestic work as "work like no other."

These distinctions came into play again in the subsequent case of *Osman v Denmark* (2011), in which the European Court of Human Rights was required to distinguish between domestic care work provided by a minor in a family context and the boundaries of human trafficking. Osman, a Somali national, had lived in Denmark from the age of seven. At the age of fifteen, she was brought by her father to Kenya and left at the Hagdera refugee camp in Northern Kenya, to care for her paternal grandmother. After two years, she left the camp and applied to be reunited with her family in Denmark. The Court found that the Danish authorities' refusal to reinstate her residence status constituted an unjustifiable interference with her rights to private and to family life.

The AIRE center, representing the applicant, had sought to argue that Osman had been subject to intra-familial human trafficking and that the state had failed in its obligation to investigate and prosecute the offense of trafficking. The Court rejected this argument, however, noting that neither the applicant nor her mother had complained of trafficking to the Danish authorities. This conclusion ignores the positive obligation on states to identify victims of trafficking, recognized as a core obligation under the Council of Europe Convention on Action Against Trafficking and an element of the positive obligations of prevention and deterrence implied by Article 4 ECHR at least since *Rantsev v Cyprus and Russia* (2010). In its judgment, the Court sought to distinguish the work done as part of everyday family life from the exploitation that constitutes an element of human trafficking offenses. Its conclusions, however, fail to acknowledge the role played by gender in determining the kind of work or harm that might be defined as exploitative, or as merely a family role. Neither does it address the wider issue of cultural expectations concerning appropriate family roles and responsibilities or the intersections of gender, race and age as overlapping axes of potential discrimination and disadvantage (Columbia Law School Sexuality and Gender Law Clinic, 2010).

The issue of intra-familial trafficking has also come before the Court in the cases of *CN and V v France* (2012) and in *CN v UK* (2012). The case of *CN and V* concerned the treatment of two sisters aged sixteen and ten years, originally from Burundi, who were living with their aunt and uncle in Paris, following the death of their parents in Burundi's bloody civil war. Both sisters were required to undertake extensive domestic work and the older sister, CN, was also required to undertake care work for the disabled son of her relatives. Reflecting again the continuum of exploitation that is frequently found in domestic work, the Court noted that it was necessary to distinguish "forced or compulsory labour" from work that could "reasonably be required in respect of mutual family assistance or cohabitation, taking into account, among other things, the nature and amount of work in issue" (para. 74). The Court noted that the older sister CN had to perform, under threat of being returned to Burundi, activities that would have been described as work if performed by a remunerated professional. In respect of her treatment, the Court concluded that France had failed to meet its positive obligations to put in place an effective legislative and administrative framework to combat servitude and forced or compulsory labor. The younger sister, V, had attended school, developing social networks that were ultimately central to the Court's finding that no violation had occurred with respect to her situation. This finding was arrived at despite the aunt having been convicted by a domestic court for aggravated assault of V. The Court's finding suggests a failure to acknowledge the relative youth of V as a key issue in assessing the reasonableness of the demands made of her and the likely impact of coercive threats.

The absence of an effective legislative and administrative framework to meet the state's positive obligations under Article 4 ECHR has arisen under a series of cases in the UK. These cases also highlight the difficulties of establishing credibility and of demonstrating the significance of the harms endured by migrant domestic workers. The case of *CN v United Kingdom* (2012) involved a Ugandan applicant who had come to the UK with the assistance of a relative to escape alleged physical and sexual violence. On arrival in the UK, her passport was taken from her by her relative and not returned. She later began work as a live-in carer for an elderly couple, having been introduced to a private recruitment agency. CN claimed not to have received any of the remuneration paid to the agent. She left her live-in carer position after several years, having fallen ill, and sought asylum. She was denied asylum, in part because of a finding of a lack of credibility. A complaint was submitted to the police concerning her treatment by her employers, but it was found that there was insufficient evidence to substantiate the allegation of trafficking, even though it was accepted that there was dispute over payment of wages and that her relative had "kept more than he should have done" (paras. 15–18). Further requests from CN's solicitor to consider prosecutions for *jus cogens* offenses of slavery or forced labor were rejected.

Of note are comments made by the police authorities that the situation was one where "one criminal (her uncle) has taken all the proceeds of their crime" (para. 25). The reference to "their crime" reveals a preoccupation with the irregularity of CN's employment. Elsewhere, the police noted that CN's identity and travel documents were false, suggesting again that the illegality of the applicant's entry to and presence in the UK somehow weakened her claims. As CN argued before the European Court of Human Rights, the suggestion that the lack of payment was no more than "an absence of honour among thieves," betrayed a fundamental disregard of the ILO's key indicators of forced labor and, "a troubling ignorance of the vulnerabilities of illegal immigrants" (para. 49). In correspondence with CN's solicitor, the police commented that they were not aware of any specific offense of forced labor or servitude in UK law, though they noted that "regulation of working conditions are controlled by such areas as health and safety legislation" (para. 30). There is no acknowledgment and perhaps not even awareness on their part that the usual protections of health and safety law so confidently invoked here do not apply to domestic workers.

The Court found the UK to have violated Article 4 ECHR. The Court's judgment on the meaning of servitude is an important one. It recognizes domestic servitude as a specific offense, distinct from trafficking and exploitation, "which involves a complex set of dynamics, involving both overt and more subtle forms of coercion, to force compliance" (para. 80). Due to the absence of a specific offense in domestic law, the Court found that the authorities were unable to give sufficient weight to these factors and to meet their obligation to carry out an effective investigation into CN's complaints. Drawing on *Ranstev*, they noted that a duty to investigate was triggered wherever a "credible suspicion" arose that rights had been violated. In this case, the Court was particularly critical of the police authorities' failure to interview key actors, notably CN's relative and the private recruitment agent. What was required under Article 4, they said, was a "thorough investigation," one premised on an understanding of "the many subtle ways an individual can fall under the control of another" (para. 80). The Court was also critical of the failure to give any weight to CN's complaints that her passport was taken from her, her wages were withheld, and she was frequently threatened with reporting to the immigration authorities. All of these were factors, as the Court noted, that came within the scope of the ILO's indicators of forced labor.

The duty of effective investigation also arose in the case of *OOO and Others v Commissioner of Police for the Metropolis* (2011). In this case four Nigerian women complained that they had been brought to the UK as children and forced to undertake extensive domestic work, including child care. Each of the women complained that they had been regularly subject to physical and emotional abuse. Although they had sought protection and assistance from the police, their complaints were not pursued. The High Court accepted that the four claimants, who had alleged treatment contrary to Articles 3 and 4 ECHR on the part of their employers, were concerned about their migration status in the UK and that this concern had impacted on their willingness to cooperate in a police investigation. The court found, however, that "reasonable sensitivity" on the part of the police authorities could have overcome this obstacle. A duty of effective investigation arose on the part of the police, they said, whenever a credible allegation was received, "however that information comes to their attention" (para. 163). The duty of effective investigation arising under Articles 3 and 4 ECHR, the court concluded, had not been met in this case.

For irregular or temporary migrants, the recognition of such a positive duty to investigate is critical. The difficulty, however, is that investigation, and the claiming of rights, may lead not to the possibility of remaining but to deportation. For those who are identified as victims of trafficking, rights to remain may be triggered (GRETA, 2012). Outside of the trafficking framework, however, deportability remains a constant limit to rights. That migrant domestic workers continue to enact rights through a process of claim making before the European Court of Human Rights reveals the continuing resonance and force of rights claims. States, employers, and others continue to resist such claims, however, and, in particular, refuse to acknowledge the nexus between denials of rights and migration status. Claiming rights through human rights litigation in domestic and international courts can lead to the creation of "contact zones," in which an "alternative legality" is presented, drawing on the transformative promise of human rights norms (De Sousa Santos, 2002). The claims presented reveal the potential to position domestic work firmly within the world of work and highlight the injustice of failing to apply generally applicable workplace and human rights norms. The obstacles to presenting such cases and claims are many, however, particularly for migrant domestic workers whose status may be tied to that of their employer, their presence within the territory of the state dependant on the goodwill of an unscrupulous employer, or perhaps irregular or illegal. The isolated and privatized nature of domestic work also limits the emergence of contact zones within which alternative legalities may be presented.

Given the high levels of irregularity and undeclared work in the domestic work sector, a key issue at the intersections of migration, gender and race is the application and enforcement of employment protections to migrant domestic workers in irregular situations. In *Hounga v Allen* (2012), the Court of Appeal held that the applicant, a Nigerian citizen employed in the UK as an au pair, could not bring a race discrimination claim against her employers as she was knowingly working unlawfully in the UK. Although the court accepted that she had suffered ill-treatment, including physical abuse in the course of her employment, they found that she was precluded from bringing forward a claim that was "clearly connected or inextricably bound up or linked with her own illegal conduct" (para. 61). On appeal, the Supreme Court (2014) reversed the Court of Appeal's findings and unanimously agreed that the illegality defense could not defeat the complaint of discrimination.[35] In a landmark judgment, the court found that the illegality was no more than the context in the respondent, Mrs Allen, perpetrated the acts of physical, verbal and emotional abuse by which, among other things, she dismissed Miss Hounga from her employment. Questioning the conclusion of the Court of Appeal that Miss Hounga was "obviously" an equal participant in the illegality of her presence, Lord Wilson was in no doubt as to who bore the greater responsibility, and questioned whether the "cruel misuse" of her perceived vulnerability would be a further justification for the defeat of Miss Hounga's complaint (para. 39). The court cited developments in international human rights law, including Article 4 ECHR and related case law, the Council of Europe Convention Against Trafficking in Human Beings (2005) and the Palermo Protocol. Ultimately the court concluded that the defense of illegality ran, "strikingly counter to the prominent strain of current public policy against trafficking and in favour of the protection of its victims" (para. 52). As such it was trumped in this case by public policy in favor of the protection of victims. Concluding Lord Wilson noted with "judicious hesitation" that, if Miss Hounga's case was not one of trafficking, it was "so close to it" that the distinction did not matter. The public policy interest in combating human trafficking trumped the defense of illegality. Ms Hounga was accepted by the court as presenting at least five of the ILO's six indicators of forced labor. Not all domestic workers subject to abuse, however, will present at the extremes of exploitation and wider questions as to the whether the ordinary protections of employment law can still be vindicated by an illegally present migrant remain.

In *Siliadin*, the European Court of Human Rights recognized states' positive obligations in the context of Article 4. It failed, however, to recognize that such obligations could extend to regularization of a victim's migration status and to positive obligations of rehabilitation (Cullen, 2006). The nexus between migration routes and states' positive obligations of prevention and protection were given more consideration in *Rantsev v Cyprus and Russia* (2010), a case involving trafficking for the purposes of sexual exploitation. Specifically the Court found that

35 [2014] WLR 2889, [2014] UKSC 47, [2014] ICR 847, [2014] Eq LR 559, [2014] 4 All ER 595, [2014] 1 WLR 2889.

Article 4 requires states to put in place adequate measures to regulate businesses used as a cover for human trafficking and to ensure that domestic legislation provides "practical and effective protection of the rights of victims and potential victims of trafficking" (para. 284). The Court found that the Cypriot government had violated Article 4 by not regulating the "cabaret artiste" industry and by maintaining a visa regime for cabaret artistes that did not provide effective protection against trafficking. On this reading, destination states may be found in breach of their Convention obligations if they continue to operate immigration schemes that put migrant domestic workers at risk of treatment contrary to Article 4.

V. Conclusion

The links between limited opportunities for legal migration for domestic workers and the high level of irregularity in the sector have been emphasized by the EU Fundamental Rights Agency, amongst others (Council of Europe Parliamentary Assembly Committee on Migration, Refugees and Population, 2011; EU Fundamental Rights Agency, 2011). Irregularity, as they note, leads to high levels of insecurity, producing susceptibility to exploitation and difficulties in accessing rights protections (Cyrus, 2008). In response to concerns of abuse and exploitation of migrant domestic workers, however, it is open to states to respond by expanding immigration controls rather than seeking to remedy the disadvantages that continue to attach to precarious migration status. As Dauvergne (2008) notes, "Once an argument is shifted to the terrain of rights, the right of the nation to shut its borders tends to overshadow the rights claims of individuals" (p. 27). The deportability of the alien persists as a constant threat to the claiming and enjoyment of rights.

The changes introduced in the ODW visa regime in the UK reveal the continuing willingness of states to limit migration options for domestic workers. Against the background of such resistance from states, the potential of human rights law to provide an effective bulwark against exclusion in the migration context must be questioned. Borders proliferate the texts of human rights law and as De Sousa Santos argues, exclusion rather than exploitation has become the central mechanism of disentitlement from law's protections. His comment appears particularly relevant to migrant domestic workers. Exclusions and exemptions that operate in employment laws, in laws and policies on access to social security, in immigration and citizenship laws, and in the scope of diplomatic immunity protections reinforce the invisibility and vulnerability of domestic workers. These exclusions take the form and shape of de-juridifications that limit the application of human rights norms to domestic work and to migration status (Blackett, 2011).

Assessing the process of law reform in the UK law, it might be argued that the position from 1998 to 2012 was an anomaly of sorts, the product of a short-lived "political moment" and a powerful advocacy campaign that successfully enacted domestic workers' rights (Ranciére, 2004). The ODW visa, though imperfect, provided a better "place in the world" (Arendt, 1986) for migrant domestic workers – a route to settlement, the possibility of changing employers, and of sponsoring family dependants. The reforms introduced by the UK government have removed these possibilities, returning migrant domestic workers again to a deeply unequal employment relationship and a precarious migration status. Is the status of the migrant domestic worker diminished then to that of "bare life?" As yet, it is unclear whether human rights law can effectively resist such processes of exclusion or whether the deployment of law continuously reproduces "categories of illegal at its boundaries" limiting the transformative promise of human rights norms (Dauvergne, 2008).

Human rights law, if it recognizes the nexus between migration status, access to safe migration routes, and the enjoyment of rights, has the potential to be transformative. States continue to resist this potential, however. The process of enacting rights, in courts and through political activism, is a difficult and uncertain one, but one that can be empowering (Benhabib, 2011). Reforms secured are contingent and reversible, as the story of the ODW visa reveals. In the context of migrant domestic workers in the UK, the limiting of a migration pathway reflects the potential for coercive exercises of state power that reverse reforms secured through sustained political activism. Such reversals, however, may yet be challenged, at which point the inescapable nexus between the state's migration laws, migration status, and human rights violations cannot be denied.

13

BAD JOBS AND GOOD WORKERS

The hiring of ex-prisoners in a segmented economy

Kristin Bumiller[1]

In an era of rising incarceration rates in the US, people who have spent time in prison face especially dismal prospects for working in the legitimate economy (Nixon et al., 2008; Travis, 2005; Western, 2008). Those exiting prison are among the most severely impacted by low job availability and often employed in the lowest tier of a segmented economy (Hudson, 2007; Wagmiller, 2007). The enormous significance to individuals and society of lost productivity, underemployment, and unemployment is yet to be fully documented, but the costs of denied access to paid labor both during and post incarceration is far greater than in other industrialized countries with lower incarceration rates (Western et al., 2001).

Coincident with mass incarceration and increasing inequality are other structural forces that disadvantage workers, including the growth of neoliberalism and the associated advent of a risk society, failures in the mechanisms of democratic governance, and the globalization of flexible labor markets (Peck, 2010b; Sassen, 2011). Moreover, the predominantly Black and Hispanic population of former prisoners is jeopardized by the erosion of liberal democratic frameworks that have previously protected workplace rights for disadvantaged groups (Kalleberg, 2009). When the formerly incarcerated seek employment, they often compete with other workers who are part of a growing class of "unemployables," including undocumented immigrants, the disabled, and persons with spotty work histories (Standing, 2011). Under these conditions, employers wield excessive power over "undesirable" prospective employees through discretionary hiring decisions and broad leeway in setting the conditions of employment.

Despite the wide-ranging structural barriers to finding work and the enormous challenges of entering the workforce through undesirable jobs, reintegration

1 George Daniel Olds Professor in Economic and Social Institutions, Amherst College. This research was funded by the Amherst College Faculty Research Award Program.

programs often focus on preparing their clients for work rather than job creation (Hallett, 2012; Martin, 2011; Wacquant, 2010). Efforts are devoted to enhancing "work readiness," skill training for interviewing and minimal job performance. These strategies follow from paradigmatic approaches in reentry programming that promote clients' success through encouraging responsibility (Bumiller, 2013). Other solutions focus on the problem of discrimination and how it impacts recidivism (LeBel, 2012; Pogarsky, 2006; Weiman, 2007).

Many advocates for the formerly incarcerated have pointed to the growing use of criminal records checks and their illegitimate use in employment decisions as ways in which the resilience of this group is further undermined. The leading edge of reform is centered on putting the formerly incarcerated on a more equal footing in the job market by "banning the box" and restricting access to public records (O'Neill, 2012; Stoll and Bushway, 2008). One of the most cited studies finds that discrimination based upon criminal records is significant, especially when the job candidate is Black (Holzer et al., 2006; Pager, 2007; but see also Holzer et al., 2006). The use of this information is largely unregulated. In fact, state laws that impose restrictions, in particular provisions that disenfranchise felons, create a considerable lack of clarity about the illegality of discrimination based on criminal record and erode the presumption that once released from prison people regain their full rights as citizens (Jacobs and Larrauri, 2012). In addition, record checks are mandated by state law for a wide range of occupations that involve contact with "vulnerable populations" (Jacobs and Crepet, 2007/2008). These exclusions are often broadly applied and have a significant impact on the range of job types to which the formerly incarcerated can aspire. Most state registries restrict the availability of criminal record information to non-authorized employers; in spite of this, information is readily available from private companies (Blumstein and Nakamura, 2009).[2]

Formal and informal workplace norms also may discourage the hiring of applicants with criminal records. Studies of organizations have documented the growing tendency for employers to adopt bureaucratic guidelines that insulate them from legal liability regarding their hiring and firing decisions (Edelman and Suchman, 1997; Edelman et al., 2011; Epp, 2009). The incentives further a risk adverse environment at all levels of society, but especially within workplace organizations which face their own vulnerability to legal liability and market pressures. Specifically, in regards to hiring people with criminal records, concerns are raised about harm to other employees and criminal activity in the workplace (for contrary findings, see Backman, 2011).

I. Investigating precarious work

While employers' aversion to employing the formerly incarcerated, concurrent racism, and growing risk aversion in workplaces are undoubtedly significant factors for employment in some types of jobs, the promise of law reform and

2 Restrictions by state governments are on the horizon. In fact, after the research phase of this project was completed, the state in which my interviews took place enacted new protections regarding the use of criminal records in employment.

instituting rights may not be fully realizable. This chapter provides a theoretical and empirical focus that attempts to capture the complexity of the barriers to sustainable workplace participation. In this research, the employment difficulties of persons exiting prisons are seen in the context of structural forces linked to the prison apparatus and declining economic opportunities for marginalized workers.

Interviewing employers about their reasons for rejecting applicants, especially in situations where these decisions are legally questionable and based upon confidential information, was not viable. This project, however, investigated the corresponding hypothesis, by exploring the factors that promote receptivity to hiring people with criminal records. In effect, this project posed a question rarely considered in studies of employment discrimination: who chooses *not* to discriminate?

The sampling area included two middle-sized cities in the Northeastern US. Both cities have substantial populations of racial and ethnic minorities and high levels of racial segregation. Prior to deciding on a sampling strategy, I gathered information about the type and variety of employers in the region and their policies regarding criminal record checks. I also attended several group meetings of two organizations focused on addressing ex-prisoners' issues and learned about their strategies for improving employment prospects for their membership. Additional information was gathered from consultations with three job counselors who specialized in working with formerly incarcerated men and women. These counselors provided extensive information about the type and location of jobs available to their clients.

My interviewees were drawn from a comprehensive sample of employers in the region willing to hire persons with criminal records. One of the job counselors, who worked as a specialist in a government employment service, provided me with her master list of 179 employers known to local agencies as showing interest in, or who had actually hired, individuals with criminal records. The list included the contact information for the person responsible for hiring decisions, usually the owner, franchise operator, supervisor, or for the few larger businesses, a human resource manager. I used a random number generator to select employers off the master list. The requests for an interview yielded a 41% response rate (out of 56 employers contacted, 23 agreed to be interviewed).

The company types include small and large manufacturers and distributors, human service agencies, small retail and service businesses, restaurants, unions, and staffing agencies.[3] All of the employers were offering jobs at entry-level wages with limited opportunity for advancement. The racial and ethnic composition of the interviewees includes disproportionally more persons identified as white than in the regional population.

These employers offer jobs that better represent the type and quality of paid work that people exiting prison will enter than a broad-based sample of all entry-level jobs. The conditions of these jobs, and importantly the perspective of the

3 More information on the data is available in the article version of this chapter, found in *Theoretical Criminology*.

employers, may differ from other entry-level jobs, including at some restaurant chains, retail pharmacies, and home improvement stores, where corporate offices routinely screen and eliminate all applicants from the pool with criminal records. This presents a more accurate picture of the restricted range of jobs realistically available to most ex-prisoners. However, it is important to recognize that the analysis presented is limited by its reliance only upon the perspective of the employers and does not draw from interviews with employees with criminal records.

The interviews with the 23 employers were conducted in person and at their place of business, each lasting approximately two hours. The interviews were tape-recorded (except in three cases in which interviewees preferred not to be recorded), fully transcribed, and manually coded. The format was semi-structured and each employer was asked the questions focused on their hiring strategies, use of criminal record checks, legal incentives/disincentives, and security/risk issues in the workplace. The data analysis process involved identifying common themes across interviews and coding all interviews for statements corresponding to one of these themes. As the following data analysis will show, my interviewees were deeply engaged with these issues but demonstrated little interest in speaking about the more formal legal processes and criteria for hiring. By far, employers were most animated by discussing a general problem evoked by the topic of hiring persons with criminal records: the difficulty of finding good workers to do bad jobs. Some interviewees were more illustrative in their description of common themes and their responses feature more prominently in the following sections of the chapter.

All of the interviews were conducted during the Great Recession, between 2008 and 2009. Both cities have suffered from long-term deindustrialization and decline of a once diversified manufacturing sector and were further affected by the economic downturn (Doussard et al., 2009). These communities are also severely impacted by trends in the economy that degrade the conditions of work, such as non-standard work arrangements (Albelda et al., 2004; Appelbaum et al., 2003; Kalleberg et al., 2000, 273). One example of this trend is the rise in the number of temporary agencies concentrated in communities with high numbers of the formerly incarcerated (Elcioglu, 2010; Peck and Theodore, 2008). Economists describe these conditions as the growth of job "precariousness," in which "most employment contracts are informal, incomplete, and shaped by social institutions and norms in addition to their formal, explicit features" (Kalleberg, 2009, p. 12).

II. Hiring at the bottom

When the employers talked about the kind of jobs they provided, it came with acknowledgment of the undesirability of the work. In fact, the work was often described as offering little satisfaction or not much interest. In terms of challenges, at most, these jobs required physical strength or dexterity and an ability to follow simple instructions. The recruiter at Fast Lane Staffing (2) put it bluntly: "it is the crappiest work there is, they're just your two hundred pounds of muscle."

Consequently, the employers conveyed low expectations about the quality of their potential employees. For example, the hiring manager for Super Parts explained:

> I'm a realist – what level of people we're hiring. People aren't making a huge living here. So I understand we're going to get people from all walks of life, people that are just coming out . . . It's all about what I'm paying them. As long as they're doing the job, this is the connection. I pay you; you do this. If you're doing that, you're worth every penny I'm paying you, maybe more.

There was a ready admission by the manager at Rent-All that "most of the people who work here would take a full-time steady job if they could get one and hold it." The owner of Ultimate Supplier made a joke about the required qualifications of their workers: "It's good if they can breathe," and "we check blood temperature and put [them] to work."

A hodgepodge workforce, ex-prisoners, immigrants, and people with gaps in their work history, filled these jobs. The employees were described as demographically representative of the ethnic and racial mix of their local communities. The manager from Rent-All made the further observation that the composition of people in local prisons closely corresponded to the demographic profile of people interested in a job of this quality and at its pay level:

> I don't really see any difference [in incarcerated men looking for jobs] than in the regular population that's out there, of people that would be interested in working here for the money and doing what we do. I mean, you go to the hiring show that the [local jail] puts on and there's a lot of minorities, probably the same percentage that's in the system are out of the system now.

Despite the ready acknowledgment about the quality of work, employers spoke of the desirable aspects of the jobs, especially for persons coming out of prison. The manager from All-in-One Supplies stated, "if you can do it, maybe, we'll let you become part of the group." The manager of Ready Services referred to the growth of friendship networks on the crew:

> That's what I like about our crew here. Even some people who came in [from jail], they had no transportation. They were taking the bus, sometimes even a taxi, sometimes walking. Within weeks of working on whatever shift they work, they've made friendships or at least a rapport with other people so that someone will say, can I give you a ride home?

This employer believed that social recognition and friendship networks, which emerged from workplace environments, provided an added benefit beyond a paycheck.

From these employers' perspective, even though the paycheck is in almost all cases well below a living wage, it serves as a placeholder in the legitimate economy, and potentially a step toward sustainable employment. Yet to some employers' chagrin, the desirability of legitimate over illegitimate employment is not always apparent and some of the most talented workers leave to work in the illegal economy, while the best employees quickly moved to better jobs. The owner of Ultimate Supplier saw himself as combining an altruistic and realistic response to this dilemma:

> But the people that come in – you do what you can to help. Sometimes you have to encourage people to leave you because they want more. I understand that, and you deserve more, you're entitled to more. You've improved. But our business can't afford that. So, still work here, find a new job, and give us two weeks' notice. Use us for a reference if you want. That's all you can do. You can't put yourself out of business trying to be a good guy.

For most of the employers, relying on personal judgment and creating a sense of trust was an essential element of workplace management. The supervisor from Downtown Parts described this as the attitude of a "lenient shop" that "allowed learning and trusted people not to take advantage." Hiring and management decisions were seen as rooted in mutual understanding and expectations and screening tactics, including criminal record and credit checks, were inconsistent with building the foundation of the future relationship. An employment manager of a large company, Book Binders, not only described record checks as impractical and unnecessary, but less reliable than his own capacity to evaluate potential employees:

> I will try to ascertain in the interview, if the person is forthright and up front with me. Say we're making [our product], and we get a call that they want 1.3 million more in the next month, sometimes it's hard to say hold up the hiring because we're going to run a [record check] on 300 people that we need. So, you use your basic instinct or your judgment, and if anything is out of line – remember they're temporary employees – we will terminate immediately.

The manager from All-in-One Supplies pronounced the importance of responding to individuals on their merits:

> I have been amazed at what my perceptions have been about all kinds of people whether they have criminal pasts or not, and the value judgments I've made by initial impression. When I find out what those people have been capable of in a positive and a negative way, it's always been a real reality check for me because I'm staggered sometimes by the false judgments we make about people, at both ends of the street. Personally, for me, my judgments are always tempered by that, because of how wrong I've been, and pleasantly, because it's been an awakening kind of experience more than one that firmed up my prejudices.

The manager at Burger Master simply relied upon a "gut feeling," rather than information about job histories and considered if an employee lasted "more than a year you're pretty lucky." As these statements make clear, reliance on personal judgment enhanced the likelihood that every potential employee would be given a chance to prove his or her worth. However, this opportunity was only made possible by an "at-will" employment situation where unsatisfactory workers are routinely fired.

While some employers invest in minimal training of a new employee, the interviewees did not use the language of rehabilitation. Desirable employees were not "created" through training, rather they arrive ready to do the job. In this regard, many of the employers believed in ex-prisoners' innate capacity for success. The managers from Helping Hands and Best Furniture expressed this sense of optimism about formerly incarcerated employees: "many people who have been incarcerated can turn out to be good employees," and "most people are able to change."

The commonsense understanding of employers was that success was most likely when contravening factors in ex-prisoners' lives are settled, making it possible for the new employee to recognize the benefits of sustaining a job. The employers refrained from making generalizations about the formerly incarcerated but rather had a more complex understanding of their barriers to working. For example, the representative from Union #44 described the problems as "no cars, there's no living arrangements, and their lives are a bit disorganized." The manager from All-in-One Supplies explicitly cited the negative impact of prison experience on an individual's capacity to hold a job:

> Unfortunately, there's a lot of the superficial bravado that comes with being incarcerated, "I can do that in my sleep," lots of promises, lots of hype, lots of "I'm going to be the best thing that's ever come in." Then, within a short period of time, the issues that have made it difficult for that person to stay employed and to be successful in whatever endeavors come back to haunt them.

A few employers explicitly mentioned the special needs of the formerly incarcerated, such as a necessity for structure or help in thinking through logistical challenges. These needs were also associated with the incapacities acquired from long-term existence within a prison environment.

Ultimately, many employers conceded that the failure rate for the formerly incarcerated is high. For example, the representative from Union #44 expected to sort through large numbers of unskilled workers and "lose about 50% of them." While employers were resigned to this reality, they still expressed the value in giving a potential employee a chance. For example, an employer from Ready Services described the satisfaction of making an unlikely hire: "When we hire them – I call them on the phone or something – and they'll say, 'Oh, my God! Really? Oh, my God!' You feel good. To me – most of it has been drugs, drugs and alcohol." The owner of Green Company suggested that whether or not it worked out for a given individual "maybe as an employer the most you can do is give someone a chance." One employer saw giving someone an opportunity against the odds as a normal aspect of hiring at the bottom and commented: "We've hired people with drug backgrounds. That's been difficult. Some worked out, some did not. It wasn't violence. They were either dealing, or using, or something, and they were stealing to get money for drugs, which is pretty standard." Overall, there was a pervasive sense of realism, not only about the undesirability of the jobs offered, but of the often-insurmountable odds of the formerly incarcerated sustaining employment.

III. Second chances, sometimes, third and fourth

The norms guiding the employers' decisions arise from the constraints of operating a business at the lowest segment of the market. Even representatives of larger companies expressed concern about having a workforce in place to meet fluctuating production demands. At the bottom, employers described themselves as having little choice about who to hire, frequently using their prerogative to fire, and exercising limited leeway in setting standards and procedures. As the manager at Handy Movers put it: "such a high turnover determines everything." In this context, employers saw themselves as making "seat of the pants" decisions rather than applying principles of personnel management.

When asked directly if they collected criminal record information from the state or private agencies, only 26% did so regularly. The employers, for the most part, imagined their employees with criminal backgrounds (if they knew this to be the case) as presenting the same issues as employees who have never gone to prison. The supervisor at Downtown Parts made this clear: "if they went to jail I know what they did wrong, but some people here, never went to jail, and it's just because they never got caught." This perception displaced the assumption that criminal background was an important factor in determining one's potential capacity to do the job:

> I actually have a person working for me now that spent eight years in jail for manslaughter. He's not my greatest employee, but he's not a discipline problem. I judge them when they get here. I mean, if I see unacceptable behavior, we get rid of them. I'm not afraid to get rid of people if they're causing me aggravation, if somebody isn't fitting in or they're causing problems out in the shop, they'll go. I don't let people's past influence what I do now. I feel everybody deserves another chance.

Employers also chose not to gather criminal record information because "everybody I would hire has a record" or "what is the use of [record checks] – what does it tell me that I don't already know?" The representative of Union #44 actually saw construction work as an opportunity for "casual" employment because "a lot of our contractors don't really care about [criminal records]. What they want to know is how many sheets a day you can do."

Those who checked criminal records were confronted with the pervasiveness of criminal backgrounds within the hiring pool, finding "problems across the board, including many people that they don't expect to have records" and "you don't know who is going to fail the screens, can't predict." The human resource manager at The Paper Mill, who gathered information, complained about not having the time to figure out what it means. Large employers were more likely than small businesses to actively weigh the consequences of hiring someone with a criminal history but still saw themselves as exercising broad discretion in deciding whether or not to hire. For example, an employer, from AAA Manufacturing explained how she made hiring decisions if the potential employee had a record:

> Absolutely, yeah, and honestly, talking to the individual, talking to the hiring manager, gathering information. I've been doing the job in Human Resources for 26 years, so I've done this a lot. Some risks are acceptable to take; some aren't, depending upon the severity of the crime, how recent it is, the pattern of it, all come into play. I'm going to have other associates being around this person. That's a very important piece, because, God forbid, that person assaults somebody, and we had in our information when hiring this person that they had this in their past, the litigation liability a company like ours or any company faces in that is astronomical.

Two of the employers were explicit that their judgments about criminal history were entirely based upon their relevance to the present:

> I judge them once they get in the door – as long as they're willing to do the work, most of the time. I happen to know about this employee because he had a tattoo, and I asked another employee, does that tattoo mean something? There's a teardrop right here. You know, me coming from suburbia, I had a feeling it meant something. So I asked somebody else and he explained it to me, what it meant. Then he actually filled in the rest of the blanks about it. I think he was a young kid at the time. He was probably in a gang. I don't get the sense that this guy could ever kill anybody. He just doesn't seem like the type of person, but he was probably caught up in the thing. But he did his time. He does his work here. He doesn't seem to have a temper or anything. So, he doesn't seem like the type.

And:

> I see it as people have made some bad mistakes in their lives, they've had poor judgment, but that doesn't mean that they should have to wear it all the time, or that they should be marked for life, or not be successful now that they've moved on. They've sort of paid the price already. What we're looking for are people that are ready to get on with what they want to do. They want to participate. They're motivated and they're mature. They know

> when to come in. They know when to let some petty things go on the job because it's really about making some money.

If an employer preferred not to hire ex-prisoners, such as the manager at Rent-All, it was motivated by logistical problems rather than perceptions about their suitability as workers:

> In some cases we've had some pre-release where they would be braceleted, and they'd have to be somewhere at a certain time, which would not allow them to work some of the hours that we needed them for. So that's been a problem in the past. What stops us from considering those people as opposed to off-the-street hires is, like I said, most of them don't have licenses.

While interviewees described numerous reasons why they would take record information into account, none of these employers (drawn from a sample of those willing to consider workers with a criminal background) treated records as a clear-cut disqualifying factor in the hiring process.

This relative openness to employing people with criminal histories, however, was usually accompanied by confidence in their ability to maintain workplace norms. Many of the employers talked extensively about their zero-tolerance policies in regards to substance abuse and workplace theft. Despite stringent regulation, the majority of employers (52%) used no drug testing or surveillance technology. Two of the staffing agencies only utilized drug testing when mandated by a placement with a specific employer. While some of the employers utilized surveillance technology, one of them admitted to having cameras just for show.

However, in a few cases the ethic of second chances was applied even to violators of workplace policies. For example, the manager of All-in-One Supplies gave the option of returning to employees who were sent home for being under the influence:

> I have a pretty good idea what people are doing and when. I tell them when they come here that they've come here for a reason. They're going to be driving a vehicle that's capable of causing incredible harm, that could put us out of business in a day, and that we're all working too hard for somebody to be that stupid, that if they have that kind of issue, they just can't be here doing it. Most of the folks that I have are folks that'll go out and get high on occasion, have a beer on occasion, do most of the things that are socially acceptable and/or not. It's just made very clear that it just doesn't happen here. What they do on their own time, they have to make their own decisions, but we're fairly perceptive and fairly intolerant of the wrong thing. We send people home. It doesn't happen very often, you know, go home, don't be here, and think about whether or not you want to come back because that kind of stuff just can't happen.

As the manager from Ready Services stated: "everybody deserves a second chance. In some cases, a third and fourth." This employer further described her willingness to make allowances to let employees resolve substance abuse and other issues:

> We know people, maybe not so much people who came to us from that program specifically, but people that have made mistakes in their personal lives, that have cost them an amount of freedom for an amount of time, court issues or whatever, that have left, sort of disappeared or said, I can't be here for a while, and we've taken them back.

While recognizing the high prevalence of substance abuse among the formerly incarcerated, she also noted that it was a problem with a broad reach across society: "I don't think there's any person in here, including myself – I'm not going to speak for you – that hasn't been affected by someone close to them having a drug and/or alcohol problem."

Despite concerns for the economic survival of their businesses, these employers often took it upon themselves to help someone overcome a challenge. A few employers talked at length about their reasons for helping an employee. For example, the hiring manager from Super Parts described such efforts as sensible:

> We've actually done people on work release from the jail. I had a shipper that was here for a long time. He'd come here from a work-release sort of thing, then he ended up being back in jail. I actually had to go pick him up in the morning because he couldn't get close enough to here on the bus. So I'd go pick him up so he could get out of jail sooner. Otherwise, he would've been there a few more. He was still in jail, but it got him out during the day. And I needed him. To me, it's like a non-issue.

The head of human resources at Book Binders went to unusual lengths for a particular employee:

> But I would say to them, "I gave you a shot. You're making me look bad." And here's what I did for someone – they were that close to being terminated. They lived a couple of blocks away from me. I said, "Because of your attendance and your tardiness, you're going to lose your job. In the morning, pick me up because I'm not going to be late. If I am late, you're out of here. Pick me up, and you're going to drop me off." You know that person's been here 35 years?

Another account from the hiring manager at AAA Manufacturing described giving someone time off to resolve his personal problems:

> I have a man now, who over the last four years has called me up twice and said, "I need to go into detox. I need some time." You know, years ago he'd

> been in trouble, and now, hasn't actually been in trouble, but has relapsed a number of times. He will call. He knows he doesn't come here under the influence.

The restaurant manager at Family Diner recounted numerous situations where giving someone a chance did not work out. The owner of Ultimate Supplier spoke of his deep disappointment:

> Obviously, part of the payback is that you feel good when you help somebody recover. And you know it. That makes you feel good. It's a self-serving thing, as well. It can be. It can be awfully painful at times. You get some people you really lose sleep over because you want to do the right thing. The fellow that I had to terminate because of the alcohol was with me for eight years. He was a recovering alcoholic. He reverted back, had a relapse. I talked with him, tried to convince him to get help. He just simply was not able to do that, and so we had to part ways. He walked out the door crying, and I walked down the hall crying because I'd lost him. What I had to do I knew was going to hurt him and his family. But I didn't want him to get hurt here, and I didn't want him to hurt anyone else here. I had to do what I had to do. Most of my decisions are not decisions I want to make but decisions that I have to make.

Questionable hires are considered worth the likely disappointment because of the possible joy arising from a success story:

> For the one out of 20 that do make it, the fact that we have high standards and they met them does make them become a success story. This one woman that I'm thinking of who is really my only success story so far in seven years, my one real success story, my 100% success story, was a single mom in her young 20s, living with her mother, couldn't hold a job. Her life was a disaster, really messed up. Now, she's been an employee for two years with living wages, health insurance, and full benefits. She's living on her own. Her life has really turned around. She's taking on more responsibilities. It's just so heartwarming to see. But, it's the exception for us, not the rule.

From these employers' perspective, finding a good worker was like waiting for an accident to happen. These accidents affirmed the power of their own intuitions, as in this case of hiring a woman right out of jail by Quick-Hire Staffing: "It was as if God was shining down on me. I think I'm a pretty good judge of character. When meeting her, I just felt it was a go. She's been here over a year now, and like I said, she's just phenomenal." The marginal conditions of the workplace are even viewed as a potential asset for an employee who needs accommodations, as the manager at The Paper Mill reasoned: "It's a small company. We're not General Motors. We have the ability to make exceptions for anybody and everybody that needs them.

I mean a doctor's appointment, take their kids somewhere, we just accommodate those things." In this situation, the employer saw himself as offering a worker the flexibility she needed. Such efforts were not necessarily framed as legal obligations, but rather as part of a strategy to keep in place potentially good employees.

IV. Normalizing risk

These employers talked about the risks associated with hiring employees with criminal records as an expected and ordinary aspect of doing business. For instance, employers often evaluated the potential risk of hiring someone with a criminal record in the context of other threats to the security and productivity of their company. Simply put by one employer who was not concerned: "there's nothing here worth stealing." The hiring manager at AAA Manufacturing explained that she was more concerned about the hassle of actually utilizing security systems, screening, and other technologies designed to reduce risk. However, she concluded: "You can't control everything but I think you have to take reasonable steps." In some cases, the greater perceived risk stemmed from not having employees in place to do the work. For example, the hiring manager at The Paper Mill argued that under these conditions it would be extremely "risky" to exclude potential employees based on criminal history because "anybody would be kidding themselves if they didn't think that every workplace could exist without somebody that's had an issue or has spent a little bit of time incarcerated or whatever – I mean, they're workforce".

The employers accepted the regularity of encountering potential employees with criminal records as a result of both the kind of work offered and the level of pay. This included the understanding that since their businesses operate in an urban setting, then "having a record" was the norm, especially for minority males. Moreover, the reliance on informal networks also brought in ex-prisoners, as people with criminal records recruit acquaintances who also have records. The owner of Ultimate Supplier described employees as coming in waves, first Vietnamese, Russians and then we "have some people that come out of the work program at the [city name redacted] College, what we affectionately call it, the prison. We have them come down, and we start them on their recovery." This employer accepted that following these "waves" was absolutely necessary in order to maintain a capable and reliable workforce over the long term.

A notable exception among some employers was heightened concern when considering hiring people who have committed violent crimes. In these cases, the employers worried about the potential for someone fighting in the workplace, selling drugs on the property, or recruiting for gangs. The owner of Green Company explicitly stated that he would not consider someone for employment who was convicted of a violent crime. He was particularly uneasy about "specific behaviors, which might cause problems in our workplace." In all, six employers specifically mentioned the importance of looking carefully at a particular individual's record if it included violent crimes. But overall, the employers conveyed a remarkable degree of perspicacity about "criminals." Stereotypical assumptions about criminals may carry less weight in a context of familiarity and when problematic employees can be easily fired. This attitude was seen in a variety of comments: "there's no significant difference with their success rate versus somebody who comes in without that background," "people go to jail for all sorts of reasons, not necessarily because they are bad people," and "[it's] not high risk taking people right out of jail – the only risk is that they could not work out." A human resources administrator from Reliable Distributions found it necessary to educate others in her company about the hazards of applying stereotypes:

> We had an individual show up in the newspaper for failing to register as an offender, a sex offender, for charges unknown to us. They had been working for us for years. I had a line of people at my office door saying, "I'm not working with this person." But they had been working with this person for years, and they'd never harmed anyone, you know. It was having to say to people, "You don't know the history. You don't know the story. You read three lines in a newspaper. This person's been here for this many years. They have a right to continue to be here. There have a right to be here free from harassment."

Her spirit of generosity reached beyond situations involving criminal records – she also pointed out that lots of people, not just people that go to jail, mess up and make regrettable, or even tragic mistakes. The hiring manager at The Paper Mill also cautioned against making judgments: "People have made choices to sell drugs to not necessarily support their habit but to support their family, when there were no other options." The manager at Best Furniture knew that she hired someone with a conviction for child pedophilia and although the company was concerned about liability, "we said okay, we're just going to accept the risk, and we did it".

V. Legality and the state

In these interviews, the employers emphasized the importance of external constraints on their decision making. Perhaps heightened by the ongoing recession, employers for both large and small businesses as well as those affiliated with national corporations or locally owned, spoke of acute pressures in the day-to-day operation. Consequently, concerns were raised about the costs of assisting people who came to them with a history of incarceration, disabilities, family problems, or other issues that affected their ability to work. Accordingly, despite concerns about employees' needs, the employers felt that they had to keep in mind the vulnerability of their business. Two employers found this agonizing:

> The biggest problem that we've had is that when we've had folks that have been incarcerated or have had little structure; they tend to need more guidance and supervision than I can sometimes offer. If we were set up differently

> and I could have somebody who could number one, constantly mentor, and number two, intervene, it would be a different kind of operation. We might have more success than we've had in the past with folks like that. There's somebody out there who will surprise us and turn into a productive member of our team and of society. There are parts of me that wish I could run a program that did nothing but. But because there's a bottom line and a set of circumstances which means I can't ever let my customers down.

And:

> We don't see them again, or in some cases, like the Labor Ready guys, they might work three hours, stop, and go get a fix. We're not able to provide them the kind of help that they need to become productive members of the workforce. We've been talking to places like [organization's names deleted] about whether somebody could do a labor-ready service for us, so when we need people, not permanent hires or placements but temporary labor, and if we knew people were being treated well when we hired them and that they were not getting abused, like, check cashing, transportation charges, no rip-off things, but that also there was someone trying to help them put the other pieces of the puzzle together.

Remarkably, two other employers spoke about their responsibility to do something to counteract the impact of the high rates of incarceration in their communities. The manager at Best Furniture noted the strong link between inadequate mental health services and the high proportion of people with mental illness ending up in jails. The hiring representative from Odds & Ends explicitly indicated the high incarceration rates in their community create a responsibility to try to hire people right out of jail.

The employers ascribed to an ethic of second chances, yet only one, a recruiter at Fast Lane Staffing, tied this ethic to the legal imperative not to discriminate. She explained, "employers either do the screen or not; and then use it or not – otherwise they would not be an equal opportunity employer – they would be making discretionary judgments using the information." In using the phrase "equal opportunity employer," she explicitly referred to her legal obligations, while the other employers described their ethic as arising from a personal sense of right and wrong.

The manager at AAA Manufacturing expressed her willingness to hire persons with criminal records as arising from her longstanding business principles: "[being a] family owned business means that we treat everyone the same." The recruiter at Acme Staffers characterized his actions as driven by "personal thought" and an administrator at Reliable Distributions simply put it as "morally and ethically the right thing to do." The administrator also considered it important to balance giving someone a chance with the wellbeing and safety of everyone in the company, but noted that "providing a person an opportunity" was always worth considering, even if the new hire ultimately failed at the job. The ethic of second chances also arose from the sense the employee's "past lives are none of my business." The hiring manager at Book Binders struck a similar theme:

> I've given more opportunity to people who've been incarcerated or who have had an issue than most people, I would think. Having grown up under circumstances, I realize which direction some people can go in at no choice of their own sometimes, and it happens. But to mar that person for life for something they did when they were 14 years old is totally, totally not correct. I could've gone that way. It could've happened to me when I was younger. Fortunately, I didn't go that way, but I grew up with people who did. I understand that, and I think everybody deserves a chance.

Although none of the employers interviewed acknowledged that they had criminal records, their commentary sometimes was suggestive of that possibility.

Only four of the employers took advantage of some kind of tax or financial incentives for hiring people with records, including funds to provide on-the-job training for new employees. Five other employers mentioned they had previously availed themselves of these benefits, but the paperwork involved made such attempts worthless. Their explanations emphasized their sense that state policy was archaic, unfruitful, and only added to the stress of operating a business. The manager at Ultimate Supplier, who never successfully utilized incentives for his small business, described his intense level of frustration:

> So, you're hiring a $50/hr accountant to do these things, to fill out the forms, and everything else. I get a letter back. I don't have that time or money to waste. It's a joke. All it does is perpetuate the state offices, the collector's stuff. There's never anything that I find that comes out of it. Now, over in the industrial area, here, in [place deleted], there are companies in there that get state funding and federal. But, they're bigger companies. They have more resources. They go after big bucks, lots of money. A company under a dozen people gets nothing. I've had people in here from the Development Commission, stuff like that and, "Well, we don't know if you qualify because of this and because of that."

In addition, when questioned specifically about how other legal requirements (as well as insurance or personnel policies) influenced their decisions to hire individuals with criminal records, the employers minimized the effects of these accountability practices. The most frequently mentioned issue was driving certifications by insurance companies. Interestingly, however, only one employer, who was subjected to homeland security regulations, found these restrictions particularly confining. Additionally, both the representative from Union #44 and the recruiter at Fast Lane Staffing noted problems resulting from the extreme measures taken in a few workplace placements, including FBI checks and terrorist watch list screenings. The overall impression from the interviewees was that personal ethics was a stronger driving force in their determinations to hire than any formal legal requirement or government benefit.

VI. Conclusion

The interviews showed that from the employers' perspective, finding a "good worker to do a bad job" was a strong motivating factor behind giving people with criminal records a chance. This desire encouraged employers to make allowances for employees with even a small degree of potential. Moreover, in the lowest tier of a segmented job market, employers were more likely to consider prior incarceration as an unremarkable indicator within a labor pool with poor prospects for meeting job demands. By their accounts, criminal background was but one of the factors that cause potential employees to be ill prepared for regular employment. Importantly, since employers would readily fire employees who were unsuccessful for any reason, giving a "second chance" was seen as a low-risk strategy with potentially high pay-off.

Under these conditions employers apply a "commonsense" approach to hiring that often relied upon their long-term experience or their gut instincts. Hiring was only minimally influenced by formal legal incentives or disincentives to employing persons with criminal records. These exceptions primarily arose when such factors had a direct impact on the basis of operating a business or where required by outsiders such as the federal government. Although a minority of businesses performed criminal record checks, formalistic methodologies for screening out high risk employees had little place in these factories and businesses. The many forms of risk experienced, including potential wrongdoing by a new employee with a criminal record, were, for the most part, considered an ordinary concern that was simply part of maintaining a business.

While this sample is drawn from companies known for hiring persons with criminal records, some of its findings might provide insight into the decision making of other employers seeking entry-level workers. Perhaps the most powerful factor in decision making was the perceived importance of labor market constraints. Of particular importance was the inability to find workers that could meet even the minimal demands of their jobs. As a result, employers were inclined to approach new employees with fair-mindedness, allowing them to prove their worth despite their criminal records. Focusing on the employers' impulse to discriminate might place too much weight on factors that these companies, and possibly others similarly situated, do not feel that they have the luxury to consider.

Yet notably, many of these employers show no propensity to discriminate. In fact, most expressed strong normative presumptions against judging persons for past mistakes and appreciation of the life difficulties their employees faced. Since employers could offer little to keep their "good workers," they recognized that trusting relationships, an element of flexibility, and small amounts of social support might go a long way to producing a reliable workforce. In a seemingly contradictory fashion, these humane measures were imparted in the context of the highly coercive conditions of non-contractual low-wage employment. But a prevailing factor limited the impact of compassionate treatment: the high employee failure and drop-out rate. Unfortunately for both employers looking for good workers and ex-prisoners seeking a place in the legitimate economy, the apparent benevolence of employers toward marginalized workers was often insufficient to counteract the obstacles to sustainable employment. Many of the employers, in fact, recognized that the challenges employees faced were far beyond what they were capable of addressing.

Employers reconciled this dilemma by emphasizing what they do offer their employees: a place to stand in the legitimate economy. These managers and supervisors saw themselves as providing an opportunity to re-establish an identity – to gain the recognition of human significance that comes with acquiring paid employment. As Zygmunt Bauman (2004) has argued, in modern capitalist society there is a lower level of being than an alienated worker – there are the wasted lives of those who have no capacity to participate (as earner or spender) in a consumer society. In their most optimistic responses, employers portrayed their jobs as an entry point into a "life of significance" – in which people might be measured by their productivity rather than their misdeeds. This research demonstrates, however, that precarious employment offers too few benefits and not enough support to sustain many if not most persons leaving prisons. The decline in adequate social services for the poor, and the formerly incarcerated specifically, accentuates the situation, as larger segments of the population suffer from problems that make them less desirable employees (including health issues, addiction, and lack of familial support). While employers may treat some of their workers with a modicum of humanity, these gestures are unlikely to counteract the overall failure of social support, and the resulting lack of resilience. In a segmented economy, where people with criminal records are already locked out of desirable jobs and compete with other "unemployables" for bad jobs, opportunities for ex-prisoners are more likely to emerge not from prohibitions on discrimination, but rather the growth in the quantity and quality of work available (Holzer, 2012) or a responsive state's investment in the resources workers need to succeed.

14

WE ARE ALL CONTINGENT

Fighting vulnerability in the US workforce

Ann C. McGinley[1] *and David McClure*[2]

I. Introduction: unemployment, underemployment and degraded work

Although the rate of unemployed persons has considerably declined in the US since the worst days of the Great Recession (Cohen, 2016; Hilsenrath, 2015), as of December 2015, there were still 7.9 million Americans who were officially unemployed; 2.1 million of these jobless individuals had been unemployed for more than six months (US Department of Labor, Bureau of Labor Statistics, 2016). The longer workers are out of work, the more difficult it becomes to re-enter the job market (Mui, 2014). Experts are concerned that a permanent class of unemployed individuals has arisen (Ghayad and Dickens, 2012; Hilsenrath, 2014; Krueger et al., 2014; Krugman, 2014). In fact, millions of people who need work have become discouraged and have stopped looking for work (Cohen, 2015). The job participation rate – the percentage of working age Americans who are employed or are looking for jobs – was 62.6% in December 2015, one of the lowest percentages in almost 40 years (Morath, 2016). In comparison, at its apex in the late 1990s, the labor participation rate was 67%; if this rate were constant today, there would be over ten million additional persons looking for work in the US (Appelbaum, 2014). Combined with the 7.9 million who are officially unemployed, the number is startling: it appears that nearly 18 million people who would prefer to work do not have jobs.

In fact, in many ways, matters for workers are even worse than the 18 million workers statistic suggests. Well before the recession, American workers experienced

1 William S. Boyd Professor of Law, William S. Boyd School of Law, University of Nevada, Las Vegas.
2 Head of Research and Curriculum Services and Associate Professor, Wiener-Rogers Law Library, William S. Boyd School of Law, University of Nevada, Las Vegas.

a sharp decline in the *quality* of jobs available. Many who are employed have had to accept low-paying full- and part-time work with minimal or no benefits. The Bureau of Labor Statistics reports that six million part-time workers say they would prefer full-time jobs, 1.4 million more than before the recession (US Department of Labor, Bureau of Labor Statistics, 2016; Rugaber, 2014). This statistic suggests that in addition to the 18 million persons who are either looking for work or who have given up looking, there are 1.4 million more workers who are underemployed. Counting the underemployed and the unemployed, some experts say that the unemployment rate is actually closer to 10% (Morath, 2016).

Jobs that formerly supported a family don't pay enough in wages or benefits. "The experience of working in America has changed profoundly and predominantly for the worse since the early 1970s" (Doussard, 2013, p. 229). It has become nearly impossible for many families to rely on one worker to support the family. In fact, as early as 1976, almost half of all families living below the poverty line had a full-time worker as the head of household (Luce et al., 2014, p. 2). Today, a day's work provides lower salaries and benefits than it used to do (Doussard, 2013, p. 229). In 2007, for example, before the Great Recession, a household in the 25th percentile earned five dollars less per hour than it did in 1973 (Doussard, 2013, p. 229). But that is not all. The same family worked ten hours more per week than it did in 1973 (Doussard, 2013, pp. 229–230). By 2011, even as the recession wound down, 28% of those in the labor market earned poverty-level wages (Luce et al., 2014, p. 2).

Wages have not kept up with expenses. The federal minimum wage was $7.25 per hour in 2012; if it had kept up with inflation, it would have been $10.52 by 2012 (Luce et al., 2014, p. 5). Had the minimum wage kept up with the increase in labor productivity, it would have measured $21.72 in 2012 (Luce et al., 2014). And, despite the efforts of President Obama and the Democrats to raise the minimum wage, at the time of this writing, the federal minimum wage still remains at $7.25 an hour for non-tipped employees (Doyle, 2016).

Moreover, many workers' pensions have gone from defined benefits to defined contribution plans, and their employer-provided health care has either disappeared or diminished in value (Doussard, 2013, pp. 229–230). In effect, while wages have degraded significantly, "*working conditions are deteriorating much more quickly than are wages*" (Doussard, 2013, p. 230).

As working conditions, wages, and benefits take a sharp turn downward, families suffer. June Carbone and Naomi Cahn (2013) explain that marriage has become a benefit open almost exclusively to the wealthy, and marriages of two well-educated partners have led to a concentration of wealth at the top. Simultaneously, they argue, it is becoming increasingly rare for working class and poor individuals to marry. All of these phenomena have undermined individual workers, their families and the society, and have created large gaps in wealth between the wealthy and the working class. Now that the 30th anniversary of the Feminism and Legal Theory Project has passed, feminist scholars should consider the ironic results of feminism: rising rates of upper middle class women with increasingly higher rates of education who live in wealthy families, while simultaneously women at the lower end of the economic spectrum experience more difficulties than ever making ends meet. Work (and marriage) prospects have changed dramatically for men as well. At the top, men are doing better than ever. Even despite the rise in women's education and employment at the upper echelons of business, law, and medicine, the gendered wage gap has increased at the top of the economic spectrum and narrowed at the bottom. But men lacking college educations do not have highly paid blue-collar job opportunities they once had, and they are making do with considerably lower salaries.

What has caused this sharp decline in employment conditions for the majority of American workers? While it may appear that a perfect storm in the form of a global economy has devastated the US workplace, that conclusion would imply that the decline is accidental and that there is no remedy for the changes. Despite the effect of global factors that to some extent may be beyond our control, there are also policy and law reforms that could improve the conditions of working Americans.

There are some positive signs. Fortunately, the economy is picking up and there is hope on the horizon in the recent popular movement to increase the minimum wage, the passage in states and localities of minimum wage legislation, and the voluntary wage hikes that some large employers have recently announced. For example, McDonald's announced in April 2015 that it would raise wages and offer new benefits to approximately 90,000 workers in the 1,500 restaurants that it owns and operates. McDonald's will increase the minimum wage of its employees to at least $1.00 over the local legal minimum wage in 2015, and even higher in 2016, and for the first time will grant paid vacation leave to part-time employees. It will also cover costs of online courses its employees and those of its franchises take toward a high school equivalency degree and will help employees pay for college tuition (Strom, 2015). Wal-Mart, too, announced in February 2015 that it would raise its minimum wage to at least $9.00 an hour in 2015, and to $10.00 an hour in 2016. It will also raise the wages of workers who are already paid above the minimum. Wal-Mart's new policies will affect about 500,000 employees (Covert, 2015). But McDonald's new wage policy will not affect the 750,000 employees who work for its franchisees in 12,500 restaurants in the US (Strom, 2015), and Wal-Mart's new pay hikes will likely be insufficient to raise all of its employees above the poverty line. Recent stories have focused on the large number of Wal-Mart employees who must resort to collecting food stamps to keep their families afloat. A small shift in the minimum wage paid will likely not solve this problem.

This chapter focuses on contingent work. It argues that nearly all Americans' work is contingent, and that what we call "contingent" work has become the norm in American workplaces. In fact, contingent or precarious work has become an institution in American society. Part II defines contingent work broadly and explains why the literature on contingent work does not always capture the essence of conditions in American workplaces. Part III of this chapter considers various sectors of our economy and examines the many causes of contingent or precarious work, while Part IV offers possible solutions. The chapter concludes that Americans must take seriously the degradation of work and make policy and legal changes necessary to improve employment prospects for all Americans.

II. Defining contingent work

Many economists and sociologists limit the definition of contingent workers to temporary employees, hired through employment agencies, "direct hire" temporary employees, and contract employees (Connelly and Gallagher, 2004; Kalleberg and Marsden, 2005; Liu and Kolenda, 2012; Marler et al., 2002). Some also include on-call work (Coverdill and Oulevey, 2007; Pedulla, 2013; Surfield, 2005). Most do not include independent contractors, part-time employees, or day laborers. There are a number of problems with these narrow definitions. First, scholars adopting the narrowest definitions have often disputed the rise of contingent or precarious working arrangements. In fact, they have concluded that there was a decrease in contingent work in the US between 1995 and 2005 (Addison et al., 2015; Surfield, 2005; von Hippel et al., 2006), and they even argued at the time that there was "little support for critics' concern of the creation of a disposable workforce" (Surfield, 2005, p. 28). At least one of these scholars, adopting a narrow definition of contingent work, disputed that employers had incentives to transfer key employee positions to contingent worker positions in order to save money (Surfield, 2005, pp. 28–29). These claims demonstrate how the narrow definition can influence and even distort how policy makers view the situation.

Second, there is a particular concern surrounding independent contractors. While scholars who omit independent contractors from their list of contingent workers would argue that independent contractors prefer these working arrangements because of the flexibility, this is not the whole story. Admittedly, there is a group of independent contractors who work at high levels and who prefer the flexibility that having their own consulting or contracting business affords them (S. Horowitz, 2011; Miller and Miller, 2012, p. 50). Management-oriented publications in particular emphasize the flexibility and independence enjoyed by both the worker and the company (MBO Partners, 2013). On the other hand, many employees who are classified as independent contractors are not independent contractors at all (Barnes, 2012a; *Ruiz v Affinity Logistics Corp.*, 2014; *Vizcaino v Microsoft Corp.*, 1996). Because many of the labor laws protecting workers cover employees and do not extend to independent contractors, and because businesses do not have to withhold income or social security taxes from payments to independent contractors, businesses, either intentionally or mistakenly, mislabel employees as "independent contractors" to avoid responsibilities that they would otherwise have under the law (Inomata, 2012). And employees appear to be unaware that they are wrongly characterized as independent contractors: many believe that if they contract to be regarded as independent contractors, they are independent contractors (Horowitz, 2014; *Mowry v DiNapoli*, 2013). This is an erroneous belief.

The legal definitions of "independent contractor" and "employee" depend largely on a list of factors developed by the Internal Revenue Service (Internal Revenue Service, 2014; Rathod and Skapski, 2013; *Vizcaino v Microsoft Corp.*, 1997). The most important factor is the control that the employer exercises over the worker. Generally, if the worker works on the employer's site, is supervised by the employer in his or her work, and uses the employer's materials and equipment, the worker is likely an employee, not an independent contractor.

To the extent that employers are wrongly identifying employees as independent contractors, these employees will often not be counted as contingent employees, even though many of them have a more precarious relationship to the employer than do those who are classified by the employer as employees. This practice leads to a serious undercount of employees who have contingent arrangements.

Third, the United States Bureau of Labor Statistics (BLS) estimated in 2005 that 4.1% of employees had contingent arrangements (Cappelli and Keller, 2013, p. 877). Theirs is also a very narrow definition, one that likely underestimates those with precarious or contingent work, in part because it relies on self-identification to determine how many contingent employees are in the labor force. The BLS categorizes as contingent workers "those who do not have an explicit or implicit contract for long-term employment" (Cappelli and Keller, 2013, p. 877; US Department of Labor, Bureau of Labor Statistics, 2005). Under the BLS definition, only about half of temporary workers hired through an agency state that they are contingent workers (Dey et al., 2010, p. 280). Research shows, however, that employees traditionally believe that they have more rights than they do have (Freeman and Rogers, 2006).

In contrast to these conservative estimates, some researchers argue that contingent workers represent up to 25 or 30% of the workforce (Bales et al., 2013; Kirk and Belovics, 2008; Parker, 2002). These estimates incorporate temporary workers which include a much higher percentage of workers without a high school diploma and who are predominately female and Black (Kirk and Belovics, 2008), and day laborers, often of Latino origin (many undocumented) who wait in groups on street corners in Western cities to be selected to work on housing construction projects and who are paid daily for their work (Parker, 2002).

Because the purpose of this chapter is to examine the conditions of and potential solutions for inequality in job pay and conditions, and we are focusing on those groups of workers who receive minimal pay and benefits, our definition of contingent workers includes an array of workers who toil under precarious conditions. Our definition, therefore, is a broad one that overlaps with the BLS definition of contingent workers, but that also includes many part-time workers, temporary workers, day laborers, and many who are now often classified as independent contractors. In fact, if we are to consider a comparative law definition of contingent work as work that is not permanent, almost all Americans who are subject to the employment at-will doctrine, except those relatively few American workers who are represented by a union with a "for cause" provision in their collective bargaining agreements, would be contingent workers (Bernhardt, 2014;

Garcia, 2012; McGlashan et al., 2003). Even though in essence we are all contingent workers, this essay focuses on the precarious nature of contingent employment relationships that has led to increasing income inequality in the US over the last forty years.

III. The decline of the US middle class

A. Lower salaries and increasing inequality

In "*The New Class Society: Goodbye American Dream*?," authors Robert Perrucci and Earl Wysong (2008) conclude that after World War II most middle class Americans had stable jobs with gradually rising real incomes. In 1973, however, the real hourly wage for nonsupervisory workers (almost three quarters of the workforce) peaked. That date began a slow decline in middle class incomes and wages and a reduction in real earnings for middle class families. In year 2000 dollars, male blue-collar workers' wages declined from $15.51 per hour in 1973 to $13.90 per hour in 2000 (Table 14.1); male service workers' wages declined from $12.89 per hour in 1973 to $11.01 per hour in 2000 (Table 14.2). Female blue-collar and service workers remained almost the same during this time period. Female blue-collar workers' wages went from $9.48 per hour in 1973 to $9.49 per hour in 2000 (Table 14.1); female service workers went from $8.14 per hour to $8.00 per hour in the same time period (Table 14.2). It is important to note that although women's salaries did not decline much or at all during this period, women continued to make significantly less per hour than the male workers to whom they are compared.

As blue-collar and service workers' salaries declined during this period, both male and female white-collar workers' salaries increased (Table 14.3). While female

TABLE 14.1 Blue-collar workers' salaries (year 2000 US$)

	Male	*Female*
1973	15.51	9.48
2000	13.90	9.49

TABLE 14.2 Service workers' salaries (year 2000 US$)

	Male	*Female*
1973	12.89	8.14
2000	11.01	8.00

TABLE 14.3 White-collar workers' salaries (year 2000 US$)

	Male	*Female*
1973	20.58	12.49
2000	22.69	15.13

TABLE 14.4 Median family incomes (year 1999 US$) and combined hours worked – husband and wife (according to race)

Year	*White/ Income*	*White/Hours worked*	*Black/ Income*	*Black/ Hours*	*Latino/ Income*	*Latino Hours*
1973	45,311		24,837		30,761	
1979		3,302		3,227		3,082
1998		3,689		3,843		3,415
1999	50,106		30,053		30,262	

salaries increased at a higher rate than male salaries did, women's salaries continued to lag behind those of white-collar male workers.

As the total combined working hours of family members (husbands and wives) rose significantly between 1979 and 1998, median family work incomes rose somewhat for white and Black families and declined slightly for Latino families from 1973 to 2000 (Table 14.4). For white and Black families, the increased work hours meant that there was no net increase in income during this period, and for Latinos, there was a significant net decline in income when factoring in the increased work hours (Perrucci and Wysong, 2003).

The overall median household income of $53,657 in 2014 demonstrates the continued stagnation of household income in the US as it hovers near 1990s levels and is significantly lower than its high of $57,843 in 1999 (Figure 14.1) (Timiraos, 2015; US Census Bureau, 2016).

At the same time, there has been a growing polarization of income between the "haves" and the "have nots" in the US. The Chief Executive Officer (CEO) to average worker pay ratio increased from 42:1 in 1980 to a high of 525:1 in 2000, and as of 2005, stood at 411:1 (Perrucci and Wysong, 2008). This pay gap between CEOs and workers continued after the Great Recession and as a wide gulf in many sectors of the economy, but is particularly expansive in the accommodation and food services sectors (Figure 14.2) (Demos, 2012).

Importantly, the losses in wages for workers were accompanied by losses in benefits. In 1980, 84% of workers in large companies (those with over 100 employees) had defined benefit plans, but by 1997, this number dropped to 50%. In small companies, the percentage of those with defined benefit plans decreased during this time period from 20% to 15% (Perrucci and Wysong, 2008). The decline in "good jobs," defined "as those that pay a minimum of $18.50 per hour and provide health insurance and retirement plans," has been significant, particularly when considering the marked increase in worker output during the same period (Table 14.5) (Wysong, Perrucci and Wright, 2014, p. 58).

B. The rise of contingent workers

Simultaneously, the contingent workforce began to grow. According to Perucci and Wysong's count, over 25% of all workers were contingent in 2005. Perhaps

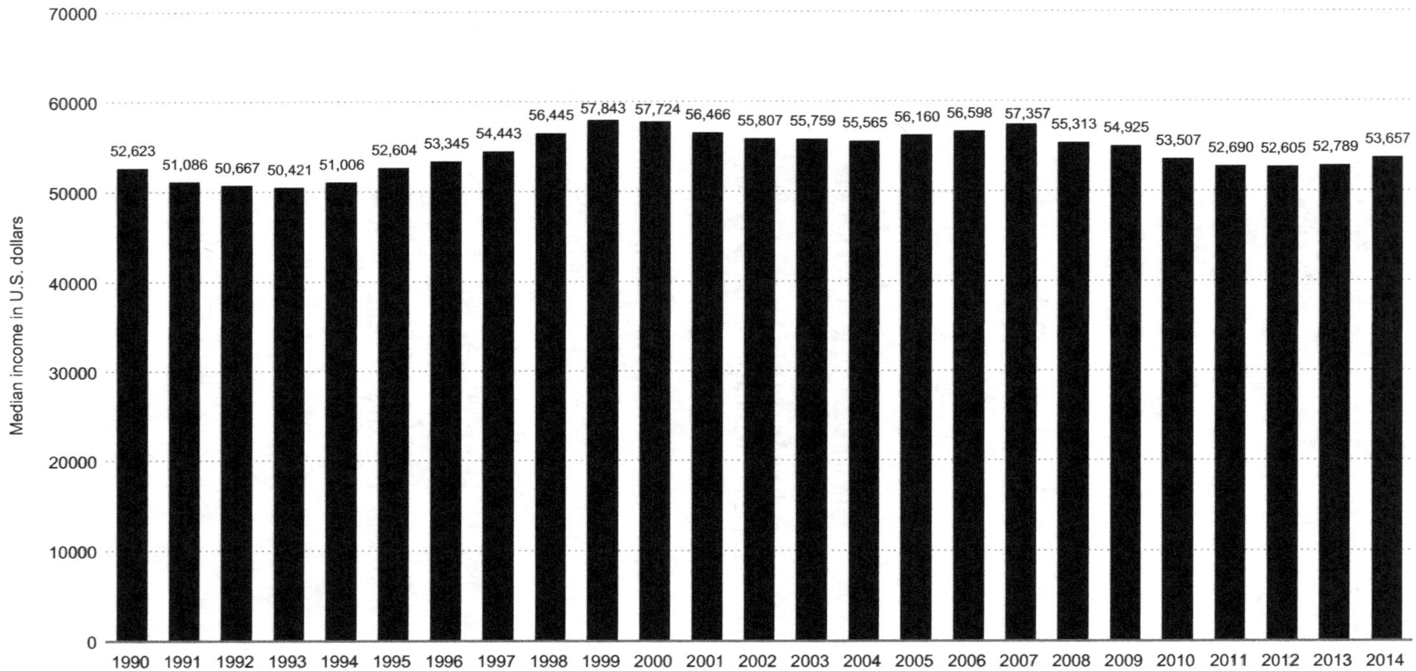

FIGURE 14.1 Median household income in the US from 1990 to 2014 (US$)

Source: © Statista 2016, US Census Bureau

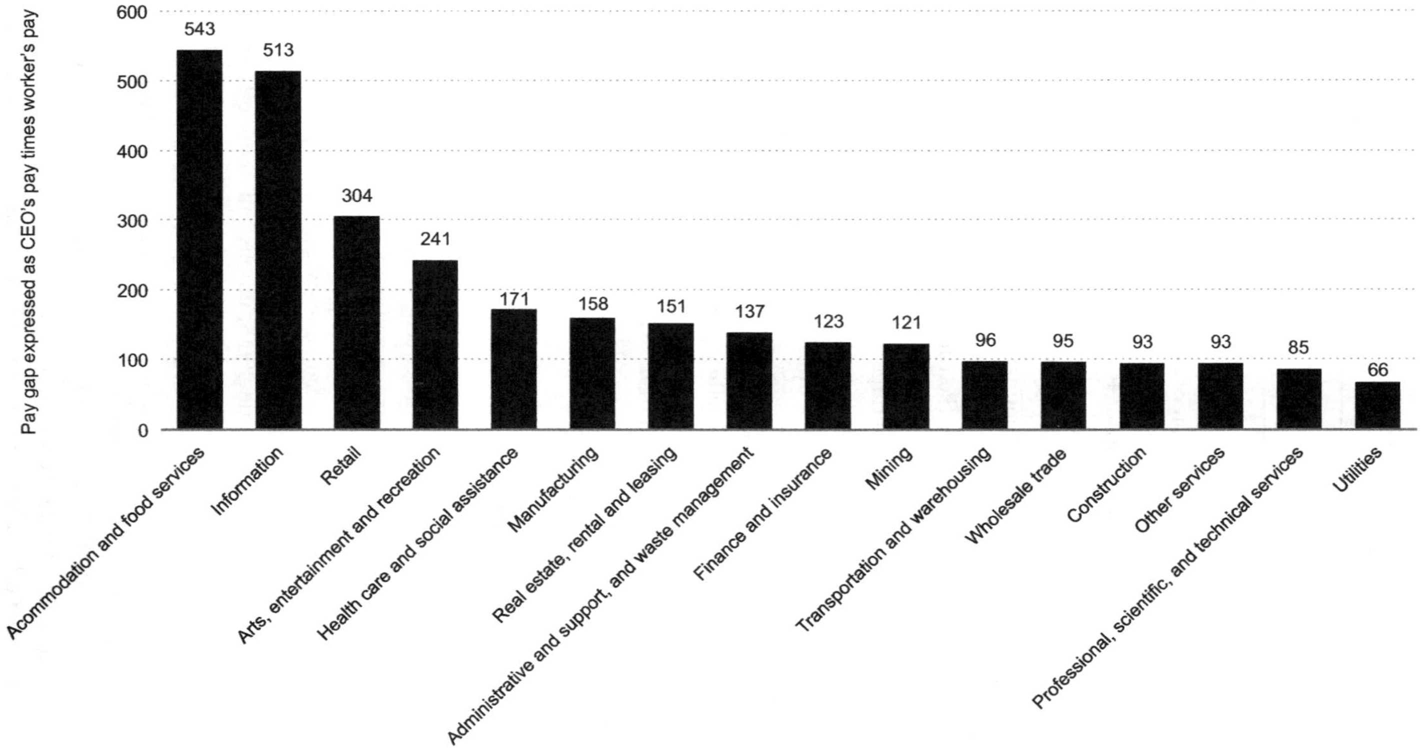

FIGURE 14.2 Pay gap between CEOs and average workers in the US in 2012, by sector

Source: © Statista 2016, Demos

TABLE 14.5 Percentage of "good jobs" and output per worker (year 2011 US$)

	"Good jobs" (%)	*Output per worker (US$)*
1979	27	69,903
2010	24	103,659

even more importantly, the distribution of contingent workers in the population is not equal. Women made up 54.7% of temporary workers in 2005; Black, Latino and younger workers were overrepresented in temporary and on-call work. Further, the pay and benefits of contingent workers do not compare to non-contingent workers. For example, in 2005, the wages of contingent workers averaged about 10% to 20% lower than those of non-contingent workers, and only a small portion of contingent workers were provided health care of any type (20.8%) or pensions of any type (22.8%) by their employers (Perrucci and Wysong, 2008).

There are numerous problems with contingent arrangements that continue today. Ordinarily the pay rate for contingent employees is lower than that for standard employees (Connelly et al., 2011), and their jobs have few, if any, benefits and no permanence. Contingent employees are considered not committed by the employer and are often separated from other employees. This separation makes it difficult for contingent employees to acquire knowledge and skills and to develop emotional attachments and trust (Connelly et al., 2011; Halbesleben and Clark, 2010). It can even lead to a decline in skills of underemployed contingent workers (Connelly et al., 2011). Finally, contingent workers may be less aware of safety issues in the workplace and more uncomfortable asking the employer about safety concerns (Collinson, 1999; Connelly and Gallagher, 2004; Luria and Yagil, 2010).

C. Globalization and a decline in unionization in manufacturing sector

A major cause of the stark inequalities between the rich and the poor and the rise of contingent work is that union representation in manufacturing and other sectors in the US has declined precipitously. Previously, manufacturing jobs were the backbone of the blue-collar economy, with unionized jobs paying significant salaries and benefits that constituted a living wage for families. Even in the conservative Mid-West in the mid-1960s, unions and union officials had considerable clout in state government and politics (Getman, 2010). With globalization and the loss of many manufacturing jobs, most notably steel, automobiles, and clothing, hundreds of thousands of well-paid union jobs were lost to the US economy, and production moved overseas (Getman, 2010; McKinnon, 2004; Wysong et al., 2014). To a large extent, unions lost the power they previously had (Getman, 2010). Even where production still takes place in this country, meatpacking and other plants are often no longer unionized, and employers hire low-paid Latino workers to take the place of union employees, leading to what Leticia Saucedo (2006) calls "the brown-collarization" of the American workplace (pp. 964–965). Such low-paid workers are often treated as a commodity and have insufficient bargaining power to change their working conditions (Garcia, 2012).

In fact, the American Labor Movement has been in a decline since the 1950s that has accelerated into a free fall since the early 1980s (Frost, 2013). In 1954, American unions represented 28.3% of the workforce in the US. By 1980, union representation had dropped to 20% and by 2012, to 11.3%, with only 6.6% unionization occurring in private workplaces today (Frost, 2013, pp. 1–2). As noted above, the drop in union representation is due in part to the loss of heavy manufacturing jobs in the US. As Americans lost jobs to cheap labor overseas, new service jobs were created in the US, but these jobs have generally not been unionized. Moreover, many of these overseas factories are "sweat shops" with unsafe working conditions and minimal pay. A recent example of such a "sweat shop" is the garment factory in Bangladesh that caught fire in November 2012, killing more than 100 workers (Bajaj, 2012; Clark, 2012).

One reason for the failure to unionize service workers is effective employer opposition. Court challenges by employers have resulted in weaker labor law protections for collective bargaining rights, giving management the advantage in resisting organizing efforts. These judicial interpretations of the labor law include decisions permitting striker replacements, which undermine the "right to strike" (Dannin, 2006; Getman, 2010, 2014; *NLRB v Mackay Radio & Tel. Col.*, 1938) and opposing secondary boycotts (Bock, 2005; *Capitol Awning Co., Inc. v Local 137 Sheet Metal Workers Int'l Assoc.*, 2010; Dannin, 2005; *Fid. Interior Const., Inc. v Se. Carpenters Reg'l Council of United Bhd. of Carpenters & Joiners of America*, 2012; Getman, 2010; *Kentov v Sheet Metal Workers' Int'l Assoc. Local 15*, 2005; *Laborers Dist. Council of Minnesota & N. Dakota v NLRB*, 2012). Moreover, employers engaged in both legal and illegal "hardball tactics" to oppose labor organizing during the late seventies and early eighties (Getman, 2010). As Professor Julius Getman states, "Our laws badly need amendment" (p. 20). While the law is increasingly weak in protecting labor rights, scholars also blame the unions themselves for their failure to counter employer opposition in union organizing (Frost, 2013; Getman, 2010). Getman argues that unions were not ready for the changes in the American economy and faults many unions for failing to focus "effort and imagination" on organizing workers. He urges unions to follow the example of the Culinary Workers, the union in Las Vegas that organized food and drink servers and bartenders in Las Vegas, Nevada. The Culinary Workers aware of the difficulties in using the law to protect union rights, used union movement tactics such as membership involvement and street protests in order to sidestep the Labor Board and successfully organize the Strip casino hotels.

As union representation fell, employers increasingly used contingent workers, reducing job stability in workplaces and the long-term job tenure of employees, as well as the median years of employees in their jobs (Wysong et al., 2014).

D. Service jobs

As manufacturing began to lose its stronghold in the US economy, economists argued that well-paid service and high tech jobs would replace the jobs lost in the manufacturing sector. To some extent, the high tech industry has created significant jobs and wealth for US workers, but the workers in the US who have good salaries and benefits in the high tech industry are generally those who are highly educated (Goel, 2014; Joint Venture Silicon Valley & Silicon Valley Community Foundation, 2014; Packer, 2013; Roush, 2014). These service jobs did not replace the highly paid blue-collar manufacturing jobs lost to factories overseas. And, as *Vizcaino v Microsoft Corp.* (1996) demonstrates, Microsoft, and other high tech companies hired large numbers of persons in the US they deemed "independent contractors" who did not receive high salaries and benefits. Apple, for example, maintains the vast majority of its manufacturing processes overseas (Duhigg and Bradsher, 2012), and most of its US positions are held by stockers and salespersons in Apple stores who earn about $25,000 per year. Relative to other retailers, these jobs are well-paid with good benefits, but many cannot afford to live very well. Moreover, when considering the amount of merchandise the workers are responsible for, they are very low-paid. For example, each Apple store employee, including non-sales stockers and salespersons brought in an average of $473,000 in sales in 2011 (Segal, 2012).

Given the ability of many manufacturing jobs to move to countries where wages are low, it makes sense to focus on service jobs as a potential replacement for well-paid jobs in the US. The successful strike by United Parcel Service (UPS) Teamsters drivers and loaders in August 1997, in which workers protested against increases in part-time workers, unhealthful working conditions, low salaries and benefits, suggested that the unions may come roaring back, at least in service sectors where there is no competition from low-paid overseas workers (Allen, 2007). Unfortunately, that was not the case. Although UPS is doing better, other non-unionized workplaces that provide services still offer poor jobs and benefits. Additionally, service jobs that were previously well-paid in the US have moved to other countries as a result of technology. Lawyers in India do discovery and research for law firms in the US, and call centers in India staff the consumer help and online sales offices for American companies (Aneesh, 2012; Hartley and Walker, 2012; Susskind, 2010; Timmons, 2010).

Many service jobs that cannot be outsourced and must be performed in the US – at fast-food companies and Wal-Mart, for example – pay extremely low wages, so low that employees qualify for food stamps and other benefits provided by the federal government (Allegretto et al., 2013; Fletcher, 2014; Gerard, 2013; Sanders, 2012). Retailers and wholesalers have cut 18.6 million full-time jobs since 2006, and have added 500,000 part-time jobs (Greenhouse, October 2012). The jobs are less predictable and stable, with hours changing weekly. In fact, many employers have sophisticated means of limiting their labor costs, with software that detects when they are busy or will be busy, and adjusts work hours to fit the expected demand. At Jamba Juice, for example, managers use software to schedule their employees. Jobs are broken down to 15-minute increments, and the software uses weather predictions to predict sales; managers schedule the employees accordingly. Consequently, some employees are scheduled for shifts of only a few hours at a time, but even worse, employees are notified only days or hours in advance of their scheduled working hours. This means that employees cannot regulate their child care or even take another part-time position in order to make a decent salary because they have no flexibility or regular working hours. Moreover in many stores, if employees are asked to work and they cannot do so, they are rescheduled in later weeks for fewer work hours. The same is true in many retail stores. A 2011 study of employees surveyed at New York City retailers that sold goods ranging from inexpensive to very expensive found that half of the employees worked part-time, only 10% of the employees had a set schedule, and 20% had to be available for call-in shifts (Greenhouse, October 2012).

With the help of local groups, employees of fast-food stores have engaged in strikes against their employers over the past two years (Choi and Matthews, 2013; Greenhouse, 2013, 2014). One of the first strikes took place in New York City in fall 2012, where employees struck in an attempt to unionize many fast-food restaurants at a time. Employees were then making between $8 and $9 per hour and were working part-time hours. On average, they worked 24 hours a week for approximately $10,000 per year and had no benefits or insurance (Owens, 2013). Despite the popular belief that fast-food restaurants hire teenagers, the vast majority of the workers were adults; many were single mothers, immigrants, and persons of color (Feuer, 2013; Jaffe, 2012).

Moreover, employees filed a number of class actions recently against McDonald's Corporation and various McDonald's franchises for violations of federal and state labor laws. The complaints alleged numerous violations ranging from wage theft to paying below minimum wage to requiring employees to wait for up to an hour or more to clock in at work in order to assure that the restaurant was sufficiently busy, and refusing to pay for the waiting time (*Beard v McDonald's Corp.*, 2014; *Hughes v McDonald's Corp.*, 2014; *Ochoa v McDonald's Corp.*, 2014; Penn, 2014; *Pullen v McDonald's Corp.*, 2014; *Salazar v McDonald's Corp.*, 2014; *Sanchez v McDonald's Rests. of Cal.*, 2014; *Wilson v McDonald's Corp.*, 2014).

Wal-Mart is the largest employer in America, the largest retailer in America, and the largest recipient of food stamps in America (Gura and Clark, 2014). Its employees are so poorly paid that many of them qualify for and collect food stamps from the US government. This means that one of the largest and richest companies in the world is subsidized by the US taxpayers. Moreover, many Wal-Mart employees actually use their food stamps to buy food at Wal-Mart markets (Bouvé, 2014). Therefore, Wal-Mart not only benefits indirectly from the government subsidy of its employees through food stamps, but also benefits directly by collecting food stamps to pay for Wal-Mart goods. Wal-Mart defends this practice of paying low salaries, arguing that it is helping the poor by keeping the price of goods low for its customers (Gura and Clark, 2014). But in a study performed at the University of California at Berkeley, researchers noted that 15% of Wal-Mart employees use food stamps and that Wal-Mart takes in about 18% of all food stamps, or $13 billion a year. In order to assure that their associates would not need food stamps, the study concluded, based on an Ohio example, that Wal-Mart would have to raise its average cashier's salary from $8.81 per hour to $13.63 per hour. In order to make up the difference, Wal-Mart would have to raise its prices by 1.4%, or for a box of Macaroni and Cheese, from 68 cents to 69 cents (Bouvé, 2014). This seems hardly a sacrifice given that Wal-Mart employees would be paid sufficiently and the federal government would not have to pay for their food stamps.

E. Globalization and immigration of cheap workers

In "The Push & Pull of Globalization: How the Global Economy Makes Migrant Workers Vulnerable to Exploitation," Neha Misra (2007) demonstrates how free trade agreements can lead to a degradation of jobs in the US and elsewhere and the exploitation of immigrant workers. She explains that implementation of the North American Free Trade Agreement (NAFTA) led to the destruction of the agricultural economy in Mexico and resulted in the displacement of 1.7 million small-scale Mexican farmers from the Mexican countryside to urban centers. Their livelihoods destroyed, these Mexican farmers moved to the cities, competed with workers for jobs, and were willing to take jobs at low salaries. As a result they displaced Mexican urban workers who then were forced to migrate to the US and other countries looking for work (Misra, 2007). Thus, NAFTA was a "push factor" in driving Mexican workers out of Mexico and into the US.

Examining the meatpacking industry in the US, Misra argues that demand for cheap labor is a pull factor for immigration. Today, the US meatpacking industry uses a majority of immigrant workers in meat and poultry plants. From the 1930s to the 1970s, she explains, the meatpacking industry was a highly paid, unionized workforce. Employees earned higher than average wages for manufacturing jobs in safe conditions. Today, in contrast, meatpackers are no longer unionized; wages are below average, and the most dangerous factory job in the US is meatpacking, with injury rates that more than double the national average (Haedicke, 2013; Kyerematteng-Amoah et al., 2014; Misra, 2007). This pattern is evident throughout the world with increasing demand for cheap migrant laborers who work without benefits. Employers see migrant workers as malleable and easy to exploit. Thus, globalization has led to an increased degradation of work, causing workers to move from formal to informal economic sectors and from permanent to temporary jobs. This movement makes workers increasingly exposed to exploitation. Unfortunately, global trade agreements, Misra argues, often encourage exploitative behavior without sufficient safeguards to protect migrant employees. And, many host countries limit the rights of immigrant labor, by guest-worker programs and sponsorship programs that link the employees to a particular employer, curtail the duration of the employees' stay in the country, and limit their abilities to bring their families to the country. The United Nations (UN) and International Labor Organization (ILO) have created international agreements for protection of the rights of migrant workers, but these instruments frequently contain no or inadequate enforcements mechanisms, and receiving states such as the US, Canada, India, Japan and the Gulf States, have not ratified either of these conventions (Misra, 2007).

IV. Legal and practical solutions to degraded work

This list of reasons for degraded work raises questions about whether there are practical and achievable solutions to the inequalities in jobs caused by globalization and other factors present in the post-modern workplace. While there are serious impediments to raising the level of workers' status and minimizing the exaggerated differences in income and benefits between the wealthy and the poor, it is imperative that we attempt to do so. The quality of jobs affects the future of our country's economy, the ability of our society to thrive, and even the viability of our union (Schoenberger, 2013).

As noted above, there is some good news. Recently, workers' groups, grass roots advocates, unions, and legal organizations have had significant success in striking, campaigning, and bringing lawsuits on behalf of workers' rights. At a time when the US Congress is unable to pass any progressive legislation, state legislatures, local councils and citizens' ballot initiatives have raised the minimum wage in a number of locations throughout the country over the past few years. The President and the Democrats in Congress have supported a federal wage bill that would raise the minimum wage from its current $7.25 per hour to $10.10 per hour after a few years, and would then index the minimum wage to inflation (US House of Representatives, Committee on Education and the Workforce Democrats, 2014). However, the Republicans did not support the bill, and it failed. A more recent bill introduced in the Senate would raise the minimum wage incrementally over the next five years, eventually reaching $12 an hour, and be indexed to inflation thereafter. It appears that there is little support for this proposal in Republican ranks (Gibson, 2015).

Much of the progressive work on behalf of workers has occurred, however, at the state and local levels, and it is important to continue to support efforts aimed at improving workers' rights locally and statewide. At the same time, workers and their advocates in particular industries – such as the fast-food industry – have engaged in strikes aimed at increasing the pay of fast-food workers throughout the country and creating an environment that is open to unionization.

As a result, in addition to specific municipalities and states that have raised their minimum wages, a number of large companies nationwide have announced that they intend to raise the wages they pay their employees. As we noted earlier, Wal-Mart and McDonald's are raising their employees' wages. Others will follow.

Moreover, private attorneys and state attorneys-general have brought lawsuits to enforce protective labor legislation. A number of successful class action lawsuits brought under both federal and state wage and hour laws have successfully challenged employers' "wage theft," a practice where employers illegally fail to pay employees for hours they worked or overtime (Penn, 2014). These lawsuits have often proved successful, and have not only redressed the wrongs committed by some employers but have also served as a warning to other employers that they need to comply with federal and state wage and hour laws (New York State Office of the Attorney General, 2014). There has been particular success in states, such as California, where the state governments have allocated significant resources to bringing these lawsuits (Lifsher, 2014).

Another successful story is the increased litigation based on misclassification of employees as independent contractors. In 2010, the Obama administration announced that it would use the Internal Revenue Service (IRS) to enforce more strictly the rules governing independent contractors. This effort has seemingly paid off. Many states have followed suit, and the business literature now invariably warns about misclassifying employees as independent contractors because of the expense if the employer is caught (Castillo, 2014; Inomata, 2012; Vilmer, 2014).

These successes demonstrate that there are many potential solutions, all of which we can work on simultaneously. Unfortunately because of space limitations, we cannot elaborate on all of these suggestions, but we encourage the reader to consider all of them. They include:

A. Continued grass roots pressure on businesses to improve wages, and on federal, state, and local governments to increase minimum wages

As noted above, grass roots efforts to influence the fast-food and other industries to increase wages have had some success, most notably at McDonald's and Wal-Mart. These efforts should continue to pressure industries dependent on low-wage workers. Moreover, campaigns to increase the minimum wage at the state and local levels have also met good success, and more campaigns in the less progressive states and cities may also improve wages in those localities. Finally, especially in light of the upcoming 2016 presidential elections, issues of wage equity, the increasing gap between the rich and the poor, and the cost of education for middle class families should dominate the debates and campaign advertisements. Research demonstrates that the vast majority of Americans believe in a higher minimum wage, which would go a long way to improving wages up the line (National Employment Law Project, 2015). Increasing the minimum wage would have significant laudatory effects on family income. Economists estimate that increasing the minimum wage to $10.10 per hour would raise 6.8 million people out of poverty (Boushey, 2014).

B. Enforcement of protective laws

Private and government attorneys should continue to bring class action lawsuits for wage theft under federal and state wage and hour laws in order to compensate victims, punish employers who have violated the acts, and deter others who are tempted to engage in these practices. Moreover, federal and state governments should continue to enforce tax laws that punish employers who have misidentified employees as independent contractors. Such enforcement actions have had significant effect in the past. For example, the US Department of Labor recovered more than $1 million in back wages and damages for 196 employees who were misclassified as independent contractors in 2013 (M. E. Wood, 2013; R. W. Wood, 2013; US Department of Labor, Bureau of Labor Statistics, 2013).

The government should also step up enforcement of laws such as the Occupational Safety and Health Act (2012). Safety enforcement is particularly important in industries, such as meatpacking, where immigrant labor predominates, and which have been identified as highly dangerous (Misra, 2007). We know that the meatpacking industry could have a much better safety record, because of the much superior record of this industry when it was unionized.

C. Reconsideration of trade agreements

There is a debate over the Trans-Pacific Partnership Free Trade Agreement (TPP) that the Obama administration recently negotiated, much of it in secrecy, with eleven Pacific Rim countries. A number of liberal Democrats in Congress, along with their union-side backers, oppose the current trade agreement because they fear it resembles NAFTA, which led to a multitude of job losses, and does not require adherence to international labor standards established by the ILO (AFL-CIO, 2015). The shroud of secrecy surrounding the TPP negotiations heightened fears that the TPP would enrich business interests without taking into account the labor rights of American workers (Srinivas, 2015). The revelation of the TPP's terms has not allayed such fears for union leaders (Hoffa et al., 2015).

The TPP faces opposition from both sides of the political aisle, but its passage will be aided by the "fast-track" approval process that Congress authorized (Calmes, 2015). Fast-track approval prohibits Congress from amending the substance of the trade agreement, but merely permits its members to vote "yes" or "no" on the final negotiated agreement (Nakamura, 2016). However, until the final vote is taken, those opposing the TPP should continue to voice their opinions and urge the government to seriously consider the labor rights of workers affected by it.

D. Federal and state labor law reform and class action reform

1. Collective bargaining rights

A number of US Supreme Court cases have significantly weakened the power of the National Labor Relations Act (NLRA) (2012), which protects the collective bargaining rights of employees (Dannin, 2006; Klare, 1978). Unfortunately,

Congress has not responded to these limiting decisions by amending the statute to overrule the Supreme Court. Political movements to encourage Congress to amend the federal act's substantive provisions and to amend the rules on preemption of state labor statutes by federal laws may create significant improvement for employee rights (Drummonds, 2009).

2. *Rights to bring class actions*

In *AT&T Mobility LLC v Concepción* (2011), the Supreme Court held that the Federal Arbitration Act (FAA) (2006) preempted California law on contract interpretation. California courts had found pre-dispute waivers of class actions unenforceable for unconscionability. The US Supreme Court disagreed, and held that the FAA preempts California law when it comes to arbitration of consumer issues. Subsequently, in *DR Horton* (2012), the National Labor Relations Board held that the Supreme Court's decision in *Concepción* is inapplicable to class actions alleging violation of workers' rights because section 7 of the NLRA protects "concerted action" of workers. A class action lawsuit, the court held, is concerted action protected by the NLRA.

On appeal, the Fifth Circuit overruled the Board, and held that employers may require employees to waive their rights to class actions (*DR Horton v NLRB*, 2013), but the Board has reasserted its *DR Horton* holding in *Murphy Oil USA, Inc. and Sheila M. Hobson* (2014), in which it decided once again that mandatory waivers of employee rights to bring a class action violate the NLRA. Even if the Board and the courts find a way to resolve their differences on this issue, it is still important for Congress to step in and bring clarity to the issue. An employer's requirement that employees waive their rights to class actions, if enforced by the courts, will undermine the rights of employees substantially and make it difficult to prevent wage theft because individual wage theft cases are relatively low-value. It would be difficult for employees to bring individual lawsuits to collect their lost wages. While governments could continue to bring such actions, class actions by the private bar are particularly important in enforcing wage and hour laws. Congress should overrule the *DR Horton v NLRB* decision legislatively by amending the FAA to prohibit employers from mandating that employees and prospective employees waive their class action rights.

E. *Creation of incentives for US companies to invest in manufacturing plants in the US*

Federal, state, and local governments should create incentives for US companies to re-establish manufacturing plants in US cities, but they should also consider regulation that would even out the disadvantages some states have for failing to have "right to work" – union hostile – laws. There are indications that companies may be inclined to bring some of their manufacturing back to the US as costs rise overseas. Moreover, it is often difficult to do business in offshore plants (Bradshaw, 2013; Evans, 2014; Northam, 2014; Rampell and Wingfield, 2012). For example, Apple intends to spend $100 million on a computer manufacturing plant in the US (Rampell and Wingfield, 2012). Other companies, too, have expressed reasons for returning their manufacturing to the US, including: (1) lower energy costs; (2) rising wages in developing countries like China and Brazil; (3) quality control issues in other countries; (4) desire to keep the supply chain close to the American market; (5) disruptions in the supply chain after natural disasters in Thailand and Japan; and (6) the US's ranking near the top of the World Bank's list for "ease of doing business" (Rampell and Wingfield, 2012, p. A3). One problem is that when companies come to the US for manufacturing, they typically build their plants in right to work states with very low union density, which means that employees earn low wages in these states. Or, companies that build their manufacturing plants back in the US contract with temporary staffing agencies for their workers. Lenovo, for example, has announced that it will begin making its Think-brand computers in North Carolina, a right to work state, and will create 115 jobs at the plant (Rampell and Wingfield, 2012). Other companies such as Nissan, Amazon, Asurion, and Dell have established warehouses in Tennessee, but they have outsourced their warehouses and call centers to staffing agencies in Tennessee. These jobs are contingent jobs, and the workers are considered temporary rather than full-time employees (DePillis, March 2014). The law should not only create incentives but also assure that the jobs that come to the US are good jobs.

F. Strengthening of anti-retaliation laws and immigration reform

One of the problems in many workplaces today is that persons of Hispanic descent suffer discrimination and harassment. Employers abuse their power against Latino employees because they know that undocumented workers are afraid to insist on their rights. There are examples of employers refusing to pay undocumented workers or calling the Immigration Control Board (ICE) when an undocumented worker sues the employer for illegal employment practices (Cho and Smith, 2013). Strengthening anti-retaliation laws, creating a barrier between government organizations enforcing employment rights and ICE, and enacting immigration reform would significantly improve the lives of low-wage undocumented workers. Adoption of fair immigration reform that permits undocumented individuals a pathway to citizenship and authorizes them to work in this country will remove the power that unethical employers lord over undocumented, and even, documented workers. Adoption of immigration reform laws would make it easier for employees to speak out about violations of labor and workplace safety laws. Even though undocumented workers have rights under the Civil Rights Act of 1964 (2012) not to be discriminated against based on their national origin, many are afraid to assert these rights. Immigration reform would make it possible to enforce these employees' rights.

G. Organizing employees of service industries

Because many services such as retailing and hospitality cannot be outsourced to foreign countries, the service industry is particularly ripe for organization of its employees. Las Vegas, for example, which has a high percentage of organized employees in the gaming and service industries, is a good example of how service industries can organize and provide good, middle class jobs to service workers (Taylor, 2014; "Union Workers," 2014). The CWA, for example, has employees working at casinos on the Strip and in downtown Las Vegas, at food service outlets in the Las Vegas airport, and in industrial laundries throughout the Las Vegas valley. CWA members work in cocktails and bell departments, and as kitchen workers, cooks, housekeepers, porters and other jobs (Culinary Workers Union Local 226 (n.d.)).

H. Passage of worker protective legislation

Federal, state, and local legislation could provide significant protection to workers. This legislation could include regulation and limitation of contingency arrangements (Borozdna and Korkin, 2014; Fedoreev and Huet, 2014; Sciarra et al., 2004; White, 2014), paid family medical leave that encourages both men and women to take a role in families (Cunningham-Parmeter, 2014), paid child care for working families, and regulation prohibiting the disruptive scheduling engaged in by many fast-food restaurants and other service jobs today (Wessler, 2014).

I. Economic and tax reform

Joseph Stiglitz (2015), the Nobel Prize-winning economist, recommends that in order to decrease inequalities, we must create jobs and growth, and the way to do that is to make long-term investments in infrastructure, technology, and education. He argues that the US should focus on public investments because they yield high returns and are labor intensive. The country should also help pay for education – states and local communities should not be laying off teachers. Education and job training are necessary for the new economy. We must, he argues, get over "deficit fetishism" by examining "both sides of the balance sheet, assets and liabilities" (p. 384). He also recommends tax increases on the wealthiest citizens and the imposition of taxes on "bad things," such as pollution. He concludes that increasing taxes at the top and lowering taxes on the bottom should lead to more consumption spending. Increasing taxes on corporations that do not invest in the US and lowering them on the corporations that do should encourage more investment in the US (p. 385). An example may be tax incentives created to bring more manufacturing back to the US and penalties for manufacturing abroad.

V. Conclusion

There is no question that there is a "great divide" between the haves and the have-nots in the US economy (Stiglitz, 2015). The contingent workforce, which is increasingly large, bears the brunt of the failed economic and labor policies that the country has followed. Only through increased attention to inequalities and the simultaneous use of the various legal, political, and economic strategies described in this essay will we create a more egalitarian society. Only through a reduced contingent workforce and improved working conditions can Americans begin once again to provide resilience to those who are unemployed and underemployed in the US.

PART IV

Limits of law

The fourth and final section of this book examines the limitations of some of the accepted strategies for improving the life of workers. Over the last 50 years, the US and many other countries have made significant changes to the workplace by enacting and enforcing laws prohibiting discrimination. Without minimizing the importance of these gains, it is important to realize that attached to the discrimination paradigm were conceptualizations that affect workplace advocacy.

First, discrimination literature often centralizes identity as the primary analytical consideration. Second, discrimination statutes and literature predominately offer equality of treatment as the primary solution. Identity and equality have come to dominate the conversation about many issues of workplace fairness. A vulnerability approach provides a different theoretical framework for thinking about workplace fairness issues – one that goes beyond identity and equality. Using vulnerability theory, the focus would change to the structure of the work relationship, the ability of workers to obtain and maintain resilience, and the responsibility of the state in regulating employment to ensure resilience.

The first author in this section critiques the modern focus on identity and formal equality from a historical perspective, arguing that early reformers' focus on equality of treatment missed an opportunity to impose meaningful regulation on employers that would have benefitted all employees. Reformers' insistence on the importance of gender equality resulted in derailing those reforms and for that reason could actually be seen as aiding the interests of employers over employees when antidiscrimination had no substantive mandates for employee protection.

The second and third chapters in this section take a more contemporary feminist approach. They still perceive the work/family conflict as implicating gender discrimination, whether because that is where it resided historically or because the conflict still has a disparate impact today. Their arguments do not urge the implementation of a regime of formal gender equality, however, looking beyond that to the underlying structures of the workplace and its incompatibility with care work. These analyses are primarily directed to one aspect of the organization of work – the balancing of the demands of work with family responsibilities.

The final chapter in this section demonstrates a broad and novel approach to workplace fairness issues that is not tied to questions of identity or gender equality and perceives the crisis in the organization of work to be a community or collective problem in need of a broad societal response.

In her chapter, "Equal by what measure? The lost struggle for universal state protective labor standards," Deborah Dinner examines the end of maternalist labor laws and the embrace of formal equality in employment law in the second half of the 20th century. She argues that while these changes advanced women's workplace interests in some ways, the end of state protective laws also posed harms for working class women. She sheds light on the overlooked story of labor feminists' struggle to realize universal labor standards and shows how a vulnerability framework can help uncover the tradeoffs involved in the adoption of the formal equality approach. Her argument recasts the end of maternalist labor standards and the defeat of the vision for universal state protective laws as a precondition for neoliberal restructuring in the relationship between the labor market, family, and state.

Elizabeth Ben-Ishai's chapter, "Improving job quality for low-wage women workers: a 21st century movement" notes that issues of discrimination have often been the focus of feminist work on labor, but that other issues, particularly the challenges of attending to both work obligations and family needs, need similar attention. Ben-Ishai examines the recent movement for improved workplace policies and argues that a rich conception of vulnerability can help feminist scholars see the potential of this movement as a site for gendered analysis of labor, as well as for re-theorizing other concepts central to feminist work, including the state, care, collective action, and others.

In her chapter, "A right to request flexible working: what can the UK teach us?" K. Lee Adams argues that the intersection of paid work and unpaid family obligations implicates underlying gender norms of work, which create structural inequality in labor markets and employment law. She examines legislation adopted by several European countries, including the UK, which provides workers with family responsibilities some degree of flexibility in paid work to accommodate family care as a possible responsive state action that could address this inequality. She concludes that a situation-sensitive right to flexible work arrangements would fit reasonably with the US Family and Medical Leave Act as a low cost, gender-neutral mechanism to promote a less gendered American workplace.

The book ends with Kenneth Casebeer's piece, "Vulnerable communities: proposing community syndicalism for distressed localities," which proposes a model for increasing the economic resilience of communities destabilized by job loss. Casebeer argues that by splitting asset ownership from enterprise ownership, it is possible to re-incentivize production for long-term stability of jobs, reduce the negative effects of globalization, and strengthen local institutions and democratic participation.

15

EQUAL BY WHAT MEASURE? THE LOST STRUGGLE FOR UNIVERSAL STATE PROTECTIVE LABOR STANDARDS

Deborah Dinner[1]

I. Introduction

The existing historical and legal literature tends to portray the end of maternalist labor laws as the dawn of a new era of sex equality. The state laws regulating women's hours, wages, and conditions of work arguably offered protection from exploitative employment conditions but also restricted women's job opportunities. Nancy MacLean (2006) presents the most powerful argument that "Title VII [of the Civil Rights Act of 1964] cut the Gordian knot" which had divided the women's rights movement between advocates of the Equal Rights Amendment (ERA) and of protective laws. MacLean argues that "[b]y promising substantive fairness" women no longer had to choose between socio-economic security and equal employment opportunity (p. 118). MacLean's argument is now dominant within the historiography. It is echoed within legal scholarship which embraces theories of sex equality premised on the goal of eliminating sex-role stereotypes under law. The anti-stereotyping principle suggests that the state discriminates on the basis of sex when it treats men as breadwinners and women as caregivers (Franklin, 2010). The principle thus imagines the primary injury rendered by sex discrimination to constitute the enforcement of female dependence within the family. If we privilege an anti-stereotyping framework, the end of a maternalist labor regime appears a triumph because it opened breadwinning opportunities to women.

By contrast, a vulnerability framework invites scholars to rethink the end of maternalist labor laws. Yes, the end of maternalism ushered in formal equality of employment opportunity. But the question is, equal in what kind of world? The dominant narrative takes insufficient account of the costs to working class women that accompanied the elimination of sex-based maternalist labor standards. As the

1 Associate Professor, Emory University School of Law.

labor movement lost power and as the workforce grew more precarious, the erosion of state protective laws represented a source of injury as well as opportunity. This was particularly true within the US system of federalism, which excluded many low-income workers – disproportionately women and people of color – from coverage under federal labor law.

In addition to neglecting the harms that the end of state protective laws posed for working class women, the prevailing narrative also overlooks labor feminists' struggle to realize universal labor standards. As Dorothy Sue Cobble (2007) shows, labor feminists advocated social rights supporting women's ability to care for their families outside of the workplace. Labor feminists fought for state protection as well as individual rights to employment opportunity. They struggled to overlay equal treatment under law over a robust legal regime of federal and state labor protections. In particular, they campaigned for a voluntary overtime law for all non-professional workers. Had states realized this ideal, it would have helped men as well as women realize work lives more compatible with robust family and civic lives. As the country transitioned from the postwar period of affluence and rights expansion to a neoliberal age, however, employers and business trade associations largely defeated labor feminists' vision to fuse employment opportunity with state protection. Furthermore, the historical record has neglected a forgotten struggle for universal state protective laws, obscuring a normative alternative to either maternalism or neoliberal conceptions of sex equality.

This chapter explodes a number of chestnuts in feminist legal history. First, it leads us to locate the legal challenge to sex-specific labor laws in the context of a rapidly changing economy. From this perspective, the supporters of maternalist labor laws appear not as the last defenders of anachronistic gender stereotypes but as canaries in the mine, sounding a warning call about the growing precarity of low-income workers. Second, vulnerability analysis asks us to reconsider the social justice objective embraced by feminist legal advocacy. It highlights the universal vulnerability of workers within capitalist systems, the institutional arrangements that made some workers more resilient than others, and the need for universal labor protections. Third, the history in this chapter identifies the ideological and institutional points of convergence between sex discrimination law and employer interests in a more flexible workplace responsive to managerial prerogatives rather than state regulation. Last, and relatedly, the analysis reveals employer's use of Title VII of the Civil Rights Act of 1964 as a deregulatory tool. In sum, this chapter recasts the end of maternalist labor standards and the defeat of the vision for universal state protective laws as a precondition for neoliberal restructuring in the relationship between the labor market, family, and state.

II. Reinterpreting the debate over maternalist labor standards: gender, class, and resilience

In 1966, the head of the Women's Department of the United Auto Workers (UAW), Caroline Davis, addressed 200 women union members. "We are against the Michigan hours law," Davis said. She was referring to a 1909 state law that restricted women's work to ten hours per day and 54 hours per week. Women workers wanted access to the overtime work widely available within the auto industry and the high wages that came with it. Limits on women's hours of work made them less able to pay for "doctor bills, children in college, and all the other [financial] demands" they faced.[2] The applause grew so deafening Davis had to halt her speech.

The UAW's fight to repeal the hours law produced a "tug of war" between Davis and Myra Wolfgang, a local leader in the Hotel Employees and Restaurant Employees and Bartenders International Union (HERE). Detroit's "two top women in labor union circles" debated whether the law deprived working women of economic opportunity or offered them vital social protection. Wolfgang argued that working class women needed protection from twelve-hour days on the job. Women who could not afford to hire substitutes for their unpaid domestic labor returned from the workplace to what contemporary sociologist Arlie Hochschild calls a "second shift" in the home (Hochschild, 2012). The hours law, Wolfgang believed, took account of the sociological "difference" between men and women's roles within the family.[3]

It is tempting to portray Davis as the embodiment of the new and Wolfgang as that of the old, but to do so would be woefully inaccurate. Instead, Davis and Wolfgang each represented how working class women differently located within the law and the labor market differently experienced dramatic transformations in the economy and in gender roles. The UAW women who demanded to gain access to overtime work illustrated the growing importance of women's workforce participation to working class families striving to enter the middle class as well as to middle class families seeking to consolidate their class position. Women's incomes helped pay for children's college education, which was fast becoming a prerequisite to well-paying jobs, for growing health care costs, and for the displays of consumption increasingly important to social status. Rising divorce rates and delayed marriage also made women's income increasingly important to familial survival (Cohen, 2003; Goldin, 1990; Stevenson and Wolfers, 2007). Increases in women's labor-market participation sparked women's rights consciousness and activism aimed at realizing equal employment opportunity.

Yet the increase in women's workforce participation also had a darker side, as it was symptomatic of the decline of union power and the end of the family wage for industrial workers. In the late-twentieth century, the industrial economy that Caroline Davis believed should contain the promise of opportunity as well as protection gave way to a service economy characterized for many workers

2 Ruth Carlton, "Women's Work – How Many Hours?," *The Detroit News*, October 19, 1967, UAW Women's Department Papers 1919–1982, Walter P. Reuther Library, Wayne State University, Detroit [hereafter UAW Women's Department Papers].

3 Helen Fogel, "Judge Tells Women to Prove that Overtime is Harmful," January 31, 1969, folder 16, box 11, UAW Women's Department Papers; Colleen O'Brien, "Angry Women Charge Secret Repeal of Law Protecting Workers," *Detroit Free Press*, October 18, 1967, folder 14, box, 11, UAW Women's Department Papers; Carlton, "Women's Work – How Many Hours?"

by low-income, dangerous, and contingent labor. Furthermore, as Myra Wolfgang observed, women's strides toward equal treatment in the workforce were not accompanied by a parallel redistribution of caregiving labor to make gender roles within the home equal. Thus, the debate between Davis and Wolfgang well illustrated the double-edged character of change in the nature of work and family: growing opportunity coupled with deepening insecurity, formal equality in the public realm without substantive equality in the domestic sphere.

The split between Wolfgang and Davis did not mean that the former embraced sex stereotypes while the latter did not. Rather, the division between these labor feminists arose from the fact that female UAW members enjoyed greater resilience within the legal and economic system than did HERE members. The UAW premised its strategic calculus – giving up maternalist protections in exchange for greater employment opportunity for women – on the basis of a strong industrial economy that promised good jobs and a powerful union that could protect its workers through collective bargaining. These premises appeared solid in the late 1960s, but by the early 1970s grew much more tenuous. By contrast, the foundational premises of the HERE's calculus – a lack of highly-remunerated jobs and the absence of powerful collective bargaining agreements – became increasingly characteristic of the labor market. Far from being a relic of the past, the defenders of maternalist labor laws were actually harbingers of the precarity that workers would face in the late 20th century.

The maternalist labor laws that were the subject of heated dispute within the women's and labor movement in the late 1960s originated in the Progressive Era. Maternalist advocates in this period and during the New Deal had pursued state support for motherhood, while at the same time reinforcing the idea of sex-differentiated gender roles central to family wage and separate spheres ideologies (Gordon, 1998; Kessler-Harris, 2001). Social feminists and their progressive allies had fought for state laws regulating women's minimum wage, work hours, and other conditions of work. They used gender ideologies to circumvent the freedom of contract doctrines deployed by Lochner Era courts. Specific laws were needed to protect working mothers from exploitation, they argued, because of women's particular vulnerability as non-unionized, low-wage workers as well as their social role as mothers (Hart, 1994; Zimmerman, 1991).

A half decade after states enacted maternalist labor laws, the passage of a federal employment discrimination law, Title VII of the Civil Rights Act of 1964, threw them into question. Reconciling Title VII with maternalist labor laws proved a vexing dilemma. Women's Bureau Director Mary Dublin Keyserling conceded that some maternalist labor laws were "exceedingly outdated." Yet she argued that "the freeing of women from employment discrimination does not demand that they all have identical treatment." She and others urged the newly formed Equal Employment Opportunity Commission (EEOC) to preserve the laws so as to allow legislatures to extend the laws to men (Pedriana, 2006).

The EEOC's 1965 guidelines stated that Title VII did not eradicate state laws that had the purpose and effect of "protecting women against exploitation and hazards." But the EEOC provided little guidance about how to answer the looming, difficult question of which laws were genuinely protective and which discriminatory. Some so-called "protective" laws clearly worked to discriminate against women. The EEOC gave the example of laws limiting the weight women workers could lift, "set at an unreasonably low level." Employers violated Title VII when they used such laws as a pretext for discrimination. Employers also violated Title VII when they refused to hire women to avoid complying with a valid protective law, such as a state minimum wage rule, that required them to extend a benefit to female employees. But employers could lawfully refuse to hire or promote women when the jobs at issue were in conflict with state laws restricting women's work hours and conditions.[4] The guidelines raised more questions than they answered. They left workers, unions, employers, and state labor departments to draw the line between valid regulations that reflected genuine protective intent and invalid regulations rooted in gender stereotypes.

In their ambivalence, the EEOC guidelines encouraged both opponents and defenders of sex-based protective laws. At a conference of state commissions on the status of women in June 1966, a number of feminist reformers expressed anger at the perceived reluctance of the EEOC to enforce the sex provision of Title VII. Betty Friedan hosted a famous midnight meeting that resulted in the formation of the National Organization for Women (NOW), dedicated in significant part to enforcing equal employment opportunity for women. Friedan declared that protective laws for women "only protect women out of a good opportunity. . . . The name of the game is equality, not protection."[5]

Friedan's statement well illustrated the manner in which class variously shaped different feminists' stance on protective laws. The phrase "long hours of work" held different meanings for unionized industrial workers and for professional women. To UAW workers, overtime was an issue of fairness – an opportunity for women, like men, to access the same much-needed extra income. But the UAW did not view overtime as an unqualified good and sought, instead, to limit work hours and maintain high wages. By contrast, professional women viewed occasional long hours as an inextricable part of their new identities as career women. Margaret Borbach, President of the Detroit Business Woman's Club, for example, explained that women had the same "responsibility" to work long hours as men.[6] Class position, workers' location within a federalist system of law, and a rapidly changing economy determined whether repeal of sex-specific protective legislation promised opportunity, injury, or some combination of both.

As NOW mobilized to influence the EEOC's interpretation of Title VII, social feminists whose political genealogy dated to the Progressive Era organized a counter-campaign in defense of maternalist labor standards. Margaret Healey,

4 29 Fed Reg 1604.1(b) (1966).

5 "New Laws for Women Workers," *The Guardian*, July 11, 1970, p. 18.

6 Letter from Charleen Knight to Willard Wirtz, November 7, 1967, folder 15, box 11, UAW Women's Department Papers. Carlton, "Women's Work – How many Hours?"

Dorothy Height, and Olya Margolin, at the respective helms of the National Councils of Catholic, Negro, and Jewish Women, took the lead. The American Civil Liberties Union and several labor unions also joined them. In the summer of 1966, these maternalists wrote to EEOC Chairman Franklin Roosevelt Jr. and Acting Chairman Luther Holcomb. "There is some misunderstanding," they wrote, of "the importance of maintaining present State labor standards for women until such time as the laws are reexamined and improved to provide good labor standards for all workers." One supporter argued that the laws' eradication would benefit "highly skilled, or favorably situated women" while harming "those with the least skill and bargaining power."[7]

Facing pressure from both camps within the women's movement, the EEOC turned the fate of the protective laws over to the federal courts and state governments. August 1966 guidelines stated that in cases involving a conflict between Title VII and state protective laws, the EEOC "would decline to make a determination of reasonable cause." Instead, the agency "would leave the charging party to judicial remedies."[8]

As some working class women began to litigate to challenge protective laws in the courts, states reevaluated their labor laws in light of Title VII. In the fall of 1967, both houses of the Michigan legislature unanimously repealed the law limiting the work hours of female employees. At the time, 43 of 50 states had a maximum-hours law for women. The UAW and, to a lesser degree, the Communication Workers of America fought these laws in a handful of states; Michigan was a frontrunner in the trend toward the repeal. Soon after it repealed the hours law for women, however, the legislature created a state Occupational Safety Standards Commission and stipulated that protective laws would remain in effect until the Commission had promulgated new labor standards. The tension between the two mandates produced "rampant" confusion within unions and on factory floors.[9]

7 Letter from Dorothy I. Height, National President, National Council of Negro Women, Inc., to Luther Holcomb, Acting Chairman EEOC July 7, 1966, p. 1, folder 25, box 10, UAW Women's Department Papers; letter from Dorothy Height to Franklin Roosevelt, July 28, 1966, letter from Mary Dublin Keyserling to Catherine Conroy, July 20, 1966, letter from Olya Margolin to Franklin Roosevelt Jr. July 30, 1965, folder 10, box 16, Catherine East Papers, Schlesinger Library, Harvard University. "National Consumers League Statement on State Protective Labor Legislation," January 1967, pp. 1–2, folder 18, box 16, East Papers [hereafter East Papers].

8 32 Fed Reg 5999 (Apr. 14, 1967).

9 Morgan O'Leary, "Women's Wrath Shakes Lansing as Males Quail," *The Detroit News*, October 21, 1967, folder 16, box 18, UAW Women's Department Papers; Helen Fogel, "Judge Tells Women to Prove that Overtime is Harmful," January 31, 1969, folder 16, box 11, UAW Women's Department Papers; memorandum from Dorothy Haener to Caroline Davis, April 8, 1967, UAW Women's Department Papers; letter from Cecelia Carrigan, International Representative Women's Department to Henry Lacayo, President, Local 887, UAW, February 27, 1967, UAW Women's Department Papers; letter from Coleman Young to Olga Madar, November 3, 1967 and letter from Gene Rayborn, October 24, 1967, folder 15, box 11, UAW Women's Department Papers; transmittal slip from Olga Madar to Caroline Davis, November 1967, folder 15, box 11, UAW Women's Department Papers.

The tenuous fate of the women's hours law catalyzed a resurgence of maternalist activism. Mary Dublin Keyserling travelled to Michigan at the invitation of HERE, the National Councils of Catholic and Jewish Women, and the Governor's Commission on the Status of Women.[10] Advocates did not make arguments on the basis of sex-role stereotypes. Rather, they premised the importance of maternalist laws on the gendered division of labor within the family and on the position of low-income, non-unionized workers under the law. The Young Women's Christian Association and the National Council of Jewish Women, for example, argued that "emancipation, while it has released [women] for work, has not released them from home and family responsibilities."[11] Defenders of maternalist labor standards took a pragmatic rather than aspirational position on gender roles. A Michigan attorney fighting to preserve the state's hours law for women was in favor of "having things equal between men and women," but emphasized her representation of women who did not "get help with the housework and baby care from their husbands." She concluded acerbically: "Until equality is something more than theory, women need protection."[12]

The competing stances of the UAW and HERE derived from their structural location within the law and economy. Variable unionization rates, the gendered system of federalism that excluded many low-income women from New Deal labor rights, and sex segregation in the labor market made the UAW women more resilient than HERE workers. To understand the debate over maternalist labor standards, therefore, it is important to examine not only the gendered discourses in which participants voiced their stances but also the structures that determined working class women's variable resilience.

As members of a powerful union, UAW women could rely on strong bargaining agreements to protect them from involuntary overtime. By contrast, 70% of Michigan's workers were not unionized. Many of these workers labored in the low-income clerical, retail, and service sectors. Myra Wolfgang of HERE argued that the repeal would leave 200,000 women at the mercy of profit-hungry employers. She accused the UAW Women's Bureau of forging an unholy alliance with the Chamber of Commerce and the General Federation of Business and Professional Women.[13]

The UAW was privileged compared to HERE, moreover, because its membership enjoyed coverage under the Fair Labor Standards Act (FLSA). Accordingly, following repeal of the Michigan law restricting women's work hours, UAW's female membership would receive extra compensation for any mandatory overtime they faced. The UAW also had strong collective bargaining agreements that provided for overtime pay. By contrast, many workers in the hotel and restaurant industries – unionized and not – lacked coverage under the FLSA. Architects of

10 Letter from Charleen Knight to Willard Wirtz.

11 "State to Scuttle Women's 54-Hr. Limit," *Hotel-Bar-Restaurant Review* 2, no. 7 (1968): 2.

12 Fogel, "Judge Tells Women."

13 O'Brien, "Angry Women"; Carlton, "Women's Work – How Many Hours?".

the FLSA had viewed the hotel and restaurant industries as confined to "intrastate" commerce and, therefore, believed that federalism required them to be regulated via state legislation. While the UAW could afford to reject maternalist state protections, HERE spoke for workers for whom these laws served as the only backstop against unfettered exploitation.

The competing stances of the UAW and HERE on sex-based protective laws also resulted from the demographic composition of these unions. In 1964, women represented only 12.5% of the UAW membership (Dekutoski, 2009). The male-dominated auto industry promised well-paying jobs, which employers restricted to men on the basis of state protective laws. By contrast, the elimination of state-based protective laws did not offer the same opportunity to women workers in highly feminized sectors of the labor market. Myra Wolfgang's Local 705, for example, had 10,000 members, of whom 85% were women.[14] In sectors such as this one, sex-based protective laws did not prevent many women from competing for "male" jobs. For HERE, the end of state maternalist labor protections threatened a return to a free contract regime reminiscent of the Lochner Era. For the UAW, it promised the hope of equal employment opportunity within workplaces subject to federal labor standards and good union contracts.

Within just over a decade, however, Wolfgang's warnings appeared a jeremiad. The industrial economy upon which the UAW premised its legal advocacy strategy – still strong in the late 1960s – would by the early 1970s begin to wane rapidly. The industrial unions that had bet their futures on the postwar grand bargain, in which employers promised good wages and benefits in exchange for labor's relinquishing of control over the production process. Yet they quickly lost ground as a result of globalization, deindustrialization, the rise of a right-to-work movement, and an increasingly hostile National Labor Relations Board. The service sector in which HERE workers toiled became the model for a new economy dominated by contingent employment relationships and a precarious workforce. Service employees comprised 60% of the American workforce in 1970; that proportion reached 70% by 1980 and only continued to increase thereafter. The kind of well-remunerated, blue-collar industrial jobs that the UAW workers held all but disappeared (Borstelmann, 2012; Cowie, 1999). As the labor movement declined both in numbers and in political power, workers lost the collective leverage necessary to bargain for improved work conditions in the absence of state protections.

III. Universal vulnerability: the campaign for a voluntary overtime law in Michigan

Within a year of their bitter contest over the elimination of the women's hours law, Davis and Wolfgang – formerly bitter enemies – had joined forces. To the surprise of almost all observers, the UAW and the Hotel and Restaurant Employees

14 Letter from Myra K. Wolfgang, January 28, 1969, folder 18, box 11, UAW Women's Department Papers.

Union forged a "united front" in a campaign for legislation that would limit the work hours of men as well as women.[15] Labor feminists and their unions interpreted the emerging principle of sex equality under law as an impetus to extend protective labor standards from women to men. Just as maternalism had acted as a wedge to crack Lochnerism, now sex equality might serve as a lever to expand protections for labor.

The campaign for universal state protective laws posed a new way out of an old and painful strategic dilemma: whether to prioritize equal employment opportunity or protection for workers. A universal hours law would offer protection to male and female workers not then covered by federal or state labor laws. Unlike sex-based hours laws, however, employers could not use a universal hours law as a justification to exclude women from job opportunities. The fight for the expansion of protective labor legislation – not the fight to strike down sex-based protective laws, as the common wisdom dictates – obviated the choice between protection and opportunity. The struggle held out the hope of fusing two strands within American liberalism: a commitment to labor protection forged in the Progressive Era and New Deal and a newer, Civil Rights Era commitment to antidiscrimination.

The limitations of the FLSA made universal hours laws especially important. Congress only had the constitutional power to regulate industries engaged in interstate commerce. Even after extensions of FLSA coverage in 1966, 430,000 women employed in hotels, motels, and restaurants nationwide remained exempt from overtime pay provisions. Of the 15.9 million women working as nonsupervisory private sector employees (excluding household workers), 39% were either excluded completely or only enjoyed partial coverage under the FLSA (Mettler, 1994).[16] The breadth of the states' police powers enabled state labor legislation to extend protections beyond workers engaged in interstate commerce.

Even for covered workers, the FLSA no longer effectuated the protections it had once promised. Congress had designed the statute to reduce work weeks and to promote full employment by mandating time-and-a-half overtime pay. By the late 1960s, however, the FLSA no longer effectively deterred employers from requiring overtime work. During World War II and in the postwar period, employers dramatically expanded fringe benefits. The cost of providing these benefits, therefore, represented a greater proportion of the total costs of employing any single worker. Mandatory overtime posed a cheaper alternative to hiring additional workers. The Big Three auto companies in Michigan, for example, kept up a competitive pace with each other by requiring overtime hours. Compulsory overtime also contributed

15 "Press Release, Coalition Spurs Senate Action on Voluntary Overtime Bill," December 9, 1970, folder 17, box 11, UAW Women's Department Papers.

16 Statement of Andrew J. Biemiller, Director, Department of Legislation, American Federation of Labor and Congress of Industrial Organizations, before the Equal Employment Opportunity Commission on "Guidelines on Discrimination Because of Sex.," June 2, 1967, p. 4, folder 28, box 10, UAW Women's Department.

to unemployment rates, especially among women, youth, older workers and racial minorities. The FLSA thus no longer fulfilled the labor movement's original aspirations: it neither deterred long hours nor advanced the goal of full employment.[17]

Furthermore, the FLSA required only that employers offer premium pay for overtime work at 1.5 times the ordinary wage rate. It did not give employees the right to refuse work beyond the standard work day or week. By contrast, the proposed law in Michigan would give workers the right to refuse overtime work, prohibiting retaliation by employers. Thus, the voluntary overtime law would compensate for the inequalities in bargaining power between employers and unorganized workers.

Other states, including Virginia, Wyoming, and Idaho, turned to premium pay for overtime as a market-based solution to the problem of the conflict between maternalist laws and Title VII. Premium pay requirements avoided the total repeal of hours laws, on one hand, as well as the extension of overtime limits to men, on the other. Proponents argued that premium pay for overtime would balance workers' interest in humane hours and management's interest in flexibility necessary "to meet production requirements." It would both broaden women's employment opportunities and foster "a positive business climate." Labor feminists, however, argued that premium pay could not "protect the worker from excessive overtime demands of employers" because the added wages fell far short of the cost of hiring additional workers.[18] In Michigan, unions' political power offered the chance to pursue a protective ideal rooted not in market incentives but rather in state responsibility to redress an imbalance of power between employers and workers.

The UAW-led coalition for a voluntary overtime law, however, faced a daunting challenge in updating maternalist rationales to argue for the extension of protections from female to male workers. The gendering of protection as feminine posed an obstacle to UAW leaders' argument that a voluntary overtime law was a moral imperative to "protect welfare, in the broadest sense *for all workers*." Dorothy Haener, a UAW activist and founder of NOW, stressed that men as well as women needed time for familial and civic life outside the workplace. Instead of emphasizing women's domestic responsibilities, she talked about workers' need for "leisure time to be with their families, for living and relaxing." Universal overtime laws would foster workers' capacity "to perform their duties as citizens."[19] Dominant conceptions of masculinity, however, were premised upon independence and

17 Letter from Stella Deakins to Willard Wirtz, October 30, 1967; "Statement Presented to Labor committee of the Michigan House of Representatives by Douglas A. Fraser, UAW Executive Board Member-at-Large," April 21, 1969, p. 2, folder 18, box 11, UAW Women's Department Papers; letter from Caroline Davis, Director, UAW Women's Department to Ken Morris, Director, UAW Region 1B (same to Marcellius Ivory, Bard Young, E S Patterson, Ken Robinson), February 26, 1969, folder 17, box 11, UAW Women's Department Papers. Statement of Andrew J. Biemiller, p. 5.

18 Memorandum to Hon. Joseph C. Fagan, Chairman; Hon. Gene A. Rowland, Commissioner; Hon. Edward E. Estowski, Commissioner, Industrial Commission of Wisconsin., pp. 8–9 1967, folder 27, box 10, UAW Women's Department Papers.

19 Statement of the International Union, UAW, August 19, 1968 at Public Hearing to the Michigan Occupational Standards Commission, 1, folder 16, box 11, UAW Women's Department Papers.

autonomy rather than universal vulnerability. The campaign for the voluntary overtime law, therefore, would require a redefinition of masculinity as well as femininity.

UAW Board Member Douglas Fraser argued that overtime laws would advance workers' self-ownership, drawing on a powerful discursive tradition that emphasized workers' independence. In the antebellum period, free-labor Republicans juxtaposed contractual labor with slavery (Foner, 1995b). In the age of emancipation, arguments about "wage slavery" reflected social anxieties about the blurry lines between free and coerced labor (Stanley, 1998). Fraser updated these arguments for the late-twentieth century. The standard forty-hour work week preserved workers' leisure time and their right to self-ownership:

> Corporations have to get away from the antiquated and inhuman concept that when a worker punches his time clock in the morning he becomes an extension of the production process, and that since the company owns the production process, the worker belongs to the company.

Drawing on Cold War metaphors, Fraser argued that a worker's capacity for self-determination – to determine how to spend his time – constituted the mark of a free society compared to a totalitarian one. He concluded, "an honest day's labor . . . cannot in itself be all-fulfilling to the total physical and spiritual needs of man."[20]

The argument that men needed protection from excessive work hours held the potential to transform gender roles as well as the employer-employee relationship. The demand for humane work hours could help enable men to assume an equal share of caregiving labor within the home. Caroline Davis made this connection explicit when she challenged the presumption underpinning sex-specific labor laws: "The home, the family, the responsibility is all theirs. What about the role of the father in the home?" In arguing for state protection of men's independence from the workplace, however, the UAW's male leadership did not challenge outright the gendered division of labor within the home. Fraser broadened the category of pursuits meriting state protection for workers' autonomy beyond motherhood, yet he did not root the argument for shorter work hours in feminists' call for a more egalitarian division of caregiving labor. Fraser did not argue that sex equality meant that men needed extra time away from the workplace to perform additional childrearing duties. He left intact the societal understanding that only women faced the necessity of working within the home. Fraser's idealized free man was one whose independence rested not only on autonomy from employers but also on the dependence of wives who performed familial caregiving.

If Fraser did not fully relinquish his commitment to a family wage system, labor feminists' campaign for a voluntary overtime law nonetheless held the potential

20 "Statement presented to Labor committee of the Michigan House of Representatives by Douglas A. Fraser, UAW Executive Board Member-at-Large," p. 2, April 21, 1969, folder 18, box 11, UAW Women's Department Papers.

to challenge that system. Their vision posed an alternative both to maternalist ideologies that reinforced gender stereotypes and to a neoliberal workplace that both reinforced sex-role stereotypes and facilitated workplace design on the basis of managerial prerogatives. Rather, labor feminists argued for universal state labor laws on the basis of all workers' entitlement to a familial, social, and civic life outside of the workplace. This argument both rested upon a more egalitarian construction of gender and also held the capacity to foster such a socio-legal transformation. Union leadership, however, stopped short of endorsing the feminist claim to redistribute caregiving labor. In part as a consequence, labor feminists faced an uphill battle striving to substitute a gender-egalitarian rationale in place of a maternalist one for state labor standards.

Labor feminists' vision encompassed far more than an antidiscrimination agenda. In advocating a voluntary overtime law, they argued that the state had a responsibility to respond affirmatively to workers' universal vulnerability. They imagined a collective solution that involved affirmative entitlements rather than an individualized, negative right allocated on the basis of identity. To understand why labor feminists' vision did not come to fruition, however, requires an historical analysis of gender. The political construction of state protective labor standards as feminine, together with the incomplete commitment of union leaders to transforming socio-legal constructions of masculinity, contributed to the defeat of the campaign to universalize state protective laws.

IV. Neoliberal sex equality: employer support for the repeal of maternalist labor laws

The Big Three automobile companies in Michigan endorsed a neoliberal conception of sex equality and opposed labor feminists' efforts to conjoin employment discrimination law with labor protection. The Big Three supported the repeal of maternalist laws, and employers across the country took the same position on their states' laws.[21] Yet the concept of sex equality had no inherent substantive content and was subject to manipulation and appropriation by employers. While endorsing repeal, employers and business trade associations vociferously opposed the use of sex equality as a rationale for extending sex-based protective laws to men.

In the eyes of the Big Three, maternalist labor standards had long gummed up the wheels of production. Repeal of the hours law in Michigan served business interests by enhancing employers' control over workers, giving management the freedom to speed up production. Now management could deny women meal

21 Memorandum from Stephen I. Scholssberg and Bernard F. Ashe to Leonard Woodcock and Ernie Moran, May 23, 1968, folder 18, box 11, UAW Women's Department Papers; letter from Duane D. Daggett, Manager, Labor Relations Department, Illinois State Chamber of Commerce to Lillian Hatcher, Letter from Duane D. Daggett, Manager, Labor Relations Department, Illinois State Chamber of Commerce to Stephen Schlossberg, General Counsel, United Auto Workers, June 14, 1967, folder 15, box 11, UAW Women's Department Papers; letter from Barbara Decaire to Caroline Davis, September 29, 1965, folder 15, box 5, UAW Women's Department Papers.

breaks and force them to work longer hours.[22] Employers welcomed repeal not out of a commitment to sex equality *per se*, but rather from the overlap between equal treatment for women and managerial flexibility over the structure of work.

Employers also welcomed the campaign for the repeal because it promised a way out of the legal uncertainty they faced. Bound by both state protective laws and Title VII, employers found themselves, in the words of one lawyer, "caught between the devil and the deep blue sea."[23] When the dust finally settled, a decisive mandate in favor of repeal would promise legal clarity, facilitate market transactions, and lower companies' legal costs. Title VII, therefore, realigned interests of the Big Three in ways that made them overlap with UAW seeking repeal of maternalist labor laws. Employers, ever mistrustful of state regulation, were much less hostile to the individualist premises of employment discrimination law than to the solidaristic tendencies of labor law.

The Big Three's stance on the voluntary overtime law starkly contrasted these companies' willingness to make job classifications formally sex-neutral. The auto companies vociferously opposed the extension of protective laws and, specifically, hours and weight limits for men. Such laws would have "dire consequences on production schedules," they claimed.[24] The Big Three, therefore, endorsed sex equality overlaid on a neoliberal labor regime but opposed equality when conjoined with a protective labor regime. Major manufacturing interests across the country echoed the claim that universal protection would come at the cost of business growth. The argument held sway over many politicians as the nation transitioned from a period of affluence to one of greater scarcity.

The proposal for voluntary overtime proved Michigan's "most controversial piece of labor legislation" during the late 1960s.[25] In 1971, the fight for overtime laws in Michigan finally succumbed to opposition from the auto lobby. This defeat marked the demise of the aspiration for state legislation that protected workers from mandatory overtime.

V. The use of title VII as a deregulatory tool: the fate of California's labor protections in courts and administrative agencies

While labor feminists sought to institutionalize both equal employment opportunity and a robust regime of labor protection, major employers and business trade associations wanted to overlay equal treatment onto a workplace liberated from

22 Marilyn Danton, "Protective Legislation and the ERA," *Workers' Power* (October 9–22, 1970): 3–4.

23 "Working Women Caught in State and Federal Law Bind," *Los Angeles Times*, November 12, 1969, folder 18, box 16, East Papers.

24 "Big Three Read from Same Script in Opposing Limits on Overtime," *Michigan AFL-CIO News*, March 26, 1969, folder 16, box 11, UAW Women's Department Papers.

25 Memorandum from Russ Leach to Caroline Davis, January 20, 1969, folder 16, box 11, UAW Women's Department Papers.

state labor regulation. Employers and business trade associations litigated under Title VII in their own interest, using the prohibition on sex discrimination to challenge maternalist protective laws. In addition, the business lobby used the advent of the egalitarian ideal to taint that of labor protection generally. Sex-neutrality emerged as a powerful instrument in the neoliberal toolbox. The defeat of the voluntary overtime law represented a lost opportunity to use Title VII to augment state labor standards. In the wake of this defeat, employers mobilized to deploy Title VII as a mechanism to reduce labor standards to a lowest common denominator.

Across the country from Michigan, a powerful labor movement in California had yielded the nation's most comprehensive maternalist labor laws, which were now at risk of invalidation under Title VII. The fate of this regime in a new civil rights era posed high stakes for California's workers. The vast majority of female employees in the state – 80% – were unorganized.[26] Lacking the protection offered by collective bargaining agreements, these workers relied on sex-based protective laws. As of 1972, 2.5 million women and minors enjoyed coverage under laws that set a $1.65 minimum wage, time-and-a-half pay for overtime work beyond eight hours, and two daily ten-minute rest periods. Although formally restricted to women, the maternalist labor regime benefitted men as well. Workplace "custom" often resulted in the extension of regulations on women's conditions of work to male employees in the same workplaces. Likewise, federal and state equal pay laws resulted in the extension of the state minimum wage for women to men. Sex-specific labor standards thus set a floor that raised the work conditions and wages of the 40% of male workers in California who did not enjoy coverage under the FLSA.[27]

The fate of protective labor laws in California illustrates the historical importance of forum and timing to legal change. Legislatures and administrative agencies gave advocates of universal protective standards the best hope of achieving their aims. Judges in federal courts, by contrast, selected remedies that struck down rather than extended sex-based labor laws. The question was whether litigation would wash away sex-based protective laws before advocates could use them as a political foothold from which to build momentum toward augmenting universal labor standards.

In October 1966, Velma Mengelkoch, a UAW spokeswoman at a North American Aviation plant in Anaheim, filed suit in federal district court alleging that California's law limiting women's work hours violated both Title VII and the

26 "Protective Laws . . . We Fought to Get 'Em, We'll Fight to Keep 'Em!!," n.d., folder 8, box 16, Union Women's Alliance to Gain Equality Records, 1971–1982, Labor Archives and Research Center at the J. Paul Leonard Library, San Francisco State University (hereafter Union WAGE Records).

27 Letter from Anne Lipow, President and Luella Hanberry, Vice President, Union WAGE to Equal Employment Opportunity Commission, July 19, 1972, box 16, folder 5, Union WAGE Records; California's Protective Laws for Women, staff report, attached to letter from Stephen Spellman to Catherine East, November 19, 1969, pp. 40–43, folder 17, box 16, East Papers.

Equal Protection Clause. Her case attracted considerable support from feminist attorneys and reformers. Not long thereafter, Leah Rosenfeld, a member of the Transportation-Communication Employees Union, filed suit challenging the state regulations that restricted the weight women could lift on the job to amounts much lower than she regularly lifted when performing heavy labor on her family ranch. Mengelkoch and Rosenfeld were brave pioneers – working class women who fought for equal rights to higher-paying jobs. An AFL-CIO economist worried, however, that while the "complaint machinery under Title VII provide[d] a built-in channel of communication" for exposing the injuries of sex-based labor standards, no similar communicative mechanism existed to highlight protective laws' importance.[28] Indeed, the historiography well illustrates the dynamic Draper feared. The scholarship celebrates women such as Mengelkoch and Rosenfeld while overlooking the disadvantages that the end of maternalist labor standards posed for non-unionized workers.

The period between 1969 and 1971 proved a turning point in the fate of sex-based protective laws. By 1972, seven states had made restrictions on women's work hours more flexible; two states declined to enforce the laws; nine exempted employees covered by Title VII; and ten more explicitly repealed the laws. In 1972, Congress passed amendments to Title VII that authorized the EEOC to bring litigation in the federal courts. The agency's new enforcement powers accelerated the demise of sex-based protective laws. By 1973, only one state retained a maximum hours law unchanged since 1964 (Woloch, 2015).

It was not inevitable that the courts, when confronted with the conflict between a sex-based labor standard and Title VII, would strike down the state law. Rather, the courts might have chosen a different remedy: extension of the state's protective standards to men. Some male workers saw Title VII as an opportunity to gain workplace benefits then restricted to women. Michael Burns of Imperial Beach, California argued that Title VII required his employer, an aerospace firm called the Rohr Corporation, to extend to men the rest periods guaranteed non-professional female workers under state law (*Burns v Rohr Corp.*, 346 F. Supp. 994, (S.D. Cal. 1972)). Burns' lawyer predicted that a ruling in Burns' favor would yield a $46.8 million judgment for the male employees of Rohr Corporation's Chula Vista and Riverside plants, who effectively worked 100 minutes unpaid overtime each week.[29]

There existed scholarly support for Burns' interpretation that the court should resolve his case by extending the sex discriminatory protective law. Law professor Leo Kanowitz argued that the US Supreme Court's role in shaping the sex-specific character of state labor regulations dictated the appropriate remedy. Freedom of

28 Letter from Anne Draper, Economist, AFL-CIO, to ACLU Equality committee Chairman, Marvin Karpatkin, March 13, 1968, quoted in memorandum from Alan Reitman and Susan Goldstein to the Board regarding Sex Discrimination, p. 5, folder 5, box 9, Anne Draper Files, 1913–1994, George Meany Memorial Archives, Silver Springs, MD.

29 "Suit Hits Rest Periods; Firm Called Unfair – to Men," *Los Angeles Times*, March 6, 1970, p. 3.

contract jurisprudence in the early twentieth century had created the necessity for a maternalist strategy by progressives and labor advocates. Kanowitz argued the court had an obligation to assume responsibility for its earlier decisions by extending state protective law that violated Title VII to men (Kanowitz, 1968).

In April 1972, the EEOC issued guidelines that suggested extension rather than invalidation as the appropriate means to resolve the conflict between Title VII and sex-based state labor laws. The guidelines stated that Title VII required employers to extend sex-based minimum wage and premium pay laws to men, without exception. Employers did not similarly have to extend other sex-based protective laws regulating work conditions if "business necessity" precluded them from doing so. The guidelines took their inspiration from a landmark Supreme Court case decided the prior year. In *Griggs v Duke Power Co.* (1971), the court held that Title VII prohibited employment practices that, even in the absence of discriminatory intent on the part of employers, had a "disparate impact" that disproportionately excluded racial minorities from employment opportunity. The EEOC's 1972 guidelines similarly interpreted Title VII broadly as a statute that, more than merely prohibiting employment practices based on discriminatory *animus* or overbroad stereotypes, might impose costs on employers. The Supreme Court had held that if plaintiffs could establish a *prima facie* case of disparate impact, then an employer would have to show that the challenged practice was related to job performance; "the touchstone [was] business necessity." In adopting this same key phrase, the EEOC's guidelines also followed *Griggs* in establishing a limiting principle to Title VII's redistributive consequences.

The US District Court for the Southern District of California remained silent about the EEOC guidelines when it ruled that the Rohr Corporation was not liable for failing to extend rest periods to male workers. The court held that the state law providing rest periods to women conflicted with Title VII. Instead of ordering Rohr Corporation to extend rest periods to men, however, the court held that Title VII preempted the state law. The court declined to follow the suggestion of Burns' attorney that "beneficial" labor regulations should be extended rather than struck down. Instead, the court found the distinction between beneficial and restrictive regulations incoherent. By limiting women's weekly work time, the state law at issue could just as easily be determined restrictive; it frustrated the purpose of Title VII by making women less competitive in the labor market. Extension was an inappropriate remedy, moreover, because it would place businesses that employed men as well as women at a competitive disadvantage with those that employed only men. Furthermore, the court reasoned that it would invalidly usurp the legislative power if it universalized a state protection that the legislature had intended to apply only to women.

A single federal court reached a different conclusion to the *Burns* court. In *Hays v Potlatch Forests, Inc.* (1972), the Eighth Circuit required an employer to comply with both Title VII and an Arkansas state law requiring premium pay for overtime work by women, by extending the premium pay to men. The EEOC filed an *amicus* brief in support of this expansive reading in *Hays* and a brief on appeal from *Burns*, urging the Ninth Circuit to overturn the district court ruling in that case.[30] The Eighth Circuit decision in *Hays* remained an outlier, however, and four years after *Hays*, the Arkansas Supreme Court held that Title VII pre-empted the overtime law because the enacting legislature could not have intended it to apply to men (*State v Fairfield Communities Land Co.*, 1976).

While male plaintiffs met defeat in their efforts to use Title VII to expand labor protections, employers across the nation deployed Title VII to dismantle maternalist labor regulations. Caterpillar Tractor and Illinois Bell Telephone litigated a successful challenge to a state maximum hours law for women. General Electric Co. and the IUE together litigated in Kentucky to win the right to give women workers overtime assignments (Woloch, 2015).

In *Homemakers, Inc. of Los Angeles v Division of Industrial Welfare* (1973), a division of Upjohn Pharmaceutical Company argued that the California law requiring overtime pay for female employees violated Title VII. The employer's motives were self-serving. Homemakers, Inc. employed an overwhelmingly female workforce who provided housekeeping and practical nursing services to individuals and local governments. The company's challenge to the overtime law could only have been motivated by a desire to pay its own employees less (Boris and Klein, 2012). California argued that its law did not conflict with Title VII; Homemakers could simply pay male employees at the same overtime rate, were it to hire men. The district court, however, held that requiring Homemakers to extend the state overtime law to men would be an exercise of legislative power beyond the institutional role of the court. Holding that Title VII superseded the state's premium pay law, the court allowed an employer to use a putative sex discrimination claim to erode real protections for low-wage women workers.

The decisions in *Mengelkoch*, *Rosenfeld*, *Burns*, and *Homemakers* stand in stark contrast to a series of Supreme Court cases in the ensuing decade that selected extension as a remedy, rather than striking down sex discriminatory legislative regimes. These decisions recognized that federal entitlements discriminated on the basis of sex, in violation of the Equal Protection Clause, when they were based on the assumption that families comprised a male breadwinner and dependent female caregiver. The Supreme Court, however, did not strike down discriminatory Social Security, military, and welfare benefits but rather made these benefit schemes formally sex-neutral.[31]

Legal scholars at the time struggled to make sense of the tension between the remedies selected in the protective labor and in the equal protection cases.

30 Letter from William H. Brown to Anne Lipow and Luella Hanberry, 1–2, folder 5, box 16, Union WAGE Records.

31 *Frontiero v Richardson*, 411 US 677 (1973) (extending automatic, non means-tested military benefits to the spouses of female servicemembers); *Weinberger v Wiesenfeld*, 420 US 636 (1975) (extending Social Security benefits to widowers as well as widows with minor children in care); *Califano v Goldfarb*, 430 US 199 (1977) (extending Social Security survivor benefits to men); *Califano v Westcott*, 443 US.76 (1979) (extending AFDC for children of unemployed mothers as well as fathers).

Legal scholar Deborah Beers (1975) found a causal explanation in the relative cost burden of the extension remedy in the state labor cases compared to the federal benefit cases. The equal protection cases in which the Supreme Court selected extension as a remedy did not impose proportionally significant costs on federal government; relatively few families defied the gender norms on which these benefit schemes were based. By contrast, extending state protective laws to men would have come with an expensive price tag for businesses. Beer's argument supports the conclusion that courts were loath to interpret Title VII in a manner that imposed significant costs on employers. The courts responded to employers' economic vulnerability in a competitive market, but not to that of employees.

Even as litigation in the federal courts struck down sex-based labor standards, labor feminists fought within California's administrative apparatus to realize universal protective laws. The Union Women's Alliance to Gain Equality, formed in 1971, understood the fight for women's equality as inextricable from the struggle for better work conditions and a more just economy. Jean Maddox, President of Local 29 of the Office and Professional Employees International Union had led a famous strike of clerical workers at food retail stores and was known as the "labor movement conscience" in the San Francisco Bay Area. Other leaders included Anne Draper, an activist in the Amalgamatted Clothing Workers and a leader in the Berkeley Independent Socialist Club, and Joyce Maupin, who wrote a column in the newspaper of the Socialist Workers Party, *The Militant.* Union WAGE conducted its first action in public hearings sponsored by the California Industrial Welfare Commission, the state administrative agency which set wages and work conditions for women. WAGE activists demanded that the Commission extend the minimum wage and protective regulations to male workers. In the spring of 1972, Union WAGE along with the California Federation of Labor realized an initial victory when the state legislature passed a bill that gave California's Industrial Welfare Commission jurisdiction over the hours and conditions of work for men as well as women.[32]

Employers and business trade associations, however, sent Governor Ronald Reagan a "heavy volume" of mail urging him to veto the bill. They reasoned, first, that universal protective legislation would impose new costs on business. Pacific Far East Line, Inc., for example, argued that extending the twenty-five pound weight restriction to male shipping workers would mean "the complete industrial complex of the United States would have to change its packaging sizes." Second, employers contended that state regulation would undermine the liberty of employers and employees to negotiate privately the terms of work. Third, the

32 Notes on History of Protective Legislation from Union WAGE Workshop, June 25, 1974, box 16, folder 8, Union WAGE Records.; Assembly Bill No. 1710, introduced by Assemblyman Brown, March 15, 1972, Amended, Governor's Vetoed Bill File, California State Archives [hereafter Vetoed Bill File].

California Manufacturers Association warned that protective laws would only increase the already alarming number of lawsuits filed by women workers.[33]

Employers and business trade associations used competing conceptions of gender to oppose giving the Industrial Welfare Commission universal jurisdiction. Some companies rested their arguments on gender stereotypes, suggesting that it would be "ludicrous" to extend maternalist protections to men. One company admonished "that since the days of Neanderthal man, the male, on the average, has grown larger and physically stronger than the female, [and] developed patterns of work capabilities which differentiated him from the female, to the advantage of the human race." Universal labor standards would thus defy nature. Other companies, by contrast, reasoned that deregulation of the labor market would advance sex equality. They maintained that the ERA had not only undermined the legal legitimacy of sex-based protective laws but had rendered these protections, themselves, "archaic."[34]

These arguments appealed to Reagan's ideals of efficient business, private markets, and a smaller state government. Reagan vetoed the legislation giving the Industrial Welfare Commission universal jurisdiction only a month after California ratified the ERA.[35] California's affirmation of formal equal treatment of men and women, coupled with the failure to expand the Commission's jurisdiction, encouraged employers to end maternalist protections in their business practices. One company stopped giving rest periods to women workers; another lowered wages to equalize them on the basis of sex; still another eliminated a taxi service previously provided to women working nights.[36]

Following the veto, Union WAGE, the California Federation of Labor, and a broad coalition of unions rededicated their efforts to vest the Industrial Welfare Commission with jurisdiction over male workers. In early 1973, the California Assembly and Senate considered revised legislative proposals that compromised

33 Enrolled Bill memorandum to Governor, Bill. No. AB 1710, December 11, 1972, letter from CT Morton, the Duncanson-Harrelson Co. to Governor Ronald Reagan, December 8, 1972, letter from DJ Haughton, Chairman of the Board, Lockheed Aircraft Corporation to Governor Ronald Reagan, December 11, 1972, p. 2, letter from Leo C. Ross, Pacific Far East Line, Inc. to Governor Ronald Reagan, December 11, 1972, letter from Howard J. Smiley, President, California Broadcasters Association, to Governor Ronald Reagan, December 1, 1972, letter from AL Libra, General Counsel, California Manufacturers' Association to Governor Ronald Reagan, December 6, 1962, p. 2, Vetoed Bill file.

34 Letter from Philip Steinberg, Regional Vice President, American Institute of Shipping, to Governor Ronald Reagan, November 22, 1972, letter from C.T. Morton, the Duncanson-Harrelson Co. to Governor Ronald Reagan, December 8, 1972, letter from Carl M. Holmes, Assistant Vice President, Pacific Telephone and Telegraph Company, to Governor Ronald Reagan, December 11, 1972, California Assembly Bill 1710 of 1972, letter from R. Di Giorgio Corporation to Governor Ronald Reagan, December 6, 1972, Vetoed Bill File.

35 *Homemakers, Inc. of Los Angeles v Division of Industrial Welfare*, 356 F supp 1111, 1113 (ND Cal April 2, 1973).

36 "E.R.A. Backfires in Los Angeles: Why?," 1973, "ERA: Equal Rights or Equal Oppression?," n.d., folder 8, box 16, Union WAGE Records.

with business interests. The new version of the bill exempted weight lifting, so that men would not be subject to the restrictions placed on women. The proposed legislation also required the Industrial Welfare Commission to "interpret . . . [the bill's] provisions in a manner which does not cause undue hardship and loss of employment opportunities in any segment of industry in California." Last, the bill invested the Industrial Welfare Commission with the option to extend protective regulations to men, but did not require the Commission to do so.[37] As a result of these concessions, the revised legislation garnered the support of business trade associations.[38] While concerned about further regulation, employers felt that sex-neutral administrative jurisdiction over labor standards would offer a means out of the legal "dilemma" caused by the conflict between Title VII and state labor laws.[39]

Reagan signed the legislation, stating that he was influenced by business support and the modest cost of the new laws. Just a few months later, the Ninth Circuit Court of Appeals affirmed the district court decision in *Homemakers*. The court based its holding in part on the possibility that under the recent legislation the Industrial Welfare Commission would "cure the defects of earlier enactments by expressly allowing the Industrial Commission" to extend overtime regulations in place for women to men (*Homemakers, Inc. of Los Angeles v Division of Industrial Welfare and Industrial Welfare Commission*, 1974). But there was no guarantee the Commission would do so. Supporters of the minimum wage for women feared that *Homemakers* undermined the economic security of two million women who had enjoyed state protection for overtime pay and affected an even greater number of men who merited the same under state and federal equal pay laws.[40]

Labor feminists' fears were not unreasonable. The legislation that vested the Industrial Welfare Commission with universal jurisdiction also enabled business to capture the Commission. The legislation required that the Commission hold public hearings before issuing new regulations and mandated that the Commission review and update its regulations every two years. These procedural requirements gave business groups a role in the administrative process; in public hearings, they could make the case that maternalist regulations should not be extended to men. In addition, when Reagan became governor in 1967 he had shifted the traditional political balance among the commissioners (two sympathetic to labor, two sympathetic to

37 AB 478-Brown as Amended 5–7–73; Hearing Date: 8–30–73; Amendments to Assembly Bill No. 478 as Amended in Assembly May 7, 1973, August 28, 1973, letter from Willie J. Brown Jr. to Governor Ronald Reagan, September 24, 1973, letter from McClung to Reagan, September 21, 1973, Senate Committee on Industrial Relations, AB 478-Brown, as Amended 9–4–73, Hearing Date 9–12–73, California State Archives, Sacramento, California [hereafter Cal State Archives].

38 Letter from Robert M. Shillito, Executive Vice President, California Retailers Association to Governor Ronald Reagan, September 21, 1973, letter from Emmonds McClung, Executive Vice President, California Manufacturers Association to Governor Ronald Reagan, September 21, 1973, Enrolled Bill Memorandum to Governor, September 24, 1973, Cal State Archives.

39 Letter from William H. Smith, Executive Vice President, Federated Employers of the Bay Area to Governor Ronald Reagan, September 19, 1973, Cal State Archives.

40 Linda Mathews, "Court Lets Limit on Overtime Pay for Women Stand," *Los Angeles Times*, January 13, 1976.

management, and one non-partisan) in favor of business interests.[41] In 1974, three of the five commissioners represented the industries that employed the largest number of female workers – agriculture, restaurants, and electronics manufacturing.[42]

That year, the Commission slashed protective regulations applicable to women workers and thereby also lowered *de facto* standards for unorganized male workers who had benefitted from the floor set by these laws.[43] The Commission increased the standard work day from eight to ten hours, reducing the overtime pay for workers in eleven industries including manufacturing, personal service, clerical, and public housekeeping, among others. The orders exempted another several million workers, mostly in the retail industries, from any overtime coverage.[44] The extension of the FLSA to agricultural and domestic workers the same year mitigated some of the political pressures on the Commission to expand state labor standards. The evisceration of these state regulations, nonetheless, devastated Union WAGE activists.

The gutting of state labor standards galvanized the formation of the Committee for Better Working Conditions, spearheaded by Union WAGE, the Asian Community Center, and the Revolutionary Union – a Marxist-Leninist group that had formed in the Bay Area to try to unify racial liberation and working class movements. Activists protested at public hearings, wearing shrouds and carrying placards and banners that read: "10 hour day - no way" and "Women need protective laws, men do too." The Committee pursued three objectives in public hearings before the Industrial Welfare Commission: an increase in the state minimum wage; overtime pay beyond the eight-hour day, and health and safety protections.[45]

Throughout the late 1970s, the pendulum of political influence in California's administrative agencies swung back and forth between labor and business. By 1979, a decade of struggle had resulted in the extension of many protective labor regulations to all workers. But union WAGE activists also reflected on the limits of the state's regulatory scheme. No law limited the hours in a work day (Kanowitz, 1980). Some Californians were burdened by overtime while others felt the sting of unemployment. Labor feminists also observed an irony: while men's declining wages had prompted women to enter the workforce, the state now used the fact of two wage-earner families as an "excuse" to keep the minimum wage low.[46]

41 Lenore Weiss, "Who Are the Commissioners?," *Union WAG.* 6, 1976, box 18, folder 2, Union WAGE.

42 The fourth commissioner was the wife of the food chain owner and the fifth a Teamsters union official. "IWC? What's That?," n.d., box 16, folder 7, Union WAGE Records.

43 "ERA: Equal Rights or Equal Oppression?," n.d., box 16, folder 8, Union WAGE Records.

44 "Fact Sheets on Action to Save Premium Overtime Pay for All Women and Men Workers," March 5, 1975, p. 3, Mel Ziegler, "No Overtime Pay for 10-Hour Day," circa 1974, box 16, folder 7, Union WAGE Records.

45 Steve Hamilton, "On the History of the Revolutionary Union (Part One)." *Theoretical Review* 13 (November-December 1979) available at www.marxists.org/history/erol/periodicals/theoretical-review/19791302.htm; Elaine Reed, "IWC Hears Women's Protest," *Oakland Tribune*, April 25, 1974, 25, box 16, folder 7, Union WAGE Records. Jackson Rannells, "Opposition to Proposed Working Rules," *San Francisco Chronicle*, June 16, 1976, box 18, folder 2, Union WAGE Records.

46 "Alert! Employers Attack California's Overtime Laws," circa 1981, box 17, folder 4, Union WAGE Records.

In the 1970s, six states – California, Michigan, Pennsylvania, Oregon, and Rhode Island – had considered voluntary overtime legislation, yet no state had passed it. In April 1978, the National Coordinating Committee for Trade Union Action and Democracy, representing eighteen international unions, met in Dearborn, Michigan to press for a shorter work week. In addition to increasing "quality of work life," advocates believed this goal would support the Humphrey-Hawkins Act in reducing unemployment.[47] But these efforts withered on the vine, as both overtime and erratic work hours became the new standard for low-wage workers.

Employers' use of the sex provision of Title VII and the ideal of sex equality more broadly to erode labor standards reveals the institutional and ideological intersections between the rise of employment discrimination law and the ascendance of neoliberal conceptions of freedom. The decade following the forgotten campaign for universal labor protections, witnessed the "opening of the American workplace" – to use historian Nancy MacLean's provocative phrase (MacLean 2006). White, male strongholds in the labor market opened to women and minorities, as historians have recognized. The relationship between management and workers was opened in new and often unbalanced ways, favoring the power of employers over workers. In a neoliberal age, freedom came to mean both individual flourishing free from discrimination and also an employment relationship free from labor regulation.

47 Brad Knickerbocker, "More Workers Balking at Compulsory Overtime," *Christian Science Monitor* (March 22, 1978): p. 7.

16

IMPROVING JOB QUALITY FOR LOW-WAGE WOMEN WORKERS

A 21st century movement

Elizabeth Ben-Ishai[1]

I. Introduction

Over the past 40 years, a growing number of women have entered the paid workforce. In 2012, more than 70% of mothers with children under 18 years of age were in the labor force (Cohn et al., 2014). In contrast, in 1975, just 55% of mothers were in the labor force, and among those with children under the age of three, only 34% participated in the labor force (US Department of Labor (US DOL), 2009). As women have increased their presence in the workforce, issues of discrimination have often been the focus of feminist work on labor. These issues remain salient; to this day, women continue to be paid significantly less than men. However, particularly over the past 20 years, another (not unrelated) set of issues is drawing attention as women's workforce participation further increases: the challenges of attending to both work obligations and family needs.

In recent years, "work/family" issues have gained attention in media and pop culture discussions, driven in part by attention to high-profile professional women's struggles to "have it all" (Sandberg, 2013; Slaughter, 2012). But the challenges of both doing one's job and caring for one's family are in many ways felt most acutely by women who are lower-wage workers, struggling to make ends meet in low-quality jobs while they scrape together sufficient resources to care for their children, often as sole or primary breadwinners. Economic changes, business trends, and public policies have created a labor market that increasingly offers temporary, part-time, low-wage, non-union jobs with few benefits and protections (Ben-Ishai and Lower-Basch, 2014). These jobs make "balancing" work and family more difficult than ever, with many workers unable to take a day off work

1 Ph.D., Senior Policy Analyst, Center for Law and Social Policy.

to care for a sick child or recover from the flu without risking losing wages or their jobs.

The number of women occupying low-wage jobs and facing such challenges has grown in part as a result of major reforms to the US welfare system in the 1990s. In the debates over welfare reform, the promise of work as a way to not only "end welfare as we know it," but also to eliminate the perceived "scourge of dependency," was a powerful rhetorical device.[2] Following the passage of the Personal Responsibility and Work Reconciliation Act (PRWORA), the Bill that enacted welfare reform under President Bill Clinton, poor mothers were pushed to take jobs – any jobs – and access to welfare benefits was drastically curbed (Weaver, 2000). With time limits imposed and diversion tactics employed, thousands of women with children flooded the low-wage job market. Those who received Temporary Assistance for Needy Families (TANF), the program that replaced Aid for Families with Dependent Children (AFDC) after the passage of PRWORA, were now often expected to work in exchange for assistance. But despite the rhetoric employed in welfare debates, which painted "work" as the panacea to a host of problems associated with poverty, the jobs poor mothers must take often pay too little to make so-called self-sufficiency possible, and are structured in a way that makes caring for a family nearly impossible. Nearly two decades later, the Great Recession and the ensuing recovery, which has disproportionately produced low-wage service sector jobs, have exacerbated these features of the labor market, with the welfare system failing to respond (National Employment Law Project, 2014).

Welfare reform implicitly devalued care work – or more specifically, unpaid care work by poor women caring for their own children – and privileged paid work in the labor force. As it did so, it pushed low-income women into a labor market that offers few protections and little of the flexibility needed to perform jobs while still meeting familial caregiving needs. In the wake of welfare reform, the major gaps in US public policy to support working parents have become more evident than ever before. While these holes are a long way from being filled, a movement in the US to improve job quality for lower-wage workers, particularly women, is starting to see success.

In this chapter, after situating it within a context of the post-welfare reform labor market, I provide an overview of this growing movement, which aims to pass laws guaranteeing access to paid sick days, paid family and medical leave, and fair job schedules. Although media attention to work/family issues often centers on middle class professional women, in fact, this movement has a heavy focus on low-wage workers, who stand to benefit the most from public policy changes. At the same time, almost all working parents would benefit from public policies to make the workplace more family-friendly. Because working parents across a wide range of economic, social, and racial groups experience a shared sense

2 For an analysis of the concept of "dependency," see Fraser and Gordon, 1994.

of vulnerability in a labor market that offers so little support for *all* caregivers, there is a universal appeal to such campaigns, which have considerable public support (and substantial business opposition). Unlike welfare reform debates, which alienate and isolate poor women, painting them as dependent non-workers, the movement for improved workplace policies highlights the shared experiences and vulnerability of women (and men) as *workers*. Feminist theorists of labor should look closely at the work/family and job quality movement as a site for gendered analysis of labor, as well as opportunities to (re)theorize numerous other concepts central to feminist work, including the state, care, collective action, and others. Central to such theorizing is a rich conception of vulnerability, which helps us to understand not only the dynamics of this particular movement and its success, but also 21st-century notions of labor more broadly. In exhorting feminist scholars to use this field as a jumping-off point for further theorizing, in the final section of the chapter, I offer several possible avenues for exploration.

II. Work/life in a post-welfare reform era: feminist considerations

Whereas prior to welfare reform, women were able to claim welfare benefits as mothers, in the post-PRWORA era, women are required to work in order to claim public benefits. But as they adopt the identity of "worker" in order to access economic supports, they are forced to take jobs that either disregard their status as mothers or actively obstruct their ability to care adequately for their children. Although work, under the conservative rhetoric of welfare reform, is meant to confer dignity and generate self-sufficiency, the working conditions, wages, and benefits available to low-wage workers are such that neither outcome is likely. Adopting the notion of "economic citizenship" from Alice Kessler-Harris, Jane L. Collins (2008) argues that though welfare reform was supposed to grant poor mothers access to this form of citizenship by turning them into workers, the increasingly prevalent share of the labor market occupied by low-quality jobs has changed the terms of economic citizenship. As it pushed many poor women to work, welfare reform "placed them on the threshold of economic citizenship at the moment that our social contract vis-à-vis work was changing" (Collins, 2008, p. 135). The Great Recession has exacerbated some of the worst aspects of the already dismal labor market these women must contend with (Lower-Basch, 2013).

The tensions between work requirements and familial obligations that many low-income women face are not surprising given the devaluation of care work that undergirds important facets of welfare reform. An examination of arguments made in favor of the reforms reveals that obscuring the value and significance of care to both women's lives and society plays a powerful role in upholding the larger arc of proponents' claims. For example, influential conservative Lawrence Mead argues that work is a crucial precursor to the status of citizenship – by engaging in work, individuals fulfill their obligations to society and are, he claims, granted the recognition that such fulfillment of civic duty commands.

Civic labor, he acknowledges, *can* take a variety of forms, so long as it is accountable to society and is done "well enough to serve a public interest" (Mead, 2005, p. 188). Although feminist writers have argued that social reproduction – "the maintenance and future of the public or common weal and the care of citizens" – ought to be seen as fulfilling societal obligations of civic labor, Mead dismisses the legitimacy of poor women's care work (Pateman, 2005, p. 35). Pointing to studies of poor outcomes for the children of low-income women, he suggests that their performance as mothers cannot be counted as civic labor (Ben-Ishai, 2012). The rhetoric surrounding welfare reform replicates this dismissal of poor women's care work, exemplifying Ellen Bravo's argument: "Whether in the home or in paid jobs caring for other people's loved ones, caregiving is consistently devalued by those in power in the ways they count most – status and compensation" (Bravo, 2007, Kindle Locations 2460–2461).

The illegitimacy of care work as civic labor has not always been the assumption of the day. Indeed, AFDC, the cash assistance program that supported very low income families (mostly single mothers) with children prior to the passage of PRWORA was founded on the assumption that mothers should not be employed in the paid labor force. The notion of women caring for their children as they relied on public assistance became increasingly unacceptable in public discourse, in part because of changing norms around women's work.[3] At the same time, the increasingly racialized conception of welfare put forward by conservatives (and some liberals) – as a program that supported unwed (and undeserving) women of color with children – likely influenced the public's sense of the acceptability of care work as a form of civic labor.

Perhaps the devaluation of care work implicit – and often explicit – in the logic of welfare reform made it easier to ignore the caregiving implications of pushing millions of mothers into the low-wage workforce. Although initially President Bill Clinton's vision for welfare reform included not only increased work requirements, but also increased funding for child care, increased minimum wage, and health care coverage, political circumstances made this package of reforms untenable. Though PRWORA increased funding for child care, with about one million additional children receiving child care assistance as a result of the initial expansions, only one in seven children who were eligible for federal subsidies were receiving them (Lower-Basch and Greenberg, 2009). The child care block grant under TANF has not been adjusted for inflation since the 1996 law passed; as a result, the grant has lost about one-third of its value. Today, the number of eligible children receiving child care assistance is at an 11-year low, with more than half of all states spending less on child care in 2013 than in 2012 (Schmit and Reeves, 2015). Only 17% of children eligible to receive child care assistance were served in 2011 – but this figure pre-dates the decline in children served from 2011–2013 (US Department of Health and Human Services, 2015).

3 See, further, DeParle, 2004.

Without adequate child care assistance, many mothers in low-wage jobs must find less than ideal care for their children while they are at work, often scrambling to piece together various arrangements with family, friends, and neighbors.[4] But even good child care does not alleviate the challenges many low-wage jobs present for working parents – when children get sick, have days off school, or need to go to medical appointments, parents need a degree of flexibility that is often elusive in the types of jobs many welfare recipients and former welfare recipients must accept. In the next section, I describe some of the features of such jobs and the enormous obstacles they present for caregivers.

A. Job quality for low-wage working women

The number of employed single mothers grew by 1.5 million between 1993 and 2000, an increase that can be explained in significant part by the exodus from welfare. Between 1994 and 2000, welfare rolls were cut in half, from 5 million to 2.4 million (Lower-Basch and Greenberg, 2009). A favorable job market also contributed to this increase in employment, but the major changes to welfare eligibility and receipt likely had the greatest impact. In addition to welfare "leavers," welfare recipients were also pushed into the labor market as they occupied "workfare" jobs – jobs subsidized by the welfare system, but through which they performed labor for private employers. Even in the wake of the Great Recession, which took a significant toll on employment rates between 2008–2011, significantly more single mothers are employed today than were prior to the reforms. Yet, though employment has gone down, TANF recipiency has not gone up in a corresponding manner. Indeed, from 2007 through 2010, as the unemployment rate increased by 88%, national TANF caseloads increased only by 14% (Zedlewski and Loprest, 2011).

What kind of jobs do these women take? By and large, they are unstable jobs with little room for advancement, few benefits and workplace protections, and, without additional support from programs like the Earned Income Tax Credit and Supplemental Nutrition Assistance Program, they typically do not pay enough to make ends meet. On average, in the years following welfare reform, women leaving welfare made between $7 and $8 per hour. Most did not work full-time in every week, and few had benefits like sick leave and health insurance (Lower-Basch and Greenberg, 2009).

The characteristics of welfare recipients' and welfare leavers' jobs are not unique to those associated with the welfare system; rather they are the characteristics of low-wage work writ large. Job quality, a set of measures that goes beyond wages, is particularly poor for low-wage workers, but has declined in many ways for workers at a variety of earning levels (Ben-Ishai and Lower-Basch, 2014; Lower-Basch, 2007). In the past twenty years, fewer employers offered health care benefits and retirement plans. For many workers, job security is limited. In 2013, the minimum

4 For an analysis of how workplace inflexibility and unpredictability affect low-wage workers with children, see Ben-Ishai et al., 2014.

wage was only 36% of what the average worker earns, only slightly above where it was in 2007 (34%) (Elwell, 2014). Even as workers grow more and more productive, their wages are not increasing.[5] Although the value of the minimum wage grew by 7.8% between 2000 and 2011, in 2009 it was still 7.8% less than its value in 1967 (in 2011 dollars), according to an analysis by the Economic Policy Institute (Mishel, 2013). Workers lack voice and autonomy in many of the most widely available entry-level jobs. Rates of union membership are extremely low; in 2014, just 6.6% of private sector workers belonged to unions (US DOL, 2015).

Few low-wage jobs offer paid leave – and paid leave is particularly crucial for workers with caregiving responsibilities. Today, only 30% of low-wage workers have access to paid sick days, compared to 84% of the top quartile of wage earners. Just 12% of all private sector workers have access to paid family leave; the numbers are even more dismal for low-wage workers, only 5% of whom have access to paid leave. Workers with less education and lower incomes are unlikely even to have unpaid leave under the Family and Medical Leave Act: fewer than half of those with a high school diploma or less, or with family incomes of less than $40,000 per year are eligible. In any case, taking unpaid leave is often too costly to be tenable for low-wage workers. Cobbling together other types of leave to accommodate one's needs is often not an option either. Nearly half of all workers in the lowest 25% of wage earners have no paid leave of any kind: no paid personal time, sick time, family leave, or vacation (US DOL, 2013). For them, even occasional child care emergencies or routine teacher professional development days at children's schools can be a major hardship.

In addition to lacking paid leave, a significant number of workers experience volatile job schedules; they are unable to predict when they will work or how many hours per week they will be assigned. A recent study estimates that at least 17% of the workforce experiences such irregular schedules (Golden, 2015). A study of early-career workers aged 26 to 32 years in hourly jobs found that more than 40% report receiving one week or less advanced notice of their job schedules for the upcoming week. Half of these workers have no input into their schedules and three-quarters experience fluctuations in the number of hours they work, with hours varying by more than eight hours per week on average. Parents of young children experience high rates of precarious schedules, with nearly 70% of mothers and 80% of fathers of children 12 or younger who work in hourly jobs receiving hours that fluctuate by up to 40% (Lambert, Fugiel and Henly, 2014). Workers with unstable schedules struggle to find child care and access child care subsidies, hold second jobs, arrange transportation, attend school or job training, and simply to pay the bills.

B. The movement – successes and campaigns

The movement for more responsive jobs that offer flexibility, predictability, and paid leave attempts to make up for some of the vast oversights of welfare reform.

5 Although productivity increased by more than 22% in 2010, typical wage earners made about the same amount per hour as in 2000 see Mishel et al., 2012).

As Bravo (2007) notes, "Given that most women end up on welfare because of problems with employment, the focus should be reform of work. Specifically, that means decent pay, flexibility for family care, universal health care, and quality childcare." Work, she writes, should be "a way out of poverty rather than another form of poverty" (Kindle Location 2633). Feminist economist Randy Albelda (2001) points out that although much focus has been on ensuring that welfare recipients are "job-ready," few jobs are "mother-ready." Increasingly, however, campaigns around the country are seeking to make the shift to jobs that are more mother-ready, or more broadly, "family-ready."

More than just addressing work/life issues in general, this movement is increasingly focused on the conditions of low-wage work. As such, the focus is on public policy to set a floor for adequate protections and workplace practices. As Albelda explains, work/life advocacy for lower-wage workers cannot be directed primarily to employer-based changes – an approach that is more prevalent in discussions of professional and managerial work. Certainly, highly skilled workers at Silicon Valley tech firms can benefit from the progressive policies of employers like Google and Facebook. However, for low-wage workers, policy change is likely the primary route to creating a labor market that does not entirely obviate the realities of workers' obligations outside of the workplace. Albelda writes, "If left to individual employers or even to individual unions, as is the case now, work/family policies will remain highly stratified, benefitting only a privileged portion of the employed population" (p. 132). In contrast, writes Albelda, universal public policies that benefit low-wage single mothers in the work force – paid sick days, paid family leave, better scheduling policies – can have a "trickle up effect." Such policies address a shared vulnerability – the stresses of balancing paid employment and caregiving – that places a heavy burden on all working parents – from the tenured professor to the university's janitorial staff. This vulnerability is felt most acutely by low-wage workers, who are least able to afford the wage loss that comes with lack of paid leave, or the potential job loss accompanying it. But better policies would benefit a wide swath of workers across economic and social categories.

Perhaps this is why the movement for paid sick days and paid family leave has been gaining momentum over the past decade, and particularly the past few years. In 2004, California passed the first paid family leave legislation, which built on the state's temporary disability insurance program (TDI) to offer leave to workers caring for sick family members or bonding with a new child. Five years later, New Jersey followed suit with a paid family leave program, and in 2014 Rhode Island became the third state to pass such a law. Both New Jersey and Rhode Island followed California's lead in using their TDI systems as the infrastructure for their paid family leave insurance programs, an option only available in the five states with TDI (Hawaii and New York are the others). In 2013, federal legislation to create a national paid family and medical leave insurance program, the Family and Medical Insurance Leave (FAMILY) Act, was introduced in Congress. With a Republican controlled Congress unlikely to move on this bill, the Obama administration has directed the US Department of Labor to fund states to study options for creating their own paid family leave programs.

Progress on paid sick days also began in California, when in 2008, by ballot initiative, San Francisco became the first city in the nation to pass a law guaranteeing workers paid time to recover from brief illnesses or care for sick family members. Since then, 21 cities and three states have also passed sick days laws, with the majority of these victories coming in 2014 (A Better Balance, 2015). Campaigns for sick days laws are active in more than two dozen cities and states across the country. Federal legislation, the Healthy Families Act, has been introduced in every Congress since 2009, but like the FAMILY Act, has not made significant progress.

A movement to establish a fair work week has also emerged in recent years, with attention to the issue of erratic job schedules erupting in 2014. After a series of *New York Times* articles drew widespread outrage across the nation, both the public and policy makers awakened to an issue that lower wage workers have increasingly grappled with (Greenhouse, 2014a; Greenhouse, 2014b; Kantor, 2014). In the 2015 legislative session, ten states introduced bills that would create minimum standards for advanced notice of job schedules, last-minute shift changes, the right to request scheduling accommodations, and more (National Women's Law Center, 2015). These bills are all new pieces of legislation, drafted for the first time for each state. San Francisco passed the nation's first comprehensive scheduling law in 2014 – a law that targets workers employed by large retailers. Federal legislation, the Schedules that Work Act, was introduced in Congress in 2014.

C. Theorizing vulnerability, theorizing work

How can examining these campaigns – and their successes – help us to theorize work and employment from a feminist perspective? Feminist and labor scholars may consider some of the following starting points:

• Universality: workers and vulnerabilities

As noted, work and family issues strike a chord across social and economic divides, in part because working mothers with quite divergent incomes, occupying a range of social classes, may share a sense of vulnerability when it comes to managing work and caregiving obligations. As Martha Fineman has noted, "Vulnerability [. . .] is both universal and particular; it is experienced uniquely by each of us." She adds, "[O]ur individual experience of vulnerability varies according to the quality and quantity of resources we possess or can command. While society cannot eradicate our vulnerability, it can and does mediate, compensate, and lessen our vulnerability through programs, institutions, and structures" (Fineman, 2010, p. 269). Although the concerns of women like Anne-Marie Slaughter and Cheryl Sandberg may seem miles away from those of mothers working in low-wage retail jobs or workfare positions, in fact, the shared vulnerability they experience as "working mothers," no matter how different, works in favor of the legislative campaigns currently underway – at least in terms of appeals to individuals (but perhaps not to employers and employer lobby groups).

Another universalizing factor is the fact that poor women appear in debates about paid family leave and paid sick days as "workers" rather than as "dependents." While the notion of the "independent worker" is mythical, nonetheless, under these auspices, poor women are not stigmatized in the same way as welfare recipients – indeed, in many ways they are sympathetic figures. A closer look at the success of the paid leave and other job quality movements currently under way may add complexity and nuance to theories of vulnerability as they apply to labor.

• *The need for state regulation and law: repairing the safety net*

One of the most significant distinctions between approaches to work and family issues for lower-wage workers and those oriented toward professional, middle class, and managerial workers is the perceived role for state intervention. Many workers in the post-welfare, low-wage work economy depend on the discretion of their employers for accommodations that enable them to care for their families while doing their jobs. But such discretion is fickle: the unreliability of such accommodations makes these jobs even more unstable. For example, in their study of welfare reform in Oregon, Morgen, Acker and Weigt (2013) note that many of the women they interviewed "relied on individual relationships with supervisors that needed to be cultivated and maintained" in order to access flexibility (p. 161). They explain, "Because this flexibility is not institutionalized, there is no guarantee that these mothers will have ongoing access to these arrangements should the condition of their jobs or their relationships with their supervisors change" (p. 161).

In debates over legislation to improve job quality, some businesses that oppose the proposed laws argue that, though they agree with the idea of paid leave, they do not think government should compel them to provide it. But the evidence is clear: few businesses do it, and when they do, it is often only for higher wage earners, instead of those who need it most. While stories of expanded family-friendly policies in big name firms garner attention in the media, these do little to help low-wage workers, unless the firm publicly supports legislative action. The businesses that typically employ those at the bottom of the wage scale are not usually influenced to improve their policies, but instead point to the deep pockets of the firms that provide such "perks" as unlimited sick time, teleworking, or condensed work weeks as justification for their differing (lesser) policies.

To address the needs of low-wage workers, particularly those with caregiving obligations, a floor must be set by government. In the case of family leave, social insurance models are most feasible, both politically and economically. Despite the vast anti-regulatory and anti-government rhetoric from conservatives in recent years, most Americans do not see paid leave legislation as "job killing;" rather, strong majorities of both Democrats and Republicans support paid sick days and paid family leave (Lake Research Partners and The Tarrance Group, 2014; Smith and Kim, 2010). Even a significant proportion of small businesses support family leave insurance programs (Small Business Majority, 2013).

For future feminist work on labor, the erosion of anti-government sentiments evidenced by broad support for work/family policies suggests that this sphere may offer unique opportunities for theorizing the role of the state. Why are people supportive of such policies, despite the frequent narratives we hear in this Tea Party-influenced era about the dangers of government intervention in the lives of citizens? Perhaps a shared sense of vulnerability contributes to this somewhat surprising finding. Or perhaps the decreasing quality of many jobs makes more Americans sympathetic to the idea of government regulation of minimum labor standards. More investigation could prove fruitful.

• *New synergies between care work and paid labor*

Debates over the relative value of care work versus paid labor seem tired, even though (or because) the media continue to dredge up the so-called "mommy wars," pitting women engaged in one type of labor against those engaged in others. The growing movement for better public policies to support working parents and families suggests that there may be opportunities to re-theorize the relationship between care and paid labor. The success of paid leave movements and the growth of a movement for a fair work week point to a possible revaluation of care without the trap of failing to recognize the constrained choices that too often bring about a life devoted solely to care work. If working mothers are increasingly seen as rights-bearing individuals worthy of public protections and economic supports – that is, worthy of recognition as citizens – perhaps a new model for thinking about care is emerging. Such a model might draw attention to the continuities between the "worker" and "mother" identities and the need to think collectively rather than individualistically.

• *Collective power in the absence of unions: organizing for change*

Frances Fox Piven and Richard Cloward (1993) describe work as the primary mechanism for establishing order in modern societies. They write, "So long as people are fixed in their work roles, their activities and outlooks are also fixed; they do what they must and think what they must" (p. 6). At the same time, according to Piven and Cloward, the stigma associated with welfare promotes the compulsion to work under any conditions, no matter how unjust or unsatisfactory with regard to meeting basic needs or respecting fundamental rights. This stigma "spur[s] people to contrive ways of supporting themselves by their own industry, *to offer themselves to any employer on any terms*" (Piven and Cloward, 1993, p. 35). Yet in what is essentially a "post-welfare" era, where citizens are no longer entitled to welfare, the dynamics of this social control model of work and welfare shift. Indeed, welfare recipients are compelled to take any job available, but this is less to avoid the stigma of welfare than as a basic survival mechanism in the absence of a safety net.

Despite the desperate circumstances that low-wage workers are facing, we are also increasingly seeing them standing up and demanding change. For example, fast-food, Wal-Mart, and a growing cadre of other low-wage workers have taken to the streets in the past year, gaining considerable public attention, even though they are not part of organized labor or protected in any way by union membership (DePillis, December 2014). Organized labor has funded a considerable portion of this action. Among the concerns voiced by these workers are those related to their inability to support families on the low wages and with the poor working conditions offered by their employers. Just as the challenges of balancing work and family resonate across economic and social divides, the situation of low-wage workers may resonate more broadly in the wake of the Great Recession. With so many people experiencing unemployment and underemployment, either directly or indirectly through family and friends, the challenges low-wage workers face may be more readily accessible to the general public.

Together, a more sympathetic public and an eroded safety net may have created conditions that make organizing and collective action, including on work/family issues, more feasible. Feminist theorists may use this opportunity to rethink the relationship between work, welfare, social control, and collective action.

III. Conclusion

This chapter offers background on the growing need for better workplace policies, such as paid leave and fair scheduling laws, for working parents, particularly low-wage parents, as well as the burgeoning and increasingly successful movement mobilizing to establish such policies. This need is in part a product of the major reforms to the welfare system in the US during the 1990s, which eroded the safety net and built a work-focused welfare system that undervalued and ignored care work. Laws that guarantee paid sick days, paid family and medical leave, and fair job schedules would help to address some of the shortcomings of welfare reform, though they are far from sufficient.[6]

At a time when most advocates for women and workers find themselves primarily in the business of defending decent public policies – often unsuccessfully – movements for paid leave are having a surprising amount of success. Of course, this success is the product of years of hard work by devoted advocates, including workers themselves, as well as investment of time and political capital by forward thinking policy makers. However, these policies are taking off in part because they have considerable public support. The success of these movements and the support they have garnered point to new opportunities to theorize work from a feminist perspective, I suggest. I have offered some initial ideas for directions such theorizing might take; more avenues of exploration surely abound.

6 Many of those worse off following welfare reform are neither working nor receiving public assistance (see Shaefer and Edin, 2013). However, improved job quality could help to address this. Many of those not working are out of the labor market in part because work is not, as Albelda puts it, "mother-ready," but others face significant barriers that demand other responses (see Albelda, 2001).

17

A RIGHT TO REQUEST FLEXIBLE WORKING

What can the UK teach us?

K. Lee Adams[1]

> *The "novel legal idea of an employee's right to flexibility . . . introduce[s] a seismic shift" in the contract of employment.*
>
> – *Collins, 2005, p. 100*

I. Equality, work, and flexibility

In the US as in other countries, most unpaid care for others is supplied by the family – as parents care for children, adult children care for aged parents, or one spouse cares for the other "for better or worse." As Martha Fineman has observed, *all* workers are vulnerable to the need for care or to the need to engage in care (Fineman, 2008, 2010). However, historically women have performed most unpaid caring labor within the family and have continued to do so despite entering the paid labor force in significant numbers. The gender disparity in caregiving can conceal this universal potential for *any* worker to become a "worker-carer" – engaged in the paid labor force while also having unpaid responsibilities to care for family members (Adams, 2005, 2014). The intersection of paid work and unpaid family obligations raises related issues: the disjunction between the demands of paid labor and the time and effort of family care; the social and economic value of care; the position of women who shoulder most unpaid caring duties; and the social norms within which care takes place. The work-family intersection implicates the underlying gender norms of work, which create structural inequality in labor markets and becomes ossified into law through the contract of employment and other mechanisms of regulating labor.

To address these gendered structural disadvantages in the labor market and increase labor force participation, several European nations have enacted legislation

1 Associate Professor, Atlanta's John Marshall Law School.

that provides workers with family responsibilities some degree of flexibility in paid work to accommodate family care (OECD, 2007a). The US does not have a national right to request flexibility in work. Instead, the US federal government has enacted only a narrow power for federal agencies to permit flexible working by employees within their agencies. Although a federal bill on flexibility was proposed in the 111th Congress, it died in Committee and never came up for a vote (Working Families Flexibility Bill, HR1274). Commentators have called for a flexible working law in the US, but at present flexible working schemes are largely governed by collectively bargained entitlements, individual contractual terms, or employer workplace policies (Arnow-Richman, 2010; Durkalski, 2009), though some US localities have introduced forms of flexibility legislation (Ben-Ishai, 2013).

The social policy choices available at a national level to mediate work-family conflict involve complex institutional impacts and cultural assumptions (Lewis, 2009). Thus, any attempt to "introduce a seismic shift" of worker flexibility into the legal regimes governing employment must fit within such legal regimes in order to be successful (Collins, 2005, p. 100). Of the current approaches to work flexibility legislation, the legislative model best suited to mesh with US federal labor legislation is the right to request flexible working as developed in the UK.

Passed in the UK originally in 2002 to provide a narrow right for parents of small children to seek flexibility in their terms and conditions of work (Employment Act, 2002 (UK) chapter 22), the right to request flexible working expanded dramatically through amendments over the following decade to include most workers who have responsibility to provide unpaid care for family members. The right to request flexible working for parents and carers eventually came to cover roughly one third of the UK workforce before being expanded to all workers by 2014. According to most empirical studies and government statistics, the UK legislation has been largely well received by both employers and workers.

This chapter argues that the US could benefit from adopting a worker-carer's right to request flexible working law modeled on the UK legislation. Given the similarities between the legal and cultural norms of the US and the UK, the structured process and light touch of the UK flexible working legislation could fit well within the US legal structure. Specifically, a process-based right to request flexibility in the terms and conditions of work would provide a much-needed complement to the US Family and Medical Leave Act of 1993 (FMLA). A formal process and "enforced" change of perspective as initially enacted in the UK may have a significant effect in diminishing structural inequality for US workers who must also provide unpaid care, permitting solutions that are adaptable, flexible, and mutually determined.

Part II of the chapter outlines the type of flexibility in work which enables worker-carers to manage concurrent work and care obligations. To contextualize the discussion of specific legislative measures, Part II then considers the typology of flexible work rights developed by Professor Hugh Collins. Part III of the chapter sets out the development and content of the UK's right to request flexible working law, focusing on the procedural rights as implemented in the legislation and critique of its provisions. Part IV suggests how a procedural right to request flexible working would fit within US labor regulation, specifically within the FMLA. The chapter concludes that a right to request flexible working is consistent with US law and employment regulation. Thus, despite potential difficulties, the US should adopt a right to request flexible working as an aid in removing structural barriers for women in the workplace and decreasing the vulnerability of worker-carers.

II. What kind of flexibility "works" for worker-carers?

Understanding the usefulness of a legislated right to request flexible working requires considering the background norms of the employment relationship, as constructed by and reflective of its legal regulation. In common law countries such as the US and the UK, the law of the contract of employment casts a long shadow over the regulation of work relationships. The common law contract of employment is currently presumed to underlie many – perhaps most – forms of exchanging labor for pay and frequently defines which legislative obligations apply to a work relationship. Hugh Collins has argued that "[c]ontrol over the time of the worker lies at the heart of the contract of employment. . . . The employer purchase[s] a worker's time rather than products of his or her labour" (2005, pp. 100–101). Collins considers that this bargain over the worker's "time" and the "absence of mutuality" in the contract of employment allows employers to respond more efficiently to their needs of production than a traditional commercial contract with greater specificity in the exchange would provide.

A. Employee-led rather than employer-led flexibility is needed for worker-carers

The common law contract of employment encompasses a considerable degree of flexibility and anticipates variation in its terms over time (Creighton and Stewart, 2010; Freedland, 2003). However, much of the flexibility of the employment contract inheres in the "management prerogative," recognized as the employer's right to control, which permits even significant terms to be altered in the contract at the employer's instigation without rising to a formal variation of terms which would require mutual agreement. The employee does not have corresponding flexibility within the contract to alter terms without the employer's agreement. If an employee seeks to change the total hours worked or the timeframe of those hours to accommodate caring obligations, for example, that would be treated as a request for a variance at common law. Absent explicit agreement by the parties to vary implied terms of the contract, the employer retains a wide scope of managerial power, backed up by the legal power of the contract, to set the place, time, and duties of work – generally referred to as the "terms and conditions of employment" (Freedland, 2003, pp. 240–250).

As Barbara Pocock has argued, "the capacity to control when, where and how one works" is crucial to the management of concurrent work and care obligations (2003, p. 204). The employer's presumed right of control both constructs and reinforces legal and social expectations about the performance of work that can be difficult for worker-carers to meet and which may often require adjustment to accommodate both work and caring obligations. The common law accordingly renders a worker-carer who is unable to conform to the obligations of hours, locations, or methods of work at risk for the employer's powerful self-help remedy of termination for breach of the contract. Thus, legislation specifically granting worker-carers an entitlement to structure their work to improve flexibility is necessary to alter the underlying fixed legal structure of the contract of employment (Adams, 2005).

Jane Lewis (2009) argues that to reduce work-family conflict, legislation must provide greater ability for the *worker* to control whether, in what circumstances, and to what degree that flexibility is exercised. She notes by way of contrast that market-provided "flexibility" may offer greater flexibility for the *employer* rather than the employee, and thus is not "family-friendly" (p. 174). For example, the "flexibility" common in management literature during the 1980s and 1990s stressed the "flexible firm" and its ability to adapt to changing market conditions by moving workers between jobs or taking on/laying off workers (Atkinson, 1986). Lewis recognizes separate policy justifications for an employee right to flexibility in work, depending on whether that right aims to improve employees' work-*life* balance or work-*family* balance (Lewis, 2009, pp. 175–176). She suggests that while the universality of work-*life* balance is attractively inclusive, it obscures both the gender equality implications and social justification for legal interference that work-*family* balance supports. Lewis notes that the UK government persistently employed the term "work-life" balance, suggesting flexibility should be universally available, although the legislatively enforced right was at the time reserved to worker-carers. The UK may have been trying to capture the public perception benefits of both policy justifications by using the ostensibly more universal term (Lewis, 2009). It is possible that the use of the universal term work-life provided a political impetus for the eventual expansion of the right to request to work flexibly to all employees in the UK.

B. Classifying flexible working rights by employer obligation

In "The Right to Flexibility," Hugh Collins notes that the EU's initial push towards flexibility in working arrangements was to enable employer-led flexibility to offer "non-standard forms" of work as a response to competitive pressures (2005, pp. 103–105). He describes a tension between managerial flexibility and the safeguards of work fairness in the form of labor entitlements that reduce employer flexibility. Collins suggests that some targeted "family-friendly" measures intended to increase sex equality or to entice women to remain in the labor force, such as publicly provided child care and paid leave rights, ultimately leave the sexual division of labor intact, and also leave in place "the legal assumption that the employer can determine unilaterally the contractual job package that is offered" (p. 114).

As an alternative, he argues that a universal right to bargain for flexibility would allow the terms and conditions of work to be "tailored to the needs of the individual, whilst . . . permitting the employer to protect its interests in productive efficiency" (p. 116). He further reasons that the critical legal change workers need to attain more universal work-life balance is a "strengthened bargaining position to demand his or her preferred diversity in the job package offered by the employer" (p. 116). Such a strengthened bargaining position would arise from a legislated employee entitlement to flexibility. Collins sets forth a typology of three different models of job flexibility schemes, depending on the "legal duty [the legislation] imposed on the employer:" (1) bargaining in good faith; (2) rejecting flexible working only on specified objective grounds; or (3) reasonably accommodating an employee's request for flexible working (pp. 118–122).

The good faith bargaining model may be exemplified by the EU's Framework Agreement on Part-time Work, which places a legal duty on employers to consider requests to transfer from full-time to part-time work. Collins regards the employer's duty in this model as weak, although it could start the parties talking. An obligation to bargain in good faith may be more effective in the context of a collective bargaining regime rather than individual bargaining, as the employer may have insufficient incentive to consider an individual proposal for flexible working carefully. Whether the employer has sufficient incentive to consider an employee's request, however, may depend on whether the legislation defines "good faith" and provides a sanction for failure to engage in good faith negotiation.

The second model operates by limiting allowable reasons for rejecting an employee's flexible working request. Collins characterizes the UK's right to request flexible working as falling within such a model, but acknowledges that the UK's grounds for employer rejection of a flexible working request are broad enough to encompass most reasons for employer resistance. The key to any improvement in employee-led flexibility through this model is in the definition of the grounds on which requests for flexibility may be rejected. If employers are permitted to take into account any costs for implementation, with no limit such as "undue" costs or a negative effect on work, then such legislation is, in Collins's view, unlikely to strengthen the employee's bargaining position beyond the market power that employee already possesses.

The most dramatic flexibility model requires the employer to "reasonably accommodate" an employee's need for flexibility. Analogizing from disability discrimination legislation, Collins suggests that this model requires reasonableness of both parties by limiting the reasons an employee is entitled to request flexibility (the employee's "need") and creating a strong presumption in favor of accepting a request for flexible work. The employers' costs in implementing flexibility might be incorporated into a reasonableness standard or a proportionality test, but in an accommodation model some costs are necessarily borne by the employer in order to allow the employee to balance work and "private life."

The reasonable accommodation model places the heaviest obligations on the employer and, as such, is the most likely to tip the scales in favor of the employee when bargaining for flexibility in the terms and conditions of work. Collins suggests that a focus on the employee's need for flexibility makes this model the least flexible in the reasons an employee might seek more flexible work terms, although he notes that a request originally framed as employee convenience may be justifiably reframed in terms of need. Additional costs and considerations may also arise within such a model. For example, in situations where the flexibility requested is a different place of work, bargaining parties will need to bargain about a larger set of matters, such as how to regulate workplace health and safety, evaluate performance, allocate costs and expenses, and other standard rights and obligations that are already provided for when workers present for work at the designated workplace.

For any of the above flexibility models, Collins suggests that where flexibility results in the employer having less control over the worker's time, an incentive to use different measures of remuneration, such as productivity, will likely result. He cautions that a move to performance-based pay may be undesirable for workers because pay for task completion "tends to transfer the risk of difficulties encountered in achieving satisfactory performance of work to the workers" (p. 123). This is, of course, already true of salaried workers, who form a significant portion of those engaged in the long-hours work culture and bear a cost in terms of reduced non-work time when difficulties in completing work reduce output during standard working time (Blau et al., 2006; Jacobs and Gerson, 2004; Schultz and Hoffman, 2006). Thus, for worker-carers, performance-based pay may be a double-edged sword. The risk of having to complete tasks on non-work time may make worker-carers worse off by simultaneously infringing on the reason they need flexibility – time for care – and reducing their pay and thus their ability to turn to the market for alternative provision of care, such as day care or housekeeping services. However, performance-based pay also holds the potential to loosen the underlying masculine time norms of work and provide an alternative objective measure for evaluating employees working within non-standard time structures (Smith, 2002).

The essence of all of Collins's models is that "right to flexibility" legislation – no matter its form – occupies some of the regulatory space formerly held by organized labor's collective bargaining in contesting employers' presumptive right to set the terms and conditions of employment. A right to request flexible working relies on individual bargaining in which a worker with preexisting low market power may not be able to achieve adequate flexibility unless the legislative model contains some detectable change in the employee's underlying bargaining power. Any infringement on management prerogative may be politically resisted by the business community and may also carry risks for workers. Yet, without a pathway to negotiate individually, many – perhaps most – worker-carers are unlikely to achieve the mix of time to work and time to care necessary to manage their unique dual responsibilities (Adams, 2005). Thus, to be effective for worker-carers, an individual right to request flexible working should be integrated into broader labor and employment laws in ways that have some teeth.

III. The UK's right to request flexible working

A. From baby steps to giant leaps: the development of UK flexible working law

The story of the incremental development of the right to request flexible working in the UK is instructive. The group of employees eligible to request flexible working was initially narrowly restricted to the neediest worker-carers. Yet coverage continued to expand over a decade through an iterative consultation process that eventually culminated in a universal employment right as of June 2014.

The right to request flexible working was introduced into UK legislation in 2002 by the Blair New Labour government, following sustained public attention from the its Work-Life Balance Campaign launched in 2000 (Anderson, 2003; Bell and Bryson, 2006) as part of a suite of measures intended to "create a society where being a good parent and a good employee are not in conflict" (DTI, 2000). A Work and Parents Taskforce suggested the initial form of the legislation (Walsh, 2008, p. 9), which provided that a narrow group of working parents – those with a pre-school aged child or a disabled child under 18 – had a "right to request" of their employer a change in the terms of their employment contracts to work more flexibly (Employment Act, 2002 (UK), chapter 22). In keeping with its sex-neutral provisions, this legislation was framed as an individual employment right for eligible workers. Thus, the UK's right to request flexible working sits alongside other legislative overlays on the minimum terms and conditions of individual employment rather than as part of an equality or collective bargaining regime (Lewis, 2009, p. 129). The original UK legislation provided a structured process that required the parties to the work relationship to consider alternatives to the typical mode of working, as well as the perspective of the other party. Eligible worker-carers could formally request flexibility in their terms and conditions of work, and this request triggered both a duty for employers to respond through a set process, subject to penalties and antidiscrimination and retaliation protections for workers who sought the protection of the statute.

From the inception of the scheme, the government intended to (and did) expand the right through incremental amendment. In early 2005, the Blair government published a consultation document (DTI, 2005a) that set forth both the social and business cases for flexible working and sought public comment. Such diverse entities as the Federation of Small Business and the Public and Commercial Services Union expressed support for the original flexible working regulations (DTI, 2005b, pp. 36–37). Opinions on whether to expand the right were predictably mixed, with the Small Business Council, among others, arguing that further regulations were not required because businesses were already going beyond what the law required, and "parents, employees, and their representatives" stating a "strong case for extending the law" to more carers (DTI, 2005b). Despite some pressure to extend the right to request flexible work to all employees, the government mid-decade expanded cautiously to "target the law to cover those who face particular challenges in balancing work and caring responsibilities" (DTI, 2005b, p. 43). As a result, the UK then substantially expanded the right to request flexible working to carers of adults, along with a suite of measures designed to beef up other "family-friendly" worker entitlements (Work and Families Act, 2006 (UK)).

The Brown Labour government considered expansion again in 2008, commissioning an independent review on extending the right to request flexible working to parents of older children (Walsh, 2008). The Walsh Review considered whether to make the right to request flexible work universal, but the legislative limitation to parents and carers was deemed an important policy statement that priority for working flexibly should go to those having the greatest need. After canvassing the options to expand the right to request only to carers of elementary school children or include secondary school children, the Walsh Review recommended the right to request should be extended in a single step to parents of children aged 16 and under. These recommendations were implemented after consultation the following year (Flexible Working (Eligibility, Complaints and Remedies) (Amendment) Regulations 2009 (UK)). Expansion of the "parent" basis of caring came into force in April 2011 for all employees with children under 18 (Flexible Working (Eligibility, Complaints and Remedies) (Amendment) Regulations 2010 (UK)). Thus, within a decade of the initial legislation, employees with a protected right to request flexible work included parents with minor children of any age and carers of adults in close relationship with them. This meant that more than one third of employees in the UK's total workforce (some 10.5 million workers) were eligible to request flexible work as worker-carers (Flexibility.co.uk, 2009).

Despite this dramatic expansion, various commentators and constituencies continued to call for further expansion of statutory eligibility (Stratton, 2010). For example, the carer definition was criticized as insufficient because workers who cared for an unrelated adult outside their household remained ineligible to invoke a right to request (James, 2006). Further targeted expansion of rights to request flexibility outside the "caring" context continued with a right to request time off work for study or training (Rodgers, 2010). Even after a change in the governing political party, the coalition government under David Cameron announced an intention to extend the right to request flexible working to all employees (Eaglesham, 2010) and a right to request flexible working, although without much of its original procedural obligations, was made universal after public consultations , along with substantial expansion and equalization of parental leave rights (DBIS, 2012a, 2012b).

Lewis suggests that flexible working was even more of a policy "balancing act" than leave or child care for the UK government (2009, p. 175). She notes that inherent tensions between economic and family welfare concerns, as well as tensions between different groups of stakeholders, are reflected in the legislation and its accompanying regulations. These tensions may be resolved to some degree by making the right to request a universal entitlement, although at the cost of losing the underlying equality justification for the law and the prominence of the social value of care as noted in the Walsh Report (Walsh, 2008). However, it is significant that the project to expand the right to request flexible working has continued under different prime ministers and different parties, suggesting a long-term and widely held social commitment to workplace change and the value of flexibility to workers.

B. How the UK's "right to request flexible working" works

1. Limits, definitions, and process

Despite the right to request no longer being limited to worker-carers, employees with a statutory right to request flexible working are still required to meet a qualifying time limit of continuous employment with the same employer for a minimum of 26 weeks (Flexible Working Regulations 2014 (UK)). The legally protected right to request remains available only to employees at common law, not to independent contractors or agency workers. Also, an employee may make only one statutory right to request in a rolling twelve-month period, calculated from the date of the last request (Employment Rights Act 1996 (UK), s 80F(4)).

Importantly, the "right to request" is just that – there is no corresponding legal duty on the employer to grant the request. As the Employment Appeals Tribunal (EAT) noted, "the Flexible Working . . . Regulations are intended to be facilitative and not mandatory: They impose no obligation on an employer to allow whatever part-time working is requested" (*British Airways v Starmer*, 2005, para. 34). The initial legislation and regulations provided that if covered employees followed certain procedural prerequisites, this created only a procedural duty for employers. Employers were bound to abide by a statutory set of procedures surrounding a request for flexible working or be subject to penalties. The procedural duties were enforceable only on narrow grounds through a complaint to the Employment Tribunal (ET, a specialized adjudicatory body for UK employment disputes), pursued within three months from a violation of the legislation or regulations. However, these specific procedural obligations were largely removed when the right to request became universal (Children and Families Act 2014 (UK), ss 131–133). The UK government now deems that the employer must consider the employee's request to work flexibly "in a reasonable manner" and make a decision within three months of the employee's request (or longer by agreement). There is no longer a requirement to hold a meeting with the employee or to provide an appeal process, although such matters may be considered in determining if an employee's request was handled in a reasonable manner.

If parties reach agreement on working flexibly, the terms should be noted in writing, as this effects a permanent change of the terms and conditions of the employee's contract of employment. According to UK government figures, 80% of requests have been agreed to, with a further 10% reaching agreement based on modifications to the employee's initial request (Walsh, 2008, p. 14). Because an agreement results in a variation to the employment contract, absent express agreement of the parties, there is no right to resume the prior terms and conditions of employment in the future. Given that a need for flexible working based on caring obligations may not be permanent, worker-carers may find themselves at a disadvantage in seeking more standard terms when the need for flexibility ends. It is worth noting in this regard that any reduction in income which comes during a period of reduced work hours while caring for another impacts not only the worker's income during that period of time but also is likely to affect the worker-carer's entitlement to raises through pro rata seniority and will affect the worker-carer's income in retirement through a pension or social security scheme. This creates a permanent financial disadvantage for worker-carers relative to workers who do not have caring obligations (Folbre, 2001). Worker-carers face a significant opportunity cost in electing to reduce hours. Creating a formal mechanism to return the worker to full or standard employment if desired in the future should become a feature of any flexibility scheme.

In the event the employer refuses a request to work flexibly, the employer may provide an "appeal" process, which before was mandatory, but this process was always quite limited. Rather than a true "appeal" to a neutral decision maker, appeals of flexible working requests provide only an opportunity for the employer, possibly including the original decision maker, to reconsider the decision to deny the request to work flexibly. Grounds for appeal were never specified within the statute or regulations.

Given tight time constraints and its underlying nature as a request for reconsideration, an opportunity to appeal is unlikely to change an employer's decision on flexible working if the scope of the employee's request remains the same. For example, in the *Craddock* case, a teacher's appeal of a refusal of her request to job share on return from maternity leave was heard by different members of the school board of governors and she was "represented by a union official," yet her appeal was still denied (*Craddock v Governing Body of Indian Queens CP School & Nursery*, 2005). Accordingly, the purpose of any appeal process in the original Flexible Working Regulations logically must have been to permit the employee seeking flexibility an opportunity to proffer an alternative plan or further information on which the employer may base a decision. Indeed, giving the employee one more try to craft a mutually congenial flexibility plan makes sense in light of the restriction on formally seeking flexible working to one request within a twelve-month period.

The UK's educational and assistance programs on the right to request flexible working provide significantly greater assistance than some commentators have reported (Durkalski, 2009, p. 389). The government provides advice and education on its website and that of the Advisory, Conciliation and Arbitration Service (ACAS) to stakeholders and the general public about the right to request flexible work, eligibility, best practices, and how to apply.[2] In addition to the ACAS

2 See www.gov.uk/flexible-working; www.acas.org.uk/.

telephone helpline, UK government assistance includes online interactive tools to help employees put together a business case for requests for flexible working and to help employers consider those requests.

2. The substance in the procedure: tribunal review and remedies

For purposes of considering the applicability of the right to request flexible working in other jurisdictions, it is useful to set out the basic procedural requirements that form the bulk of the right to request. To trigger the employer's duty, the employee seeking flexible working had to make a dated, written request to the employer, referencing the right to request flexible working (Flexible Working Regulations (Eligibility, Complaints and Remedies) 2002). This request was required to specify the employee's requested change to work terms and conditions, the date the employee proposed the change to begin, and how the employee met the definition of relationship to the person requiring care (Employment Act, 2002 (UK) s 80F(2)). Importantly, the written request also had to explain the effect that "the employee thinks the change applied for would have on [the] employer and how . . . any such effect might be dealt with" (Employment Act, 2002 (UK) s 80F(2)(c)). This requirement remains in the current iteration of the legislation. The worker's statutory requirements have been interpreted strictly, with the ET determining that it lacked jurisdiction to hear complaints where these requirements were not satisfied (*Hussain v Consumer Credit Counseling*, 2005).

Refusal of a request to work flexibly still is limited to the grounds provided in the original legislation. On refusing a request for flexibility, the employer's written notice of the decision has to state the applicable grounds for refusal and explain why those grounds apply. Employers may only refuse a properly made application for flexible working on certain business grounds:

(i) the burden of additional costs,
(ii) detrimental effect on ability to meet customer demand,
(iii) inability to re-organize work among existing staff,
(iv) inability to recruit additional staff,
(v) detrimental impact on quality,
(vi) detrimental impact on performance,
(vii) insufficiency of work during the periods the employee proposes to work,
(viii) planned structural changes, and
(ix) such other grounds as the Secretary of State may specify by regulations.[3]

(Employment Act, 2002 (UK)80G(1)(b);
Employment Rights Act 1996 (UK), s 80G(1)(b))

Although limited, these grounds are drawn broadly and represent the most common reasons employers would raise in resistance to granting flexible work (Collins,

3 No additional grounds were ever created via the regulations.

2005, p. 120). As such, the grounds themselves do not pose a significant intrusion on the employer's business decision making. While they do represent some limit on the exercise of management prerogative, because of their breadth they limit only the employer's common-law "right" to act arbitrarily in dealing with an employee's request for flexibility (Fischl, 2002, pp. 259–261). Further, the grounds are not attached to any absolute or balancing standard, such as the originally proposed standard that flexible working may be refused if it causes harm to the business or the objective justification defense available under equality law (Anderson, 2003, p. 37). The employer's business decision is essentially unreviewable.

An employee could complain under Flexible Working to the ET only if: (1) the employer did not comply with its procedural obligation under the legislation; (2) the employer based the decision to reject the application on "incorrect facts;" (3) the employee was discriminated against because of exercising the right to request; or (4) the employee was dismissed for exercising the right to request flexible working (Employment Rights Act 1996 (UK), s 80H). These grounds also remain the ET's limited review standard in the current form of the legislation. Collins has called the anti-victimization and retaliation protections against detriment and dismissal for exercise of the right to request a necessary component of any flexibility legislation (2005, p. 117). Although ET complaints have been described as having "minimal requirements," the claims process could present real hurdles to employees who may be proceeding *pro se* (*Badra v Gardiner & Theobald LLP*, 2010). Before proceeding to the tribunal, the employee must notify ACAS of their intention and allow an attempt at conciliation through the ACAS dispute resolution scheme.

Substantively, review by the ET is also problematic. Lewis opines that the ET process provided "no effective right of appeal," given the limited nature of flexible working review, and notes that other scholars have called the UK's right to request "anaemic" (2009, pp. 112, 185). Freedland argues that employers have a "concrete duty [under Flexible Working] to exercise discretion in favour of the worker, in the absence of justification for refusal" (Freedland, 2003, p. 289). However, the ET was never empowered to overturn an employer's decision to refuse flexible working. The real teeth in ET review occurs with claims of sex discrimination or unfair dismissal.

Some commentators were concerned that the omission of any power for the ET to overturn a refusal to work flexibly rendered the law a toothless tiger (Anderson, 2003). Yet the ET gave some teeth to its consideration of "incorrect facts" on which an employer bases a decision in the case of *Commotion v Rutty*. Ms. Rutty, a warehouse packer who had the care of her granddaughter, sought under the flexible working law to reduce her hours to work three days per week. Her employer refused the request on the grounds that they wanted all warehouse employees to work the same standard hours because a uniform working day "promote[s] good team spirit" and that shortening her working hours would have a "negative impact on overall warehouse performance" (paras. 5–7). Ms. Rutty complained to the ET, which awarded her a substantial amount, albeit on the grounds of discrimination and unfair dismissal rather than flexible working. On appeal, the employer argued that the tribunal exceeded its authority by making an "objective assessment of the assertion [of grounds for refusal] which the employer made" and considering "whether [the refusal] was objectively justified" (para. 36). The EAT held that the grant of jurisdiction to consider whether a refusal to permit flexible working was "based on incorrect facts" gave the tribunal authority to "investigate the evidence" to determine the basis of the decision, and that the tribunal was not bound to accept the employer's stated ground of refusal without "investigation of the correctness or accuracy or truthfulness of that ground" (paras. 37–39). The EAT suggested that while the scope of review under Flexible Working did not encompass a full enquiry into whether "the employer has acted fairly, reasonably, and sensibly in putting forward that ground [for refusal]," it was appropriate for the tribunal to consider the employer's asserted ground for refusal of flexible working and determine if it was "factually correct" or was the genuine reason for the refusal (Anderson, 2003). Such an enquiry legitimately included examining evidence as to the surrounding circumstances of the application for flexible working, including the potential effect of granting the application. In considering evidence of the basis for the refusal of flexible working, the ET was limited to "assessing the correctness of the employer's assertion" rather than considering whether that assertion was "fair," "reasonable," or "justified" (Anderson, 2003).

The EAT appeared to accept that the employer bears some burden of production of evidence supporting the reason for the refusal and that the request was not feasible, at least in cases where the "industrial experience" of the tribunal would suggest that flexible work was possible to achieve while meeting the employer's needs. Based on the EAT's reasoning, the employer needed to be prepared to produce evidence of having considered and investigated whether the flexible working request could, in fact, be coped with. Such an obligation supports the frequent characterization of the employer's duty under Flexible Working as a duty to "seriously consider" the request. A burden of production here is not unlike the *McDonald-Douglas/Burdine* shift in the burden of production of evidence in US employment discrimination cases, where the employer is required to put forth evidence of a legitimate, non-discriminatory reason for a detrimental employment action which is challenged as discriminatory (*McDonnell-Douglas Corp v Green*, 1973; *Texas Department of Community Affairs v Burdine*, 1981).

Given its link to discrimination, it is important to understand the legal context of the issue of justification raised in *Rutty*, due to multiple claims brought in the case. Justification is an affirmative defense in UK antidiscrimination law and is not directly relevant under the Flexible Working Regulations. However, by contrasting the EAT's factual review under Flexible Working with the scope of the tribunal's inquiry into justification under an indirect discrimination claim (similar to a US disparate impact claim), the EAT demonstrates a difference between the two inquiries which further defines the ET's permissible review under Flexible Working. Justification is an available defense in indirect discrimination when the employer can demonstrate a legitimate business purpose for a policy that has a detrimental effect on workers with a protected characteristic. To determine whether a practice or policy is justified, the tribunal is to weigh the employer's business purpose achieved by the challenged practice against the detriment to those in the employee's position, to determine whether, objectively, the employer's practice is a "proportionate means of achieving a legitimate aim" (Equality Act, 2010 (UK), s 19(2)(d)). *Rutty's* distinction between the two inquiries suggests that the employer's obligation under Flexible Working to supply evidence of the reasons for refusal is a burden of production of evidence only, rather than the burden of persuasion carried by an affirmative defense. The burden to produce evidence is logically placed on the employer as the party who holds such information rather than placing on the employee an obligation to refute any possible objections to the proposal. The tribunal inquiry is then limited to examining: (1) whether the employer's reason was legitimate (permitted by the statute and regulations) and the genuine reason for the refusal, and (2) if the reason for the refusal is supported by the facts, in the form of evidence before the tribunal from either party. The genuineness of the employer's reason emerges as an appropriate tribunal inquiry from the *Rutty* decision rather than the statute or regulations directly, but it is a logical corollary to confining the employer to the statutorily permissible reasons, since if the employer's decision was not based on the enumerated permitted grounds, the decision was necessarily impermissible. Importantly, however, in contrast to a justification defense, the tribunal's consideration under Flexible Working does not carry with it an objective inquiry of whether the employer's reason for the refusal outweighs the detriment to the employee as in indirect discrimination claims such as *Barry v Midland Bank* (1999) and *British Airways v Grundy* (2008).

Under the original Flexible Working Regulations, if it found an employer in violation of its obligations under Flexible Working, the ET could award an employee "just and equitable" compensation of up to eight weeks' pay (Employment Rights Act 1996 (UK), s 80I; Flexible Working (Eligibility, Complaints and Remedies) Regulations 2002 (UK), ss 6, 7). This remedy remains in place despite the dramatic reduction in procedural requirements (Flexible Working Regulations, 2014, s 6). The limitation on monetary compensation was "another extremely hard fought lobbying point," with compensation limits being set far closer to those desired by employers (four weeks) than by unions (52 weeks) (Anderson, 2003, p. 41). The low caps on compensation and the inability of the ET to make orders such as a trial period of flexible work provide little incentive for the stubborn employer determined to avoid workplace change to comply with the Flexible Working Regulations. The big stick was and still remains with sex discrimination claims rather than the sex-neutral right of flexible working. For example, although the claimant was awarded over £14,000 in *Rutty*, she received no award under the head of flexible working, inasmuch as her recovery under discrimination and dismissal law exceeded the compensation caps for flexible working (*Commotion v Rutty*, 2005). Conversely, despite compliance with the Flexible Working Regulations, employers who denied requests to return from maternity leave part-time have nevertheless been held to have indirectly discriminated against female employees (*Caswell v Advance Travel Partners UK*, 2004; Slater, 2005a, 2005b; *Webster v Princes Soft Drinks*, 2005).

3. Does the UK's flexible working scheme work for worker-carers?

Under the Collins typology, the UK legislation bears some features of all three types of flexible work entitlements. The legislation initially limited its operation to employees who "need" flexibility for caring obligations as in Collins's Type 3 model but stopped short of requiring employers to reasonably accommodate that need. The initial Act and regulations did not define "care" nor limit the eligibility of an employee on the basis of the type or degree of care required, such as by confining the right to primary carers. Apparently there was substantial consensus that care was required for a pre-school or disabled child as provided in the original legislation. As eligibility was expanded, some groups suggested that care should be defined to prevent abuse of the right to request flexible work or that employees should be prepared to provide the employer with evidence of the need to undertake the care (DTI, 2005b, 2006). However, the government rejected this suggestion, noting abuse of the right had not been a problem. The government reasoned that employees would be unlikely to seek a permanent change to their terms and conditions of work lightly and expressed concern that requiring evidence of need or circumscribing the definition of care would result in some employees with legitimate needs being deemed ineligible and promote disputes on whether the definition had been met in particular cases (DTI, 2006). As there was no requirement to prove a need for care, employees did not have to establish that a caring need was reasonable and no employer duty to accommodate such a reasonable need arose. Thus, even the original UK legislation would not be among the most intrusive legislative mechanisms to the contract of employment.

Instead, the legislation sets forth limited reasons an employer may reject the request for flexible working, as consistent with Collins's Type 2 scheme. While the obligation for the employer to treat requests in a reasonable manner may be suggestive of a Type 1 "good faith bargaining" model, the removal of clear procedural obligations and the lack of incentivizing sanctions suggest that the scheme is not likely driven by such a bargaining standard. Accordingly, the universally available scheme now available places the UK right firmly within the Type 2 scheme, which is dependent upon objective legislative content to create a shift in employee bargaining power. Having now no procedural obligations or even small sanctions to induce compliance, the UK legislative right to request intrudes little on employer authority or the underlying assumptions of the employment contract.

Impact on carers in the workplace

Since the enactment of the flexible working law, UK government surveys report an increase over time in the percentage of employees surveyed who had one or more flexible working arrangement available to them (Hooker et al., 2007). Employees report that 60% of requests to work flexibly were fully agreed to, and another 18% were partially agreed to (Hooker et al., 2007, p. 4).[4] A significant percentage (39%) of employees reported that flexibility was important to them in deciding to work with their current employer, some indication that workers "vote with their feet" (Hooker et al., 2007, p. 84). In 2007, 21% of employees said they did not make a flexible working request because they did not think that it would be successful, although this was down from the previous survey in 2003 (Hooker et al., 2007, pp. 5, 98). Although there is some evidence to suggest that the rate of unmet demand to work flexibly is falling (Lewis, 2009), this does not take into account carers who are not now working and would wish to work flexibly provided they could maintain adequate income.

Surveys generally indicate that employers are reasonably satisfied with the light touch regulation of the right to request law, although some employers have argued that it is too costly and results in resentment by employees not given the right to request under the law (Confederation of British Industry, 2006). As the scope of the law widened, more employers expressed discontent with the law, fearing that all workers would seek flexible work. There is some evidence that the business case for flexible working may be increasingly recognized as a result of the flexible working law. Studies show an increase in the number of firms who provide formal options for flexible working, but, predictably, workplaces with a predominately female workforce were the most likely to provide for flexible working (Hegewisch, 2009; Lewis, 2009).

As to empirical evidence of success, Lewis (2009) cautions that the data across the government's different Work-Life Balance surveys are not comparable, so it is difficult to draw clean conclusions. These government surveys are also deficient in the limited nature of their questions and in collecting subjective rather than objective data, relying on self-reporting of impressions that may not necessarily be accurate. In addition, it has been noted that several gaps exist in the British survey data on the consequences of a request (Hegewisch, 2009). Yet, if the outcomes of cases are an indication, the demands of family care can be so inelastic that lack of flexibility in work renders simultaneous engagement in the labor force impossible for worker-carers at some times. A review of cases before the ET and EAT in which employees' requests for flexible working were refused indicates that employees seeking greater flexibility for family responsibilities may be apt to resign in the face of employer refusals (*Clarke v Telewest Communications*, 2005; *Giles v Geach*, 2005; *Ministry of Defence v DeBique*, 2009; *Network Rail Infrastructures Ltd. v Gammie*, 2009; *Shaw v CCL Ltd.*, 2007). This pattern suggests that worker-carers seek formal alterations to work terms as a last resort in juggling work and family responsibilities. Further empirical research is needed into the prevalence of resigning in the face of refusal to work flexibly, and more targeted policies should be developed to prevent the loss of these worker-carers from the labor force in the future.

4 These figures are considerably lower than the data reported by the Walsh survey the following year, and the anomaly was not adequately addressed.

The UK's legislation is open-ended about what terms or conditions may be the subject of flexibility requests or negotiations. Compared to approaches of other nations that focus only on working time, the potential breadth of working flexibly in the UK is a strength. More available options may permit solutions which are workable for both employers and employees. Yet, the data suggests that most flexible working requests are to reduce the number of hours and days worked. This may reflect that, in view of the long-hours work culture of the UK, time is the primary need of its worker-carers (Jacobs and Gerson, 2004). Alternatively, it may reflect a certain lack of imagination or willingness in the parties to approach mediating conflicting demands with novel solutions.

Despite the lack of firm legislative content and indeterminate evidence of workplace change, perhaps simply naming and claiming the right to seek changes in the terms and conditions of work goes some way towards shifting ossified social roles. Lewis agrees to some degree with Collins that providing a right of work-life flexibility to all workers may have the desirable effect of "eroding expectations" of an ideal worker model (Lewis, 2009, p. 176). After all, the legislation does provide that employers "shall only refuse" a request to work flexibly on commonly asserted business grounds (Employment Rights Act, 1996, s 80G(1)). This public statement that employers should accede to a worker's request for flexibility absent a clear business reason not to do so may induce change based on what stakeholders expect rather than what the law forces them to do (Smith, 2002). That such a dynamic is already occurring is suggested by data indicating some employers offer flexible working to workers who are not statutorily eligible to assert the right to request.

Impact on sex equality

Another key feature by which to evaluate the UK's right to request flexible working is its impact on sex equality. The sex-neutral availability of the right to request is a positive aspect of the legislation. Lewis has noted that, outside the Scandinavian countries, "gender equality in and for itself is rarely a priority" in flexibility law, and the UK has "striven for gender neutrality" (Lewis, 2009, p. 18). Lewis suggests that this approach is consistent with Nobel laureate Amartya Sen's "equal capabilities" conception of equality and leads to a focus on the ability of an individual (male or female) to undertake "genuine choice" about the appropriate mix of work and care obligations for that person (Lewis, 2009, p. 18).

Operationally, however, the sex-neutrality of the legislation is not enough by itself to shift gender roles. Predictably, more female than male employees have sought to make a formal request for flexible working (Hooker et al., 2007, pp. 3–4). This is possibly due to the initial limitation to carers. Women workers have been found twice as likely to have caring responsibility for an adult as men workers (Hooker et al., 2007, p. 7). Additionally, 43% of women who requested flexible working sought flexibility to meet child care needs, although only 17% of men did so – an amount equal to men's flexible working requests for "more free time"

(Lewis and Campbell, 2008, p. 536). Worryingly, it appears that gender also plays a role in employer acceptance of flexible working requests: 23% of men had requests to work flexibly declined, although only 13% of women did (Hooker et al., 2007, p. 5). This gender disparity in seeking flexible working has persisted since the right to request law was implemented (Holt and Granger, 2005).

Grace James has criticized the operation of the right to request law within the context of sex-based disparities in parental leave rights (2006; 2009). James has pointed out that the UK system of leave rights is tilted in favor of the mother as primary carer, inasmuch as her rights to maternity/parental leave, including pay during leave, are more secure and generous than the fathers' (2006). As such, it is no surprise that the take-up of flexible working has been largely by mothers (Lewis, 2009), and father's requests are refused more frequently than those of mothers. However, the expansion of "shared" parental leave, available from 2015, may go some way towards alleviating the concern of the effect of sex-neutral laws operating within a highly gendered paradigm (Children and Families Act 2014 (UK), Part 7). It is unclear whether a right to request flexible working for any reason, coupled with parental leave rights that are more attractive for fathers, will result in a greater shift in the gendered nature of caregiving or of flexible working in the UK. It seems clear, however, that many worker-carers need access to both job-protected leave and work flexibility to cope with the demands of family care. Flexible working may be necessary but not sufficient alone as a measure to generate large-scale shifts in the gendered nature of caring.

IV. How would a right to request flexible working fit with the FMLA?

For several reasons, the UK's right to request flexible working would fit well within the US regulatory scheme. The conception of the right to request as a basic employment right, its complement to existing US legislation, its sex-neutral availability, limited intrusion on management prerogative, low cost, and research supporting its palatability and effectiveness for the business community all suggest that a right to request flexible working could operate comfortably in the US alongside a similar sex-neutral statute which was intended to improve gender equality – the Family and Medical Leave Act of 1993 (FMLA) (US). The aims and operation of the FMLA would be forwarded by the addition of a right to request flexible working.

A. Flexibility is needed to provide wider protections than caring leave

The FMLA has been the principal legislative method in the US of directly addressing work-family conflict. The slogan "workers should not have to choose between their jobs and their families," was repeatedly made part of the incentive to pass the FMLA (Clinton, 1992; 139 Cong Rec H225–01, 1993; 139 Cong Rec H319–02,

1993; 139 Cong Rec S1355–01, 1993). The US has no other broad, nationally applicable legislated leave than FMLA and depends on private sector employers' policies, individual contract, collectively bargained agreements, or applicable state or local law to define most workers' leave rights beyond FMLA. Neither family responsibilities, caregiving, nor family status is a protected class under US national antidiscrimination legislation (EEOC, 2007), and legislative rights to flexibility in the US are quite narrow in scope and underdeveloped.

The FMLA does provide some ability to structure work to accommodate care by permitting a covered employee in limited cases not to perform work. However, leave rights are at best only a temporary accommodation of the concurrent demands of work and care. Leave in general and FMLA leave in particular do not fully address the issue of structuring work to combine work and family responsibilities.

Aside from birth, and adoption, FMLA leave addresses only urgent needs of worker-carers to minister to *serious* medical needs of family members (29 USC 2612(a)(1)(C)). FMLA is of limited use when caring for persons beyond infancy. Further, the ability of workers to use FMLA leave in a flexible way – in short, discrete periods of two, one, or even half-days – is quite narrow, which reduces its usefulness to the worker-carer (Hein, 2005). Thus, the majority of worker-carers' needs for flexibility go unmet through FMLA leave. Scholars have called for an expansion of mandatory rights to parenting leave in the US to allow for more everyday caring needs, such as taking parents, children, or spouses to medical appointments (Friedman and Greenhaus, 2000). Since FMLA leave is unpaid (although employers can require employees to take paid leave to which they are entitled concurrently with FMLA leave (29 USC 2612(d)), FMLA does not address the economic needs of worker-carers to provide adequate income while caring for their families. A right to request flexible working law could fill those gaps.

Flexible working offers a necessary complement to FMLA leave rights, because flexible working can be tailored to individual circumstances, is more economically advantageous for both worker and employer, and offers solutions to a broader range of caring needs. First, the UK right to request flexible working leaves the type of flexibility open to be mutually determined by the parties to the work relationship (Hegewisch, 2009). Although most stakeholders negotiate around working time, parties are free to negotiate the work site, method of pay, or any other term or condition of work as the subject of flexibility. Greater choice to craft the mix of work terms and conditions which works for their families' needs would improve the options available to worker-carers.

Importantly, an option to request flexible working also provides worker-carers with greater income security. Given that seeking flexible work is not a protected right in the US, any worker who seeks flexibility now risks "mommy-tracking," retaliation, or worse. All families are vulnerable to a loss of income simply because of caring obligations when worker-carers are left with no options but unpaid leave, jeopardizing job security, or resignation. Flexible working alternatives such as job sharing, compressed hours, or annualized hours may permit worker-carers to spend needed time caring for family members and yet maintain income. At the same time, agreed upon flexibility allows an employer to preserve that worker's productivity and plan more predictably (Rapoport et al., 2002). Ultimately, protected flexible working options can reduce the vulnerability of both worker-carers and employers.

B. A right to request flexible working is consistent with FMLA aims and operation

A right to request flexible working would fit with the US FMLA and work towards a less gendered American workplace. The FMLA was characterized as a "minimum labor standard" "directly addressing" an intractable social problem – the necessity and difficulty of combining paid work and family care (139 Cong Rec HR Rep 103–8(I), 1993; 139 Cong Rec S Rep 103–3, 1993). The FMLA was never considered the complete solution to problems of combining work and care – far from it. As the House of Representatives report on the FMLA stated:

> The role of the family as primary nurturer and care-giver has been fundamentally affected by these [demographic] changes in the work force. Often families must struggle to fulfill the traditional role of bearing and caring for children and providing emotional and physical support during times of great need. When families fail to carry out these critical functions, the societal costs are enormous.
>
> Yet our workplaces are still too often modeled on the unrealistic and outmoded idea of workers unencumbered by family responsibilities. . . . Workers whose family needs are accommodated at the workplace are more likely to stay, and to be productive in their jobs.
>
> *(139 Cong Rec HR Rep 103–8(I), 1993, pp. 20–21)*

Proponents of the FMLA were motivated by the needs of workers and families in general but also specifically raised the issue of increasing numbers of working women with families in their speeches (139 Cong Rec H447–06, 1993; 139 Cong Rec S1355–01, 1993).

The FMLA is intended to serve as a floor, rather than a ceiling, of employee entitlements (29 USC 2652(b)). The FMLA is located in the Labor section of the United States Code, along with the New Deal era Fair Labor Standards Act of 1938 (FLSA), which regulates minimum wages and maximum hours of employment, and the National Labor Relations Act (NLRA), which governs collective bargaining and unfair labor practices. These three statutes fall under the administrative governance of the US Department of Labor (DOL). The DOL is given administrative authority to investigate and attempt to resolve complaints and may also bring civil actions (29 USC 2617(b)). Commentators have concluded that FMLA enforcement is intended to fit within the scheme of basic labor regulation in the US, expressive of minimum standards of employment (where it applies) (Rothstein, 1994). This is the precise niche which the right to request flexible working occupies in the UK. Moreover, the FMLA has a fairly simple structure, which provides a limited leave entitlement for a defined group of eligible workers, prohibits discrimination on the basis of the leave entitlement, prescribes compliance mechanisms such as notice requirements, and provides for the pursuit of legal claims in the event of violation. The UK's right to request flexible working is structured much the same.

In its emphasis on procedural rights and stakeholder bargaining against a market background, a right to request flexible working would harmonize with the NLRA as well. Commentators have praised a focus on fair process as a mechanism of achieving workplace cooperation (Arnow-Richman, 2007). An individual right to a good faith bargaining process is consistent with long-established rights in the collective bargaining arena under the NLRA. Such process-based rights are well understood and reasonably well accepted, so long as they leave the ultimate outcomes to the parties. The UK's right to request flexible working does not impose a substantive solution – indeed a tribunal cannot overturn the employer's business judgment – but the process does concentrate on getting the parties to consider the impact of their position. In the UK legislation, this is accomplished by requiring the employee's request for flexibility to consider the effect on the employer's business and how that effect might be mitigated, as well as the employer's reciprocal duty to reasonably consider the employee's request and confine refusal to acceptable business reasons. However, parties are not required to come to an agreement about flexible working. This structure is much like the collective bargaining regime in the NLRA, in which parties are to bargain in good faith over the terms and conditions of employment but neither party is "legally obligated to yield" and is free "to agree or not to agree" (*NLRB v Wooster Div. of Borg-Warner Corp.*, 1958, p. 349).

C. A gender-neutral mechanism may not shift sex roles

The UK's sex-neutral approach to flexibility rights is also consistent with the US policy of sex-neutrality in the provision of FMLA leave and the US Supreme Court's holding that the sex-neutrality of the FMLA scheme was a necessary component in the achievement of sex equality in work and care. The stated purposes of the FMLA provide that leave is available "on a gender-neutral basis" (29 USC 2601(a)(6)). The proponents of the FMLA considered that availability to "not only women of childbearing age, but all employees, young and old, male and female" was important to insure equality:

> The FMLA addresses the basic leave needs of all employees. . . . A law providing special protection to women or any defined group, in addition to being inequitable, runs the risk of causing discriminatory treatment. H.R. 1, by addressing the needs of all workers, avoids such a risk. Thus H.R. 1 is

> based not only on the Commerce Clause, but also on the guarantees of equal protection and due process embodied in the Fourteenth Amendment.
>
> *(139 Cong Rec HR Rep 103–8(I), 1993, p. 30)*

The US Supreme Court opinion in *Nevada v Hibbs* (2003), which upheld the gender equality basis of the FMLA, insisted that caring leave from work must be available on a gender-neutral basis in order to secure equality for women. Otherwise, the court reasoned, employers would have a reason to discriminate against women workers and the gender differences in work and care would have no incentive to equalize over time. These were similar motives for the sex-neutral availability of the right to request flexible working in the UK. In addition, of course, a right to request for all worker-carers recognizes that many worker-carers are male and removes a potential barrier to males shouldering more of the family care burden. As such, a sex-neutral right to request flexible working would be consistent with both the FMLA and the equality basis of the larger US legal scheme.

The UK's Right to Request Flexible Working – and any transplant of this scheme to the US – will likely have complex effects on sex equality in work and care. While the law provides a needed buttress to the ability of worker-carers (who are primarily women) to seek flexibility in their terms and conditions of employment, this right is located within industrial legislation and is thus unmoored from sex equality principles. Although the UK law's divorce from equality legislation may have positive benefits of re-norming work expectations, a right to request by itself does little to shift the relative duties of work and care between the sexes. To have a significant effect on gender equality in work and care, care would need to be made both more acceptable and more financially feasible for men to undertake. Placement of a right to request flexible work within an industrial law framework may have the effect of normalizing the worker-carer and increasing the visibility of this segment of the work force, but more would be needed to shift old cultural patterns and support the economic security of worker-carers. Right to request legislation in the US should begin with targeted groups phased in over time through a consultative process, as was undertaken in the UK. Employers would remain free to broaden the scheme to all their employees if they wished.

Further, while the breadth of worker-carers covered is a strength of the UK law, its limitation to employees at common law does not address the needs of some of the most disadvantaged workers in industrialized society – contingent workers, who are more likely to be female than are full-time employees (Fudge and Owens, 2006). Many women, in fact, are engaged in less secure contingent work because they have moved in and out of the labor force in order to manage caring responsibilities.

V. The new normal

Despite an insistence on self-reliance in US culture, awareness of universal vulnerability does break through. As the character of A D Skinner said in the popular TV show *X-Files*: "Every life, every day, is in danger. That's just life" (Morgan and

Wong, 1994). While the universal nature of vulnerability is intrinsic to the human condition and to all workers, there are nevertheless structures we can put in place to increase resilience for families, and a right to request flexible working is one of those structures. The right to request flexible working would fit within US labor and employment regulation and plug a gap presently existing in our protections for worker-carers.

While the UK's right to request flexible working has been expanded to be available regardless of need, if transplanted to the US, eligible employees should be limited to worker-carers. The limitation to carers reinforces the equality dimension of the right and underscores the importance of family care. Offering a right to request flexible working to all workers removes a right to request flexibility from its equality roots and justification, thereby making it "just" another labor right to be bartered away, like leave and pay, rather than recognition of a distinct need stemming from universal human vulnerability and the importance of families to our social structure.

Considering the power of the law to shape and structure social expectations and behaviors, a right to request flexible working law may help dislodge entrenched expectations that all workers must behave as a "ideal workers" in order to be productive and valuable (Williams, 2000). A right to request flexible working as enacted in the UK may include little substantive content in the law, but it offers an important device both enabling worker-carers to fulfill their dual tasks and deconstructing the institution of the ideal worker. Making multi-tasking the "new normal" is a necessary step towards sexual equality and flexibility for those who work and care. The US could benefit from adapting the UK's initial model to take concrete steps towards sex equality by addressing structural inequalities in work.

18

VULNERABLE COMMUNITIES

Proposing Community Syndicalism for distressed localities

Kenneth M. Casebeer[1]

> *The economic renewal will be moral or it will not exist. The moral revolution will be economic or it will not take place.*
>
> (*Don Jose Maria Arizmendiarrieta*)[2]

Individuals are not the only subjects who are vulnerable. Increasingly, communities are becoming distressed areas as a result of plant closings, offshoring of jobs, and deep recession. Local communities and regional populations in the US have destabilized, and even collapsed, with many attendant social problems (Foster, 2010; Swinney and Metzgar, 1986). Of course, all structural economic change will be accompanied by dislocations associated with local economies; however, recent dislocations due to job loss have not proven to be subject to temporary readjustments. A recent study by Greenstone and Looney (2010) shows that twenty years after the 1980s recession:

> The net loss to a displaced worker with six years of job tenure is approximately $164,000, which exceeds 20 percent of the average lifetime earnings of these workers. These future earnings losses dwarf the losses associated from the period of unemployment itself. . . . [J]ob loss also has negative economic and noneconomic effects on workers' health, their families and their communities. Men with high levels of seniority when they are displaced from their jobs experience mortality rates in the year after unemployment 50 to 100 percent higher than otherwise would be expected. . . . These elevated rates of mortality are still evident even twenty years after the job

1 Professor of Law Emeritus, University of Miami Law School.

2 Founder of Mondragon Cooperatives, Basque, Spain, quoted in William Foote Whyte & Kathleen King Whyte, *Making Mondragon: The Growth and Dynamics of the Worker Cooperative Complex*, Volume 14. Cornell University Press, 1991).

> loss and may reduce these workers' life expectancies by twelve to eighteen months for a worker who loses his job at age forty.

The children of these workers also appear to suffer. Children whose fathers were displaced have annual earnings about 9% lower than similar children whose fathers did not experience an employment shock. The collapse of the mortgage market as a result of the bursting of the securitized mortgage bubble has worsened the personal welfare of workers in declining communities by making their houses unsellable, making relocation to communities with available jobs of any kind infeasible.

Economic globalization is a fact and a material condition of modern society. There will be no going back to purely local economies. At the same time, the future of participatory democracy depends upon "localizing" leverage within this global market. Otherwise, community autonomy will be ephemeral. As Graeber (2009, p. 239) argues:

> Temporary bubbles of autonomy must gradually turn into permanent, free communities. However, in order to do so, those communities cannot exist in total isolation; neither can they have a purely confrontational relation with everyone around them. They have to have some way to engage with larger economic, social or political systems that surround them.

Such leverage will depend upon new economic and moral changes embodied in new economic and legal institutions. Such institutions will depend on a more authentic model of human behavior, a rationality rooted in interdependence and thus socially constructed and not the product of atomated individualism (Casebeer and Whalen, 2011, p. 177). Harvey (2012) posits:

> At the heart of all this [. . .] lies a simple structural dilemma: How can the left fuse the need to actively engage with, but also create an alternative to, the capitalist laws of value determination on the world market, while facilitating the associated laborers' ability democratically and collectively to manage and decide on what they will produce and how? This is the central dialectical tension.

One possible practical response for distressed communities is Community Syndicalism – local community finance and operating credit for industrial production linked with, but separate institutionally from, democratic worker ownership and control of production – in short, investment capital assets separate from enterprise ownership and control. Community Syndicalism would increase investment directly for production, retain jobs in existing population centers, promote job skilling, and retain tax bases for local services and income supporting local businesses, at the same time increasing support for authentic political democracy by rendering the exploitive ideology of the public/private distinction superfluous.

After analyzing Community Syndicalism as a moral and economic model, this chapter explores the future viability of worker ownership or cooperatives in the US. It analyzes the law affecting their viability, identifies necessary legal changes in US law, and outlines the global legal and political impacts of Community Syndicalism.

I. Structural challenges to developed economies embedded in financial globalization

Threatening developed economies, the Great Recession resulting from the globalization of finance capitalism created two structural labor crises for developed economies:

(1) The investment conundrum: the channeling of substantial investment into non-productive, speculative, paper commodities, due in large part to hyper-inequalities in wealth, and entailing reduced growth of production for use and therefore reduced available aggregate job creation in the developed economies. When the finance bubbles burst, more than 11,800,000 jobs were lost in the US alone, and this jobs gap is not closing with the financial sector bail out and recovery. At present, optimistic, projected job creation rates (which are about double current job creation rates), it will take over 12 years to return to pre-recession employment levels according to Greenstone and Looney (2010).

(2) The exportation problematic: The continued exportation of industrial jobs from the US to other "lower-cost-of-production" nations, and the outsourcing, automation, "just-in-time" production, and speed-ups associated with investments, spurring dispersion of global supply chains to create excess global productive capacity according to Foster (2010).

Beyond short-term corporate incentives (greed) to exploit low-wage, underdeveloped regions, excess capacity will reinforce lower standardized wages worldwide. In turn, this will make new investment in production, and therefore jobs, in developed countries more unlikely in the future.

There are two reasons to care. The first is economic. Stabilizing production to some extent in developed economies slows the now frenetic race to the bottom of labor standards promoted by capital managers playing developing countries against each other. The second is moral. An economic enterprise model needs to be established and proven that changes the priority of incentives based on production for use. The goal is not profit maximization but economic stabilization. The first reason is both macro-economic and morally distributive in the long run. The second reason is micro-economic in incentives and rationality but moral as well in redefining rights to work, mutuality of relations, equality, and democratic participation. What is required is a change in economic agency, not the abandonment of markets at this time.

II. Community Syndicalism as a moral/economic response to structural dislocation

Community Syndicalism will not be a quick fix. The key to breaking the conceptual roadblock to reversing local economic decline is to institutionalize the incentive to invest in job maximizing production that maximizes long-term stability and continuity of those jobs, and minimizes short-term profit seeking at the expense of long-term stability. Investment incentives must be turned upside down. Furthermore, these new investments largely will have to be from the distressed locality to that same locality. Outsiders won't be interested. Furthermore, regarding hoped-for economic spinoff of new local production, known as the local strategy of import substitution, Whyte and Whyte (1991, p. 59) cite the experience with Mondragon is that "the base for the healthiest and most sustainable growth is the development of increasing numbers of firms that buy from and sell to one another as they create a labor market with increasingly skilled workers and technical and professional people." Thus, first, the incentive to invest needs to be collectivized locally so that investment flows are not solely directed by short-term return to individualized investors. Friedman observes that this phenomenon will continue, "[S]o long as we treat the public good of investment as a private for-profit activity coordinated by individual banks and investment companies. 'Speculative finance' [Hyman] Minsky argues, is the problem; reliance on financial markets creates economic instability and discourages real innovation and investment" (p. 345).

In Community Syndicalism, local community start-up finance and operating credit for industrial production combines with, but is separate from, linked democratic worker ownership and control of production. Community funding and ownership, coupled with worker control, was the intent behind the closest attempt proposed in the US thus far – the Steel Valley Authority's (SVA) attempt to use the public power of eminent domain to acquire and municipally operate failed industrial plants in the Pittsburgh region during the 1980s, as explained by Hornack and Lynd (1986–87). Community Syndicalism differs in two important aspects: first, the aim is not takeover of failing or closing plants as with SVA; second, splitting community investment in and ownership of capital assets from worker ownership and democratic control of the enterprise contribute synergistically to long-term viability. In such situations Simon (1991) concludes that both the community which wants a stable economic base, and the workers, who want sustainable jobs, desire stabilization in the labor market. The "private" capitalist economy may be driven by short-term maximization of return, but Community Syndicates assume long-term viability.

How can this new model be generated? Start with the economic problem. Local communities or regional populations have been devastated by the decline of industrial production, whether the disappearance of enterprise that formed the economic base of those communities resulted from competitive failure or from outsourcing of some or all of the production from the affected area. Community economics, of course, are not limited to the base firm. Hundreds of small businesses, community non-profits, local taxes for services, even big-box retailers, and supply chain production, depend upon resident incomes. Looney and Greenstone (2010, p. 3) show how "[a] dearth of good jobs in distressed communities leads to high unemployment and stagnant wages. Evidence shows that certain place-based policies can help attract business investment to targeted areas and can boost the productivity and wages of workers in those areas." The key is jobs, and not just minimum-wage jobs, but jobs that approximate the number and wage level of the production drain. Moreover, to rekindle the local economy, new jobs need to be anchored to the community. According to Olson (1986–87, p. 242):

> Employee ownership helps anchor capital in local communities because employee-owners usually reside in the community in which they work and their interests, as residents and employee-owners, coincide with those of the community. Employee ownership is therefore a valuable tool for aiding economic development strategies which value both the geographic stability and the quality of employment opportunities created.

For a counter example, computerized service jobs can always be easily relocated to another community. What is needed is the formation of new production creating large numbers of jobs within modern, flexible production modalities. Existing capital formations are unlikely candidates as the source of the necessary new investment.

Will it work? There is reason to believe from Ansley (1993) that much deindustrialization and job exportation is driven by short-term profit and inability to compete in world financial markets.

Many plants are closed not because they fail to make a profit, but because they fail to make *enough* profit to hold the decision maker's interest when compared to some other marginally more profitable opportunity. When management fails to reinvest and modernize, productivity and profit margins most often *do* decline, thereby reinforcing the initial, casual decisions whose rhetoric often either places blame at the feet of labor, or speaks of these developments as if they constituted some natural and inevitable evolutionary path beyond anyone's control.

High wages, retained earnings, but no profit requirement as demanded by outside private capital investors, coupled with high productivity, could allow such syndicates to be market competitive and achieve long-term supply chain relations, especially within non-profit global production networks.

Those left behind thus have strong economic incentive to act but no clear agency. For example, Greenstone and Looney (2010) demonstrate that the economic spillover effects on community economies are not captured by the private investor market. The community or region needs capital pooling. Traditional sources include local industrial revenue bonds, state abatements or investment funds, and grants from non-profits. Brecher (1986) reports the Naugatuck Valley Project in Connecticut created a revolving fund to support worker buyouts from credit unions, churches, unions, and other institutions. These sources, however, have been substantially diminished since the initial enthusiasm for financing worker buyouts of failing industries in the early 1980s waned. State and local tax incentives to private enterprise may result in initial private enterprise investment but have not captured those enterprises long-term because such incentives do not change community against community race to the bottom dynamics, either economically or legally. Yet, there may still be unused land or buildings available in unfinished local industrial parks. The Tri-State Conference on Steel in Pittsburgh has proposed land trusts owning land and buildings, leasing to private enterprises.

More likely, capital contributions would have to be raised by rolling but not permanent taxes on business franchises in the area. Local private banks may be induced to participate by providing long-term, low interest loans if local residents are willing to withdraw personal and business accounts from banks declining to participate. Businesses paying franchise taxes might not object to participating in pooled leverage because they are already "paying" in another way, as Stout (1986, p. 20) shows:

> When you lose 1,000 manufacturing jobs, you lose an additional 1,000 jobs in the service economy. You put the following service companies out of business: 17 eating places, 13 food stores, 11 gas stations, 6 apparel shops, 3 automobile dealerships, 2 hardware stores, 2 drug stores, 1 sports store, 1 jewelry store, 17 doctors and 5 dentists, and an unknown number of teachers, government employees, etc.

III. The community in Community Syndicalism

First, a local mechanism is needed for taxing those enterprises expected to benefit from new production and jobs in advance of those benefits to provide for initial investment. This is difficult where the workforce is divided into local municipalities, sometimes crossing state borders. After long negotiations, this obstacle was overcome via a unique provision of state law under the Tri-State Steel Valley Authority in the 1980s. The authority was empowered to acquire failing steel plants through eminent domain and continue production through an agreement to fund acquisitions agreed to by nine supporting communities. Some plants were targeted, but none were ultimately operated by the authority. Initial steel plants targeted for eminent domain takeovers by the authority ultimately were not purchased because of a failure of funding, particularly for investing in new plant equipment to make the plants competitive, because reinvestment had been ignored by prior private ownership bent on milking the plants until the inevitable end. Building up an ongoing tax value capture structure, admittedly, will be difficult politically given the collective need to bet on the future, but in an economically declining community there is little real choice other than abandonment.

A special tax and borrowing jurisdiction would be needed. Such specialized political institutions have frequently been established to govern water distribution in the Western US. This local community investment fund under democratic elected management, legally limited to investing in local syndicates would control pooled resources. Initial capital needs would likely be great because the purchase of production technology would be necessary to generate sufficient numbers of jobs. It is key to making the investment fund debt obligations minimal. Furthermore, after start-up, additional capital must be raised to provide operating credit. Raising the capital pool and creating the community district to hold the capital assets would solve the main barriers to entry for successful industrial worker ownership cooperatives by separating investment capital needs from enterprise returns and providing a reliable source for ongoing credit draws. These twin market barriers of preventing the directing of capital investment solely to specific qualifying enterprises and denying access to continuing funding after start-up, according to Curl (2012), have led to most worker ownership and control market failures in the US.

It is crucial that the politics of governing the investment pool funds should be institutionally separated from short-term changes in political party leadership of the community in general. Many Community Development Agencies (CDAs) have foundered by succumbing to short-term political forces structured into the enterprises that were developed by the CDAs. The short-term demands and political log rolling involved in general policy making should not intrude on the single-minded, long-term resolve of enterprise stability. In instances where local entities have sat on the boards of cooperatives in return for funding support, the results for the cooperatives have not been positive, except perhaps in the housing area. The special district should be restricted to using its funds in support of local, cooperative enterprises. Funds must be available for both asset investment and operating capital lines of credit. Perhaps a minimal amount of funds could be authorized for other investments in order to assure funds for the district's own operational needs. Leasing of the district's assets must be guaranteed for the duration of the enterprise in order to prevent the district from withdrawing capital assets earlier on purely political grounds. Criteria for the determination of the point of enterprise failure triggering district asset recapture would either have to be specified in creating the district or in the terms of the lease requirements.

Why would communities want to generate substantial capital pooling? Most directly, for survival: to recreate a tax base, to save small businesses and community organizations such as churches, and to reduce the servicing costs of social morbidity. While lacking economic agency to support worker ownership, political agency for worker enterprises is longstanding. Swinney (1985, pp. 106–7) notes, "This [cooperatives] movement includes community organizations, urban political organizations, religious organizations, unemployed organizations, and others who are responding to the reality of very high levels of unemployment." Secondarily, the community would acquire new assets in the form of land, buildings, and machinery. The investment fund would have title to these capital assets unless bought from it later by the worker enterprises themselves. In the case of enterprise failure, the fund would have these basic assets to begin anew. Eventually, it might be hoped that worker and enterprise deposits would grow to support a subsidiary mutual bank that might be the source of future investments without taxing the community. In 1959, four years after the first cooperative was established in Mondragon, Spain, the corporation created the Caja Laboral Popular, which has grown to become the fourth largest bank by assets in Spain.

IV. The syndical in Community Syndicalism

Splitting asset ownership from enterprise ownership is the conceptual advance of Community Syndicalism. Once planning by political communities and potential worker groups have identified a viable long-term market niche, an investment pool can be initiated. At this point or shortly thereafter, worker organizations may form coalitions to "bid" (by virtue of viability of proposed business plans) on the value of the enterprise. The capital assets of the fund would be "leased" at nominal value for the period of the enterprise's existence. The workers initially or subsequently employed would own the enterprise on a one share, one vote basis and generate any necessary management committee by democratic choice. Worker ownership and control not only permits, but is crucial to, stability. Hyde (1993, p. 748) convincingly argues, "If employees own the firm, they will not shut it, or move it to Mexico, after a disappointing quarter, or a failure to meet a growth target, or simply because they have failed to attain a 30 per cent market share." There should be no incentives created to allow the local community to pull out capital assets or for workers to view participation as a transitory job rather than continuing ownership of the enterprise. Thus, day-to-day management could be delegated under periodic democratic oversight meetings. This organizational model worked reasonably well in the Northwest plywood cooperatives.

To structure the legality of worker enterprise ownership, little needs to be done. As the most well-known of legal reformers for worker ownership, Ellerman and Pitegoff (1982–83) report that virtually all states have already modified their incorporation statutes to allow licensing of cooperative ownership. Modifications of organizational management subject to owner control useful to the specific enterprise can be established voluntarily in corporate bylaws. Long-term nominal leases of assets and provision of financing in subsidy of local production is also standard practice. There is no policy reason except resistance by private enterprises to new competition to prevent the extension of favorable national and local tax treatment given to other employee ownership forms, such as Employee Stock Ownership Plans (ESOPs).

By eliminating the need of the enterprise for more than variable cost coverage, which would include relatively high monthly distributions to workers (replacing wages) plus some retained earnings for production improvement and flexibility, the enterprise should gain cost competitiveness against private enterprises forced to produce world competitive (not minimum) short-term profits for investors and the coverage of initial asset investments for start-ups. This should be true even where competitors gain their advantage from low-wage labor exploitation.

Following the Mondragon experience, a parallel "social council" structure (or union) would mediate any differences arising between workers as owners and workers as workers. However, such differences, while perhaps inevitably about short-term value distributions as opposed to long-term retained earning reinvestment, are likely also to be reduced by eliminating the ownership/employee legal separation.

Another and linked problem to be addressed legally involves maintaining worker management, which has proven problematic in production cooperatives in the US. Hansmann (1990) has predicted the failure of industrial production enterprises managed democratically based on the substantial coordination costs of large corporation management. The more specialized and hierarchical the internal division of labor, and the greater the number of workers involved in industrial production, the greater the coordination costs (informational and divisional) occasioned by democratic forms. He is willing to concede that consumer service delivery and shop-based small-scale firms can more easily overcome these transaction costs and survive if their capitalization costs are also relatively low, because everyone tends to do the same thing and debt can be retired more quickly, easing turnover problems. But small-scale enterprise is not the aim here. Undoubtedly, there is some truth to the argument that there are transaction costs of democratic decisions, and that is why direct democratic micro-management of day-to-day production decisions is impossible. However, Hansmann discounts offsetting productivity gains due to worker input and productivity gains due to ownership and loyalty stakes in the enterprise. Historically, Jackall and Levin (1984, p. 7) report, "For the same level of capital investment, the cooperatives had far higher labor productivity than comparable capitalist firms." In the plywood cooperatives, worker owners often were rotated through different stages of production in order to educate each owner about the enterprise as a whole.

The Mondragon cooperatives engage in extensive worker education and also utilize interacting and overlapping hierarchies of democratic decision making. Of course, this is costly, particularly in terms of time, and generally goes without full compensation of management decisions. Just as maximizing short-term profit is not necessarily the most important goal of economic life unless we choose to embed it in law, so is absolute minimization of transaction costs not inscribed naturally. Nothing more has been established but that democracy and equality have some allocation costs.

Related to firm management, a more technical legal problem is workforce transitions or enterprise labor turnover. The main benefit of enterprise ownership is job stability and perhaps an increase in the number of stable jobs. Indeed, one of the aims of separation of asset ownership and enterprise ownership is to remove the incentive of any cohort of worker owners to liquidate the capital assets of the enterprise and cash out. Alternatively, enterprise value is mostly found in the income stream. This, in turn, reduces the magnitude, but does not eliminate the problem of share transfer. In the past, cooperatives have sometimes repurchased owner shares at current market value for owners who were leaving, retiring, or deceased. The purchased shares are then sold to new workers or retained by the enterprise with returns apportioned to remaining owners pro rata. However, market repurchase can escalate to prohibitive prices, particularly related to capital asset appreciation. Escalating market value of shares often forced sales to non-worker shareholders, and over time the enterprise returned to ordinary stock corporations. Given split ownership, that is not a cognizable option for community syndicates. Other cooperatives, such as Mondragon, have stabilized the share price for long-standing and new jobholders, but created undistributed share accounts for each owner that increase with longevity or value contribution. When a shareholder eventually severs their connection to the cooperative, the accumulated individual fund is paid out. In some sense the worker's accumulation operates similarly to a defined contribution pension fund in the US, although Mondragon workers also have an additional pension fund. This plan allows movement in and out of the cooperative but also has drawbacks. This approach does not consider risks undertaken by early worker owners and fails to compensate owners for the appreciation in the value of the enterprise over time except as accumulation based on labor time. It thus depends on a strong culture of commitment to cooperation that may be diminishing among younger entrants.

The project of job stability based on enterprise stability should not incentivize easy exit. An assumption of lessened mobility is part of the tradeoff justifying replacement of lost local jobs. If the community has bought in, the worker owner can be expected to make a similar commitment, foregoing some degree of mobility. Simon (1991, p. 1393) posits, "Legal and economic arrangements that make it more difficult or costly for parties to withdraw from the relationship may serve as safeguards that induce firm-specific human capital investments by reducing the risk of subsequent opportunistic withdrawal." Of course, this idea cannot justify involuntary servitude. But perhaps a sliding scale exit penalty reducing market value repurchase payout could be justified based on length of service to the firm, at least if exit is not due to retirement or incapacity. Nothing prevents an enterprise generating surplus revenues successfully earned above costs or periodic and generous distributions from also funding defined payment accumulation accounts. Also, there is justification for some share appreciation for well-established enterprises, because new entrant worker owners are taking less risk and early workers are more likely to have made sacrifices in distributions stemming from early debts incurred in establishing supply chain connections and reputation. Furthermore, the lack of appreciation of share value equity may be less disruptive within the Mondragon core area because of the extensive acculturation of workers before they join a cooperative enterprise. Share control and turnover can be part of the enterprise bylaws, but some limitation on transferability may need to be legislated to respect community capitalization and aggregate job stabilization.

The new enterprises should not be thought to be static. In fact, production flexibility should be planned into the enterprise from the beginning to adapt production inputs, process, and products to changing markets. Worker owners whose jobs are eliminated or technologically changed should be retrained and reassigned within the enterprise, with costs covered by normal attrition. That too will enhance labor force stability.

V. The past failures of worker cooperatives in the US is largely a problem of access to capital

Worker cooperatives have historically only been able to succeed in the US in limited sectors for limited periods. The longest surviving cooperatives have clustered in small, service delivery or small-scale consumer production firms. Curl (2009) estimates that there are roughly 300 worker cooperatives currently operating in the US. In such firms, initial capitalization may be low and coordination of management costs among a small number of workers also low, with little hierarchy associated with specialization.

Attempts to sustain large industrial cooperatives have failed most directly for three reasons. The first is the economics of start-up. In the 1970s, worker ownership, sometimes as cooperatives, was pushed as a way of buying out failing industries where no other buyer emerged to continue the enterprise, and thus the workers' jobs. This was cooperative by desperation. Predictably, failing industries usually failed, sometimes because former ownership had stripped assets or neglected reinvestment or had paid investor dividends instead of retaining earnings.

The second reason for failure relates to access to operating capital. Early cooperatives in the 19th century and more recent industrial attempts have failed not because initial capital could not be found, but because additional, conventional credit lines could not be secured for short-term production costs or modernization. Private banks, by and large, have more profitable short-term loans available, or at least perceive other loan options as less risky. Levin (1984, pp. 245–246) notes:

> One of the major difficulties faced by worker cooperatives and worker owned firms has been access to financial capital. Without the ability to borrow for purposes of meeting short-term cash flow needs or long-term expansion, these firms have faced substantial difficulties in surviving and competing in the marketplace.
>
> Both some truth and some self-fulfilling prophecy lead to bank choices.

The third reason for failure is legal inflexibility in transition. Large cooperatives in particular face difficult issues with labor attrition or turnover. Existing laws and the accompanying economic incentives often force marketable worker ownership shares to revert to non-participant shareholders. Over time the cooperative reverts to a public stock corporation. This was the fate for many of the plywood cooperatives in the Northwest US. These three problems are barriers to the success of any large worker owned and democratically managed enterprises.

This chapter does not consider individual worker stock purchases or the sham ownership involved in the increasing number of ESOPs, even those owning (but not controlling) a majority of stock shares. By splitting ownership by workers from control, which remains with management, ESOPS have been primarily used as anti-takeover or last-ditch capital raising devices, often in failing enterprises.

The political structure of federalism in the US makes past successful organizational examples of worker ownership elsewhere more or less inapplicable to what would be needed in the US, as well. This chapter thus casts some doubt on the universalization of the Mondragon experience in other country contexts, while applauding the Mondragon example, sharing its aims, and adapting its practices where context is favorable. In contrast, Community Syndicalism:

(1) would be located in locally distressed and deindustrialized communities;
(2) would not be subsidized from the regular state budget;
(3) would most likely be aimed initially at creating single enterprises aside from cooperative networks;
(4) would not raise capital from workers, who after all are unemployed in distressed communities;
(5) would still depend on the state budget for pensions and social insurance for workers;
(6) would require all employees to be or to become owners;
(7) would be established with no connection to the educational system, and aside from being in distressed communities, face hostility from the larger capitalist society; and
(8) would promote different, more cooperative relations contrasted to the adversary nature of the larger culture's normal management/worker hostility.

One concern might be that if this model catches on, communities not in decline might turn to Community Syndicalism and by competition reduce the value of the new model. Such a defeat is devoutly to be wished for – despite the great success of the Mondragon system, cooperatives have comprised less than 1% of the Spanish economy. Three results would follow. First, economic incentives would switch to maximize long-term stability, which is better for the world and earth. Second, the public versus private realm distinction underwriting massive worldwide wealth concentration and inequality would be undermined. Public subsidy in "profitable" private corporations communities would then have to compete in direct political tradeoff with Community Syndicates dedicated solely to job creation and community stability. Third, the experience of something approaching full democratic participation at work is likely to be a spreading malady leading to greater democratizing of political participation in non-market arenas. As Whyte and Whyte (1991, pp. 59–66) conclude, "Clearly, a strong case can be made for bringing greater democracy into the workplace in order to create a citizenry that participates in all of the major areas affecting its daily circumstances and its future." Too many tears would not be shed for private capital. Furthermore, traditional short-term competitive return may well be appropriate for high-risk production, research and development, organizational or product innovation, and other economic sectors, and thus it is likely to continue.

Some leaders in the labor movement decry worker ownership because worker owned firms are claimed to pacify workers as owners and undercut union wages. However, this outcome is unlikely to follow where worker-managed enterprises are (1) created to inhabit long-term market niches generating relatively high wage jobs, and (2) generated in failing communities, particularly where unionized employment has previously fled. Ownership of democratically managed enterprise may well, in fact, increase *social* militancy.

Such a development becomes more practicable, of course, with the expansion of networks of such firms, for example in Basque Spain. Azevedo and Gitahy (2010, p. 5) report that as of 2008, the network of cooperatives centered in Mondragon, Spain contained "106 cooperatives, with 97,773 workers, and a total invoice of 15.6 billion euros." However, even with a single enterprise in a local community, extensive planning and market analysis by independent intellectual cadres would be necessary to support workable community syndicates, given the costs of potential failure of such enterprises, the inability to easily diversify, and the need to build in production flexibility and adaptation for long-term job preservation. The major difficulties in reaching systemic networked outcomes are mainly political, the currently non-marketizable coordination costs of multi-location divisions of enterprise labor within global supply chains. These coordination issues have been of great recent concern to the Mondragon cooperative network.

VI. Conclusion: building resilient communities

Community Syndicalism is not a panacea for local communities destabilized by job loss. It is simply an alternative model of economic enterprise organization that is as yet untried. The US cannot simply replicate Mondragon, given the lack of an established internal bank or financing mechanism from within a larger cooperative structure, outside any existing cooperative network or cultural experience, and facing hostility from an educational system committed to replicating capitalism under separate federal jurisdictions, and within an adversarial society also committed to individualistic capitalism. But within the margins of desperately distressed communities, under available local legal mechanisms, it may be possible to demonstrate a different moral-economic alternative, paralleling the Mondragon strategy. By splitting asset ownership from enterprise ownership, it is possible to re-incentivize production for long-term stability of aggregate jobs; refocus on production for use; provide the tax and economic base for local institutions; localize participation in globalization of product markets and reduce the race to the bottom of labor standards; increase the experience of democratic participation affecting other areas of social life; and put the lie to the fictional public/private distinction underwriting inequality. Even under Tea Party control of current politics, it is not a utopian project to begin what will follow. We need to make persuasive and feasible what is to be done.

COMBINED BIBLIOGRAPHY

AARP Bulletin, 54(2), (2013) 36 (the study is by the Center on Budget and Policy Priorities).

Adams, K. L. (2005). "Indirect discrimination and the worker-carer: It's just not working". *Law Context: A Socio-Legal Journal*, 23, 18–44.

Adams, K. L. (2014). "The family responsibilities convention reconsidered: The work-family intersection in international law thirty years on". *Cardozo Journal of International and Comparative Law*, 22, 201.

Addison, J. T., Cotti, C. D., & Surfield, C. J. (2015). "Atypical jobs: Stepping stones or dead ends? Evidence from the NLSY79". *The Manchester School*, 83(1), 17–55. doi: 10.1111/manc.12052.

AFL-CIO (2015). *Trans-Pacific Partnership Free Trade Agreement.* Retrieved from: www.aflcio.org/Issues/Trade/Trans-Pacific-Partnership-Free-Trade-Agreement-TPP.

Age UK (2015). *Later Life in the United Kindgom.* Retrieved from: www.limeconsultancy.net/wp-content/uploads/2015/01/Later_Life_UK_factsheet.pdf. Age UK, London.

Agency of Labor (2009). *Ny matchmodel – hvorfor og hvordan?* Brief from the Agency of Labor, 2009–000–2943. Copenhagen: Agency of Labor.

Agency of Labor (2013). *Kontanthjælpsreformens betydning for voksne samt unge under 30 år med en erhvervskompetencegivende uddannelse.* Copenhagen: Agency of Labor.

Agustín, L. M. (2007). *Sex at the Margins: Migration, Labour Markets, and the Rescue Industry.* London, UK: Zed Books.

Ahmed, S. (2010). Orientations matter. In D. Coole & S. Frost (eds), *New Materialisms: Ontology, Agency and Politics.* Durham and London: Duke University Press, pp. 234–257.

Ahn, I. (2014). *Religious Ethics and Migration: Doing Justice to Undocumented Workers.* New York: Routledge.

Alaimo, S. & Hekman, S. (2008a). Introduction: Emerging models of materiality in feminist theory. In S. Alaimo & S. Hekman (eds), *Material Feminisms.* Bloomington and Indianapolis: Indiana University Press, pp. 1–22.

Alaimo, S. & Hekman, S. (eds.). (2008b). *Material Feminisms.* Bloomington and Indianapolis: Indiana University Press.

Albelda, R. (2001). "Welfare-to-work, farewell to families? US welfare reform and work/family debates". *Feminist Economics*, 7(1), 119–135.

Albelda, R., Drago, R. W. & Shulman, S. (2004). *Unlevel Playing Fields: Understanding Wage Inequality and Discrimination.* Cambridge, MA: Economic Affairs Bureau.

Allegretto, S., Doussard, M., Graham-Squire, D., Jacobs, K., Thompson, D. & Thompson, J. (2013). *Fast Food, Poverty Wages: The Public Cost of Low-Wage Jobs in the Fast-Food Industry.* Retrieved from UC Berkeley, Center for Research and Education website: http://laborcenter.berkeley.edu/fast-food-poverty-wages-the-public-cost-of-low-wage-jobs-in-the-fast-food-industry/.

Allen, J. (2007). When big brown shut down: The UPS strike ten years on. *International Socialist Review*, 55. Retrieved from: http://isreview.org/issues/55/55.shtml.

Anderson, B. (1983). *Imagined Communities.* London: Verso.

Anderson, B. (1993). *Britain's Secret Slaves.* London: Anti-Slavery International.

Anderson, B. (2000). *Doing the Dirty Work? The Global Politics of Domestic Labour.* London, UK: Zed Books.

Anderson, B. (2010a). "Migration, immigration controls and the fashioning of precarious workers". *Work, Employment & Society*, 24(2), 300–317, p. 312.

Anderson, B. (2010b). "Mobilizing migrants, making citizens: Migrant domestic workers as political agents". *Ethnic and Racial Studies*, 33(1), 60–74.

Andersen, J. (2013). *Socialforvaltningsret.* Copenhagen: Nyt Juridisk Forlag.

Andersen, N. Å. (2003). *Borgerens kontraktliggørelse.* Copenhagen: Hans Reitzels Forlag.

Anderson, L. (2003). "Sound bite legislation: The Employment Act 2002 and new flexible working "rights" for parents". *Industrial Law Journal*, 32, 37.

Andrees, B. Linden, van der, & Mariska, N. J. (2005). "Designing trafficking research from a labour market perspective: The ILO experience". *International Migration*, 43(1–2), 55–73.

Aneesh, A. (2012). "Negotiating globalization: Men and women of India's call centers". *Journal of Social Issues*, 68, no.3, 514–533. doi: 10.1111/j.1540-4560.2012.01761.x.

Ansley, F. (1993). "Standing rusty and rolling empty: Law, poverty and America's eroding industrial base". *Georgetown Law Journal*, 81, 1757, 1764.

Appelbaum, B. (2014, March 13). Labor market slack: A guide for the perplexed. *The New York Times Economix* [web log post]. Retrieved from: http://nyti.ms/1fu2ATg.

Appelbaum, E., Bernhardt, A. D. & Murnane, R. J. (eds). (2003). *Low-Wage America: How Employers Are Reshaping Opportunity in the Workplace.* New York: Russell Foundation.

Araki, T. (2002). *Labor and Employment Law in Japan.* Tokyo: Japanese Institute of Labor.

Araki, T. (2013). New forms of dispute resolution: Japan's labor tribunal system. In K. V. W. Stone & H. Arthurs (eds), *Rethinking Workplace Regulation: Beyond the Standard Contract of Employment.* New York: Russell Sage Foundation.

Arendt, H. (1986). *The Origins of Totalitarianism.* Andre Deutsch.

Arendt, H. (1998/1958). *The Human Condition.* Chicago: University of Chicago Press.

Arnow-Richman, R. (2007). "Public law and private process: Toward an incentivized organizational justice model of equal employment quality for caregivers". *Utah Law Review*, 25.

Arnow-Richman, R. (2009). "Response to working group on chapter 2 of the proposed restatement of employment law: Putting the restatement in its place". *Employee Rights and Employment Policy Journal*, 13, 143.

Arnow-Richman, R. (2010). "Incenting flexibility: The relationship between public law and voluntary sction in enhancing work/life balance". *Connecticut Law Review*, 42, 1081.

Arthurs, H. (2013). Cross-national legal learning: The uses of comparative labor knowledge, law, and policy. In K. V. W. Stone & H. Arthurs (eds), *Rethinking Workplace Regulation: Beyond the Standard Contract of Employment.* New York: Russell Sage Foundation, pp. 353–364.

Artz, M. (2012). "Beyond Wisconsin: Public employee union rights amidst attacks on public sector collective bargaining". *American University Labor & Employment Law Forum*, 2, 131–143.

Atkinson, C. & Lucas, R. (2013). "Policy & gender in adult social care work". *Public Administration*, 91, 159–173.

Atkinson, J. (1986). *Changing Work Patterns: How Companies Achieve Flexibility to Meet New Needs.* London: National Economic Development Office.

Avisen.dk (2016). *Er sagsbehandleren på jobcentret uddannet frisør eller tømrer?* Retrieved from: www.avisen.dk/er-din-sagsbehandler-paa-jobcenteret-uddannet-frisoe_391167.aspx.

Azevedo, A. & Gitahy, L. (2010). "The cooperative movement, self management, and competitiveness: The case of Mondragón Corporación Cooperativa". *Working USA*, 13, 5.

Backman, C. (2011). "Vocabularies of motive among employers conducting criminal background checks". *Acta Sociologica*, 54(1), 27–44.

Baines, D. (2004). "Caring for nothing: Work organization and unwaged labour in social services". *Work, Employment & Society*, 18, 267–295.

Bajaj, V., "Fatal fire in Bangladesh highlights the dangers facing garment workers," *The New York Times*, 26 November, 2012, p. A4.

Bakst, D. & Taubman, P. (2010). "From the great depression to the great recession: Advancing women's economic security through tough economic times and beyond". *Women's Rights Law Reporter*, 32(25), 40–41.

Bales, R. A., Hirsch, J. M. & Secunda, P. M. (2013). *Understanding Employment Law* (2nd edn). New York, NY: LexisNexis.

Ballam, D. (1996). "Exploding the original myth regarding employment-at-will: The true origins of the doctrine". *Berkeley Journal of Employment & Labor Law*, 17, 91–130.

Banerjee, S. (2012). *Time Trends in Poverty for Older Americans between 2001–2009*, Employee Benefits Research Institute (EBRI).

Bankovsky, M. (2012). *Perfecting Justice in Rawls, Habermas an Honneth: A Deconstructive Perspective.* London: Bloomsbury Academic.

Barad, K. (1998). "Getting real: Technoscientific practices and the materialization of reality". *Differences*, 10(2), 87–128.

Barad, K. (2008). Posthumanist performativity: Toward an understanding of how matter comes to matter. In S. Alaimo & S. Hekman (eds). *Material Feminisms.* Bloomington and Indianapolis: Indiana University Press, pp. 120–154.

Barnes, H. (2012, November 24). Organized labor's newest heroes: Strippers strip employers bare: Win unprecedented $13 million settlement [web log post]. Retrieved from: www.granted.com/blog/2012/11/24/organized-labors-newest-heroes-strippers-strippers-strip-employers-bare-win-unprecedented-13-million-settlement/.

Barnes, M. (2012). *Care in Everyday Life.* Bristol, UK: Policy Press.

Bartlett, K. (2009). "Making good on good intentions: The critical role of motivation in reducing implicit workplace discrimination". *Virginia Law Review*, 95, 1893, 1895–1896.

Bassiouni, M. C. (1996). "International crimes: Jus Cogen and Obligatio Erga Omnes". *Law and Contemporary Problems*, 59(4), 63–74.

Bauman, Z. (2004). *Wasted Lives: Modernity and Its Outcasts.* Cambridge: Polity.

Beecroft, A. (2011). *Report on Employment Law.* Department of Business, Innovation and Skills, HM Gov.

Beede, D., Julian, T., Langdon, D., McKittrick, G., Khan, B., & Doms, M. (2011). *US Dept. of Commerce, Women in STEM: A Gender Gap to Innovation.* Retrieved from: www.esa.doc.gov/sites/default/files/reports/documents/womeninstemagaptoinnovation8311.pdf.

Beers, D. (1975). "Extension versus invalidation of underinclusive statutes: A remedial alternative". *Columbia Journal of Law & Social Problems*, 12, 128–131.

Befort, S. (2002). "Labor and employment law at the Millennium: A historical review and critical assessment". *Boston College Law Review*, 43, 351.

Bell, A. & Bryson, C. (2006). Work-life balance: Still a "women's" issue? In A. Park, J. Curtice, K. Thomson, C. Bromley, M. Phillips, & M. Johnson (eds), *British Social Attitudes: The 22d Report*. London: Sage, 2005, p. 33.

Ben-Ishai, E. (2012). The new paternalism: Rethinking state intervention and autonomy. In E. Ben-Ishai (ed.), *Fostering Autonomy: A Theory of Citizenship, the State, and Social Service Delivery*. University Park, PA: Pennsylvania State University Press, pp. 43–68.

Ben-Ishai, E. (2013, October 23). San Francisco's new workplace law signals a shift. *Women's Enews*. Retrieved from: http://womensenews.org/story/equal-payfair-wage/131022/san-franciscos-new-workplace-law-signals-shift#.U0sB0KL6-pp.

Ben-Ishai, L. & Lower-Basch, E. (2014, August 28). A job creation and job quality agenda for labor day. Retrieved from: www.clasp.org/resources-and-publications/publication-1/A-job-creation-and-job-quality-agenda-for-Labor-Day-1.pdf.

Ben-Ishai, L., Matthews, H. & Levin-Epstein, J. (2014, March). Scrambling for Stability: The Challenges of Job Schedule Volatility and Child Care. Retrieved from: www.clasp.org/resources-and-publications/publication-1/2014-03-27-Scrambling-for-Stability-The-Challenges-of-Job-Schedule-Volat-.pdf.

Benhabib, S. (2011). *Dignity in Adversity: Human Rights in Troubled Times*. Malden, MA: Polity Press.

Berman, P. (2012). *Global Legal Pluralism: A Jurisprudence of Law beyond Borders*. Cambridge: Cambridge University Press.

Bernhardt, A. (2014, January 11). Labor standards and the reorganization of work: Gaps in data and research (UC Berkeley Institute for Research on Labor & Employment Working Paper No. 100–14). Retrieved from: http://escholarship.org/uc/item/3hc6t3d5.

Bernhardt, A., Milkman, R., Theodore, N., Heckathorn, D., Auer, M., DeFilippis, J., Gonzalez, A. L., Narro, V., Perelshteyn, J., Polson, D. & Spiller, M. (2009). Broken laws, unprotected workers: Violations of employment and labor law in America's cities. Retrieved from: www.unprotectedworkers.org/index.php/broken_laws/index.

Bessa, I., Forde, C., Moore, S., & Stuart, M. (2013). The national minimum wage, earnings and hours in the domiciliary care sector. *University of Leeds and Low Pay Commission*. Retrieved from: www.researchgate.net/profile/Mark_Stuart/publication/259574414_The_National_Minimum_Wage_Earnings_and_Hours_in_the_Domiciliary_Care_Sector/links/00b7d52caa84be30ef000000/The-National-Minimum-Wage-Earnings-and-Hours-in-the-Domiciliary-Care-Sector.pdf.

Best, R., Edelman, L., Krieger, L. & Eliason, S. (2011). "Multiple disadvantages: An empirical test of intersectionality theory in EEO litigation". *Law and Society Review*, 45, 991.

A Better Balance (2015). *Overview of Paid Sick Time Laws in the United States*. Retrieved from: www.abetterbalance.org/web/images/stories/Documents/sickdays/factsheet/PSDchart.pdf.

Bird, R. (2004). "Rethinking wrongful discharge: A continuum approach", *University of Cincinnati Law Review*, 73, 517.

Bird, R. (2005, Fall). "Employment as a relational contract", 8 *University of Pennsylvania Journal of Labor and Employment Law*, 149, 162.

Bisom-Rapp, S. (2011). "Learning from troubled times: Pursuing equality outside an antidiscrimination law frame by rethinking the promotion of safe work during the bush administration". *University of San Francisco Law Review*, 45, 603.

Bisom-Rapp, S. & Malcolm, S. (2014). "It's complicated: Age, gender, and lifetime discrimination against working women – the United States and the UK as examples". *Elder Law Journal*, 22, 1.

Bisom-Rapp, S. & Sargeant, M. (2016). *Lifetime Disadvantage, Discrimination and the Gendered Workforce*. Cambridge: Cambridge University Press.

Bjørnholt, M. (2013). "Vulnerability as a basis for justice and equality in the Nordic countries: Introduction". *Retfærd, årgang*, 36, 1–8.

Blackett, A. (2011). "Introduction: Regulating decent work for domestic workers". *Canadian Journal of Women & Law*, 23, 1.

Blades, L. (1967). "Employment at will vs individual freedom: On limiting the abusive exercise of employer power". *Columbia Law Review*, 67, 1404, 1433–1434.

Blaine, B. E. (2013). *Understanding the Psychology of Diversity*. (2nd edn). Thousand Oaks, CA: Sage Publications, pp. 177–178.

Blau, F. D., Ferber, M. A. & Winkler, A. E. (2006). *The Economics of Women, Men, and Work*. (5th edn). New York: Pearson Education.

Blau, F. D., Peter, B. & Albert, Y. H. L. (2012, April). *Trends in Occupational Segregation by Gender – 1970–2009: Adjusting for the Impact of Changes in the Occupational Coding System 27*. IZA Discussion Paper Series. *Demography* 50(2), 471–492.

Block, R. (1997). "Rethinking the National Labor Relations Act and zero-sum labor law: An industrial relations view". *Berkeley Journal of Employment & Labor Law*, 18, 30–55.

Blumrosen, A. (1978). "Strangers no more: All workers are entitled to just cause protection under title VII". *Industrial Relations Law Journal*, 2, 519.

Blumstein, A. & Nakamura K. (2009). "Redemption in the presence of widespread criminal background checks". *Criminology*, 47(2), 327–359.

Bock, R. A. (2005). "Secondary boycotts: Understanding NLRB interpretation of section 8(b)(4)(b) of the National Labor Relations Act". *University of Pennsylvania Journal of Labor and Employment Law*, 7(4), 905–969.

Bohan, M. (2011). Steering committee for equality between women & men, Council of Europe. *Study on 'Combating Gender Stereotypes in Education*, (December 2011), Retrieved from: www.coe.int/t/dghl/standardsetting/equality/03themes/gendermainstreaming/CDEG_2011_16_GS_education_en.pdf.

Bolton, S. C. & Wibberley, G. (2013). "Domiciliary care: The formal and informal labour process". *Sociology*, 48, 682.

Boris, E. & Jennifer, K. (2012). *Caring for America: Home Health Care Workers in the Shadow of the Welfare State*. New York: Oxford University Press.

Bornstein, S. (2012). "The law of gender stereotyping and the work-family conflicts of men". *Hastings Law Journal*, 63, 1297, 1334.

Borozdna, J. & Korkin, A. (2014, June 2). B2B: New law bans temporary agency work, but allows for secondment. *The Moscow Times*. Retrieved from: www.themoscowtimes.com/business/business_for_business/article/b2b-new-law-bans-temporary-agency-work-but-allows-for-secondment/501305.html.

Borrus, A., McNamee, M. & Zegel, S. (2002, June 10). "Corporate probes: A scorecard". *Business Week*, 3786, 42.

Borstelmann, T. (2012). *The 1970s: A New Global History from Civil Rights to Economic Inequality*. Princeton, NJ: Princeton University Press.

Bosniak, L. (2006). *The Citizen and the Alien: Dilemmas of Contemporary Membership*. Princeton, NJ: Princeton University Press.

Bouffard, A. (1986). "Emerging protection against retaliatory discharge: A public policy exception to the employment at-will doctrine in Maine". *Maine Law Review*, 38, 67, 70.

Boushey, H. (2014, March 12). Testimony before US Senate Committee on Health, Education, Labor, and Pensions on *From Poverty to Opportunity: How a Fair Minimum Wage Will Help Working Families Succeed* [video file]. Retrieved from: www.help.senate.gov/hearings/hearing/?id=51f3cf01-5056-a032-5266-935ef3b78cc9.

Boushey, H. & Glynn S. J. (2012, November). "There are significant costs to replacing employees", *Center for American Progress*, 16.

Bouvé, A. (2014, April 3). What if Wal-Mart paid its employees more? [video file]. *Marketplace*. Retrieved from: https://www.marketplace.org/2014/04/03/wealth-poverty/secret-life-food-stamp/video-what-if-wal-mart-paid-its-employees-more.

Bowden, P. (2000). "An 'ethic of care' in clinical settings: Encompassing 'feminine' and 'feminist' perspectives". *Nursing Philosophy*, 1, 36.

Bowman, J. & West, J. (2007). Ending civil service protections in Florida government: Experiences in state agencies. In J. S. Bowman & J. P. West (eds), *American Public Service: Radical Reform and the Merit System*. Boca Raton, FL: CRC Press, pp. 123–149.

Boydston, J. (1990). *Home & Work: Homework, Wages and the Ideology of Labour in the Early Republic*. Oxford: Oxford University Press.

Bradshaw, T., "Onshoring: Manufacturers capitalise on goods 'made in the USA'." *Financial Times*, 16 October, 2013, p. 2.

Bravo, E. (2007). *Taking on the Big Boys: Or Why Feminism Is Good for Family, Business, and the Nation*. CUNY: The Feminist Press. Kindle file.

Bravo, K. (2009). "Free labor! A labor liberalization solution to modern trafficking in humans". *Transnational Law and Contemporary Problems*, 18 (1), 545–618.

Brecher, J. (1986). "If all the people are banded together: The Naugatuck Valley Project". *Labor Research Review*, 1(9), 11.

Bredgaard, T. & Larsen, F. (2010). "External and Internal Flexicurity: Comparing Denmark and Japan", *Comparative Labor Law & Policy Journal*, 31, 745.

Brøgger, K. (2015). *The Faceless Masters of Higher Education. Governing Through Standards: The Bologna Process and the New Realities of Higher Education* (PhD dissertation). Danish School of Education, Aarhus University.

Brooks, J. (2003). Vulnerability, risk and adaptation: A conceptual framework, Tyndall Centre Working Paper no. 38, September 2003.

Brooks, J. (2012). Radio interview/article. Retrieved from: https://ww2.kqed.org/news/2012/06/28/interview-nancy-pelosi-on-health-care-decision/

Bronfenbrenner, K. (2005). Organizing women: The nature and process of union organizing efforts among US women workers since the mid-1990s. *Work and Occupations*, 32(4), 1–23. Retrieved from: http://digitalcommons.ilr.cornell.edu/articles/3.

Bronshtein, N. (n.d.). 200 Years of Immigration to the US. *Insightful Interaction*. Retrieved from: http://insightfulinteraction.com/immigration200years.html.

Brown, W. (2005). Neoliberalism and the end of liberal democracy. In *Edgework: Critical Essays on Knowledge and Politics*. Princeton: Princeton University Press, pp. 37–59.

Brown, W. (2015). *Undoing the Demos: Neoliberalism's Stealth Revolution*. New York: Zone Books.

Bumiller, K. (2013). Incarceration, welfare state, and the labor market nexus: The increasing significance of gender in the prison system. In B. Carlton & M. Segrave (eds), *Women Exiting Prison: Critical Essays on Gender, Post-Release Support*. London: Routledge, pp. 13–33.

Bureau of Labor Statistics (2014, May 22). Foreign born workers: Labor force characteristic – 2013. Retrieved from: www.bls.gov/news.release/pdf/forbrn.pdf.

Bureau of Labor Statistics (2015, January 23). Union members summary. Retrieved from: www.bls.gov/news.release/union2.nr0.htm.

Calmes, J., "Pacific Nations and US Endorse Giant Trade Pact," *The New York Times*, October 6, 2015.

Campbell, I., Whitehouse, G., & Baxter, J. (2009). Australia: casual employment, part-time employment and the resilience of the male-breadwinner model. In L.F. Vosko, M. MacDonald, I. Campbell (eds), *Gender and the Contours of Precarious Employment*. London: Routledge, pp. 60–75.

Campbell, I. & Peter, B. (2005). "Relative advantages: Casual employment and casualization in Australia and New Zealand". *New Zealand Journal of Employment Relations*, 30, 33.

Canetto, S. S. (2001). Older adult women: Issues, resources, and challenges. In R. K. Unger (ed), *Handbook of Psychology of Women and Gender*. Hoboken, NJ: John Wiley, p. 183.

Cantalupo, N. C. (2012). "Comparing single-sex and reformed coeducation: A constitutional law analysis". *San Diego Law Review*, 49, 725.

Capelli, P. H. & David N. (2001). "Do "high performance" work practices improve establishment-level outcomes?" *Industrial & Labor Relations Review*, 54, 737.

Cappelli, P. H. & Keller, J. (2013). "A study of the extent and potential causes of alternative employment arrangements". *Industrial & Labor Relations Review*, 66 (4), 874–901. doi:10.1177/001979391306600406.

Carens, J. (2008). "Live-in domestics, seasonal workers, and others hard to locate on the map of democracy". *Journal of Political Philosophy*, 16(4), 419.

Carbone, J. & Cahn, N. (2013). "Is marriage for rich men?" *Nevada Law Journal*, 13(2), 386–409.

Carr, H. (2013). Housing the vulnerable subject in law and politics. In M. A. Fineman, & A. Grear (eds), *Vulnerability: Reflections on a New Ethical Foundation for Law and Politics*. London, UK: Routledge, pp. 107–113.

Carlson, R. (2001). Why the Law Still Can't See an Employee When It Sees One and How It Ought to Stop Trying. *Berkeley Journal of Employment & Labor Law*, 22, 295.

Carstens, A. (1998). *Aktivering: Klientsamtaler og socialpolitik*. Copenhagen: Hans Reitzels Forlag.

Caruso, B. (2001). Decentralised social pacts, trade unions and collective bargaining – how labour law is changing. In M. Biagi (ed), *Towards a European Model of Industrial Relations? Building on the First Report of the European Commission*. The Hague, The Netherlands: Kluwer Law International, p. 193.

Caruso, B. (2013). The employment contract is dead! Hurrah for the work contract! A European perspective. In K. V. W. Stone & H. Arthurs (eds), *Rethinking Workplace Regulation: Beyond the Standard Contract of Employment*. New York: Russell Sage Foundation, pp. 95–112.

Casebeer, K. (1987). "Holder of the pen: An interview with Leon Keyserling on drafting the Wagner Act". *University of Miami Law Review*, 42, 285.

Casebeer, K. & Whalen, C. (2011, Faii). "Taking interdependence and production seriously: Toward mutual rationality and more useful law and economics". *University of Miami Law Review*, 66, 141–156.

Castles, S. & Miller, M. (2009). *The Age of Migration* (4th edn). New York: Guilford Press.

Castillo, M. K. (2014). "Independent contractor misclassification penalties under the Affordable Care Act". *Houston Journal of International Law*, 36(2), 323–340.

Caswell, D., Greg, M. & Jørgen, E. L. (2010). "Unemployed citizen or 'at risk' client? Classification systems and employment services in Denmark and Australia". *Critical Social Policy*, 30(3), 384–404.

Cauthen, N. (2007, October 2). Improving work supports: Closing the financial gap for low-wage workers and their families. *EPI Briefing Paper*. Retrieved from: www.sharedprosperity.org/bp198.html.

Cavico, F. (1992). "Employment at will and public policy". *Akron Law Review*, 25, 497, 502.

Chafer, C., "The government must find a way to enable parents to work," *The Guardian* (online), 29 August, 2010. Retrieved from: www.guardian.co.uk/commentisfree/2010/aug/29/woring-hours-childcare.

Chait, J. (2015). Stalin, Mao, Kristol. *The New Republic*, March 24, 2010 [blog last viewed on June 15, 2015]. Retrieved from: https://newrepublic.com/article/75148/stalin-mao-kristol.

Chang, G. & Kim, K. (2007). "Reconceptualizing approaches to human trafficking: New directions and perspectives from the field(s)". *Stanford Journal of Civil Rights and Civil Liberties*, 3(2), 317–345.

Charlesworth, S. (1997). "Enterprise bargaining and women workers: The seven Perils of flexibility". *Labor and Industry*, 2, 101.

Charny, D. (1996). "The changing workplace: The employee welfare state in transition". *Texas Law Review*, 74, 1601–1643.

Cho, E. H. & Smith, R. (2013, February). *Workers' Rights on ICE: How Immigration Reform Can Stop Retaliation and Advance Labor Rights – California Report*. Retrieved from National Employment Law Project website: http://nelp.org/content/uploads/2015/03/Workers-Rights-on-ICE-Retaliation-Report-California.pdf.

Choi, C. & Matthews, K., "Fast-Food Strikes Set for Cities Nationwide," *The Capital* (Annapolis, MD), August 29, 2013, p. A3.

Chuang, J. A. (2006). "The United States as Global Sheriff: Using unilateral sanctions to combat human trafficking". *Michigan Journal of International Law*, 27(2), 441–494.

Chuang, J. A. (2010). "Rescuing human trafficking from ideological capture: Prostitution reform and anti-trafficking law and policy". *University of Pennsylvania Law Review*, 158(1), 1655–1725.

Chuang, J. A. (2014). "Exploitation creep and the unmaking of human trafficking law". *American Journal of International Law*, 108(4), 609–649.

Clark, K., "US retailers see fallout from Bangladesh factory fire," *Marketplace*, 28 November, 2012. Retrieved from: https://www.marketplace.org/2012/11/28/world/us-retailers-see-fallout-bangladesh-factory-fire.

Clayton, G. (2012). *Immigration and Asylum Law*. (5th edn). Oxford: Oxford University Press.

Clinton, W. J. (1992). The New Covenant, Democratic presidential nomination acceptance speech, 1992 Democratic National Convention. Retrieved from: www.americanrhetoric.com/speeches/wjclinton1992dnc.htm.

Cobble, D. S. (2004). *The Other Women's Movement: Workplace Justice and Social Rights in Modern America*. Princeton: Princeton University Press.

Cobble, D. S. (2007). Introduction. In D. Cobble (ed), *The Sex of Class: Women Transforming American Labor*. Ithaca: Cornell University Press, pp. 1–12.

Cohen, L. (1990). *Making a New Deal: Industrial Workers in Chicago, 1919–1939*. Cambridge, UK: Cambridge University Press.

Cohen, L. (2003). *A Consumers' Republic: The Politics of Mass Consumption in Postwar America*. New York: Alfred A. Knopf.

Cohen, P., "March data shows signs of slowing in job gains," *The New York Times*, April 4, 2015, p. B1.

Cohen, P., "December Gains Wrap Up 2 Years of Strong Hiring," *The New York Times*, January 9, 2016.

Cohn, D., Livingston, G. & Wang, W. (2014, April 8). After decades of decline, a rise in stay-at-home mothers. Retrieved from: http://www.pewsocialtrends.org/2014/04/08/after-decades-of-decline-a-rise-in-stay-at-home-mothers/.

Colish, M. (1985). *The Stoic Tradition from Antiquity to the Middle Ages*. vol. 1. Leiden: Brill.

Colish, M. (1990). *The Stoic Tradition from Antiquity to the Middle Ages*. vol. 2. Leiden: Brill.

Collins, H. (2005). The right to flexibility. In J. Conaghan & K. Rittich (eds), *Labor Law, Work, and Family 99*. Oxford: Oxford University Press, pp. 99–124.

Collins, J. (2008). The specter of slavery: Workfare and the economic citizenship of poor women. In B. Williams, & M. Leonardo (eds), *New Landscapes of Inequality: Neoliberalism and the Erosion of Democracy in America*. Santa Fe, NM: SAR Press, pp. 131–151.

Collinson, D. L. (1999). "'Surviving the rigs': Safety and surveillance on North Sea oil installations". *Organization Studies*, 20, 579–600. doi: 10.1177/0170840699204003.

Columbia Law School Sexuality and Gender Law Clinic (2010, May). *Sent Away: The Trafficking of Young Girls and Women Within the Family Unit.* Retrieved from: http://www.law.columbia.edu/sites/default/files/legacy/files/sent_away_columbia_sglc_may_2010.pdf.

Colvin, A. (2013). Employment conflict in a post-standard contract world. In K. V. W. Stone & H. Arthurs (eds), *Organizational Primacy: Employment Conflict in a Post-standard Contract World.* New York: Russell Sage Foundation, pp. 194–210.

Compa, L. (2000). Unfair advantage: Workers' freedom of association in the United States under international human rights standards. *Human Rights Watch.* Retrieved from: http://digitalcommons.ilr.cornell.edu/cgi/viewcontent.cgi?article=1332&context=articles.

Confederation of British Industry (2006, April). *Response to Draft Regulation on Maternity and Adoption Leave and Flexible Working.* Retrieved from: www.berr.gov.uk/consultations/page24647.html.

Congressional Budget Office (2014, February). *Labor Market Effects of the Affordable Care Act: Updated Estimates.*

Connelly, C. E. & Gallagher, D. G. (2004). "Emerging trends in contingent work research". *Journal of Management*, 30, 959–983. doi: 10.1016/j.jm.2004.06.008.

Connelly, C. E., Wilkin, C. L. & Gallagher, D. G. (2011). Understanding underemployment among contingent workers. In D. C. Maynard & D. C. Feldman (ds), *Underemployment: Psychological, Economic, and Social Challenges.* New York, NY: Springer, pp. 145–162.

Coole, D. & Frost, S. (eds). (2010). *New Materialisms: Ontology, Agency and Politics.* Durham and London: Duke University Press.

Countouris, N. & Horton, R. (2009). "The Temporary Agency Work Directive: Another Broken Promise?" *Industrial Law Journal*, 38, 329.

Council of Europe Parliamentary Assembly Committee on Migration, Refugees and Population. *Report on Protecting Migrant Women in the Labour Market*, Doc. 12549, 24 March 2011.

Cover, R. (1982). "The Supreme Court, 1981 term – foreword: Nomos and narrative". *Harvard Law Review*, 97, 4.

Coverdill, J. E. & Oulevey, P. (2007). "Getting contingent work: Insights into on-call work, matching processes, and staffing technology from a study of substitute teachers". *The Sociological Quarterly*, 48(3), 533–557. doi: 10.1111/j.1533-8525.2007.00088.x.

Covert, B. (2015, February 19). Walmart will raise its minimum wage to $10 an hour. *ThinkProgress.* Retrieved from: http://thinkprogress.org/economy/2015/02/19/3624666/walmart-minimum-wage-increase/.

Cowie, J. (1999). *Capital Moves: RCA's Seventy-Year Quest for Cheap Labor.* Ithaca, NY: Cornel University Press.

Crain, M. & Matheny, K. (2001). "Labor's identity crisis". *California Law Review*, 89, 1767–1846.

Creighton, B. & Stewart, A. (2010). *Labour Law* (5th ed). Sydney: Federation Press.

Crenshaw, K. (1991). "Mapping the margins: Intersectionality, identity politics, and violence against women of color". *Stanford Law Review*, 43(6), 1241.

Crowley, M. (2014). "Being beyond politics, with Jean Luc Nancy". *Qui Parle*, 22(2), 123–145.

Crown Prosecution Service, Legal Guidance (2009). *Slavery, Servitude and Forced or Compulsory Labour.* Retrieved from: www.cps.gov.uk/legal/s_to_u/slavery_servitude_and_forced_or_compulsory_labour/.

Culinary Workers Union Local 226 (n.d.). *Our Union.* Retrieved from: www.culinaryunion226.org/union.

Cullen, H. (2006). "*Siliadin v France*: Positive obligations under article 4 of the European Convention on Human Rights". *Human Rights Law Review*, 6, 585.

Cunningham-Cook, M., "Chicago teachers push back against neoliberal education reform," *The Nation*, 11 September, 2012. Retrieved from: www.thenation.com/article/169859/chicago-teachers-push-back-against-neoliberal-education-reform.

Cunningham-Parmeter, K. (2014). "(Un)equal protection: Why gender equality depends on discrimination". *Northwestern University Law Review*, 109(1), 1–56.

Cunningham-Parmeter, K. (2016). From Amazon to Uber: defining employment in the modern economy. *Boston University Law Review*, 96, 1673.

Cunningham, P. (2014). "Artists benefit from obamacare". *Politico*, March 31. Retrieved from: www.politico.com/story/2014/03/self-employed-artists-actors-benefit-obamacare-105179.

Curl, J. (2012). *For all the People: Uncovering the Hidden History of Cooperation, Cooperative Movements, and Communalism in the United States*. Oakland, CA: PM Press, pp. 351–352.

Cyrus, N. (2008). Being illegal in Europe: Strategies and policies for fairer treatment of migrant domestic workers. In Lutz (ed), *Migration and Domestic Work: A European Perspective on a Global Theme*. New York: Ashgate, pp. 177–194.

Danhard, E. (2006). *Individual and Collective Dismissals in Labour Law and Productive Decentralization – Sweden: Outsourcing of Work and Labour Hiring*, XVIII World Congress of Labour Law & Social Security.

Dannin, E. (2005). "NLRA values, labor values, American values". *Berkeley Journal of Employment & Labor Law*, 26(2), 223–274.

Dannin, E. (2006). *Taking Back the Workers' Law: How to Fight the Assault on Labor Rights*. Ithaca, NY: Cornell University Press.

Dannin, E. (2012). "Privatizing government services in the era of ALEC and the Great Recession". *University of Toledo Law Review*, 43, 503–531.

Dauvergne, C. (2008). *Making People Illegal: What Globalization Means for Migration and Law*. Cambridge: Cambridge University Press.

Dauvergne, C. & Marsden, S. (2012). "The ideology of temporary labour migration in the post-global era". *Citizenship Studies, 18*(2), 224–242.

Dekutoski, D. A. (2008). Olga M. Madar: Lifelong activist. Doctoral dissertation, Wayne State University.

DeParle, J. (2004). The accidental program: Washington, 1935–1991. In *American Dream: Three Women, Ten Kids, and a Nation's Drive to End Welfare*. New York: Viking, pp. 85–100.

DePillis, L., "This is what a job in the US's new manufacturing industry looks like," *The Washington Post Wonkblog*, 11 March, 2014. Retrieved from: https://www.washingtonpost.com/news/wonk/wp/2014/03/09/this-is-what-a-job-in-the-u-s-new-manufacturing-industry-looks-like/.

DePillis, L., "It's not just fast food: The fight for $15 is for everyone now," *The Washington Post*, 4 December, 2014. Retrieved from: www.washingtonpost.com/news/storyline/wp/2014/12/04/its-not-just-fast-food-the-fight-for-15-is-for-everyone-now/.

DeWitt, L. (1996). *Research Note #1: The Origins of the Three-Legged Stool Metaphor for Social Security*, SSA Historian's Office. Retrieved from: www.ssa.gov/history/stool.html.

De La Torre, M. (2009). *Trails of Terror and Hope*. Maryknoll: Orbis.

De Sousa, S. (2002). *Toward a New Legal Common Sense: Law, Globalization, and Emancipation*. Cambridge: Cambridge University Press.

De Ville, J. (2011). *Jacques Derrida: Law as Absolute Hospitality*. New York: Routledge.

Demos (2012). Pay gap between CEOs and average workers in the United States in 2012, by sector. In *Statista – The Statistics Portal*. Retrieved from: www.statista.com/statistics/318102/ceo-to-worker-compensation-ratio-in-the-us/.

Department for Business, Innovation and Skills (DBIS) (2012a). *Consultation on Modern Workplaces, Government Response on Flexible Working*, November 2012. Retrieved from: www.gov.uk/government/consultations/consultation-on-modern-workplaces.

Department for Business, Innovation and Skills (DBIS) (2012b). *Consultation on Modern Workplaces, Government Response – Equality Impact Assessment (EQIA) on Flexible Parental Leave and Flexible Working*, November 2012. Retrieved from: https://www.gov.uk/government/consultations/consultation-on-modern-workplaces.

Department of Health (2016). *Care and Support Statutory Guidance.* Retrieved from: http://webarchive.nationalarchives.gov.uk/+/www.dh.gov.uk/en/SocialCare/Socialcarereform/Personalisation/Directpayments/DH_076522.

Department of Health (2009). *Guidance on Direct Payments for Community Care, Services for Carers and Children's Services.* Retrieved from: http://webarchive.nationalarchives.gov.uk/+/www.dh.gov.uk/en/SocialCare/Socialcarereform/Personalisation/Directpayments/DH_076522.

Department of Health (2010, November). *A Vision for Adult Social Care: Capable Communities and Active Citizens.* Retrieved from: www.cpa.org.uk/cpa_documents/vision_for_social_care2010.pdf.

Department of Trade and Industry (DTI) (2000). *Work and Parents: Competitiveness and Choice*, Stationery Office. Retrieved from: www.tsoshop.co.uk/bookstore.asp?Action=Book&ProductId=9780101500524.

Department of Trade and Industry (DTI) (2005a). *Work and Families: Choice and Flexibility: A Consultation Document*, DTI, 2005. Retrieved from: http://webarchive.nationalarchives.gov.uk/20060715135645/dti.gov.uk/files/file16317.pdf.

Department of Trade and Industry (DTI) (2005b). *Work and Families: Choice and Flexibility: Government Response to Public Consultation*, DTI 2005. Retrieved from: www.berr.gov.uk/files/file16317.pdf.

Department of Trade and Industry (DTI) (2006, November 9). *Draft Flexible Working Regulations: Summary of Responses and Government Response to the 2006 Consultation.*

Derrida, J. (2005). *On Touching – Jean Luc Nancy.* Stanford: Stanford University Press.

Devisch, I. (2006). The sense of being (-) with Jean Luc Nancy. *Culture Machine*, 8. Retrieved from: http://www.culturemachine.net/index.php/cm/article/view/36/44.

Devisch, I. (2011). "Doing justice to existence: Jean Luc Nancy and 'The size of humanity.' " *Law Critique*, 22, 1–13.

Devisch, I. & Wynn, F. (2010). "Meeting a patient as a singular event: A philosophical reflection". *Aporia: The Nursing Journal*, 2(1), 18–23.

Dey, M., Houseman, S. & Polivka, A. (2010). What do we know about contracting out in the United States? Evidence from household and establishment surveys. In K. Abraham, J. R. Spletzer & M. J. Harper (eds), *Labor in the New Economy.* Chicago, IL: The University of Chicago Press, pp. 267–308.

Dimatteo, L., Bird, R. C. & Jason, A. (2011). "Colquitt: Justice, employment, and the psychological contract". *Oregon Law Review*, 90, 449, 459.

Donald, C. C. (2012). "At-will employment: The arc of justice bends towards the doctrine's rejection". *University of San Francisco Law Review*, 46, 655.

Dottridge, M. (2006). Introduction. In Global Alliance Against Traffic in Women (eds), *Collateral Damage: The Impact of Anti-trafficking Measures on Human Rights Around the World* (1–27). Retrieved from: www.gaatw.org/Collateral%20Damage_Final/singlefile_CollateralDamagefinal.pdf.

Dottridge, M. (2007) Introduction. In *Collateral Damage: the Impact of Anti-Trafficking Measures on Human Rights around the World* 17 (Global Alliance Against Traffic in Women edn).

Doussard, M. (2013). *Degraded Work: The Struggle at the Bottom of the Labor Market.* Minneapolis, MN: University of Minnesota Press.

Doussard, M., Peck J. & Theodore, N. (2009). "After deindustrialization: Uneven growth and economic inequality in "postindustrial" Chicago". *Economic Geography*, 85(2), 183–207.

Doyle, A. (2016, January). Federal and state minimum wage rates for 2016. *About Careers*. Retrieved from: http://jobsearch.about.com/od/compensation/fl/minimum-wage-rates-2016.htm.

Drago, R. & Fazioli, J. (2003, March 27). Unions and work and family integration, a Sloan work and family encyclopedia entry. *Sloan Work and Family Research Network*. Retrieved from: http://wfnetwork.bc.edu/encyclopedia_entry.php?id=259&area=All.

Draus, P. J., Roddy, J. K. & Greenwald, M. (2010). "A hell of a life: Addiction and marginality in post-industrial Detroit". *Social & Cultural Geography*, 11(7), 663–680.

Drummonds, H. H. (2009). "Reforming labor law by reforming labor law preemption doctrine to allow the states to make more labor relations policy". *Louisiana Law Review*, 70(1), 97–191.

Duhigg, C. & Bradsher, K., "How US lost out on iPhone work," *The New York Times*, 22 January, 2012, p. A1.

Duncan, Jr. J. (1999). "The indentured servants of academia: The adjunct faculty dilemma and their limited legal remedies". *Indiana Law Journal*, 74, 513–586.

Durkalski, J. A. (2009). "Fixing economic flexibilization: A role for flexible work laws in the workplace policy agenda". *Berkeley Journal of Employment and Labor Law*, 30, 381.

Eaglesham, J., "Flexible work rule lays wisp of a cloud on positive mood," *The Financial Times*, London, 26 May, 2010. Retrieved from: www.ft.com.

Edelman, L. B., Abraham, S. E. & Erlanger, H. S. (1992). "Professional construction of law: The inflated threat of wrongful discharge". *Law and Society Review*, 26(47), 61–67, 79–80.

Edelman, L. B., Krieger, L. H., Eliason, S. R., Albiston, C. R. & Mellema, V. (2011). "When organizations rule: Judicial deference to institutionalized employment structures". *American Journal of Sociology*, 117(3), 888–954.

Edelman, L. B. & Suchman, M. C. (1997). "The legal environments of organizations". *Annual Review of Sociology*, 23(1), 479–515.

Edwards, H. (2010). In particular at chapter 4, equality and non-discrimination on the basis of sex. In *Violence against Women under International Human Rights Law*. Cambridge: Cambridge University Press, pp. 140–197.

Edwards, H. & Seitz, V. (1998). From labor law to employment law: What next?. In M. Neufeld & J. McKelvey (eds), P. Zamoiski (assoc ed). *Industrial Relations at the Dawn of the New Millennium*. Ithaca: New York State School of Industrial and Labor Relations, Cornell University, pp. 162–179.

Eigen, Z., Menillo, N. F. & Sherwyn, D. S. (2012). "Shifting the paradigm of the debate: A proposal to eliminate at-will employment and implement a "Mandatory Arbitration Act"." *Indiana Law Journal*, 87, 271.

Eisenberg, D. T. (2010). "Shattering the Equal Pay Act's glass ceiling." *SMU Law Review*, 63, 17.

Eisenberg, D. T. (2012). "*Wal-mart stores v Dukes*: Lessons for the quest for equal pay". *New England Law Review*, 46, 229.

Elcioglu, E. F. (2010). "Producing precarity: The temporary staffing agency in the labor market". *Qualitative Sociology*, 33(2), 117–136.

Ellerman, D. & Pitegoff, P. (1982–1983). "The democratic corporation: The new worker cooperative statute in Massachusetts". *N.Y.U. Review of Law & Social Change*, 11, 441.

Elster, J. (1983). Exploitation, freedom, and justice. In J. R. Pennock & J. W. Chapman (eds), *Marxism: Nomos XXVI*. New York: NYU Press, pp. 277–304.

Elwell, C. K. (2014, January 8). *Inflation and the Real Minimum Wage: A Fact Sheet*. Retrieved from: www.fas.org/sgp/crs/misc/R42973.pdf.

Entmacher, J., Robbins, K. G., Vogtman, J. & Frohlich, L. (2013). *Insecure & Unequal: Poverty and Income among Women and Families 2000–2012*. National Women's Law Center. Retrieved from: https://nwlc.org/resources/insecure-unequal-poverty-among-women-and-families-2000-2012/

Epp, C. R. (2009). *Making Rights Real: Activists, Bureaucrats, and the Creation of the Legalistic State.* Chicago, IL: University of Chicago Press.

Epstein, R. (1984). "In defense of the contract at will". *University of Chicago Law Review,* 51, 947.

Equal Employment Opportunity Commission (EEOC) (2007). Enforcement guidance: Unlawful disparate treatment of workers with caregiving responsibilities (23/5/07). Retrieved from: www.eeoc.gov/policy/docs/caregiving.html; EEOC Notice # 915.002.

Eskelinen, L, Olesen, S. P. & Caswell, D. (2010). "Client contribution in negotiations on employability – categories revised?" *International Journal of Social Welfare,* 19, 330.

Eskow, R. (2015). *5 Reasons We Need Medicare for All,* Issue paper on candidate's website. Retrieved from: https://berniesanders.com, posted July 21, 2015.

Estes, C., O'Neill, T. & Heidi, H., Inst. for Women's Pol'y Res. et al. (2012, May). *Breaking the Social Security Glass Ceiling: A Proposal to Modernize Women's Benefits.* Retrieved from: https://iwpr.org/publications/breaking-the-social-security-glass-ceiling-a-proposal-to-modernize-womens-benefits/.

Estlund, C. (2002). "How wrong are employees about their rights, and why does it matter?" *N.Y.U. Law Review,* 77(6), 8.

EU Fundamental Rights Agency (2011). *Migrants in an Irregular Situation Employed in Domestic Work: Fundamental Rights Challenges for the European Union and Its Member States (EU FRA).* Retrieved from: http://fra.europa.eu/en/publication/2012/migrants-irregular-situation-employed-domestic-work-fundamental-rights-challenges.

European Commission (2004). *Final Report Precarious Employment in Europe: A Comparative Study of Labour Market Related Risks in Flexible Economies.* Retrieved from: https://cordis.europa.eu/pub/citizens/docs/kina21250ens_final_esope.pdf.

European Commission (2013). Tackling the Gender Pay Gap in the European Union. Retrieved from: http://ec.europa.eu/justice/gender-equality/files/gender_pay_gap/gpg_brochure_2013_final_en.pdf.

European Foundation for the Improvement of Living and Working Conditions (2009). *Temporary Agency Work and Collective Bargaining in the EU.* Retrieved from: www.eurofound.europa.eu/sites/default/files/ef_publication/field_ef_document/ef0899en.pdf.

Evans, M. (2014, February 27). Trickle of jobs returning to US shores could soon become a torrent. *Forbes* [web log post]. Retrieved from: www.forbes.com/sites/allbusiness/2014/02/27/trickle-of-jobs-returning-to-u-s-shores-could-soon-become-a-torrent/.

Ewins, J. (2015, December 16). *Independent Review of the Overseas Domestic Worker Visa.* Retrieved from: www.gov.uk/government/uploads/system/uploads/attachment_data/file/486532/ODWV_Review_-_Final_Report__6_11_15_.pdf (accessed on 2016, February 2).

Fairchild, A. (2003). *Science at the Borders: Immigrant Medical Inspection and the Shaping of the Modern Industrial Labor Force.* Baltimore: The Johns Hopkins University Press.

FairWork Ombudsman *Long Service Leave.* Retrieved from: https://www.fairwork.gov.au/leave/long-service-leave.

Fedoreev, V. & Huet, C. (2014, June 3). New law bans outstaffing and sets a framework for the regulation of temporary employment and intragroup secondments. *Lexology.* Retrieved from: www.lexology.com/library/detail.aspx?g=d7eefccb-e6a7-4875-84f2-92b9f9107b9f.

Feinberg, L., Susan, C. R., Ari, H. & Rita, C. (2011, June). AARP Public Pol'y Inst. *Valuing the Invaluable: 2011 Update – The Growing Contributions and Costs of Family Caregiving.* Retrieved from: https://assets.aarp.org/rgcenter/ppi/ltc/i51-caregiving.pdf.

Feuer, A., "Life on $7.25 an hour." *The New York Times,* 1 December, 2013, p. MB1.

Fienman, J. M. (1976). "The development of the employment at will rule". *American Journal of Legal History,* 20, 118.

Fineman, J. (2008). "The inevitable demise of the implied employment contract". *Berkeley Journal of Employment and Labor Law*, 29, 345.

Fineman, J. (2013a). "Cronyism, corruption, and political intrigue: A new approach for old problems in public employment law". *Charleston Law Review*, 8, 51.

Fineman, J. (2013b). "The vulnerable subject at work: A new perspective on the employment at-will debate". *Southwestern Law Review*, 43, 275.

Fineman, M. A. (1995). *The Neutered Mother, the Sexual Family, and Other Twentieth Century Tragedies*. New York, Routledge.

Fineman, M. A. (2004). *The Autonomy Myth*. New York: The New Press.

Fineman, M. A. (2005). *The Autonomy Myth: A Theory of Dependency*. New York: The New Press.

Fineman, M. A. (2008). "The vulnerable subject: Anchoring equality in the human condition". *Yale Journal of Law and Feminism*, 20, 1–23.

Fineman, M. A. (2010). "The vulnerable subject and the responsive state". *Emory Law Journal*, 60, 251–275.

Fineman, M. A. (2012). "Beyond identities: The limits of an antidiscrimination approach to equality". *Boston University Law Review*, 92, 1713.

Fineman, M. A. (2013a). " 'Elderly' as vulnerable: Rethinking the nature of individual and societal responsibility". *Elder Law Journal*, 20, 71–111.

Fineman, M. A. (2013b). Equality, autonomy and the vulnerable subject in law and politics. In M. A. Fineman & A. Greer (eds), *Vulnerability: Reflections on a New Ethical Foundation for Law and Politics*. Farnham: Ashgate, pp. 13–27.

Fineman, M. A. (2013c). "Feminism, masculinities, and multiple identities". *Nevada Law Journal*, 13, 619.

Fineman, M. A. (2015). "Equality and difference – the restrained state". *Alabama Law Review*, 66, 23.

Fineman, M. A. & Grear, A. (eds). (2013). *Vulnerability: Reflections on a New Ethical Foundation for Law and Politics*. Farnham: Ashgate.

Fink, L., "What's the matter with Indiana?" *Salon*, 7 February, 2012. Retrieved from www.salon.com/2012/02/07/whats_the_matter_with_indiana/.

Finnis, J. (2010). "Law as idea, ideal and duty". In *Jurisprudence*, 1.2, 245–251.

Finnis, J. (2011a). *Natural Law and Natural Rights*. Oxford: Oxford University Press.

Finnis, J. (2011b). *Collected Essays of John Finnis*. 4 volumes. Oxford: Oxford University Press.

Firestein, F. & Dones, N. (2007). Unions fight for work and family policies – not for women only. In D. Cobble (ed), *The Sex of Class: Women Transforming American Labor*. Ithaca: Cornell University Press, pp. 140–154

Fischl, R. M. (2002). A domain into which the King's writ does not seek to run: Workplace justice in the shadow of employment-at-will. In J. Conanghan, R. M. Fischl & K. Klare (eds), *Labor Law in an Era of Globalization: Transformative Practices and Possibilities*. Oxford: Oxford University Press, p. 253.

Fisk, C. & Chemerinsky, E. (2013). "Political speech and associational rights after Knox v SEIU, local 1000". *Cornell Law Review*, 98, 1023.

Fiss, O. M. (2001). The autonomy of law. *Yale Journal of International Law* 26, 517.

Fitzpatrick, P. (2004). "Juris-fiction: Literature and the law of the law", *Ariel: A Review of International English Literature* 35, 1–2.

Fletcher, M. A., "Minimum wage hike would cut food stamp spending by $4.6 billion a year," *The Washington Post*, 5 March, 2014. Retrieved from: https://.washingtonpost.com/business/economy/report-minimum-wage-hike-would-cut-food-stamp-spending-by-46-billion-a-year/2014/03/04/150e4bfa-a3db-11e3-a5fa-55f0c77bf39c_story.html?utm_term=.97c434e636d4.

Fletcher, M. & Sullivan, S. (2012, December 11). "Michigan enacts right-to-work law, dealing blow to unions". *Washington Post.* Retrieved from: www.washingtonpost.com/business/economy/michigan-enacts-right-to-work-law-dealing-blow-to-unions/2012/12/11/bb9f8e5a-43ad-11e2–9648-a2c323a991d6_story.html.

Fletcher, R., Marie, F. & Julie, M. (2008). "Legal embodiment: Analysing the body of healthcare law". *Medical Law Review,* 16, 321–345.

Flexibility.co.uk (2009, April 6). *10 Million Parents Now Have "Right to Request" Flexible Working.* Retrieved from: www.flexibility.co.uk/flexwork/general/flexible-right-to-request-2009.htm.

Folbre, N. (2001). *The invisible heart: Economics and family values.* New York: The New Press.

Folbre, N. (2013, August 26). *Full Time, Part Time, Good Jobs, Bad.* N.Y. Times Economix. Retrieved from: https://economix.blogs.nytimes.com/2013/08/26/full-time-part-time-good-jobs-bad/?_r=0.

Foner, E. (1995a). *Free Soil, Free Labor, Free Men: The Ideology of the Republican Party before the Civil War.* New York: Oxford University Press.

Foner, E. (1995b). The idea of free labor in nineteenth century America. In *Free Soil, Free Labor, Free Men.* New York: Oxford University Press, pp. ix–xiii.

Forbath, W. (1991). *Law and the Shaping of the American Labor Movement.* Cambridge, MA: Harvard University Press.

Forbath, W. (2001). "The new deal constitution in exile". *Duke Law Journal,* 51, 165.

Foster, J. B. (2010). "The financialization of accumulation". *Monthly Review,* 62(5), 1–17.

Franklin, C. (2010). "The anti-stereotyping principle in constitutional sex discrimination law". *New York University Law Review,* 85, 84–172.

Frantz, J. (1997). "Market ordering versus statutory control of termination decisions: A case for the inefficiency of just cause dismissal requirements". *Harvard Journal of Law and Public Policy,* 20, 555, 560.

Fraser, N. & Gordon, L. (1994). "A genealogy of dependency: Tracing a keyword of the US welfare state". *Signs,* 19(2), 309–336.

Freed, M. G. & Polsby, D. D. (1989). "Just cause for termination rules and economic efficiency". *Emory Law Journal,* 38, 1097.

Freedland, M. (2003). *The Personal Employment Contract.* Oxford: Oxford University Press.

Freeman, R. B. & Rogers, J. (2006). *What Workers Want.* (Updated ed.). Ithaca, NY: Cornell University Press.

Friedman, G. (2010). "The crisis and the economists: A guide to the perplexed". *Labor History,* 51, 345, 352.

Friedman, M. (1962). *Capitalism and Freedom.* Chicago, IL: University of Chicago Press.

Friedman, S. & Greenhaus, J. H. (2000). *Work and Family – Allies or Enemies? What Happens When Business Professionals Confront Life Choices.* Newyork: Oxford University Press.

Frost, A. C. (2013). Introduction: Collective bargaining under duress. In H. R. Stranger, P. F. Clark, & A. C. Frost (eds), *Collective Bargaining under Duress: Case Studies of Major North American Industries.* Ithaca, NY: Cornell University Press, pp. 1–8.

Fudge, J. (2011). "Global care chains, employment agencies, and the conundrum of jurisdiction: Decent work for domestic workers in Canada". *Canadian Journal of Women & Law,* 23, 235.

Fudge, J. (2012). "Global care chains: Transnational migrant care workers". *International Journal of Comparative Labour Law and Industrial Relations,* 28(1), 63.

Fudge, J., Mccrystal, S. & Sankaran, K. (2012). *Challenging the Legal Boundaries of Work Regulation.* Hart Publishing.

Fudge, J. & Owens, R. (eds) (2006). *Precarious Work, Women, and the New Economy: The Challenge to Legal Norms.* Oxford: Hart Publishing.

Fuller, L. (1969). *The Morality of Law* (revised edn). New Haven: Yale University Press, 159–171.

Fuller, M. & Goriunova, O. (2012). Worse luck. In B. Rosi & P. Pisters (eds), *Revisiting Normativity with Deleuze*. London and New York: Bloomsbury Academic.

Galotti, M. (2009). The gender dimension of domestic work in Western Europe, No. 96 International Migration Papers, International Labour Office, Geneva, in particular, pp. 9–13. Retrieved from: https://ec.europa.eu/anti-trafficking/publications/gender-dimension-domestic-work-western-europe_en.

Gallagher, A. T. (2009). "Human rights and human trafficking: Quagmire or firm ground? A response to James Hathaway". *Virginia Journal of International Law*, 49(4), 789–848.

Gallagher, A. T. (2013). "Counteracting the bias: The department of labor's unique opportunity to Combat human trafficking". *Harvard Law Review*, 126(4), 1012–1033.

Garcia, R. J. (2012). *Marginal Workers: How Legal Fault Lines Divide Workers and Leave Them without Protection*. New York, NY: New York University Press.

Garden, C. (2011). "Citizens, united and citizens united: The future of labor speech rights?" *William and Mary Law Review*, 53, 1.

Garden, C. & Leong, N. (2013). "So closely intertwined: Labor and racial solidarity". *George Washington Law Review*, 81, 1135–1210.

Gardiner, L. (2015). The scale of minimum wage underpayment in social care. *Resolution Foundation*. Retrieved from: www.resolutionfoundation.org/publications/the-scale-of-minimum-wage-underpayment-in-social-care/.

Gerard, L. W., "America feeds the rich," *The Huffington Post*, 17 June, 2013. Retrieved from: www.huffingtonpost.com/leo-w-gerard/america-feeds-the-rich_b_3450749.html.

Getman, J. G. (2010). *Restoring the Power of Unions: It Takes a Movement*. New Haven, CT: Yale University Press.

Getman, J. G. (2014). "Boeing, the IAM, and the NLRB: Why US labor law is failing". *Minnesota Law Review*, 98(5), 1651–1681.

Ghayad, R. & Dickens, W. (2012), *What Can We Learn by Disaggregating the Unemployment-Vacancy Relationship?*, Public Policy Briefs No. 12-3. Boston, MA: Federal Reserve Bank of Boston. Retrieved from: https://www.bostonfed.org/publications/public-policy-brief/2012/what-can-we-learn-by-disaggregating-the-unemployment-vacancy-relationship.aspx.

Gibson, K. (2015, May 1). Bill aims to hike US minimum wage to $12. *CBS Moneywatch*. Retrieved from: www.cbsnews.com/news/bill-aims-to-hike-u-s-minimum-wage-to-12-dollars-an-hour/.

Glenn, E. N. (2010). *Forced to Care: Coercion and Caregiving in America*. Cambridge: Cambridge University Press.

Global Forum on Migration and Development (2012a). *Checklist to Support and Protect Domestic Workers*, Mauritius GFMD 2012. Retrieved from: http://www.gfmd.org/files/documents/DomesticWorkerChecklist-Final6.pdf.

Global Forum on Migration and Development: Background Paper (2012b). *Protecting Migrant Domestic Workers – Enhancing Their Development Potential*, Prepared for Mauritius GFMD 2012. Retrieved from: www.gfmd.org/files/documents/gfmd12_mauritius12_rt_3-3-background_paper_en.pdf.

Glynn, S. J. & Nancy, W. (2013, April 9). The gender wage gaps differ by occupation. Center for American Progress. Retrieved from: www.americanprogress.org/issues/labor/news/2013/04/09/59698/the- gender-wage-gap-differs-by-occupation/.

Glynn, T. P. (2011). "Taking the employer out of employment law? Accountability for wage and hour violations in an age of enterprise disaggregation". *Employee Rights and Employment Policy Journal*, 15, 201.

Goel, V., "The two silicon valleys: One of haves, one of have-nots," *The New York Times Bits* [web log post], 4 February, 2014. Retrieved from: http://bits.blogs.nytimes.com/2014/02/04/the-two-silicon-valleys-one-of-haves-one-of-have-nots/.

Goldberg, J. (2014, February 7). Freedom for the job-locked: Dems' desperate defense of Obama-induced unemployment. *National Review*. Retrieved from: http://www.aei.org/publication/freedom-for-the-job-locked/.

Golden, L. (2015, April). Irregular work scheduling and its consequences. Retrieved from: http://s2.epi.org/files/pdf/82524.pdf.

Goldin, C. (1990). *Understanding the Gender Gap: An Economic History of American Women*. New York: Oxford University Press.

Gomberg-Muñoz, R. (2011). *Labor and Legality: An Ethnography of a Mexican Immigrant Network*. New York: Oxford University Press.

Goodin, R. (1988). *Reasons for Welfare: The Political Theory of the Welfare State*. Princeton: Princeton University Press.

Gordolan, L. & Lalani, M. (2009). *Care and Immigration: Migrant Care Workers in Private Households*, Kalayaan, September 2009. Retrieved from: http://www.kalayaan.org.uk/documents/Kalayaan%20Care%20and%20Immigration%20Report%20280909%20e-version.pdf.

Gordon, C., Mailman, S. & Yale-Loehr, S. (2004). Immigration law and procedure. In S. Legomsky (2005) (ed), *Immigration and Refugee Law and Policy* (4th edn). New York: Foundation Press.

Gordon, L. (1992). "Social insurance and public assistance: The influence of gender in welfare thought in the United States, 1890–1935". *American Historical Review*, 97, 1.

Gordon, L. (1998). *Pitied but Not Entitled: Single Mothers and the History of Welfare, 1890–1935*. Cambridge, MA: Harvard University Press.

Gottrup, R. (2011). *Officialprincippet og sagsoplysning*. Copenhagen: Jurist- og Økonomforbundets Forlag.

Graeber, D. (2009). *Direct Action: An Ethnography*. Chico, CA: AK Press.

Grant, D. (2011). Older women, work and the impact of discrimination. In M. Sargeant (ed), *Age Discrimination and Diversity: Multiple Discrimination from an Age Perspective*. Cambridge, MA: Cambridge University Press, pp. 41, 48.

Grear, A. (2011). "The vulnerable living order: Human rights and the environment in a critical and philosophical perspective". *Journal of Human Rights and the Environment*, 2(1), 22, 43, 44.

Grear, A. (2013). Vulnerability, advanced global capitalism and co-symptomatic injustice: Locating the vulnerable subject. In M. Fineman & A. Grear (eds), *Vulnerability: Reflections on a New Ethical Foundation for Law and Politics*. Farnham: Ashgate, pp. 41–60.

Green, R., Forbis, R., Golden, N. S. & Robinson, J. (2006). "On the ethics of at-will employment in the public sector". *Public Integrity*, 8, 305.

Greenberg, M. (2011, October 13). *Preserving Mental Health During Unemployment, Psychology Today*. Retrieved from: www.psychologytoday.com/blog/the-mindful-self-express/201110/preserving-mental-health-during-unemployment.

Greenstone, M. & Looney, A. (2010). *The Great Recession's Toll on Long-Term Unemployment, Brookings*. Retrieved from: www.brookings.edu/blogs/jobs/posts/2010/11/05-jobs-greenstone-looney.

Greenhouse, S., "A part-time life, as hours shrink and shift," *The New York Times*, 28 October, 2012, p. A1.

Greenhouse, S., "In drive to unionize, fast-food workers walk off the job," *The New York Times*, 28 November, 2012. Retrieved from: www.nytimes.com/2012/11/29/nyregion/drive-to-unionize-fast-food-workers-opens-in-ny.html?_r=0.

Greenhouse, S., "Wage strikes planned at fast-food outlets," *The New York Times*, 2 December, 2013, p. B2.

Greenhouse, S., "Fast-food protests spread overseas," *The New York Times*, 15 May, 2014, p. B1.

Greenhouse, S., "A push to give steadier shifts to part-timers," *New York Times*, 15 July 2014a. Retrieved from: www.nytimes.com/2014/07/16/business/a-push-to-give-steadier-shifts-to-part-timers.html.

Greenhouse, S., "Part-time schedules, full-time headaches. *New York Times*," 18 July 2014b. Retrieved from: www.nytimes.com/2014/07/19/business/part-time-schedules-full-time-headaches.html.

Gregg, P. and Gardiner, L. (2015). A Steady Job? The UK's Record on Labour Market Security and Stability since the Millenium. Resolution Foundation.

GRETA (2012, September 12). Report concerning the implementation of the Council of Europe Convention on Action against Trafficking in Human Beings by the United Kingdom, Strasbourg. Retrieved from: https://rm.coe.int/168067a080.

Greve, B. (2002). "Skøn og ret – historie og nutid i dansk socialpolitik". *Uden for nummer*, 4, 3. Årgang. Retrieved from: www.socialraadgiverne.dk/Files/Filer/10-Publikationer/UdenForNummer/UdenForNummer4-SkoenOgRet_HistorieOgNutidIDanskSocialpolitik.pdf.

Griffith, K. L. (2009). U.S. migrant worker law: the interstices of immigration law and labor and employment law. *Comparative Labor Law & Policy Journal*, 1, 125.

Gross, K. (2005/2006). "Separate to unite: Will change to win strengthen organized labor in America". *Buffalo Public Interest Law Journal*, 24, 75–130.

Grundy, L. & Firestein, N. (1997). Work, family, and the labor movement. *The Labor Project for Working Families*. Retrieved from: www.working-families.org/publications/workfamily_labormovement.pdf.

Guldager, J. (2011). "Helhedssynet i socialt arbejde – er det stækket af de senere års socialpolitiske tiltag?" *Social Politik*, 6, 20–25.

Gura, D. & Clark, K. (2014, April 3). Food stamps: A reporter's notebook. *Marketplace*. Retrieved from: https://www.marketplace.org/2014/04/03/wealth-poverty/secret-life-food-stamp/food-stamps-reporters-notebook.

The Guardian. Retrieved from www.theguardian.com/us-news/2015/apr/21/obama-trans-pacific-partnership-deal-democrats.

Haedicke, M. A. (2013). "From collective bargaining to social justice certification: Workers' rights in the American meatpacking industry". *Sociological Focus*, 46(2) 119–137. doi: 10.1080/00380237.2013.766877.

Haipeter, T. (2013). Erosion, exhaustion, or renewal? New forms of collective bargaining in Germany. In K. V. W. Stone & H. Arthurs (eds), *Rethinking Workplace Regulation: Beyond the Standard Contract of Employment*. New York: Russell Sage Foundation, pp. 115–134.

Halbesleben, J. R. B. & Clark, S. K. (2010). "The experience of alienation among temporary workers in high-skill jobs: A qualitative analysis of temporary firefighters". *Journal of Managerial Issues*, 22(4), 531–545.

Hallett, M. (2012). "Reentry to what? Theorizing prisoner reentry in the jobless future". *Critical Criminology*, 20(3), 213–228.

Handler, J. F. (2004). *Social Citizenship And Workfare in the United States and Europe: The Paradox of Inclusion*. Cambridge: Cambridge University Press.

Hansen, I. B., Nørrelykke, H., Sjelborg, H. & Bundesen, P. (2015). *Borgerinddragelse og retssikkerhed i socialt arbejde*. Copenhagen: Hans Reitzels Forlag.

Hansen, F. K. (2004). Socialpolitik og fordeling. In J. E. Larsen, & I. H. Møller (eds), *Socialpolitik*. Copenhagen: Hans Reitzels Forlag, pp. 344–356.

Hansen, F. K., Abrahamson, P., Posborg, R., Grostøl, M., Petersen, A., Rasmussen, N., Askgaard, L., Sørensen, H. & Hansen, H. (eds). (2015). Social Årsrapport. In *Social Årsrapport*. Copenhagen: Socialpolitisk Forening og Center for Alternativ Samfundsanalyse, CASA.

Hansmann, H. (1990). "When does worker ownership work? ESOPS, law firms, codetermination, and economic democracy". *Yale Law Journal*, 99, 1749.

Harkinson, J. (2014, November 28). Walmart is seeing its biggest Black Friday protests ever today. *Mother Jones*. Retrieved from: www.motherjones.com/politics/2014/11/walmart-protests-black-friday.

Harrison, J. (1984). "The "new" terminable-at-will employment contract: An interest and cost incidence analysis". *Iowa Law Review*, 69, 327.

Hart, V. (1994). *Bound By Our Constitution: Women, Workers, and the Minimum Wage*. Princeton: Princeton University Press.

Hartley, M. & Walker, C. (2012, December 16). The culture shock ofIndia's call centers. *Forbes* [web log post]. Retrieved from: www.forbes.com/sites/morganhartley/2012/12/16/the-culture-shock-of-indias-call-centers/.

Harvey, D. (2005). *A Brief History of Neoliberalism*. Oxford: Oxford University Press.

Harvey, D. (2012). *Rebel Cities: From the Right to the City to the Urban Revolution*. London: Verso, p. 126. Retrieved from: http://abahlali.org/files/Harvey_Rebel_cities.pdf.

Haas, R. de (1998). "Business law: Employee benefits: Vizcaino v. Microsoft". *Berkeley Technology Law Journal*, 13, 483–498.

Hathaway, J. C. (2008). "The human rights quagmire of "Human Trafficking" ". *Virginia Journal of International Law*, 49(1), 1–59.

Hayes, L. J. B. (2015). "Care and control are the national minimum wage entitlements of homecare workers at risk under the Care Act 2014?" *Industrial Law Journal*, 44, 492–521.

Hayes, L. J. B. (2017). *Stories of Care, a Labour of Law: Gender and Class at Work*. Basingstoke: Palgrave Macmillan.

Hayes, L. J. B. & Moore, S. (2016). Care in a time of austerity: The electronic monitoring of working time in homecare. *Gender, Work & Organization*.

Hegewisch, A. (2009). Equality and human rights commission research report. *Flexible Working Policies: A Comparative Review*. Retrieved from: https://www.equality humanrights.com/en/publication-download/research-report-16-flexible-working-policies-comparative-review.

Hegewisch, A., Hannah, L., Jeffrey, H. & Heidi, H., Institute for Women's Policy Research (2010). Separate but not equal? Gender segregation in the labor market and the gender wage gap. Retrieved from: https://iwpr.org/publications/separate-and-not-equal-gender-segregation-in-the-labor-market-and-the-gender-wage-gap/

Hein, C. (2005). *Reconciling Work and Family Responsibilities: Practical Ideas from Global Experience*. Geneva: International Labour Office.

Hekman, S. (2008). Constructing the ballast: An ontology for feminism. In S. Alaimo & S. Hekman (eds), *Material Feminisms*. Bloomington and Indianapolis: Indiana University Press, pp. 85–119.

Henneberger, M., "Millions of Italians take to the streets in a general strike," *New York Times*, 17 April, 2002, p. A3.

Henson, C. (2012). "Title VII works – that's why we don't like it", *University of Miami Race & Social Justice Law Review*, 41, 2.

Hernandez, V., Federica, O., Manuela, S. L. & Luis, T. (2008). Dreaming of a permanent job: The transitions of temporary workers in Italy and Spain. In R. Muffels, (ed), *Flexibility and Employment Security in Europe*. Cheltenham, UK: Edward Elgar, pp. 79–86.

Heyer, K. (2012). *Kinship across Borders: A Christian Ethic of Immigration*. Washington: Georgetown University Press.

Hielmcrone, N. von og & Schultz, T. (2007). Større retssikkerhed i socialt arbejde? Tendenser i reguleringen af socialt arbejde. In M. A. Nissen, L. K. Uggerhøj (eds), *Magt og forandring i socialt arbejde.* Akademisk Forlag, pp. 93–115.

Higham, J. (2002). *Strangers in the Land: Patterns of American Nativism, 1860–1925.* New Brunswick: Rutgers University Press.

Hill, J. (2010). "Can unions use worker center strategies? In an age of doing more with less, unions should consider thinking locally but acting globally". *FIU Law Review*, 5, 551–591.

Hilsenrath, J., "More gloom for the long-term unemployed, from Alan Krueger," *Wall Street Journal Real Time Economics* [web log post], 22 May, 2014. Retrieved from: http://blogs.wsj.com/economics/2014/05/22/more-gloom-for-the-long-term-unemployed-from-alan-krueger/.

Hilsenrath, J., "Fed poised to raise rates in end of era," *Wall Street Journal*, December 16, 2015.

Hippel, C. von, Bendapudi, V., Tansky, J., Greenberger, D. B., Mangum, S. L. & Heneman, R. L. (2006). Operationalizing the shadow workforce: Toward an understanding of the participants in nonstandard employment relationships. In S. E. Gleason (ed), *The Shadow Workforce.* Kalamazoo, MI: W.E. Upjohn Institute for Employment Research, pp. 29–63.

Hirschmann, N. J. & Liebert, U. (2001). *Women and Welfare: Theory and Practice in the United States and Europe.* New Brunswick, NJ: Rutgers University Press.

Hochschild, A. & Machung, A. (2012). *The Second Shift: Working Families and the Revolution at Home.* (3rd edn). New York: Penguin Books.

Hoff, K. (2009). Aktivering. In R. Posborg, H. Johansen, H. Antczak, R. Posborg, B. Kjærgaard, H. Fehmerling, H. Nørrelykke & K. Hoff (eds), *Socialrådgivning og socialt arbejde.* Copenhagen: Hans Reitzel, pp. 165–190.

Hoffa, J. P., Gerard, L. W. & Williams, D., "It's time to take a stand for workers on TPP," *Huffington Post The Blog* [Web log post], December 7, 2015. Retrieved from: http://www.huffingtonpost.com/james-p-hoffa/labor-unions-tpp_b_8740856.html.

Holmes, J. (2015). *An Overview of the UK Domiciliary Care Sector.* UK Homecare Association, Wallington. Retrieved from: www.ukhca.co.uk/pdfs/DomiciliaryCareMarketOverview2015.pdf.

Holmes, S. (2013). *Fresh Fruit, Broken Bodies: Migrant Farmworkers in the United States.* Berkley: University of California Press.

Holt, H. & Granger, H. (2005). *Results of the Second Flexible Working Employee Survey.* DTI Employment Relations Research Series No. 39. Retrieved from: file:///Users/kirstenwidner/Downloads/flexible_working_july05_tcm77-160026%20(1).pdf.

Holzer, H. J. (2012). "Better skills for better jobs". *Issues in Science and Technology*, 28(2), 31–40.

Holzer, H. J., Raphael, S. & Stoll, M. A. (2006). "Perceived criminality, criminal background checks, and the racial hiring practices of employers". *Journal of Law and Economics*, 49(2), 451–480.

Hooker, H., Neathey, F., Casebourne, J. & Munro, M. (2007). *Third work-life balance employee survey: main findings.* DTI Employment Relations Research Series No. 58. Retrieved from: http://citeseerx.ist.psu.edu/viewdoc/download?doi=10.1.1.460.7315&rep=rep1&type=pdf.

Hornack, J. F. & Lynd, S. (1986–1987). The steel valley authority. *N.Y.U. Review of Law & Social Change*, 15, 113, 114–116.

Horowitz, C. A. (2014, March). "Civil penalties for misclassification of independent contractors". *Los Angeles Lawyer*, 37(1), 8–10.

Horowitz, S. (2011, September 1). The freelance surge is the industrial revolution of our time. *The Atlantic.* Retrieved from: www.theatlantic.com/business/archive/2011/09/the-freelance-surge-is-the-industrial-revolution-of-our-time/244229/.

Hotchkiss, J. L., Pitts, M. M. & Walker, M. B. (2011). To work or not to work: The economics of a mother's dilemma 1, Federal Reserve Bank of Atlanta, Working Paper 2011–2012. Retrieved from: www.frbatlanta.org/pubs/wp/11_02.cfm.

HSCI (2012). Community Care Statistics, Social Services Activity, England, 2011–2012, Final Release.

HSCI (2016). Personal Social Services: Staff of Social Services Departments, England, as at Sept 2015.

Hudson, K. (2007). "The new labor market segmentation: Labor market dualism in the new economy". *Social Science Research*, 36(1), 286–312.

Hunt, G. & Bielski, B. M. (2007). The lesbian, gay, bisexual, and transgender challenge to American labor. In D. Cobble (ed), *The Sex of Class: Women Transforming American Labor.* Ithaca: Cornell University Press, pp. 81–98.

Hyde, A. (1993). "Ownership, contracts, and politics in the protection of employees against risk". *University of Toronto Law Journal*, 43, 721, 748.

IFO Institute (2013). *The Gender Wage Gap in OECD Countries 69.* Retrieved from: www.cesifogroup.de/ifoHome/publications/docbase/details.html?docId=19083499.

IFSW (2012). Statement of ethical principles. International Federation of Social Workers. Retrieved from: http://ifsw.org/policies/statement-of-ethical-principles/.

Ingraham, P. (1995). The foundation of merit: Public service in American democracy. Baltimore, MA: Johns Hopkins University Press, pp. 55–56.

Inomata, R. (2012). Perils of misclassification of workers as independent contractors. In M. Downey, R. Inomata, R. P. Brooks, B. Y. Freeman, A. S. Gutierrez, J. N. Gross, *Complying with Employment Regulations: Leading Lawyers on Analyzing Legislation and Adapting to the Changing State of Employment Law.* Boston, MA: Aspatore, pp. 23–34.

Internal Revenue Service (2014). Independent contractor (self-employed) or employee? Retrieved from: www.irs.gov/Businesses/Small-Businesses-&-Self-Employed/Independent-Contractor-Self-Employed-or-Employee.

International Labour Office (2009). The cost of coercion: global report under the follow-up to the ILO Declaration on Fundamental Principles and Rights at Work 59, 1–3.

International Labour Organization (2001). Stopping forced labour: Global eport nder the follow-up to the ILO Declaration on the Fundamental Principles and Rights of Work. Retrieved from: www.ilo.org/wcmsp5/groups/public/@dgreports/@dcomm/documents/meetingdocument/kd00014.pdf.

International Labour Organization (2007). *ABC of Women Workers' Rights and Gender Equality* (2nd edn), p. 146. Retrieved from: www.ilo.org/wcmsp5/groups/public/---dgreports/---gender/documents/publication/wcms_087314.pdf.

International Labour Organization (2008). Rights, jobs and social security: New visions for older women and men. Retrieved from: http://www.ilo.org/wcmsp5/groups/public/---dgreports/---gender/documents/publication/wcms_098930.pdf.

International Labour Organization (2009a). The cost of coercion: Global report under the follow-up to the ILO Declaration on Fundamental Principles and Rights at Work. Retrieved from: http://www.ilo.org/global/topics/forced-labour/publications/WCMS_106268/lang--en/index.htm.

International Labour Organization (2009b). Operational indicators of trafficking in human beings: Results from a Delphi survey implemented by the ILO and the European Commission. Retrieved from: www.ilo.org/wcmsp5/groups/public/@ed_norm/@declaration/documents/publication/wcms_105023.pdf

International Organization for Migration (2009). Irregular migration and mixed flows: IOM's approach, IOM Doc. No. MC/INF/297. Retrieved from: www.iom.int/jahia/webdav/shared/shared/mainsite/about_iom/en/council/98/MC_INF_297.pdf.

Immigration Policy Center (2011, March 29). Employment-based immigration to the United States: A fact sheet. Retrieved from: www.immigrationpolicy.org/printpdf/1971.

Irwin, T. (2007). *The Development of Ethics*. Oxford: Oxford University Press.

Jackall, R. & Levin, H. M. (1984). "Work in America and the cooperative movement". *Worker Cooperatives in America*, 3, 7.

Jackson, J. (2012). *A Reply to Nimer Sultany*. Retrieved from: www.harvardcrcl.org/sultanycolloquium.

Jackson, J. (2016). "Not yet an end: Neoliberalism, the jurisprudence of Obamcare, and the welfare-state left". *Theory & Event*, 19, 2.

Jacobs, J. & Crepet, T. (2007–2008). "The expanding scope, use, and availability of criminal records". *New York University Journal of Legislation and Public Policy*, 11(1 January), 177–213.

Jacobs, J. A. & Gerson, K. (2004). *The Time Divide: Work, Family, and Gender Inequality*. Cambridge, MA: Harvard University Press.

Jacobs, J. B. & Larrauri, E. (2012). "Are criminal convictions a public matter? The USA and Spain". *Punishment & Society*, 14(1), 3–28.

Jacobs, M. (2005). *Pocketbook Politics: Economic Citizenship in Twentieth-Century America*. Princeton: Princeton University Press.

Jacobsen, J. P. & Laurence, M. L. (1996). "Effects of intermittent labor force attachment on women's earnings". *Monthly Labor Review*, 14, 14–19.

Jacoby, S. M. (1985). *Employing Bureaucracy: Managers, Unions, and the Transformation of Work in American Industry, 1900–1945*. New York, New York: Columbia University Press.

Jaffe, S., "McJobs should pay, too: Inside fast-food workers' historic protest for living wages," *The Atlantic*, 29 November, 2012. Retrieved from: www.theatlantic.com/business/archive/2012/11/mcjobs-should-pay-too-inside-fast-food-workers-historic-protest-for-living-wages/265714/.

James, G. (2006). "The Work and Families Act 2006: Legislating to improve choice and flexibility?" *Industrial Law Journal*, 35, 272.

James, G. (2009). "Mothers and fathers as parents and workers: Family-friendly employment policies in an era of shifting identities". *Journal of Social Welfare & Family Law*, 31, 271.

Japan Institute for Labour Policy and Training (2006). *Labour Situation in Japan and Analysis/Detailed Exposition*. Retrieved from: http://www.jil.go.jp/english/lsj/index.html.

Japan Ministry of Labor, Health, and Welfare (2006). *Japanese Working Life Profile, 2007/2008*. Retrieved from: www.jil.go.jp/english/jwl/2007-2008.pdf.

Jarman, J., Robert, M. B. & Girts, R. (2012). "The dimensions of occupational gender segregation in industrial countries". *Sociology*, 46, 1003.

Joint Venture Silicon Valley, & Silicon Valley Community Foundation (2014). *2014 Silicon Valley Index*. Retrieved from: http://siliconvalleyindicators.org/pdf/index2014.pdf.

Judt, T. (2010). *Ill Fares the Land*. New York: Penguin Books.

Jydebjerg, C. S., Rosenberg, C. & Nielsen, T. (2016 (in prep)). *Borgerinddragelse i jobcentret mellem pligt og ret*.

Kaiser Family Foundation (2013). "Medicaid expansion under The Affordable Care Act". *Journal of the American Medical Association*, 309, 12, 1219.

Kalleberg, A. L. (2009). "Precarious work, insecure workers: Employment relations in transition". *American Sociological Review*, 74(1), 1–22.

Kalleberg, A. L., Reskin, B. F. & Hudson, K. (2000). "Bad jobs in America: Standard and nonstandard employment relations and job quality in the United States". *American Sociological Review*, 65(2), 256–278.

Kalleberg, A. & Marsden, P. (2005). "Externalizing organizational activities: Where and how US establishments use employment intermediaries". *Socio-Economic Review*, 3(3), 389–416. doi:10.1093/SER/mwi017.

Kanowitz, L. (1968). "Constitutional aspects of sex based aiscrimination". *Nebraska Law Review*, 48, 170–171.

Kanowitz, L. (1980). ""Benign" sex discrimination: Its troubles and their cure". *Hastings Law Journal*, 31, 1379–1395.

Kantor, J., "Working anything but 9 to 5: Scheduling technology leaves low-income parents with hours of chaos," *New York Times*, 13 August, 2014. Retrieved from: www.nytimes.com/interactive/2014/08/13/us/starbucks-workers-scheduling-hours.html?_r=1.

Karlamangla, S., "Actors, musicians are big beneficiaries of Obamacare," *Los Angeles Times*, 23 May, 2014. Retrieved from: www.latimes.com/business/la-fi-actors-insurance-20140523-story.html

Katz, H. C. & Owen, D. (2000). *Converging Divergences: Worldwide Changes in Employment Systems*. Ithaca: Cornell University Press.

Kellough, J. E. & Nigro, L. (2010). "Dramatic reform in the public service: At-will employment and the creation of a new public workforce". *Journal of Public Administration Research and Theory*, 16(3), 447.

Kemmerling, A. & Oscar, B. (2006). "New politics in German labor market policy? The implications of the recent Hartz reforms on the German welfare state". *West European Politic*, 29, 90.

Keren-Paz, T. (2013). *A Private Law Response to Human Trafficking*. New York, NY: Routledge.

Kesby, A. (2012). *The Right to Have Rights: Citizenship, Humanity, and International Law*. Oxford: Oxford University Press.

Kessler-Harris, A. (2001). *In Pursuit of Equity: Women, Men, and the Quest for Economic Citizenship in 20th-Century America*. New York: Oxford University Press.

Kessler-Harris, A. (1982). *Out to Work: A History of Wage-Earning Women in the United States*. Oxford: Oxford University Press.

Keune, M. (2007). Flexicurity: The new cure for Europe's labour market problems. In C. Degryse & P. Pochet (eds), *Social Developments in the European Union*. Brussels: ETUI-REHS, pp. 92–98.

Kim, K. (2011). "The coercion of trafficked workers", *Iowa Law Review*, 96(2), 409–474.

Kim, K. & Hreshchyshyn, K. (2004). "Human trafficking private right of action: Civil rights for trafficked persons in the United States". *Hasting Women's Law Journal*, 16(1), 1–36.

King, D. & Ross, F. (2010). Critics and beyond. In F. G. Castles, S. Leibfried, J. Lewis, H. Obinger, C. Pierson (eds), *The Oxford Handbook of the Welfare State*. Oxford: Oxford University Press, pp. 45–60.

Kingsmill, D. (2014). The Kingsmill Review: Taking Care. *An Independent Report into Working Conditions in the Care Sector.*

Kirby, P. (2006). *Vulnerability and Violence: The Impact of Globalization*. London: Pluto Press.

Kirby, P. (2011). "Vulnerability and globalisation: Mediating impacts on society". *Journal of Human Rights and the Environment*, 2(1), 86–105.

Kirk, J. J. & Belovics, R. (2008). "A look into the temporary employment industry and its workers". *Journal of Employment Counseling*, 45(3), 131–142. doi: 10.1002/j.2161-1920.2008.tb00052.x.

Kitchen, R. K. (2011). "Eradicating the mothering effect: Women as workers and mothers, successfully and simultaneously". *Wisconsin Journal of Law, Gender & Society*, 26, 167, 171–173.

Klare, K. E. (1978). "Judicial deradicalization of the Wagner Act and the origins of modern legal consciousness, 1937–1941". *Minnesota Law Review*, 62, 265–339.

Klausen, J. (2002). *Offentlig Forsørgelse*. Copenhagen: Jurist- og Økonomforbundets Forlag.

Klausen, J., Schultz, T. & von Hilemcrone, N. (2015). *Socialret: Forsørgelse og Beskæftigelse.* Copenhagen: Jurist- og Økonomforbundets Forlag.

Klein, N. (2007). *The Shock Doctrine: The Rise of Disaster Capitalism.* New York: Picador.

Kochan, T. & Shulman, B. (2007, February 22). A new social contract: Restoring dignity and balance to the economy. *Economic Policy Institute Briefing Paper #184.* Retrieved from: www.sharedprosperity.org/bp184/bp184.pdf.

Koehler, I. (2014). Key to Care. *Report of the Burstow Commission on the Future of the Home Care Workforce.* Retrieved from: http://www.lgiu.org.uk/2014/12/02/key-to-care-report-of-the-burstow-commission-on-the-future-of-the-home-care-workforce/.

KQED interview: Jon Brooks, "Pelosi on Health Care Mandate: 'Goodbye to the Free Riders'; Interview with Scott Shafer," June 28, 2012 (www.kqed.org).

Kremer, W. & Hammond, C. (2013, July 4). "Hikikomori: Why are so many Japanese men refusing to leave their rooms?" *BBC World Service.* Retrieved from: www.bbc.com/news/magazine-23182523.

Krueger, A. B., Cramer, J. & Cho, D. (2014). "Are the long-term unemployed on the margins of the labor market?" *Brookings Papers on Economic Activity,* Spring, 229–299. doi: 10.1353/eca.2014.0004.

Krugman, P., "Op-ed: The jobless trap," *The New York Times,* 22 April, 2014, p. A21.

Kulow, M. D. (2013). "Beyond the paycheck fairness act: Mandatory wage disclosure laws – a necessary tool for closing the residual gender wage gap". *Harvard Journal on Legislation,* 50, 385.

Kurz, K., Buchholz, S., Schmelzer, P., Blossfeld, H-P. (2008). Young people's employment changes in flexible labor markets: A comparison of changes in eleven modern societies. In Blossfeld, H-P., Buchholz, S., Bukodi, E., Kurz, K. (eds), *Young Workers, Globalization and the Labor Market: Comparing Early Working Life in Eleven Countries.* Northampton, MA: Edward Elgar. pp. 352–353.

Kyeremateng-Amoah, E., Nowell, J., Lutty, A., Lees, P. S. J. & Silbergeld, E. K. (2014). "Laceration injuries and infections among workers in the poultry processing and pork meatpacking industries". *American Journal of Industrial Medicine,* 57(6), 669–682. doi: 10.1002/ajim.22325.

Lake Research Partners and The Tarrance Group (2014, November). *National Partnership for Women & Families/Rockefeller Family Fund Elective Eve/Night Omnibus.* Retrieved from: www.nationalpartnership.org/research-library/work-family/lake-research-and-tarrance-group-2014-midterm-election-omnibus-poll-results.pdf.

Lalani, M. for Kalayaan (2011, May). *Ending the Abuse: Policies That Work to Protect Migrant Workers.*

Lambert, S. J., Fugiel, P. J. & Henly, J. R. (2014, July 17). Schedule unpredictability among early career corkers in the US labor market: A national snapshot. Retrieved from: http://ssascholars.uchicago.edu/einet/files/lambert.fugiel.henly_.executive_summary.b.pdf.

Larsen, F. (2013). Active labor-market reform in Denmark. In E. Z. Brodkin & G. Marston (eds), *Work and the Welfare State: Street-Level Organizations and Workfare Politics.* Copenhagen: Djøf Publishing, pp. 103–124.

Larson, L. S. (1986). "Why we should not abandon the presumption that employment is terminal at will". *Idaho Law Review,* 23, 219.

Las Vegas Sun Staff (2014). "Union workers reach agreement with two more downtown casinos as strike date nears," *Las Vegas Sun,* 27, May, 2014. Retrieved from: http://lasvegassun.com/news/2014/may/27/union-workers-reach-agreement-two-more-downtown-ca/.

LeBel T. P. (2012). "If one doesn't get you another one will: Formerly incarcerated persons' perceptions of discrimination". *The Prison Journal,* 92(1), 63–87.

Lee, S. (2014). *The Workplace Constitution: From the New Deal to the New Right*. New York: Cambridge University Press.

Leonard, A. (1988). "A new common law of employment termination". *North Carolina Law Review*, 66, 631.

Levin, H. (1984). "ESOPS and the financing of worker cooperatives". *Worker Cooperatives in America*, 245, 245–246.

Levinson, S. (2006). *Our Undemocratic Constitution*. Oxford: Oxford University Press.

Lewis, D. (2010). "Modern presidents and the transformation of the federal personnel system". *The Forum*, 7(4).

Lewis, J. (2009). *Work-Family Balance, Gender and Policy*. Cheltenham, UK: Edward Elgar Publishing.

Lewis, J. & Campbell, M. (2008). "What's in a name? "Work and family" or "Work and life" balance possibilities in the UK since 1997 and the implications for the pursuit of gender equality". *Social Policy and Administration*, 42, 524.

Lewis, J. & West, A. (2014). "Re-shaping social care services for older people in England: Policy development and the problem of achieving "Good Care"". *Journal of Social Policy*, 43, 1.

Libenson, D. (2006). "Leasing human capital: Toward a new foundation for employment termination law". *Berkeley Journal of Employment and Labor Law*, 27, 111, 126.

Librett, J. S. (2015). Sense. In P. Gratton & M. E. Morin (eds), *The Nancy Dictionary*. Edinburgh: Edinburgh University Press, pp. 213–215.

Lichtenstein, N. & Howell, J. H. (1993). *Industrial Democracy in America: The Ambiguous Promise*. Cambridge, UK: Cambridge University Press.

Lieberwitz, R. (2005). Contingent labor: Ideology in practice. In M. Fineman, & T. Dougherty (eds), *Feminism Confronts Homo Economicus*. Ithaca: Cornell University Press, pp. 324–337.

Lifsher, M., "State cracks down on wage theft: California's controller is seeking restitution from firms suspected of cheating workers," *The Los Angeles Times*, 24 October 2014, p. B1.

Liptak, A., "Corporations find a friend in the Supreme Court," *New York Times*, 13 May, 2013. Retrieved from: www.nytimes.com/2013/05/05/business/pro-business-decisions-are-defining-this-supreme-court.html?nl=todaysheadlines&emc=edit_th_20130505&pagewanted=all&_r=0.

Liu, C. Y. & Kolenda, R. (2012). "Counting and understanding the contingent workforce: Using Georgia as an example". *Urban Studies*, 49(5), 1003–1025.

Livengood, C. & Ferretti, C., "Judge: EM lawsuit can proceed on racial grounds," *The Detroit News*, 19 November, 2014. Retrieved from: www.detroitnews.com/story/news/politics/2014/11/19/judge-michigan-em-lawsuit-can-proceed-racial-grounds/19273435/.

Livingston, G. & D'Vera Cohn, Pew Research Ctr. (2010). Childlessness up among women; down among women with advanced degrees 1. Retrieved from: http://www.pewsocialtrends.org/2010/06/25/childlessness-up-among-all-women-down-among-women-with-advanced-degrees/.

Livingston, G. & Parker, K., Pew Research Ctr. (2010). Since the start of the recession, more children raised by grandparents. Retrived from: www.pewsocialtrends.org/2010/09/09/since-the-start-of-the-great-recession-more-children-raised-by-grandparents/.

Looney, A. & Greenstone, M. (2010, October 8). *Leave No Community behind, Brookings*. Retrieved from: www.brookings.edu/opinions/leave-no-community-behind/.

Lower-Basch, E. (2007, September). Opportunity at work: improving job quality. Retrieved from: www.clasp.org/issues/body/0374.pdf.

Lower-Basch, E., "A shredded safety net," *The American Prospect*, 31 May, 2013. Retrieved from: http://prospect.org/article/shredded-safety-net.

Lower-Basch, E. & Greenberg, M. H. (2009). Single mothers in the era of welfare reform. In A. Bernhardt, H. Boushey, L. Dresser, & C. Tilly (eds), *The Gloves-Off Economy: Workplace Standards at the Bottom of America's Labor Market.* Champaign, IL: Labor and Employment Relations Association.

Luce, S., Luff, J., McCartin, J. A. & Milkman, R. (2014). Introduction. In S. Luce, J. Luff, J. A. McCartin, & R. Milkman (eds), *What Works for Workers? Public Policies and Innovative Strategies for Low-Wage Workers.* New York, NY: Russell Sage Foundation, pp. 1–16.

Luria, G. & Yagil, D. (2010). "Safety perception referents of permanent and temporary employees: Safety climate boundaries in the industrial workplace". *Accident Analysis & Prevention*, 42(5), 1423–1430. doi:10.1016/j.aap.2009.02.016.

Lutz, H. (2002). "At your service madam! The globalization of domestic service". *Feminist Review*, 70, 89.

Lutz, H. (2010). "Gender in the migratory process". *Journal of Ethnic and Migration Studies*, 36(10), 1647.

MacGillvary, J. & Firestein, N. (2009). Family-friendly workplaces: Do unions make a difference? *UC Berkeley Labor Center Project for Working Families.* Retrieved from: http://laborcenter.berkeley.edu/jobquality/familyfriendly09.pdf.

McGlashan, K., Ellis, R. & Glasgow, D. (2003). Flexible employment in the USA. In O. Bergström, & D. Storrie (eds), *Contingent Employment in Europe and the United States.* Northampton, MA: Edward Elgar, pp. 163–194.

McGovern, P. (2012). "Inequalities in the (de-)commodification of labour: Immigration, the nation state, and labour market stratification". *Sociology Compass*, 6, 485–498.

Mcgrath, S. & Defilippis, J. (2009). "Social reproduction as unregulated work". *Work, Employment and Society*, 23, 66–83.

Mackenzie, C. (2012). The importance of relational autonomy and capabilities for an ethics of vulnerability. In C. Mackenzie, W. Rogers, & S. Dodds (eds), *Vulnerability: New Essays in Ethics and Feminist Philosophy.* Oxford: Oxford University Press, pp. 33–59.

MacLean, N. (2006). *Freedom Is Not Enough: The Opening of the American Workplace.* Cambridge, MA: Harvard University Press.

Maitland, I. (1989). "Rights in the workplace: A Nozickian argument". *Journal of Business Ethics*, 8, 951.

Malin, M. (2012). "Life after Act 10? Is there a future for collective representation of Wisconsin public employees?" *Marquette Law Review*, 96, 623–658.

Maloney, C. B., Joint Econ. Comm. (2010). *The Earnings Penalty for Part-Time Work: An Obstacle to Equal Pay.* Retrieved from: www.jec.senate.gov/public/index.cfm/democrats/reports1?ID=D6034BC5-9247-4B08-91F3-A41E86B3A0D0.

Mantouvalou, V. (2015). "'Am I free now?' Overseas domestic workers in slavery". *Journal of Law and Society*, 42(3), 329.

Manzano-Diaz, S. (2011, April 12). Where's My 20? Work in Progress – The Official Blog of the US Department of Labor.

Markotic, N. & McRuer, R. (2012). Leading with your head: On the borders of disability, sexuality, and the nation. In R. McRuer & A. Mollows (eds), *Sex and Disability.* Durham: Duke University Press, pp. 165–182.

Marler, J. H., Barringer, M. W. & Milkovich, G. T. (2002). "Boundaryless and traditional contingent employees: Worlds apart". *Journal of Organizational Behavior*, 23(4), 425–453. doi: 10.1002/job.148.

Marshall, T. H. (1965). Citizenship and social class. In *Class, Citizenship, and Social Development.* New York: Anchor Books, pp. 71–135.

Martin, L. (2011). "Debt to society: Asset poverty and prisoner reentry". *The Review of Black Political Economy*, 38(2), 131–143.

Marx, K. (1843). *On the Jewish Question*. Retrieved from: www.marxists.org/archive/marx/works/1844/jewish-question/.

Marx, K. (1850). *Address to the Central Committee of the Communist League*. Retrieved from: www.marxists.org/archive/marx/works/1847/communist-league/1850-ad1.htm.

Marx, K. (1978). The German ideology. In R. C. Tucker (ed), *The Marx-Engels Reader* (2nd edn). New York: Norton, pp. 146–200.

Marx, K. & Engels F. (1978) Manifsto of the Communist Party. In R. C. Tucker (ed), *The Marx-Engels Reader* (2nd edn). New York: Norton (1978), pp. 469–500.

Matthews, D. (2014). "From jurisdiction to juriswriting: At the expressive limits of law". *Law Culture and the Humanities*, 1–21.

Matthews, D. (2015). On the law of originary sociability or writing the law. In T. Mulqueen & D. Matthews (eds), *Being Social. Ontology, Law, Politics*. Oxford: Counterpress.

MBO Partners (2013). *The State of Independence in America: Third Annual Independent Workforce Report*. Retrieved from; http://info.mbopartners.com/rs/mbo/images/2013-MBO_Partners_State_of_Independence_Report.pdf.

McKinnon, R. I. (2004). "Government deficits and the deindustrialization of America". *The Economists' Voice*, 1(3), Art. 1, 1–6. doi: 10.2202/1553-3832.1029.

Mead, L. M. (2005). Welfare reform and citizenship. In L. M. Mead & C. Beem (eds), *Welfare Reform and Political Theory*. New York: Russell Sage Foundation.

Melick, M. D. (2003). The relationship between crime and unemployment. *The Park Place Economist*, 30. Retrieved from: http://digitalcommons.iwu.edu/parkplace/vol11/iss1/13.

Merkle, J. A. (1980). *Management and Ideology: The Legacy of the International Scientific Management Movement*. Berkeley, CA: University of California Press.

Mettler, S. B. (1994). "Federalism, gender & the Fair Labor Standards Act of 1938". *Polity*, 26(4), 635–654.

Meurs, P. & Devisch, I. (2015). The meaning of sense. In T. Mulqueen & D. Matthews (eds), *Being Social: Ontology, Law, Politics*. Oxford: Counterpress Oxford, pp. 47–57.

Milkman, R. (2007). Two worlds of unionism. In D. Cobble (ed), *The Sex of Class: Women Transforming American Labor*. Ithaca: Cornell University Press, pp. 63-80.

Milkman, R. & Voss, K. (2004). Introduction. In R. Milkman & K. Voss (eds), *Rebuilding Labor: Organizing and Organizers in the New Union Movement*. Ithaca: Cornell University Press, 1–16.

Miller, C. C. & Liz, A., "Why US women are leaving jobs behind," *New York Times the Upshot*, 12 December, 2014. Retrived from: www.nytimes.com/2014/12/14/upshot/us-employment-women-not-working.html.

Miller, J. G. & Miller, M. (2012). "The rise of the supertemp". *Harvard Business Review*, 90(5), 50–59.

Miller, A. & Stewart, A. N. (1998). "Report from the roundtable on the meaning of 'trafficking in persons': A human rights perspective." *Women's Rights Law Reporter*, 20(1), 11–19.

Milligan, C. & Wiles, J. (2010). "Landscapes of care". *Progress in Human Geography*, 34, 736–754.

Ministry of Labor (2004). Vejledning til bekendtgørelse om visitation og det individuelle kontaktforløb, VEJ nr. 9628 af 01/12/2004.

Ministry of Social Affairs (2001). Vejledning om ændrede rådigheds- og sanktionsregler m.v. for kontanthjælpsmodtagere, VEJ nr. 49 af 24/04/2001.

Ministry of Social Affairs (2006). Vejledning om retssikkerhed og administration på det sociale område, vejledning nr. 73 af 3/10 2006.

Mishel, L. (2013, February 21). Declining value of the federal minimum wage is a major factor driving inequality. Retrieved from: www.epi.org/publication/declining-federal-minimum-wage-inequality/.

Mishel, L., Bernstein, M. & Allegretto, S. (2006/2007). *The State of Working America 2006/2007.* Economic Policy Institute, Ithaca: Cornell University Press.

Mishel, L., Bivens, J., Gould, E. & Shierholz, H. (2012). *The State of Working America.* (12th edn). Economic Policy Institute, Ithaca: Cornell University Press.

Misra, N. (2007). "The push and pull of globalization: How the global economy makes migrant workers vulnerable to exploitation". *Human Rights Brief,* 14(3), pp. 2–4.

Møller, I. H. (2004). De fire socialreformer i moderne tid. In L. J. Elm & M. I. Hornemann (eds), *Socialpolitik.* Copenhagen: Hans Reitzels Forlag, pp. 80–109.

Moomaw, R., Kent W. O., William M. & Michael A. (2009). Economics and Contemporary Issues 308 (8th edn). Higher crime rate linked to low wages and unemployment, study finds; Ohio State University Research News. Retrieved from: http://researchnews.osu.edu/archive/crimwage.htm.

Moore, J. (2002). "Utility and humanity: The quest for the *Honestum* in Cicero, Hutcheson and Hume". *Utilitas,* 14, 365.

Moore, S. (2007). "Age as a factor defining older women's experience of labour market participation in the UK". *Industrial Law Journal,* 36, 383.

Moore, A. E. (2015, April 1). From Brothel to Sweatshop? Questions on labour trafficking in Cambodia. *Open Democracy.* Retrieved from: www.opendemocracy.net/beyondslavery/anne-elizabeth-moore/from-brothel-to-sweatshop-questions-on-labour-trafficking-in-camb.

Morath, E., "Hurdles Persist Despite Job Gains," *Wall Street Journal,* January 9, 2016.

Morgan, S., Acker, J. & Weigt, J. (2013). *Life after Welfare: The Costs of Low-Wage Employment: Stretched Thin: Poor Families, Welfare Work, and Welfare Reform.* Ithaca, NY: Cornell University Press.

Morgan, G. & Wong, J. (1994). *One Breath,* Season 2, Episode 8, X-Files (Fox Television, 11 November, 1994).

Morin, M.-E. (2012). *Jean Luc Nancy.* Cambridge: Polity Press.

Moss, S. (2005). "Where there's at-will, there are many ways: Redressing the increasing incoherence of employment-at-will". *University of Pittsburgh Law Review,* 67, 295, 361–364.

MPI: Migration Policy Institute (n.d.). US immigrant population and share over time, 1850-present. Retrieved from: www.migrationpolicy.org/programs/data-hub/charts/immigrant-population-over-time.

Ms. Foundation for Women (2013, January 16). More to do: The road to equality for women in the United States. Retrieved from: http://forwomen.org/content/143/en/publications-and-resources.

Muffels, R. (2008). Flexibility and employment security in Europe: Setting the scene. In R. Muffels (ed), *Flexibility and Employment Security in Europe: Labour Markets in Transition.* Cheltenham, UK: Edward Elgar, pp. 3–30.

Mui, Y. Q., "Work elusive for long-term jobless," *The Washington Post,* 19 April, 2014, p. A1.

Munger, F. (2004). "The new economy and the unraveling social safety net: How can we save the safety net?" *Brooklyn Law Review,* 69, 543–581.

Munro, V. & Scoular, J. (2012). "Abusing vulnerability? Contemporary law and policy responses to sex work in the UK". *Feminist Legal Studies,* 20, 189–206.

Murphy, E. F. & Graff, E. J. (2005). *Why Women Don't Get Paid Like Men – And What To Do about It.* New York, Touchstone.

Nakamura, D., "Hundreds of Advocacy Groups ask Congress to Block Obama's Pacific Rim Trade Pact", *The Washington Post,* January 7, 2016. Retrieved from: https://www.washingtonpost.com/news/post-politics/wp/2016/01/07/hundreds-of-advocacy-groups-ask-congress-to-block-obamas-pacific-rim-trade-pact/.

Nakamura, K. & Michio, N. (2013). Organizing nonstandard workers in Japan: Old players and new players. In K. V. W. Stone & H. Arthurs (eds), *Rethinking Workplace Regulation: Beyond the Standard Contract of Employment*. New York: Russell Sage Foundation, pp. 253–270.

Nancy, J. L. (1991). Of being in-common in miami theory collective. In The Miami Theory Collective (eds), *Community at Loose Ends*. Minneapolis: University of Minnesota Press, pp. 1–12.

Nancy, J. L. (1993). *The Birth to Presence*. Stanford: Stanford University Press.

Nancy, J. L. (1993b). *The Experience of Freedom*. Stanford: Stanford University press.

Nancy, J. L. (1997). *The Sense of the World*. Minneapolis: University of Minnesota Press.

Nancy, J. L. (2000). *Being Singular Plural*. Stanford: Stanford University Press.

Nancy, J. L. (2007). *The Creation of the World or Globalization*. Albany: State University of New York Press.

Nancy, J. L. (2015). *Identity: Fragments, Frankness*. New York: Fordham University Press.

National Alliance for Caregiving and AARP (2009). Caregiving in the US. Retrieved from: https://assets.aarp.org/rgcenter/il/caregiving_09_fr.pdf.

National Audit Office (2016, May 11). Ensuring employment comply with national minimum wage regulations. Department for Business, Innovation and Skills: HM Revenue and Customs.

National Employment Law Project (2014, April). The low-wage recovery: Industry employment and recovery four years into the recovery. Retrieved from: www.nelp.org/page/-/Reports/Low-Wage-Recovery-Industry-Employment-Wages-2014-Report.pdf?nocdn=1.

National Employment Law Project (2015, May). *Minimum Wage Basics: Public Opinion on Raising the Minimum Wage*. Retrieved from http://www.nelp.org/content/uploads/Minimum-Wage-Basics-Polling.pdf.

National Equal Pay Task Force (2013). Fifty years after the Equal Pay Act: Assessing the past, taking stock of the future. Retrieved from: https://obamawhitehouse.archives.gov/sites/default/files/equalpay/equal_pay_task_force_progress_report_june_2013_new.pdf.

National Labor Relations Board Office of Public Affairs (2014, August 4). NLRB officials ratify agency actions taken during period when Supreme Court held board members were not validly appointed. Retrieved from: http://nlrb.gov/news-outreach/news-story/nlrb-officials-ratify-agency-actions-taken-during-period-when-supreme-court.

National Women's Law Center (2015, April). *Fact sheet: Recently introduced and enacted state and local fair scheduling legislation*. Retrieved from: www.nwlc.org/sites/default/files/pdfs/recently_introduced_and_enacted_state_and_local_fair_scheduling_legislation_apr_2015.pdf.

New York City Bar Justice Center (2014). Spotlight on 150 human trafficking cases. Retrieved from: www2.nycbar.org/citybarjusticecenter/images/stories/pdfs/cbjc-iwc-human-trafficking.pdf.

New York State Office of the Attorney General (2014, March 18). A.G. Schneiderman announces $500k settlement with seven McDonald's restaurants in Manhattan [press release]. Retrieved from: www.ag.ny.gov/press-release/ag-schneiderman-announces-500k-settlement-seven-mcdonalds-restaurants-manhattan.

Ngai, M. (2004). *Impossible Subjects: Illegal Aliens and the Making of Modern America*. Princeton: Princeton University Press.

Nielsen, M. H. (2015a). Socialpolitikkens to virkeligheder – et essay om beskæftigelsesrettet socialpolitik fra henholdsvis politikerens og borgerens perspektiv. In *Social Årsrapport*. Copenhagen: Socialpolitisk Forening og Center for Alternativ Samfundsanalyse,

CASA. pp. 43–48. Retrieved from: http://vbn.aau.dk/da/publications/socialpolitikkens-to-virkeligheder(a9330ff4-e20b-4d33-b8a4-235cadaf32cb)/export.html.

Nielsen, M. H. (2015b). "Det aktive menneskes triumf?: En analyse af de omfattende forand. Et ringer af kategoriseringen af kontanthjælpsmodtagere". *Tidsskrift for Arbejdsliv*, 17(1), 43–48.

Nixon, V., Clough, P. T., Staples, D. Nixon, V., Ticento Clough, P., Staples, D., Johnson Peterkin, Y., Zimmerman, P., Voight, C. & Pica, S. (2008). "Life capacity beyond reentry: A critical examination of racism and prisoner reentry reform in the U.S.". *Race/ Ethnicity: Multidisciplinary Global Perspectives*, 2(1), 21–43.

Noll, G. (2010). "The laws of undocumented migration". *European Journal of Migration and Law*, 12(2), 143.

Northam, J. (2014, January 27). As overseas costs rise, more US companies are 'reshoring'. *NPR* [web log post]. Retrieved from: www.npr.org/blogs/parallels/2014/01/22/265080779/as-overseas-costs-rise-more-u-s-companies-are-reshoring.

Notice and Invitation to File Briefs in Miller & Anderson, Inc. Retrieved from: https://www.nlrb.gov/cases-decisions/invitations-file-briefs/archived-notices-briefs-and-invitations.

Nussbaum, K. (2007). Working women's insurgent consciousness. In D. Cobble (ed), *The Sex of Class: Women Transforming American Labor.* Ithaca: Cornell University Press, pp. 159–176

Nyström, B. (2006). *Trade Liberalization And Labour Law, National Report Sweden*, XVIII World Congress of Labour Law & Social Security. Retrieved from: http://islssl.org/wp-content/uploads/2013/01/Swedenenglish-Nystrom.pdf.

Obama, B. (2012, September 23). *Remarks by the President to the Clinton Global Initiative.* Retrieved from: www.whitehouse.gov/photos-and-video/video/2012/09/25/president-obama-speaks-clinton-global-initiative-annual-meeting#transcript.

Obama, B. (2014, November 20). *Remarks by the President in Address to the Nation on Immigration.* Retrieved from: www.whitehouse.gov/the-press-office/2014/11/20/remarks-president-address-nation-immigration.

O'Brien, E., Ke Bin Wu & David B., AARP Public Policy Institute (2010). Older Americans in poverty: A snapshot 12 (2010, April).

O'Brien, R. (2005). *Bodies in Revolt.* New York: Routledge.

O'Donnell, A. (2013). Safety nets and transition assistance: Continuity and change in a liberal welfare state. In K. V. W., Stone & H. Arthurs (eds), *Rethinking Workplace Regulation: Beyond the Standard Contract of Employment.* New York: Russell Sage Foundation, pp. 273–291.

OECD (2007a). Babies and bosses: Reconciling work and family life: A synthesis. Paris: OECD. Retrieved from: http://www.oecd.org/els/family/babiesandbosses-reconciling workandfamilylifeasynthesisoffindingsforoecdcountries.htm.

OECD (2007b). Workers in the global economy: Increasingly vulnerable? Retrieved from: https://www.oecd.org/els/emp/38597305.pdf.

OECD (2015). In it together: Why less inequality benefits all. Paris: OECD Publishing.

Office of the Assistant Secretary for Planning and Evaluations, US Department of Health and Human Services (2015, February). Retrieved from: http://aspe.hhs.gov/hsp/15/ChildCareEligibility/ib_ChildCareEligibility.pdf. As cited in Ben-Ishai, L., Matthews, H. & Levin-Epstein, J. (2014, March). Retrieved from: http://www.clasp.org/resources-and-publications/publication-1/2014-03-27-Scrambling-for-Stability-The-Challenges-of-Job-Schedule-Volat-.pdf.

Olson, D. G. (1986–87). "Employee ownership: An economic development tool for anchoring capital in local communities". *New York University Review Law & Social Change*, 15, 239, 242.

Omori, M. & Shelley A. S. (2006). Women's occupational mobility after work interruption, 4 *Soc. Today*, Retrieved from: www.ncsociology.org/sociationtoday/v41/women.htm.

O'Neill, H. (2012). "Thinking outside the box". *Workforce Management*, 91(1), 3.

Orren, K. (1991). *Belated Feudalism: Labor, the Law, and Liberal Development in the United States*. Cambridge: Cambridge University Press.

Owens, C. (2013, August 29). Trying to raise a family on a fast-food salary [Reuters: The Great Debate Web log post]. Retrieved from: http://blogs.reuters.com/great-debate/2013/08/28/trying-to-raise-a-family-on-a-fast-food-salary/.

Oxfam and Kalayaan (2008). The new bonded labour? The impact of the proposed changes to the UK immigration system on migrant domestic workers. Retrieved from: http://policy-practice.oxfam.org.uk/publications/the-new-bonded-labour-the-impact-of-proposed-changes-to-the-uk-immigration-syst-112374.

Packer, G. (2013, May 27). "Change the world". *The New Yorker* 89(15), 44–55.

Pager, D. (2007). *Marked: Race, Crime, and Finding Work in an Era of Mass Incarceration*. Chicago, IL: University of Chicago Press.

Pahl, R. (2005). "Are all communities communities in the mind?" *Sociological Review*, 53, 621.

Parashar, A. (2008). "Re-conceptualizing regulation, responsibility and law". *Macquaire Law Journal*, 8, 59–77.

Parker, R. E. (2002). The global economy and changes in the nature of contingent work. In B. Berberoglu (ed), *Labor and Capital in the Age of Globalization*. Lanham, MD: Rowman & Littlefield, pp. 107–123.

Passavant, P. (2005). "The strong neo-liberal state: Crime, consumption, and governance". *Theory & Event*, 8, 3.

Passel, J. & Cohn, D. (2015, March 26). Share of unauthorized immigrant workers in production, construction jobs falls since 2007: In states, hospitality, manufacturing and construction are top industries. *Pew Research Center*. Retrieved from: www.pewhispanic.org/files/2015/03/2015-03-26_unauthorized-immigrants-passel-testimony_REPORT.pdf.

Pateman, C. (2005). Another way forward: welfare, social production, and a basic income. In L. M. Mead & C. Beem (eds), *Welfare Reform and Political Theory*. New York: Russell Sage Foundation.

Peck, C. J. (1979). "Unjust discharges from employment: A necessary change in the law". *Ohio State Law Journal*, 40(1), 1.

Peck, J. (2010a). *Constructions of Neoliberal Reason*. Oxford: Oxford University Press.

Peck, J. (2010b). "Zombie neoliberalism and the ambidextrous state". *Theoretical Criminology*, 14(1), 104–110.

Peck, J. & Theodore, N. (2008). "Carceral Chicago: Making the ex-offender employability crisis". *International Journal of Urban and Regional Research*, 32(2), 251–281.

Pedriana, N. (2006). "From protective to equal treatment: Legal framing processes and the transformation of the women's movement in the 1960s". *American Journal of Sociology*, 111(2006), 1718–1761.

Pedulla, D. S. (2013). "The hidden costs of contingency: Employers' use of contingent workers and standard employees' outcomes". *Social Forces*, 92(2), 691–722.

Penn, B. (2014, March 28). Class actions against McDonald's allege 'systemic' wage theft in three states. *BNA Class Action Litigation Report*, 15, 281. Retrieved from: http://bna.com.

Perrucci, R. & Wysong, E. (2003). *The New Class Society: Goodbye American Dream?* (2nd edn). Lanham, MD: Rowman & Littlefield.

Perrucci, R. & Wysong, E. (2008). *The New Class Society: Goodbye American Dream?* (3rd edn). Lanham, MD: Rowman & Littlefield.

Phillips, M. (1992). "Toward a middle way in the polarized debate over employment at will". *American Business Law Journal*, 30, 441, 443.

Pierce, E. & Dworkin, T. (1988). "Workers' compensation and occupational disease: A return to original intent", *Oregon Law Review*, 67, 649, 653.

Piven, F. & Cloward, R. (1993a). *Regulating the Poor: The Functions of Public Welfare* (2nd edn). New York: Vintage.

Piven, F. & Cloward, R. (1993b). The welfare explosion of the 1960s. In *Regulating the Poor: The Functions of Public Welfare* (2nd edn). New York, NY: Vintage Books, pp. 183–199.

Player, M. (2004). *Federal Law of Employment Discrimination in a Nutshell* (4th edn). St. Paul: Thomson/West.

Pocock, B. (2003). *The Work/Life Collision: What Work Is Doing to Australians and What to Do about It.* Sydney: Federation Press.

Pogarsky, G. (2006). "Criminal records, employment, & recidivism". *Criminology & Public Policy*, 5(3), 479–482.

Pollert, A. & Charlwood, A. (2009). "The vulnerable worker in Britain and problems at work". *Work, Employment & Society*, 23**,** 343–362.

Poo, A. J. & Kim, E. T. (2011). "Organizing to transform ourselves and our laws: the New York domestic workers Bill of Rights campaign". *Clearinghouse Review*, 44, 577–580.

Pope, J. (1997). "Labor's constitution of freedom". *Yale Law Journal*, 106, 941.

Pope, J. G. (2004). "How American workers lost the right to strike, and other tales". *Michigan Law Review*, 103, 518.

Pope, J. G. (2010a). "Contract, race, and freedom of labor in the constitutional law of "involuntary servitude" ". *Yale Law Journal*, 119, 1474.

Pope, J. G. (2010b). "A free Labor approach to human trafficking". *University of Pennsylvania Law Review*, 158(6), 1849–1875.

Porter, E., "Inequality undermines democracy," *The New York Times*, 20 March, 2012. Retrieved from: www.nytimes.com/2012/03/21/business/economy/tolerance-for-income-gap-may-be-ebbing-economic-scene.html.

Porter, N. B. (2010). "Why care about caregivers? Using communitarian theory to justify protection of "real" workers". *University of Kansas Law Review*, 58, 355.

Portes, A. & Borocz, J. (1989). "Contemporary immigration: Theoretical perspectives on its determinants and modes of incorporation". *International Migration Review*, 23, 606–630.

Posner, R. (1989). "Hege and employment at will: A comment". *Cardozo Law Review*, 10, 1625.

Powell, B. (2012, May 17). "Op-Ed: The law of unintended consequences: Georgia's immigration law backfires". *Forbes*. Retrieved from: www.forbes.com/sites/realspin/2012/05/17/the-law-of-unintended-consequences-georgias-immigration-law-backfires/.

Power, R. (1983). "A defense of the employment at will rule". *St. Louis University Law Journal*, 27, 881.

Procacci, G. (1998). Against exclusion: The poor and the social sciences. In M. Rhodes, & Y. Mény (eds), *The Future of European Welfare: A New Social Contract?* New York: MacMillan Press, pp. 63–78.

Public Accounts Committee (2014). Sixth report – adult social care in England. 2 July 2014. Retrieved from: www.publications.parliament.uk/pa/cm201415/cmselect/cmpubacc/518/518.pdf.

Quadagno, J. (1984). "Welfare capitalism and the Social Security Act of 1935". *American Sociological Review*, 49, 5.

Raday, F. (1999). "The insider-outsider politics of labor-only contracting". *Comparative Labor Law & Policy Journal*, 20, 413–445.

Rampell, C. & Wingfield, N., "In shift of jobs, apple will make some Macs in US," *The New York Times*, 7 December, 2012, p. A1.

Ranciére, J. (2004). *Disagreement: Politics and Philosophy*. Minneapolis, MN: University of Minnesota Press.

Rapoport R., Bailyn, L., Fletcher, J. K. & Pruitt, B. H. (2002). *Beyond Work-Family Balance: Advancing Gender Equity and Workplace Performance*. San Francisco: Jossey-Bass.

Rasmussen, N. & Hansen, H. (2015). Trygheden i de sociale ydelser er faldet siden 1970'erne. In Hansen, F. K., Abrahamson, P., Posborg, R. et al. (eds) *Social Årsrapport*. Copenhagen: Socialpolitisk Forening og Center for Alternativ Samfundsanalyse, CASA, pp. 27–37. Retrieved from: www.casa-analyse.dk/wp-content/uploads/2016/08/2014-Social-%C3%85rsrapport-2014-Sociale-ydelser-og-ulighed.pdf.

Rasnic, C. D. (2013). "Shootout at the ECJ corral: Management 4, Labor 0; European Labor Dispute Law after Viking Line", *South Carolina Journal of International Law & Business*, 9, 353.

Rathod, J. M. & Skapski, M. (2013). "Reimagining the law of self-employment: A comparative perspective". *Hofstra Labor and Employment Law Journal*, 31(1), 159–192.

Regalia, I. (2013). Regional and local experiments for labor market policy in Europe. In K. V. W. Stone & H. Arthurs (eds), *Rethinking Workplace Regulation: Beyond the Standard Contract of Employment*. New York: Russell Sage Foundation, pp. 155–173.

RESPECT Network (2009). Introduction and key recommendations for an ILO Convention on Domestic Work (May 2009). Amsterdam: Briefing Paper.

Richards, K. (2004). "The trafficking of migrant workers: What are the links between labour trafficking and corruption?" *International Migration*, 42(5), 147–168.

Rodgers, L. (2010). "Time to train rights: A new impetus for skills development in the workplace?" *Industrial Law Journal*, 39, 312.

Rodgers, W., Horowitz, S. & Wuolo, G. (2014). "The impact of client nonpayment on the income of contingent workers: Evidence from the freelancers union independent worker survey". *Industrial & Labor Relations Review*, 67, 702–732.

Rogers, B. (2010). Toward Third-Party Liability for Wage Theft. *Berkeley Journal of Employment & Labor Law*, 31, 1.

Rogers, J. (1990). "Divide and conquer: Further "reflections on the distinctive character of American labor laws."" *Wisconsin Law Review*, 1990, 1–147.

Rooks, D. (2004). Sticking it out or packing it in? Organizer retention in the new labor movement. In R. Milkman & K. Voss (eds), *Rebuilding Labor: Organizing and Organizers in the New Union Movement*. Ithaca: Cornell University Press, pp. 195–224

Rothstein, M. A. & Liebman, L. (1994). *Employment Law, v.1*. New York: West Publishing.

Rothstein, M. & Liebman, L. (2004). *Employment Law*. (3d edn). New York: Foundation Press Thomson/West.

Roush, W. (2014, March 21). The missing middle class: jobs in the second machine age. *Xconomy*. Retrieved from: www.xconomy.com/national/2014/03/21/the-missing-middle-class-jobs-in-the-second-machine-age/.

Rubery, J., Grimshaw, D. & Hebson, G. (2012). "Exploring the limits to local authority social care commissioning: Competing pressures, variable practices and unresponsive providers". *Public Administration*, 91, 419.

Rubery, J., Grimshaw, D. Hebson, G. & Ugarte, S. (2015). "'It's All About Time' time as contested terrain in the management and experience of domiciliary care work in England". *Human Resource Management Journal*, 54(5), 743.

Rubery, J. & Urwin, P. (2011). "Bringing the employer back in: Why social care needs a standard employment relationship". *Human Resource Management Journal*, 21, 122.

Rugaber, C. S. (2014, October 4). "Surge of hiring cuts US jobless rate to 5.9 pct". *Daily Ledger* (Canton, IL), p. A10.

Sachs, B. (2012). "Unions, corporations and political opt-out rights after citizens united", *Columbia Law Review*, 112, 800.

Sadker, D., Sadker, M. & Zittleman, K. R. (2009). Still failing at fairness: How gender bias cheats girls and boys in school and what we can do about it. New York: Scribner.

Sandberg, S. (2013). *Lean in: Women, Work, and the Will to Lead.* New York, NY: Random House.

Sanders, K., "Many Wal-Mart workers depend on government support," *Tampa Bay Times*, 9 December, 2012, p. 1D.

Sangalis, T. R. (2011). "Elusive empowerment: Compensating the sex trafficked person under the trafficking victims protection act". *Fordham Law Review*, 80(1), 403–439.

Sassen, S. (2000). *Guests and Aliens.* New York: The New Press.

Sassen, S. (2011). "An emerging global market". *Harvard International Review*, 33(2), 48–53.

Satz, A. (2011). "Fragmented lives: Disability discrimination and the role of "environment-framing" ". *Washington & Lee Law Review*, 68(1), 187–252.

Saucedo, L. M. (2006). "The employer preference for the subservient worker and the making of the brown collar workplace". *Ohio State Law Journal*, 67, 961–1021.

Saucedo, L. M. (2008). "A new "U": Organizing victims and protecting immigrant workers". *University of Richmond Law Review*, 42(4), 101–165.

Schenker, M. (2011, October 11). Migration and occupational health: Understanding the risks. *Migration Information Source.* Retrieved from: www.migrationpolicy.org/article/migration-and-occupational-health-understanding-risks.

Schliebner, C. & Peregoy, J. (1994). "Unemployment effects on the family and child: Interventions for counselors". *Journal of Counseling & Development*, 72, 368.

Schmidt, G. (2008). Sharing risks: On social risk management and the government of labour market transitions. In R. Rogowski (ed), *The European Social Model and Transitional Labour Markets: Law and Policy.* Farnham, UK: Ashgate, pp. 29–60.

Schmit, S. & Reeves, R. (2015, March). *Child Care Assistance in 2013.* Retrieved from: www.clasp.org/resources-and-publications/publication-1/Spending-and-Participation-Final.pdf.

Schoenberger, T. M. (2013, October 22). When the quality of jobs is more important than the quantity [CNN iReport web log post]. Retrieved from: http://ireport.cnn.com/docs/DOC-1051586.

Schultz, T. (2004). *Retsanvendelse og skøn.* Copenhagen: Jurist- og Økonomforbundets Forlag.

Schultz, V. & Hoffman, A. (2006). The need for a reduced workweek in the United States. In J. Fudge & R. Owens (eds), *Precarious Work, Women, and the New Economy: The Challenge to Legal Norms.* Oxford: Hart Publishing, pp. 131–152.

Schwab, S. J. (1993). "Life-cycle justice: Accommodating just cause and employment at will". *Michigan Law Review*, 92(8), 8.

Schwab, J. (2001). "Predicting the future of employment law: Reflecting or refracting market forces". *Indiana Law Journal*, 76, 29, 36.

Schwenken, H. (2005). "Domestic slavery" versus "workers rights": Political mobilizations of migrant domestic workers in the European Union. Retrieved from: https://ccis.ucsd.edu/_files/wp116.pdf.

Schwenken, H., Prügl, E., Schwenken, H., Pabon, R., Hobden, C. & Ally, S. (2011). "Conversations". *International Feminist Journal of Politics*, 13(3), 437.

Sciarra, S., Davies, P. & Freedland, M. (eds) (2004). *Employment Policy and the Regulation of Part-Time Work in the European Union.* New York, NY: Cambridge University Press.

Segal, D. (2012, June 24). "Apple's retail army long on loyalty but short on pay". *The New York Times*, p. A1.

Seitz, V. (1984). "Legal, legislative, and managerial responses to the organization of supervisory employees in the 1940's". *American Journal of Legal History*, 28(3), 199–243.

Selberg, N. & Wegerstad, L. (2011). Interview with Professor Martha Albertson Fineman. In Retfærd Årgang 34 2011 NR. 4/135.

Shaefer, H. L. & Edin, K. (2013). "Rising extreme poverty in the United States and the response of federal means-tested transfer programs". *Social Service Review*, 87(2), 250–268.

Shamir, H. (2012). "A labor paradigm for human trafficking". *UCLA Law Review*, 60(1), 76–136.

Shelton, A. AARP Public Pol'y Inst. (2013, August). Social security: A key retirement resource for women. Retrieved from: www.aarp.org/content/dam/aarp/ppi/2016-03/social-security-key-retirement-source-for-women-AARP-PPI.PDF.

Sheppard, C. (2011). Multiple discrimination in the world of work 1 (Int'l Labour Org., Working Paper No. 66).

Sikkink, K. (2011). *The Justice Cascade: How Human Rights Prosecutions Are Changing World Politics*. New York: WW Norton & Co.

Simon, W. H. (1991). "Social-republican property", *UCLA Law Review*, 38, 1335.

Singer, A. (2012, March 15). Immigrant workers in the US labor force. *Brookings*. Retrieved from: www.brookings.edu/~/media/research/files/papers/2012/3/15-immigrant-workers-singer/0315_immigrant_workers_singer.pdf.

Singer, N., "In executive pay, a rich game of thrones," *The New York Times*, 7 April, 2012. Retrieved from: www.nytimes.com/2012/04/08/business/in-chief-executives-pay-a-rich-game-of-thrones.html.

Silver, B. (2003). *Forces of Labor: Workers' Movements and Globalization Since 1870*. New York: Cambridge University Press.

Skills For Care (2015). *The Size and Structure of the Adult Social Care Sector and Workforce in England*. London: Skills for Care.

Slater, H. (2005a, October 1). "Refusal of half-hour-a-day reduction unjustified". *Equal Opportunities Review*, 146. Retrieved from: www.eortrial.co.uk/default.aspx?id=1093655.

Slater, H. (2005b, October 1). "Risk of inefficiency does not outweigh discrimination in refusing flexible working". *Equal Opportunities Review*, 146. Retrieved from: www.rubensteinpublishing.com.

Slater, J. (2000). "The court does not know "What a labor union is": How state structures and judicial (mis)constructions deformed public sector labor law". *Oregon Law Review*, 79, 981.

Slater, J. (2004). *Public Workers: Government Employee Unions, the Law, and the State, 1900–1962*. Ithaca: Cornell University Press.

Slater, J. (2007). "The "American rule" that swallows the exceptions". *Employee Rights and Employment Policy Journal*, 11, 53.

Slater, J. (2012). "Collective bargaining in the public sector under Obama: Public-sector labor in the age of Obama". *Indiana Law Journal*, 87, 189–229.

Slater, J. (2013). "The strangely unsettled state of public-sector labor in the past thirty years". *Hofstra Labor & Employment Law Journal*, 30, 511.

Slaughter, A. (2012, June 13). "Why women still can't have it all". *The Atlantic*. Retrieved from: www.theatlantic.com/magazine/archive/2012/07/why-women-still-cant-have-it-all/309020/.

Small Business Majority. (2013, September 27). Opinion poll: Small businesses support family medical leave. Retrieved from: www.smallbusinessmajority.org/small-business-research/downloads/092713-Family-Medical-Leave-poll-report.pdf.

Smith, A. (2007). *Welfare Reform and Sexual Regulation*. Cambridge: Cambridge University Press.

Smith, B. (2002). "Time norms in the workplace: Their exclusionary effect and potential for change". *Columbia Journal of Gender and Law*, 11, 271.

Smith, T. & Kim, J. (2010, June). *Paid Sick Days: Attitudes and Experiences.* Retrieved from: www.nationalpartnership.org/research-library/work-family/psd/paid-sick-days-attitudes-and-experiences.pdf.

Snyder, S. (2012). *Asylum-Seeking, Migration and Church.* Farnham: Ashgate.

Soifer, A. (2012). "Federal protection, paternalism, and the virtually forgotten prohibition of voluntary peonage". *Columbia Law Review*, 112, 1607.

Sokoloff, W. (2005). "Between justice and legality". *Political Research Quarterly*, 58(2), 341–352.

Spencer, S. & Pobjoy, J. (2011). The relationship between immigration status and rights in the UK: Exploring the rationale. Centre on Migration, Society and Policy Working Paper No. 86. Oxford: Oxford University Press.

Srinivas, S., "Trans Pacific partnership: Obama ready to defy Democrats to push secretive trade deal," *The Guardian*, 20 January, 2015. Retrieved from: www.theguardian.com/business/2015/jan/20/barack-obama-trans-pacific-partnership-republicans.

Stanley, A. D. (1998). *From Bondage to Contract: Wage Labor, Marriage and the Market in the Age of Slave Emancipation.* Cambridge: Cambridge University Press.

St. Antoine, T. J. (1988). "A seed germinates: Unjust discharge reform heads toward full flower". *Nebraska Law Review*, 67, 56, 67.

Standing, G. (2011). *The Precariat: The New Dangerous Class.* London: Bloomsbury Publishing.

Stevenson, B. & Wolfers, J. (2007). "Marriage and divorce: Changes and their driving forces". *The Journal of Economic Perspectives*, 21(2), 27–52.

Stiglitz, J. E. (2015). *The Great Divide: Unequal Societies and What We Can Do About Them.* New York, NY: W.W. Norton & Company.

Stoll, M. A. & Bushway, S. D. (2008). "The effect of criminal background checks on hiring ex-offenders". *Criminology & Public Policy*, 7(3), 371–404.

Stone, K. (n.d.). The decline of the marsupial: the end of the Australasian form of employment regulation [unpublished manuscript, on file with author].

Stone, K. (n.d.). Flexibility in Japan: New institutions of work and new conceptions of the social contract [unpublished manuscript, on file with author].

Stone, K. (1974). "The origins of job structures in the steel industry". *Review of Radical Political Economics*, 6.2, 113–173.

Stone, K. (1981). "The postwar paradigm in American labor law". *Yale Law Journal*, 90 (7), 1509–1580.

Stone, K. (2004). *From Widgets to Digits: Employment Regulation for the Changing Workplace.* Cambridge: Cambridge University Press.

Stone, K. V. W. (2013). The decline of the standard contract of employment in the United States: A socio-regulatory perspective. In K. V. W. Stone, & H. Arthurs (eds), *Rethinking Workplace Regulation: Beyond the Standard Contract of Employment.* New York: Russell Sage Foundation, pp. 58–77.

Stone, K. & Arthurs, H. (2013). The transformation of employment regimes: A worldwide challenge. In K. V. W. Stone & H. Arthurs (eds), *Rethinking Workplace Regulation: Beyond the Standard Contract of Employment.* New York: Russell Sage Foundation, pp. 1–12.

Stone, K. & Cummings, S. (2011). Labor activism and local politics: From CBS to "CBAs". In G. Davidov & B. Langille (eds), *The Idea Of Labour Law.* Oxford, UK: Oxford University Press, pp. 273–293.

Story, A. (1995). "Employer speech, union representation elections, and the First Amendment", *Berkeley Journal of Employment & Labour Law*, 16, 356.

Stout, M. (1986). "Reindustrialization from below: The steel valley project". *Labor Research Review*, 9, 19.

Stratton, A., "Minister calls for wider flexible working rights," *The Guardian* (online), 29 January, 2010. Retrieved from: www.guardian.co.uk/money/2010/jan/28/flexible-working-extension-labor-plans.

Streeck, W. (2010). Re-forming capitalism: institutional change in the german political economy. Oxford, UK: Oxford University Press.

Strom, S., "McDonald's to raise pay at outlets it operates," *The New York Times*, 2 April, 2015, p. B1.

Studdert, D. (2006). *Conceptualising Community: Beyond the State and the Individual.* London: Palgrave MacMillan, pp. 10–20.

Sudipto, B. (2012, April). "Time trends in poverty for older Americans between 2001–2009". *Employee Benefits Research Institute*, 13.

Sukert, A. (2000). "Marionettes of globalization: A comparative analysis of legal protections for contingent workers in the international community". *Syracuse Journal of International Law & Commerce*, 27, 431–477.

Summers, C. (1976). "Individual protection against unjust dismissal: Time for a statute". *Virginia Law Review*, 62, 481.

Sumner, A. & Mallett, R. (2013). "Measuring multidimensionality: What does a human wellbeing conceptual framework add to the analysis of vulnerability?" *Social Indicators Research*, 113, 671–690.

Supiot, A. (2001). *Beyond Employment: Changes in Work and the Future of Labour Law.* New York, NY: Oxford University Press.

Surfield, C. J. (2005). "The contingent workforce". *Journal of Economics and Economic Education Research*, 6(1), 23–36.

Susskind, R. (2010). *The End of Lawyers? Rethinking the Nature of Legal Services.* (Rev. edn). New York, NY: Oxford University Press.

Swinney, D. (1985). "Worker ownership: A tactic for labor". *Labor Research Review*, 6, 99, 106–107.

Swinney, D. & Metzgar, J. (1986). "Expanding the fight against shutdowns". *Labor Research Review*, 9, 99, 102.

Tataryn, A. (2015). Labour and migration in the suspended step. In T. Mulqueen & D. Matthews (eds), *Being Social: Ontology, Law, Politics.* Oxford: Counterpress Oxford, pp. 90–100.

Tavernise, S., "Soaring poverty casts spotlight on 'Lost Decade'," *The New York Times*, 13 September, 2011. Retrieved from: www.nytimes.com/2011/09/14/us/14census.html.

Taylor, J., "Unions call for June 1 strike at nine downtown casinos," *Las Vegas Sun*, 21 May 2014. Retrieved from: http://lasvegassun.com/news/2014/may/21/unions-call-june-1-strike-downtown-casinos/.

Thornley, C., Jeffreys, S. & Appay, B. (2010). Introduction: Globalization and precarious forms of production and employment. In C. Thornley, S. Jeffreys, & B. Appay (eds), *Globalization and Precarious Forms of Production and Employment: Challenges for Workers and Unions.* Cheltenham, UK: Edward Elgar, pp. 1–9.

Tien, M. T. (2013). "Human trafficking: The missing male victim". *Public Interest Law Reporter*, 18(3), 207–214.

Timiraos, N., "US Incomes Edged Lower in 2014," *Wall Street Journal*, September 16, 2015. Retrieved from http://www.wsj.com/articles/u-s-household-incomes-fell-in-2014-1442413964.

Timmons, H., "Due diligence from afar," *The New York Times*, 5 August, 2010, p. B1.

Tiraboschi, M. (2005). "The Italian labour market after the Biagi reform". *International Journal of Comparative Labor Law and Industrial Relations* 21, 149.

Tollenaar, A. & Ridder, K. de (2010). Administrative justice from a continental European perspective. In M. Adler (ed), *Administrative Justice in Context.* Oxford and Portland: Hart Publishing, pp. 301–320.

Ton, Z. (2012, January). "Why good jobs are good for retailers". *Harvard Business Review*, 2012 Jan–Feb; 90(1-2), 124–131.

Tong, R. (2013). Vulnerability and aging in the context of care. In C. Mackenzie, W. Rogers & S. Dodds (eds), *Vulnerability: New Essays in Ethics and Feminist Philosophy*. Oxford: Oxford University Press, pp. 288–308.

Travis, J. (2005). *But They All Come Back: Facing the Challenges of Prisoner Reentry*. Washington, DC: Urban Institute Press.

TUC Commission On Vulnerable Employment (2008). Hard work, hidden lives. Retrieved from: www.vulnerableworkers.org.uk/files/CoVE_full_report.pdf.

Turner, B. (2006). Vulnerability and Human Rights. University Park, PA: Pennsylvania State University Press.

Tushnet, M. (1984). "An essay on rights". *Texas Law Review*, 62, 1363.

Unger, R. M. (1998). *Democracy Realized: The Progressive Alternative*. London: Verso Press.

UK Border Agency (2008, June). Government response to the consultation on visitors.

UK Border Agency (2011, June). Employment-related settlement, tier-5 and overseas domestic workers: A consultation.

UKHCA (2010). The homecare pledge: A challenge to national and local politicians. *UK Homecare Association*. Retrieved from: http://www.ukhca.co.uk/pdfs/thehomecarepledge.pdf.

UK Home Office (2006). A points-based system: Making migration work for Britain.

UN Office on Drugs & Crime (2009). Global report on trafficking in persons. Retrieved from: www.unodc.org/unodc/en/human-trafficking/global-report-on-trafficking-in-persons.html.

United States Citizenship and Immigration Service (2015, April 15). Executive actions on immigration. Retrieved from: www.uscis.gov/immigrationaction.

United States Department of Labor, Bureau of Labor Statistics (2009). Current population survey, women in the labor force: A databook 2008 edition [data set]. Retrieved from: www.bls.gov/opub/ted/2009/jan/wk1/art04.txt.

United States Department of Labor, Bureau of Labor Statistics (2013a). National compensation survey: Employee benefits in the United States, March 2013 [Table 32: Leave benefits: Access, private industry workers]. Retrieved from: www.bls.gov/ncs/ebs/benefits/2013/ownership/private/table21a.htm.

United States Department of Labor, Bureau of Labor Statistics (2013b). National compensation survey: Employee benefits in the United States, March 2013 [Table 46: Paid leave combinations: Access, private industry workers]. Retrieved from: www.bls.gov/ncs/ebs/benefits/2013/ownership/private/table44a.htm.

United States Department of Labor, Bureau of Labor Statistics (2015, January 23). Union membership (annual) news release [data sets]. Retrieved from: www.bls.gov/news.release/union2.htm.

United States Department of Labor, Wage and Hour Division (2016). Misclassification of Employees as Independent Contractors. Retrieved from: http://www.dol.gov/whd/workers/misclassification (last checked April 25, 2016).

United States, National Labor Relations Board, Legislative History of the National Labor Relations Act, 1935.

US Census Bureau. Median household income in the United States from 1990 to 2014 (in US dollars). In *Statista – The Statistics Portal*. Retrieved from: http://www.statista.com/statistics/200838/median-household-income-in-the-united-states/.

US Department of Commerce, Economics and Statistics and Executive Office of the President Office of Management and Budget, Women in America: Indicators of social and economic well-being (2011). Retrieved from: https://obamawhitehouse.archives.gov/the-press-office/2011/03/01/white-house-releases-first-comprehensive-federal-report-status-american-.

US Department of Labor (2011). Women's employment during the recovery. Retrieved from: www.dol.gov/_sec/media/reports/FemaleLaborForce/FemaleLaborForce.pdf.

US Department of Labor, Bureau of Labor Statistics (2013). National compensation survey: Employee benefits in the United States, March 2013. [data set]. Retrieved from http://www.bls.gov/ncs/ebs/benefits/2013/ownership/private/table44a.htm.

US Department of Labor, Bureau of Labor Statistics (2015, January 23). Union membership (annual) news release [data set]. Retrieved from: http://www.bls.gov/news.release/union2.htm.

US Department of State (2004). Trafficking in persons report. Retrieved from: www.state.gov/j/tip/rls/tiprpt/2004/.

US Department of State (2010). Trafficking in persons report. Retrieved from: www.state.gov/j/tip/rls/tiprpt/2010/.

US Department of State (2012). Trafficking in persons report. Retrieved from: www.state.gov/j/tip/rls/tiprpt/2012/.

US Department of State (2014). Trafficking in persons report. Retrieved from: www.state.gov/j/tip/rls/tiprpt/2014/.

US Department of Labor, Bureau of Labor Statistics (2005, July 27). Contingent and alternative employment arrangements (news release). Retrieved from: www.bls.gov/news.release/pdf/conemp.pdf.

US Department of Labor, Bureau of Labor Statistics (2013, May 9). US Department of Labor recovers more than $1 million in back wages and damages for 196 employees misclassified as independent contractors. [news release]. Retrieved from: www.dol.gov/opa/media/press/whd/WHD20130745.htm.

US Department of Labor, Bureau of Labor Statistics (2016, January 8). The employment situation – December 2015 [news release]. Retrieved from: http://www.bls.gov/news.release/archives/empsit_01082016.pdf.

US Department of State (2013). Report of the Visa Office 2013. Retrieved from: http://travel.state.gov/content/dam/visas/Statistics/AnnualReports/FY2013AnnualReport/FY13AnnualReport-TableVI.pdf.

US Government Accountability Office, GAO-12–699 (2012, July). Retirement security: Women still face challenges.

U.S. House of Representatives, Committee on Education and the Workforce Democrats (2014, October 1). Miller applauds rule to raise minimum wage for federal contractors, calls on Congress to act [press release]. Retrieved from: http://democrats-edworkforce.house.gov/media/press-releases/miller-applauds-rule-to-raise-minimum-wage-for-federal-contractors-calls-on-congress-to-act.

Vance, S. (2002). "Trying to give private sector employees a break: Congress's efforts to amend the fair Labor Standards Act". *Hofstra Labor and Employment Law Journal*, 91, 311, 312–314.

Vandervelde, L. (1989). "The labor vision of the thirteenth amendment". *University of Pennsylvania Law Review*, 138, 437.

Varia, N. (2011). "Labour and migration in international law: Challenges of protection, specialization and bilateralim, remarks by Nisha Varia". *Proceedings of the Annual Meeting (American Society of International Law)*, 105, 410.

Vilmer, M. (2014, June 9). "Employers beware of IRS worker classification breakdown". *Law 360.* Retrieved from: www.law360.com/articles/545670/employers-beware-of-irs-worker-classification-crackdown.

Visser, J. (2013). Flexibility and security in post-standard employment relations: The Netherlands. In K. V. W. Stone & H. Arthurs (eds), *Rethinking Workplace Regulation: Beyond the Standard Contract of Employment.* New York: Russell Sage Foundation, pp. 135–154.

Voegelin, E. (1957). *Order and History III.* Baton Rouge: Louisiana State University Press.

Wacquant, L. (2010). "Prisoner reentry as myth and ceremony". *Dialectical Anthropology,* 34(4), 605–620.

Wagmiller, R. L., Jr. (2007). "Race and the spatial segregation of jobless men in urban America". *Demography,* 44(3), 539–562.

Waldinger, R., Erickson, C., Milkman, R., Mitchell, D., Valenzuela, A., Wong, K., & Zeitlin, M. (1998). Helots no more: A case study of the justice for janitors campaign in Los Angeles. In: K. Bronfenbrenner, S. Friedman, R. Hurd, R. Oswald, & R. Seeber (eds), *Organizing to Win: New Research on Union Strategies.* Ithaca: ILR Press, pp. 102–119.

Walkerdine, V. (2010). "Communal beingness and affect: An exploration of trauma in an ex-industrial community". *Body & Society,* 16, 91–116.

Walpole-Hofmeister, E. (2001, May 11). "FLSA: Perdue farms settles overtime suit, will pay chicken catchers $1.7 million". *Daily Labor Report,* 92, A-1.

Walsh, I. (2008). Right to request flexible working: A review of how to extend the right to request flexible working to parents of older children (Dept. for Bus. Enter. & Regulatory Reform May 2008).

Walsum, S. van (2012). Labour, legality and shifts in the public/private divide (Paper presented at seminar on Gender, Migration and Human Rights, EUI Florence, 18–20 June 2012), p. 9 (copy on file with authors Mullally and Murphy).

Wasem, R. (2010). Immigration visa issuances and grounds for exclusion: Policy and trends. *Congressional Research Service report R41104.*

Waters, L. & Moore, K. A. (2002). "Predicting self-esteem during unemployment: The effect of gender, financial deprivation, alternate roles, and social support". *Journal of Employment Counseling,* 39, 171.

Weiman, D. F. (2007). "Barriers to prisoners' reentry into the labor market and the social costs of recidivism". *Social Research,* 74(2), 575–611.

Weaver, R. K. (2000). *Ending Welfare as We Know It.* Washington, DC: Brookings Institution Press.

Weaver, J. D. (2013). "Grandma in the White House: Legal support for intergenerational caregiving". *Seton Hall Law Review,* 43, 1.

Weeks, K. (2011). *The Problem with Work: Feminism, Marxism, Antiwork Politics, and Postwork Imaginaries.* Durham, NC: Duke University Press.

Weiler, P. (1983). "Promises to keep: Securing workers' rights to self-organization under the NLRA". *Harvard Law Review,* 96, 1769–1827.

Weiner, M. (1995). *The Global Migration Crisis: Challenge to States and to Human Rights.* New York: HarperCollins College.

Weiss, M. (2009). "Human rights and global economy: The centrality of economic and social rights", *Maryland Journal of International Law,* 24, 257.

Welch, T. (2004). "A primer on texas public employment law". *Baylor Law Review,* 56, 981, 983–988.

Wessler, S. F., "Shift change: 'Just-in-time' scheduling creates chaos for workers," *NBC News,* 2 May, 2014. Retrieved from: http://nbcnews.to/1gkjsgS.

Western, B. (2008). "Criminal background checks and employment among workers with criminal records". *Criminology & Public Policy,* 7(3), 413–417.

Western, B., Kling, J. R. & Weiman, D. F. (2001). "The labor market consequences of incarceration". *Crime & Delinquency,* 47, 410–427.

White, M. C., "For many Americans, 'temp' work becomes permanent way of life," *NBC News,* 20 April, 2014. Retrieved from: www.nbcnews.com/feature/in-plain-sight/many-americans-temp-work-becomes-permanent-way-life-n81071.

Whyte, W. F. & Whyte, K. K. (1991). *Making Mondragon: The Growth and Dynamics of the Worker Cooperative Complex.* Ithaca: Cornell University Press.

Wilentz, S. (1984). *Chants Democratic: New York City & the Rise of the American Working Class, 1788–1850*. New York: Oxford University Press.

Williams, J. (2000). *Unbending Gender*. New York: Oxford University Press.

Williams, F. (2010). "Migration and care: Themes, concepts and challenges". *Social Policy & Society*, 9(3), 385.

Williams, F. (2011). "Markets and migrants in the care economy". *Soundings*, 47, 22.

Williams, J. C., Devaux, R. & Petrac, P. AARP Public Pol'y Inst. (2012, August). Protecting family caregivers from employment discrimination. Retrieved from: www.aarp.org/home-family/caregiving/info-08-2012/insight-protecting-family-caregivers-from-employment-discrimination-AARP-ppi-health.html.

Williams, J. C. & Segal, N. (2003). "Beyond the maternal wall: Relief for family caregivers who are discriminated against on the job". *Harvard Women's Law Journal*, 26, 77, 78.

Williams, R., "Behind closed doors: The plight of the UK's domestic workers," *Guardian* online, 15 June, 2011. Retrieved from: www.guardian.co.uk/lifeandstyle/the-womens-blog-with-jane-martinson/2011/jun/15/domestic-workers-uk-obstructive [last accessed 5 June 2012].

Woloch, N. (2015). *A Class by Herself: Protective Laws for Women Workers, 1890s–1990s*. Princeton, NJ: Princeton University Press.

Wood, M. E., "Victims of misclassification [opinion]," *The New York Times*, 16 December, 2013, p. A25.

Wood, R. W., "Feds and New York State jointly target 'independent contractor' misclassification," *Forbes* [web log post], 19 November, 2013. Retrieved from: http://onforb.es/I0DemY.

Woodhouse, B. (2009). "A world fit for children is a world fit for everyone: Ecogenerism, feminism, and vulnerability". *Houston Law Review*, 46, 817.

Woodman, S., "Labor takes aim at Walmart – again," *The Nation*, 4 January, 2012. Retrieved from: www.thenation.com/article/165437/labor-takes-aim-walmart-again.

Wysong, E., Perrucci, R. & Wright, D. (2014). *The New Class Society: Goodbye American Dream?* (4th edn). Lanham, MD: Rowman & Littlefield.

Zedlewski, S. & Loprest, P. (2011). "What role is welfare playing in this period of high unemployment". *Urban*. Retrieved from: www.urban.org/sites/default/files/alfresco/publication-pdfs/412378-What-Role-is-Welfare-Playing-in-this-Period-of-High-Unemployment-.PDF.

Zietlow, R. & James, G. P. (2011). "The auto-lite strike and the fight against "wage slavery"". *University of Toledo Law Review*, 38, 839 (2007), reprinted in American Labor Struggles and Law Histories, Kenneth M. Casebeer (ed), pp. 211–224.

Zimmerman, R. (1991). "The jurisprudence of equality: The women's movement, the first equal rights amendment, and *Adkins v Children's Hospital*, 1905–1923". *Journal of American History*, 78(15), 188, 199.

Zolberg, A. (2006, June 1). Rethinking the last 200 years of US immigration policy. *Migration Information Source*. Retrieved from: www.migrationpolicy.org/article/rethinking-last-200-years-us-immigration-policy.

Statutes and statutory materials

35 Congressional Record 5757–66 (1902) (remarks of Representative Shattuc).

139 Congressional Record H225–01 (1993) (remarks of Representative Reynolds).

139 Congressional Record H319–02 (1993) (remarks of Representative Pastor).

139 Congressional Record H447–06 (1993) (remarks of Representative Richardson).

139 Congressional Record HR Rep 103–8(I) (1993) 1993 WL 30779.

139 Congressional Record S1355–01 (1993) (remarks of Senator Mitchell).
139 Congressional Record S Rep 103–3 (1993) 1993 WL 22195.
1971 Immigration Act Statement of Immigration Rules for Control on Entry. EEC and Other Commonwealth Nationals. Laid before the Houses of Parliament on 25 January 1973 (HC 81).
Anti-Peonage Act, chap. 187, 14 Stat. 546, 546 (1867) (codified as amended at 18 USC § 1581 (2006) and 42 USC § 1994 (2006)).
Appeal No. UKEAT/0553/10/DM, Judgment of 8 December 2011.
Children and Families Act 2014 (UK).
Chinese Exclusion Act (1882). *Statutes at Large*, 22, 58–61.
Civil Rights Act of 1964 (Title VII), 42 USC 2000e et seq. (US).
Civil Rights Act of 1964, 42 USC §§ 2000a to 2000h-6 (2012).
Civil Service Reform Act of 1978 (October 13, 1978, Public Law 95–454, 92 Stat. 1111).
Committee for the Elimination of All Forms of Racial Discrimination, General Recommendation No. 30 on Discrimination against Non-Citizens, 10 January 2004.
Committee for the Elimination of All Forms of Discrimination Against Women, General Recommendation No. 26 on Women Migrant Workers, 5 December 2008, CEDAW/C/2009/WP.1/R (2008).
Committee on the Protection of the Rights of All Migrant Workers and Members of Their Families, General Comment No. 1 on Migrant Domestic Workers, 23 February 2011, CMW/C/GC/1 (2011).
Consolidation Act on Active Labor Market Measures. Law no. 419 of 10/6 2003, jf. lovbekendtgørelse nr. 807 af 1/7 2015 with later changes.
Consolidation Act on Active Social Policy. Law no. 455 af 10/6 1997, jf. lovbekendtgørelse nr. 468 af 20/5 2016 with later changes.
Consolidation Act on Legal Protection and Administration in Social Matters. Law no. 453 of 10/6 1997, jf. lovbekendtgørelse nr. 1052 af 8/9 2015 with later changes.
Council of Europe, Convention on Action against Trafficking in Human Beings. 16 May 2005, C.E.T.S. No. 197. Retrieved from http://conventions.coe.int/treaty/en/Treaties/Html/197.htm.
Convention Concerning Decent Work for Domestic Workers, (No.189) International Labour Organization, Adopted at the 100th session of the International Labour Conference, Geneva, 2011 (ILO Domestic Work Convention).
Coroners and Justice Act 2009 (UK).
Emergency Quota Act 1921, Public Law 67–5, Statutes at Large, 42, 5–7.
Employment Act 2002 (UK).
Employment Act 2008 (UK).
Employment Relations Act 2004 (UK).
Employment Rights Act 1996 (UK), s 80F et seq.
Employment Rights (Increase of Limits) Order 2011, SI 2011 No. 3006.
Equal Pay Act, 29 USC § 206(d).
Equality Act 2010 (UK).
False Claims Act, 31 USCA §§ 3729–3730; 18 USCA § 287.
Family and Medical Leave Act of 1993 (FMLA), 29 USC 2601 et seq. (US).
Federal Arbitration Act, 9 USC. §§ 1–16 (2006).
Federal Employees Flexible and Compressed Work Schedules Act of 1982, 5 USC § 6120–6133 (2011) (US).
Fair Labor Standards Act of 1938 (FLSA), 29 USC 201 et seq. (US).
Flexible Working (Eligibility, Complaints and Remedies) (Amendment) Regulations 2002 (UK).

Flexible Working (Eligibility, Complaints and Remedies) (Amendment) Regulations 2006 (UK).

Flexible Working (Eligibility, Complaints and Remedies) (Amendment) Regulations 2009 (UK).

Flexible Working (Eligibility, Complaints and Remedies) (Amendment) Regulations 2010 (UK).

Flexible Working (Procedural Requirements) Regulations 2002 (UK).

Flexible Working Regulations 2014 SI 2014/1398 (UK). Retrieved from: www.legislation.gov.uk/uksi/2014/1398/pdfs/uksi_20141398_en.pdf.

Government response to the report from the Joint Committee on the Draft Modern Slavery Bill: Session 2013-14 HL Paper 166 /HC 1019, Cm 8889, June 2014, p. 28.

Hart-Cellar Act 1965, Public Law 89–236. Statutes at Large, 79, 911–22.

Home Affairs Select Committee, The Trade in Human Beings: Human Trafficking in the UK, 2008–9, H.C. 23-I, Para 59 (UK).

ILO, Decent Work for Domestic Workers, Report IV(2A), International Labour Conference, 100th Session, Geneva, 2011.

ILO, Recommendation Concerning Decent Work for Domestic Workers, (ILO Recommendation No. 201) Geneva, 16 June 2011.

Immigration Act 1924, Public Law 68–139. Statutes at Large, 43, 153–70.

Inter-American Court of Human Rights Advisory Opinion on the Juridical Condition and Rights of the Undocumented Migrants (Advisory Opinion OC-18/03, 17 September 2003, Inter-Am. Ct HR (Ser. A) No. 18 (2003)).

International Covenant on Civil and Political Rights, 16 December 1966, 999 UNTS 171.

International Covenant on Economic, Social and Cultural Rights, 16 December 1966, 993 UNTS 3.

International Convention on the Protection of the Rights of All Migrant Workers and Members of their Families 1990, 2220 UNTS 3.

International Labour Conference, 99th session 2010, Report on Decent Work for Domestic Workers (Report IV(1)).

International Labour Organization, Report of the Committee on Domestic Workers, Provisional Record No. 15, International Labour Conference, 100th session, Geneva, June 2011.

International Labour Organization. (June 11, 2014). Text of the Protocol to the Forced Labour Convention, 1930. Retrieved from www.ilo.org/wcmsp5/groups/public/--ed_norm/--relconf/documents/meetingdocument/wcms_246615.pdf.

Joint Resolution to Aid in Relieving from Peonage Women and Children of the Navajo Indians, HR Con Res 83, 40th Cong (1868).

Labor Disputes Act, Hearing on H.R. 6288 Before the H. Comm. on Labor, 74th Cong. 1 (1935) (testimony of William Green, President of Am. Fed'n of Labor).

Labor Management Relations Act, 29 USC §§ 401–531.

National Labor Relations Act of 1935 (NLRA), 29 USC 151 et seq. (US).

National Labor Relations Act, 29 USC §§ 151–169 (2012).

Nr LSF 228 (1996), Forslag til Lov om retssikkerhed og administration på det sociale område, 1996/1 LSF 228.

Nr LSF 230 (1997), Forslag til Lov om aktiv socialpolitik, 1996/1 LSF 230.

Occupational Safety and Health Act, 29 USC §§ 651–678 (2012).

Padrone Act, an Act to Protect Persons of Foreign Birth against Forcible Constraint or Involuntary Servitude, chap. 464, 181 Stat. 251 (1874) (codified as amended at 18 USC § 1584 (2006)).

Page Law (1875), Statutes at Large, 18, 477–78.

"Empowering the People: The Privatization of Social Security in Chile," Jose Pinera, Testimony before the Subcommittee on Social Security, House Ways and Means Committee (September 18, 1997).

Protocol Against the Smuggling of Migrants by Land, Sea and Air, Supplementing the United Nations Convention against Transnational Organized Crime, November 15, 2000, 2241 UNTS 480, 512-13.

Protocol to Prevent, Suppress and Punish Trafficking in Persons Especially Women and Children, supplementing the United Nations Convention against Transnational Organized Crime (2000).

Report of the Joint Select Committee on the Modern Slavery Bill, para. 227, citing written evidence from Human Rights Watch, available at www.publications.parliament.uk/pa/jt201314/jtselect/jtslavery/166/16610.htm. (8 April 2014).

Report of the Special Rapporteur on contemporary forms of slavery, including its causes and consequences, Gulnara Shahinia, UN Doc A/HRC/15/20 (18 January 2010).

Report of the Special Rapporteur on the Human Rights of Migrants, Commission on Human Rights, 16th session E/CN.4/2004/76 (January 2004).

Sarbanes-Oxley Act of 2002, 18 USCA §§ 1514A.

The Flexible Working Regulations 2014 SI 2014/1398 (UK), available at: http://www.legislation.gov.uk/uksi/2014/1398/contents/made.

The Stockholm Programme – An Open and Secure Europe Serving and Protecting Citizens (2010/C 115/01).

Taft-Hartley Act, chap. 120, § 14(b), 61 Stat. 136, 151 (1947) (codified as amended at 29 USC § 164(b) (2006)).

Title VII of the Civil Rights Act of 1964 (Title VII), 42 USC § 2000e et seq. (2006).

Trafficking Victims Protection Act of 2000, Public Law No. 106–386, § 102(b)(22), 114 Stat. 1464, 1468.

Trafficking Victims Protection Act of 2000 (TVPA), Public Law No. 106–386, div. A, 114 Stat. 1466 (codified as amended in sections of 8, 18, and 22 USC), amended by Trafficking Victims Protection Reauthorization Act of 2003 (2003 TVPRA), Public Law No. 108–193, 117 Stat. 2875 (codified in sections of 8, 18, and 22 USC), Trafficking Victims Protection Reauthorization Act of 2005 (2005 TVPRA), Public Law No. 109–164, 119 Stat. 3558 (2006) (codified in sections of 18, 22, and 42 USC), William Wilberforce Trafficking Victims Protection Reauthorization Act of 2008 (2008 TVPRA), Public Law No. 110–457, 122 Stat. 5044 (codified in sections of 6, 8, 18, 22, and 42 USC), Trafficking Victims Protection Act of 2013 (Title XII of the Violence Against Women Reauthorization Act of 2013), Public Law No. 113–4, 127 Stat. 54.

UN Protocol to Prevent, Suppress and Punish Trafficking in Persons, Especially Women and Children, Supplementing the United Nations Convention Against Transnational Organized Crime, 15 November 2000, 2237 NTS 319.

Universal Declaration of Human Rights, GA Res 217A (III), Art. 23(a), UN Doc. A/810 (10 December 1948).

Whistleblower Protection Act of 1989, Public Law 101–12 as amended.

Work and Families Act 2006 (UK).

Working Families Flexibility Bill, HR 1274, 111th Cong (2009–2010) (US).

Cases

Abood v Detroit Board of Education, 431 US 209 (1977).

Adair v United States, 208 US 161 (1908).

American Federation of State, County, and Municipal Employees, AFL-CIO ("AFSCME") v Woodward, 406 F 2d 137 (8th Cir 1969).
Appeal No. UKEAT/0553/10/DM, Judgment of 8 December 2011 ("EAT judgment").
AT&T Mobility LLC v Concepción, 563 US 333 (2011).
Atkins v City of Charlotte, 296 F Supp 1068 (WDNC 1969).
Badra v Gardiner & Theobald LLP [2010] UKEAT 0191_10_2409.
Barry v Midlands Bank [1999] IR 859 (1997).
Beard v McDonald's Corp, No. 1:14-CV-01664 (E.D.N.Y. 13 March 2014).
Belline v K-Mart Corp. 940 F.2d 184 (7th Cir. 1999).
British Airways v Grundy [2008] EWCA 875.
British Airways v Starmer [2005] UKEAT 0306_05_0607.
Browning Ferris Industries 362 NLRB No. 186 (2015).
Burlington Indus. v Ellerth, 524 US 742, 760–66 (1998).
Burns v Rohr Corp., 346 F Supp 994, 996 (SD Cal 1972).
C.N. v France, App. No. 67724/09 Eur. Ct. H. R. (2012).
C.N. v The United Kingdom, App. No. 4239/08 Eur. Ct. H. R. (2012).
Capitol Awning Co., Inc. v Local 137 Sheet Metal Workers Int'l Assoc., 698 F Supp 2d 308 (EDNY 2010).
Carpenter v Secretary of State for the Home Department, C-60/00 [2002] ECR I-6279.
Carter v Carter Coal Co., 298 US 238 (1936).
Caswell v Advance Travel Partners UK, UKET Case No 2304832/2000 (2004).
Chellen v John Pickle Co., 446 F Supp 2d 1247 (ND Okla 2006).
Citizens United v FEC, 558 US 310 (2010).
Clarke v Telewest Communications [2005] UKET Case No. 1301034/2004 (7 June 2005) (unpublished).
Commotion, Ltd v Rutty [2005] UKEAT 0418_05_1310, [2006] IRLR 171 (EAT).
Communications Workers v Beck, 487 US 735 (1988).
Coppage v State of Kansas, 236 US 1 (1915).
CPSU (Community and Public Sector Union) v CSL, Ltd [2002] AIRC, PR921278 (3 June 2002).
Craddock v Governing Body of Indian Queens CP School & Nursery [2005] UKEAT 0367_05_1912.
Cumbria County Council v Dow [2008] IRLR 91 EAT.
Digiacinto v Ameriko-Omserv Corp., 69 Cal Rptr 2d 300, 304 (Ct App 1997).
DH and Others v the Czech Republic, European Court of Human Rights Application no. 57325/00, 7 February 2006.
Doe v Nestle, SA, 748 F Supp 2d 1057 (CD Cal 2010).
D.R. Horton, Inc., 357 NLRB 2277 (2012).
DR Horton, Inc. v NLRB, 737 F 3d 344 (5th Cir 2013).
Dubuque Packing Co. (1991) 303 NLRB 386, enforced, 1 F.3d 24 (DC Cir 1993).
Fid. Interior Const., Inc. v Se. Carpenters Reg'l Council of United Bhd. of Carpenters & Joiners of America, 675 F 3d 1250 (11th Cir 2012).
First National Maintenance Corp. v NLRB, 452 US 666 (1981).
Friedrichs v California Teachers Association, 136 S Ct 1083 (2016).
Garrity v New Jersey, 385 US 493 (1967).
Gibson v Sheffield City Council [2010] EWCA Civ 63.
Giles v Geach [2005] ET 3100720/05.
Griggs v Duke Power Co., 401 US 424 (1971).
Gonzalez ("Cotton Fields") v Mexico, Inter-American Court on Human Rights, Judgment of 16 November 2009.
Hague v CIO, 307 US 496 (1939).

Hammer v Dagenhart, 247 US 251 (1918).
Harris v Quinn, 134 S Ct 2618 (2014).
Hays v Potlatch Forests, Inc., 465 F 2d 1081 (8th Cir 1972).
Heart of Atlanta Motel v US, 379 US 241 (1964).
Homemakers, Inc. of Los Angeles v Division of Industrial Welfare, 356 F Supp 1111 (ND Cal 1973).
Homemakers, Inc. of Los Angeles v Division of Industrial Welfare and Industrial Welfare Commission of the State of California, 509 F 2d 20, 23 (9th Cir 1974).
Hounga v Allen, [2012] EWCA Civ 609.
House v Carter-Wallace, Inc., 232 NJ Super. 42, 556 A.2d 353, certification denied, 117 NJ 154, 564 A 2d 874 (1989).
HS Care LLC, d/b/a Oakwood Care Ctr., 343 NLRB 659 (2004).
Hughes v McDonald's Corp. et al., No. RG14717085 (Cal Super Ct Alameda County 12 March 2014).
Hussain v Consumer Credit Counseling, UKET Case No. 1804305/2004 (12 January 2005) (unreported).
JI Case v NLRB, 321 US 332 (1944).
Lenahan J.,(Gonzales) v United States, Inter-American Court on Human Rights, Judgment of 21 July 2011.
Kentov v Sheet Metal Workers' Int'l Assoc. Local 15, AFL-CIO, 418 F 3d 1259 (11th Cir 2005).
Keyishian v Board of Regents, 385 US 589 (1967).
Knox v SEIU, Local 1000, 132 S Ct 2277 (2012).
Laborers Dist. Council of Minnesota & N. Dakota v NLRB, 688 F.3d 374 (8th Cir 2012).
Lochner v NY, 198 US 45 (1905).
McDonnell-Douglas Corp. v Green, 411 US 792 (1973).
McLaughlin v Tilendis, 398 F.2d 287 (7th Cir 1968).
Ministry of Defence v DeBique [2009] UKEAT/0048/09/MAA and 0049/09/MAA (19 May 2009).
Mowry v DiNapoli, 976 NYS 2d 577 (NY App Div 2013).
Murphy Oil USA, Inc. and Sheila M. Hobson, 361 NLRB No. 72 (October 28, 2014).
Nambalat v Taher & Ors (2012); Nambalat v Taher & Anor: Udin v Pasha & Ors [2012] EWCA Civ 1249).
Network Rail Infrastructures Ltd v Gammie [2009] UKEAT/0044/08/BI (6 March 2009).
Nevada Department of Human Resources v Hibbs, 538 US 721 (2003).
NFIB v Sebelius, 132 S Ct 2566 (2012).
NLRB v Health Care and Retirement Corp. of America,511 US 571(1994).
NLRB v Kentucky River Community Care Inc., 532 US 706 (2001).
NLRB v Mackay Radio & Tel. Co., 304 US 333 (1938).
NLRB v Noel Canning, 134 S Ct 2550 (2014).
NLRB v Truitt Mfg. Co., 351 US 149 (1956).
NLRB v Wooster Div. of Borg-Warner Corp., 356 US 342 (1958).
In re Oakwood Healthcare, Inc., 348 NLRB 686 (2006).
Ochoa v McDonald's Corp. et al., No. RG14717102 (Cal Super Ct Alameda County 12 March 2014).
OOO & Others v Metropolitan Police [2011] EWHC 1246 (QB).
Opuz v Turkey, European Court of Human Rights Application No. 33401/02, Judgment of 9 June 2009.
Osman v Denmark, European Court of Human Rights Application No. 38058/09, Judgment of 14 June 2011.
Pollock v Williams, 332 US 4 (1944).

Pugh v See's Candies, Inc., 171 Cal. Rptr 917 (Ct App 1981).
Pullen v McDonald's Corp. et al., No. 5:14-CV-11081 (ED Mich 13 March 2014).
Rantsev v Cyprus and Russia, ECHR Application No. 25965/04, Judgment of 7 January 2010.
Reynolds v Sims, 377 U.S. 533 (1964).
Ruiz v Affinity Logistics Corp., 754 F.3d 1093 (2014).
Salazar v McDonald's Corp. et al., No. RG14717081 (Cal Super Ct Alameda County 12 March 2014).
Sanchez v McDonald's Rests. of Cal, No. BC499888 (Cal Super Ct Los Angeles County 13 March 2014).
Shaw v CCL Ltd [2007] UKEAT 0512_06_2205 (22 May 2007).
Siliadin v France (2006) 43 EHRR 16.
Smith v Arkansas Highway Employees Local 1315, 441 US 463 (1979).
State v Fairfield Communities Land Co., 260 Ark 277, 538 SW 2d 698, cert. denied, 429 US 1004 (1976).
Texas Dept. of Community Affairs v Burdine, 450 US 248 (1981).
Thomas v Collins, 323 US 516 (1945).
Thornhill v Alabama, 310 US 88 (1940).
United States v Gasanova, 332 F 3d 297 (5th Cir 2003).
United States v Juan Ramos, 2002 US App LEXIS 10396 (2002); 130 Fed Appx 415 (2005).
United States v Lueleni Fetongi Maka, 237 Fed Appx 225 (9th Cir Haw 2007) 283 Fed Appx 547 (9th Cir Haw 2008) 2008 US Dist LEXIS 60823 (D Haw 8 August 2008).
United States v Nantawat Naovasaisri, 150 Fed Appx 170 (3rd Cir 2005).
United States v Timothy Bradley, 390 F 3d 145 (2004); 545 US 1101 (2005); 426 F 3d 54 (2005).
United States v Zheng et al., 538 F 3d 1078 (ND Mariana Isld 2006).
United Steelworkers of America v Warrior & Gulf, 363 US 574, 581 (1960).
Victoria v Schou [2004] VSCA 71.
Vizcaino v Microsoft Corp., 97 F 3d 1187 (9th Cir 1996).
Vizcaino v Microsoft Corp., 120 F 3d 1006 (9th Cir 1997) (en banc).
Wal-Mart Stores, Inc. v Dukes, 131 S Ct 2541 (2011).
Webb v EMO Air Cargo [1992] 4 All ER 929.
Webster v Princes Soft Drinks, UKET Case No. 1803942/2004 (17 February 2005) (unreported).
Wickard v Fillburn, 317 US 111 (1942).
Wilson et al. v McDonald's Corp. et al., No. 2, 14-CV-11082 (ED Mich 13 March 2014).
Wisconsin Education Association Council v Walker, 2013 WL 203532 (CA 7 2013).
Wolff Packing Co. v Court of Industrial Relations, 262 US 522 (1923).

INDEX

For Product Safety Concerns and Information please contact our EU
representative GPSR@taylorandfrancis.com
Taylor & Francis Verlag GmbH, Kaufingerstraße 24, 80331 München, Germany

www.ingramcontent.com/pod-product-compliance
Lightning Source LLC
LaVergne TN
LVHW021246011026
849160LV00010BA/752

* 9 7 8 1 1 3 8 6 9 8 8 2 6 *